ADOLESCENT EDUCATION

Library of Congress Cataloging-in-Publication Data

Adolescent education: a reader / edited by Joseph L. DeVitis,
Linda Irwin-DeVitis.
p. cm. — (Adolescent cultures, school, and society; v. 45)
Includes bibliographical references.
1. Urban youth—Education (Secondary) —United States.
2. Youth with social disabilities—Education (Secondary) —United States.
3. African American youth—Education (Secondary)
4. Urban youth—United States—Social conditions.
I. DeVitis, Joseph L. II. Irwin-DeVitis, Linda.
LC5131.A36   373.73—dc22   2010007224
ISBN 978-1-4331-0505-0 (hardcover)
ISBN 978-1-4331-0504-3 (paperback)
ISSN 1091-1464

Bibliographic information published by **Die Deutsche Nationalbibliothek**.
Die Deutsche Nationalbibliothek lists this publication in the "Deutsche
Nationalbibliografie"; detailed bibliographic data is available
on the Internet at http://dnb.d-nb.de/.

Editors' photo by Amanda R. Hall
Cover photo by Amanda R. Hall

The paper in this book meets the guidelines for permanence and durability
of the Committee on Production Guidelines for Book Longevity
of the Council of Library Resources.

© 2010 Peter Lang Publishing, Inc., New York
29 Broadway, 18th floor, New York, NY 10006
www.peterlang.com

Printed in the United States of America

To Leigh Garrett Irwin,

who has brought joy to us
before, during, and after adolescence.

Contents

SOCIAL AND CULTURAL PERSPECTIVES

PEDAGOGICAL PERSPECTIVES

Preface

We are living in a time of unbearable dissonance between promise and performance; between good politics and good policy; between professed and practiced family values; between racial creed and racial deed; between calls for community and rampant individualism; and between our capacity to prevent and alleviate human deprivation . . . and our political and spiritual will to do so.
—MARIAN WRIGHT EDELMAN, PRESIDENT, THE CHILDREN'S DEFENSE FUND

In 1997, Linda Irwin-DeVitis and I launched the Peter Lang Publishing book series, Adolescent Cultures, School & Society. (We thank Chris Myers, managing director, and Shirley Steinberg, Education series editor, for their confidence in us and for encouraging us to undertake this project.)

Adolescent Education: A Reader offers a fitting testimony to the importance of analyzing adolescent lives and their contexts differently from the jaundiced preconceptions that have scolded youths in recent times. This book is both a celebration and a call for renewal of our original intent: focusing on the plethora of adolescent cultures that exist in contemporary postindustrial societies without blinders of blame or condemnation.

We first embarked on that critical journey because we had been deeply concerned about the mean-spirited conservative backlash that dominated political and educational discourse, policy, and practice at the end of the last century. An insidious, hurtful, and grossly unfair campaign of myths and lies had been spread about America's teenagers. The propaganda was simple and deadly in its force and coarseness: adolescents were deemed a prime cause of many of our nation's social ills. A similar charge was leveled against our public schools and their teachers—one that has re-appeared throughout the history of the United States. In short, both schools and youths have long been targeted as scapegoats in a society far too prone to neglect larger social problems.

Meanwhile, a media rampage blared purple prose of drugs, sex, violence, teen pregnancy, and various, and sundry other "immoral" behavior by our youths. However, such over-embellished cries seldom met the pen or voice of concerted challenge, defense, or contestation. Thus came our own efforts to take a small step toward presenting public counterpoints against adult myth-making and the immature bombast and blaming-the-victim mentality fostered by many politicians, think tanks, policy-makers, and, yes, even some educators.

We sought to chart a more complex course that portrayed the messy contradictions and confusion surrounding adolescence in American culture and education. Unlike our more extreme conservative friends, we continue to share the reality that many teenagers inhabit—a world in "psycho-historical dislocation," that is, "the break in the sense of connection men (and women) have long felt with vital and nourishing symbols of their cultural traditions—symbols revolving around family, idea systems, religions, and the life cycle in general."[1]

For several decades now, our perceived "realities" have been framed largely by metaphors and discourses alien to the idea of developing teenagers in humane, life-generating fashion. Instead, the universe of adolescence has often been inundated by shrill calls for obedience, discipline, punishment, and "tough love," what George Lakoff terms the "strict father model" of child-rearing. This compendium of essays implicitly adopts Lakoff's alternative model: that of the "nurturing mother." The latter emphasizes empathy, equity, caring, goodness, mutual respect, and the willingness to question.[2]

Those who have contributed to this book do not expect to lead our readers on a blithe excursion to pure peace and happiness for adolescents. Established patriarchal norms have long dominated our perceptual and cultural lenses. They are deep-rooted and exceedingly difficult to change. As Morrie Schwartz, the dying college teacher in *Tuesdays with Morrie*, puts it: "The culture we have does not make people feel good about themselves. We're teaching the wrong things. And you have to be strong enough to say if the culture doesn't work, don't buy it."[3] Nevertheless, each of these essays invites us to question and battle to alter entrenched ideologies and practices that weaken our propensity to care for and respect our youths and their promise for the future. "Mothering" power is unabashedly strong and vital in the chapters that follow.[4]

We present the knotty complications of adolescence in three parts, none of which are really distinct and separate from one another: developmental, social and cultural, and pedagogical perspectives. Part One explores theoretical discourse on adolescent development—its trajectories, detours, and refusals. Individual identity formation, family and peer influences, racial differences, and gender issues are particularly highlighted. Each of those crucial factors is not easily disentangled, nor should they be. They form the fading fabric of American institutions either at outright war or partial peace with their children. Part Two focuses on those sociocultural forces that directly impinge upon, and often circumscribe, the social and educational well-being of our youths. They help explain much of the alienation and disengagement of today's teenagers. They also teach us why and how teachers and teenagers have too often been unfairly branded as "culprits" in society's nasty blame game. In addition, they prod us, as citizens, to challenge politicians and policymakers to re-frame "educational" problems as deep-seated structural problems within our social, economic, and political systems. That lesson is especially important to learn in those teacher preparation courses that minimize the fact that what goes on *outside* the classroom tends to reproduce what occurs *inside* the bare bricks and mortar. Lastly, Part Three brings readers back to the pedagogy of the schoolhouse—but one that is rebuilt in more caring, compassionate, yet critical, patterns. Whether the authors refer to subject-matter content or the processes of teaching and learning, they aim their presentations and recommendations in reframed directions. They remind us of the significance of education in youth-full lives and the innovative ways it can be shared by both adolescents and instructors alike. Moreover, they view both teachers and students as participant-creators who can and should work in genuine collaboration for mutually rewarding means and ends.

Ultimately, each contributor to this volume yearns for more health and happiness within the minds and hearts of our whole community, including children, adolescents, and adults. Our educational institutions can certainly aid our development as human beings who can grow individually, yet contribute consciously and simultaneously to each other's growth. As we enter this dialogue toward community, we hope, together, that we can make a better world.

JOSEPH L. DEVITIS

Notes

1. Robert Jay Lifton, *Boundaries: Psychological Man in Revolution* (New York: Random House, 1970), p. 43.
2. George Lakoff, *Moral Politics: How Liberals and Conservatives Think* (Chicago: University of Chicago Press, 2002), pp. 143–176.
3. Morrie Schwartz, as quoted in Mitch Albom, *Tuesdays with Morrie: An Old Man, a Young Man, and Life's Greatest Lesson* (New York: Doubleday, 1997), p. 35.
4. *See* Nancy J. Chodorow, *The Reproduction of Mothering: Psychoanalysis and the Sociology of Gender* (Berkeley: University of California Press, 1999).

PART ONE

Developmental Perspectives

CHAPTER ONE

Theoretical Overview

Adolescent Culture and the Culture of Refusal

BRETT ELIZABETH BLAKE

> In the best of circumstances, the tasks and striving of adolescence are tumultuous . . . purposelessness and rolelessness create a heightened sense of despair and an increased risk of disaster. Add to this the devastating effects of poverty, violence, and drugs, and the passage of adolescence becomes absolutely treacherous (Ayers, 1997, p. 140).

The onset of adolescence is a critical period of biological and psychological change for every child involving dramatic transitions in one's physical as well as one's social environment. These "transitions" have become more difficult in recent years as a combination of socio-economic factors has led to an "erosion" of the traditional social-support networks (schools, family, and community) upon which adolescents so desperately depend. And yet, little, if any, work done on adolescence prior to the 1980s has focused on the implications of the loss of these support systems. And, further, little, if any, work since the 1980's has taken into account the dramatic effects that gender, race, and class have on adolescence, nor has any examined these intersections within the context of such a rapidly changing, and increasingly violent, social environment. Simply put, we know far too little about the relationship between adolescence, ethnic identity, and the perceptions and expectations of multiply-marginalized youth, the youth Ayers (1997) so eloquently describes as having a "treacherous" ride into adulthood.

In this chapter, I will first historically situate commonly-held theories on adolescence and individual development, beginning with Freud (1978), Erikson (1963, 1968) and Kohlberg (1981,1987) and moving on to Gilligan (1982, 1990) and the "new literature" on boys (Faludi, 1999; Garbarino, 1999; Pollack, 1998; Real, 1997). I will then examine some of the cultural and social factors at play in adolescents' lives, emphasizing the roles of family and community as crucial contexts in which adolescents develop. With this in mind, I will examine recent literature that points toward the "staggering array of guises" (Strauss, p. vii) that violence takes among adolescents, and the importance of recognizing that violence, too, can best be understood by placing it in socio/cultural and historical contexts. And finally, I will turn toward a discussion of the notion of "adolescence as social policy" as I explore the role of the school, examining, in particular, how and why multiply-marginalized youth share "precious little with other [adolescent] groups" (Strauss, p. 4). Exacerbated by institutionalized racism and fueled by the reality of the poverty and the lack of opportunity within the outside community, school simply becomes another place where these adolescents experience loss, precipitously entering a "culture of refusal."

Historical Settings: Individual Development

At the turn of the 20th century, adolescence was believed to be a time of "ambiguous and prolonged transition" (Straus, p. 4) in part because of an intense interplay between sexual and moral life (Freud, 1978) that needed to be resolved. In fact, this dichotomous notion of adolescence as a time period in which sexuality interrupted one's moral reasoning and thereby one's subsequent successful transition into adulthood remained firmly entrenched in the work of psychologists well into the 1980s and still can be found today in selected pieces of research on the topic.

Kaplan (1984), for example, centered much of her discussion on the physical manifestations of adolescence, including, most notably, work on the harmful effects of masturbation. If unchecked, she claimed, adolescent masturbation would "serve regression and *impede* the forward-moving aspects of adolescent development" (p. 201) as well as "threaten[ing] the needs of the larger social community" (p. 196).

At the same time, researchers were re-visiting the notion of "turmoil theory" to explain the rite of passage of adolescents. Led by Erikson (1963, 1968), turmoil theory, re-coined as "identity crisis theory," posited that adolescents were not able to function well until they encountered a series of struggles that would help them form their own identities. The primary task of the adolescent, therefore, was to develop an "ego identity," as he or she struggled with developing "basic" skills that included literacy, intimacy, and problem solving. This was predicated, however, on the premise that adolescents had an overall sense of "personal safety." If adolescents were unable to develop this sense of self within a safety network they then would fall prey to "role confusion" and become dangerously vulnerable to "delinquency, peer pressure, and . . . severe psychological disturbances" (Straus, 1994, p. 3). Erikson, importantly, too, was one of the first researchers to link personal identity and its evolution with the changing nature of culture and social change. Kohlberg (1981, 1987), on the other hand, reframed Freud's original work on the connections between identity development and moral development. Essentially, Kohlberg claimed that in order for adolescents to develop any sense of personal identity, thereby gaining entrance into adulthood, they needed to adopt a common understanding of a "*singular*" notion of morality.

Based on a longitudinal study of 84 boys (almost all white and middle class) over a period of 20 years, Kohlberg (1981) developed a model of "normal" cognitive development that included an acceptance of a code in which "moral dilemmas are discussed and resolved in a manner which will stimulate normal behavior" (p. 675), i.e., an "ethic of justice." Because young women (and presumably young men who were not middle class and white) did not see right and wrong in the same way as young men in the study did (i.e., they did not always hold an "ethic of justice" as central to a notion of morality and moral behavior), they experienced an abnormal transition into adulthood. Young women (and young men) who did not articulate an ethic of justice, therefore, were presumed to have critical gaps in their abilities to conduct moral reasoning and exhibit moral behavior.

In her crucial work of the 1980s, however, Gilligan (1982) presented an alternative theory of adolescent development that examined, specifically, a *female* model of transition. In this model, "morality is conceived in interpersonal terms and goodness is equated with helping and pleasing others" (p. 18). Grounded in opposition to the "ethic of justice" that served the white male privilege so well, this "ethic of care" firmly re-centered young women's (and others') cognitive and moral development within a stable, balanced and thereby "normal" framework. Gilligan's work, for the first time, had begun to shift the understandings of adolescent transitions to include more perspectives and voices. Interestingly, although Erikson (1963, 1968) had attempted to make connections between his theories of identity development to the changing nature of society, it was not until Gilligan's work that any notion of discussion of identity development was discussed outside of the "normal white male" range.

Adolescent Girls and a Loss of Voice

According to Gilligan (1990), it is absolutely crucial at the early adolescent stage (usually considered to begin around the fifth grade or at 10 years of age) for girls not to separate formal education from other powerful out-of-school learning experiences. As young women learn to deal with evolving emotional issues such as connection and relationship and learn to deal with the perceived validity of these evolving emotions, they require guidance, role models, and confirmation to further their emotional development. Instead, however, because formal education has traditionally centered on other issues—i.e., autonomy, independence, detachment, and separation—adolescent girls not only begin to "observe where and when women speak and when they are silent" (Gilligan, 1990, p. 25), but also begin to learn precisely how to separate formal educational experiences from their other learning experiences. In other words, girls learn, and internalize, that what they consider to be central to their learning and knowledge lies, in fact, outside of any formal school realm. Girls understand that the image of the nice girl is so persuasive that they learn to modulate, silence, or appropriate others' voices altogether.

Feminist researchers (Belenky et al., 1986; Fine 1987, 1991a; Gilligan, 1982, 1990; Gilbert, 1989, 1991) see an appropriation of voice as extremely problematic for girls. Because girls have traditionally held few positions from which to speak (Gilbert, 1989), they typically learn to do what these researchers have called "doubling their voices. This doubling of voice is considered to be a direct response to a situation of a "deeply-knotted dilemma of being at once inside and outside of the world they are entering as young women" (Gilligan, 1982, p. 148). In other words, girls feel they must present separate voices depending on the context, audience, purpose, and theme for both speaking and writing.

Fine's (1987) work among urban adolescent girls supports the notion that girls learn to develop two or more separate voices. "Good" girls trained themselves to speak and produce in two voices, one academic, and one at the margin. While the academic voice was one that denied class, gender, and race and "reproduced ideologies about hard work success, and their 'natural' sequence; and stifled the desire to disrupt?" (p. 163), the marginal voice expressed more private experiences and snuggles such as those that *revolved around* discussions of gender, race, and class. This particular two-voice dilemma was often more permanently resolved by "creative, if ultimately self-defeating strategies" (p. 164) such as dropping out of school.

One major result of this emphasis on the differing experiences of girls' transitions into adulthood has been to re-examine boys' development, finally, perhaps, from within the socio-cultural perspective so desperately lacking in any early studies.

The New Literature on Boys: A Loss of Heart

Recently, both psychologists and educators (Faludi, 1999; Gilligan, 1982; Garbarino, 1999; Pollack, 1998; Real, 1997) have begun to write that "a national crisis of boyhood" (Hall, 1999, p. 33) is upon us. Tragically realized before much of the research reached the mainstream public (see news accounts on the school shootings by adolescent males in Littleton, Jonesboro, Springfield, and Columbine High School in Colorado, 1998 and 1999), the crisis has now captured the attention of the general public. In a desperate attempt to ascribe blame, however, policy and law-makers seem to have obscured (or discounted) the very real challenges inherent in the volatile social environment that adolescents are faced with at the beginning of the 21st century. And yet, as a result of the school tragedies (and partly fueled by the AIDS epidemic), a new "masculine ideology" (Pleck, 1988) has emerged from the literature. Called the "new literature" on boys, this ideology measures risk for dangerous sexual behavior, substance use, educational problems, and encounters with law enforcement and the criminal justice system by the degree to which males subscribe to traditional roles (e.g., a need for physical toughness; a reluctance to talk about problems; an unwillingness to do things "feminine," such as housework or childrearing; and an undying need for respect of masculinity). That is, boys who have difficulty reconciling the traditional values of their fathers and other older male relatives with a feminist culture that celebrates sensitivity and girls' voices are in danger of becoming "un-done."

According to Real (1997), for most boys, becoming a man is not so much an acquisition of something good, but a disavowal of something bad. He explains:

> When researchers asked girls and women to define what it means to be feminine, the girls answered with positive language: to be compassionate, to be connected, to care about others. Boys and men, on the other hand, when asked to describe masculinity, predominantly responded with double negatives. Boys and men did not talk about being strong so much as about not being weak. They do not list independence so much as not being dependent. They did not speak about being close to their fathers so much as about pulling away from their mothers. In short, be[coming] a man generally means not being a woman. As a result, boys' acquisition of malehood is a negative achievement. . . . Masculine identity development turns out to be not a process of development at all but rather a process of elimination, a successive unfolding of loss. (p. 130)

This successive unfolding is undoubtedly exacerbated by the effects of race and class. In an adolescent world already fraught with strife and confusion, multiply-marginalized adolescent males, in particular, attempt to make the transition into adulthood amidst social systems designed to segregate and punish, rather than include and support.

Cultural and Social Settings: Family and Community Roles

The family remains the primary group from which adolescents learn the norms and social expectations of human behavior, as well as the most important source from which children receive emotional nurturance. In fact, much like the development research on the individual, family life-cycle theories address the various stages that adolescents must complete from within the familial structure itself, a structure that, once again, must be perceived as "safe." And yet, family life-cycle theories become distinct from individualistic theories in that here the development, that is the emotional and economic stability of the family, directly impacts adolescents' growth.

Today, one in four adolescents is raised in a single-parent household where 70% of the mothers in those households are working and 46% of those households are poor, with a median income of only $9,000. Adolescents are greatly over-represented among poverty populations of all races, but among Blacks that figure mirrors the general populace at 46.1%; among Latinos it is slightly lower, at 40.9%. (As a single parent of a 15-year-old son who, along with family and friends, has raised him exclusively since he was two years old, I cringe when I hear that "single mothers" are to blame for societal ills, and I, therefore, in no way mean to imply that children cannot be "successful" in single parent households.) Further, there is a strong positive correlation between poverty, i.e., economic stability, and "delinquency" and violence. Children raised in poverty, with parents who are either working long or unusual hours or who have become too isolated and disenfranchised to care for children on a level that white mainstream society sees fit, often find that they have little to depend on both emotionally and financially within their homes. Lacking resources and the ability to tap into the support systems available to other adolescents, poor adolescents often react to the victimization they endure by engaging in "anti-social" or violent behavior. (A caveat here, too: obviously there are other important factors at work besides poverty as evidenced, again, by the school shootings in white middle-class and upper-middle-class communities.)

Fifty thousand adolescents—a number equivalent to all of those Americans who died in the Vietnam War—have been killed in violent acts in the United States since 1979 (Strauss, 1994, p. xiv). Although typically violence flourishes where familial abuse, neglect, poverty and societal and institutional racism and inequities abound, putting urban, poor adolescents most at risk, recent research (Dryfoos, 1990) claims that violence in the 2000s will cut across social and economic lines. A staggering one in four adolescents today will experience a form of violence so severe that they "have little chance of becoming responsible adults." In fact, Dryfoos (1990) sees the problem so overwhelming that she states:

> a new class of untouchables is emerging in our inner cities, on the social fringes of suburbia, and in some rural areas: young people who are functionally illiterate, disconnected from school, depressed, prone to drug abuse and early criminal activity, and eventually, parents of unplanned and unwanted babies (p. 3).

Violence in adolescence is primarily the result of the profound economic, social, and political inequalities that many adolescents are faced with on a daily basis. In a society dominated and controlled by an entrenched patriarchy, poor adolescents, in particular, find few adults whom they can look up to and on whom they can model their behavior. Violence, therefore, becomes an adaptive, and often a sole, coping mechanism.

Adolescence as Social Policy: School, Cultural Compatibility Theory and a Culture of Refusal

The violence so prevalent in our communities today makes it an unrealistic expectation that schools alone can prepare adolescents for work, further education, and life in general. The debilitating living conditions that so many of our youth encounter as routine make it a difficult task indeed for these adolescents to succeed in a traditional school setting. Incongruent with their life experiences and unprepared to give the support these adolescents so desperately need, middle or junior high schools typically become the very sites where delinquency develops.

At the turn of the 20th century it was thought that all adolescents' lives and experiences were incongruent with the way schools have been set up and run. Therefore, it was decided that schooling for adolescents needed to be re-conceptualized, and thus, the idea of the junior high school was born. Essentially, the junior high school was established to differentiate, and isolate, as well as to help society create a means and a context in which to not only "protect" but also to help "sort" adolescents for future work and careers. At the same time, three major social policy changes were being enacted to coincide with the invention of the junior high school. These were mandatory high school, the juvenile justice system (see Ayers' 1997 account), and federal legislation against child labor (Strauss, 1994, p. xi). These social policies, coupled with a new vision for the schooling of this age group, established "adolescence" as a bona fide developmental period between childhood and adulthood over which the government had much control. Out of policy makers' favor from the 1930s to the 1960s, junior high schools enjoyed a revival that eventually led to the modern-day creation of middle schools, the places where, it was believed, both the educational and developmental needs of adolescents could truly be met (Hechinger, 1993).

Today's middle schools, however, are still ill-defined. Seen as places where the transition could be eased from childhood to adulthood (and from elementary school to high school), where the notion of incongruence could be addressed and soothed, a lack of understanding (by teachers, administrators, and other support personnel, including parents) of what constitutes this transition is apparent. In fact, the middle school has been described as the "breeding ground for behaviors and attitudes that cause many students to drop out of school" (Takanishi, 1993, p. 73).

Realistically, though, we still know far too little about how these "incongruent" worlds "combine in the day-to-day lives of adolescents to affect their engagement in educational settings" (Phelan, Davidson, & Yu, 1998, p. 3). If we, for example, believe, as Giroux (In Jipson et al., 1995, p. x) would have us believe, that "schools function as cultural sites actively engaged in the production of not only knowledge but also social identities," then we might come to understand how poor youth, in particular, seek to develop their social identities outside of school, where cultural space and expectations of everyday life are in line with their daily experiences.

Cultural compatibility theory seeks to describe and explain this incongruence and lack of common cultural space between minority youths' lives and experiences at home and their lives and experiences at in school. Cultural compatibility research not only draws on observational data to document the important differences between home and school for minority youth but also describes in detail the rich, though different, home and school learning environments within which these students live and learn. Much of what we have learned from cultural compatibility theory has provided us with empirical evidence that supports the claim that "problematic" interactions in schools [among minority youth] are, in fact, related to cultural differences (Heath, 1983; Trueba, Guthrie, & Au, 1981; Trueba & Delgado-Gaitan, 1988).

The notion of cultural differences as a major factor in the challenge of the poor, urban adolescent's development is found in recent research that strongly posits that school is simply not "enveloping" enough to help these (and similar) adolescents approximate success. In a work entitled "Schools Are Not the Answer," Traub (2000) argues that "school . . . as we understand it now, is not as powerful an institution as it seems." In effect, poor (urban) students' educational inequality, he claims, is not rooted in the school; rather, it is deeply entrenched in the existing social, cultural, and economic problems and challenges of the urban community. Coleman (in Traub, 2000) elaborates:

> the inequalities imposed on children by their home, neighborhood and peer environment are carried along to become the inequalities with which they confront adult life at the end of school. (p. 55)

Coleman continues by saying that it is an "impossibility" to expect that school can provide all of what he calls the "child's human and social capital," terms invented by social scientists in the 1960s to "describe and quantify" the effects of family, community, and school on the developing child. Human capital refers to all human capabilities that are passed along from family to their children, accumulating like other capital, and "produced," in part by school. Social capital is defined as "the norms, the social networks, the relationships between adults and children that are of value for the children . . ." (Coleman in Traub, 2000). Because of the enormous influence of the human and social capitals, "the effects of home and community *blotted out* (emphasis mine) almost all those of school" (p. 57). The imbalance, therefore, once seen as being firmly entrenched in the lack of connections between home and school, is now regarded as being situated on much larger continua. Where schooling, the resources of the local community, and the needs of the larger society in today's global, technological workplace become at odds—where the school is not providing the extra support missing from the family, the community is not providing the extra support missing from both the family and the school, and the larger society offers no support in the form of work—multiply-marginalized adolescents, in particular, become effectively engulfed in the *incongruence* of their lives. This incongruence leads, then, precipitously to a culture of refusal, where it is believed that the lack of support systems are unnecessary, unwanted, and certainly undermining of adolescents' true needs and desires.

Adolescence was invented for specific reasons at a particular point in history; its roots, therefore, are both social and political, and so, too, especially is the hopelessness, joblessness, and violence associated with it (Straus, 1994, xiv). Contrary to the days where unskilled work could be found in the industries of mass production, today's high-tech society requires finely-tuned skills, particularly in what the *New York Times* once called "the manipulation of letters and symbols." Further, the obsolescence of our traditional learning systems as well as a changing, global economy that depends increasingly more on human resources has, in fact, most adversely affected poor and minority students.

Undoubtedly, school remains a "pivotal institution" in adolescents' lives. Along with the other major factors (e.g., family and community) that strongly influence the adolescent's transition into adulthood, schools, too, remain notoriously ineffective in attending to "the social meanings of ethnicity and the identity development of minority adolescents" (Takanishi, 1993, p. 56). Indeed, much of the current research states that "the real damage gets done in middle school" (Hall, 1999, p. 35). Being an adolescent in this society is intrinsically stressful, but among multiply-marginalized adolescents, the transitions into adulthood may be particularly so as race, class, and gender intersect to produce different and more pronounced patterns of anxiety and challenge.

We have a great need for continuity in schools (i.e., curricular and developmental) and congruence among social institutions (i.e., families, communities and community organizations, and schools). In essence, to begin, we need to give students the "cultural space within dominant arenas" (Ferrell, 1997, p. 22) where, "among marginalized kids, battles over cultural space, are . . . more intense . . . [as the] creation and contestation of cultural space shape expectations/experiences of everyday life." Without such spaces, I argue, schools, as one crucial support system needed for adolescent development, fail the adolescent.

Multiply-marginalized adolescents, just like all adolescents, are "avid seekers of moral authenticity" (Ayers, 1997, p. 139), and yet they come face-to-face with a society that disdains them, i.e., does not legitimize their understandings of themelves and their perspectives of their social world. Like the girls about whom Brown & Gilligan (1992) write, marginalized adolescents learn, too, to separate their formal education experiences—to refuse their formal educational experiences—for more powerful learning experiences in out-of-school contexts, taking their voices, their cultural spaces, and their literacies underground, to that place I call "a culture of refusal."

QUESTIONS TO CONSIDER

1. The author claims that traditional psychological theories have failed to provide adequate socio-cultural perspectives on adolescent development. How convincing is her argument? Why or why not?

2. What is meant by "a national crisis of boyhood"? If true, what has contributed to that "crisis"? How valid is the assessment of the purported "crisis?"

3. In what ways have economic, social, and political inequities affected violent youth behavior? Give examples.

4. Has the transition from "junior high school" to "middle school" effected significant change in adolescent development? Why or why not?

5. How does "cultural compatibility theory" explain the dissonance in youths' daily lives, both in and out of school? How do race, class, and gender contexts contribute to that theory?

This chapter originally appeared in Shirley R. Steinberg and Joe L. Kincheloe (eds.), *19 Urban Questions: Teochlng in the City* (New York, Peter Lang, 2007).

References

Ayers, W. (1997). *A kind and just parent: The children of juvenile court.* Boston, MA: Beacon Press.

Belenky, M.F., Clinchy, B.M., Goldberger, N.R. & Tarule, J.M. (1986). *Women's ways of knowing: The development of self, voice, and mind.* New York: Basic Books.

Brown, L.M. & Gilligan, C. (1992). *Meeting at the crossroads: Women's psychology and girls' development.* Cambridge, MA: Harvard University Press.

Dryfoos, J. (1990). *Adolescents at risk.* New York: Oxford University Press.

Erickson, E. (1963). *Childhood and society.* New York: Norton.

Erickson, E. (1968). *Identity: Youth and crisis.* New York: Norton.

Faludi, S. (1999). *Stiffed: The betrayal of the American man.* New York: Morrow & Co.

Ferrell, J. (1997). *Youth, crime, and cultural space.* Social Justice, 24, 4, 21–38.

Fine, M. (1987). *Silencing in the public schools.* Language Arts, 64, 157–175.

Fine, M. (1991). *Framing dropouts.* Albany, NY: SUNY Press.

Freud, S. (1978). *Basic works of Sigmund Freud.* Franklin Center, PA: The Franklin Library.

Garbarino, J. (1999). *Lost boys: Why our sons turn violent and how we can save them.* New York: Free Press.

Gilbert, P. & Taylor, S. (1991). *Fashioning the feminine: Girls, popular culture, and schooling.* North Sydney, Australia: Allen & Unwin.

Gilbert, P. (1989). *Writing, schooling, and deconstruction: From voice to text in the classroom.* London: Routledge.

Gilligan, C. (1982). *In a different voice: Psychological theory and women's development.* Cambridge, MA: Harvard University Press.

Gilligan, C. (1990). *Teaching Shakespeare's sister: Notes from the underground of female adolescence.* In Gilligan, C., Lyons, N.P., & Hanmer, T. J. (Eds.), Making connections: The relational worlds of adolescent girls at Emma Willard School. Cambridge, MA: Harvard University Press.

Hall, S. H. (1999) *The troubled life of boys: The bully in the mirror.* (August, 22). The New York Times Magazine. Pp. 31–35.

Heath, S. B. (1983). *Ways with words: Language, life, and work in communities and classrooms.* New York: Cambridge University Press.

Hechinger, F.M. (1993). *Schools for teenagers: A historic dilemma.* In Takanishi, R. (Ed.) Adolescence in the 1990's: Risk and opportunity. New York: Teachers College Press.

Jipson, J., Munro, P., Victor, S., Froude Jones, K., Freed Rowland, G. (1995). *Repositioning feminism and education: Perspectives on educating for social change.* Westport, CT: Bergin & Garvey.

Kaplan, L. J. (1984). *Adolescence: The farewell to childhood.* New York: Simon & Schuster.

Kohlberg. L. (1981). *The philosophy of moral development: Moral stages and the idea of justice.* San Francisco: Harper & Row.

Kohlberg, L. (1987). *Child psychology and childhood education: A cognitive-developmental view.* New York: Longman.

Phelan, P., Davidson, A.L. & Yu, H.C. (1998). *Adolescents' worlds: Negotiating family, peers, and school.* New York: Teachers College Press.

Pleck, J. H. (1988). *1988 Survey of adolescent males.* Urbana-Champaign: University of Illinois.

Pollack, W. (1998). *Real boys: Rescuing our sons from the myths of boyhood.* NY: Henry Holt.

Real, T. (1997). *I don't want to talk about it: Overcoming the secret legacy of male depression.* New York: Scribner.

Straus, M.B. (1994). *Violence in the lives of adolescents.* New York: Norton.

Takanishi, R. (Ed.) (1993). *Adolescence in the 1990's: Risk and Opportunity.* New York: Teachers College Press.

Traub, J. (2000). *Schools are not the answer: What no school can do.* (January). The New York Times Magazine. 52-57, 68, 81, 90, 91.

Trueba, Guthrie, & Au, K. (1981). (Eds.) *Culture and bilingual education: Studies in classroom ethnography.* Rowley, MA. Newbury House Publishers.

CHAPTER TWO

Who Is Included in the Urban Family?

KATIA GOLDFARB

The *ideal* family conjures up an image of a mom, a dad, and two children—preferably, one boy and one girl, in that order. As we continue conjuring, we envision a stylish home surrounded by trees and, of course, enclosed in a white picket fence. The mother has a career, but she has chosen to stay home until the children grow up. Her position will be waiting when and if she decides to go back to work. The father happily leaves for the commute to his job every morning, as part of his conscious decision; life in the city is not the best environment to raise a family.

Families who have the economic resources to entertain this decision are the only ones who can fulfill the above mythical image of family living. Urban families are either wealthy enough to offer their members the necessary experiences to compensate for the suburban context, such as private schools, periodic vacations, and modern and spacious apartments, or they are stuck with life in the city as their only viable option. In this chapter, I will describe some of the most crucial contextual issues affecting urban families with children of low socioeconomic status and limited formal education.

The Pathologization of Families from Minority Groups

One of the most important of these contextual issues involves the right-wing pathologization of urban families of minority groups. Deploying the concept of "family values," right-wing operatives have argued that there is little we can do for urban students because they come from pathological families. The urban student signified in such representations is, of course, of color. This is accompanied by a concurrent deployment of the concept of "urban troubles," used to signal the existence of gargantuan unsolvable problems in contemporary cities. The causes of these insurmountable problems involve the demographic changes of the last 40 years. As nonwhites constituted a larger percentage of urban dwellers, they began to manifest their own family pathologies. Along with these domestic people of color, a rash of non-European immigrants (so proclaim right-wing leaders) have brought family pathologies with them to American cities that "threaten the historic identity of the United States as a 'European' country, thus endangering the country's 'character' and 'value structure'" (Bennett, Dilulio, Jr., and Walters, 1996). Thus, urban institutions such as schooling were pathologized by "these people."

In this right-wing world, crime is caused by this degraded family life, not by poverty. Thus, political and educational policies in this ideological construct see no reason to address poverty or formulate attempts to alleviate it. The best thing we can do is to bring pathological family members to Christ, many conservative politicos argue. Through Him we can restore family values and begin the process of improving urban family life for poor people and especially poor people of color. Until such salvation occurs, however, right-wing analysts such as William Bennett, John Dilulio Jr., and John Walters maintain that urban areas and their schools will be victimized by ultraviolent superpredators, the worst criminals any society has ever known. As Cornel West (1993) argues, the right-wing's use of terms such as *superpredator* and *feral, presocial beings* caters to the worst types of racial prejudice found in the United States. What is wrong with African American and Latino families, these critics contend, is a manifestation of moral poverty. Moral poverty causes criminal behavior—a tautology that can be neither proved nor disproved. The only thing virtuous white people can do in this circumstance is to punish perpetrators—lock 'em up and throw away the key in "three strikes and you're out" policies or execute them. Moral poverty is an excellent twenty-first-century way to say that the bad parenting of black and Latino parents causes socially irresponsible behavior (Bennett, Dilulio, Jr., and Walters, 1996).

In this explosive context, the pathologization of the family is central to the right-wing position. Morally impoverished black and Latino superpredators have never been exposed to loving parents who can teach them good from evil, to stay away from drugs, or to resist violence. This family collapse is a single-bullet theory of urban minority poverty and school failure. Bombarded by such crypto-racism, many educators have been induced to complain: "How can we teach these children when their parents don't care about them?" Unfortunately, many white middle- and upper-middle-class Americans don't know very much about their poor nonwhite fellow countrymen and countrywomen. As an example, contemporary popular wisdom fueled by right-wing talk shows and think tanks posits that poor minority women produce huge numbers of "illegitimate" babies. Actually, birth rates among single African American women, for example, over the last three decades have fallen by 13 percent. Incidentally, during the same decades, the birth rates for single white women increased 27 percent. Such data might induce right-wing spokespeople to tone down their descriptions of black mothers living in poverty as "brood mares" and "welfare queens" (Coontz, 1992).

As the rate of financial polarization grew in the last portion of the twentieth century, of course problems emerged in poor urban neighborhoods that worry all of us. Violence is of concern to all Americans, though African American and Latino poor suffer far more than anyone else. The right-wing effort to lay the cause of such problems exclusively at the doorstep of the alleged moral poverty of urban nonwhite people with their broken families, high divorce rates, unwed pregnancies, family violence, and drug and alcohol abuse is misleading. In this context, Joe Kincheloe (1999) argues:

The same problems confront families whose members serve as police officers or in the military, yet most Americans refrain from blaming them for their dysfunctionality. Typically, we have little trouble understanding that the context in which police officers and soldiers operate is in part responsible for such pathologies. Work stress from danger and conflict can produce devastating results. With this in mind, it is not difficult to imagine the stress that accompanies living for just one week in an inner-city war zone. Now imagine living there with no hope of getting out. (p. 243)

The right-wing view of poor urban African American and Latino families as corrupt and morally bankrupt is not the only perspective on this matter. Many educators, sociologists, and urban studies scholars argue that such families are often very resilient, hard working, and self-sufficient, are in possession of loving kinship networks, and value education for their children (Hill, 2003). Many researchers have pointed to the strength of the extended African American family, for example (Wicker, 1996; Ashworth, 1997). The power of such families often succeeds in maintaining the lives of its individual members despite overwhelming problems and travails. To not understand the ways that cousins, grandparents, great-grandparents, aunts, and uncles provide support when times are bad is to miss a profound dimension of urban black family life. Thus, there is a dialectic of strength and weakness of African American and other poor urban families from minority groups in contemporary America. It would be misguided to argue that racism, class bias, and the ravages of poverty do not tear the fabric of such families and create profound problems for them. Concurrently, it is amazing how the inner strengths of urban minority families work to help their members persevere in spite of some extremely difficult situations.

Urban Families in Historical Context

As with any other family, urban families interact with their natural and human-built environments. Their lives are affected by the available emotional and material resources. They have to interrelate with their immediate context such as extended family, workplace, school, welfare system, and health system. They have to coordinate communication between these organizations. Their lives are influenced by policy and laws often endorsed by politicians far removed from their realities. And every day, they have to fight against the negative image held by mainstream society of low-income urban families.

The creation of this particular group of families can be traced to the capitalistic industrialization of the United States following the American Civil War. The Industrial Revolution brought a reorganization of work. Different social groups had access to different jobs that held extremely different statuses and earning possibilities. The national economy moved from the traditional colonial agricultural family-based system to a wage economy. An increasing number of goods and services were produced and rendered outside the family.

Rural migrants and high numbers of European immigrants settled in cities growing around mill towns, steam- and later oil- and electricity-powered factories, and sweatshops. Within this process, a middle class based on ownership of business and industry and a working class based on low-pay and low-status jobs were created. These economic and social changes were lived very differently by varied groups. Slave society developed into a distinctive African American culture, and Native Americans have had numerous structures of family living. These groups did not share the same context as that of the old and new European immigration. However, the ideal image of the family, even though its origin can be found in the patriarchal structure of the New England colonies, is still regarded as the family form to be used in judging any other form of family living.

As cities grew, families who had the economic resources started to migrate out of the urban areas in search of what was called a "better standard of living." The odors, noises, crowds, limited personal space, traffic, and what was defined as low educational standards were among the issues used as reasons to leave the cities and build more homogeneous, stable, and private communities. The new immigrants and the working poor remained.

Parallel to these economic and social changes, the roles within the family were also reorganized. A clear differentiation between the private and public worlds was created in which the private/family domain belonged to the woman and the public/work domain belonged to the man. Working-class women and children from poor families did not have the privileges these developments were offering (Chavkin, 1993; Cherlin, 1988; Redding & Thomas, 2001).

In the present times, there are additional social forces influencing families and individuals. There is a growing production of new technologies that is changing the economy to a service / information-based system. The United States is rapidly pressing for a global economy. Big corporations are merging and/or relocating and/or investing outside the country. Lastly, there is a growing trend in which corporations are shifting from manufacturing to being knowledge-based institutions. Within these processes, low-income urban families with children are facing bigger and more rapid social and economic changes. Their situation is aggravated by specific issues influencing their daily live. Some of these areas are: increasing and permanent poverty, medical care, overcrowding, mobility and loss of extended family network, immigration, language, diversity in family structure, work/family influences, violence, stress, environmental problems, access to cultural life and enrichment activities, the family/school relationship, and, of course, the class and race issues previously discussed (Ruiz-de-Velasco & Fix, 2000; Delgado-Gaitan, 2001).

The Wages of Poverty

The lack of economic resources greatly impacts the dynamics of urban families. There is a constant struggle for the basic necessities. Since the working adults are dependent on weekly or monthly wages, any drastic change in the economy will have immediate repercussions. These families may face fluctuating times when they will need government assistance, requiring from them the use of their time and energy to access the necessary services. By having very limited job opportunities, children and adults will have extremely low possibilities of receiving adequate and continuous medical care. The prompt diagnosis of chronic illness will be hindered. The implications of a deteriorating health status for the responsible adult(s) will create a vicious and difficult-to-break cycle in which unemployment becomes a regular part of living. As for the children, research has shown that one of the most important issues affecting readiness to learn is the nutrition and health status of the child. Families in turn rely on the emergency room for medical care.

Overcrowding has been a constant issue in urban settings, whether it is within the household or as part of city life. Immigrant families especially find themselves sharing small physical spaces. In the attempt to help family or members of the community, people will be willing to sacrifice their personal space in the assumption that more economic resources will open up for the family system. In situations like this, there may be growing frictions among members and increasing frustration. Outside the household, cities also feel crowded. There are fewer and smaller public spaces. There are fewer and smaller natural spaces. Buildings are tall, imposing, cluttered in repetition. The feeling as you walk through the city is that you are moving within a contingency of people.

As economic and living issues become increasingly problematic, family members may decide to move in search of better job opportunities. Working-class families have relied on extended-family members for child care, economic help, and emotional support. Extended family is a crucial resource for the sustainability of low-income urban families and the well-being of the children (Ruiz-de-Velasco & Fix, 2000; Trumbull, Rothstein-Fish, Greenfield, and Quiroz, 2001).

Immigration and Language in Urban Family Life

Immigration and language are becoming increasingly crucial areas in understanding urban families. Immigration is one of the most important economic and social changes. The current immigration is influencing society not only because of its numbers but also because of its diversity. As in the past, new immigrants tend to settle in established communities of people from their own national origin. This traditional trend influences issues such as access to education, availability of jobs where fluency in English is not required, and the offering of basic services (such as health care, education) in the appropriate language. The issue of immigration has been part of the antagonism between minority groups struggling for the same scarce resources. Division and hostility are also part of the problematic between immigrants and the powerful mainstream society. They challenge the exclusive ownership and access to social goods.

One hundred years ago, 90 percent of immigration to the United States was from European countries; today, 90 percent is from non-European, mainly Latin American and Asian, countries. Therefore, there are going to be drastic changes on the face of the nation. This increases the number of U.S. residents who are foreign born and also the number of their children. Currently, in major urban settings like New York, Los Angeles, and Chicago, minority groups make up the majority in numbers but not in sociopolitical power. The United States is witnessing birth rates of racial minorities increase faster than that of the majority population. In the year 2000, Latinos outnumbered African Americans. It is clear that immigration is one of the most important issues facing major metropolitan areas.

For families, immigration implies a series of social, economic, and familial adjustments. Immigrants are entering the country in a moment of economic difficulties. There are fewer jobs available, and social and economic mobility will not be as easy as it was for prior waves of immigrants. Since the current immigration is not from European countries, new arrivals will face social and institutional discrimination. Immigrants will face the option to blend in as soon as possible, reject the dominant culture, increase and strength ethnic ties, or develop bicultural or multicultural forms of family and community living (Kincheloe & Steinberg, 1997; Dickinson & Tabors, 2001).

Different Types of Families

Currently in the United States there is an increase in the diversity of family structures. As with any other group, low-income urban families are also facing an increase in the number of family structures that do not resemble the ideal image. There are single-parent houses with different custody arrangements; homes in which the parent has remained single by choice or as the result of divorce, separation, or death; families with two cohabitating adults and children; multi-generational families; two-parent homes of same-sex couples. There may be members of the extended family or of another, unrelated family living in the house. There are families with one child and families with many children. The low-income urban family with children is not a monolith or beyond the diversity of family structure, and we find urban families from bicultural or multicultural backgrounds.

Work/family influences are also shared by any family who has at least one member in the workforce. Low-income urban families with children face the increasing need to find permanent and well-paying jobs. Some families have to resort to two jobs, which may mean leaving the children alone for longer periods of time. There are going to be increased challenges for the adults in trying to keep up with different sets of work-related expectations. The majority of the time, the jobs that adults from low-income urban families can find are not personally satisfying. They are usually labor intensive, not stimulating, and low-paying, which only aggravates an already stressful situation. The mother or father will have a stronger probability of carrying his or her frustration from one world to the other (Grigorenko & Sternberg, 2001).

Families and Violence

Violence is an endemic problem facing low-income urban families. There is violence at the institutional level. Minority groups (ethnic/racial, gender, age, sexual orientation, social class) face constant violence in our social institutions: such as the legal system, in which African Americans are disproportionately incarcerated; the schools, where children are labeled "slow learners" because they do not speak English; and government organizations whose policies exacerbate the struggles of families with small children to keep jobs and have their children in quality day care. Children are exposed to drugs, gang activity, alcohol, and homicides. These problems are not exclusive to poor neighborhoods, but when access to quality and appropriate education does not exist, when safety in these neighborhoods is not supported, and when you can make a lot more money selling drugs than going to school to get a high school diploma, the ground is fertile for the proliferation of violence.

Environmental Dimensions of Urban Family Life

As mentioned before, families are influenced by their natural environment. The access to clean water, clean air, peace and quiet, and open spaces should be a right for all human beings. As if low-income urban families with children do not have enough to contend with, their physical and natural environments add to the challenges. Usually, these families live in multistory or high-rise apartment buildings with numerous other families, with little or no recreational space. Their neighborhoods are often located close to airports, busy intersections, commercial, and/or industrial zones, or neglected areas. Their apartments are often in need of repair. Children and adults are still exposed to lead-based paint. Buildings are not fumigated. These conditions prevent healthy development.

Access to Urban Educational and Cultural Resources

Minority and low socioeconomic status also hinders access to entertainment and enrichment activities. Shows, restaurants, movies, plays, museums are often beyond the economic reach of low-income urban families, even though they may live just a few blocks from them. All the extracurricular activities that enrich the education and the cognitive, emotional, and physical development of children may be out of reach for urban families with tight budgets unless the services are provided by a community center and sponsored by local or federal funds. Children and parents from all socioeconomic backgrounds are interested in meaningful and accessible experiences offering the optimal environment for growth.

Right-Wing Subversion: Efforts to Help Urban Families Undermined by Family-Values Ideology

All of these urban family issues are colored by the right-wing ideology of family values, with its pathologization of poor families of color. Such a way of seeing maintains that all the social and educational programs in the world cannot help such families. This is the same argument made by Richard Herrnstein and Charles Murray in *The Bell Curve*—poor people of color are genetically inferior, lacking intelligence and moral fiber, and are thus beyond salvation. We do not need more money to help them, the argument goes; they need simply to acquire more family values (SOCQRL, 2003). Indeed, in the right-wing ideological universe, it is assumed that poor black and Latino parents don't want to work to provide for their families and thus don't merit help.

In addition, the conservative use of the "absence of family values" argument has served as a convenient smoke screen to obscure the public's view of the poverty caused by free-market economics over the last 25 years. Using a "politics of nostalgia," the right wing has successfully reconstructed America's view of its family history. The perspective paints a misleading picture of a past in which extended families worked together, pious mothers protected little boys and girls from exposure to adult issues, virginal newlyweds consummated their marriages after religious nuptials, and faithful husbands devoted much of their time to familial needs (Kincheloe, 1999).

The legislation that has come out of this right-wing ideology has exerted a negative effect on the efficacy of urban families of color over the last couple of decades. The welfare reform legislation of the 1990s limited aid to the poorest families to merely five years in a lifetime and required mothers to work in order to get any assistance—even mothers with babies as young as three months. Education and job training for poor mothers are discouraged in this legislation, and states have the prerogative to deny aid for a wide range of reasons. Because of these stipulations, poor women have been forced to take low-paying, dead-end jobs instead of improving their education (Stafford, Salas, Mendez, & Dews, 2003). As poor women take these jobs, they enter into a vicious circle. Child care is hard to find in poor urban communities—especially high-quality child care (Covington Cox, 2003). Mothers who choose to stay at home with their children have their benefits cut off, while those who take jobs often face the prospect of having to leave children alone at certain times. These mothers are often charged with child neglect.

Another result of the right-wing legislation has been the rise in the numbers of poor urban African American women and Latinas in prison. Right-wing drug policies have placed disproportionate numbers of poor urban African American and Latino men and women in prison—this taking place while there is no evidence of higher rates of illegal drug use by this population. In this context we are struck by statistics such as the rate of drug-related imprisonment of black and Latino males being 30 to 40 times higher than that for white males (Drucker, 2003). The effect of this mass incarceration on poor urban black and Latino families is devastating. The sponsors and supporters of the legislation responsible for these outcomes have expressed little concern for the families affected by mothers and fathers in jail. Prisoners' families must get by any way they can. Drucker (2003) concludes that the mental and physical health of families of prisoners is so damaged that the very conditions that create the tendency toward crime are exacerbated. Such legislation serves to devalue families in the name of family values. Teachers in schools in low-socioeconomic urban areas will be forced to deal with the damage caused by such social policies, as poor children of color may be the ones most victimized by such draconian measures.

Conclusion: Poor Urban Families Face Great Challenges

The above descriptions are only some of the issues that low-income urban families with children face. High levels of stress are a constant in all of these areas. Stress influences all aspects of human development. It impacts our physical and emotional health. It can serve as an impediment to self and family realization. Natural and adequate levels of stress should help us perform better. Excessive stressors tend to result in crisis, and if the appropriate material and emotional resources (existing and new) are not available, family living is disrupted.

The family/school relationship is a common experience for all families with children. In the specific case of low-income urban families, the issues presented above permeate the context of this relationship. The quantity and, most important, quality of interaction between schools and families directly influence the development of children. It has been documented that a positive communication between schools and families improves students' achievement, especially in families from minority and immigrant groups. Although there are political, ideological, theoretical, and practical differences in the ways the partnership between schools and families is carried out, this relationship is a recurrent theme in educational reform.

The issues affecting schooling, the role of the family, and the family's relation to formal education have taken many permutations. We have defined the role of the family as "the enemy," in which parents, family, and guardians are to be blamed for everything that goes wrong with the children. We have relegated their participation to fund-raising by allowing families to be involved within the schools as long as they keep their participation connected to bringing material goods. Educational and curriculum issues are viewed as the prerogative of the experts, teachers, and school administrators.

The type of family involvement is directly connected to the school's tacit and explicit policies, which are usually supported by district policies. Regardless of the rules and regulations set by the decision makers, access to information and extent of family involvement depend on the openness of the school to maintain a genuine dialogue with families for the benefit of the children. If we continue basing the need for family involvement in school on the sole concern of improving students' academic achievement, we are in danger of removing parents from helping in problems to whose solutions they can contribute the most.

Research suggests that there is nothing to lose and everything to gain from mandating and implementing school/family partnerships. It has been found that standardized test scores are higher. In terms of family outcomes, there is evidence of a more positive self-concept, acquisition of skills, and positive attitudes. Also, such a partnership affects the school and school district by showing an increase in student attendance and reductions in the rates of dropout, delinquency, and teen pregnancy. The responsibility for educating the children should be shared. None of the current social institutions can carry out alone the enormous challenge of educating the future generation. For example, if it is not demanded that businesses (particularly those offering low-paying, low-status jobs) enact flexible and family-friendly policies, society cannot blame mothers and fathers for neglecting their children. Families are not able to attend parent/teacher conferences and other school-based activities because such attendance usually involves losing a day's pay—an unacceptable outcome for poor families.

In the context of immigrant families, it has been found that language and prior experiences are the real reasons for lower levels of family involvement. The majority of our urban children are being educated by middle-class white female teachers who often do not speak the students' language(s). Such families get the hidden message that they are not important in the formal educational process of their children. A common practice in schools is to use the children as translators for their parents and in family interactions at school—by so doing, research shows, there is a potential for conflict in the role reversal between children and adults and the perception that cultural practices are not being respected by school personnel. Another barrier to immigrant families' involvement in schools is the lack of understanding of the American educational system. Immigrants are neither tutored nor expected to become active decision makers in the process of schooling their children. Another reason for the ostensible lack of involvement is that different cultural practices give to the teacher the honor of establishing communication, as the expert (Hiatt-Michael, 2001).

Most of the adult immigrants in low-income urban families were not able to go to school past the third grade. They feel that they do not have the knowledge or the language skills to engage in meaningful communication with the teachers and school administrators. It has been found that often, the school administrators and teachers view such parents' absence from the school as a lack of interest in the education of their children (Britto and Brooks-Gunn, 2001).

Educators at all levels should be trained to understand the importance of working *with* and not *on* the community and the families. Families should be seen as equal partners in the education of their children. Their voices should be heard and respected. We live in difficult times of war, economic troubles, violence, racism, class bias, and terrorism. As educators, we are not sufficiently prepared to recognize and deal with the overwhelming influence that social, cultural, and linguistic contexts have in the life of our children. We need families and communities to face the challenges of educating the next generation.

This chapter originally appeared in Shirley R. Steinberg and Joe L. Kincheloe (eds.), *19 Urban Questions: Teachlng in the City* (New York: Peter Lang, 2007).

References

(Websites accessed November 18, 2003)

Ashworth, Pam (1997). POS334-L: The race and ethnicity book review discussion list. [Book review of *Tragic failure: Racial integration in America*]. http://lilt.ilstu.edu/gmklass/pos334/ archive/wicker.htm

Bennett, William J. & Dilulio, Jr., John & Walters, John. (1996) *Body Count: Moral Poverty and How to Win America's War Against Crime and Drugs.* Simon and Schuster.

Britto, Pia Rebello, & Brooks-Gunn, Jeanne (Eds.) (2001). *The role of family literacy environments in promoting young children's emerging literacy skills.* San Francisco: Jossey-Bass.

Chavkin, Nancy F. (1993). *Families and schools in a pluralistic society.* Albany: State University of New York Press.

Cherlin, Andrew J. (Ed.) (1988). *The changing American family and public policy.* Washington, DC: Urban Institute Press.

Coontz, Stephanie (1992). *The way we never were: American families and the nostalgia trap.* New York: Basic Books.

Covington Cox, Kenya (2003). *The effect of childcare imbalance on the labor force participation of mothers residing in highly urban-poor counties.* http://www.nul.org/documents/ all_abstracts.doc

Delgado-Gaitan, Concha (2001). *The power of community: Mobilizing for family and schooling.* Lanham, MD: Rowman and Littlefield Publishers.

Dickinson, David K., & Tabors, Patton O. (Ed.) (2001). *Beginning literacy with language: Young children learning at home and school.* Baltimore: P. H. Brookes Publishing.

Drucker, Ernest M. (2003). *The impact of mass incarceration on public health in black communities.* http://www.nul.org/ documents/all_abstracts.doc

Grigorenko, Elena L., & Sternberg, Robert J. (Eds.) (2001). *Family environment and intellectual functioning: A life-space perspective.* Mahwah, NJ: Lawrence Erlbaum Associates.

Hiatt-Michael, Diana B. (Ed.) (2001). *Promising practices for family involvement in school.* Greenwich, CT: Information Age Publishing.

Hill, Robert B. (2003). The strengths of black families revisited. http://www.nul.org/documents/ all_abstracts.doc

Kincheloe, Joe L. (1999). *How do we tell the workers? The socioeconomic foundations of work and vocational education.* Boulder, CO: Westview.

Kincheloe, Joe L., & Steinberg, Shirley (1997). *Changing multiculturalism.* Buckingham (UK) and Philadelphia: Open University Press.

Redding, Sam, & Thomas Lori G. (Eds.) (2001). *The community of the school.* Lincoln, IL: Academic Development Institute.

Ruiz-de-Velasco, Jorge, & Fix, Michael (2000). *Overlooked and underserved: Immigrant students in U.S. secondary schools.* Washington, DC: Urban Institute.

SOCQRL [Sociology Quantitative Research Laboratory] (2003). *Cycle of unequal opportunity.* http://www.socqrl. niu.edu/forest/SOCI270/UequalCycle.html

Stafford, Walter; Salas, Diana; Mendez, Melissa, & Dews, Angela (2003). *Race, gender and welfare reform: The need for targeted support.* http://www.nul.org/documents/all_abstracts.doc

Trumbull, Elise; Rothstein-Fish, Carrie; Greenfield, Patricia; & Quiroz, Blanca (2001). *Bridging cultures between home and school: A guide for teachers: With a special focus on immigrant Latino families.* Mahwah, NJ: Lawrence Erlbaum Associates.

West, Cornel (1993). Race Matters. New York: Vintage Books.

Wicker, Tom (1996). *Tragic failure: Racial integration in America.* New York: William Morrow and Co.

QUESTIONS TO CONSIDER

1. What does Goldfarb mean by the "pathologization of the urban family"? She claims that such a portraiture is central to conservative assaults on low-income groups. Do you agree or disagree with her assessment? Why?

2. How does low socio-economic status affect how families live on a daily basis? Give examples.

3. How can linguistic differences and immigration influence how low-income families cope with changing cultural and social circumstances? Give examples.

4. Goldfarb lists several examples of diverse family structures in the United States. What are some of those different compositions, and how do they affect individual families?

5. The author contends that low-income urban families face unusual levels of violence and environmental difficulties. Give examples of those problems.

6. How has governmental policy been detrimental to urban families over the past several decades? Explain your response.

7. What can be done to assure greater school success for youth coming from low-income backgrounds? Give reasons and examples to support your case.

CHAPTER THREE

"Who You Think I Am Is Not Necessarily Who I Think I Am"

The Multiple Positionalities of Urban Student Identities

REBECCA A. GOLDSTEIN

Introduction

"There are a lot of stereotypes out there right now. And when you fit a stereotype, you are really not given a chance for people to find out who you are just because they look at your skin color. And a lot of opportunities, you do not get to have because people look at your skin color" (Gina, age 14).

When I first met Gina, she was a ninth-grade student attending a large comprehensive high school in a mid-sized city in the northeastern United States.[1] Like many of her peers, Gina struggled with different aspects of who she was, not just because she had recently entered a new school, but because she was also acutely aware of how others—peers, adults, and the wider community—viewed her and made decisions about who she was. Gina was trying to figure it out for herself, to become somebody who she wanted to be, in spite of what was going on around her and who others expected her to be. However, she was frustrated because she encountered many assumptions about who she was because of her race, gender, and the community from which she came. People assumed who she was before they got to know her and expected somebody very different from the intelligent, thoughtful, goal-oriented young woman she was.

Too often when people conduct research on adolescent identity, they view high schools as logical places in which to collect their data. On the surface it makes sense to conduct research in such a manner, because one is then able to work with a population of young people who are more or less held captive by societal norms and expectations about who they are and how they behave, and what role public schooling ought to play in creating active American citizens out of them.[2] But there is also a corresponding danger, particularly for students of color and other marginalized groups, because of who ultimately benefits from such research.[3] What happens when researchers use the high school as a mere repository of adolescent bodies from which to collect data without exploring the complex set of meanings that students construct about and for themselves and others within the physical confines of school? And, perhaps more important-ly, what do researchers overlook when they expect to see a certain set of behaviors or meanings associated with adolescent identity development and only look for those constructs? What hap-pens when one strips data of the subjective positions—the lived experiences of race, class, gen-der, sexuality, language, and culture—of students and others and use it to define who young people are? The most important question of all: What happens to students like Gina?

Such questions are particularly important for those who work with urban students and com-munities. Regardless of whether we (e.g., those who work with urban students) are from those communities or not, learning to listen to urban students, and expanding our own understand-ings of how they come to understand who they are in (and in spite of) the world requires us to acknowledge the complexity of how people come to understand themselves. This chapter will illustrate how one might read adolescent development and identity formation differently to explore how urban students might construct identities for themselves. How we do so involves moving away from the modern concept of universalism, to a critical understanding of culture and identities in which we recognize positionality in such a way that understanding adolescence involves a much closer examination of how urban young people become the people they are. Positionality refers to people's many subjectivities in action, and concerns how people engage in the lived experiences/subjective positions of race, class, gender, sexuality, physical ability, etc. Doing so enables us to move beyond seeing urban student identity development as being deviant or oppositional, to seeing it as strategic and empowering in light of the political and power strug-gles in which young people engage.

Universalist Theories and Identity Construction

When many people think about adolescence, they envision a time of turbulent emotions, phys-ical and emotional changes, and a stage that young people must simply get through in order to become healthy, normal adults. Theories that posit that young people must move through var-ious stages successfully on their way to becoming individuated adults are referred to as stage the-ories, and have become among the most common and powerful ways that many people understand how adolescent development occurs.[4] Nakkula's discussion of Erickson's theory of psychosocial development is particularly useful here. Erickson's theory of psychosocial develop-ment posits that people's identities are formed as a result of experiencing and successfully rec-onciling crisis (or not). Further, as Nakkula points out, Erickson views development as a process that occurs across the life span, from birth to adulthood, so that quite literally "adolescence pro-vides that best last chance to rework some of the prior crises, and thus reset the course for pos-itive subsequent development."[5]

Erikson's contribution to psychology and education represents a theoretical model that holds universalism as a fundamental lens through which one ought to view the world. Universalism implies that what is good for one person is good for everyone, and what holds true for one individual or a group holds true for everyone else. In addition, what people come to know and understand about others and themselves is independent of place and time. As a result of this modernist belief in universalism, people have conducted research on identity development looking to confirm that young people do, in fact, pass through various uniform stages to become normal, healthy adults. Once they draw and apply their conclusions to all groups, researchers then conduct additional research to examine those who do not fall into the normal ranges of development, and pose ways to remediate, that is fix, those who fail to develop normally.[6]

Of particular concern regarding the universalist approach to adolescent identity development is the notion that people can apply what they have learned from one group of young people to all other young people because adolescent identity formation is viewed to be culturally and politically, and value neutral. Identity research in the first half of the twentieth century was conducted on populations of middle-class boys of European descent, and even though other groups did not share the same cultural and social (racial, socio-economic, and gender-based) experiences, researchers believed their findings and theoretical views could and should be applied to all groups. The result? Individuals or groups who did not fit the models evolving from this research were labeled deviant, abnormal, and in need of remediation, whether through education or psychological intervention. In other words, because the universalist approach to identity formation excludes things like race, class, gender, sexuality, and culture (because it views those differences as inconsequential), people who do not fit the norm (e.g., white, middle-class, heterosexual, Western European male) may fail to develop healthy identities from this perspective.

As a result, places like school have evolved to ensure that students develop "normally."[7] But, how do we define "normal"? Those who work in schools have been historically expected to prepare students to become active members of society. Coincidentally, students are not only expected to acquire attributes to maintain the status quo in society, but also to ensure that universalist theories of development and identity construction remain the defining concepts used to construct who is normal or deviant. For urban adolescents who do not fit the middle class, male of European descent profile mentioned above, constructing one's identity can be problematic. In many cases, urban adolescents are expected to assimilate the values, behaviors, and norms that the dominant society espouses.[8] These values, behaviors, and norms reflect the interests of a predominantly white, middle-class, heterosexual masculine society. Simultaneously, these norms construct who people ought to and ought not to be, as well as what their place in society will be.

If we return to Gina, the young woman to whom I referred at the beginning, the dominant culture and society expected her to fit a stereotype: to be poor, ignorant, a high school dropout, pregnant, and a drain on society—all because she was a fourteen-year-old black girl from the inner city. However, the sum of who Gina was and what she was becoming was much more than a stereotype. Not only was she aware of that, but she was also aware of how complex it all was.

> [Stereotypes make] them (black students) feel like there is nothing better to do. If they (whites and people outside of the city) are saying that about us, we might as well live up to that stereotype, which is like the most stupidest thing to think. You should never prove somebody right when you know they are wrong. If you just prove them right, then that just means you have no self-esteem for yourself or for anyone else. Because it's bad enough that the media is, what's the word . . . is exaggerating the facts, and then you gotta come and live up to them. That makes it even more ridiculous, and makes yourself look bad.

What options does a universal theory of adolescent development and identity present urban youths like Gina? Gina's statement captures the conflicts that students of color from urban communities struggle with on a daily basis when they are boxed into or box themselves into a universalist perspective. They have the either/or choice of assimilating into the dominant group in terms of behavior and norms (though they will never "look like" those of the dominant group), or they can resist and develop an oppositional culture.[9] Through such resistance, students may construct identities that are self-affirming; however, these same identities may further marginalize them from the mainstream. And, depending on which avenue they choose, urban adolescents may be seen as not quite a member of the dominant group or sell-outs within their home communities.

Breaking Away from the Stereotypes: Critical Identities in Action

The interplay between stereotypes and the beliefs and actions of urban students is an example of how urban students come to support and perpetuate the struggle between dominant class ideas, and struggle with those ideas on the part of those who are not part of the dominant class. This is because the common sense ideas and beliefs, or ideologies, that groups have about themselves and others are believed to be natural and simply a function of the ways things are.[10] And, because they are common sense, many people accept an ideological position as a natural truth because they do not consciously think about it or where it comes from. Gina recognized that students "living up to that stereotype" were examples of such buy-in and lack of awareness of an ideology, even though it ultimately hurt the student. However, according to Gina, living up to such an expectation was also a matter of poor self-esteem or having no self-respect, which, on a certain level, is also an ideological belief. In Gina's mind, if students only felt better about themselves, things would be OK. Thus, Gina felt that students themselves were in part responsible for the perpetuation of such stereotypes as well as the unequal treatment minorities received. So, even as she recognized how larger social forces shaped her experiences and how people viewed students like her, Gina still relied on many of those common sense beliefs that defined who she and her peers were and ought to be.

Another ninth-grade student, Jen, provided a provocative example of how complicated it can be when stereotypes play out in the lives of urban youth. Jen played in a local youth basketball league during the high school off-season. To be a member, each woman had to "try-out," and was accepted based upon her ability to play. Once on the team, players were expected to maintain a strong academic record, or face removal. Playing on the team also meant a great deal of travel during the summer months and exposure to college scouts. Jen was the only member from the city on her team. In contrast, most of her teammates were from the outlying suburbs. When asked about her experiences on the traveling youth team, she related:

> So they ask me where I am from and I tell them "Urban." And they're like, "Oh you from Urban? You can't be playing on this team; you don't have the grades." And when I tell them I get good grades, and that I'm not a bad student they don't believe me . . . they think that because I'm black, all I can do is play ball. But that's not true. I'm smart. I get the grades. But they think that all I can do is play ball.

Jen's ability to play basketball was never questioned. She made the youth league team so she must be a competent, if not outstanding, player. And, this must be especially true because of the stereotypes about black athletes. Her academic abilities were in doubt, also because of the stereotypes of black athletes. Even after she told them that she was eligible to play on the team, they still doubted her, hinted that the league made an exception (e.g., she needed the "enriching experience") and allowed her to play even though she might not have been a good enough student. Regardless of their real academic and athletic ability, students like Jen were automatically constructed as deviant or deficient when it came to what others thought about them.

There were other ways in which Gina and Jen experienced stereotypes that affected their school experiences. Both women noted that in addition to being under suspicion when they played tournaments outside the city, their peers in school paid attention to their every move. Even as they were a source of pride for the school (the women's basketball team had a winning season), people were suspicious of their abilities *because they were girls*. Even though they were talented athletes, there was something decidedly not-girl-like about their abilities. You could not be good at sports and still be feminine.

> JEN: It's really frustrating because we are good, like better than we have been in a long time. And so, suddenly there's this rumor going around that we (the girls' team) are gay.
> RG: (REBECCA GOLDSTEIN) Why do you think people are spreading this rumor?
> JEN: I think the boys (team) be spreading it because they angry at us. They don't want us getting all the recognition here, so they are telling people we are gay.

Again, no one questioned their athletic ability; they attacked the women's sexuality, because real girls should not be able to play basketball better than the boys. Kimmel notes that this is one way that homophobia works to create fear in students. For male students, using homophobic language strips them of their masculinity, thus negating a large part of who they are.[11] For girls, such language functions essentially the same way. If a girl is good at sports, and is therefore not feminine, she cannot be a woman in the true sense of the word, no matter how she might try to navigate being an athlete and being feminine.[12] Like homophobia functions for boys, it did so for girls, creating for girls a fear of being called too masculine. The girls on the team could not be both good athletes and "good" girls (e.g., sexually appealing and thus, socially acceptable among their peers). Only the boys could be the athletic stars. The girls were supposed to watch and cheer on the boys, not infringe on a world normally relegated to male athletes.[13]

The rumors and stereotypes about the girls' basketball team had disastrous consequences for one of their teammates. Both Jen and Gina related that one young woman was sent to live with a relative when her mother heard about the rumor. It did not matter whether it was true or not. The rumor took on a life of its own:

> Gina: The girls on the basketball team have a reputation. They act a certain way. You know people say things like, "Look at her, she's on the basketball team, she dresses in baggy jeans, she acts that way." So she must be a certain way. She fits a stereotype.
> RG: What stereotype is that?
> Gina: Well, she must be bi- or gay.
> RG: Why?
> Gina: If you play basketball, and you dress in baggy clothes, and you're good on the court, they think, "Oh you dress like a boy, you act like a boy, you must be a dyke." Now, I wear the baggy jeans and shirts because they are comfortable. I know there are a lot of girls in this school that wear the tight jeans, the high heels, the shirt, and they're that way (a lesbian). But because they don't dress like a boy, nothing is said.

Gina once again referred to the notion of a stereotype, a category of meaning that functioned to produce her as someone she was not. Because some girls on the basketball team wore baggy clothes and were strong athletes, they did not "act" like girls (however it was that girls "were supposed to act"). Rather, because they were athletes, and dressed like boys, they must want to be a boy, or they must be gay (even if they were not).

Gina's above point is critical. Some of the girls on the team wore "fashion" that was symbolic within the peer community of what lesbians supposedly wore. That, combined with the fact that the women on the team were strong players, confirmed the stereotypes for others, true or not. However, Gina noted that there were a number of girls who dressed in tight jeans, high heels, and tight shirts, girls who dressed "like girls," and were gay, just as there were girls who dressed in baggy clothes who were not. However, they seemed to fall below the radar in many cases, or because they were not as high-profile as their athlete peers, they escaped the most vocal ridicule:

RG: Are there a lot of girls who are like that (e.g., lesbians) here?
Gina: There are some. But only the ones who dress like a boy are called 'dyke' and given a hard
             time.
RG: What about the stereotype of the team? Is that true?
Gina: Yeah, there are some, but there are lots who aren't.
RG: So you think that the way the girls dress has a lot to do with the way they are treated.
Gina: Yeah, if they dress like a boy, they are called out. But if they dress all feminine and like a girl
             nobody says anything to them.
RG: Because they fit the image of being a girl.
Gina: Yeah, so nobody really knows that they are into that.

Clearly, the relationship between fashion, sexuality, and athletics was not lost on the young women I interviewed. Whether they dressed like a "boy" in baggy clothes, or like a "girl" in tight jeans or a skirt, students like Jen and Gina noted that how girls dressed ended up representing gender roles and sexuality. Reflecting upon these two young women's comments, I am struck by how clearly they articulated the fact that students who "fit the image" (e.g., feminine, heterosexual woman) became that image and were able to "pass for straight." On the other hand, it did not matter whether a female student was gay or not, because if she was an athlete or dressed the part (in baggy clothes "like a lesbian"), her peers determined her identity based upon the stereotypes and ideologies regarding gender and sexuality. The girls who dressed like girls were not nearly as suspect and may have been safer from other students' harassment. How young people use the activities, symbols like clothing, music, technology, and positionality to define themselves come together not simply as a series of layers that create uniform and permanent identities. Rather, they are woven together with threads of contradictory meaning, power relationships, and ambivalence that ultimately shape the identity trajectories of urban adolescents' lives.

Reading Urban Adolescence Critically

If one were to continue an analysis of the above narrative from a universalist perspective, one might fail to consider the strategic and political aspects of identity formation that make up an important part of this conversation. Critical psychological perspectives enable those who work with young people to think about how students come to be the people they are in much more complex ways. At its most basic level, critical psychological theory acknowledges the influence of culture, power, and ideology, and challenges the universalist perspective, the Western European belief that time, progress, and scientific study are neutral. Further, critical perspectives focus on the notion that just as our understandings of adolescence are constructed in relation to culture, power, and the subjectivities of race, class, gender, and sexuality, so too is the individual adolescent. In this sense, how "adolescence" and "the adolescent" are constructed involves unequal power relations that enable some to define both the healthy and the unhealthy adolescent. Finally, critical psychology requires us to rethink what we think we know about identity construction for *all* students.

What people might begin to see is that students use their own definitions of difference—in this case gender and sexuality—as a means to "other" or marginalize students and to reproduce various terrorizing and oppressive power relations within the school, even as they challenged others. On one level, one might "read" Gina's comments as homophobic because she defended her right to wear comfortable clothing and not "be that way." Clearly, Gina did not want other students to challenge her sexuality, nor did she want them to think she was gay. When asked about her feeling regarding sexuality, Gina noted, "To me it's a personal thing," which in and of itself ignores larger social and political aspects of sexuality. In her mind, what one did in private was done in private; it had no impact beyond the bedroom. However, she made no connection to larger political struggles that were defined by how young people viewed "what goes on in the bedroom." At the same time, Gina showed a great deal of critical insight into how athletics and fashion relate to gendered and sexual discourses. She connected gender and sexuality to the symbolic and cultural economy, that is, who and what urban students and athletes are and what power they have, and how it became part of students' physical bodies at Urban High. In effect, students' bodies were the cultural medium through which students enacted and performed their identities, and not only on how they appropriated that physical and symbolic space. Fashion became an important symbol that students used to define who they were, in terms of being "urban," having or pretending to have money, and perhaps most importantly, identified females students' availability to and objectification of the male gaze. If a female student was a strong athlete, she might not be available to validate male students' masculinity and power, and fashion became a large part of students trying to figure out who they were supposed to be. For some it maintained the status quo relationship; for others like Gina, it served as a means to reject certain norms.

If one employs a critical psychological perspective to explore how students like Gina navigate positionalities like sexuality, it is necessary to look at how Gina maintained as well as challenged the association of fashion and sexuality in order to protect herself. While she noted that clothing did not connote sexuality, Gina made evident her own discomfort with sexuality through language. She was "not that way" (e.g., a lesbian, a "dyke") and did not want people to think she was. She noted that it was "fine for other people" to be gay, lesbian, or bisexual, but that it was not who or what she was. Thus, she uncritically brushed sexuality aside, implicating herself in, while simultaneously protecting herself from, the heterosexist language and practices of her peers. While it was not OK to label students because of the clothing they wore, or to associate being gay or straight with certain clothes, Gina was clearly ambivalent about sexuality. For Gina, being outspoken about choice of clothing was particularly important because it also served as a means for self-preservation. After all, not only was she an outstanding athlete, she preferred to wear baggy clothing. Female students were expected to be "heterosexual girls" and dress the part, yet these same young women also wanted to be able to dress and act the way they wanted to, including play sports and be academically successful. They thus struggled to balance who they wanted to be with who others expected them to be in regard to their dress, athletics, and their sexuality. In some cases they downplayed their athletic abilities, in others perhaps they chose to dress in more stereotypically feminine ways than they might have otherwise.

In contrast to universalist perspectives regarding adolescent development, a critical psychological perspective requires those of us who work with young people to consider that students struggle with who they are becoming in ways that are non-linear relative to the discourses of progress that we might expect to see. Jen and Gina's voices clearly indicate that the processes of identity construction in which they are engaged involved multiple issues: not just race or class or gender, but all of the above *as well as* sexuality. How all of this played out for these young women depended on who had power in the school and who did not.

Learning to Teach from the Margins

So how is it that those of us working with urban adolescents or working with teachers of urban adolescents might come to a better understanding of the important issues related to identity construction? First, we must critically examine what we believe to be true about urban young people. In that regard, we must really look at our assumptions, what Gina and Jen called "the stereotypes," that people sometimes use to define urban adolescents. However, it is not enough to simply look at them; we must ask ourselves where these beliefs, good or bad, come from and how they might shape the teaching and learning that goes on in classrooms. Looking inward is a definite starting point, but alone it is insufficient in terms of understanding how urban young people come to be who they are.[14]

Second, it is important for us to move away from what we may have believed or been taught about adolescent development in our educational programs. We can no longer assume that one size fits all. Adolescent identity construction is a function of many experiences, both personal and cultural, in which young people create meanings about themselves and the world in which they live. Further, as Jen and Gina's comments above illustrate, who they are becoming is also very political in nature. For Jen, her experiences as a student and an athlete were shaped by race, and what others believed about her because of the discourses of race. In addition, because Jen was from an urban community, that too carried particular connotations that outsiders used to determine who she was, what her abilities were, and what if any future she had. For Gina, athletics, sexuality, and gender shaped who she was becoming in political ways particularly in ways related to the power she had both in school and out. Taking a critical psychological perspective acknowledges "how psychology locks us into descriptions of who we are, descriptions which reiterate and reinforce patterns and relations of social power."[15] Thus, those who work with youths can begin to see how others' expectations of students of color shape their experiences in and out of school in ways that can be destructive to their well-being.

While culturally, adolescence in United States schools is supposed to be a period in which students find themselves, how they do so occurs in such diverse contexts that those who work with young people cannot assume that their experiences will be similar. Nor can they assume that these experiences will affect all young people in the same manner. It is crucial for those of us who work with students from urban communities to rethink how we interpret what they say about themselves as well as how they behave in and out of school. Instead of asking, "What's the matter with kids today?," people should be asking, "What is right about kids today?" That Jen and Gina chose to be critical of the ways in which they were viewed, both by people outside their home communities and their peers from within, should be viewed as a positive rather than a negative. Both Jen and Gina began to see through the transparent power relations related to their lived experiences as African American adolescent women from the inner city, and challenged what was assumed about them and who they ought to be. From this perspective, a critical psychological reading enables us to understand that their resistance was by no means self-defeating; it was an expression of strategic agency that enabled students like Jen and Gina to find strength in who they were becoming, challenge the oppressive status quo, and come to a deeper understanding of who they were according to them, not others.

QUESTIONS TO CONSIDER

1. The author emphasizes "positionalify" instead of "universalist" assumptions in studying adolescent identity. What does she mean by "positionality," and do you agree that it offers stronger research perspectives than a moral universalist approach? Why or why not?

2. Goldstein is skeptical of the notion of "normality" and the use of stereotypes in assessing and explaining teen behavior. Show how and why her skepticism may be prudent through the use of examples from the lives of Gina and Jen.

3. How does Goldstein define "critical psychological theory," and how does it help elucidate culture, power, and ideology in the construction of adolescent identity?

4. How does one's belief system shape what one brings to the classroom situation? How can it influence teachers' reactions to student resistance and those who challenge the status quo?

This chapter originally appeared in Joe L. Kincheloe and kecia hayes (eds.), *Teaching City Kids: Understanding and Appreciating Them* (New York, New York: Peter Lang, 2007).

Endnotes

1   A pseudonym. All names, except the author's are pseudonyms to protect the privacy of individuals.

2   Norms are relations that describe who people are, ought to be and how they should behave. They further define what all people should be like, regardless of race, class, gender, sexuality, and ableness, and exclude those who do not fit the Western European middle-class model.

3   S. SooHoo, "Crossing cultural borders into the inner city," in The Social Justice Consortium with S. SooHoo, ed. *Essays on Urban Education: Critical Consciousness, Collaboration and the Self* (Cresskill: Hampton Press, 2002), pp. 163–180.

4   N. Lesko, *Act Your Age! A Cultural Construction of Adolescence* (New York: Routledge/Falmer, 2001).

5   M. Nakkula, "Identity and possibility: adolescent development and the possibility of schools," in M. Sadowski, ed. *Adolescents at School: Perspectives on Youth, Identity, and Education* pp. 7–18 (Cambridge: Harvard Education Press, 2003), p. 11.

6   D. Hook, "Critical psychology: the basic co-ordinates," in D. Hook, ed. *Critical psychology* (Lansdowne: University of Cape Town Press, 2004), pp. 10–23.

7   K. B. deMarrais and M. D. LeCompte, *The Way Schools Work: A Sociological Analysis of Education* 3rd ed. (New York: Longman, 1999).

8   B. Tatum, *Why Are All the Black Kids Sitting Together in the Cafeteria? and Other Conversations About Race* (New York: Basic Books, 1997).

9   R.P. Solomon, *Black Resistance in High School: Forging a Separatist Culture* (Albany, New York: State University of New York Press, 1992).

10   K.B. deMarrais and M.D. LeCompte, *The Way Schools Work: A Sociological Analysis of Education 3rd ed.* (New York: Longman, 1999).

11   M.S. Kimmel, "'I am not insane; I am angry': adolescent masculinity, homophobia, and violence," in M. Dadowski, ed. *Adolescents at School: Perspectives on Youth, Identity, and Education* (Cambridge: Harvard University Press, 2003), pp. 69–78.

12   S. K. Carney, "Body work on ice: the ironies of femininity and sport," in L. Weis and M. Fine, eds. *Construction Sites: Excavating Race, Class, and Gender Among Urban Youth* (New York: Teachers College Press, 2000), pp. 121–139.

13   N. Lesko, *Act Your Age! A Cultural Construction of Adolescence* (New York: Routledge/Falmer, 2001).

14   K.M. Zeichner and D.P. Liston, *Reflective Teaching: An Introduction* (Mahwah, NJ: Lawrence Erlbaum, 1996).

15   D. Hook, "Critical psychology: the basic co-ordinates," in D. Hook, ed. *Critical Psychology*, pp. 10–23 (Lansdowne: University of Cape Town Press, 2004), p. 19.

CHAPTER FOUR

Tween Social and Biological Reproduction

Early Puberty in Girls

ELIZABETH SEATON

In 1997, the publication of a major study in the journal *Pediatrics* caused a nationwide media storm in Canada and the United States. The research offered compelling evidence that North American girls were experiencing the onset of puberty one or two years earlier than their counterparts had 30 years ago (Hermann-Giddens et al. 1997). This phenomenon of early puberty—termed "precocious sexual development" by the medical establishment—became the causal underpinning for a new generation of media panics and normative social representations of girls. With varying degrees of scientific fact and inflammatory rhetoric, *Time Magazine, Newsweek, The New York Times*, countless other dailies, talk shows and web-magazines described "a generation in fast forward" . . . of girls who are "8 going on 25" and "becoming sexually active at an alarmingly early age" (*Newsweek* 1999: 17). For all those parents and teachers who had long suspected that young girls were becoming more mature overnight, there was now scientific 'proof' that the age of puberty was plummeting. More fortuitously for target marketers, ad types and the media, it could now be claimed that there was a biological veracity to what remains an invention of marketing and cultural representation: the 'tween' girl.

'Precocious sexual development' provides an especially rich ground for inquiry into the discursive embodiment of social identity. Having captured the imaginations of both 'legitimate' (medical and social scientific) sources and unauthorized (popular) audiences, it lends important insights into the discursive frameworks which construct notions of a body, its sex, gender and age, and the assumptions of value and causality which support these. But perhaps more intriguing is the way in which 'precocious sexual development' appears to move in fidelity with our radically shifting social, cultural and natural environments. And in this respect, it begs the question, "Does discourse simply stop at flesh and bone?" Or does the social interact reciprocally with the physical in ways both contrived and accidental? What manner of fluid interchanges—discursive, material and physical—exists among social, cultural, and natural environments?

"Childhood," as James, Jenks, and Prout describe it, "is less a fact of nature than an interpretation of it" (1998: 62). Certainly, these changing bodies tell us much about the changing conceptions and social values attached to the identities of children. Children act as important symbolic and mediating figures for society: they serve as both the nostalgic reserves of 'fond childhood memories' and as the corporeal agents of society's future; they delineate both the maturity and rationality of 'adulthood' and the irrational and asexual 'nature' of childhood. Girls may be even more sensitive to such discursive shaping, for they are held within doubled dualisms which posit children as 'animalistic' or 'primitive' and females, by virtue of their physiology, as 'closer to nature' than men. Yet, the phenomenon of 'precocious sexual development' raises the possibility that not all is what it is meant to be: that even while we may refute the naturalization of arbitrary social identities upon a body, we are also constantly faced with its residual, morphological, 'nature'. These changing bodies thus strongly gesture to the oblique and dialectical interplay of biological and social reproduction.

The past three decades have seen dramatic changes to the economic, political, and social structures of North American society, many of which directly affect the present and future of young people. The 'liberalizations' of global trade laws and the digitalized speed and efficiencies of 'fictive' finance capital have resulted in the massive exportation of manufacturing jobs to countries believed to have more compliant and cheap labor pools.[1] With jobless futures (Aronowitz and DiFazio 1995) have also come deteriorating social benefits—from pensions to quality health care to welfare and social security—which were once viewed as immutable and sacrosanct (in Canada at least) but now are increasingly under attack. In this respect, the prospects for employment, and the progressive forms of citizenship and value offered to young people in North America have become far more limited.[2]

The abstractions of a 'fictive' finance capitalism, which amasses wealth through exchange and replication, are matched by the ascension of a pervasive consumer culture fashioned within the mantra of synergy, duplication, and disposability (Baudrillard 1988; Rifkin 2000). We are no longer enticed but rather swarmed by commercial culture. Desire has become unhinged, replaced by the more "unfastened and licentious" 'wish' as the motivating force of consumption (Bauman 2001: 14). Zygmunt Bauman (ibid.) argues that 'the wish' perfectly corresponds to a time in which nothing of consequence transpires beyond the immediate moment: nothing of lasting duration, nothing contextualized by history.

These times, too, are marked by high anxiety. Not too long ago, the constant fear of an unknown danger was the purlieu of the self-important or the self-delusional. Today this fear is dispersed, democratized, and commodified (Seaton 2001). No doubt, the demise of social protections under a 'liberalized' economy has added to the prevalence of social insecurities. So too do the new commodities of fear—the police forces, both private and public, the monstrous Hummers, the armed and alarmed houses, gated communities and surveillance cameras, the War on Terror, the new identity documents, and the smug visage of G.W. Bush—which, like all media, impart particular messages about the state of the world and how we should live in it.

Something too has gone terribly amiss in the relationship between humanity and nature. We are now in the midst of a full-blown environmental crisis, which, even for the cosseted occupants of a 'society of abundance', is impossible to ignore. And as the natural environment mutates, changes texture and temperature and finally vanishes under the weight of human excess, its only remaining value is as a spectacle or experience for consumption. Nature is no longer itself. Even those ontological certainties once supported by the blueprint of natural history are rendered null and void, as genomic maps are re-written, sheep are cloned, human fetuses are 'resourced,' and the food we eat is genetically engineered. We seem to be witnessing the dramatic alteration of life itself.

'Precocious sexual development' may thus act as a touchstone for more distant and impersonal forces. The ambivalence and discomfort with which we may experience these changes—whose effects are as intimate as they are remote—speak to a more subtle perception that life, labor, and language are becoming undone, realigned, and re-made by forces beyond our control. What happens to young bodies when their future becomes uncertain?

There are thus two broad focal points to this investigation into 'precocious sexual development.' The first concerns the discursive premises and powers that shape its representation. *How* is the problem of precocious sexual development socially produced within regimes of power and knowledge? What epistemological and ontological premises guide the various hypotheses of its scientific investigation, and from what historical conditions do these premises arise? And how are its different referential components—childhood, puberty, adolescent girls, etc.—held within networks of control that are at once both disciplinary and pleasurable? The second part of this investigation seeks to understand precocious sexual development as the result of a mutually generative relationship between human beings and their social and cultural environments. A common sentiment forwarded (either implicitly or explicitly) in much of the writing on early puberty is that it is the physiological effect, or incorporation, of culture. If this is so, how is it so? And if it is so, may not early puberty affect the world as much as it is affected? Can it be seen as a strategic reaction to the social environment?

Competing Hypotheses

The research project on precocious sexual development was principally authored by Dr. Marcia Hermann-Giddens, who, in collaboration with the American Academy of Pediatrics, undertook a major study of 17,077 girls aged 3–10 across the United States (Hermann-Giddens et al. 1997).[3] Six percent of the girls were African-American, and 90.4% were white. The results of the study were surprisingly consistent. For white girls, the mean age of the on-set of puberty was 9.96 years. For African-American girls, that age was 8.87 years. At every age, African-American girls were shown to be more advanced in puberty than white girls were. At age eight, 48.3% of African-American girls and 14.7% of white girls showed pubertal maturation. At age seven, 27.2% of African-American girls, and 6.7% of white girls had begun development. Close to one-third of the African-American girls showed pubertal characteristics by their seventh birthday (puberty here measured by appearance of breast-buds or pubic hair). These girls are in their second-grade of grammar school.

Since 1969, medical textbooks and pediatricians have commonly cited the expected normative age for the start of puberty in young girls as 11 and by these standards, pubescent girls younger than eight would be considered 'precocious' sexual developers.[4]

It is important to note that the incidence of early onset of puberty does not necessarily mean the early onset of menstruation. In fact, the majority of girls who begin puberty early progress through this stage slowly and tend to reach first menstruation at the same age (13 years) as their cohorts. In this respect, puberty is not so much accelerated as it is elongated (from 18 months to 3 years).

On its own, the development of puberty for girls stands as a significant event, as it signals the onset of profound changes in a girl's life and impacts the give and take of family control. Yet, such changes also resonate within more expansive social parameters. This is because puberty involves not just the physiological modifications taking place within an adolescent body but the ways in which these changes are socially understood and the changing social contexts in which these understandings are formed. As child-centered ethnographies have shown (e.g., James 1993), bodies are of great importance to children in the creation of self and social identity. A child's size, shape, gender, sex, and any number of other visible characteristics (spectacles and skin, hair or eye color) are all crucial markers of social distinction. And as her own body constantly changes through on-going and varying forms of development—of which puberty is only one instance—a child's sense of self and her perception of others are re-created as well.

In a like manner, so too does a child's changing body affect, as it is affected by, social perception. Children, more than any other age group, are held to strict normative limits and controls. A great deal of attention is paid to a child's 'proper' development—as the archival documents of growth charts, school records, vaccination histories and family photo albums attest. As Kovarik (1994) has argued, childhood is temporally and spatially structured into 'stages and scripts': a child's given age, from infant to toddler to preschooler to school-ager to adolescent and teenager, involves different expectations about the capabilities of different bodies and their different types of independent movement and access to different social spaces. Puberty is obviously perceived as a most important marker within this genealogy. It signals a girl's imminent entrance into the social and temporal spaces of adult life—and therefore her entry into the complex social, political, and economic relations of gender and sexuality.

Girls come of age in a patriarchal culture. The concessions paid as the price of this admission can be seen in the behavioral changes from childhood to adolescence. Girls begin to learn that their lives will always be shaped by the constraints of gendered power relations. These lessons are made concrete in instances of economic inequality or dependence, in shared peer group assumptions about appropriate gendered behavior, and in the simple, and sometimes violent, day-to-day affirmation of the subordinate values males place upon females as sexual beings (McRobbie 1991; Friedman 1994; Pipher 1994). Yet, such determinations are not without their contradictions. Girls are also portrayed as impertinent and powerful (e.g., Lolita or Grrrrl culture)—an image which bolsters, as it ostensibly belies, a sexualized and commodified image of adolescent girls as precocious, delinquent and deviant.

Puberty is therefore shaped by a whole concatenation of personal, physical, and political forces. Deviations from such markers of normal development—such as early puberty—can cause a great deal of social anxiety. Early maturing girls are not sticking to the temporal and spatial script.

Such societal concerns have undoubtedly contributed to the popular and professional interest that Hermann-Giddens' study has provoked. The research not only appears to show an increase in sexual maturation in young girls in the United States but a quite dramatic racial distinction in the rate of maturation. Underlying these findings is the provocative question of why these changes are taking place *now*. While much is known of the varying consequences which early puberty may have for a girl, relatively little has been concretely determined about the social, psychological, and physiological antecedents of these consequences. Instead, there are competing hypotheses that attempt to account for the accelerated maturation of young girls.

Body weight is crucial for the timing of sexual development. It is commonly accepted that overweight girls tend to menstruate early, while for severely underweight girls the onset of menses begins late if at all. This is because menstruation is triggered by body weight—it starts when a girl is heavy enough (has enough body fat) to support a pregnancy—which is virtually always at 105 lbs or 17% body fat. Eighty years ago, menstruation began at age 16 and now, because of the substantive increase in the quality of nutrition, it begins on average at age 13.

Hermann-Giddens' research compared the weight and height of study girls against a national sample of race-specific data from the first and second national Health and Nutrition Examination Surveys (HANES). The girls in Hermann-Giddens study were found in general to be larger than in the HANES sample, especially as age increased. Moreover, "[study] girls who had one or more secondary sexual characteristics [evidence of breast development or pubic hair] were larger and heavier than sexually immature girls" (Hermann-Giddens et al. 1997: 508). Hermann-Giddens et al. proposed two factors that may have bearing on these findings. Because the HANES data are approximately 20 years old, girls in general today may be taller and heavier. Moreover, the report cites several studies undertaken in the United States in the 1970s and 1980s that found African-American girls to be taller, heavier, and maturing earlier than white girls of the same age. Nonetheless, Hermann-Giddens et al. were unable to offer an "explanation for the discrepancy in timing sequence between the African-American and white girls for either the on-set of puberty and subsequent menses or appearance and spacing of the secondary sexual characteristics. Neither [could they] explain the earlier development among African-American girls in general" (ibid.: 510).

Still, the association of early puberty with heaviness has grown apace with recent concerns regarding the weight and health of children in the United States and Canada.[5] Twenty-five percent of children under the age of 19 in the U.S. are obese or overweight. Twenty-five percent of children in the U.S. also live in poverty (in Canada, 1 in 5 children lives in poverty). Obesity is crosscut with the politics of class and race. It is the urban working poor and their increasing need for cheap and fast meals as they run from home to job, from job to job, or from school to home, that has fuelled the growth of fast-food empires such as McDonalds or Wendy's (Townsend et al. 2001).

Food is also a culprit in another popular theory, which argues that the presence of growth hormone additives in dairy products (or even the nutritional make-up of cow's milk itself) causes 'precocious sexual development.' Today, there is many a mother who will not allow her daughter to consume industrial dairy products, in the fear that "she will have the body of a grown woman by the time she is ten" (Belkin 2000: 41). While there has yet to be any strong epidemiological evidence pointing to milk as the cause of accelerated maturation, nonetheless, this theory remains perhaps the most compelling to a popular audience.

Hormones have long been associated with puberty and its rages, as puberty begins when estrogen levels are at a peak. Hormones are 'chemical messengers'—the natural secreting products of endocrine glands found in plants, animals, and humans. In higher vertebrates, they travel through the blood stream, where they affect the tissues and organs they come into contact with. In binding with cells, hormones influence the regulation, growth, and equilibrium of body function. Key endocrine glands are the hypothalamus, pituitary, thyroid, parathyroid, pancreas, adrenal, ovary, and testes.

The fears associated with hormone-ridden cattle are also connected to the more dispersed, and increasingly more deadly, consequences of our degraded environment. In 1997, the U.S. Environmental Protection Agency reported, "evidence has been accumulating that humans and domestic and wild species have suffered adverse health consequences resulting from exposure to environmental chemicals that interact with the endocrine system" (EPA 1997: vii). These chemicals are believed to mimic the effects of the body's own natural hormones, such as estrogen, and thus produce a cascade of developmental problems, including hormone-sensitive cancers such as breast, ovarian, cervical and testicular cancers and, potentially, early puberty. At least fifty chemicals have been identified as possible hormone disruptors, the majority of which are found in pesticides, fungicides, herbicides, insecticides, and nematocides. They can also be found in solvents, sunscreen lotions, plastic bottles, hair straighteners, nail polish and in the lining of food cans— in short, the everyday ingredients of our Chemical Age. Billions of pounds of these chemicals are released into the environment every year—exposing plants, humans, and animals to any number of chemical compounds at every point of the globe.

While there are, as yet, no hard evidentiary claims linking endocrine disruptors to early puberty, those studies investigating the linkage have strengthened the possibility. A research team of pediatric endocrinologists led by Jean-Pierre Bourguignon of Belgium found that girls who immigrated to Belgium from countries such as India or Colombia were 80 times more likely to begin puberty before the age of eight. The researchers found high levels of DDE (a derivative of DDT and a well-known estrogenic pesticide) in the blood of these children (M. Krstevska-Konstaninova et al. 2001). In the U.S., an on-going study at Emory University has found that girls born to women exposed to the chemical polybrominated biphenyl (PBB) in 1973—inadvertently mixed with cattle feed in one of the largest food contamination accidents in U.S. history—started menstruating one-half to a full year earlier than others (Blanck et al. 2000). Research published in 1994 suggests that hair products containing estrogen may be related to the increasing prevalence of early puberty amongst African-American girls (Tiwary 1994: 135, 108A). These studies that investigate endocrine disruptors are especially compelling because they forward notions of an 'unseen' yet prevalent danger preying upon children while they are fetuses in utero or while they work or play in agricultural fields.

Not surprisingly, social scientific studies have also contributed to the causal hypotheses regarding 'precocious sexual development.' One of these is "the absent-father hypothesis" proposed by developmental psychologists (Ellis et al. 1999). Expanding from evolutionary psychology's contention that early family environment has the capacity to shape reproductive behavior; the absent-father hypothesis suggests that the quality of a father-daughter relationship has important consequences for a daughter's age of puberty and that the greater the level of supportive and positive interactions between father and daughter, the later the onset of puberty. However, if the biological father is absent in a daughter's early life, then the earlier the puberty (cf. Jones et al. 1972; Moffitt et al. 1992; Wierson et al. 1993). Moreover, if there is an unrelated male in the household, this maturation is further accelerated. One of the principal researchers of this study has proposed that this may be due to the influence of pheromones from the unrelated male (Ellis and Garber 2000).

The Attractions of Vulnerability

My interest lies less in the veracity of each of these competing explanations, than the way in which they are folded within and are articulated to both each other and to other locations of societal concern. Explanations of 'precocious sexual development,' as with most scientific claims, are based upon the strength of association among variables rather than upon a direct causal relationship. And it is the degree of concern with which we attend to such variables—the ways in which we respond to and regard the relations of poverty, television, fast food, endocrine additives, or the break-up of marriages and absent fathers, especially as these are culled through the sieve of North American class, gender and racial ideologies—that builds the strength of these associations. This acknowledgment of the historical and social construction of epistemic value guides us to expand the question of 'precocious sexual development' onto a multi-layered milieu of substances, qualities, forces and events, rather than one of origins. If we accept that causal hypotheses are the product of social conditions, then we may also begin approaching this question (hopefully somewhat) free from reductionist traps. As feminist sociologist Christine Delphi once argued:

> When we connect gender and sex, are we comparing something social to something natural or are we connecting something social with something which is also social (in this case, the way that a given society represents biology to itself)? (1993: 5)

How now does society represent the biology, the bodies, of its children to itself? What is being made meaningful in the stories told about 'precocious sexual development'?

In his 1967 work, *Coldness and Cruelty*, Gilles Deleuze notes that medicine is comprised of three different activities: "symptomatology," which is the study of signs of illness and the grouping of these "signs" into "symptoms"; etiology, which is the search for causes; and therapy, which is the development and application of treatment. Deleuze argues that etiology, "which is the scientific or experimental side of medicine, must be subordinated to symptomatology, which is its literary, artistic aspect" (1989: 133). Thus, it is the signifying capacity of 'precocious sexual development' that takes precedence over and guides the search for antecedent causal factors. The narrative told by this syndrome is far more compelling than the 'scientific proof.'

A recurring figure in the majority of hypotheses concerning early puberty is the 'vulnerable' child, impoverished or assailed by unseen outside forces. This premise of vulnerability offers a most compelling narrative. Something is changing the bodies of children. (Although, it is not one thing, but many things: a number of multi-causal factors.) Regardless of what *it* is, there is the consistent and implicit assumption that it comes not from within but from without. It is a foreign body acting upon the bodies of the innocent.

Representations of modern childhood are heavily reliant upon the idea of 'innocence'; a term which rose from the Industrial Revolutions of the 18th and 19th centuries, and today gains its efficacy from a number of complex material, economic, and semiotic registers (Ariés 1962; James, Jenks and Prout 1998; Giroux 2000). Childhood is commonly represented as a 'natural' state, a kind of 'never-land' temporally and spatially removed from the 'real' world of adults. Ideally, children should be shielded from the instrumental relations of economics and the productive sphere. Their social worth then lies not in the ability to generate surplus value as workers but in being objects of expressive or "sentimental value" (Zelizer 1994). As those who are 'innocent' of the exigencies of economics, history and politics, children are posited as pre-social beings who act upon instinct and unreason and are not yet reined to, or ruined by, the conventions or corruptions of the social. In this respect, the modern child is closely linked to historical conceptions of 'the primitive Other,' that "creature without speech" (Soper 1995: 76) who inhabits a pristine natural state.

Innocence, however, is a gilded cage. The non-economic appeal of children allows for its own exploitations, and it is a conceptual apparatus that excludes some children as it captures others within its grasp. With its signifiers of nostalgia, comfort and stasis, the concept of 'innocence' tends to halo white upper-middle class children, whilst leaving poor children and children of color in another, less pure and thus less worthy state. Moreover, the obligations of a protected and 'priceless' childhood safely removed from the corruptions of labor ironically remove children from their own experiences of autonomy and agency (Giroux 2000). Children are to be the real, everyday equivalent of Anne Geddes' perverse photographs of children guised as vegetables: immobile, mute and something to be picked up at the market. Economically worthless, but symbolically priceless, the child becomes wholly dependent upon the adult for any designation of value. As James Kincaid puts it, "[innocence] makes you vulnerable—badly in need of protection" (1998: 54).

Threats to the state of innocence are dealt a swift paternal hand. Children are kept in custody, locked indoors and entertained by the commercial predations of television perhaps, but away from the predatory reach of child molesters. And children themselves are carefully watched for any infractions of 'purity.' A child's non-economic appeal is dependent upon his or her ability to remain attractive as an emotional object—an often-difficult task, given the difficulties of child development in general. A child should always be pleasant, playful, and compliant, and transgressions of this code are often strictly enforced. No doubt, the violence meted out to children on a weekly (if not daily) basis is a result of the frustrations experienced by those stifled within the confines of domesticity and childhood innocence.[6] The structural passivity and powerlessness of school and home lend themselves to practices of discipline and enforcement, often to the level of abuse.

There is a great deal of ideological work performed under the auspices of this historically recent, and Western concept, of childhood. It aids the legitimation of the sexual and spatial separation of work from home—thus normalizing wage labor and the sequestering of women and children into the emotional, domestic sphere. It defines adulthood in so far as it is the innocence of childhood that constructs its antithesis. It universalizes childhood. Childhood innocence is constituted as an innate, essential part of *all* children, an ontological trick which renders the lives of children homogenous despite their social-economic, racial and cultural differences and thus excludes those who have 'fallen from innocence' by virtue of these differences. Lastly, childhood innocence allows for the conceptualization of children as passive, commodified, and sexualized objects. It is a short distance from adoration to exploitation.

Michel Foucault spoke of the ways in which inhibition also always circulates back upon a pleasurable incitement. The productivities of discourse, especially as they "trace around bodies and sexes," revolve in "perpetual spirals of pleasure and power" (1990: 45). As that which is free from the corruptions of adult society, innocence is also *always potentially corruptible*, and so it is constantly shadowed and shaped by its future debasement. What begins as a negation ultimately begins again as an enticement. In this respect, it is interesting that the term 'precocious sexual development' turns so readily to its eroticized twin: 'the sexually promiscuous child.' The vulnerable is not only to be protected but also promoted.

In his acerbic analysis of the culture of child molesting—the media spectacles, the endless and ongoing talk on talk shows, the hypocrisies—James Kincaid writes:

> Few stories in our culture right now are as popular as those of child molesting. . . . Why do we generate these stories and not others? What rewards do they offer? Who profits from their circulation and who pays the price? (1998:3)

The United States has long been besotted with the matter of child abuse. Its global cultural industries are vehicles in which girl children are frequently trafficked—the Olsen twins, the 5-year-old 'beauty queen' JonBenet Ramsey, or the more 'intermediate' Britney Spears (she who is 'not a girl, not yet a woman') are only a few of its more recent commodities. However, it is also a place that regards an erotic response to children as a heinous crime. In other words, it professes to prohibit that which it also perpetrates. Its denunciations are always and only just further deployments of desire. As Kincaid puts it (in a manner which evokes Foucault's "repressive hypothesis"): "When we speak of the unspeakable, we keep the speaking going" (ibid.: 21).

Both the representations of precocious sexual development and the cultural industry of child molestation are premised upon an image of the vulnerable child: an innocent whose protection has failed. In this provocative story of the violation of innocence, the character of the violating agent is always foreign. And yet, harm is perpetrated within the more familiar limits of nation and home. It results from those social policies and political economies that allow for the continuation of childhood poverty, junk food, chemicals in the environment, hormones in cow's milk, and little girls dressed up as Joan Collins. 'Innocence' is a fetishistic tale serving to deflect attention away from the harm that a society systemically inflects upon its children. As Henry Giroux has argued, "innocence . . . makes children invisible except as projections of adult fantasies—fantasies that allow adults to believe that children do not suffer from their greed, recklessness, perversions of will and spirit and that adults are, in the final analysis, unaccountable for their actions" (2000: 40).

The attractions of vulnerability speak to the paradoxical times we inhabit. The economic restructuring of the past twenty years has indeed made us more susceptible. The replacement of long-term and binding agreements of employment with short-term, tendered services has got us used to the idea that mutual obligations are no longer to be expected and that only an uncertain future lies ahead. At the same time, the ideologies of self-interest and individualism accompanying the 'structural adjustments' of neo-liberalism cast us as so many autonomous competitors: each one fighting for our own piece of propertied enrichment, each one "utterly, unqualifiedly responsible for [our]selves" and yet at the same time, "dependent upon conditions which completely elude [our] grasp" (Beck 1992: 137). We are left with the paradoxical situation of a society experiencing an 'enforced' vulnerability, and those people and things which purport to protect us—tax cuts, downsizing, privatization of social services, ethnic profiling, pre-emptive strikes and regime change—are also those which perpetuate harm. Vulnerability no longer has to refer to any real referent of injury or actual suffering. It has become a heuristic device for social control.

A Habitus of Some Uncertainty

Surely, a nation's political and social landscape becomes a child's experience, as she must travel through it in so many various ways. Following the work of Pierre Bourdieu, it may be argued that this contemporary landscape constitutes an entirely different "field" of objective social conditions, within which children variously occupy different "structuring structures" or "habitus." In a dialectic of internal and external relations, the 'field' supplies those objective conditions which structure the 'habitus', while the 'habitus'—through the embodiment of meaningful social action—is constitutive of the 'field' (Bourdieu 1977: 72). Habitus describes that generative location, system, and time whereby the social—ingrained, taken-for-granted assumptions and social inequalities—is incorporated into the corporeal and psychological dispositions of individuals. In this respect, 'habitus' importantly involves the reproduction of class and gender relations. Yet, this is more of a generative than strictly determinative process. Bourdieu places a temporal accent upon 'habitus,' opening up its accepted practices to contingency and historical change. As Lois McNay describes it, the embodied responses of habitus are not just repetitive acts of social reproduction but "a creative anticipation of future uncertainty on the part of social actors" or a "practical reference to the future" (1999: 102).

Habitus is realized in *le sens pratique* ('feel for the game'), a mode of knowledge that involves the habitual or 'instinctual' responses of a body without conscious thought, a form of behavior which is automatic because it is engrained in bodily practice (Bourdieu 1990: 52). For instance, a primary distinction of small child from adult is the latter's internalized performance of bodily practices in a socially prescribed manner, such as eating or defecating in the right way and at the right time. But, while such learned social behavior may be 'automatic,' it is also strategic, as it involves the manipulation of the tempo (the pace of time unfolding) of the habitual response of a body. What implications, then, may the current objective structures of society hold for girls in Canada and the U.S.—not only in terms of their life conditions (which have already been found to suffer[7])—but also for the manner and *the pace* with which they now conduct themselves? Does early puberty involve a habituated and strategic response to the uncertain terrain of neoliberalism?

Lately, a number of cultural analysts have focused their attention upon the recent changes wrought by neo-liberal society in the conceptualization, evaluation, and treatment of children in North American society (e.g., Giroux 2000; Lee 2001; Grossberg 2001). In varying ways, each of these writers finds that recent shifts towards less stable economic and political arrangements, and the free-run of a consumer ethos, have been deleterious for children. In an essay that convincingly argues that the United States is engaged in a "war on children," Larry Grossberg links neoliberalism's "radical devaluation of labor" to a diminished appraisal of children. Labor and the social inclusion and citizenship that accrue from it are crucial components of modernity and as such are also articulated to its key concepts of progress, the dynamic movement of time, and the investment in the future. Grossberg argues that, "by placing finance capital at the centre, [neoliberalism] is attempting . . . to negate—or at least amend and partially retreat from—the assumption of labor as the source of value" (2001: 131). Children and youth have long acted as privileged signifiers for the continuation and progress of society into the future. Yet, in the shift from industrial commodity capital to a 'fictive' finance capital, youth is no longer of value (to put it in Althusserian terms) for the reproduction of the conditions of production. Or, as Grossberg puts it, youth have lost their value as "the trope of the universal faith in futurity" (ibid.: 133). In fact, they have become so de-valued to the point of being erased. They have become adults before their time.

The telescoping of childhood into adulthood neatly parallels concern paid to the synchronic position of contemporary children. A popular nostalgic representation portrays childhood as a time of idleness; an 'endless summer' of slowly moving bodies and hours. Today, the rhythms of childhood are believed to have sped up dramatically, keeping pace with the tempo of contemporary life in which time is a precious commodity. Recent ethnographic research commissioned by the Girl Scouts of the U.S.A. finds that girls of "middle childhood" (ages 8–12) "seem to be pressured to deal with typically 'teenage' issues years before they reach their teens" (2000: 5). The research supports parents' beliefs that child development is becoming "hurried" or "compressed" (ibid.). Similarly, Allan Mirabelli, executive director of the Vanier Institute of the Family in Ottawa, comments that, "Our children do suffer from what Daniel Elkind characterizes as the "hurried child syndrome," as they rush, at younger and younger ages, to emulate and imitate adults and their behaviors. It is more convenient to us if our children grow up quickly so that they become less dependent upon us" (Fulsang 2002: L1). Given the economic necessity of working parents and government cutbacks to funding of schools, most children's lives today are far more shaped by regimen and discipline than those of a previous generation were. School time now segues onto structured (and paid for) after-school activity, and family evenings have become a tyranny of school-assigned duties. School-aged children are given the appearance of miniature flight attendants as they wheel suitcases, instead of knapsacks, to carry home their heavy burdens. The rigid structure and stressful obligations of the parent have become shared by the child.

Are girls not only addressed by society's synchronic rhythms, social policies, and ideological reproductions as adult females but also responding to these mediations in embodied ways? If discourse (pace Foucault) creates its own productivities, what new bodies are produced by advanced capitalism? Here's one deterministic and rather crude answer: Perhaps young girls are becoming the only thing of value in this new world of de-valued laboring bodies—the value of commodified sexual objects? This is a response which is evocative of Henry Giroux's contention that "corporate culture's promotion of the sexualization of children has shortened the distance between childhood and adulthood" (2000: 16). Similarly, this response echoes the parental panics ensuing from the current 'pop-tart' look of bared midriffs, 'junior thong' underwear, and hip-hugger jeans cut down to the pubis favored by pre-teen girls (Fulsang 2002). However, such answers are too expedient and not explanatory enough. They do not go far enough in attempting to deal with the multi-faceted milieu that revolves around this troublesome subject.

Despite the fact that young people now occupy a social order in which employment or social services can no longer be taken for granted, their responses to such uncertainty cannot be generalized as reactionary or pessimistic. In fact, in the midst of a widespread attenuation of security and life choices, young people are found to adopt a highly individualist approach to life that emphasizes choice and agency. As Johanna Wyn and Rob White have recently discovered, there is a growing gap "between the structural position of young people, in terms of schooling, employment and income, and the experiences and perceptions of young people as they attempt to deal with new social constraints and opportunities" (2000: 165). This makes some sense too. Young people today have little or no experience with an expansionary welfare state, life-long employment, and collective society. They have come to know a completely different world, which prioritizes a 'rationalized economy' and 'the entrepreneurial self' as ideological 'commonsense.' 'Self-possession' and 'self-confidence' have become the panacea for the intense competition that occupies society today. While it may seem contradictory to acquire a highly individualistic perspective about one's life circumstances when such circumstances would be better understood in terms of the structural conditions of neo-liberalism, such an "epistemological fallacy" (Furlong and Cartmel 1997) may also be read as a strategic response. The dispositions of habitus emerge from a "practical evaluation of the likelihood of success of a given action in a given situation . . ." (Bourdieu 1977: 77).

Precociousness may be read as a type of strategic reaction—a 'becoming adult,' becoming self-possessed—for a society that no longer has time for children. Perhaps precocious sexual development can be understood in a similar way. The class and gender-specific conditions of socialization that girls occupy today are fraught with contradiction: stressing both conventional, if not reactionary, gender roles and the necessity of accumulating economic capital. Why not grow up quickly? But something, again, interrupts this smooth equation.

Recall that precocious sexual development involves less an accelerated maturation than the *elongation of the time* of puberty. Girls are not becoming women earlier—in terms of reaching menses—but rather become pubescent earlier and remain that way for extended durations. The distinction is important—as one signifies an attainment of adulthood (at least in a physiological respect) while the other signifies an anticipation of adulthood. If we are to read early puberty as an 'embodied social practice,' then this important temporal dimension to the encounter of habitus and field cannot be overlooked. For again, it is the tempo or pace of a social action that lends it its strategic qualities: the brushing up against ambiguity and contradiction as it moves through space and time.

Jacques Deleuze and Felix Guatarri once wrote, "We are not *in* the world, we *become with* the world" (1987: 169). The ways in which a child grows into and occupies the world are dependent upon the ways in which the world grows into and occupies her. Not only are these through the signs and languages of an external world but also the manner in which these signs and languages *sound* to her, the means by which they resonate against her body with different degrees of intensity, or what Greg Seigworth (1999) describes as "the slow, steady and continual accumulation of seeming insignificances." How a body is affected is also how a body is connected—to moments of space and time and the composition and conjunction of these moments. The images and languages of our social world are influential beyond the signifying productions of ideology—they entail *affect*, in addition to effects. May not precocious sexual development be the result (as one part of a multiple) of affects—a body affected by the different shifting resonances and tempo of this new social terrain?

QUESTIONS TO CONSIDER

1. The author argues that the discovery of "precocious sexual development? has triggered significant changes in how we view puberty in our social, cultural, and natural worlds. In what ways is this the case?

2. Analyze the various hypotheses used to explain the phenomenon of precocious sexual development. Which one(s) make the most sense to you? Why?

3. How does our society convey certain narratives about precocious sexual development, and how beneficial or harmful are they in children's lives? Give examples.

4. Seaton speaks of "vulnerability" as an instrument of social control over adolescents. What does she mean, and do you agree with her analysis? Why or why not?

5. The author portrays youth as being de-valued in our culture and society. In what ways does this appear to be the case? Give examples.

6. Seaton claims that social immaturity is ironically prolonged in the age of precocious sexual development. Explain her argument. Do you find it compelling? Why or why not?

Notes

This chapter originally appeared in Claudia Mitchell and Jacqueline Reid-Walsh (eds.), *Seven Going on Seventeen: Tween Studies in the Culture of Girlhood* (New York: Peter Lang, 2005).

I acknowledge financial and course-release support from the Social Sciences and Humanities Research Council (SSHRC), the Faculty of Arts at York University, and the York University Research Development Fellowship towards the researching and writing of this project.

1. Wal-Mart, which, as the world's largest corporation, makes $220 billion a year in revenues, is also the largest importer of Chinese-made products in the world, buying $10 billion worth of merchandise from several Chinese factories annually (Hightower, *The CCPA Monitor*, November 2002, 10–11).

2. The gap between rich and poor in Canada is now dramatic. *Statistics Canada*'s most recent survey (1994) shows that while Canadians hold $2.4 trillion in personal wealth (averaging an impressive $199,664 for each family

unit), the actual distribution of this wealth is anything but equitable. "The wealthiest 10% of family units in Canada held 53% of the personal wealth, and the top 50% controlled an almost unbelievable 94.4% of the wealth. That left only 5.6% to be shared amongst the bottom 50%" (Kerstetter, *The CCPA Monitor*, November 2002, 1).

3. This study was conducted via the American Academy of Pediatrics (AAP) Pediatric Research in Office Settings (PROS) network. The goal of the study was to describe the prevalence of secondary sexual characteristics and occurrences in U.S. girls aged 3–12 as seen in pediatric office practice. Data were collected from July 1992 to Sept. 1993 from 17,077 girls who were seen for a health supervision (well-child) visit, or a problem (e.g., abdominal pain, fatigue) that according to office routine would require a complete physical examination. Although it was recognized that a study drawn from office practice would not represent a population-based sample, it was believed that findings from such a study would provide more relevant norms for U.S. girls than currently exist. Of the 17,077 girls, 9.6% were African-American and 90.4% were Caucasian.

4. Because nationally representative data on the subject were lacking up until the publication of Hermann-Giddens et al. 1997 (see below), clinicians largely relied on Marshall and Tanner's classic study on pubertal changes in girls, published in 1969. See Marshall and Tanner 1969.

5. There has been a dramatic increase in overweight and obese children in the United States over the past 20 years, and a concurrent rise in incidence of Type 2 diabetes in youth. See Shinha et al. 2002.

6. Despite widespread awareness and condemnation of child abuse, a 1995 study (Giles-Stiles et al. 1995: 170–176), offers evidence that a majority of parents in the U.S. physically punish their children. Interviews with mothers showed that 61% had spanked their pre-schooler in the past week. Twenty-six percent had spanked their pre-schooler three or more times over the past week. It is estimated that a pre-schooler receives over 150 spankings a year. The physical punishment of children also continues to enjoy state and institutional sanction: 22 states in the U.S. still allow corporeal punishment in schools.

7. In 1989, when the Parliament of Canada vowed to eliminate child poverty by the year 2000, 15% of the nation's children (or one in seven) were living in poverty. Since then, 400,000 more Canadian children have become poor, increasing Canada's child poverty rate by 39%. One in five, or 20% of all children in Canada now live in poverty. Food bank use has also increased in Canada since 1989. The largest group of people served by food banks is single-mother-headed families (Canadian Association of Food Banks, *2001 Hunger Count Survey*, March 2001).

References

Ariés, P. *Centuries of Childhood: A Social History of Family Life*. Translated by R. Baldick. New York: Alfred A. Knopf, 1962.

Aronowitz, S., and W. DiFazio. *The Jobless Future: Sci-Tech and the Dogma of Work*. Minneapolis: University of Minnesota Press, 1995.

Baudrillard, J. *The Ecstasy of Communication*. Translated by B. Schutz and C. Schutz. New York: Semiotexte, 1988.

Bauman, Z. "Consuming Life." *Journal of Consumer Culture* 1, no.1 (2001): 9–29.

Beck, U. *Risk Society Toward a New Modernity*. Translated by M. Ritter. London: Sage, 1992.

Belkin, L. "The Making of an 8 Year Old Woman." *New York Times Magazine*, December 24, 2000, 38–43.

Blanck, H. M., M. Marcus, P. E. Tolbert, C. Rubin, A. K. Henderson, V. S. Hertzberg, R. H. Zhang, and L. Cameron. "Age at Menarche and Tanner Stage in Girls Exposed in Utero and Postnatally to Polybrominated Biphenyl." *Epidemiology* 6 (November 11 2000): 641–647.

Bourdieu, P. *The Logic of Practice*. Cambridge: Polity Press, 1990.

———. *Outline of a Theory of Practice*. Cambridge: Cambridge University Press, 1977.

Butler, J. *Bodies That Matter: On the Discursive Limits of Sex*. London: Routledge, 1993.

———. *Gender Trouble: Feminism and the Subversion of Identity*. London: Routledge, 1990.

Canadian Association of Food Banks. *2001 Hunger Count Survey*, March 2001.

Caspi. A., and T. E. Moffitt. "Individual Differences are Accentuated During Periods of Social Change: The Sample Case of Girls at Puberty." *Journal of Personality and Social Psychology* 61 (1991): 157–168.

Deleuze, G. *Coldness and Cruelty. A Discussion of 'Venus in Furs' by Leopold von Sacher-Masoch*. New York: Zone Press, 1989.

————. *Essays Critical and Clinical*. Translated by D. Smith and M. Greco. Minneapolis: University of Minnesota Press, 1997.

Deleuze, G., and F. Guattari. *A Thousand Plateaus: Capitalism and Schizophrenia*. Translated by B. Massumi. Minneapolis: University of Minnesota Press, 1987.

Delphi, C. "Rethinking Sex and Gender." *Women's Studies International Forum*, 16, no. 1 (1993): 1–9.

Ellis, B. J., S. McFayden-Ketchum, K. Dodge, G. Pettit, and J. Bates. "Quality of Early Family Relationships and Individual Differences in the Timing of Pubertal Maturation in Girls: A Longitudinal Test of an Evolutionary Model." *Journal of Personality and Social Psychology* 77, no. 2 (1999): 387–401.

Ellis, B. J., and J. Garber. "Psychological Antecedents of Pubertal Maturation in Girls: Parental Psychopathology, Stepfather Presence, and Family and Marital Stress." *Child Development* 71 (2000): 485–501.

Environmental Protection Agency (EPA). *Special Report on Environmental Endocrine Disruption: An Effects Assessment and Analysis*. Washington, D.C.: U.S. EPA, 1997.

Foucault, M. *The History of Sexuality, Vol. 1: An Introduction*. New York: Vintage Books, 1990.

Friedman, S. *Girls in the 90's*. Vancouver, Canada: Salal, 1994.

Fulsang, D. "Mom, I'm Ready for School." *The Globe and Mail*, Saturday September 28, 2002, L1.

Furlong, A., and F. Cartmel. *Young People and Social Change*. Buckingham: Open University Press, 1997.

Fuss, D. *Essentially Speaking: Feminism, Nature, Difference*. New York: Routledge, 1989.

Giles-Sims, J., M. A. Straus, and D. B. Sugerman. "Child, Maternal and Family Characteristics Associated with Spanking." *Family Relations* 44, no. 2 (1995): 170–176.

Girl Scout Research Institute, (2000) *Girls Speak Out: Teens Before Their Time*. New York: Girl Scouts of the USA, 2000.

Giroux, H. *Stealing Innocence: Youth, Corporate Power and the Politics of Culture*. New York: St. Martin's Press, 2000.

Grossberg, L. "Why Does Neo-Liberalism Hate Kids?: The War on Youth and the Culture of Politics." *The Review of Education/Pedagogy/Cultural Studies* 23, no. 2 (2001): 111–136.

Grosz, E. *Volatile Bodies: Towards a Corporeal Feminism*. London and New York: Routledge, 1994.

Hermann-Giddens, M., E. Slora, R. Wasserman, C. J. Bourdony, M. V. Bhapkar, G. Koch, and C. M. Hasemeier. "Secondary Sexual Characteristics and Menses in Young Girls Seen in Office Practice: A Study from the Pediatric Research in Office Settings Network." *Pediatrics* 99, no. 4 (1997): 505–512.

Hightower, J. "How Wal-Mart Is Re-Making the World." *The CCPA Monitor* 9, no. 6 (2002): 10–12.

James, A. *Childhood Identities: Self and Social Relationships in the Experience of a Child*. Edinburgh: Edinburgh University Press, 1993.

James, A., C. Jenks, and A. Prout. *Theorizing Childhood*. Cambridge: Polity Press, 1998.

Jones, B., J. Leeton, L. McLeod, and C. Wood. "Factors Influencing the Age of Menarche in a Lower Socio-Economic Group in Melbourne." *Medical Journal of Australia* 2 (1972): 533–535.

Kampert, J. B., A. S. Whittemore, and R. S. Paffenbarger. "Combined Effects of Childbearing, Menstrual Effects and Body Size on Age-Specific Breast Cancer Risk." *American Journal of Epidemiology* 128 (1988): 962–979.

Kerstetter, S. "Rags and Riches." *The CCPA Monitor* 9, no. 6 (2002): 1,7.

Kincaid, J. R. *Erotic Innocence: The Culture of Child Molesting*. Durham and London: Duke University Press, 1998.

Kovarik, J. "The Space and Time of Children at the Interface of Psychology and Sociology." In *Childhood Matters: Social Theory, Practice and Politics*, edited by J. Qvortrup, M. Bandy, G. Sgritta and H. Wintersberger. Aldershot: Avebury, 1994.

Krstevska-Konstantinova, M., C. Charlier, M. Craen, M. DuCaju, C. Heinrichs, C. deBeaufort, G. Plomteux, and J. P. Bourguignon. "Sexual Precocity after Immigration from Developing Countries to Belgium: Evidence of Previous Exposure to Organochlorine Pesticides." *Human Reproduction* 16, no. 5 (2001): 1020–1026.

Lee, N. *Childhood and Society: Growing Up in an Age of Uncertainty*. Buckingham: Open University Press, 2001.

Lukacs, G. *History and Class Consciousness: Studies in Marxist Dialectics*. Translated by R. Livingstone. Cambridge, Mass.: MIT Press, 1971.

Manlove, J. "Early Motherhood in an Intergenerational Perspective: The Experiences of a British Cohort." *Journal of Marriage and the Family* 59 (1997): 263–279.

Marshall, W. A., and J. M. Tanner. "Variations in the Pattern of Pubertal Changes in Girls." *Archives of Diseased Child* 44 (1969): 291–303.

McNay, L. "Gender, Habitus and the Field: Pierre Bourdieu and the Limits of Reflexivity." *Theory, Culture and Society* 16, no. 1 (1999): 95–117.

McRobbie, A. *Feminism and Youth Culture*. Boston: Unwin Hyman, 1991.

Moffitt, T. E., A. Caspi, J. Belsky, and P. A. Silva. "Childhood Experience and the Onset of Menarche: A Test of a Sociobiological Method." *Child Development* 63 (1992): 47–58.

Ness, R. "Adiposity and Age of Menarche in Hispanic Women." *American Journal of Human Biology* 3 (1991): 41–48.

Pipher, M. *Reviving Ophelia: Saving the Selves of Adolescent Girls.* New York: Ballentine, 1994.

Rifkin, J. *The Age of Access: The New Culture of Hypercapitalism Where All of Life Is a Paid-For Experience.* New York: Putnam Books, 2000.

Seaton, E. "The Commodification of Fear." *Topia* no. 5 (2001): 1–15.

Seigworth, G. "Sound Affects." CultStud-L List, September 5 1999. Available from www.cas.usf.edu/communication/rodman/cultstud/columns.

Shinha, R., G. Fisch, B. Teague, W. Tamborlane, B. Banyas, K. Allen, M. Savoye, V. Rieger, S. Taksali, G. Barbetta, R. Sherwin, and S. Caprio. "Prevalence of Impaired Glucose Tolerance Among Children and Adolescents with Marked Obesity." *The New England Journal of Medicine* 346, no. 2 (2002): 802–810.

Soper, K. *What Is Nature?: Culture, Politics and the Non-human.* Oxford: Blackwell, 1995.

Tiwary, C. M. "Premature Sexual Development in Children Following the Use of Placenta and/or Estrogen Containing Hair Products." *Pediatric Research* 135 (1994): 108A (abstract).

Townsend, M. S., J. Person, B. Love, C. Achetenberg, and S. Murphy. "Food Insecurity Is Positively Related to Overweight in Women." *Journal of Nutrition* 131 (2001): 1738–1745.

Wierson, M., P. J. Long, and R. L. Forehand. "Toward a New Understanding of Early Menarche: The Role of Environmental Stress in Pubertal Timing." *Adolescence* 28 (1993): 913–924.

Wyn, J., and R. White. "Negotiating Social Change: The Paradox of Youth." *Youth and Society* 32, issue 2 (2000): 165–183.

Zelizer, V. *Pricing the Priceless Child: The Changing Social Value of Children.* Princeton, New Jersey: Princeton University Press, 1994.

CHAPTER FIVE

The Body of Evidence

Dangerous Intersections between Development and Culture in the Lives of Adolescent Girls

MARY K. BENTLEY

As I was walking through a major department store in our local mall I was stopped dead in my tracks by a mannequin in front of me. I'm sure many of you have had the experience of being "snuck up on" by a mannequin, but the reason for my fear was not its placement, its wild hair, or strange dress, it was the mannequin itself. It (it was a she) looked sick, emaciated, as if it could hardly stand under the burden of its own weight. I stood there gawking at this shocking image, with disbelief and concern about the message it conveyed, when I heard two young women commenting on the dress worn by this mannequin. Their conversation, with this form looming above them, went something like this:

GIRL #1: I love that dress.
GIRL #2: Me too, but I would have to lose forty pounds to wear it.
GIRL #1: You! Look at my gut, I am a huge hog. I should never eat.
GIRL #2: You know Jenn, in fourth period, she didn't eat for two days and her stomach was totally flat.

As I peered around the display, I saw two girls about twelve or thirteen years old strolling toward the cosmetic department, clutching plastic bags and drinking Diet (in large letters) Cokes. Neither one of them was overweight. They looked like healthy middle school girls. This scene bothered me so much that I decided to go back to the store with a measuring tape and actually take the measurements of this form. When I attempted this, I was stopped by a sales clerk who wished to direct me to the rack where I could find the dress on display. I tried to explain the situation to her, but she got very uncomfortable and called the manager. After explaining to three different people that I was contributing to a book on adolescent girls and I was interested in knowing the proportions of the mannequins they used in their displays, I was finally told that I could not disturb the display and was referred to the corporate office. I called the corporate office. After some additional explanation, I was given the phone number of a man who is in charge of dressing displays. A brief phone conversation with him led to a visit.

He was a wealth of information and gave me a fascinating account of the historical evolution of the mannequin. He explained that mannequins have gone through many incarnations over the past thirty years. He was very animated in his descriptions of mannequins that had exaggerated body parts, like cinched waists and large hips and breasts in the 1950s, mannequins that were actual body casts of models complete with genitalia in the 1970s, and the advent of the girlish flat-busted form of the 1980s. The mannequins he currently uses for displays are generally very thin. He explained: "The waif-like heroin addict is the look that dominates most of the young women's displays." He further added that in some of the displays they now "add a substantial breast to the form, the Pamela Anderson kind of thing, for more provocative displays."

He was in the process of dressing two mannequins and agreed to measure them for me. The first was 5'8" tall. Her measurements were 30" bust (she had no pads on, a la Pamela Anderson), 23" waist, and 32" hips. The second was 6 ft. tall with a 32" bust, 23" waist, and 31" hips. They both had 18" thighs and upper arms of less than ten inches. When I asked how the proportions of the mannequins were determined, he replied: "They were made so the clothes fit right and look the way they are supposed to." Perhaps even more disturbing were his projections about the future evolution of the female form in displays. He replied by saying that display dressers were going toward a complete abstraction of the forms to display clothing. He cited designers who were "just using two sticks" or "abstract metal cross-like forms." At that point we both just looked at each other, mouths open, and said, "Wow," at the same time.

A mannequin is by definition a life-sized model of the human body, used to fit or display clothes. If the forms he measured were real bodies, there would be very little life in them. The average woman in the United States is a size 14. According to international sizing charts, this means she has a 38–39" bust, 29–31" waist, and 39–40" hips, more than 6 inches larger than this mannequin (32–23–31). Strange as it seems, the girls were right. They *would* have to lose forty pounds.

Learning about Being Female

> Young women are engaged with questions of "being female"; that is, who will control, and to what extent they control, their own bodies.
>
> —MICHELLE FINE, *DISRUPTIVE VOICES*

Girls are constantly barraged by images of women from a wide array of cultural sources. From these many sources girls begin to understand the implications of power, prestige, wealth, and male attention that are bestowed upon women who are culturally defined as "attractive." Consequently, their value is measured by physical attraction.

In an extensive study looking at how adolescent boys and girls rate their self-worth, Stephanie Harter concluded that physical appearance is the most important domain contributing to children's and young adolescents' sense of self-worth, outpacing social acceptance, scholastic and athletic competence, and behavioral conduct. This seemed to be particularly true for girls

(Harter 227). So where does an adolescent girl get the idea that how she looks determines her worth?

A primary source of attractiveness messages for girls can be found in widely read magazines targeted to this population, such as *Seventeen* and *YM*. Numerous studies have documented the fact that these magazines focus primarily on beauty and fashion (Duffy and Gotcher, Peirce), weight loss and physical attractiveness (Guillen and Barr), physical self-improvement (Evans, Rutberg, Sather and Turner), and the link between being physically beautiful and sexually attractive to males (Durham).

In addition, there is evidence that one of the strongest, most pervasive sources of such messages is television, specifically commercials. Television commercials strongly reinforce the importance of appearance and attractiveness. In the mid-1980s, Chris Downs and Sheila Harrison examined 4,294 network television commercials and found that 1 out of 3.8 featured an attractiveness-based message, (17). They estimated that children and adult viewers were, at that time, exposed to an average of 14 of these messages each day. They proposed several reasons why television advertising acts as a primary disseminator of attractiveness stereotypes. Perhaps the most significant of these is that attractiveness messages are not critiqued by the viewer. In fact, the authors claim that it is television that makes this attractiveness norm "real," particularly for children and adolescents, since they most often believe that what they see on TV is "the real world." These researchers concluded: "Overall then there are compelling reasons to suspect that television acts as a salient source of 'attractiveness oriented socialization'" (14).

More recently the effect of television advertising on body image distortion in young women was examined. Phillip Myers and Frank Biocca found that watching as little as thirty minutes of television programing and advertising had an effect on how women evaluated their bodies. "There may be some cumulative effect of all these messages. It is reasonable to imagine that each of these body image messages is just one strike on a chisel sculpting the ideal body inside a young woman's mind" (111).

Like the mannequins in the mall, models who embody the ideal female form also have an effect on the ways in which girls learn to evaluate their attractiveness, and hence their worth, in the culture. Mary Martin and Patricia Kennedy asked girls in grades eight and twelve to answer questions about their physical attractiveness, the way they rated themselves, and their overall self-esteem. They found that as girls get older they tend to compare themselves with fashion models more often. This comparison was even more pronounced for girls with lower scores on measures of self-perceptions of physical attractiveness and/or self-esteem. Remarkably, the researchers found "even one-time exposure to highly attractive advertising models raises comparison standards for physical attractiveness in 8th and 12th graders" (527).

According to Myra and David Sadker: "As girls move into adolescence, being popular with boys becomes overwhelmingly important. It is the key to social success because the boys measure the girls' physical attractiveness. They (girls) look to males for esteem, hoping to see approval and affirmation in their eyes" (85). In this difficult time they learn that the labels of popular and pretty are handed out by the boys and reinforced by both the girls and the boys. It is these labels that will, to a large extent, determine who will be successful. So girls learn to self-monitor their food intake, their exercise, and the appearance of their bodies as a necessary measure to achieve social, economic, and relational success.

In fact, obese girls and women often suffer a myriad of cultural/social sanctions for their unacceptable physical appearance. Numerous studies have demonstrated that obese women are most likely to suffer from job discrimination and a hostile work environment, are less popular, and less successful with dating and marriage opportunities (Margolin and White, Wooley and Wooley cited in Fredrickson and Roberts 177–179). For obese females there is little or no consideration for the genetic/metabolic indicators that are major etiological factors in obesity. The culture condemns them as "women who have let themselves go," who are "lazy," "inactive," and, most importantly unattractive, hence of little value (Fredrickson and Roberts 179). This phenomenon plays out differently for women than it does for men. "For women, positive self-concept hinges on perceived physical activeness, whereas for men, it hinges on perceived physical effectiveness" (Lerner, Orlos, and Knapp cited in Fredrickson and Roberts 179).

We must remember, however, that cultural ideals of attractiveness are subject to dramatic changes. What was considered attractive and desirable in one decade may change dramatically in the next. Marilyn Monroe was considered the ideal of feminine beauty in the 1950s and was a size 12 in her movies only through constant dieting. For most of her life she was a size 16 (Nadelson). In contemporary culture the yardstick by which girls self-monitor is an extraordinarily thin, unhealthy, and in most cases unobtainable ideal, like the mannequin. But this cultural ideal is so pervasive that it becomes each individual girl's responsibility to "make herself right." In this regard there is an expectation that a girl "should" reduce her size and change the appearance of her body through the restriction of food intake or dieting. Part of being the "perfect girl" is being a thin girl, and that means taking control of her unruly body and appetites. The problem is that when girls are learning this female responsibility, they are also experiencing profound changes—that is to say they are developing a woman's body: "[S]ensing something amiss at adolescence, they sought the answer in their individual biology. Their bodies were changing, becoming curvy and fuller, taking on the shape of a woman. They [girls] were changing, in a way over which they had no control—they did not know whether they would be small breasted and large hipped or whether their bodies would eventually end up as the teenagers in *Seventeen*" (Orbach 168).

Growing into Girls: Development

> Like the tightening of a corset, adolescence closes around these precocious, authoritative girls. They begin
> to restrict their interests, confine their talents, pull back on their dreams.
> -SADKER AND SADKER, *FAILING AT FAIRNESS*

In elementary grades girls possess a strong sense of themselves, of what they can be and who they can become. They exist side by side with boys, inviting new challenges, eager to try anything, interacting with the world, physical, vital. For many girls, this freedom is short-lived as they begin to understand what it means to be female in a world that objectifies and devalues the feminine.

Girls often learn to censor themselves and present the "nice girl," the "perfect girl" to those from whom they need approval. This means abandoning aspects of their former selves, the bravado and zest for life, leaving behind all their knowledge about self and the world learned through this way of being. As their bodies change, so do their identities. For girls, adolescence is not only a time of changing body shapes, but a time they are mandated by the culture to change their identities, the essence of who they are and how they take in the world. Girls must transform themselves into the role of the feminine in our culture, which means being nice, sweet, pretty, and thin. These are the things that we have come to know as "feminine." These are also the characteristics that make it difficult for girls to be agents on their own behalf as they perpetuate objectification and passivity.

There is also significant evidence that as girls enter adolescence they experience a marked drop in self-esteem (Sadker and Sadker 77–78). If, as the aforementioned research points out, physical attractiveness is the yardstick by which girls will be measured, then it follows that their self-worth would diminish as their bodies grow out of control and away from this very thin cultural standard. Self-esteem is not only a vital sign of mental health, it is also a connection to academic achievement and a direct link to career goals and hope for the future (Sadker and Sadker 78–79). Learning to be female in our culture not only diminishes a girl's potential, it also, and rather suddenly, reduces her worth in the larger culture. She is reminded through constant body and behavioral monitoring whether or not she is meeting the perfect girl standard. It is this very standard that pushes her away from authentic relationships, which are critical to healthy growth and development, and into relationships where she learns to play the role of nice girl.

In their book *Failing at Fairness*, Sadker and Sadker asked middle schoolers this question: "Suppose you woke up tomorrow and found you were a member of the opposite sex? How would your life be different?" (83–85). Many of the girls (42 percent) came up with very good things about being male, like having more respect and more money and being less worried about what other people think. Boys, however, were often repulsed by the notion of being female. Only 23 percent of them could come up with any benefits, and 16 percent came up with desperate fantasies about how to get out of the female form, mostly involving suicide. "I would kill myself right away by setting myself on fire so no one knew." "I'd wet the bed, then I would throw-up. I'd probably go crazy and kill myself." After reading hundreds of boys' essays, the researchers were "shocked at the degree of contempt expressed by so many" (Sadker and Sadker 85).

Taking Control?

Given this playing field, where boys are so repulsed by the notion of being female, it is difficult to determine how a young girl could successfully negotiate her changing world. What would control over her body, perhaps one of the only sources of control available to her, mean? For most girls dieting becomes a way of life. Approximately 50 percent of adolescent and young women are dieting at any one time, while half of these individuals are at or below normal weight (Centers for Disease Control). Despite many of the media-generated claims to the contrary, dieting simply does not change a girl's morphology, or body type. In fact, dieting in normal weight individuals can have detrimental psychological and physiological effects, with weight fluctuation, not permanent weight loss, as the most prevalent result. According to the Centers for Disease Control, "one third to two thirds of the weight lost during dieting is regained within one year, and almost all is regained within five years" (2811).

While girls may believe that dieting will increase their sense of power, self-esteem, success, and control, diets, and the weight fluctuation that is most often the end result, do just the opposite. Weight fluctuation has been strongly associated with negative psychological effects in normal weight and obese individuals (Foreyt). So if a girl diets and the diet fails to change her body into the ideal one, she may have an even further diminished sense of worth.

One of the most widely cited surveys on body image was conducted in 1972 and 1985 by *Psychology Today*. In 1997 they again asked their readers to respond to more than five pages of items related to how they see, feel, and are influenced by their bodies (Garner). The first 4,000 respondents were included in the analysis. Most were white (87 percent), female (86 percent), college graduates (62 percent), and heterosexual (93 percent). Women seemed to be more dissatisfied with their bodies than ever before with 89 percent wanting to lose fifteen pounds or more. Among young women ages 13–19, 62 percent claimed they were dissatisfied with their weight. When asked about the origins of this discontent, most women (58 percent) claimed it was their personal feeling about weight, 44 percent, claimed it was from being teased by others, and 23 percent claimed they had been influenced by movie or TV celebrities. In the extremes of weight management, 23 percent of women reported vomiting and 50 percent reported cigarette smoking. Fifteen percent claimed they would sacrifice more than five years of their lives to be thin, while 24 percent were willing to sacrifice three or more years of their lives. "We can confidently conclude that a significant minority of you believe life is not worth living if you are not thin" (Garner 30).

Strategies for Control?

[A]lthough young women today enjoy greater freedom and more options than their counterparts of a century ago, they are also under more pressure, and at greater risk, because of a unique combination of biological and cultural forces that have made the adolescent female body into a template for much of the social change of the twentieth century.

—JOAN BRUMBERG, *THE BODY PROJECT*

With 62 percent of the young women responding that they are dissatisfied with their weight (Garner), and an overwhelming number of girls who consider themselves overweight or anorexic/bulimic, it becomes clear that they are responding to some kind of cultural demand. The experience of girls as they move into adolescence can be seen as a kind of cultural mirror, reflecting back strategies for coping with the increasingly loud messages they are receiving about who the culture demands they should be. There appear to be three strategies young girls use to take control of their lives and hence their bodies: dieting, overeating, and anger. The first two have led to an increase in young girls with eating disorders, the third to young girls being rebellious.

The first strategy is best described by Hilde Bruch in her book *The Golden Cage: The Enigma of Anorexia Nervosa*. Although this book is more than twenty years old, it continues to be a relevant source for describing this disorder. Here she describes what the extreme end of self-imposed restriction means to the girls who live with it and the way it gives them a sense of control. "[N]ot to give in to any bodily demand becomes the highest virtue. Most vigorously denied is the need for food. However painful the hunger, to tolerate it for one more hour, to postpone even the smallest amount, becomes a sign of victory" (62). She further describes that this detachment from internal body signals also applies to body fatigue: "Hunger is not the only bodily demand that is denied: not giving in to fatigue rates equally high. Swimming one more lap, running one more mile, doing ever more excruciating calisthenics, everything becomes a symbol of victory over the body" (63).

Louise Perimenis describes this extreme control in terms of what it means about the cultural context of being female: "Anorexia nervosa is an expression of the construction of gender in American society; it is both a ritual of self-effacement and a ritual of empowerment for women and girls par excellence. In a visceral way it allows women and girls to experience (and display) what it means to be inferior—hence, unentitled members of society—through the physical pain of constant hunger" (49).

In *The Body Project*, Joan Brumberg suggests this obsession with the body has become so culturally indoctrinated that it is used as a proxy to measure mental health. "The increase in anorexia nervosa and bulimia in the last thirty years suggests that in some cases the body becomes an obsession, leading to recalcitrant eating behaviors that can also result in death. But even among girls who never develop full-blown eating disorders, the body is so central to definitions of the self that psychologists sometimes use numerical scores of 'body esteem' and 'body dissatisfaction' to evaluate a girl's mental health" (xxiv).

A second strategy for resolving these cultural dilemmas is practiced by girls who compulsively overeat. Anorexics share with compulsive overeaters a conscious desire to control their world. Overeating may be a way to avoid being sexually objectified. It is a way to take yourself out of competition with other girls and to be left alone by boys. This makes authentic relationships, with both boys and girls, more likely. These girls are safer, easier to be real with. They can also be seen as a reminder that they will not be controlled. They will eat what they want and wear it, literally. "The crucial difference for anorexics and for overweight women is that the kind of attention they do attract is of a different nature, outside the status of a sex object. Broadly this means men will dismiss her and other women will relax in her presence" (Orbach 174)

A third strategy, particularly among those who also experience discrimination and oppression in addition to those imposed by gender, is that of anger. These girls act out their anger both physically and verbally with an "in your face" attitude. In more than six years of listening to the stories of adolescent girls in detention centers and juvenile facilities in both New Mexico and New York, I have heard very clearly and very loudly these voices of resistance. These girls are not "nice." They are not "sweet." They are "bad girls," rejecting the feminine by acting out their anger and assuming the role of the male—being one of the guys. In a chapter co-written with Pat McPherson, Michelle Fine wonderfully describes this strategy, gleaned from conversations with four self-defined "bad girls":

> The behavior, clothing and values associated with such identification with boys and sports suggests both a flight from femininity they collectively described as "wearing pink," "being prissy," "being Barbie," and "reinforcing guys all the time,"—and an association of masculinity with fairness (vs. cattiness), honesty (vs. backstabbing), strength (vs. prissiness, a vulnerability whether feigned or real), initiative (vs. deference or reactionary comments), and integrity (vs. the self-doubt and conflicting loyalties dividing girls). The four's risk-taking behaviors—driving fast, sneaking out at night—reinforced identities as "one of the guys." Such are the bad girls. (Fine 196–197)

This strategy of rejecting the feminine by being "one of the guys" may also be evidenced in the numbers of girls who are committing violent crimes. Take notice of the growing numbers of girls in corrections and detention facilities, just like the boys.

Offering Alternatives

The question becomes: In a culture that trains adolescent girls to be quiet, nice, thin, and invisible to the point of incarceration or anorexia, what supports are necessary to help them negotiate this developmental period and come out intact? That is, how can we help them come through adolescence with a clearer sense of who they are and what forces have shaped them? We need to cultivate strategies that offer alternatives to playing the role of the "perfect girl," who is primarily concerned with how attractive she is. Alternative means to achieving cultural success and opportunities for relationships need to be established and maintained within institutional structures so girls have a wider array of options available from which to learn who they are and what they could become during this important developmental period.

A Critical Lens

First, girls need to learn how to identify and critique cultural messages. Identification is the first essential step. The mannequin, for example, is a clear cultural message that contributes to an unrealistic ideal. The act of taking the measurements, of critically assessing how unrealistic this form is, is healthy and self-affirming. Acts such as these help girls to understand the magnitude of the conspiracy afloat. The translation of the message from the unconscious mind to a conscious realization of the effect these images have is an essential skill for girls. This skill needs to be taught in all manner of ways, in public (schools, community groups) as well as private (family, relational) spaces. All youth need to learn to critique the messages that inundate them by measuring these messages against their lived experiences, not the "real" as depicted by television, advertisements, magazines, and mannequins. This kind of vigilance gives girls a tool, a way to sift through the images and messages, and make meaning of them in a conscious way. This is an active process of taking in the world that allows girls a chance to be agents on their own behalf, so that the objectification girls experience in their daily lives does not lodge so firmly in their collective brains. Girls need to understand that the option to critique and reject some of these images is as strong a possibility as the options of dieting, anorexia, obesity, violence, and diminished sense of self. Susan Faludi, in her book *Backlash*, writes about the cultural backlash against women saying: "It [the backlash] is most powerful when it goes private, when it lodges inside a woman's mind and turns her vision inward, until she imagines the pressure is all in her head, until she begins to enforce the backlash too, on herself" (xxii).

Safe Spaces

Second, girls need safe spaces. Girls need a chance to experience their bodies and their voices in spaces where they will not be held to the cultural restrictions of the "feminine." They need places where they can run, play, and explore, without self-censoring, silencing, and monitoring. This may mean having girls-only spaces, or spaces where girls can interact with women who are committed to letting girls be rather than insisting they conform to the cultural stereotype.

These spaces will have to be outside of the traditional spaces where girls interact with the larger culture. School is one of the most dangerous places for girls to be authentic. It is where the rules for being a girl are most strongly enforced. Instead, .athletics, organized clubs, and out-door trips where girls are measured by what they can do provide spaces where girls can excel on their own terms. Girls need opportunities where they can see what their changing bodies can do. They need spaces where they can know what they know and try new identities without self-censoring. Without safe spaces, girls will not be fully able to discover who they are and who they would like to become.

Voice Lessons

Third, girls need models of women and of other girls who have had the courage to speak up, to use their voices on their own behalf, with positive, self-affirming results. This requires women to challenge the silence in their own psyches and become examples of courage. Girls need to see women in their daily lives who summon the courage to speak and who insist on taking up space, in both public and private spaces. They need to know the consequences of surrendering their voic-es and taking on the voice of the "perfect girl." They need to understand that depression and sui-cide, as well as anorexia, unintended pregnancies, smoking, HIV, and a whole host of other dangerous situations are all consequences of "lost voice." Perhaps it is best said by the very coura-geous Audre Lorde: "My silence has not protected me. Your silence will not protect you. . . . In the case of silence, each of us draws the face of her own fear—fear of contempt, fear of censure, of some judgment, of recognition, of challenge, of annihilation. But most of all I think, we fear for the very visibility without which we cannot truly live" (Lorde 20–21).

Reflecting on a series of dinnertime conversations with a group of four girls from a variety of racial and socioeconomic backgrounds, Michelle Fine and Pat MacPherson (Fine 185) com-ment: "They (the girls) are often reminded of their bodies as a public site (gone right or wrong), commented on and monitored by others—male and female. But as often, they reminded us, they forcefully reclaim their bodies by talking back and by talking feminist. 'It'd be harder not to talk,' Sophie thinks. 'It'd be harder to sit and swallow what people are saying.'"

Voice is not without consequence. Detention centers and juvenile facilities are full of girls who speak out in anger. Many of these girls refused to be invisible, refused to be mute. These girls underscore the need not only for safe space but also for guidance, like "voice lessons." It is critical to have the opportunity to practice, to learn when it is safe, when there is support, and when there is not. There is no question that as the world becomes an increasingly unsafe place, there are times when it is not in the best interest of an individual girl to resist those who are unjust. Voice lessons involve learning a variety of ways to use tone, pitch, and volume. So that girls won't be taken out of the discourse by falling mute from a diminished sense of self, being locked up from acting out, or disappearing altogether from anorexia, it is critical for girls to learn and prac-tice the full range of voice possibilities as strategies to stay intact, as a path for nurturing self, and increasing opportunities.

When writing a speech for a feminist gathering, Audre Lorde was contemplating her fear of using her voice, of her move from silence: "And of course I am afraid, because the translation of silence into language and action is an act of self-revelation, and that always seems fraught with danger. But my daughter when I told her of my topic and my difficulty with it, said, 'Tell them about how you're never really a whole person if you remain silent, because there is always that one little piece inside you that wants to be spoken out, and if you keep ignoring it, it gets madder and madder, and hotter and hotter, and if you don't speak it out one day it will just up and punch you in the mouth from the inside'" (8).

We as women (mothers, aunts, sisters, daughters, friends), and all those who want girls to learn to honor and respect themselves, those of us who know the lost potential in our own lives, need to better understand the dilemmas that girls navigate each day and help them develop strategies within and around them. Perhaps this way fewer of us will be punched in the mouth, from the outside or the inside. Perhaps then we can better navigate these *dangerous intersections*.

QUESTIONS TO CONSIDER

1. How apt is the author's analogy of the mannequin to the female image? What realities and fantasies are expressed in that analogy?

2. Which media sources seem most significant in conveying images of the "female form"? How do such images change over time? Give examples.

3. Trace the development of girls from childhood to adolescence. Some research shows that girls typically face "cultural devaluation" as they grow into their teens. What evidence do you perceive to confirm or disconfirm such an assessment?

4. In what ways do young girls attempt to gain mastery and control over their bodies and lives? Give examples.

5. Bentley describes the school as "one of the most dangerous places for girls to be authentic." Do you agree with that characterization? Why or why not?

6. What parallels do you draw from the "nice girl/perfect girl" image and the fear of speaking out? How can adolescent girls develop their voice "as a path for nurturing self"?

This chapter originally appeared in Sharon R. Mazzarella and Norma Odom Pecora (eds.), *Growing Up Girls: Popular Culture and the Construction of Identity* (New York: Peter Lang, 1999).

Works Cited

Bruch, Hilde. The *Golden Cage: The Enigma of Anorexia Nervosa*. Cambridge: Harvard University Press, 1978.

Brumberg, Joan Jacobs. *The Body Project: An Intimate History of American Girls*. New York: Random House, 1997.

Centers for Disease Control. "Leads from the Morbidity and Mortality Weekly Report." *Journal of the American Medical Association* 266 (1991): 2811–2812.

Downs. Chris, and Sheila K. Harrison. "Embarrassing Age Spots or Just Plain Ugly? Physical Attractiveness Stereotyping as an Instrument of Sexism on American Television Commercials." *Sex Roles* 13 (1985): 9–19.

Duffy. Margaret, and J. Micheal Gotcher. "Crucial Advice on How to Get the Guy: The Rhetorical Vision of Power and Seduction in the Teen Magazine *YM.*" *Journal of Communication Inquiry* 20 (1996): 32–48.

Durham, Meenakshi G. "Dilemmas of Desire: Representation of Adolescent Sexuality in Two Teen Magazines." *Youth and Society 29* (1998): 369–389.

Evans, Ellis D., Judith Rutberg, Carmela Sather, and Charlie Turner. "Content Analysis of Contemporary Teen Magazines for Adolescent Females." *Youth and Society* 23 (1991). 99–120.

Faludi, Susan. *Backlash: The Undeclared War against Women.* New York. Doubleday Books, 1991.

Fine, Michelle. *Disruptive Voices: The Possibilities of Feminist Research.* Ann Arbor: University of Michigan Press, 1992.

Foreyt, James. "Psychological Correlates of Weight Fluctuation." *International Journal of Eating Disorders* 17 (1995): 263–275.

Fredrickson, Barbara, and Tomi-Ann Roberts. "Objectification Theory: Toward Understanding Women's Lived Experiences and Mental Health Risks." *Psychology of Women Quarterly* 21 (1997): 173–206.

Garner, David. "The 1997 Body Image Survey Results: An In-Depth Look at How We See Ourselves." *Psychology Today* Feb. 1997: 30–44, 75–84.

Guillen. Eileen O., and Susan I. Barr. "Nutrition, Dieting, and Fitness Messages in a Magazine for Adolescent Women, 1970–1990." *Journal of Adolescent Health* 15 (1994): 464–472.

Harter, Stephanie. "The Determinants and Mediational Role of Global Self-Worth in Children." *Contemporary Issues in Developmental Psychology.* Ed. Nancy Eisenberg. New York: John Wiley and Sons, 1987. 18–72.

Lorde. Audre. *Sister Outsider: Essays and Speeches.* Trumansburg, NY: crossing Press, 1984.

Martin, Mary C., and Patricia Kennedy. "Advertising and Social Comparison: Consequences for Female Preadolescents and Adolescents." *Psychology and Marketing* 10 (1993): 513–530.

Myers, Phillip N., and Frank Biocca. "The Elastic Body Image: The Effect of Television Advertising and Programming on Body Image Distortions in Young Women." *Journal of Communication* 42 (1992):108–136.

Nadelson, Robert. "Marilyn Monroe: Was She Really a Size 16?" *Style Magazine* Sept. 1995: 88–91.

Orbach, Susie. *Fat Is a Feminist issue.* New York: Berkeley Books, 1978.

Peirce, Kate. "A Feminist Theoretical Perspective on the Socialization of Teenage Girls through *Seventeen Magazine.*" *Sex Roles* 23 (1990): 491–500.

Perimenis, Louisa. "The Ritual of Anorexia Nervosa in Cultural Context." *Journal of American Culture* 14 (1991): 49–59.

Sadker, Myra, and David Sadker. *Failing at Fairness: How Our Schools Cheat Girls.* New York: Touchstone/Simon and Schuster, 1994.

CHAPTER SIX

Urban African American Female Students and Educational Resiliency

VENUS EVANS-WINTERS

As raced, classed, and gendered subjects, urban African American female students are multiply affected by racist, sexist, and classist research paradigms and their resulting educational policies. Needless to say these racist and sexist frameworks have affected research on or about Black girls and women, as researchers and the researched. In the lives of African American girls and women, racism, sexism, and classism are three interdependent control systems. Simultaneously and interdependently, White racism has suppressed urban Black girls within racialized identities; patriarchy has subordinated them and deemed them powerless; concurrently their lower-income and working-class status has forced them to the periphery of society. Their raced, classed, and gendered bodies have made them both invisible and hyper-surveillanced in educational policy and within the urban school system.

Because African American females experience the intersection of race, class, and gender simultaneously, they become easy targets in the subordination and legitimation process in Western society.[1] As articulated by Patricia Hill Collins,[2] "Portraying African American women as stereotypical mammies, matriarchs, welfare recipients, and hot mommas, helps justify US Black women's oppression".[3] Collins further states that these socially constructed images are designed to make racism, sexism, and poverty, and other injustices appear to be a normal part of life.[4] Politicians, the media, social service personnel, religious groups, and researchers tend to focus on teenage pregnancy and high school dropout rates among urban African American adolescent girls. The generalized depressing statistics about poor minority girls erase the role of discriminatory practices in education and other social structures.[5] Very rarely do we hear discussions about the majority of Black girls from urban and inner-city communities that graduate high school and college. There is a need for more urban education research and pedagogical reform efforts that look at how urban girls are resilient despite their risks and vulnerabilities.

Resiliency Research

Resiliency studies ask questions pertaining to the motivation and persistence of students. Research on resilience is more likely to ask the following question: What resources do students identified as "high-risk" have in place to support educational achievement? Resiliency is the ability to recover from or adjust to problems, adversities, and stress in life.[6] For women and African Americans, academic achievement has been associated with social and economic mobility. However, very little research has focused on factors that enhance positive educational development among African American females. Instead, the majority of research on Black female students focuses on social problems, such as school dropouts, drug and alcohol use, welfare dependency, and teenage pregnancy.[7] The discussion below focuses on educational resiliency in the lives of a group of African American female students living in a midsize urban city in the Midwest.

Researching processes of resiliency

The results reported below are based on a three-year ethnography that followed five students from their eighth grade school year to their junior year in high school.[8] Data was gathered in the form of field observations in family homes, neighborhoods, and schools, as well as open-ended interviews. The original purpose of the study was to look at how the interaction of racism, classism, and sexism impacted the school experiences of urban African American female adolescents. However, after implementing the study, the theme of resiliency dominated the theme of subjugation in the lives of the selected students. I learned from the most educationally resilient students that support from the family, community, and school simultaneously buffered adversity and fostered school resiliency. Three of the five students were found to be educationally resilient, as measured by school persistence.

All the students in the study lived in low-income and working class neighborhoods. They also attended the more high-risk middle schools and local high school, which were identified as such by their high student dropout rate, high mobility rate, and the number of low-income students who attended the school. I found that resilient students in the study did not dichotomize or order the significance of their stressors. Most of the stressors that the students experienced occur at the intersection of their race, class, and gender. Consequently, these stressors have affected the young women's educational experiences. In the discussion following, I attempt to extract out the stressors and support systems that the resilient students experience as urban girls.

Context-specific stressors

Four of the five students experienced some kind of medical problem that impeded on the schooling process. For example, one student, Nicole, reported that she was hospitalized for pneumonia, and as a result required home schooling for the first three years of her education. She also reported that she was diagnosed as having Attention Deficit Hyperactivity Disorder, prior to entering middle school. To cope with her medical problems, Nicole and her mother were required to integrate their resources from the Department of Children and Family Services

(DCFS) and the school, which included at-home tutoring provided by the school and paid for by DCFS. In Nicole's case, the family, community, and school came together to help her achieve academically.

Likewise, another student, Zora, reported that teachers thought she had a learning disability, because she had refused to talk at school for a period of time. Obviously, it is not known if a student's environment, income status, or biology caused any of their health conditions. However, from other research it is known that there exists a relationship between poverty, health problems, and student deficits at school.[9] Zora eventually thrived, despite the circumstances that may have caused her speech delays. Two of the students who were found not to be educationally resilient, but resilient nonetheless, left school due to early pregnancies.

Other stressors that the students in the study reported encountering were racism and classism in the larger community, police or government intervention in family affairs, violence and drug trafficking in their neighborhoods, hostile school environments, etc. All the students described how negative media perceptions of their school have affected students' interactions with teachers and staff. As Zora explained about her high school, "It's like every year, they get a new rule, and it gets stricter and stricter." Using the pregnant body as a point of reference, Pillow explains how the female body is a "site of paradoxical social attention and avoidance."[10,11] Like the pregnant body, the bodies of African American female adolescents have always been sites monitored, avoided, and scrutinized by those holding power. Whether the power holders are caregivers, slave masters, legal/political bodies, or school officials, the Black female adolescent body has been the targeted culprit.[12] Zora is conscious of her and her female peers' targeted bodies.

Many of these factors had not only affected the Black girls' individual (micro-level) school experiences, but it had managed to affect them on a broader (macro) level. For example, the students in the study were affected by teacher shortages and were less likely to have an African American female as a teacher. Yet, they were more likely to be educated by bitter White teachers, who found themselves with low pay, few resources, and teaching in an environment that was "culturally" different from their own. I can only presume that these were the "prejudiced" teachers the students described in their life stories. As for resilience, the most resilient students located resources that countered prejudicial behavior. For instance, Nicole located an African American teacher at school, who she felt understood her emotional needs growing up as an urban girl. The third resilient student, Yssis, who had more trouble finding solace in the school building, located a mentor through a community organization. Zora, on the other hand, found solace in her own acquired skills, by interacting with and mentoring students who were considered outsiders by their peers.

Another example of gender and cultural-specific stress that is linked to their context, is that the young women in the study also found themselves being surveillanced by policies that dictated what they learned, how they dressed, and how they behaved. For example, all the girls in the study complained of school policies that appeared to allude to the sexual messages in their styles of dress (i.e., girls were not permitted to wear sleeveless blouses or tank tops). Most of the girls alleged the policies served to try to prevent sexual molestation or rape by controlling young women's behaviors. These policies are racist and sexist in thinking. First of all, the policies are targeting the potential victim's behavior. Second, the policies assume there is going to be a victim. As we hear from the girls, many of the policies at their schools were put into place because the larger community views them as uncivilized heathens, who need to be contained. Even more, it is assuming that the Black girls in the school building are jezebels, who tempt the potential rapist (or, some may conclude, the girls' victim).

Fortunately, the most resilient students in the study were conscious of how the images held by members of the larger community and society affected the rules and discipline policies of their local school buildings. What is even further interesting is that the most resilient students attempted to guard against "tainting" their own images. They strived to maintain the "good girl/good student" image by avoiding sexual relationships with boys and participating in the labeling of "those girls" who fit the "loose girl/bad girl/bad student" stereotype. These gender-specific resilient strategies have worked to the advantage of the resilient students.

In sum, all the gender and cultural-specific stress, derived from their families, communities, and schools, only caused more stress between the students themselves. Therefore, it was even difficult for students to turn to their peer group for support. Only one of the three students, Zora, expressed a somewhat high attachment to other students attending her high school. None of the students reported spending time with peers located in their immediate neighborhoods. In the case of the resilient young women, community organizations and extracurricular activities at school at least provided a supportive environment for the opportunity to foster peer relationships. All the girls had participated in community and school student groups.

I argue that the stressors that the young women experienced throughout their educational career are related to their race, class and gender, and where they live and attend school. I also argue that these gender and cultural-specific stressors required the most resilient students to draw on gender and cultural-specific resiliency fostering supports.

Resilience and African American female students

After reading the stories of the most resilient students, we are able to begin to answer the following questions: Who are the students who are more likely to stay in school? What factors contribute to students staying in school? When were the profiled African American female students at their most resilient? What are the historical, economic, and political conditions that affect their schooling process? And, how do the most resilient African American female students cope with, resist, or buffer adversity?

I found that the most resilient students were those young women who received support from their family, community, and schools simultaneously. Because the young women's stressors could not be dichotomized, neither could their support systems. For example, in the conversation below, Nicole's words demonstrate how outside forces affect the schooling process.

> N: It was kind of hard when I was in kindergarten, because my mom, we got taken from her, and all that kind of stuff. So, it was kind of hard for us. For me, because I was the baby in kindergarten. It was hard. We would like go to the courthouse almost everyday. They come pick us up from school and stuff.

It appears that those families and students, who were more adept at blurring the boundaries between family, community, and school, were the most resilient, for their stressors were very rarely easily divisible; thus, their resources were not stratified either. The more a student was able to utilize resources at home and in the community, the more likely she was to stay psychologically (measured by school involvement in extracurricular activities) and physically (measured by school attendance) attached to the school building.

Community support

Community resources that assisted in educational development usually included after-school programs like tutoring, mentoring, or group-related activities. In most cases, community participation usually depended on its relevance to school. Participation in religious services was the exception. Most students attended church, because they had family members who attended the church, they felt it was the "right thing to do," or simply to worship. However, church appeared to be very important to all three resilient students. Educational resilience many times was also reinforced at the community level, by programs that offered the young women temporary job opportunities during the summer or after school. Even in the community work programs, the most resilient students still took preferred job assignments that focused on education or learning in some capacity (i.e., tutoring younger students or providing childcare).

Besides, most of the resilient students associated out-of-school interns or work programs as learning opportunities. For example, Nicole tutored children, because she thought that it gave her the chance to see what it would be like to be a teacher who cared. Another example includes Yssis' decision to continue working at her summer job with children, because it offered a college scholarship incentive to long-term employees.

It is important to restate that in some cases lines were blurred between stressors and resources. For example, Zora and Nicole both received intervention services through DCFS, which may be categorized as potential stressors or distractions to student education and development. Postmodern tenets remind us that we must avoid binarial thinking that would force us to order stressors and buffers, because the two may actually be working bi-directionally. For example, I found that all the resilient students were very concerned with their grades. The student's over-concern with grades may actually produce more stress and strain in her life, while also encouraging her to work harder as a student. Looking at stressors, support systems, and individual agency simultaneously, reminds us that resiliency-fostering factors are dynamic in nature.

In this particular study, the resilient students and their families utilized community resources as a mediating entity as they negotiated a space of their own in the realm of education. The resilient student understood that community resources assisted in their educational development by providing networking opportunities (i.e., community mentors), and needed resources such as paid work, community mentors, tutoring services, or a safe space beyond their schools and homes. Yssis sums up the role of community organizations in the lives of resilient Black girls. When I asked Yssis how her community could help her with school, she responded:

> Well, they do got a lot of programs and stuff around, but all the commotion around the neighborhood . . . I think that we should move somewhere, like away from this drama. People fighting every day, arguing, saying stuff that kids don't need to hear . . . But, it's a lot of programs around the neighborhood that'll help you with your school and stuff. If you need to just talk, somebody always there to talk to you.

School support

Like with community resources, the most resilient students were keen at taking advantage of resources available to them at the school itself. For instance, all three of the resilient students in this study at some point sought tutoring in at least one subject. Moreover, the resilient students were also more likely to participate in extracurricular school activities that supported their long-term goals. Because all the young women had planned on completing high school and going on to college, all three participated in Junior Recruitment Officer Training Corp (JROTC), with the goal of receiving a college scholarship. Resiliency studies show that students who are involved in school activities are more likely to be academic achievers and to complete school on time; thus, these students early on had increased their chances of completing high school.[13]

Furthermore, the resilient students appreciated stern but understanding teachers. Also, all the resilient students voiced the need for Black female teachers. I do not believe that the girls necessarily felt an African American female teacher could teach them more or any better than a White teacher. My hypothesis is that the students associated African American female teachers as being stern and empathetic to their needs and the adversities they faced in life (qualities similar to their mothers). As pointed out by Lisa Delpit,[14] some African American teachers bring a teaching style to the classroom that is congruent with the parenting styles that some African American children are accustomed to at home. It too was assumed by the students that African American teachers had the potential of mixing caring and sternness to provide an ideal learning environment. Moreover, the students welcomed those teachers, regardless of race, who were fair.

In contrast to other ethnographies, this study also found that even the resilient young women were in opposition to unjust school policies and discipline procedures. Oppositional behavior was displayed in "talking back" to teachers and other school staff, refusing to carry out a punishment, or simply choosing to ignore a school rule or policy. Different from other studies on resistors, the resilient young women continued to attend school and soon enough decided to conform to what it took to graduate from high school. Their conformity was marked by their advocacy for more school programs and extracurricular activities that made education fun, like it was prior to high school.

Even though all the resilient students generally had a negative attitude about their schools' environment (staff and other students), most had positive feelings about at least one adult in their school. A positive feeling toward an adult in the school was usually a result of one-on-one contact, such as after school tutoring. For example, Nicole, an honor roll student, stated, "those teachers don't understand us ghetto children." When I asked her to explain her comment further she explained, "We need some Black teachers. The teachers are prejudiced. Get us some books." Interestingly, this same resilient student named her White resource teacher as the one person who has helped the most at school with her schoolwork. As a side note, Nicole also mentioned the emotional support that she received from an African American female in her school, who was not a teacher. Therefore, research on gender and cultural-specific resilience programs might emphasize that the race of a teacher is less important than the caring nature of the teacher and the ability of the teacher to understand the cultural experiences of the students.

These findings on teachers' caring attitudes toward students are consistent with Valenzuela's work with Mexican and Mexican American students' perceptions of schoolteachers.[15] As Valenzuela found in her research:[16]

> The individual histories that teachers and students bring to classroom encounters necessarily influence the chances for successful relationship building. Still, in most cases, there is likely to be some room to maneuver that is, if the situation is approached literally "with care."[17]

Because caring relationships with teachers were not very frequent, the family members of the students also contributed to support school persistence. Although all the students' families had experienced crisis of their own at some point in their child's educational career, they were able to meet the educational needs of their child. Most of their crisis situations were related to their social and economic positions in the city in which they lived. For example, Yssis's family had survived a divorce and the incarceration of her father; Nicole's biological mother had lost custody of her children; and Zora experienced the death of her biological mother in the middle of her freshman year of high school. Ironically, none of the students lived with both their (biological) mother and father during the time of the study. Yet, all of the resilient students named a family member as their main source of support. More specifically, the young women named their female caregiver as the one person who has helped them "get this far" in school.

Familial support

In my view, family support was the most dynamic in nature amongst the resilient qualities of students. Family support defied almost everything I have ever learned in sociological theory about educational resilience. For instance, most hypotheses state that those students who come from two parent (heterosexual) families are going to be more competent in society. However, I learned that the most resilient or competent students were those students who felt love in their family. Although Yssis and Nicole admitted having missed building a relationship with their fathers, none of the resilient students felt that living in a single-parent household (or not with their biological parents) negatively affected their education. All three of the resilient young women felt that their parents cared about their educational accomplishments and wanted them to do well in school. More importantly, all the students reported that a family member helped them directly with some aspect of their schooling, like completing a homework assignment or providing assistance with studying for an examination. In the dialog below, Yssis, as a junior, discusses her mother's role in her educational development:

V: Tell me who has helped you get this far in school?

Y: Mainly, my mom, because she really like pushed me to get good grades and stuff. Like if I ever brought home like a "D" or something, she'll be like, "Well, you just gotta work more in this subject" or whatever. Then, I'll probably get an "A" in it the next week. She helps me a lot too.

Aside from emotional support (i.e., girls reported that mother is "there for me when I need her"), or financial support (i.e., providing housing or clothing), family support also included monitoring school participation (i.e., intervening with discipline problems at school or even punishing a student for not doing well in school). Nevertheless, very high attachment to a female caregiver was very significant in the resiliency process. For example, the forms of support listed above were more likely to come from a primary female caregiver, such as a mother, grandmother, or aunt. The study found that relationships between maternal caregivers and students fostered resilience, when students experienced a "muse" relationship with their mothers.

Muse relationships are relationships that are more natural in nature, as opposed to mentoring relationships, where an adult guide is usually assigned to a student. With muse relationships, students are able to choose their own role model, who usually is someone from a similar background or community as their own.[18] Furthermore, muse relationships, like the ones that appeared to have been more worthwhile and effective for the resilient students, teach girls life lessons by sharing from one's own experience. This study found that female caregivers, who were reportedly more open and honest with their daughters about their life experiences, produced stronger mother–daughter relationships. Even more, it was also found that regardless of other available mentors or role models, resilient students always named their female caregiver as the main source of support.

Individual Agency

Although support from the family, community, and school is significant in fostering educational resilience, students' individual intentions and motivations also play a significant role in school persistence. For instance, all the resilient students in the study looked forward to completing high school and eventually going on to college and having a long-term career. In fact, the most resilient students had already developed a plan for their life course. For example, in the eighth grade, Zora's goals were to go to high school, get into the nursing academy, and get involved in school activities, graduate from high school, and go to college. Of course, not all of the girls' goals worked out as planned, but it is still important to mention that the most resilient students had some type of plan in place. Maybe their articulated goals actually served as a buffer to school failure.

Grades also appear to be very important to the most resilient students. The most resilient students seemed to be always conscious of their grade evaluations, and usually strived to do better in school or in a particular class. I found grade evaluations to be a stressor for all the resilient young women, instead of serving as a reward or positive reinforcement. Regardless of the level of real or perceived stress, the resilient students asked for help or sought out useful resources in their family, community, or schools. Despite their ability to seek out social and academic resources in the community, the most resilient students were also those who had low attachment to their community neighborhoods. Yssis, for instance, simply chose not to associate herself with any of her peers at school or in the neighborhood. Nicole and Zora's parents simply forbade them to hang out in their neighborhoods. Definitely, the most resilient students were not "social butterflies" in their immediate neighborhoods, by choice or by force. Notwithstanding their low attachment to their immediate neighborhoods, the most resilient students and their families were more likely to have a low mobility rate. Nicole and Zora have lived in the same neighborhood and homes from kindergarten through high school, and Yssis from approximately fourth grade through high school. Therefore, low mobility was also a supporting factor in the students' resiliency.

Another significant finding to point out about the character of the most resilient students is that these young women were also very attuned to and vociferous about intimate relationships with boys, sex, and the possible negative consequences of an early unplanned pregnancy. The resilient young women rationalized from the experiences of others around them (i.e., peers, neighbors, or family members) that sexual activity was a potential threat to their educational and career goals. In other words, intimate relationships with boys and pregnancy were viewed as a threat to their long-term goals, and were behaviors that they were almost always conscious of and articulated often in their educational stories.

Also, it is important to mention that resilience is a process. The most educationally resilient students did not necessarily display the qualities listed above all at once or all the time. Just like any other skill, building relationships with adults, asking for help, and participation in extracurricular activities, require skills that we are more adept or comfortable with at a particular time. For instance, some students in the study had to work on improving their school attendance, or others ended their participation in a school organization. Yssis, for example, had decided that she no longer felt comfortable participating in after-school activities offered at a local community organization. Similarly, Zora's relationship with a boyfriend interfered with her attendance record, and Nicole found that her plans for joining the cheerleading team had to be altered. What is more important about the resilient students is that they showed resilience over time. The most resilient students had the motivation and resources to access the available support systems that were necessary to bounce back from adversity.

Implications for Urban Education Reform

Not only does structural inequality shape the specific stressors in urban girls' lives, but it also shapes the systems of support that Black girls depend on to cope. Unfortunately, current literature on resiliency does not acknowledge the interaction of race, class, and gender, or the influence of individual agency and social structures on African American female students' educational development. A new and more inclusive cultural and gender-specific look at school resilience has the potential of having a transcending effect on school reform. For example, this new focus in resilience research can assist reformers in producing more cultural and gender-specific resiliency programs. Also, this new perspective may bring cultural and gender-specific issues (i.e., concerns that Black feminists have traditionally addressed) to education policy and pedagogy discourse altogether. Resilience research has the potential of assisting policymakers in identifying the impact of race, class, and gender oppression on educational experience and outcome. Many researchers in urban education have studied the impact of race and class discrimination on urban education,[19] but very few have studied gender oppression in urban education. Even more important is the fact that little or no research has focused on the ways in which women of color cope with and overcome many forms of gender, race, and class oppression, and maintain resilience in the face of adversity.

Rigsby reminds us that resilience is contextually bound in time and place and culture.[20] African American female students' educational experiences are impacted by their race, class, and gender status. Their educational experiences are also influenced by where and how they live.

Multiple identities and multiple oppressions require that minority females draw on unique cultural and gender-specific systems of support. From past research with African American females, their families, and their communities, we are able to recognize resilience-fostering factors.[21] We also realize the need for a more inclusive definition of resilience and a need to reconstruct resilience. Finally, gender- and culture-specific resilience research has the potential to help facilitate progress in urban education reform initiatives. Resilient African American female students struggle against race, class, and gender oppression. For instance, African American female students are more likely to attend schools in urban neighborhoods with high poverty, unemployment, and high crime rates than their white counterparts,[22] and to live in a world that privileges White over Black, male over female, and wealth over poverty. In spite of social and institutional racism and sexism, the majority of African American females have been able to achieve academically. More resilient adolescents may obtain support from the family, community, and/or school, that serve as protective factors against academic failure.

QUESTIONS TO CONSIDER

1. How does the author define "resiliency," and how does she claim resiliency research is a different kind of research?

2. What is meant by "culture-specific" and "gender-specific" resilient strategies? What can be their positive and negative effects? Give examples.

3. Which students in the study were more likely to cope with psychological, physical, and educational stressors? Which resources were most beneficial in their coping strategies?

4. How did the most resilient students use school policies and practices to their advantage? Give examples.

5. What seem to be the most important ingredients in familial support? Are any of those factors surprising to you? If so, why?

6. Evans-Winters uses the term "agency." What does it mean, and how is that concept played out in the lives of some of the resilient youth in her study?

NOTES

This chapter originally appeared in Joe L. Kincheloe and kecia hayes (eds.), *Teaching City Kids: Understanding and Appreciating Them* (New York: Peter Lang, 2007).

1   L. F. Miron, *The Social Construction of Urban Schooling: Situating the Crisis* (Cresskill, NJ: Hampton Press, Inc., 1997).

2   P.H. Collins, *Black Feminist Thought: Knowledge, Consciousness, and the Politics of Empowerment* 2nd ed. (New York: Routledge, 2000).

3   Ibid., p. 69.

4   Ibid.

5   B.J.R. Leadbeater and N. Way, *Urban Girls: Resisting Stereotyping, Creating Identities* (New York: New York University Press, 1996).

6   J.B. Ashford, C.W. LeCroy and K.L. Lortie, *Human Behavior in the Social Environment: A Multidimensional Perspective* (Pacific Grove, CA: Brooks/Cole, 1997).

7   Ibid.

8   V.E. Evans-Winters, *Reconstructing Resilience: Including African American Female Students in Educational Resilience Research.* Unpublished Dissertation. (Urbana-Champaign: University of Illinois at Urbana-Champaign, 2003).

9   I.A. Canino and J. Spurlock, *Culturally Diverse Children and Adolescents: Assessment, Diagnosis, and Treatment* (New York: The Guilford Press, 1994).

10 W.S. Pillow, "Exposed methodology: The body as a deconstructive practice," in E.A. St. Pierre, and W.S. Pillow, eds. *Working the Ruins: Feminist Poststructural Theory and Methods in Education* (New York: Routledge, 2000), pp. 199–222.

11 Ibid., p. 201.

12 A.Y. Davis, *Women, Race, and Class* (New York: Random House, 1981); D. Roberts, *Killing the Black Body: Race, Reproduction, and the Meaning of Liberty* (New York: Random House, Inc., 1997).

13 M.C. Wang and E.W. Gordon, *Educational Resilience in Inner-City America* (Mahwah, NJ: Lawrence Erlbaum, 1994).

14 L. Delpit, *Other People's Children: Cultural Conflict in the Classroom* (New York: The New Press, 1995).

15 A. Valenzuela, *Subtractive Schooling: U.S. Mexican Youth and the Politics of Caring* (New York: University of New York Press, 1999).

16 Ibid.

17 Ibid., p. 73.

18 A. M. Sullivan, "From mentor to muse: Recasting the role of women in relationships with urban adolescent girls," in B.J.R. Leadbeater and N. Way, eds. *Urban Girls: Resisting Stereotypes, Creating Identities* (New York: New York University Press, 1996), pp. 226–254.

19 J. Anyon, *Ghetto Schooling: A Political Economy of Urban Educational Reform* (New York: Teachers College Press, 1997); C.M. Payne, *Getting What We Ask For: The Ambiguity of Success and Failure in Urban Education* (Westport, CT: Greenwood Press, 1994); R. Taylor, "Risk and resilience: Contextual influences on the development of African American adolescents," in M.C. Wang, and E.W. Gordon, eds. *Educational Resilience in Inner-City America: Challenges and Prospects* (Mahwah, NJ: Lawrence Erlbaum, 1994), pp. 119–130.

20 L.C. Rigsby, "The Americanization of resilience: Deconstructing research practice," in M.C. Wang, and E.W. Gordon, eds. *Educational Resilience in Inner-City America: Challenges and Prospects* (Mahwah, NJ: Lawrence Erlbaum, 1994), pp. 85–96.

21 C.A. Bagley and J. Carroll, "Healing forces in African American families," in H.I. McCubbin, ed. *Resilience in African American Families* (Thousand Oaks, CA: Sage, 1996); A. M. Cauce, Y. Hiraga, D. Graves, N. Gonzales, K. Ryan-Finn and K. Grove, "African American mothers and their adolescent daughters: Closeness, conflict, and control," in B.J.R. Leadbeater, and N. Way, eds. *Urban Girls: Resisting Stereotypes, Creating Identities* (New York: New York University Press, 1996), pp. 100–116; M.L. Clark and D. Scott-Jones, "The school experiences of black girls: The interaction of gender, race, and economic status," *Phi Delta Kappan, 67* (1986): 520–526; A. Henry,

"Invisible and womanish: Black girls negotiating their lives in an African-centered school in the USA," *Race, Ethnicity, and Education, 1(2)* (1998): 151–170; J.A. Ladner, "Introduction to tomorrow's tomorrow: The black woman," in S. Harding, ed. *Feminism and Methodology* (Bloomington: Indiana University Press, 1987).

22   J. Anyon, *Ghetto Schooling: A Political Economy of Urban Educational Reform* (New York: Teachers College Press, 1997); M. Fine, *Framing Dropouts: Notes on the Politics of an Urban Public High School* (NY: SUNY Press, 1991); W.J. Wilson, *When Work Disappears: The World of the New Urban Poor* (New York: Random House, 1996).

CHAPTER SEVEN

Making a Way Out of No Way

Black Male Students at City High School[1]

GARRETT ALBERT DUNCAN & RYONNEL JACKSON

Introduction

The Schooled Lives of Black Male Students in Post-Civil Rights America

Established in 1972 in a mid-sized metropolitan setting in the Mid-west United States, City High School (CHS)[2] has a national reputation as a racially integrated public school that emphasizes a rigorous curriculum and that produces first-rate students. In addition to its curriculum, CHS is also known for its "caring" ethic, which was instituted by the school's founding principal and is codified in the school's mission statement. Anyone who visits CHS will conclude that its reputation for being a caring, high-achieving school is indeed merited. However, not unlike other fragmented communities that at first glance appear to be internally coherent,[3] CHS has demographic fractures that marble a school that, observed from a distance, appears to be a paragon of academic excellence and educational equity. Black male students, for instance, have not fared as well as their peers at CHS. For example, although the school is racially balanced, females outnumber males by a ratio of 2:1 as a direct result of the dearth of black male students. The absence of these students was realized most poignantly in 1998, a term that the school ranked first on the state's high-stakes examination. The school year concluded with only one black male student, from an initial cohort of 15, walking with his graduating class at commencement time.

Conventional wisdom in society suggests that the exclusion and marginalization of black males from schools such as CHS is a normal, albeit problematic, aspect of the education of this population of students. Studies in the United States and the United Kingdom seem to provide support for this pervasive belief.[4] Most studies describe how adolescent black males and/or their families contribute to the problem of underachievement, while others also point out the roles of schools in creating these outcomes.

For example, in her study of a predominately black urban high school, Fordham (1996) posits that black families, especially mothers, largely contribute to the problem of underachievement and maladjustment of black male students by encouraging them to embrace a "two-fold contradictory formula" in their approach to academic and social decision-making. In other words, parents encourage their sons "to concurrently accept subordination and the attendant humiliation (for survival in the larger society), and preserve gender domination (for survival in the black community)" (p. 148). What this means is that black parents urge their sons to downplay the significance of racism in their lives even as they encourage them to adopt patriarchal attitudes and behaviors "to be both non-dominating and successful in a racialized patriarchy" (p. 149). Fordham notes that the formula, however, is complicated by the contradictory status of what it means to be both black and male in North American society. She concludes that black males largely reject their subservient place in the gender hierarchy of schools and appropriate alternative forms of black masculinity that "further stigmatize them, reproducing the patriarchy and their consignment to secondary domination" (p. 165). This is not really a short comment though, perhaps in other words? In other words, Fordham surmises that black families contribute to the educational woes of black male students by providing them with untenable strategies for negotiating hostile academic climates, and that black males further contribute to their problems by appropriating attitudes and behaviors that exacerbate their marginalization and exclusion in schools.

Other ethnographic studies describe how race and gender converge on and through black male students in schools to shape their social and academic experiences, and often to their disadvantage. For example, Ferguson describes the daily interactions between black pre-adolescent male students, their peers and teachers, that illustrate "a disturbing tautology [where] transgressive behavior is that which constitutes [black] masculinity.[5] Consequently, African American males in the very act of identification, of signifying masculinity, are likely to be breaking the rules" (p. 170). Similarly, in a study of a boys' comprehensive school in Britain, Sewell argues that teachers and peers impose sexualized perceptions on black boys and that black boys appropriate "normative notions of masculinity that act as an oppressive and repressive agent on their schooling."[6] Sewell explains that schools do not exist in a vacuum though, and that influences from the wider society, including forms of popular culture such as music, also influence how black boys are perceived and perceive themselves. Likewise, Mac an Ghaill examines the production of heterosexual masculinities in his study of an English secondary school.[7] He posits that black male students, their peers, and teachers construct these compulsory identities within complex sets of power relations that have particular references to class, race, and ethnicity.

Black Male Students: Strange or Estranged?

One may conclude from the overviewed studies that, for black male students, school success comes at a great personal loss, both real and imagined. In short, the literature frames the issue of their schooling in terms of a dilemma where black male students are damned if they do and damned if they do not achieve academically. Unsurprisingly, the typical orientation of psychological, sociological, and anthropological research on black male students is toward explaining the motivational, affective, or cognitive bases of their actions, or on explicating the cultural resources that they bring to bear in making academic and social decisions in school. In addition, researchers devote considerable attention to identifying interventions and strategies to rehabilitate and to incorporate black males more fully into schools; most pedagogical, policy and programmatic responses to the problems of these young men are similarly focused. However, as we describe in the sections that follow, responses to the purported crisis of black males, even when they are guided by the best intentions, do little to enhance their experiences in schools and, in some instances, reinforce their marginalization.[8] We posit that the intransigent nature of the problems black male students encounter in schools is indicative of populations that are socially constructed as fundamentally different from those who are deemed normal in society. Such constructions result in conditions for these populations in which they become estranged from the rest of society.

In previous publications,[9] we argued that the values that typically inform inquiries into the lives of estranged groups, such as black male students, derive from curiosity and control.[10] The aim of such inquiries is to understand better these groups and to determine effective ways to integrate them into institutions, or to devise compensatory programs to support them in attaining some measure of success within these social structures. However, as we noted, critics of "problem-solving approaches" argue that this orientation leaves institutions unexamined for their complicity in reproducing a racist social order,[11] and reinforces notions that members of oppressed groups are strange.[12] In other words, marginalized populations possess values and attitudes that require explication and clarification because they are fundamentally different from those of the rest of society.

It is in this way that society tacitly constructs black males as a strange population and contributes to the widespread perception that their plight in schools is unremarkable: the dominant frame, or storyline, suggests that black males are too different from other students, and oppositionally so. Moreover, it comes as no surprise that they have difficulty in schools, especially in those with high-powered academic programs and codes of conduct that rely on student consent and compliance for their enforcement. Thus, despite the intentions of the researchers who employ it, the problem-solving orientation in research on black male students tends to gloss over the conditions of their estrangement and reinforces the perception of their strangeness, which only contributes to their further marginalization in school and society.

Beyond Love at City High[13]

As we suggest above and describe in previous writings,[14] even well-intentioned "interventions" for black male students function in some ways to reinforce the dominant storyline about their academic engagement and to marginalize them even as they seek to ameliorate their conditions. For example, after one of the initial visits by the first author to CHS in the spring of 1999 to talk with members of the mentoring program that the school's administration created for black male students, one of the younger adult mentors, a 25-year-old black male, shared the following observations:

> Some of the more recent speakers have come speaking to our students as if they have the solutions to ALL of their problems (including [a prominent black educator that had recently conducted an all-day professional development workshop at CHS]), and after the presentation, their problems would be solved. . . . These younger brothers don't need a speech or series of speeches, they need positive and conscious Black men like ourselves to be honest with them, guide them, and truly listen to them. (4/29/99)

The views of this mentor are not unlike Nel Noddings's observation that "our claim to care must not be based on a one-time, virtuous decision but rather on continuing evidence that caring relations are maintained."[15] To address their concerns: "they need the continuing attention of adults who will listen, invite, guide, and support them."[16]

Data from this study indicate that black male students encounter at CHS a school climate that, for them, is characterized by a form of indifference, or estrangement, that contributes to their marginalization and oppression. This point is best illustrated in the contradictory effect of a mentoring program that was established to stave the attrition rate of the black male student population. For instance, during an all-school assembly on the first day of the 2000–2001 school year, the first author scanned the audience for the faces and expressions of black male students during an announcement regarding the mentor program. During the announcement he experienced that "peculiar sensation," described by W. E. B. Du Bois, that is brought on by "a world that looks on in amused contempt and pity."[17] For the most part, the young men he observed either looked down or straight ahead, in ways to suggest that they were shutting out the announcement. Their behavior was cause for me to wonder what the program meant to them. In terms of what the program signified for some of their peers is best captured in the following account by a research assistant, composed from field notes and observational data, that portrays an exchange between students in a hallway during a passing period that indicates disdain for the perceived dependency of black males on others at the school:

> When the bell rings to indicate the end of class I notice this white girl, standing next to an African American female student, shouting "hello" to many other students. Her social interactions interest me, so I ease over to listen in on her conversations. At this point, she is leaning over the balcony, shouting to a friend in the cafeteria.
>
> "Hey, are you joining the black male mentor program?" she calls down to an African American male.
>
> "Naw, I don't need that," he answers. There is no hint that he is either startled or offended by her question.
>
> "Well, I'm starting a female Caucasian group," she screams back. She laughs and seems to be unconcerned that she may have offended either of her friends. Neither of the students responds to her last comment and the three take up separate conversations with other students. (02/16/01)

With respect to those for whom the intervention was intended to benefit, all the young men we interviewed stated that they found the mentoring sessions to be helpful. However, the boy's response in the previous exchange and, more generally, the low and inconsistent attendance of black male students at meetings suggested that the program represented something more complicated in their lives at school. Indeed, during sessions, mentors sometimes conveyed contradictory messages to the mentees: they encouraged them to do well academically but also blamed the young men for the stereotypical attitudes that their teachers had of them. For example, on one such occasion during the spring of 2000, Jack, the second author, conducted a group interview at CHS with members of the mentoring group. However, older adult mentors who were present interjected themselves into the conversation. On the one hand, they counseled and encouraged the young men, yet, on the other hand, they peppered their advice with comments that apologized for uncaring teachers and that blamed the young men for their conditions at CHS.

At the same time, the video record of the session captured the young men strategically rolling and closing their eyes as well as glancing at the clock on the wall. We use the term "strategically" because these actions were often embedded in others, such as reaching for a buffalo wing, sipping soda from a cup, stretching, and shifting one's weight in the chair. The mentors, who regularly chastised the students for what they deemed to be disrespectful or inappropriate behavior, never remarked upon and appeared to not notice what the young men were doing, further supporting our view that the young men were engaged in clandestine activities. The boys also appeared to be communicating with one another, not only through eye contact but also through auditory cues, such as synchronized coughs and throat-clearings. A full transcript and analysis of this session are provided elsewhere [18]

The Cultural Resourcefulness of Adolescent Black Males; or, How Aquil Flipped the Script and Lived to Tell About It

Piqued by what we observed in the video footage, we organized a session to conduct stimulated recall interviews with some of the mentees who were present at the mentoring session. This interview session involved reviewing the video tape of the mentoring session. In addition, it was video taped with Aquil and Roger, two students from the mentoring session, at the university. During the university session, Aquil repeated the concerns that his peers raised in the earlier session, namely that adults at the school treat black males unfairly. Specifically, he complained that teachers and other adults at CHS who have marked him as having an "attitude problem" constantly picked on him. Aquil, however, recast "attitude" as an adult problem, as opposed to a black male problem. "Definitely," he contended, "they have an attitude toward us. People like . . . people like have an attitude problem toward us." Aquil also set the record straight about what teachers perceive to be his attitude problem: "She would say, 'that boy has a . . . Aquil has a smart mouth,' I don't got a smart mouth, I just 'respond'—I respond to questions! She asked me a question and I was like, 'huh? What happened? Like, you going to sue me? I ain't got no money. . . .'"

Mark Tappan and Lyn Mikel Brown suggest that the key to understanding the complexity of moral situations is found not only in the relationship between the cognitive and affective dimension, but also in the conative dimension of how individuals construct their experiences.[19] The conative dimension focuses on what people do and, along these lines, of particular relevance to this paper, are aspects of the stories that Roger and Aquil told during the recall interview that provide insight into strategies they employ when they feel authority figures are disrespecting them and when it appears that they have no way out of the situation—where they are outnumbered and outgunned. In the following story told during the recall session, Aquil describes how he got out of a situation at CHS when he felt that he was being unfairly targeted for reprimand by the school's security guard. In doing so, he illustrated how the use of a strategy similar to those that he and his peers also appeared to have employed during the previous mentoring session helped him to survive a testy situation. Aquil recounted the story as follows:

Well, wait a minute, I was running through the hallway, right? He was chasing me, yeah, he was chasing me because I said something to him. I think I told him that his pants were too [ ] or something. And I ran past this, what was that, uh Mephistopheles, right? [group laughter] straight up, right? And I run past her, right? She looks and I'm like, "whatever." Then I kept on running and then I came back, she said, "Come here. Now, if you would have ran into me, I would have sued you for assault." And I was like, "huh?" She said, "yeah, I could have just sued you for assault." "Aw, sue me what?" "You were running in the hallway. If you had bumped into me, I would have sued you." I was like, "whatever, can I go?. . . ." She was like, "No I want to talk to you." "No," I was like, "I got to go to class . . ." She was like, "I want to talk to you right now . . ." "No, I'm going to be tardy bye." That was all I did. I haven't said nothing to her since. I ain't said nothing else to her at all since then. I would have took her on Judge Judy and sued for some pennies, now. Straight up. But Judge Judy would do that type of stuff, too.

Aquil retold this episode in response to Jack's follow-up inquiry exploring students' complaints about double standards at the school. It was obvious to Aquil that the security guard was subjecting him to a double standard; however, as indicated elsewhere, he was also aware at the time that she perceived him as having an "attitude" problem—recall that "Aquil has a smart mouth." But passive acquiescence is not an option for this young man, as suggested in his words above. At the same time though, Aquil could not directly call the security guard on her unfair treatment of him for, having been in this situation a number of times, Aquil knew that the airing of his legitimate concern would only get him into more trouble. Hence, he is confronted with a dilemma: "Do I do right and suffer, or do I do wrong and get ahead?"[20]

In his version of events, Aquil reconstructed his story with a variety of indirect languages. Marcyliena Morgan argues that the use of indirection, as demonstrated by Aquil, "has to do with the development of a speech economy in which 'ways of speaking' inherited directly from Africa have been reshaped by the historical experience of Afro-Americans in America."[21] According to Morgan, the African American counterlanguage of the sort that Aquil employed is an expansion of indirect speech in the U.S. that signals "both the social reality of antisociety as well as solidarity among African descendants."[22] The initial use of this counterlanguage is evident in Aquil's reference to the security officer: "And I ran past this, what was that, uh Mephistopheles, right? [group laughter] straight up, right?" The laughter of the group may be interpreted any number of ways. On the one hand, just the use of the term Mephistopheles in the context of this conversation is cause for laughter. However, the laughter in the room, especially as it came from Roger, was more of the sort that said, "I cannot believe that you just went there!," to which Aquil replies, "straight up," or "I sure did!" His use of Mephistopheles illustrates one way that Aquil appropriates a tool borrowed from school for his own end and is also consistent with Bakhtin's view of language. For Bakhtin:

> Any word exists for the speaker in three aspects: as a neutral word of a language, belonging to nobody; as an other's word, which belongs to another person and is filled with echoes of the other's utterance; and, finally, as my word, for since I am dealing with it in a particular situation, with a particular speech plan, it is already imbued with my expression. . . .
>
> These words of others carry with them their own expression, their own evaluative tone, which we assimilate, rework, and re-accentuate.[23]

Clearly, Aquil assimilated, re-worked, and re-accentuated a word that carried with it its own expression and evaluative tone. Mephistopheles, for instance, represents the personification of evil forces, or the devil in Goethe's *Faust,* a book that is required reading for sophomores at CHS. The video footage and transcript suggest that Aquil, cognizant of the fact that his voice and image were being recorded, was rather purposeful in selecting a specific term that would convey his sentiments in a way that elicited laughter and that lent itself to deniability. Clearly the reaction of Roger and Jack indicated that they heard Aquil call the white security guard a *devil.* Although we are inclined to agree with Robin D. G. Kelley who would likely argue that the main purpose of Aquil's choice of words was to get a laugh from his peers, we also posit that his choice has an historic dimension, described by Morgan, that clearly links his narrative across time and space with others throughout the African Diaspora in North America.[24] His use of counterlanguage here employs the style of Martin Luther King Jr., who used snake metaphors to convey essentially the same sentiments as Aquil. This specific use of counterlanguage is in contrast to its use by, say, Malcolm X or Frederick Douglass who explicitly referred to white people as devils in their public speeches and writings.

In addition to Mephistopheles, Aquil also appropriated another official tool of the school. However, this particular use occurred within the actual context of his interaction with the security guard. Here, in the tradition of Nat Turner, Aquil appropriated the use of a tool that school personnel often used against him for his own ends. Specifically, Aquil employed the school's tardy policy to flip the script, so to speak, on the security guard. Although the tardy policy is rarely enforced on this open campus where students come and go as they please and enter and leave class without permission, authority figures selectively enforce it against black males in the same way that the rule against running in the hallway was selectively enforced in this incident. Moreover, Aquil places the security officer in an awkward position by suggesting that she, whose main job it is to enforce school rules, is contributing to the delinquency of a minor.

Conclusion

The aforementioned example is typical of the linguistic and interpersonal resourcefulness that we found among black male students as they sought to "make a way out of no way" at a school where they were always outnumbered and always outgunned. Overall, the experiences of the young men in the broader project evince evidence of unjust conditions at school; they also illustrate the strategies these students employ to negotiate their academic and social lives within these institutions. To what extent may their experiences inform educational practice and policy? The data tell us something about the nature of schooling and even about ourselves as teachers and researchers, that runs counter to conventional wisdom about public education. For instance, if it is true that knowledge is to be found in the relationship between the knower and the known,[25] the analysis in this study may offer alternatives to the pervasive notion that the post-Civil Rights era plight of black males in public schools is simply an expression of anti-intellectualism, academic disengagement, or oppositional identities. Indeed, such an analysis of schooling may also point to more endemic problems related to oppression and domination that place all students at risk and may provide insights on how to reform schools in more fundamental ways.

Along these lines, we posit that the domination and oppression that black male students encounter at CHS are organizational features of schools in general. Problems of domination and oppression are about relationships and, thus, are moral in nature. If this is the case, and we believe that it is, liberation should be the primary term for conceptualizing remedies to the problems that students and the schools they attend encounter. A notion of liberation in this sense fosters cultural democracy,[26] or the nurturing of group differences. As Iris Marion Young suggests, group differentiation, or what we commonly call diversity, "is both an inevitable and desirable aspect of modern social processes. This alternative view of social justice then, requires not the melting away of differences, but institutions that promote reproduction of and respect for group differences without oppression."[27]

Optimistically, we found that a significant minority of students and adults at CHS forged relationships that support the academic success of students without respect to race, ethnicity, gender, or class. Our on-going research suggests that teachers and administrators that support black male students at the school share affiliations with social movements or a commitment to egalitarian ideologies. Further, some of the students at the school also demonstrated their willingness to mobilize around the concerns of black male students to promote change at CHS.[28] These findings suggest to us the possibilities of bringing about the conditions of social justice grounded in the affirmation of, and respect for, group differences. Such conditions will not only foster the academic achievement of black male students but that of their peers as well.

QUESTIONS TO CONSIDER

1. How do the authors argue that past research on black male students has mitigated against their growth and has served to increase their marginalization? Do you agree or disagree with their assessment? Why?

2. What examples and illustrations advance the authors' notion of indifference, or estrangement, among black male youth at City High?

3. Why is it important that we study and understand the "conative dimension of how individuals construct their experiences"? What is meant by that recommendation, and how closely was it followed at City High? Explain and elaborate.

4. What coping strategies did black male students use to navigate the world of City High? Give examples.

5. The authors contend that domination and oppression are "organizational features" of most schools. What do they mean? Do you agree or disagree with their claim? Why?

Notes

This chapter originally appeared in Joe L. Kincheloe and kecia hayes (eds.), *Teaching City Kids: Understanding and Appreciating Them* (New York: Peter Lang, 2007).

1   Earlier versions of this chapter were presented at the 24th Annual Ethnography in Education Research Forum, Center for Urban Ethnography, University of Pennsylvania, PA, USA, March, 2003, and at a forum sponsored by the International Writer Center, Washington University in St. Louis, St. Louis, MO, USA, March 20, 2003. We would like to thank Cleo Brooks for her research assistance and the IES/AERA Grants Program for a 2002–2004 research grant awarded to the first author, and the generous support of the Washington University Graduate School of Arts & Sciences for funding various stages of this project.

2   All names of institutions and persons used in this section are pseudonyms.

3   M. Fine and L. Weis, "Writing the "wrongs" of fieldwork: Confronting our own research/writing dilemmas in urban ethnographies," in *The Unknown City: The Lives of Poor and Working-Class Young Adults* (Boston: Beacon Press, 1998), pp. 264–288; see also C. West, "Black leadership and the pitfalls of racial reasoning," in T. Morrison ed. *Race-ing Justice, En-Gendering Power: Essays on Anita Hill, Clarence Thomas, and the Construction of Social Reality* (New York: Pantheon Books, 1992), pp. 390–401.

4   See, e.g., M. Blair, *Why Pick on Me? School Exclusion and Black Youth* Stoke on the Trent (UK: Trentham Books, 2001); M. C. Brown and J. E. Davis, eds., *Black Sons to Mothers: Compliments, Critiques, and Challenges for Cultural Workers* (New York: Peter Lang, 2000); L. Davis, ed., *Working with African American Males: A Guide to Practice* (Thousand Oaks, CA: Sage Publications, 1999); J. Davis, "Black boys at school: Negotiating masculinities and race," in R. Majors, ed. *Educating Our Black Children: New Directions and Radical Approaches* (London and New York: Routledge/Falmer, 2001), pp. 169–182; G. Dei, J. Mazzuca, E. McIsaac, and J. Zine, *Reconstructing "drop-out": A Critical Ethnography of the Dynamics of Black Students' Disengagement from School* (Toronto: University of Toronto Press, 1997); G. Duncan, "Racism as a developmental mediator," *The Educational Forum, 57(4)* (1993): 360–370; G. Duncan, "Educating adolescent black males: Connecting self-esteem to human dignity," in L. Davis, ed. *Working with African American Males: A Guide to Practice* (Thousand Oaks, CA: Sage Publications, 1999), pp. 173–186; G. Duncan, "Beyond love: A critical race ethnography of the schooling of adolescent black males," *Equity and Excellence in Education, 35(2)* (2002a): 131–143; A. Ferguson, *Bad Boys: Public Schools in the Making of Black Masculinity* (Ann Arbor: The University of Michigan Press, 2000); B. Harry and M. Anderson, "The disproportionate placement of African American males in special education programs: A critique of the process," *Journal of Negro Education, 63(4)* (1994): 602–619; R. Hopkins, *Educating Black Males: Critical Lessons in Schooling, Community, and Power* (New York: State University of New York Press, 1997); M. Mac an Ghaill, *The Making of Men: Masculinities, Sexualities and Schooling* (Buckingham: Open University Press, 1994); K. Meier, J. Stewart and R. England, *Race, Class, and Education: The Politics of Second-Generation Discrimination* (Madison, WI: The University of Wisconsin Press, 1990); P. Noguera, "Preventing and producing violence: A critical analysis of responses to school violence," *Harvard Educational Review, 65(2)* (1995): 189–212; V. Polite and J.E. Davis, eds., *African American Males in School and Society: Practices and Policies for Effective Education* (New York: Teachers College Press, 1999); T. Sewell, *Black Masculinities and Schooling: How Black Boys Survive Modern Schooling* (Stoke on the Trent, UK: Trentham Books, 1997).

5. A. Ferguson, *Bad Boys: Public Schools in the Making of Black Masculinity* (Ann Arbor: The University of Michigan Press, 2000).

6. T. Sewell, *Black Masculinities and Schooling: How Black Boys Survive Modern Schooling* (Stoke on the Trent, UK: Trentham Books, 1997).

7. M. Mac an Ghaill, *The Making of Men: Masculinities, Sexualities and Schooling* (Buckingham: Open University Press, 1994).

8   P. Noguera, "Preventing and producing violence: A critical analysis of responses to school violence," *Harvard Educational Review, 65(2)* (1995): 189–212; B. Hamovitch, "More failure for the disadvantaged contradictory African American student reactions to compensatory education and urban schooling," *The Urban Review, 31(1)* (1999): 55–77.

9   G. Duncan, "Beyond love: A critical race ethnography of the schooling of adolescent black males," *Equity and Excellence in Education, 35(2)* (2002): 131–143; G. Duncan and R.Jackson, "The language we cry in: Black language practice at a post-desegregated urban high school," *GSE Perspectives on Urban Education, 3(1)* (2004) (This article may be retrieved from < http://www.urbanedjournal.org/ articles/article0014.html>

10 J. Laible, "A loving epistemology: What I hold critical in my life, faith, and profession," *Qualitative Studies in Education, 13(6)* (2000): 683–692; P. Parker, *To Know As We Are Known: Education As a Spiritual Journey* (New York: Basic Books, 1993); R. Williams, "The death of white research in the black community," *Journal of Non-White Concerns in Personnel and Guidance* (1974, April): 116–131.

11 Laible, "A loving epistemology: What I hold critical in my life, faith, and profession"; Williams, "The death of white research in the black community"; D. Bell, *Faces at the Bottom of the Well: The Permanence of Racism* (New York: Basic Books, 1992); D. Bell, *Afrolantica Legacies* (Chicago: Third World Press, 1998); R. Delgado, *The Rodrigo Chronicles: Conversations About America and Race* (New York: New York University Press, 1995); K. Crenshaw, N.Gotanda, G. Peller and K. Thomas, (Eds.). *Critical Race Theory: The Key Writings That Formed the Movement* (New York: Routledge, 1995); M. Matsuda, *Where Is Your Body? And Other Essays on Race, Gender, and the Law* (Boston: Beacon Press, 1996); M. Matsuda, C. Lawrence, R. Delgado, and K. Crenshaw, *Words That Wound: Critical Race Theory, Assaultive Speech, and the First Amendment* (Boulder, CO: Westview Press, 1993).

12 Delgado, *The Rodrigo Chronicles: Conversations About America and Race;* P. Tillich, *Love, Power, and Justice: Ontological Analysis and Ethical Applications* (Oxford: Oxford University Press, 1954).

13 Our interpretive framework draws on critical ethnographic and discourse analyses that examine the layers of meanings and multiple viewpoints that are brought to bear on the academic and social experiences of black male students in the study. See, e.g., P. Carspecken, *Critical Ethnography in Educational Research: A Theoretical and Practical Guide* (New York: Routledge, 1996), and L. Chouliaraki and N. Fairclough, *Discourse in Late Modernity: Rethinking Critical Discourse Analysis* (Edinburgh: Edinburgh University Press, 1999). The larger portion of the field research was conducted from the spring of 1999 through the spring of 2003. Data for the study discussed in this paper were obtained from black male students using loosely structured conversations, semi-structured, open-ended question and answer sequences, and stimulated recall interviews; both individual and focus group sessions were conducted. The authors and research assistants collected the interview data reported in this chapter. Additional data were obtained from interviews with other students, and faculty and staff members. Data related to the culture of the school were collected through systematic participant observations of classrooms and corridors and during assembly sessions and other school-related activities and meetings. Data were recorded in field notes and on digital videotape and audiotape. Data related to demography, standardized testing, attendance, and graduation rates, and documents related to the historical, ideological, and programmatic features of the school augmented the interview and participant observation data in the larger study. Finally, we collected both participant observation and textual (e.g., written assignments) data from an ethics course the first author taught at the school during the 2000–2001 academic year.

14 Duncan, "Beyond love: A critical race ethnography of the schooling of adolescent black males"; Duncan and Jackson, "The language we cry in: Black language practice at a post-desegregated urban high school."

15 N. Noddings, "Care, justice, and equity," in M. Katz, N. Noddings, and K. Strike, eds. *Justice and Caring: The Search for Common Ground in Education* (NewYork: Teachers College Press, 1999), p. 14.

16 Noddings, "Care, justice, and equity," p. 13.

17 W. E. B. Du Bois, *The Souls of Black Folk* (Chicago: A.C. McClurg & Co., 1903).

18 Duncan and Jackson, "The language we cry in: Black language practice at a post-desegregated urban high school";

19 M. Tappan and L. Brown, "Stories told and lessons learned: Toward a narrative approach to moral development and moral education," in C. Witherall, and N. Noddings, eds. *Stories Lives Tell: Narrative and Dialogue in Education* (New York: Teachers College Press, 1991), pp. 171–192.

20 W. Mosley, *Always Outnumbered, Always Outgunned* (New York: Washington Square Press, 1998); W. Mosley, *Workin' on the Chain Gang: Shaking off the Dead Hand of History* (New York: The Ballantine Publishing Group, 2000).

22 M. Morgan, "The Africanness of counterlanguage among Afro-Americans," in S.S. Mufwene, ed. *Africanisms in Afro-American Language Varieties* (Athens and London: The University of Georgia Press, 1993), pp. 423–435.

22 Morgan, p. 427.

23 M. Bakhtin, C. Emerson and M. Holquist, V. McGee, Trans., (Eds.) *Speech Genres and Other Late Essays* (Austin: University of Texas Press, 1986), pp. 88, 89.

24 M. Morgan, "The Africanness of counterlanguage among Afro-Americans," in S.S. Mufwene, ed. *Africanisms in Afro-American Language Varieties* (Athens and London: The University of Georgia Press, 1993), pp. 423–435; R. D. G. Kelley, *Yo' mama's Disfunktional!: Fighting the Culture Wars in Urban America* (Boston: Beacon Press, 1997).

25 P. Parker, *To Know As We are Known: Education As a Spiritual Journey* (New York: Basic Books, 1993); P. Carspecken, *Critical Ethnography in Educational Research: A Theoretical and Practical Guide* (New York: Routledge, 1996).

26 A. Darder, *Reinventing Paulo Freire: A Pedagogy of Love* (Boulder, CO: Westview Press, 2002).; M. Ramírez and A. Castañeda, *Cultural Democracy, Bicognitive Development, and Education* (Orlando, FL: Academic Press, 1974).

27 I. Young, "Five faces of oppression," in T. E. Wartenberg, ed. *Rethinking Power* (Albany: State University of New York Press, 1992), p. 180.

28 G. Duncan, "At the risk of seeming ridiculous": A post-critical approach to researching the schooled lives of adolescent black males, an unpublished manuscript, 2002.

CHAPTER EIGHT

Between a Danger Zone and a Safe Space

LGBTQ Youth and the Challenge of Democratic Education

DENNIS CARLSON

I have for some years taught a graduate level course on multicultural education and diversity, primarily for teachers and soon-to-be teachers, and whenever I introduce the topic of sexual and gender diversity, I immediately face the problem of naming. Who are the people about whom I am speaking, and how do I name them? In my multicultural education and diversity class for teachers I often use the term "queer youth," and this invariably gets a reaction from some of the teachers, particularly older teachers. One teacher thought it offensive for me to refer to gay youth as queer youth, "because queer is a derogatory term, like the 'n' word." I told her that when I was a child in the 1950s, queer was indeed a derogatory term to refer to homosexuals, or more typically gender non-conforming boys, but that a new generation of young people was beginning to embrace the word "queer" and use it in a positive sense. Some use "queer" to refer to a broad spectrum of LGBTQ (lesbian, gay, bisexual, transgendered, and questioning) people, as a name that brings groups together across their differences to fight *homophobia* and *heteronormativity*. Queer is also a term that implies a challenge to the "old" binary oppositional identities of the modern era in the United States: straight-gay, and masculine-feminine. These binary oppositional identities were also understood to overlap, with homosexuals represented as feminized men or masculinized women. Now, these categories are being "queered" by critically minded young people, that is, understood as socially constructed, related to power relations of privilege and subordination, and open to being performed in new, more empowering ways.

This does not mean we are moving beyond categories of sexual orientation and gender, only that these categories are (at least among some) becoming less fixed in their meaning and less defined in terms of binary oppositions. For all of these reasons, I now find myself using the word "queer" more often in class, although the first time I use the term I usually get a look of alarm from some of the teachers in the room who—usually those over 50 years old—who, like me, were raised in an era when the word "queer" was a derogatory term and the worst thing you could call someone, which only goes to show how much the process of renaming LGBTQ people has a political agenda, and that as names become stigmatized, they fall out of usage. Once the word "gay" was used along with "pride," in an effort to create a new word for homosexual that would not carry the negative connotations of "queer." Now it seems that "queer" must do service again as the word "gay" has become a derogatory word and a general putdown, as in "that's so gay."

If all of this is confusing, it is because identity is a social construction, and the social context of sexual identity formation and identity naming is always shifting. Whatever names are used to mark sexual difference, it is clear that as a culture we are moving very rapidly to accept homosexuals and transgendered people as "normal," and this means that public education will be pushed to provide a context for the development of a positive queer identity. At the same time, public education will need to help young people question identity, especially when it takes for granted an uncrossable border that separates the self from its opposite, the "Other." To affirm identity, but in ways that "trouble" and question identity borders and boundaries, is the great challenge of our age, and of a public education that is democratically reconstructive rather than merely reformist.[1]

One fact of life has not changed significantly through all this renaming. Public schools historically have not been, and unfortunately still are not, safe spaces for queer youth. In fact, most schools have been and continue to be the opposite—danger zones where LGBTQ youth face formidable odds in affirming their sexual identities and where many still seek safety in the "closet," hiding who they are and attempting to get through their middle and high school years with as few psychic and physical wounds as possible. Public schools are not safe spaces for LGBTQ youths because, along with conservative religious institutions and the traditional, patriarchal family, schools have played an important role in socializing young people into *heteronormativity*—the presumption that everyone is, or ought to be, exclusively heterosexual, and that those who deviate from this norm need to be stigmatized, silenced, and/or made invisible as much as possible.[2] To live in a heteronormative school culture as a "gay" person is to constantly be aware of one's absence in the educational conversation, one's invisibility in the textbook, and one's marginalization and isolation in the social world of the school. I have sometimes been told by well-meaning heterosexual friends that gay people do not have to face discrimination because they can always "act straight" and get treated just like "normal" people. What this actually communicates is that everything would be fine, and there would be no reason to discriminate against them, if LGBTQ people just acted like "normal" people. Of course, this argument has in fact been used against black people and women when they "complain" that they face discrimination or are being marginalized in the workplace or the school. If they would just "act white," or "act like a man," they would be accepted. This is nonsense, of course, for a number of reasons, but it is particularly offensive when it is applied to queer youths, for hiding a part of who we are always comes at a psychic cost, and it is unfair to ask someone to bear the burden of this cost. When principals tell LGBTQ teachers and students to just "keep it quiet," and everything will be okay, they are participating in the construction of what Eve Sedgwick has called the "epistemology of the closet," the construction of a world in which it is "normal" to hide yourself if you happen to not be heterosexual.[3] "Don't ask, don't tell" is the credo of heteronormativity, and we must not think we are countering homophobia by pursuing this approach as a formal or informal policy, either in the military or the public schools.

In what follows I want to suggest how progressive-minded educators might begin to deconstruct and unpack heteronormativity in their schools and classrooms, and in the process reconstruct the public school as a safe space for LGBTQ and other youths marginalized by class, race, gender, and other markers of difference and identity. To do so I want to turn first to developmental theories of adolescence, focusing on the idea that marginalized young people need a "safe space" to affirm positive identities. This concept implies two things: separate spaces where queer and queer-friendly young people can meet and serve as a support group and network, and the entire school space reimagined as a safe environment for queer youths. I then want to provide an example of a student-led movement, the Gay-Straight Alliance (GSA) that is actively working in high schools and on college campuses to construct both types of safe spaces. A safe space as a separate space is, one might say, a pragmatic, here-and-now response to the situation queer young people face in the homophobic, toxic school environment; but that toxic environment must also be interrogated and reconstructed to move schools in the direction of safe spaces for all young people.

Adolescent Identity Development and LGBTQ Youth

To use developmental theories of adolescence to argue that schools be reconstituted as safe spaces for LBGTQ youth is, I must say at the outset, a somewhat contradictory project. For the very idea of "adolescence" emerges out of a developmental discourse in the early twentieth century in the United States that was deeply heteronormative and homophobic, as well as racist and sexist.[4] We need to remember that the word "adolescence" was invented by the educational psychologist Granville Stanley Hall in his 1904 text, *Adolescence*.[5] Before then, people were considered children until they became adults, and they were treated as adults in many ways after they reached puberty. This wasn't always good, of course. It meant that many young people got married early, were working 60 to 70 hours a week, and never got a chance to pursue an education or follow their dreams. Even childhood was an abbreviated age, with young people expected to take on many of the responsibilities and burdens of adults at an early age. In a sense, the category of "adolescents" was invented by Hall to change all this. He argued that young people in their teenage years were in a developmentally distinct phase of life between childhood and adulthood, a phase characterized by *Sturm* and *Drang*—emotional storm and stress, longings, and impulses. Hall argued that unless young people could be carefully guided through this stage, under the watchful eye of professional educators, they could fall prey to all sorts of maladjustments and bad influences that would stunt their "normal" development. The high school was thus envisioned by Hall as a safe space, where young people could be kept from "bad" influences and allowed to sublimate their emerging sexuality through sports and organized boy-girl activities (like the prom).

By the "normal" development of the adolescent, Hall meant the development of adolescents into genetically fit breeding stock that would advance the evolution of the "race" (and he always made it clear that he was referring to the "white" race). Hall largely accepted the notion that young people enter puberty in a "stage of relative undifferentiation [by gender or sexual orientation] . . . and that it is at this point that heterosexuality makes itself manifest. . . . in the higher romantic and idealizing sense of the word."[6] Homosexuality was, from this perspective, a maladjustment, caused by an over-repressive and moralistic upbringing by both parents and teachers (and here Hall blamed "prudish" mothers and female school teachers in particular), who moralistically condemned the "natural expression of the sex instinct. . . ."[7] Here we have a restatement of what was already becoming a popular refrain among psychologists and psychoanalysts in the early twentieth century, the idea that a male homosexual orientation resulted from over-protective and moralistic mothering which retarded the "normal" sexual development of the adolescent and turned individuals narcissistically toward their own gender. A homosexual orientation among boys was further encouraged, according to Hall, by the tendency in the culture to de-sexualize the female and hide her natural beauty: "dress and modesty have tended to divert this [heterosexual] interest into many unusual directions, and . . . may have tended to homosexuality."[8] Hall sympathized with the poor unfortunates who could not achieve "normal" heterosexual identities for one reason or another and records the observations of a psychologist friend, for example, who had treated many sexually "abnormal" men.

> One typical youth of good heredity and otherwise normal decided that he would not go to college, was ruined and must soon inevitably become insane. Another bought a revolver and planned, after a farewell visit to his mother in a distant town to shoot himself in despair. Another selected a spot at the river where he would drown himself . . . Another young man selected a cord, which he carried in his pocket for a long time, trying to muster the courage to hang himself.[9]

One must presume that Hall felt sorry for these young men, but perhaps also secretly wished they had the courage to remove themselves from the racial gene pool, for the good of everyone. What we have here is an historical record of a phenomenon that has, unfortunately, a long history—suicide and attempted suicide among LGBT youth, a suicide that Hall's developmental theory seems to almost sanction as the inevitable result of sexual "degeneracy" and "abnormality." One might agree with Hall that prudishness about sexuality, and what Michelle Fine has called the "missing discourse of desire," has resulted in serious sexual dysfunctions later in life.[10] However, we now know, or ought to know, that a homosexual orientation or preference is not one of them, that it is not the result of something going wrong in upbringing but rather the result of a natural diversity within the human population, that people are born with a sexual predisposition or orientation, and that their sexual orientation or preference cannot be significantly altered at any age.

If we could untangle developmental theory from the roots established by Hall and other early developmentalists, then it might be possible to recuperate developmental theory in a way that would allow us to speak of adolescence as a time in which queer or LGBTQ youth develop self-affirming sexual identities, as part of the process of "becoming somebody."[11] This is just what a number of developmental theorists began doing in the 1970s and 1980s, and their work has continued to be influential today in shaping thinking among youth advocates and professional educators who work with adolescents. These models were first identified as "homosexual identity development" models, and this concept opens them to the criticism that they overlook the special experiences of bisexual, transgendered, and questioning young people and do not differentiate between the experiences of LGBT youths positioned as different by race, class, and gender. With these limitations in mind, the models of homosexual identity development do represent a major advancement in the professional literature in education. For the first time, the attainment of a stable gay identity is viewed positively rather than negatively, and schools are called upon to become safe spaces for LGBTQ youths. To the extent that these models are useful, it is because they suggest that the ethos of the public school must be transformed in far-reaching ways in order to become safe spaces for the development of LGBT youths.

Erik Erikson has had the most influence on recent developmental theories of adolescence. Although his work dates from the 1950s and 1960s, all models of homosexual identity formation are variations on Erikson's basic model.[12] Erikson had argued that each phase in the normal development of the individual throughout life was characterized by a conflict and challenge that had to be resolved if the individual was to successfully move on. He defined adolescence as the age of "identity versus role diffusion." Individuals faced the challenge of deciding who they were, as opposed to who their parents were or wanted them to be, and sometimes this took the form of experimenting with alternative lifestyles and values. Young people, Erikson argued, needed a "moratorium" on making decisions about their future or deciding exactly what they would do with their lives. As a time of moratorium, adolescence was at best a time of exploration, leading—by the end of adolescence—toward a fairly fixed and stable sense of self in relation to others (or "identity" in Erikson's terms). Young people emerge from adolescence, hopefully with some coherent sense of identity as to from whom they are apart but in relationship to others around them. If, by the end of adolescence, young people do not achieve "identity," Erikson believed that they fell victim to "role diffusion," looking to others—parent figures or peer groups—to conform in terms of dress, behavior, values, and so on. Unable to "find themselves," they follow others and seek refuge in the crowd. This is Nietzsche's "herd" mentality, and Erich Fromm's "authoritarian personality," associated with deference to authority figures in personal and political life.[13]

Thus, in Erikson's model of adolescent development, the individual who "steps to the beat of a different drummer" is represented as developmentally more mature than her or his peers, and this certainly could be said of "out" LGBTQ young people in public schools—that they have achieved identity and do not feel the need to conform anymore. In real life, of course, it is never quite as easy as achieving identity or falling into role diffusion. The "out" gay or lesbian adolescent may step to the beat of a different drummer in some ways, but in other ways may conform quite narrowly to the dress codes and lingo of his or her queer subgroup, and may need to in order to establish a positive sexual identity. The most influential homosexual development models are all very similar, and so I want to focus on only one here. Vivienne Cass's influential model includes six stages, beginning with "identity confusion," in which young people recognize that their actions, thoughts, and feelings could be defined as homosexual.[14] The conflict in this stage is between accepting at least the possibility that one could be homosexual or queer, and rejecting the possibility entirely—this latter choice foreclosing the possibility of developing a positive homosexual identity. If young people are presented with only negative, stigmatizing images of "gayness," or no images at all and if the school is an alien space for those who feel different in any way from what is considered "normal," then schooling poses a significant danger to queer youth at this stage, and if they foreclose the possibility of developing a positive queer identity, then suicide or alienation is a real possibility, as is a commitment to leading a closeted or double life, and hiding behind a "straight" mask. If young people can see the possibility of being happy and no longer hiding who they are, they advance to Stage Two: "identity comparison." This is a time in which queer youth compare themselves with straight youths and develop coping mechanisms for dealing with their alienation and difference. This may involve beginning to reach out to other queer youth. In the "identity tolerance" stage that follows, young people acknowledge that they are probably gay or queer and seek the company of other gay people out of necessity, to fulfill social, sexual, and emotional needs—without necessarily affirming a public gay identity. In this stage, young people often live compartmentalized lives, with LGBT friends and "straight" friends, the public and the private self kept carefully apart. If this stage is successfully negotiated, the individual enters into the state of "identity acceptance," marked by an effort to reconcile public and private selves and to "come out" more broadly within the family and among friends. Next comes the stage of "identity pride," in which a political sense of "us" versus "them" develops, and individuals strongly identify with LGBT causes. "Identity synthesis" comprises the final stage; in it the individual recognizes that being queer is only one part of a self that is multiply-positioned and evolving. In this final stage, one might say, the individual is no longer merely positioned by one axis of identity formation (say, sexual orientation), but rather by multiple, overlapping and even contradictory (in terms of power and privilege) subject positions of class, race, gender, sexuality, and other markers of difference. This concept suggests that one becomes more able to see connections between struggles of different groups, to understand social injustice because as women, black, Latino/a, Muslim, and/or queer people, or as members of the new working poor, we have been there and need to know that we can only be free, can only have power, when we can see the common threat of injustice across different struggles. This social justice interpretation of the "identity synthesis" stage is not there, to be sure, in Cass's interpretation. However, it is one of the cultural implications of developing a more polyvocal, multi-dimensional sense of identity. In this regard, it is perhaps noteworthy that Cass and other developmental theorists leave it as a possible last stage, but one not typically associated with adolescents. For adolescents, achieving identity acceptance and identity pride is the real challenge, and sometimes this means seeking a safe space within a heteronormative and homophobic institution, where LGBT young people can support each other and work for change.

Creating a Safe Space for Identity Development

The presumption in homosexual development theory that LGBTQ young people, in the process of developing a self-affirming identity, need a safe space of their own to gain support from each other, is very similar to the presumption in African American developmental theory, as applied, for example, by Beverly Tatum in *Why Do All the Black Kids Sit Together in the Cafeteria?* Tatum argued that, during adolescence, black students attending predominantly white high schools need each other's support and a safe space for blackness within the hegemonic white culture of their schools—hence the "black table" in the cafeteria. If black youth are to forge a self-affirming racial identity, according to Tatum, they need—during adolescence—to affirm their blackness through immersion in black culture, styles, and linguistic codes, and this means conforming in significant ways to codes of "acting black." In adolescence, black youth "turn to each other for the much needed support they are not likely to find anywhere else."[15] Along with this reciprocal support, "certain styles of speech, dress, and music, for example, may be embraced as 'authentically' Black."[16] Sometimes, black youths assert their racial identity and culture in an "in your face" way which may be experienced as threatening within the school, but as Tatum argued, this behavior needs to be recognized for what it is—a coping mechanism in the face of stress and a positive affirmation of racial pride in a culture that frequently puts down blackness. There are, however, alternatives to the "safe space" of the black table in the cafeteria, and Tatum suggests schools need to explore after-school clubs and even special classes oriented toward black students. This kind of environment would provide them with the opportunity to develop a positive black identity.

Cass makes a very similar argument with regard to homosexual youths. According to Cass, during the "identity acceptance" and "identity pride" stages homosexual youth need space and time to form support networks. She writes:

> The individual in this [identity pride] stage becomes immersed in gay life, which means that they spend little time interacting with heterosexual people. There can be anger at heterosexual people during this stage. Usually the individual believes that heterosexual people cannot be allies and probably should not be trusted.[17]

Trust cannot be forced, according to Cass, which means schools should provide a safe space for queer adolescents to explore being different and even oppositional to "normal" kids—especially for those who are most "out" and/or face the most harassment and marginalization in the school. This space apart can also be a space where queer youths mobilize to take action to confront homophobia in the school and thus reengage in the school community as active participants in change.

An influential model of making the school a safe space for LGBTQ young people along these lines is that associated with the Gay-Straight Alliance (GSA) movement. Currently, there are over 4,000 GSAs nationally, most of them also affiliated with the Gay, Lesbian, and Straight Education Network (GLSEN). Aside from promoting tolerance and discussion of gay-themed issues in the school curriculum, GSA establishes after-school organizations and support groups for queer students, along with children from LGBTQ families and supportive heterosexual students. A safe space is, of course, never fully safe, but it is a place where queer youths can combat the negative effects of verbal and physical violence, alienation, and other forms of homophobia and heteronormativity in a support group setting. Los Angeles' Project Ten is often pointed to as one of the first efforts to establish such a safe space in a public school setting, and it has served as a model for the GSA movement that followed. Organized in 1984 at Fairfax High School in Los Angeles Unified School District, Project Ten got its name from the estimated ten percent of the population who are exclusively or primarily homosexual (a figure widely attributed to Kinsey). Project Ten also established an activist orientation early on that has continued in the GSA movement. Activism has taken the form of sponsoring or participating in national campaigns to raise awareness of LGBTQ issues, including: a National Day of Silence, a National Coming Out Day, and a No Name Calling Week. In 1993 the State of Massachusetts adopted the GSA model as part of its "Safe School Program," and this led to its broader acceptance throughout the country. Since the 1998 murder of Matthew Shepard, an openly gay student at the University of Wyoming, the GSA has been involved in helping publicize and stage "The Laramie Project," an educational play about the trial of Shepard's killers, in which local high school and college students perform parts. This play, though, is controversial, and it is noteworthy that a high school teacher in Wyoming was recently fired for staging the play. To perform such a play in the public schools is still very much an act of activism and resistance. Also in 1999, the federal district court of Utah, in *East High Gay/Straight Alliance v. Board of Education of Salt Lake City School District*, ruled that denying a Gay-Straight Alliance access to school meeting rooms after school violated the federal Equal Access Act.

If progress has been made, it is clear that much more needs to be done to make public schools safe spaces for LGBTQ youths. This is clear from a 2007 GLSEN report: The National School Climate Survey.[18] That survey of 6,209 middle and high school students found that nearly 9 out of 10 LGBTQ students (86.2%) experienced harassment at school in the past year, three-fifths (60.8%) felt unsafe at school because of their sexual orientation, 44.1% reported being physically harassed, and 22.1% reported being physically assaulted at school in the past year because of their sexual orientation. Furthermore, 73.6% heard derogatory remarks such as "faggot" or "dyke" frequently or often at school. More than a third (38.4%) felt unsafe because of their gender expression. If there was any good news in the survey, it was that in high schools with Gay-Straight Alliances, there were fewer homophobic remarks and less harassment and assault because of sexual orientation and gender expression. Students also were more likely to trust school staff in schools with GSAs and thus were more likely to report incidents of harassment and assault to school staff.

In working to make public schools safe spaces for diversity and establishing GSAs in local high schools, progressive educators and community groups must expect to face some resistance, even considerable resistance from religious conservatives and fundamentalists. How progressives respond to this opposition is important in the effort to re-imagine public schools as democratic safe spaces. A recent court case provides a good example of the challenges LGBTQ groups and movements face in making public schools safe spaces, and it also raises questions about how we should respond. In *Harper vs. Poway Unified School District* (2006), the court was presented with a complex case involving competing claims to freedom of speech and protection from the effects of hate speech. Harper was a sophomore at Poway High School in 2004 when the local GSA announced its annual "Day of Silence." The year before, there had been disruptions and conflicts over the Day of Silence, and the administration wanted to make sure it proceeded smoothly this time. On the Day of Silence, while some gay and gay-supportive students wore masking tape over their mouths, Harper showed up for school in a t-shirt on which he had placed masking tape, across which he had written in black marker: "Be ashamed, our school embraced what God has condemned," and "Homosexuality is shameful." When Harper refused to take off the T-shirt, the principal kept Harper out of class and assigned him to do homework in a conference room for the rest of the day. He was not suspended from school. The California Ninth Circuit found that the school district had not violated Harper's First Amendment rights of freedom of expression. The district's dress code stated that unacceptable attire includes clothing that promotes or portrays "violence or hate behavior including derogatory connotations directed toward sexual identity." The district's policy on freedom of speech and expression recognizes students' rights to express ideas and opinions but cautions against speech that might "incite students so as to create a clear and present danger . . . of unlawful acts . . . or of the substantial disruption [of the school day]."[19] In sum, hate speech which could cause some young people to direct their anger or resentment against LGBT students, is no longer legally protected speech in many schools, and that means the days when the word "faggot" could ring through the halls with no teacher speaking up are also limited, as are the days when rituals of bullying are taken for granted and thus never questioned. At the same time, one cannot help but wonder what might have happened if school officials had reacted less out of fear of possible conflict and more in terms of using this situation as an opportunity to start a complicated conversation about sexual identity, respect for difference, and privilege and marginalization. Because public educators continue to be so afraid of conflict and debate, they react less out of a sense of protecting queer students than out of a sense of protecting order and authority in the school.

Conclusion

We have, as a culture and as public educators, come a long way from the developmentalism of Hall, when it was impossible to even imagine well-adjusted homosexual adolescents, to a queer developmentalism that is about growth toward self-affirming LGBTQ identities in adolescence. However, if young people are to develop along these latter lines, the schools—as I have argued—will have to be re-imagined and reconstructed as safe spaces for differences of all sorts, in which people are brought together in particular and overlapping interpretive communities, where there is respect for difference within the conversation, and conflict is approached as an opportunity to educate and learn rather than something to be avoided at all costs. Public educators have traditionally sought to avoid conflict as if it were the plague—conflict of any sort. That is one of the reasons why young people in schools are not given a chance to discuss the most pressing issues of their day and of their lives.[20] It might be better to engage uncomfortable speech, even hate speech (or what feels like hate speech if you are on the receiving end of it), rather than simply silencing it in the interests of maintaining control and making sure no one deviates from the state-approved lesson plan. This dynamic, in turn, suggests the need, long ignored, to teach young people the skills of civic and civil discourse in a democracy. Only when we can have such a discourse, or conversation, in our schools on sexual identity and gender difference can we expect significant progress in making schools safe spaces for all young people. We cannot confuse safe schools with highly-disciplined or policed schools, or schools that adopt one version or another of a zero tolerance policy on intolerance. Schools that are safe for LGBT youth, and black and Latino/a youth, and young women of all backgrounds, and the poor and the handicapped, must emerge out of ongoing self-reflection and dialogue, and openness to others. In such a dialogue, conflict is both inevitable and the mechanism for change and growth. At the same time, and as the dialogue continues, queer young people have a right to have their rights protected—the right to not be harassed and bullied, the right to be included in the curriculum, and the right to be recognized for who they are.

To side with youth as public educators is to help fight the legacy of heteronormativity and homophobia that, unfortunately, has a long history in public education. This long history may make it seem that little can be done within public schools to challenge commonsense beliefs and fears. I hear again and again from teachers and administrators, "I would like to do something, but. . . ." I understand these fears, although I believe that the role of educators is to face fears and take stands that will not always be popular. As educators, we can stand up against bullying and verbal harassment and insist that our schools commit themselves to becoming inclusive communities of difference. This is the work of social justice education, and it links the battle against heteronormativity to the battle against racism, sexism, and classism. It may be too much to expect that the public schools will become suddenly gay-friendly, given that they are responsive to organized community groups that want the schools to teach traditional, religious, "family values." However, at least committed public educators can take action to make their schools and classrooms safer spaces for queer and gay-friendly youths. They can assume responsibility for responding rather than remaining quiet and uninvolved. The very idea of a democratic public school as reflective of the diversity of a wider American community, where no one is silenced, closeted, or marginalized, is at stake if we do not respond to this call of responsibility toward social justice and inclusiveness in every aspect of our school lives.

QUESTIONS TO CONSIDER

1. In what specific ways, based on your own experiences and memories, were there danger zones or safe spaces for LGBTQ youth at your middle school and high school?

2. In what ways is Hall's developmental theory of the "normal" heterosexual and the homosexual as the "abnormal" sexual degenerate still taken for granted among young people, teachers, parents, and other members of the community?

3. For each stage of Cass's homosexual identity formation model, explore ways in which schools can be organized so as to promote a successful resolution and movement to the next stage.

4. How are the school, the "hidden curriculum," and the official school curriculum organized to support and maintain heteronormativity?

5. What policies and practices might be adopted in schools and school districts to make schools safe spaces for LGBTQ youth?

Notes

1. See Dennis Carlson, *Making Progress: Toward a New Progressivism in American Education and Public Life* (New York: Routledge, 2003), see especially chapter 3: "Recognizing Ourselves: Hegel and the Master/Slave Struggle in Education," 69–98.
2. See Eve Sedgwick, *Epistemology of the Closet* (Berkeley: University of California Press, 2008).

3. Sedgwick, *Epistemology of the Closet*.

4. See Bernadette Baker, *In Perpetual Motion: Theories of Power, Educational History, and the Child* (New York: Peter Lang, 2001).

5. Granville Stanley Hall, *Adolescence* (New York: Arno Press, 1969).

6. Hall, *Adolescence*, p. 450.

7. Hall, *The Pedagogical Seminary* (Seattle: Old Classics, Amazon Digital Services, Kindle Edition, 2009), 394.

8. Hall, *Adolescence*, 451.

9. Hall, *Adolescence*, 452.

10. Michelle Fine, "Sexuality, Schooling, and Adolescent Females: The Missing Discourse of Desire," *Harvard Educational Review* 58, no. 1 (1988): 29–53.

11. See Philip Wexler, with the assistance of Warren Crichlow, June Kern, and Rebecca Martusewicz, *Becoming Somebody: Toward a Social Psychology of School* (Washington, D.C.: Falmer Press, 1992).

12. Erikson focused on adolescence as a stage of life in, Erik Erikson, *Identity: Youth, and Crisis* (New York: W. W. Norton, 1968).

13. Friedrich Nietzsche, *A Genealogy of Morals*, trans. William A. Haussmann (New York: Macmillan, 1897); Erich Fromm, *Escape from Freedom* (New York: Rinehart & Company, 1941).

14. Vivienne Cass, "Homosexual Identity Formation: A Theoretical Model," *Journal of Homosexuality* 4 (1979): 219–35; "Homosexual Identity Formation: Testing a Theoretical Model," *Journal of Sex Research* 20 (1984): 143–67; and "Sexual Orientation Identity Formation: A Western Phenomenon," in *Textbook of Homosexuality and Mental Health*, ed. R. P. Cabaj and T. S. Stein (Washington, D.C.: American Psychiatric Press, 1996), 227–51.

15. Beverly Tatum, *"Why Are All the Black Kids Sitting Together in the Cafeteria?,"* (New York: Basic Books, 1997), 60.

16. Tatum, *"Why Are All the Black Kids Sitting Together in the Cafeteria?"* 61.

17. Cass, "Homosexual Identity Formation: A Theoretical Model," 231.

18. *The 2007 National School Climate Survey: Key Findings on the Experiences of Lesbian, Gay, Bisexual, and Transgender Youth in our Nation's Schools* (Washington, D.C: The Gay, Lesbian, and Straight Education Network, 2007).

19. 365Gay.com Newscenter Staff. "Anti-Gay T-Shirt Battle Heads to Supreme Court," http://365gay.com/Newscon06/10/102806tshirt.htm (accessed October 30, 2006)

20. Linda McNeil, *Contradictions of Control: School Structure and School Knowledge*. (New York: Routledge, 1988).

CHAPTER NINE

What About Adolescent Curiosity and Risk Taking?

THOMAS G. REIO, JR.

Curiosity, the desire for new information and sensory experience that motivates exploratory behavior, is the fuel of learning, development, and adaptation throughout the lifespan (Reio, 2008). Curiosity is praised by parents and educators and has been investigated to a limited degree by researchers, yet most curiosity research involves only children. Curiosity indeed may be a powerful children's learning motivator, but we have little information about curiosity motivation during adolescence and how it might influence learning. This knowledge gap is troubling, considering that student motivation for academic work in general decreases from elementary to middle to high school (Marks, 2000; Reeve, 1989). In high-stakes testing contexts, student motivation decreases are even more pronounced, with accompanying increases in frustration and anxiety; and these effects are not limited to adolescents in U.S. schools (Smith, 2004).

Curiosity and exploration and the learning it motivates can be productively understood in light of taking risks. As Dewey (1916) noted, "Since [sic] the situation in which thinking occurs is a doubtful one, thinking is a process of inquiry, of looking into things, of investigating. . . . It is seeking, a quest, for something not at hand. . . . It also follows that all thinking involves a risk. Certainty cannot be guaranteed in advance" (p. 148). Thus, through the process of being curious and taking positive, adaptive risks for curiosity's sake, significant thinking and learning occur (Dewey, 1916; Reio, 2007a; Reio & Lasky, 2007). Answering the call for more information about student motivation in adolescence (Flum & Kaplan, 2006), I focus then on curiosity. The aim of this chapter is to explore the possible links among adolescent curiosity, risk taking, and exploration, and how teachers can foster each on behalf of learning and development.

What Is Curiosity?

There are two major types of curiosity: cognitive and sensory (Reio, Petrosko, Wiswell, & Thongsukmag, 2006). Cognitive curiosity is the desire for information and knowledge, while sensory curiosity is linked to wanting new thrills and experiences (Malone, 1981). Both types of curiosity motivate exploratory behavior for its resulting satisfaction. Cognitive curiosity stimulates observation, consultation, and directed thinking (specific exploration) that result in information acquisition and learning (Berlyne, 1960, 1978). It is linked to convergent thinking, which is finding the one solution to a question. On the other hand, sensory curiosity, which is aroused by boredom and a need for stimulation, kindles explorations of the environment through experimentation with novel physical (e.g., rock climbing) and social (e.g., going to a party to meet someone new) thrills and experiences (diversive exploration; Berlyne, 1960; Zuckerman, 1994, 2007). This type of curiosity is related to creativity and divergent thinking, that is, finding an array of pertinent answers to a question. Information acquisition and learning do occur through sensory curiosity, but they are not its main purpose; instead, the primary intent is to experience new thrills and sensations. Both types of curiosity interact to foster learning and development, and continuous adaptation to pressing environmental contingencies (Piaget, 1952; Reio et al., 2006).

Working in tandem with curiosity and exploration, risk taking is required if learning is to occur (Dewey, 1916; Reio & Lasky, 2007). Learning, then, requires appropriate risk. As Biesta (2007) noted,

> . . . even if one engages in neatly organized forms of learning, there is always a risk. Not only is there a risk that you will not learn things you wanted to learn. There is also the risk that you will learn things you couldn't have imagined you would learn or that you couldn't have imagined that you would have wanted to learn. . . . To engage in learning always entails the risk that learning may have an impact on you, that learning may change you. This means that [learning and therefore] education only occurs when the learner is willing to take a risk. (p. 10)

Risk taking is related to a combination of the chance for loss, the possibility of significant loss, and uncertainty (Ponticell, 2003). Like curiosity, it is vital for successful learning, adjustment and growth throughout the lifespan (Reio & Lasky, 2007). If the chance for loss is perceived to be acceptable, the significance of the possible loss is not strongly valued (and sufficient gain is likely), and if the uncertainty level is not overwhelming, risk taking and its related exploratory behavior (e.g., testing new ideas, evaluating new approaches, creating) are likely to increase. In classroom contexts, for instance, adaptive risk-taking occurs when the benefits of an activity may outweigh the potential hazards (e.g., volunteering to solve a geometry problem in front of the class); on the other hand, risk-taking is maladaptive when the activity's hazards outweigh any benefits (e.g., screaming a profanity at a teacher; Byrnes, Miller, & Schafer, 1999).

Cognitive curiosity is linked to risk taking in that, if the adolescent is curious to know more about a novel topic, she or he must risk admitting not knowing something in the face of being considered uninformed. For example, although prominent female artists were relatively rare in the twentieth century, Georgia O'Keeffe was identified in class as one of the major American artists of that time. The surprising new information might arouse the adolescent's desire to know more, but she or he might not be willing to openly ask for more information if the risk of publicly not knowing is perceived to be too great. However, taking the risk of asking questions and being exploratory in class can be adaptive when the benefits (i.e., *learning* more about the intriguing artist) outweigh the hazards (i.e., looking uninformed in front of one's peers or teacher).

Sensory curiosity is also connected to adolescent risk taking. Researchers tend to focus on this area because taking physical and social risks for the sake of new thrills and experiences is closely related to maladaptive risk-taking such as drug experimentation, smoking cigarettes, driving too fast, and engaging in unprotected sex, among others (Rudasill, Reio, Kosine, & Taylor, in press; Zuckerman, 1994, 2007). These types of maladaptive risks can have profound short- and long-term health-related outcomes, with their concomitant societal costs (Rudasill et al., in press). In a classroom context, maladaptive risk-taking might include cheating on an exam merely for the thrill, skipping class to see if one can get away with it, and skirting classroom rules to test the teacher's patience. In spite of the fact that these types of behaviors occur, risk taking associated with sensory curiosity can be adaptive and beneficial. When faced with a novel classroom problem-solving activity (e.g., in civics class, how to introduce a bill in the legislature), sensory curiosity might impel students to be more divergent in their thinking by perhaps collaborating with someone new, experimenting with diverse combinations of data sources, and creating new procedures to monitor and evaluate the success of completing the task appropriately. Consequently, the individual may become a better thinker and problem solver and learn more if she or he is willing to accept the challenge and take the risk of stepping beyond comfort zones when faced with such classroom situations.

Curiosity During Adolescence

Stereotypes abound that adolescents are simply incurious or at best ambivalent about almost everything related to learning. One wonders how this can be. Curiosity and exploration are vital for learning and development across the lifespan not only during childhood. Bowlby (1969, 1973) and Ainsworth, Blehar, Waters, and Walls (1978) noted how an infant's curiosity and exploration (exploratory system) motivates the infant to learn more about its surroundings if the infant feels a sense of secure attachment (i.e., feeling a sense of security) with its caregiver; curiosity and exploration were much less likely among infants who were insecurely attached. Mikulincer (1997) extended attachment theory to include curiosity or searching for information with adolescents and adults. He found that secure people are actively curious, open to new information, confident about being able to deal with social and informational ambiguity, and willing to change their minds in view of new evidence. They also have positive attitudes toward opportunities for information processing and learning. Insecure persons, in contrast, were less likely to explore novel stimuli and be open-minded in the face of new information. Erikson (1968) theorized exploration to be especially important during adolescence; without being appropriately curious and exploratory, and by extension willing to take risks for their sake, healthy identity formation would be less sure. In his theory of emerging adulthood (age 18–25 years), Arnett (2000), too, identified the exploration of life's possibilities as being essential to forming a healthy identity.

In may be that adolescents are just as curious as children or adults, but with an interesting twist. In earlier research (Reio & Choi, 2004), I examined curiosity from adolescence to late adulthood with interesting results. With a relatively large sample of working adults and college students, the 17- to 20-year-olds had the lowest cognitive curiosity scores, but the highest sensory curiosity scores. The sensory curiosity results were similar to those found in previous research (Zuckerman, 1979, 1994), but the cognitive curiosity scores left me curious. By the time our children reach adolescence, have we as parents and educators succeeded in crushing their natural curiosity and their desire to learn? Perhaps the surveys themselves were problematic in some way. Interestingly, when examining the cognitive curiosity scales, many of the items were related to school kinds of learning (e.g., I like "Reading a book entitled *How Things Work*" or "Analyzing a theory to see if it is a good one"). Adolescents scored relatively low on those two questions, and other similar ones such as "Being excited about the prospects of learning new things," "Figuring out how a light meter works," "Being fascinated by a piece of complicated machinery," and "Trying to figure out the meaning of unusual statements."

I designed a much larger study including additional curiosity measures in a university context. The Reio and White (2005) study included two state curiosity (measures curiosity as a temporary cognitive state) instruments, but also a lie detection scale to control for possible social desirability effects. Indeed, it is plausible that certain adolescents expect their peers to not be cognitively curious to maintain group norms. The reverse could be true for sensory curiosity. After statistically controlling for social desirability, the results still mirrored the first; thus, cognitive curiosity was lowest among the adolescents, as was their state of curiosity. Sensory curiosity was highest in the adolescent and young adult groups. The results of this research and the Reio and Choi (2004) study stimulated my own curiosity further about measuring and understanding adolescent curiosity. Again, I am convinced that adolescents should be as curious as any other age group, but it is possible that current curiosity measures, which have not been validated with adolescent samples, are not measuring the essence of adolescent curiosity. With this in mind, I designed a small pilot study to ask a select group of adolescents about their curiosities. With the data emerging from the semi-structured interviews, I hoped that the beginning of a refined understanding of adolescent curiosity could be gained from the eyes of adolescents. Of course, to facilitate the generalization of my research, I will need to secure additional data from larger samples in future studies, with balanced representation from those representing a variety of different socioeconomic, cultural, and ethnic backgrounds.

Pilot study participants

The four participants ranged in age from 16 to 20, with similar socioeconomic, school, ethnic, and religious backgrounds. The participants for this pilot study were volunteers selected to represent a range of ages. "Franklin" (age 16) and "Summer" (17) attended high school, while "Esther" (19) and "Gloria" (20) attended college.

Answering the pilot study's semi-structured interview questions

When asked if they agreed with the stereotype that adolescents were not terribly curious, the adolescents strongly disagreed, although Summer did note it was possible that some adolescents "don't know enough to be curious about all kinds of different things." This supports Piaget's (1952) moderate novelty principle that if something is too novel or too familiar, curiosity is less likely. Berlyne (1960) also reported that too much or too little novelty would not appreciably motivate curiosity. Gloria suggested that adolescents' curiosity focused mostly on "social types of information, such as interpersonal relationships," "what others think about my appearance," and "finding out about yourself and what your strengths and limitations might be." Similarly, Esther indicated the importance of social curiosity but stressed that adolescents also "tend to be curious about new places and in what jobs they might excel." Finally, Franklin mentioned adolescents were curious, too, about "short- and long-term relationships, sports, cars, girls, politics, and the future."

I also inquired about whether they thought there was a dark side to curiosity. The research literature in general supports a very positive view about curiosity and exploration (e.g., Flum & Kaplan, 2006; Reio et al., 2006), but we must acknowledge that curiosity can be a vice (Berlyne, 1978). Curiosity can lead to nosiness, the gobbling of trivial information without meaning, the search for sensation through experimentation with drugs and sex, and scientific experiments that harm life (Gross, 1975; Reio, 2008). Each of the participants thought, like Gloria, that they did not "really see it [curiosity] as dark per se." Summer acknowledged, though, that curiosity "could lead to trying things where the outcomes could be bad," but she was quick to add that "without taking the risk to try something new we would still be cavemen." Gloria also suggested that it could be used "for controlling people," which she found most distasteful.

Curiosity has been linked to a state of arousal that leads to a pleasant feeling when satisfied (Berlyne, 1960; Flum & Kaplan, 2006). Other motivational theorists such as Deci and Ryan (self-determination; 1991) and White (effectance motivation; 1959) have linked curiosity and exploration to subjective states of uncertainty and ambiguity, which when satisfied are linked to positive affect. Because little research has examined that fascinating notion with adolescents, I probed the participants about how they felt while being curious. Summer stated that when she was curious, she was "motivated to find out more" and "intrigued," yet at the same time "kind of antsy." Franklin, when curious, also felt "nervous, but excited" because there was a "feeling of the unknown." Likewise, Gloria felt "not so nervous," but "excitement" and "satisfied once I got the answer." These findings support motivation theory and prior research in that, when a situation is ambiguous or uncertain, the adolescents' curiosity is aroused, creating a state of discomfort. Once the uncertainty is removed through answering a question, the discomfort disappears, resulting in satisfaction or positive affect.

In response to my question about whether they would be willing to take a risk to pursue a curiosity, all participants claimed they would do so, but as Esther noted, "find ways to minimize the risk" to be safe. When I probed a little further about their willingness to take risks in classroom contexts when curious, all suggested they would quickly risk raising their hands if they had a question, but only if there was a safe climate where failure was treated as a learning opportunity, not as a cause for ridicule. Moreover, Franklin and Summer both pointed out that they would take risks for both social and intellectual ends, in that they would risk volunteering to assist a struggling classmate because, not only was it the right thing to do, but that kind of activity was a way to learn.

Subsequently, I asked them to tell me what they might be curious about on a typical day. The answers ranged from "What do I need to do today?" to the weather, looking for the latest news, what clothes to wear, what was going to be on television that night, dinner, and what friends and family might be doing. It is interesting to note that none reported being curious specifically about school-related topics. I also investigated whether they were as curious currently as they were at any other time in their life. Each indicated they were roughly as curious as ever, but Gloria strongly claimed she was "braver" and Esther indicated she was more "willing to take chances" than when she was younger. This finding is consistent with research examining females in late adolescence in that they are more likely to engage in sensory curiosity and its related risks at that time (Reio et al., 2006; Zuckerman, 2007). Arnett (1994, 2000), for example, suggested that higher sensory curiosity among 18- to 21-year-old females may be the result of a socialization effect in that females are socialized to engage less in sensory curiosity and physical and social risk taking. Once outside the home, adolescent females' risk taking increases markedly, but it decreases significantly after the college years. At no time in their lives, however, do females as a group engage in more risk taking behavior than males. This phenomenon is consistent across cultures and ethnic groups (Zuckerman, 2007).

Finally, I asked how attending school had influenced their curiosity. Each participant suggested that school had sometimes increased his or her level of curiosity. Indeed, Summer observed that she became "more curious as she learned about the things she wanted to learn," especially if the "learning was on my own terms." Franklin focused on how his introduction to government stimulated his ongoing curiosity about the economy. Gloria noted how her curiosity was aroused by being "introduced to new subjects and that's a good thing." Summer, Esther, and Gloria also indicated that teachers sometimes "sparked" their curiosity about a topic in general, but the teachers were just as likely to "kill" their curiosity through bad teaching. For one, Summer gave a poignant example when she lamented, "Bad kids tend to get picked on and they eventually drop out." She also listed other "bad teacher traits" such as "being mean" and "putting no effort into making things fun or interesting so students want to learn." She was particularly upset about the poor teaching she received in chemistry and math. Esther was very emotional about "drill and kill" teaching practices that subdued "my creativity and desire to think outside the box." Even though they were college students, both Esther and Gloria still were very aggravated about their standardized testing experiences in high school. They resented greatly that pressured, harried teachers in testing situations projected their frustration and anxiety onto the students, and over periods of months. Their comments concerning high-stakes, standardized testing ranged from "We get no credit for it!" and "They push too hard!" to "It's a waste of time!" and "They never explained the importance of the tests to us!" Gloria summed up the state of affairs related to testing well when she stated, "My curiosity was stifled by [high-stakes, standardized] testing."

These pilot data preliminarily support the notion that adolescents are indeed curious about many things, but not necessarily school-related topics or subjects. The adolescents demonstrated a healthy curiosity about their friends, interpersonal relationships, sport teams, and many other things not directly linked to school learning. These adolescents saw a possible dark side to being curious, yet acknowledged that they must take risks, within reason, to learn and grow (i.e., adaptive risk-taking). Additionally, they noted they felt a little anxious when they were curious; however, obtaining the answer to a curiosity-driven question was in turn satisfying and pleasant. All claimed they were as curious as they ever were, but they tended to be curious about a greater diversity of things than when they were younger. Last, the participants had few encouraging words about their standardized testing experiences, notwithstanding acknowledging that school had stimulated their curiosity about certain subjects.

In sum, my quantitative studies indicate that something is amiss with adolescents' curiosity because their cognitive curiosity scores are lowest among all the age groups examined. Follow-ups through qualitative inquiry suggested that adolescents are certainly curious, but about a wider variety of things, both inside and outside of school. The students I interviewed also indicated the willingness to take risks for the benefit of learning and helping others learn in safe classroom conditions. The need for including social and interpersonal curiosity scales in future adolescent curiosity research became apparent, as well as how high-stakes, standardized testing could be a serious detriment to being curious and maintaining interest in school-related learning.

Adolescent Curiosity and Risk Taking in a High-Stakes Testing Context

In the high-stakes, high-pressure testing context in today's schools, curiosity and other intrinsic motivators of learning seem to have little value (Anderman, 2004; Reio, 2004, Reio & Lasky, 2007). In an interview with Scherer (2002) for *Educational Leadership*, for instance, motivation theorist Mihaly Csikszentmihalyi noted that "To the extent that [high-stakes] tests are taken seriously, testing worries me." He stressed, "One should not take any test very seriously because test results don't really tell us anything" (p. 14). He went on to remark that he was unaware of any research that scores on high-stakes tests were positively linked to happiness or success in life. Still, national legislation such as No Child Left Behind (NCLB) or state legislation such as the Kentucky Education Reform Act (KERA) and its accompanying high-stakes testing continues unabated. Unfortunately, such legislation puts little emphasis on developing students' positive motivational beliefs and orientations to learning, despite ostensibly being designed to support student learning and academic achievement. Instead of developing both the expertise and learning motivation of students who one day will embrace learning for the sake of learning, today's teaching increasingly focuses on coaxing student performance on high-stakes tests. In general, it is a prolonged period of drudgery for students, parents, teachers, and administrators. In this unfortunate state of affairs where testing seems to be the end all of learning performance, evaluation continues unabated, regardless of considerable evidence that attainment of well-meaning high-stakes testing goals have been elusive at best.

What Can Teachers Do?

Developing curious, self-motivated learners who are competent and confident enough to take reasonable, adaptive risks for the sake of learning throughout the lifespan is the *sine qua non* of teaching (Reio, 2005). I must acknowledge, though, that creating a learning climate where curiosity, exploration, and risk taking are embraced at school will be no easy task. As Brophy (2004) suggests, school is compulsory and curriculum content and learning activities are for the most part based on what society thinks students should know instead of what students would like to know. There are time constraints and standardized testing pressures as well. Because of that kind of school context, students tend to focus far more on project completion than on the skill or knowledge development the activity was designed to enhance. Student concerns about how task performance will be evaluated tend to predominate over learning and learning how to learn. Brophy strongly asserts that it is simply "unrealistic to adopt intrinsic motivation [e.g., curiosity] . . . as the model of student motivation . . . to maintain on an all-day, everyday basis" (p. 14).

I beg to differ with Brophy (2004) because, in my view, virtually any subject, despite being externally mandated, can be taught in such a way as to arouse students' curiosity and exploration, and their willingness to take risks to do so—and consistently so. The issue is that we, as teachers, must embrace a teaching philosophy that student learning can and must be motivational from the eyes of the student. Approaching curiosity-motivated learning as merely "something nice" rather than a non-negotiable objective guiding every learning endeavor (within reason) may not be in the best interest of our students. Again, that charge is not so easy, but through thoughtful instructional designs and planning, and considerable practice, we can better meet both the "felt" and "real" learning needs of our students by generating and sustaining student curiosity.

Wlodkowski's (1993) time continuum motivation model is but one example of effective teaching models embracing the concept of enhancing student motivation to learn. In his model, through addressing student attitudes and needs at the "beginning" of a learning endeavor, stimulation and affect throughout the "during" phase, and finally, competence and reinforcement in the "ending" phase, motivational learning and achievement can be attained. He proposes 68 useful strategies aligned with the three phases to assist teachers in both their individual and group learning efforts.

Borrowing from Berlyne's (1960) collative motivational variables, Reeve (1996) proposed five strategies to facilitate curiosity in the classroom: guessing and feedback, suspense, playing to a student's sense of knowing, contradiction, and controversy. By asking students to make predictions about a topic and demonstrating that existing knowledge may be insufficient to attain some goal, curiosity can be ignited, and exploration ensues. In turn, the curiosity can be developed into enduring interest in the topic or subject (Dewey, 1910; Reio et al., 2006). All this curiosity-induced learning activity hinges, however, on being stimulated and nurtured in a context where adaptive risk taking is encouraged appropriately. We must be reminded, too, that both the cognitive and sensory types of curiosity are vital to learning, not just one or the other.

As teachers, then, we must create a classroom climate where curiosity and risk taking are supported as desirable learning motivators, not something to be ignored. Thus, students must feel safe expressing their curiosity by asking questions or guessing in class and consulting with more knowledgeable peers or adults when faced with a knowledge gap or a problem. We should foster a classroom context, therefore, where adolescents feel comfortable expressing what they learned after a self-directed learning quest, motivated by his or her curiosity about a topic. We cannot overlook, too, the usefulness of trial-and-error experimentation as a productive exploratory means to answering questions and thus satisfying their curiosity. Reflection is also an exploratory behavior, far too often disregarded, where puzzling information can be pondered for the benefit of solving a problem.

Moreover, we must teach our adolescent students how to be appropriately curious, exploratory, and open to taking adaptive risks for learning through modeling such behaviors in an array of meaningful contexts (Reio, 2008). For instance, the teacher needs to model how to act when faced with the excited student's questions, but she also needs to take that situation as a teachable moment to patiently explain that perhaps rudely interrupting someone during a class conversation is not the best way to express one's curiosity. Modeling cognitive curiosity might also entail sharing with students what was learned in a professional development workshop, academic conference, or a college class. Sensory curiosity could be modeled by communicating how volunteering at a local recycling shelter, exploring a new nature trail, and meeting someone from a different culture were such personally satisfying endeavors. In addition, the teacher can ask students to reveal what they learned from reading a newspaper, book, or magazine over the weekend. Encouraging students to disclose how they learned from a recent failure might be another useful means to modeling curiosity. In each case, by modeling how to be curious through taking adaptive risks in the context of a safe classroom climate, a teacher can promote optimal learning.

We cannot overlook the extensive evidence that learners with special educational needs tend to demonstrate the greatest diversity in motivation (Rudasill et al., in press). These learners include those who are developmentally delayed, possess learning disabilities, lack proficiency in their mother tongue, possess advanced cognitive development, and exhibit social, emotional, and behavioral challenges. Further, non-majority culture males and students from low socioeconomic backgrounds have been shown consistently to possess lower levels of school-related learning motivation (e.g., curiosity) and suffer the greatest risk of failing and dropping out of school (Rudasill et al., in press). For those most at risk for not completing school, focusing on developing student curiosity, exploration, and risk taking seems especially promising in relation to the potential short- and long-term individual and societal costs.

As the pilot study results suggest, there is a strong rationale for finding what students really want to learn about and the activities they enjoy, and subsequently building them into the daily classroom learning endeavor. Adolescents are surely curious and want to learn, even in the school-mandated subject areas, but a little more on their own terms. Adolescent learning motivation need not decline throughout school, as Marks (2000) and Smith (2004) so clearly demonstrate it does. We simply cannot afford not to address our students' motivational needs if we are to keep our students learning and to make sure they continue to enjoy it, even within the context of high-stakes testing pressures. Stimulating and building upon student curiosity and exploration is the key.

QUESTIONS TO CONSIDER

1. Describe the role that curiosity plays in the day-to-day learning of adolescents.

2. Provide some examples of how you might stimulate adolescent curiosity (both cognitive and sensory) in an English, math, or physical education class.

3. Should high school teachers embrace curiosity and risk taking in their classrooms even in times of high-stakes testing? Why or why not?

4. Discuss what you might do to promote adaptive risk taking in your classroom.

5. Discuss how you might set up a group of adolescents to model being appropriately curious to their peers.

6. Local community leaders recently proposed paving over a two-acre grassy area (favored by teenagers for sports and recreation) to relieve parking pressures in the neighborhood. How might you use the teens' curiosity and risk taking to productively contest this community proposal?

References

Ainsworth, M. D. S., Blehar, M. C., Waters, E., & Wall, S. (1978). *Patterns of attachment: A psychological study of the strange situation*. Hillsdale, NJ: Erlbaum.

Anderman, E. (2004). Implications of motivation research for learning and assessment. In R. N. Ronau & R. Shapiro (Eds.), *Proceedings of the University of Kentucky/University of Louisville Collaborative Research Conference* (pp. 139–149). Lexington, KY: University of Kentucky Press.

Arnett, J. (1994). Sensation seeking: A new conceptualization and a new scale. *Personality and Individual Differences, 16*, 289–296.

Arnett, J. J. (2000). Emerging adulthood: A theory of development from the late teens through the twenties. *American Psychologist, 55*, 469–480.

Berlyne, D. E. (1960). *Conflict, arousal, and curiosity*. New York: McGraw-Hill.

Berlyne, D. E. (1978). Curiosity and learning. *Motivation and Emotion, 2*, 97–175.

Biesta, G. (2007). The problem of "learning." *Adults Learning, 18*(8), 8–11.

Bowlby, J. (1969). *Attachment and loss: Attachment*. New York: Basic Books.

Bowlby, J. (1973). *Attachment and loss: Separation, anxiety, and anger*. New York: Basic Books.

Brophy, J. (2004). *Motivating students to learn* (2nd ed.). Mahwah, NJ: Erlbaum.

Byrnes, J. P., Miller, D. C., & Schafer, W. D. (1999). Gender differences in risk taking: A meta-analysis. *Psychological Bulletin, 125*, 367–383.

Deci, E., & Ryan, R. M. (1991). A motivational approach to self: Integration in personality. In R. Dienstbier (Ed.), *Nebraska symposium on motivation* (pp. 237–288). Lincoln: University of Nebraska Press.

Dewey, J. (1910). *How we think*. Lexington, MA: D.C. Heath.

Dewey, J. (1916). *Democracy and education*. New York: Free Press.

Erikson, E. H. (1968). *Identity: Youth and crisis*. New York: Norton.

Flum, H., & Kaplan, A. (2006). Exploratory orientation as an educational goal. *Educational Psychologist, 41*, 99–110.

Gross, D. W. (1975). Curiosity in context. *Childhood Education, 51*, 242–243.

Lee, V. E., & Burkam, D. T. (2003). Dropping out of high school: The role of school organization and structure. *American Educational Research Journal, 40*, 353–393.

Malone, T. W. (1981). Toward a theory of intrinsically motivating instruction. *Cognitive Science, 4*, 333–369.

Marks, H. M. (2000). Student engagement in instructional activity: Patterns in the elementary, middle, and high school years. *American Educational Research Journal, 37*, 153–184.

Mikulincer, M. (1997). Adult attachment style and information processing: Individual differences in curiosity and cognitive closure. *Journal of Personality and Social Psychology, 72*, 1217–1230.

Piaget, J. (1952). *The origins of intelligence in children.* New York: International Universities Press.

Ponticell, J. A. (2003). Enhancers and inhibitors of teacher risk taking: A case study. *Peabody Journal of Education, 78*, 5–24.

Reeve, J. (1989). The interest-enjoyment distinction in intrinsic motivation. *Motivation and Emotion, 13*, 83–103.

Reio, T. G., Jr. (2004). Further implications of motivation research for learning and assessment. In R. N. Ronau & R. Shapiro (Eds.), *Proceedings of the University of Kentucky/University of Louisville Collaborative Research Conference* (pp. 149–154). Lexington, KY: University of Kentucky Press.

Reio, T. G., Jr. (2005). Emotions as a lens to explore teacher identity and change: A commentary. *Teaching and Teacher Education, 21*, 985–993.

Reio, T. G., Jr. (2007). Exploring the links between adult education and human resource development: Learning, risk-taking, and democratic discourse. *New Horizons for Adult Education and Human Resource Development, 21*(1/2), 5–12. http://education.fiu.edu/newhorizons

Reio, T. G., Jr. (2008). Primary source materials and curiosity: Making history come alive. In D. M. McInerney & A. D. Liem (Vol Eds.), *Standards in education:* Vol. 8. *Teaching and learning: International best practice* (pp. 169–190). Charlotte, NC: Information Age Publishing.

Reio, T. G., Jr., & Choi, N. (2004). Novelty seeking across the lifespan: Increases accompany decline. *The Journal of Genetic Psychology, 165*, 119–133.

Reio, T. G., Jr., & Lasky, S. L. (2007). Teacher risk taking changes in the context of school reform: A sociocultural and cognitive motivational perspective. In D. M. McInerney & S. Van Etton (Eds.), *Standards in education*: Vol. 7. *Research on sociocultural influences on motivation and learning.* (pp. 13–32). Charlotte, NC: Information Age Publishing.

Reio, T. G., Jr., & White, K. H. (2005, April). *Understanding curiosity beyond the realm of childhood: Cognitive curiosity and the adolescent.* Paper presented at the 2005 biennial meeting of the Society for Research in Child Development, Atlanta, GA.

Reio, T. G., Jr., & Petrosko, J. M., Wiswell, A. K., & Thongsukmag, J. (2006). The measurement and conceptualization of curiosity. *The Journal of Genetic Psychology, 167*, 117–135.

Rudasill, K. M., Reio, T. G., Jr., Kosine, N., & Taylor, J. E. (in press). Temperament and student-teacher relationship quality as predictors for risky behavior. *Journal of School Psychology*.

Scherer, M. (2002). Do students care about learning? A conversation with Mihaly Csikszentmihalyi. *Educational Leadership, 60*, 12–17.

Smith, L. (2004). Changes in student motivation over the final year of high school. *Journal of Educational Enquiry, 5*, 64–85.

White, R. W. (1959). Motivation reconsidered: The concept of competence. *Psychological Review, 66*, 297–333.

Wlodkowski, R. J. (1993). *Enhancing adult motivation to learn: A guide to improving instruction and increasing learner achievement.* San Francisco: Jossey-Bass.

Zuckerman, M. (1979). *Sensation seeking: Beyond the optimal level of arousal.* New York: Cambridge University Press.

Zuckerman, M. (1994). *Behavioral expressions and biosocial bases of sensation seeking.* New York: Lawrence Erlbaum Associates.

Zuckerman, M. (2007). *Sensation seeking and risky behavior.* Washington, DC: American Psychological Association.

CHAPTER TEN

Understanding Adolescent Suicide

A Psychological Interpretation of Developmental and Contextual Factors

PEDRO R. PORTES, DAYA S. SANDHU, & ROBERT LONGWELL-GRICE

Suicide is a complex problem with ideology or beliefs as a common element that interacts idiosyncratically with any number of emergent identities pressing on the individual. One factor underlying suicide concerns the failure to construct a healthy identity. Much of the research on this issue focuses on adolescence, the period of time when individuals are most engaged in developing a healthy identity (Erikson, 1968; Coleman & Remafedi, 1989; Bar-Joseph & Tzuriel, 1990; Newton, 1995). Erikson (1968) noted that in extreme instances of delayed and prolonged adolescence, complaints of "I give up" and "I quit" are more than signs of mild depression—they are expressions of despair. Erikson acknowledged that suicide itself is an identity choice for some adolescents. Furthermore, suicide is increasingly occurring among people who are not adolescents, which may have to do with the inability to master Erikson's stages of development throughout the lifespan, beginning early in life.

Accomplishing developmental tasks in a given cultural context requires a sense of connectedness. As the institution of the family, which is the primary engine for healthy socialization, has weakened in modern society, individuals' risk for disturbances in identity formation mounts. For suicidal individuals, the family and society may have failed to provide the necessary conditions for sound development.

New trends in suicide are emerging for practically all ages and walks of life. Children, adolescents, and young adults appear to share in this "mis-solution," yet for quite different reasons. The purpose of this paper is to examine, within an Eriksonian framework, the different motives for and contexts of suicide among these three groups, to identify specific school-age populations that are vulnerable to suicide, and to discuss implications for school counselors and others. In so doing we will also look at how firearms and gender differences relate to suicide in the United States.

Suicide within an Eriksonian Framework

The reasons for suicide vary, but seem to cluster around disruption of specific developmental tasks, vulnerability of the individual, and risk conditions in the immediate situation of the individual, such as lack of emotional support. From a sociocultural perspective, new norms may emerge (e.g., legalization of assisted suicide). Both the characteristics of the individual and the culture appear to interact in suicide ideation and attempts. This interaction becomes particularly life threatening when identity formation is obstructed in ways that the individual considers impossible to resolve.

Individuals who take their own lives vary in age. What prompts a 16-year-old to commit suicide as opposed to a 60-year-old? We need to recognize the different motives and life situations among children, adolescents, adults, and the elderly. According to Erikson (1963, 1968), there are eight stages in the lifespan, each of which poses conflicts or crises that need to be resolved positively and in a prosocial manner. Failure to do so may impact a person's personality development in a negative and cumulative way. Such failure may be understood as an important risk factor in the etiology of suicide and violent behavior.

Erikson was among the first theorists to indicate the importance of social context in understanding individual development. He witnessed the violence that took place during much of the twentieth century, and conflict resolution figured prominently in his work as he sought to establish a nexus between the individual and society. Some extensions of his work and other cultural-context models are presented here, with a focus on suicide. It is hoped that this will provide a means for understanding the socioemotional disturbances influencing life-threatening behavior.

Preadolescents

Research by Greene (1994) dispels many myths surrounding the suicide of children. Greene showed that children under the age of six experience true depression and that they are cognitively and physically able to implement a suicide plan. As Pfeifer (1993, 1994) shows, children are not too young to consider death. However, the exact mediating circumstances remain unclear from a theoretical perspective.

According to Erikson, how each developmental task is resolved (e.g., infancy: trust versus mistrust; early childhood: autonomy versus doubt and shame; preschool age: initiative versus guilt; school age: industry versus inferiority) defines to a considerable extent how healthy or unhealthy the person becomes and how well he/she is able to deal with future tasks or crises. The developmental history of the person varies depending on the extent to which trust was established in early attachments, a view that is currently well established (Bowlby, 1988). Failure to establish trust contributes to insecurity and poor adjustment in later life. Similarly, failure to establish autonomy leaves the individual subject to shame and doubt, which again can be carried over to the next stage. These may be seen as part of the maladjustment problems of children who internalize or externalize their anger. Anger emerges when socioemotional needs are not met in the contexts where development takes place, and this anger precedes violence. The antecedents of life-threatening behavior thus appear related to what may be regarded as a developmental sequence or syndrome rather than to any one specific experience.

If during this period prior to adolescence children are able to develop confidence by doing something well (i.e., learn to be competent and productive), they will be more likely to carry that confidence into the future. If during this time they fail at their endeavors and do not have a nurturing environment to give them support, they will more than likely carry feelings of inferiority and low self-esteem into their future developmental tasks. Parental separation and family dysfunction are generally associated with violent behavior at this age, particularly where conflict and anger have been present in the child's experience.

In our view, failure to resolve preadolescent crises successfully does appear to present a cumulative risk for suicide. This failure generally signals interference in the bonding process.

Adolescents

According to Erikson, individuals attempt to resolve the issue of identity versus role confusion during the teenage years. Adolescents try to answer the question "Who am I?" so as to establish an identity in the sexual, social, ideological, and career domains. They often experience considerable stress in a variety of contexts as they attempt to forge an identity (Lock & Steiner, 1999). For example, the changing sex roles of men and women may exacerbate identity confusion. In addition, environmental stressors such as parental pressure for academic achievement, family mobility, the availability of drugs, and peer pressure can lead to depression (Capuzzi, 1994). Suicide seems to occur when stress, cognitive immaturity, and lack of emotional bonding interact and overwhelm an individual's ability to cope and to reason clearly. In one study, adolescents who had attempted suicide reported significantly more stress related to parents, lack of adult support outside the home, and sexual identity than did control groups (Wagner, Cole, & Schwartzman, 1995). Mood disorders are generally found in this population (Archer & Slesinger, 1999).

Some teenagers come from families with high expectations which, when coupled with identity confusion, feelings of inferiority, biological changes, and low self-esteem, are often too much to handle. In one study, school professionals were asked to identify individual, familial, and sociocultural factors which might make adolescents more vulnerable to suicide. Of 450 responses, half focused on the impact of the family; lack of parental support and alienation from and within the family were considered key risk factors (Grob, 1983). In the literature, parental absence or unavailability, poor communication between family members, conflict within the family, high parental expectations for achievement, and overt family pathology are generally considered the main risk factors.

Suicidal ideation is related to psychosocial distress, drug involvement, family stress, and unmet school goals (Thompson, 1994). Many adolescents become involved with drugs or alcohol in an attempt to reduce tension. Further, many adolescents who commit suicide are heavy users of alcohol or drugs (Laws & Turner, 1993). This suggests a two-factor process. First, drugs may provide some initial relief from distress. However, in masking distress chemically, the individual's cognitive development is undermined just as he or she may be beginning the difficult transition to formal operations. Drugs also tend to alienate the individual from his or her sources of social support. This leads to exacerbation of the crisis, overwhelming the individual's resources and making suicide seem the only option.

In discussing motives for suicide, Adler (1964) considered adolescents to be irrational, unrealistic, and illogical: "In dismissing interest in life and committing suicide, adolescents are able to accomplish something no one else is able to do. A person who considers himself or herself too weak to overcome life's difficulties acts 'intelligently' according to his or her goal of coping with the difficulties of life". Adolescents' intellectual functioning is in a state of transition and instability, and their ability to project themselves and others into the future is often limited. Elkind (1978) has referred to this unevenness in thought as "pseudostupity." It can be observed in people who fail to take into account the consequences of a successful suicide, particularly the effects on their families. Typically, the stressful situation that precipitates suicidal action is of a transitory nature and will abate over time (for example, the loss of a girlfriend or boyfriend); however, the adolescent's egocentric, rigid here-and-now perspective reflects an inability to utilize his or her growing cognitive competencies.

Young Adults

During the early adult years, according to Erikson, the conflict of intimacy versus isolation is the predominant developmental issue. Individuals at this time seek companionship and love, which puts them at risk for rejection. Once rejected, they may become fearful of attempting closeness again. Not wanting to be hurt again, they may isolate themselves, which can lead to depression. Efforts by others to help is often met with anger or avoidance (McNeely, 1977). This decreases the social feedback available, compounding cognitive and emotional dissonance. In general, these persons have not achieved a positive identity in adolescence. The clinical literature supports the view that the less successful adolescents and young adults are in establishing healthy identities and intimacy, the more at risk they are for self-destructive behavior.

Suicide has been extensively studied among college students. Although research has shown that the overall suicide rate for this population is lower than it is for the population as a whole (Silverman, Meyer, Sloane, Raffel, & Pratt, 1997), there has been a dramatic increase in suicide among college students since 1950 (Lipschitz, 1995) and for those aged 15–24 in general (Hirsch & Ellis, 1993). Strang and Orlofsky (1990) reported that nearly 61% of college students experience some suicidal ideation during their college years—a frightening statistic.

It has been found that suicidal students have poorer parent relationships than do nonsuicidal students (Strang & Orlofsky, 1990) and come from families that are more rigid in their values, attitudes, and beliefs (Carris, Sheeber, & Howe, 1998). Associated with this rigidity, college students who feel that others have unrealistically high expectations of them are more likely to commit suicide (Dean, 1996). Adolescents from rigid families with unrealistic expectations often have problem-solving deficits and are unable to see a way out of perceived crises. Jones (1991) found that depression, hopelessness, helplessness, and loneliness were usually present in college students who attempted suicide, with hopelessness the best predictor of more lethal behavior. Certain personality types are more likely to be suicidal among college students, with introverts at higher risk than extraverts (Street & Komrey, 1994).

Issues surrounding the intimacy versus isolation conflict are key determinants of whether young adults will attempt suicide. Crucial to the resolution of this conflict are the problem-solving skills that young adults learn (or fail to learn) in earlier stages of life.

Gender Differences

Not only do the dynamics of each developmental period affect adolescents' response to suicide ideations, there are also gender-based issues that need to be considered. What differentiates males from females who commit suicide?

In general, males learn to suppress their feelings (i.e., to keep their emotions inside), while females are encouraged to express them (i.e., that it is acceptable to cry, vent, and reach out to others). Suicide attempts are often a cry for help.

Suicide rates increase sharply at adolescence, starting significantly earlier for boys than girls (Aro, 1993). The adolescent male often acts quickly, using more violent means. Females, for the most part, use passive means of self-destruction: poison, gas, or pills (they have greater access to prescribed drugs through more frequent use of medical services). As Grollman (1971) noted, they prefer not to shed their blood or disfigure their bodies. Changes in gender roles may reduce the gap between males and females in suicide rates, as women are increasingly encouraged to take on more male-oriented characteristics.

Risk Factors and Firearm Availability

Social learning theory (Bandura, 1977) is informative regarding adolescent suicide. Research has found that individuals whose parents had attempted suicide were more likely to attempt suicide than those without a family history of suicide. This is supported by social learning and cultural historical theory (Vygotsky, 1978). Grollman (1971) also reported that adolescents with a family history of suicide are more likely to take their own lives. However, how such patterns become established in the first place requires further research.

Some experts feel that suicide should not be discussed lest there be a "chain reaction." Often, when there is a suicide in a particular geographical area, others follow. This "solution" to an adolescent's problems seems driven by identification with the model or the model's situation. Males and females alike may also have a desire to "get back" at someone through suicide. The permanency of death may not be comprehended.

Each suicide attempt has an underlying message, and suicide completion indicates that the message was not received. Most people who attempt suicide threaten to do so beforehand, with over 80% of those contemplating suicide verbalizing their thoughts. Seventy-seven percent of adolescents state that if they were contemplating suicide they would first turn to a friend for help (King. 1999).

Whether a suicide attempt is successful often depends upon the method chosen. When someone uses a firearm, death is almost certain. Suicide by firearm is currently the third leading cause of death for adolescents and young adults in the United States (Duker, 1994), and 80% of suicides by older males are committed with firearms (Kaplan, 1994). Men tend to use firearms to kill themselves more often than do women, and this is attributed to the socialization of males in American society. For example, most males raised in the South have shot a gun before their thirteenth birthday. Females are less likely to be socialized to guns, and suicide by firearms is much less prevalent among them, except in the South, where female firearm suicide rates are highest. Recent studies, however, have shown an increase in the acceptance of firearms as a method of committing suicide for women (Adamek, 1996).

Conclusions

In attempting to understand suicide, it is difficult to specify a single pattern because those who commit suicide come from all walks of life and vary in background and motives. However, rates of suicide generally increase with age (Bingham, 1994) and males are more likely than females to commit suicide.

Suicide among the adolescent population is of major concern. The failure to resolve developmental crises, as described by Erikson, can lead to the belief that suicide is an acceptable solution to seemingly insurmountable problems.

Taking into account increasing economic difficulties for some, exposure to drugs and alcohol, and greater social alienation, suicide rates may continue to rise. Intervention needs to be multidimensional as well as developmentally differentiated. Research on suicide prevention (among adolescents in particular) indicates that there is a continuum of self-destructive behavior (Wolfle & Siehl, 1992). Pfeifer (1994) argues that a multifactorial approach that considers developmental concerns in all phases of life must be utilized to limit suicidal behavior.

Intervention, including screening, should begin early. Jackson, Hess, and van Dalen (1995) suggest that suicide intervention should begin at preadolescence. School counselors should be alert to the types of personal difficulties that could lead students to attempt suicide, and take appropriate and timely action. Awareness of the signs and symptoms of suicidal ideation should be a priority in the schools and in the community. Teachers and family members can work in partnership with school counselors to intervene when needed.

A family approach to intervention is especially important in light of recent evidence suggesting that parents may actually precipitate a child's suicide (Jacobson, Rabinowitz, Popper, & Solomon, 1995). A cost-effective strategy would involve educating parents in such areas as communication, problem-solving skills, and knowledge of child development, in an effort to avoid problems rather than merely react to them.

Interventions that help connect people and that improve an individual's self-worth can reduce potential suicides. These interventions can be conducted in a supportive social setting, such as the school. To the extent that families can be educated with regard to developmental issues, we may succeed in reducing individual vulnerability to maladjustment and neutralize external stressors. Further, families can be strengthened by macro-level economic policies.

A psychosocial model, focusing on the resolution of crises that constitute serious risk for suicide over the lifespan, offers direction to school counselors, psychologists, and teachers. This area is fertile for additional theory-driven research. Cross-cultural contrasts may also provide insights for suicide prevention and social promotion of psychological health. It is clear that there is a social learning component to self-destructive behavior and that the availability of guns interacts with unhealthy identity development. Thus, prevention is linked to the development of healthier conditions for positive identity development.

QUESTIONS TO CONSIDER

1. How do the authors show how Erik Erikson's theory of adolescence is relevant to the study of suicide in youth? Could you pose alternative explanations for suicidal behavior? Compare Erikson's notions in this article with those of his in Ch. 1 (pp. 4–5) in this text.

2. According to the authors, what are some of the precipitating causes of suicide in the pre- adolescent years? How might those factors carry on into adolescence?

3. Which interacting factors seem especially germane in explaining suicidal ideation and actions in adolescence?

4. What are Alfred Adler's psychological contributions to the theory of adolescent suicide? How do they differ from those of Erikson? Which theorist is most convincing to you? Why?

5. Which developmental, familial, and gender issues are typically at play in the suicidal inclinations of young adults and college students? How do the authors use Eriksonian theory to address those concerns?

6. Which psychological models and strategies do the authors recommend for the prevention of suicide?

This chapter originally appeared in *Adolescence*, Vol. 37, No. 148 (Winter, 2002).Published here with permission of Libra Publishers.

References

Adamek, M. (1996). The growing use of firearms by suicidal older women, 1979–1992: A research note. *Suicide and Life-Threatening Behavior*, 26(1), 71–78.

Adler, A. (1964). Brief comments on reason, intelligence, and feeblemindedness. In H. L. Ansbacher & R. R. Ansbacher (Eds.), *Superiority and social unrest: A collection of later writings* (pp. 41–49). Evanston, IL: Northwestern University Press.

Amato, P. R., & Keith, B. (1991). Parental divorce and the well-being of children: A meta-analysis. *Psychological Bulletin*, 110, 26–46.

Archer, R. P., & Slesinger, D. (1999). MMPI-A patterns related to the endorsement of suicidal ideation. *Assessment*, 6, 51–59.

Aro, H. (1993). Adolescent development and youth suicide. *Suicide and Life Threatening Behavior*, 23, 359–365.

Bandura, A. (1977). *Social learning theory*. Englewood Cliffs, NJ: Prentice Hall.

Bar-Joseph, H., & Tzuriel, D. (1990). Suicidal tendencies and ego identity in adolescence. *Adolescence*, 25, 215–223.

Bingham, C. R. (1994). An analysis of age, gender and racial differences in recent national trends of youth suicide. *Journal of Adolescence*, 17(1), 53–71.

Bowlby, J. (1988). *A secure base: Parent-child attachment and healthy human development*. New York: Basic Books.

Capuzzi, D. (1994). *Preventing adolescent suicide* (ERIC Document Reproduction Service No. 383 964).

Carris, M., Sheeber, L., & Howe, S. (1998). Family rigidity, adolescent problem-solving deficits, and suicidal ideation: A mediational model. *Journal of Adolescence*, 21, 459–472.

Coleman, E., & Remafedi, G. (1989). Gay, lesbian and bisexual adolescents: A critical challenge to counselors. *Journal of Counseling and Development*, 68, 36–40.

Cotton, R. C., & Range, L. M. (1993). Suicidality, hopelessness, and attitudes toward life and death in children. *Death Studies*, 17, 185–191.

Dean, P. (1996). The escape theory of suicide in college students: Testing a model that includes perfectionism. *Suicide and Life-Threatening Behavior*, 26, 181–186.

Duker, L. (1994). *Youth suicide and guns* (ERIC Document Reproduction Service No. 378 459).

Elkind, D. (1978). *The child's reality: Three developmental themes*. Hillsdale, NJ: Erlbaum.

Erikson, E. (1963). *Childhood and society (2nd ed.)*. New York: W. W. Norton.

Erikson, E. (1968). *Identity: Youth, and crisis*. New York: W. W. Norton.

Evans, R. I. (1973). *Jean Piaget: The man and his ideas* (Eleanor Duck-worth, Trans.). New York: E.P. Dutton.

Feenstra, J. S., Banyard, V. L., Rines, E. N., & Hopkins, K. R. (2001). First-year students' adaptation to college: The role of family variables and individual coping. *Journal of College Student Development*, 42, 106–114.

Garber, R. J. (1991). Long-term effects of divorce on self-esteem of young adults. *Journal of Divorce and Remarriage*, 17, 131–137.

Gilligan, C. (1982). *In a different voice: Psychological theory and women's development*. Cambridge, MA: Harvard University Press.

Greene, D. B. (1994). Childhood suicide and myths surrounding it. *Social Work*, 39, 230–232.

Grob, M. C. (1983). The role of the high school professional in identifying and managing adolescent suicidal behavior. *Journal of Youth and Adolescence*, 12, 163–173.

Grollman, E. (1971). *Suicide: Prevention, intervention, postvention*. Boston: Beacon Press.

Hirsch, J., & Ellis, J. (1993). *Family support and other social factors precipitating suicidal ideation*. (ERIC Document Reproduction Service No. 373 276).

Jackson, H., Hess, P., & van Delen, A. (1995). Preadolescent suicide: How to ask and how to respond. *Families in Society*, 76(5), 267–279.

Jacobsen, L., Rabinowitz, I., Popper, M., & Solomon, R. (1995). "Interviewing prepubertal children about suicidal ideation and behavior": Reply. *Journal of the American Academy of Child and Adolescent Psychiatry*, 34, 701.

Jones, J. W. (1991). *Suicidality among college and university students: Contributing factors and preventive response* (ERIC Document Reproduction Service No. 333 249).

Kaplan, M. S. (1994). Trends in firearm suicide among older American males. Gerontologist, 34, 59–65.

King, K. A. (1999). Fifteen prevalent myths concerning adolescent suicide. *Journal of School Health*, 69, 159–161.

Laws, K., & Turner, A. (1993). *Alcohol and other drug use: The connection to youth suicide. Abstracts of selected research* (ERIC Document Reproduction Service No. 362 818).

Lipschitz, A. (1995). Suicide prevention in young adults (age 18–30). Suicide *and Life-Threatening Behavior*, 25, 155–170.

Lock, J., & Steiner, H. (1999). Gay, lesbian and bisexual youths' risks for emotional, physical, and social problems: Results from a community-based survey. *Journal of Child and Adolescent Psychiatry*, 1, 297–304.

McNeely, J. (1977). The student suicide epidemic. *Today's Education*, 66(3), 71–73.

Newton, M. (1995). *Adolescence: Guiding youth through the perilous ordeal*. Scranton, PA: W. W. Norton.

Pfeifer, C. (1993). Too young to consider death? Think again. *PTA Today*, 19(2), 14–16.

Pfeifer, C. (1994). Developmental issues in child and adolescent suicide: A discussion. *New Directions for Child Development*, 64, 109–114.

Silverman, M., Meyer, P., Sloane, F., Raffel, M., & Pratt, D. (1997). The Big Ten Student Suicide Study: A 10-year study on suicides on Midwestern university campuses. *Suicide and Life-Threatening Behavior*, 27, 285–303.

Strang, S., & Orlofsky, J. (1990). Factors underlying suicidal ideation among college students: A test of Teicher and Jacob's model. *Journal of Adolescence*, 13, 39–52.

Street, S., & Komrey, J. D. (1994). Relationships between suicidal behavior and personality types. *Suicide and Life-Threatening Behavior*, 24, 282–292.

Thompson, E. (1994). Discriminating suicide ideation among high-risk youth. *Journal of School Health*, 64, 361–367.

Vygotsky, L. S. (1978). *Mind in society*. Cambridge, MA: Harvard University Press.

Wagner, B., Cole, R., & Schwartzman, P. (1995). Psychosocial correlates of suicide attempts among junior and senior high school youth. *Suicide and Life-Threatening Behavior*, 25, 358–372.

Wolfle, J., & Siehi, P. (1992). Case *study of early personality traits of 10 adolescent suicides* (ERIC Document Reproduction Service No. 377 423).

PART TWO

Social and Cultural Perspectives

CHAPTER ELEVEN

Framing Adolescents, Their Schools and Culture

Contested Worldviews

LINDA IRWIN-DEVITIS

Across America today, adolescents are confronting pressures to use alcohol, cigarettes, or other drugs and to have sex at earlier ages. Many are depressed: about a third of adolescents report they have contemplated suicide. Others are growing up lacking the competence to handle interpersonal conflict without resorting to violence. By age seventeen, about a quarter of all adolescents have engaged in behaviors that are harmful or dangerous to themselves and others: getting pregnant, using drugs, taking part in antisocial activity, and failing in school. Altogether, nearly half of American adolescents are at high or moderate risk of seriously damaging their life chances. The damage may be near term and vivid, or it may be delayed, like a time bomb set in youth.

—THE CARNEGIE COMMISSION ON ADOLESCENCE (1995)

How we think about adolescents is shaped by deeply held, largely subconscious worldviews about family. Worldviews about family inform our belief systems and values; and they influence the ways we relate to adolescents in the family, school, agency, or any other setting. The argument I am making in this chapter—and the challenge for us all—is to examine our beliefs and predispositions and their foundations. I will build upon George Lakoff's work on family-based worldviews and how the values privileged by a worldview inform current policies toward adolescents, their schools, and their cultures. How do our worldviews impact our professional roles and relationships with adolescents (as well as our parenting)?

The chapter explores our understanding of adolescence and adolescent policies within the context of theories of family worldviews, and overarching frames that shape thinking across a wide variety of issues, including adolescence and education. Finally, the chapter explores what might happen if we bring deeply held worldviews to the surface, consciously deconstruct those frames, worldviews and values, and begin a conversation on a progressive "reframing" of adolescence and adolescent policies. Such a reframing has the potential to bring changes many progressive educators and other professionals believe are needed. Progressive policies whose purpose is to increase the well-being, aspirations and outcomes of all adolescents, their families, and communities are possible within the American value system. These progressive policies encourage the development of students and citizens who are engaged and well-prepared for creating ful-filled, productive lives in caring communities (as will be discussed in chapter 24 of this reader).

Worldviews, Adolescents, and Social Policy

"What is happening to our young people? They disrespect their elders; they disobey their par-ents. They ignore the law. They riot in the streets inflamed with wild notions. Their morals are decaying. What is to become of them?" Plato's words are not much different from those voiced in editorials, frustrated conversations in teachers' break rooms, and many portrayals of teens in print, movies, television, and newer media.

How we think of adolescents, individually and collectively, is influenced by the historical con-text and popular culture; but our views of teens and 'tweens are primarily shaped by deeper frames that shape our worldview. There are distinctive worldviews (meta-frames) that shape and divide our individual opinions, beliefs, and actions. These worldviews predispose our willingness to see young people as either basically worthy of adult mentoring and second chances or to punish them as adults deserving retribution for disobedience. The tensions among worldviews and our con-ceptions of adolescence are reflected in dysfunctional and contradictory impulses not only in descriptions of adolescent psyches, but also in our policies, and too often in unyielding disagree-ments about what is in the best interests of young people.

When we think of an adolescent, a teen, or a 'tween, what images and words come to mind? Those thoughts and words are evidence of the frame(s) we use to think about adolescents. The collective frames regarding adolescents are very powerful in shaping the actions of parents, teach-ers, and policymakers whose decisions influence the lives and futures of young people who are within their sphere of influence. The frames defining adolescents are influenced by larger frames or worldviews, largely unconscious to the individual, held by adolescents themselves, as well as their parents, their teachers, and policymakers. These worldviews influence and define most, if not all, aspects of a person's values, beliefs and understandings (Lakoff, 2002, 2004).

Linguistic framing activates the generally unconscious mental structures that shape our understandings of a topic, a concept, a role, and a worldview. The skillful, sometimes invisible, use of frames is a key aspect of work in marketing, politics, and any type of persuasion. In order to create social change, George Lakoff (and other scientists who investigate the linguistic aspects of cognition and belief systems) indicates that social activists must "reframe" their argu-ments. The next section of this chapter explores Lakoff's notion of family worldviews more fully, applies it to understandings of adolescence, and concludes with some suggestions for reframing our understandings of adolescence, and social policies and practices that shape American ado-lescent education.

Frames, Family Metaphors, and Worldviews

In his most popular book exploring the ubiquity of frames, *Don't Think of an Elephant!* (2004), Lakoff asks his readers to try not to think about an elephant after reading the book title. He reiterates, "Whatever you do, do **not** think of an elephant" (p. 3). As he notes, and as you are experiencing currently, once a "frame" such as "elephant" is activated, you cannot force yourself not to see the big, heavy animal with its ivory tusks, huge eyes, and long trunk. We each have our own set of frames about elephants and, once those are activated, our minds fall into those frames without any conscious effort—and getting out of the frame is extremely difficult once it is activated.

Lakoff's earlier work focused on metaphors (Lakoff & Johnson, 1980) as central to our ability to make meaning. Drawing upon that work, Lakoff attempted to find the metaphors (organizing ideas, meta-narratives) that would explain the seemingly unrelated positions of American conservatives and liberals on key issues. Lakoff (1996) eventually began to see divergent family metaphors that could explain the seemingly incoherent pastiche of political views that unite people as conservatives (or progressives) and sometimes divide them from each other. Lakoff's primary interest in these metaphors was understanding seemingly contradictory and inconsistent political stances on issues that unite conservatives and liberals: "I remembered a paper that one of my students had written some years back that showed that we all have a metaphor for the nation as a family. We have Founding Fathers. The Daughters of the American Revolution. We "send our sons" to war. . . . Given the existence of the metaphor linking the nation to the family, I asked the next question: If there are two different understandings of the nation, do they come from two different understandings of family?" (2004, p. 5.)

Lakoff found that divergent moral and political views could originate in the potent metaphor of nation/government as family.[1] These divergent metaphors of family (and nation/government) embody certain values and beliefs that form the basis for moral reasoning. The first of the family metaphors that provides the foundation of conservative thought is the *strict father family*. The other metaphor, the *nurturing parent family*, explains and unifies most progressive positions and understandings.[2]

The *strict father family model* is built upon the notion of a traditional family with an authoritative father supporting and protecting the family, i.e., setting and enforcing rules. The mother is responsible for the care of children and home and upholding the father's rules. Children must respect and obey their parents. Such obedience will enable children to be accountable and self-reliant. Parental love is part of the strict father model, but it never outweighs parental authority. Successful children become self-reliant and independent. Thus adolescents/young adults are to be independent, make their own way, and parents are no longer to meddle in their lives since parental work is done (Lakoff, 2002, p. 33). Moral strength and authority are primary in the patriarchal family. Nurturance and empathy are also important, but they are never allowed to interfere with the strict father's moral strength and authority. In this family metaphor, the pursuit of self-interest coming from self-discipline allows one to achieve self-reliance. Meritocracy is a central pillar of "strict father" worldviews—one earns and gets what one deserves on the basis of individual talent and work.

In the *nurturing parent family model*, empathy, nurturance, and love are dominant, and parenting is shared, not hierarchical. It is expected that being cared for, nurtured, and demonstrating and expecting empathy and respect will enable children to become responsible and self-disciplined. Nurturing families teach and model respect for those within and beyond the family. Nurturance also implies protection, support, and strength from both parents who share responsibilities for all aspects of family life and child-rearing. Dialogue and explanations between parents and children are crucial since children need to understand parental decisions. Nurturing parenting requires understanding children as individuals, including their interests, values, and right to individuality. In this model, the moral pursuit of self-interest and fulfillment can only be realized by the practice of empathy and nurturance of others. In fact, empathy and nurturance are the basis of self-fulfillment and moral authority (Lakoff, 2002, p. 34)

Lakoff, while clearly identifying himself as a progressive, does not discuss these different family models as right or wrong, better or worse. Rather, he explores their explanatory power to make sense of a variety of outwardly contradictory positions and stances. Using Lakoff's competing views of family, one can examine the competing frames of adolescence and the resulting policies and practices regarding adolescence. These divergent family metaphors provide a theoretical base to explore the boundaries and contradictions that competing frames impose on parents, teachers and policy-makers.

A recent example of the "strict father model" is making the news. Congress and the media are engaged in debating the abortion provisions in the health care reform bill. The "strict father model" may be seen in the statement from the Catholic Diocese of Washington, DC, about the health care reform bill. The bishop of the Washington diocese said if the bill pays for abortion services as part of the public option,[3] the social services work of the DC Catholic Charities will be suspended. This threat clearly exemplifies the "strict father" model, i.e., valuing obedience to church doctrine on abortion more than empathy for those in need. This position puzzles or outrages those, both Catholic and not, who value empathy in the "nurturing family model" over the obedience demanded by "the strict father."

The model of obedience to the "father" also elucidates the reluctance to offer sex education or contraception. Furthermore, the strict father's authority explains policies requiring parental notification for adolescents seeking abortions. Drug, alcohol, and tobacco addictions are seen as "disobedience" and a "failure of self–discipline," and the key intervention is punishment in a "strict father" worldview. The adolescent's opinion is not sought and often ignored or cut off when offered. The failure is within the adolescent, the punishment is the father's duty, and the future is solely up to the adolescent to work out herself. While the "nurturing family" view strongly supports protecting adolescents from these destructive forces, the responses are more likely to include counseling, support, rehabilitation, and nurturance in addition to or in place of punishment. When punishment is involved, the "nurturing" model involves the adolescent in discussion and strategizing how to change behavior and collaboratively explores the kinds of support the adolescent herself identifies as important to her future success.

In education policy, we encounter some interesting examples of this conflict between worldviews. "Strict father" approaches are being seen in Arne Duncan's and President Obama's words and policies, which are generally consistent with those of President George W. Bush, albeit better funded. A "strict father" worldview promotes the top down setting of policy we are seeing in the criteria for "Race to the Top (RTTT)." RTTT affirms high-stakes testing, although with more realistic and psychometrically valid ways of measuring individual students, schools, districts, and states. There are still "report cards" that demonstrate obedience, or lack thereof, to the top-down mandates and competition in which both schools and states are winners and losers. In President Obama's controversial speech televised to the nation's school children, the themes of "individual responsibility" and "personal accountability" far outweighed a more nuanced discussion of a social contract with America's young people. A social contract is based upon mutual responsibility (by student, family, school, and society) and goes far beyond tests, report cards, and increasingly empty promises of "the American Dream."

Similarly, in Secretary Duncan's relentless attacks on teacher education, he plays the role of the strict father who is reprimanding the "mother" who is charged with carrying out his dictates obediently and without any expectation of input. There is no doubt that ardent supporters of education from both "strict father" and "nurturing family" perspectives expect high achievement and rigorous standards. The differences most often lie in choosing a set of strategies to achieve those goals and sometimes in the motives underlying them.

These policies are distressing at face value; more importantly, they are incompatible with what we know about successful schools. Schools that are able to educate all children, close the achievement gap, and attract and keep great teachers and leaders are nurturing schools. Schools that live the values in John H. Lounsbury's *This We Believe* (2003) are wonderfully written examples of the nurturing family model for educating adolescents in middle schools. The vision of middle schools as nurturing places for adolescents was, at best, incompletely enacted in our nation's schools over the last several decades. That nurturing vision met vigorous opposition from the Education Department under President George W. Bush. *This We Believe* violated the "strict father" views of NCLB. NCLB emphasized teacher-centered classrooms implementing a curriculum and standards set by the "father" (state departments and district offices) and enforced through standardization, regulation, and sanctions. NCLB mandates left little time for student-centered democratic classrooms and schools. NCLB contains no provisions for students' exploration of their talents, roles, and place in society. *This We Believe,* rather than prescribing outcomes, promoted team-centered schools with democratic structures that honored teachers' professionalism, collaboration, and input in school-wide policies and procedures. Schools based upon *This We Believe* and a nurturing family worldview work to ensure student success in a climate that values relationships and models responsibility and empathy in addition to protecting students with an orderly environment. Such schools facilitate students' increasing self-governance and place less emphasis on inflexible, "zero tolerance" rules. Research on effective high schools has highlighted the importance of commitments to strong relationships among all stakeholders (leaders, teachers, students, parents, and community), mutual respect, individualized curricula, participatory decision-making, and high expectations. These school characteristics were associated with the highest levels of achievement and satisfaction among students, teachers, and leaders. However, such nurturing family values collide with NCLB's test-driven accountability, school report cards, and sanctions. RTTT, Obama's major initiative, only affirms the top-down, "strict father" model of educational reform with its emphasis on competition among the states for better tests, stricter accountability, and repetition of the perennial call for better teachers and better teacher preparation.

Family Metaphors as They Shape Views of Adolescents in Popular Culture, Education, and Social Policy

The implications of these disparate views of family are reflected in the debates that frame the views of adolescence in our culture and in policy debates:

	Strict Father Model	Nurturing Family Model
Adolescents	Accepting need for obedience; needing discipline; conforming to rules and to the "strict father" model; working to win in a competitive world with winners and losers; growing up self-reliant; expecting punishment for disobedience.	Being encouraged to explore; developing empathy and respect; developing confidence and self-reliance; participating in decisions and nurturing discussion and inquiry; growing up self-confident, committed to the well-being of self and others; expecting to know reasons for discipline and to be asked for explanations prior to disciplining.
Family dynamics	Acknowledging the authority of the father; recognizing the mother's role as supporting the father's decisions; modeling obedience within the hierarchy; refusing to tolerate questions that can be seen as challenging authority; expecting children to replicate the model or risk exclusion as a result of their disobedience or "failings."	Participating in decision-making as a family; encouraging discussion and negotiation; modeling responsibility and empathy; encouraging and answering questions even when they are difficult; encouraging children to replicate the model, but communicating empathy and nurturing acceptance as primary values.
Popular culture	Supporting strict limits on alcohol and tobacco sales to minors; protecting of minors from certain movies and books, including; censoring print and Web access; restricting access to contraception, including parental notification in abortion; banning exposure to ideas and options inconsistent with the strict father family's values.	Negotiating rules and responsibilities; modeling and expecting democratic and respectful discussion of issues in family relations with empathy, flexibility and active listening; emphasizing adolescent apprenticeship in decision-making and recognition of adolescent voice in decision-making.
Adolescent development	Advocating firm guidance and boundaries with strict consequences to protect adolescents from mistakes and from straying beyond their appropriate role in the strict father family, i.e., being obedient and unquestioning; Designating LBGT as deviant behavior, as something to be corrected, as a personal failing, and a practice for which an adolescent can be forced to leave the family.	Suggesting adolescents need to experiment within safe contexts, make mistakes without adult consequences, negotiate boundaries with parents and adults, and explore and challenge as they practice independent thought; Honoring difference in a variety of ways, including LBGT youth.
Textbooks on adolescence and parenting guides	Discussing adolescent pathologies, stress and the turmoil of identity formation and physical change; suggesting "tough love" approaches.	Emphasizing identity development, experimentation, and freedom to explore roles and new responsibilities.
Purpose for adolescent education	Preparing adolescents and the nation to win in a tough world; creating standards to assure businesses that graduates are going to be valuable workers; requiring students to understand American history	Preparing adolescents to be engaged citizens; providing opportunities for adolescents to develop empathy for others; encouraging students to ask questions, even about national priorities;

	from a traditional American perspective and the world from a nationalist point of view.	exploring the possibilities of global citizenship.
Education policy	Setting standards; implementing high-stakes assessments; using graduation tests; tracking; making early decisions on vocational versus college—bound tracks; establishing a clear hierarchy with rules and enforcement in the hands of adults; enforcing zero tolerance; emphasizing top-down decision-making and curriculum mandates; emphasizing teacher- dominated classroom management with rule-dominated adult supervision rather than promoting student self-management and democratic approaches to discipline.	Practicing "middle school philosophy," which values relationships and individualism; creating small schools movement; using a student-centered curriculum; practicing democratic decision-making with significant student voice in classroom management and curriculum.
Educational funding and support	Defining equity as equal standards for students and schools; de-emphasizing the role of funding inequities; paying teachers for performance (principally test scores or value-added outcomes); using tax dollars to choose schools (public or private) to insure individual success.	Promoting funding for supplemental education, including early education; educational, health and social support needed for students who are "at risk"; funding teacher development, learning communities, and collaborative achievement within a school; using funds to achieve equitable education for democratic participation as well as career participation.
Classroom management	Focusing on teachers and school principal as authorities who make and enforce the rules.	Focusing on student self-governance with democratic rule-making.
School and district management	Recognizing a hierarchical structure that privileges top-down decision-making; discouraging teacher voice, independence, and innovation; implying a view of teacher as technician who implements policies and procedures determined at a higher level.	Aspiring to a democratic, flatter structure in which teacher voice is strong; innovating and challenging are tolerated, if not welcomed; recognizing teacher expertise and professionalism.
Criminal justice	Trying adolescents as adults; reluctance to remove adolescents from the family, even in cases of parental abuse and neglect.	Emphasizing rehabilitation; welfare of the adolescent and adolescent voice as well as parental rights.
Religious belief	Requiring adherence to the parental religion (while the model is found in families from all religious traditions and those who have no religion at all, it is most common in fundamentalist faiths).	Supporting exploration of different types of religion and spirituality with the expectation that the adolescent will eventually have a choice.

Implications for Teachers of Adolescents

The vast majority of adolescents, in families and schools that are nurturing, navigate their 'tween and teen years without major trauma. The voices of adolescents who do not "fit the model" of expectations fare very differently, depending on the schools and classrooms where they are expected to learn and grow (see chapter 34 by Camille Daniel-Tyson & Lianna Nix in this book). Those voices, and other research, strongly suggest that teachers of adolescents, who work with their students, respect them as individuals, and provide nurturance, are able to motivate students to far greater achievement, self-confidence, and aspirations. These voices come from school professionals (individual and, more importantly, collectively) who understand that certain students have, or lack, privileges, thus rendering meritocracy as a dubious model and indeed a potentially dangerous one when students come from vastly different backgrounds, cultures, languages, discourses (Gee, 2008), homes, and neighborhoods. Those educators are able to create "nurturing" instructional climates and teach communities that are conducive to greater learning and better social and psychological outcomes for all adolescents.

Implications for Adolescent Advocates

In many ways, this chapter reflects the assumption that you, the reader, will evaluate the research, claims, and logical consistency of the arguments I have presented, judge their worth, and, if they are found worthy, they may have some impact on your thinking and practice. That assumption, applied to you, may be accurate; but educational progressives who hold the "nurturing family" value system are finding that their arguments have little actual impact in policy or practice.

If you responded to the ideas presented with an "ah-ha" reaction and a feeling of re-affirmation, it is likely you share many of the values of the "nurturing family." If you found yourself questioning the argument, disagreeing with its assumptions, doubting the research presented and the conclusions drawn, it is likely that you do not share the "nurturing family" worldview and my contention that "nurturance" is key to good adolescent education and policy. This understanding leads back to George Lakoff's seminal work on how we make decisions—largely on our basic worldview and the hierarchy of values that we hold as individuals, and only secondarily on evidence as filtered through worldview frames and their associated values.

In many ways, Lakoff's work on the power of values over logic, worldviews over specific issues, and the relative failure of progressive educators to respond effectively to conservative educational policies of the last decade complements current work in cognitive psychology and behavioral economics (Ariely, 2009; Levitt & Dubner, 2005; Thaler & Sunstein, 2009; Brafman & Brafman, 2009; Lehrer, 2009) that challenges the Enlightenment view of rational individuals operating to maximize self-interest. In this new realm of cognitive science Willingham (2009), we are far from rational, i.e., not designed primarily to think, but rather to operate on a series of scripts, frames, and memories that shape our responses and behavior in ways that are largely unconscious. "Discourses" (Gee, 2008)—ways of believing, thinking, talking, and being— are similar to the scripts and memory sequences cited by Willingham. Both "Discourses" and memory scripts are largely unconscious and do not require or invite "thinking." The scripts that Willingham (2009) describes are being researched through MRI work; however, "Discourses" lend themselves to linguistic analysis both by researchers and, to some extent, by teachers, other professionals, parents and adolescents themselves. I suggest that a person's "Discourses" can be examined, reflected upon, embraced, or discarded to some degree. However, those Discourses operate within the family worldview that is dominant (and largely operating below consciousness) for the individual, i.e., the dominant family metaphor is lived in specific sets of beliefs and behaviors. These dominant worldviews, strict father or nurturing parent, are so strongly and deeply held that they override "rational" analysis and logical argument. Research and theories that contradict these deeply held views rarely have the impact needed to make or accept the changes advocated.

Well-written, cogent issue analysis (the forte of many progressives and academics) will not be sufficient. Critiques of conservative adolescent policies, no matter how well argued, will only reinforce the conservative frames that dominate current policies and discussions. By arguing for a different or more effective type of accountability, we are using a conservative frame and reinforcing the argument that the major flaw of adolescent education is lack of accountability. By citing the research that graduation tests disproportionately have a negative impact on high school graduation by low-income, minority students through the use of statistics and graphs, we are not challenging the "personal responsibility," "meritocracy," and "accountability" motifs of the "strict father" family. In reality, I am merely pointing to results that are acceptable and deserved within that worldview. By citing recidivism rates for "boot camps" and early incarceration, we are arguing for more empathy, which works with other progressives, but is trumped by perceived lack of "obedience" and "personal responsibility" in the "strict father" model. By arguing for protection of LBGT adolescents and acceptance of families that are not "traditional," we are assaulting the very foundation of the "strict father" family worldview.

When these worldviews, deeply held and largely below the level of conscious and rational thought, are challenged, it is clear that the Enlightenment view of human beings as rational actors is inaccurate. Research-based arguments have had modest impact on federal education policies. When qualitative, historical, and ethnographic research contradicted the "strict father" worldview, it was officially ousted from recognition as valid research for guiding educational policy. The textbook example is the "scientifically-based reading instruction" (SBRI) push in Reading First. Though purportedly based on the National Reading Panel Report, a close reading of the report itself and an examination of the implementation of federal and state regulations put forth in the name of the report produce little consistency and many contradictions. Adolescent literacy programs were expected to adapt to SBRI findings that were never intended for use with students who were not beginning readers, and in many cases were inconsistent with the findings of the NRP report itself. The appeal of SBRI, the stipulated authority prescribing interventions for an admittedly serious problem of inadequate literacy performance, was the "answer" coming from above which supposedly merely needed consistent implementation by classroom teachers. The reality is that even many original SBRI supporters, including the arch-conservative Grover Whitehurst (in Manzo, 2008) admitted that, while the model had robust implementation, sufficient time to demonstrate impact, and a rigorous longitudinal evaluation, Reading First failed to improve the reading skills of beginning readers. The multi-billion-dollar Reading First Initiative certainly made no impact on the older students who lacked the literacy skills needed for success.

Current research from Harvard (Hill, quoted in Viadero, 2009) on parent involvement also indicates that the NCLB requirement for parental involvement, modeled on meta-analysis largely comprised of elementary school research, has not been successful in improving adolescents' success. Hill's findings on parent involvement in secondary schools suggest that adolescents benefit most by parental communication of high expectations for achievement, fostering career aspirations, and linking school learning to real life. This research also indicates that the transition from middle to high school is a key time and that communication between schools, parents, and adolescents is an important factor. Again, we have a "strict father," top-down policy over-generalizing the research available from elementary school studies and tying school accountability to parent involvement without a carefully researched, nuanced understanding of what kind of involvement is most appropriate for parents, teachers, tweens, and teens.

Reframing Adolescent Education and Policy

Given current top-down accountability, high-stakes assessment and the move toward federal curriculum mandates, which are all based upon a "strict father" model, how can progressive educators be heard? *Adolescent Education: A Reader* is likely to have the same limited impact as the many progressive, well-researched, scholarly, and popular arguments going back to John Dewey. If George Lakoff's (2004, 2008) work has any salience, perhaps the most important message for adolescent advocates is that we must make "nurturing family" arguments based on American values that have persisted since the earliest days of our country. Only through consistent and ubiquitous narratives emphasizing such values will progressives find the arguments and language frames that will be persuasive, that will unify diverse issues in a larger vision, and that will be influential in policymaking and the re-shaping of the "common wisdom."

By connecting individual issues, arguments, and policy positions to a common set of values, we can be more effective advocates. These values are not solely "contested" values, and they are shared to some degree by almost every American. Some examples of such shared progressive values are: the American commitment to public education as necessary for an engaged and informed citizenry; protection of our children and adolescents; adolescents' ability to practice engaged citizenship by participating in democratic decision-making, collaborative goal-setting, teamwork, and reflection upon their own behaviors, understandings, needs and wants; the crucial lessons of our founding fathers that we find success in shared efforts and common commitments; unity and a sense of common purpose, as Franklin D. Roosevelt so eloquently inspired in his fireside chats; and, perhaps most importantly, the nurturance, caring, and empathy that are pre-eminent in all major religious, spiritual, and moral traditions.

These values, while often contested, prevailed in the Civil Rights Movement of the 1950s and 1960s, the New Deal, and Lyndon Johnson's Great Society. While all of those movements had flaws, both in their conception and implementation, they were endorsed by the majority of Americans because they invoked basic values associated with the nurturing family worldview: empathy, community, caring, an equal playing field, the right to be different (Kumashiro, 2008); safety and security through common purpose; creating engaged and active citizenry through public education; and measuring success through the growth of individuals and communities in health, happiness, and security, as well as economic strength. This list is doubtless incomplete and in need of word-smithing. It is meant as a first step, wading into the moral issues inherent in adolescent policy in education, criminal justice, and other social arenas and anchoring our arguments in values that are clear and powerful. Adolescent advocates must set a progressive agenda, a unifying narrative in which powerful research and analysis, including the variety of issues raised in this book and others, can penetrate the "strict father" worldview. That agenda includes head-on challenges to the pre-eminence of economic goals as the purpose of education, educational policy, and educational practice.

The "strict father" worldview has led to policies that are detrimental to many adolescents, families, communities, and the professionals who work with them. The "strict father" worldview contradicts the deeply held moral convictions of many Americans who continue to fight or subvert the system. As policies become more entrenched and representative of the "strict father" worldview, and more instantiated in poor and minority institutions deemed "failing," resultant "strict father" policies will lead many to resist and drop out. Others will learn obedience in a top-down hierarchy with little opportunity for democratic participation, little modeling of empathy and compassion, and a restricted sense of who they are and what they might become.

If this dynamic is to change, progressives must reach out to the vast majority of Americans who value both empathy and obedience. Progressives must create a narrative elevating the long tradition of progressive values in American thought and policy—freedom, prosperity, empathy and compassion, equity, and social justice for all through democratic models of nurturance, community, and engaged citizenship.

QUESTIONS TO CONSIDER

1. What circumstances and events might lead to the dominance of the "strict father" worldview in educational and social policy?

2. What physical aspects of a school might be interpreted as examples of either the "strict father" or the "nurturing mother" family worldview?

3. If worldviews largely operate below the level of consciousness, can a person's views on an issue be changed? Why or why not?

4. Do these worldviews have implications for preparing teachers and school leaders?

5. Most people are not strict adherents of one worldview in every area, but rarely are they exactly in the middle. How would you identify your own worldview? Can you think of at least one issue on which you deviate from your predominant worldview? Explain how and why.

Notes

1. Lakoff does not equate *parenting* and *political views*. He also warns that individuals may vary between the views depending upon the issues and that their views may also vary over time. Even with these important caveats, Lakoff still makes a persuasive case that these guiding views of *family* and by extension *nation* have important explanatory power to elucidate political beliefs and values.

2. For a fascinating, popular, and accessible exploration of these family metaphors in American politics, read Lakoff's (2004) *Don't Think of an Elephant!: Know Your Values and Frame the Debate*. For a more scholarly examination, *Moral Politics* (2002) provides a thorough, research-based examination.

3. The Hyde Amendment already bars the use of government money for abortions.

4. Since *A Nation at Risk* in 1983, there has been an increasing focus on economic rationales for education: workforce development has become the mantra from not only business interests, but also educators and education policymakers; and it has had the greatest impact on the shape of adolescent education. Historically, the American notion of "common schools" was to prepare a citizenry (although largely restricted to white males) who would be prepared to assume their rightful roles in a democratic republic.

   Linking outcomes of adolescent education to economic dominance of the nation is again in vogue. *Tough Choices or Tough Times: The report of the new commission on the skills of the American workforce* (2006) states: "We have failed to motivate most of our students to take tough courses and work hard, thus missing one of the most important drivers of success in the best-performing nations." Our morality, our national security, and everything in-between seem to rest on the shoulders of the adolescents in our society. Scholars challenge the conclusions of these recurrent exhortations with their scapegoating and over-wrought language of crisis, but their work is largely unknown to the public and ignored by the media. Therefore, the progressive rebuttal has little impact on policy or perception. There are strong rebuttals about the ability of our society to produce high-paying positions for all students, even if they achieve a postsecondary education (Aronowitz & DeFazio, 1994; Gee, 1996). Bureau of Labor data (2009) tell us that the greatest job growth (in real numbers) in 2008–2009 was in the fields of personal and home health and care aides (773,000) that require only short-term training. In fact, of the new jobs created, 52% require short to moderate on-the-job training, another 6% require an associate's degree or specialized post-high school training, 35% require a bachelor's degree, and 7% require an advanced degree.

References

Ariely, D. (2009). *Predictably irrational: The hidden forces that shape our decisions*. New York: Harper.

Aronowitz, S. & DiFazio, W. (1994) *The jobless future*. St. Paul: University of Minnesota Press.

Brafman, O., & Brafman, B. (2009). *Sway: The irresistible pull of Irrational behavior*. New York: Broadway Business.

Bureau of Labor Statistics. (2009). *Occupational outlook handbook*. As retrieved December 14, 2009 from http://www.bls.gov/oco/oco2003.htm

Carnegie Commission on Adolescence. (1995). *Great transitions: Preparing adolescents for a new century*. New York: Carnegie Corporation of New York.

Gee, J. P., Lankshear, C. & G. Hull (1996) *The new work order: Behind the language of the new capitalism*. Boulder, CO: Westview Press.

Gee, J. P. (2008). *Social linguistics and literacies: Ideology in discourses*. (3rd ed.). New York: Routledge.

Kumashiro, K. K. (2008). *The seduction of common sense: How the right has framed the debate on America's schools*. New York: Teachers College Press.

Lakoff, G. (1996) *Moral politics: What conservatives know that liberals don't*. Chicago: University of Chicago Press.

Lakoff, G. (2002). *Moral politics: How liberals and conservatives think,* (2nd ed.). Chicago: University of Chicago Press.

Lakoff, G. (2004). *Don't think of an elephant! Know your values and frame the debate*. White River Junction, VT: Chelsea Green Publishing.

Lakoff, G. (2008). *The political mind: A cognitive scientist's guide to your brain and its politics*. New York: Penguin.

Lakoff, G. & Johnson, M. (1980). *Metaphors we live by*. Chicago: University of Chicago Press.

Lounsbury, J. H. (2003). *This we believe*. Westerville, OH: National Middleschool Association.

Lehrer, J. (2009). *How we decide*. Boston: Houghton Mifflin.

Levitt, S. D., & Dubner, S. D. (2005). *Freakonomics: A rogue economist explores the hidden side of everything*. New York: Morrow.

Males, M. A. (1996). *Scapegoat generation: America's war on adolescents*. Monroe, ME: Common Courage Press.

Manzo, K. K. (2008, June 3). Kamil questions the results of latest Reading First Impact Study. *Education Week*, retrieved December 14, 2009, from http://ed.stanford.edu/suse/faculty/displayFacultyNews.php?tablename=notify1&-id=828

National Commission on Excellence in Education. (1983). *A nation at risk: The imperative for educational reform*. Washington, DC: National Institute for Education.

National Institute of Child Health and Human Development. (2000). *Report of the National Reading Panel. Teaching children to read: An evidence-based assessment of the scientific research literature on reading and its implications for reading instruction* (NIH Publication No. 00–4769). Washington, DC: U.S. Government Printing Office.

New Commission on the Skills of the American Workforce. (2007). *Tough choices or tough times*. Washington, DC: National Center on Education and the Economy.

No Child Left Behind Act of 2001, Pub.L. No. 107–110, 115 Stat. 1425 (2002).

Thaler, R. H., & Sunstein, C. (2009). *Nudge: Improving our decisions about health, wealth and happiness*. New York: Penguin.

Viadero, D. (2009, November 17). Scholars: Parent-school ties should shift in teen years. *Education Week*, retrieved December 14, 2009 at http://www.edweek.org/login.html?source=http://www.edweek.org/ew/articles/2009/11/18/12parent_ep.h29.html&destination=http://www.edweek.org/ew/articles/2009/11/18/12parent_ep.h29.html&levelId=2100

Willingham, D. T. (2009). *Why students don't like school: A cognitive scientist answers questions about how the mind works and what it means for the classroom*. San Francisco: Jossey-Bass.

CHAPTER TWELVE

Stigma Stories in the Media

Four Discourses about Teen Mothers, Welfare, and Poverty

DEIRDRE M. KELLY

That [newspaper] lady totally twisted what we said because she wanted it to sound worse. I wrote her a letter and said, "If you weren't going to write what we said, why did you waste your time and our time? You might as well just have sat home, made up the story yourself—not even bother us if you weren't going to use the facts."

—MOLLY, MOTHER, AGE 17, LA FUENTE[1]

Feminist and other critical researchers have produced studies that have challenged conventional wisdom about teen mothers causing, and being produced by, poverty. But critical feminist research has been taken up infrequently by the mainstream media—and rarely as authoritative. Although ideas about teen sexuality and "alternative" family structures may have become less rigid over the last 25 years, the mainstream media's representations of teen mothers remain for the most part stigmatized, albeit within updated constructs.

Although the social stigma about teen pregnancy is popularly perceived to have lessened in recent times, I have shown that it is still quite prevalent, although its manifestations are evolving. Over the last 25 years, the forms taken by the stigma have been far more openly contested by various social and political groups. This contest is waged among those who continue to believe that adolescent pregnancy should be stigmatized as a deterrent to early sexual activity and welfare dependence and those with rival interpretations of the meaning of teen pregnancy and motherhood. This contest is making headlines in the United States at a moment when teen pregnancy and birth rates are leveling out at non-epidemic proportions after a slight increase in the late 1980s, although the percentage of teen births that are out of wedlock has increased steadily since 1960. The same debates rage today in Canada, where, with the exception of the past few years, teen pregnancy and birth rates have declined in almost every province over the last 20 years.[2] This contest can be seen as a clashing of discourses, an ongoing struggle over public definitions of deviance.

In the waging of this "stigma contest" (Schur, 1980), the mass media constitute a key arena. Within this arena, print media—newspapers and magazines—are key cultural texts. The print media frequently provide broadcast journalists with story ideas, and politicians and other members of the elite favor the quality newspaper as a source of news (Ericson, Baranek, & Chan, 1991, pp. 31–32, 45). It is within the print media, then—and at a moment when teen mothers are increasingly portrayed as the nexus of most major social ills—that I have focused my analysis of the discourses about teen mothers.

In this chapter I will present: (a) a framework for analyzing the discourses around teen pregnancy and motherhood and (b) reflections based on an analysis of print media coverage of teen mothers in Canada since 1980. As I compare and contrast discourses, I attempt to reveal the ideological agendas inscribed in particular representations of teen mothers.

Media and Discourse Theory

I focused on newspaper and magazine articles that addressed the topic of teen mothers, located through a search of the Canadian News Index for the years 1980–1992, the Alternative Press Index,[3] and a personal clipping file collected from the mainstream, alternative, and right-wing press (both in the United States and in Canada) over the last 8 years. As I analyzed the over 700 articles, I found a pragmatic model of discourse theory to be useful. Drawing on Foucault, among others, Fraser (1992, p. 185) describes the pragmatic model thus:

> Discourses are historically specific, socially situated, signifying practices. They are the communicative frames in which speakers interact by exchanging speech acts. Yet discourses are themselves set within social institutions and action contexts. Thus, the concept of a discourse links the study of language to the study of society.

More specifically, Griffith and Smith (1991, p. 90) define discourse as

> an organization of relations among people participating in a conversation mediated by written and printed materials. A discourse has a social organization of authorities, sites, production processes, etc. . . . The term does not just refer to the "texts" of this conversation and their production alone, but also to the ways in which people organize their activities in relationship to them.

These definitions direct attention not just to statements and texts but also to the variety of discursive practices, their interconnections, and the many ways people make sense of texts in everyday life. Experts in universities and policy think tanks conduct research that provides categories and language that news reporters and magazine editors appropriate and popularize in their stories; these stories, in turn, encourage readers (not always successfully) to think about teen mothers, for instance, in certain ways and not in others.

A number of discourses coexist and compete with each other; there is no "single, monolithic 'symbolic order'" (Fraser, 1989, p. 10). But the discourses do not compete as equals; some carry little weight and are marginalized, while others are considered to be authoritative and dominant. In Canada, as in other late capitalist societies, social groups have unequal access to power, status, and resources, including the discursive arena of the mass circulation media (Fraser, 1989, p. 165).

Within each discourse, media writers, social activists, professionals, and researchers use various frames to help their audiences make sense of phenomena or events. Sociologist Amy Binder (1993) explains: "Frames and frameworks are 'schemata of interpretation that enable individuals to locate, perceive, identify, and label' events they have experienced directly or indirectly" (p. 754). These frames, composed of arguments and images, are selected and constructed from larger sets of cultural beliefs; they serve "an ideological function when the frames reinforce unequal social relations by those institutionally empowered to do so" (p. 755).

Ideologies are partial accounts of the world constructed from within particular historical contexts, and they operate to serve particular economic, political, and social interests. An anti-racist, feminist ideology, for example, would point to the gender and racial subtexts of the dominant discourse about teen mothers (subtexts are what remains unsaid that is often central to a text's meaning). Although dominant ideologies downplay conflicts of interest and perspectives that challenge prevailing power relations, I am not suggesting that a position exists outside of ideology that is "innocent." This does not mean, however, that all truth claims are relative. As Hawkesworth (1989) states:

> standards related to the range of human cognitive practices allow us to distinguish between partial views (the inescapable condition of human cognition) and false beliefs, superstitions, irrebuttable presumptions, willful distortions. . . . informed judgments can be made. (p. 555)

A Critical Feminist Interpretation of the Scholarly Research on Teen Mothers, Welfare, and Poverty

My admittedly partial view is that teen mothers provide a convenient scapegoat for those who would ignore the structural causes of poverty. I thus participate in what I describe below as an oppositional discourse about teen mothers. Before turning to an analysis of the discourses constructed and disseminated by the print media, I will summarize here a growing body of research that calls into question a number of widely held assumptions about teen mothers, welfare, and poverty.

First, poverty is not a straightforward cause of early motherhood; there appear to be many other precipitating factors. Research done mainly in the United States suggests that "[l]iving in poverty is associated with both early sexual activity and early pregnancy" (Miller & Moore, 1990, p. 1030). This, however, begs the question of causation. Phoenix (1991a) reviewed the research in North America and England and concluded:

> While many young people experience poverty and do not have "proper jobs," most young women who lack money do not become mothers. Poverty is thus the context within which the overwhelming majority of instances of motherhood under 20 occur, rather than a causative factor. (p. 90)

Second, adolescent pregnancy and childbearing do not necessarily cause poverty. To examine the long-term economic outcomes associated with female adolescent marriage and childbearing, Grindstaff (1988) looked at women who were 30 in the 1981 Canadian census. As expected, he found that women who became mothers at a young age obtained less formal schooling, but in terms of income, the early-childbearing women did not have substantially less than the women who became mothers at a later age. The timing of marriage and childbearing was "secondary to the overriding issue of whether the woman has a child" (p. 54). In other words, today's economy does not easily accommodate women of any age who combine childrearing and paid work. The data also showed that at least some teen mothers eventually do quite well economically.

Third, studies do not show that welfare payments entice women to become pregnant. Most of the research in this area has been done in the United States. Wilson and Neckerman (1987, cited in Phoenix, 1991a, p. 87) reviewed U.S. studies that explored the connection between welfare policies, levels of welfare benefits, and the incidence of teen motherhood and single motherhood; they found no relationship between welfare provision and low-income women's childbearing.

In Canada, a few provincial governments have investigated the claim that availability of welfare benefits encourages teen pregnancy and found it to be without merit (on Alberta, see "Study," 1989; on Nova Scotia, see Clark, Dechman, French, & MacCallum, 1991). In fact, an international study found that countries with some of the highest welfare benefits, such as Sweden, have the lowest teen pregnancy rates (Jones et al., 1986).

Fourth, researchers have not established that teen motherhood is a prime cause of welfare dependency. To show such causation, one would need to design longitudinal studies, which are costly to do and thus rarely done. More often, researchers conduct statistical analyses of large extant data bases; these studies have found strong correlations between teen motherhood, school dropout, reduced earnings, and welfare status. Yet new research suggests that these earlier cross-sectional studies may have overstated the negative socioeconomic consequences of teen childbearing (Geronimus & Korenman, 1992).

A common problem with non-longitudinal studies is that the researchers, the various consumers of the research (such as policymakers, advocacy groups, news reporters), or both go beyond the research findings to make unwarranted generalizations and predictions. On the basis of a non-random, snowball survey[4] of 79 teen mothers in Vancouver, British Columbia, for example, a researcher reported that only 20% had finished Grade 12 and that 46% had completed Grade 9 or less, while 77% were on social assistance (Fallon, 1979, Appendix A, pp. 22, 25). Citing only this study, a practitioner who worked with teen mothers concluded: "Eighty per cent of adolescent mothers never complete their education, become welfare dependent, and endure lives of desperate poverty and futility" (Billung-Meyer, 1982, p. 28). Thus, the fate of all teen mothers was discerned from a sample confined, by its design, to a disproportionately poor segment of teen mothers, who had been interviewed only once, at a point in their lives that was too early to show how they would fare.

The few longitudinal studies that exist tend to paint a much less bleak portrait of teen mothers and their children. Pozsonyi (1973) did a longitudinal study of unmarried, first-time mothers who kept their children and who were clients of a Family and Children's Services agency, checking back with the mothers at six-month intervals for the first eighteen months after the baby's birth. At the last face-to-face interview, only 30% were receiving welfare and 26% had married. Pozsonyi concluded: "The majority of unmarried mothers and their children were found to fare well in the community" (p. 59; see also S. Clark, 1999).

Studies in the United States have followed women who became teen mothers over decades;

they have refuted the stereotype of teen mothers as chronic welfare recipients (Furstenberg, Brooks-Gunn, & Morgan, 1987; Harris, 1997). Over time, many of the women in these studies obtained paid work, achieved more education, and increased their levels of employment. The lack of affordable child care services, however, often hindered them (Harris, 1997).

Finally, reducing the number of teen mothers would not mean a big cut in welfare spending. According to a recent Statistics Canada report, single-parent families (male-led and female-led) made up only 13% of all families in 1991, and only 6.4% of families led by female single parents were led by young women (aged 15 to 24) (Mitchell, 1993). Further, if the ranks of teen mothers were to somehow thin significantly, that alone would not result in commensurate savings to taxpayers. Luker (1991) summarizes the findings of U.S. policy analysts Richard Wertheimer and Kristin Moore, who "have estimated that if by some miracle we could cut the teen birth rate in half, welfare costs would be reduced by 20 percent, rather than 50 percent, because many of these young women would still need welfare for children born to them when they were no longer teens" (p. 80).

This conclusion is underscored by a group of U.S. studies that have used innovative ways to assess whether young women who are already disadvantaged by having grown up in poverty and so forth (i.e., those most likely to become teen mothers) are further disadvantaged by teen motherhood in and of itself. Geronimus and Korenman (1992) compared a national sample of sisters and found no correlation between teen childbearing and high school graduation or subsequent family income. They cite a study by Corcoran and Kunz that

> found teen mothers to be no more likely to be welfare recipients after age 25 than their sisters who became mothers at older ages. So too, Joseph Hotz et al. comparing teens who gave birth to those who miscarried in recent data from the National Longitudinal Survey of Youth concluded that a teen mother is no more likely to participate in welfare programs, to have her labor market earnings reduced, or to experience significant losses in spousal earnings, than the same woman would have experienced if she had delayed childbearing. (Geronimus, 1997, p. 5; see Hoffman, 1998 for a more critical and cautionary review of this new literature)

To be sure, some women spend extended periods of time receiving government assistance. They tend to be those who have troubled childhoods, leave school before getting pregnant, and face multiple and severe barriers to paid employment—beyond those that result from teen motherhood. As sociologist Frank Furstenberg has written in the U.S. context, "State government can remove them from the welfare rolls but it will not help them make the transition into the labor force without intensive and extensive assistance that certainly costs more than the modest funding provided by AFDC [Aid to Families with Dependent Children], as we presently know it" (1997, pp. x–xi). Further, women who grow up in poverty, as many teen mothers have, face long odds against doing well later in life whether or not they become pregnant early in life.

Stigma Contest: Discourses about Teen Mothers

Given the research cited above, why aren't the same conclusions commonly drawn by liberal technocrats and social service providers, two groups cited often in most mainstream media accounts and a sector that usually places such faith in social science? The irony, as I explain below, is that this group of bureaucratic experts, one that contests the more traditional stigmatizers, has incentives to tell its own stigma stories about teen mothers.

People are not always so explicit about what should be stigmatized or denounced and what should be defended or advocated. Instead, they talk about "needs." Nancy Fraser (1989) has argued that when the late capitalist welfare state undertakes to satisfy social needs, the definition of the needs in question is often taken for granted. But let us consider the "needs" of a teen mother. Does she need earlier abortion and adoption counseling? Or does she need more incentives to keep her child? Does she need publicly funded day care and training? Or does she need it to be easier to stay home with her infant? Does she need more self-esteem that comes with independence or the support that comes with marriage or family ties? Perhaps her needs are not so self-evident after all—and which needs a person identifies as paramount locates that person politically within the stigma contest surrounding teen mothers.

Fraser calls for a recasting of the dominant policy framework to highlight the "politics of need interpretation." In her discussion of women and welfare policy, she identifies three major, competing "discourses about needs" that are associated with bureaucratic experts, conservatives, and oppositional social movements.[5] How, then, has the stigma contest over teen mothers been waged by each group in North America?

Bureaucratic Experts: The Wrong-Girl Frame

In the late 1960s, popular and academic journals began to frame teen pregnancy as less a moral problem and more a technical one related to the creation of intergenerational welfare dependency and poverty (Arney & Bergin, 1984). Rather than attend to the conditions of poverty and frame the social psychology as rooted in the problems of the powerless, however, "experts" have tended to focus attention on the psychological motivations of girls who become pregnant and decide to keep their babies. Once the "problem" is located within the individual, the technical solution often amounts to therapy and monitoring.

In the same vein as the "girl nobody loved" construct, the two most prominent psychological explanations of teen motherhood both infantilize these mothers and cast suspicion on their families. The first argues that these young women, many of whom are said to come from "broken" homes themselves, have babies out of an unfulfilled need for somebody to love them: "An adolescent's decision to raise a child, for example, is often determined by such egocentric desires as the wish to . . . receive unconditional love from a dependent object, in this case, the baby" (D. Gordon, 1990, p. 349). This expert discourse then gets translated for a popular audience as it was in the *Vancouver Sun:* "The teen mother is usually a child who looked for love or acceptance, and instead found herself thrown into adulthood before her mind and body were ready" (Krangle, 1980, p. A1).

The second psychological explanation holds that the young women have been abused (sexually or otherwise) and that motherhood may help them escape a bad family situation. Boyer and Fine (1992) investigated the links between prior sexual abuse and adolescent pregnancy. They hypothesize that the "developmental process" of children who are sexually abused may become arrested. Further, "a link between sexual victimization and adolescent pregnancy may also illuminate . . . child maltreatment by adolescent parents" (p. 5). Or as the Canadian Press (1990) put it: "Experts in child care worry about the ability of many teenage parents to put the needs of their children ahead of their own. . . . The children are seen as especially vulnerable to abuse, neglect and slow development, what child-care workers call 'failure to thrive'" (p. 12).

These two psychological explanations are not, of course, mutually exclusive. In both versions, the teenager's having her baby tends to be seen as a "personal tragedy," in part because "adolescent pregnancy breeds poverty" (e.g., Schlesinger, 1982, pp. 45–46); she has made a mistake—not so much a moral mistake in this discourse, as an error in timing—and she needs help to set it right. The difficulty, according to these experts, is that she may not realize she has made a mistake in "forsaking her childhood and jumping the adolescent bridge into adulthood too soon." Indeed, "she may be unable—simply unable—to see that she has made a mistake and that she could be helped to put it right" (Hudson & Ineichen, 1991, p. 55).

Defining teen mothers in this way, as girls from flawed backgrounds who are making tragic mistakes, leads quite naturally to the analysis that the wrong girls are having and keeping babies. This indeed is the view of many university-based researchers and people who staff the various programs that deal with teen mothers. As is common practice, these bureaucratic experts are the first people the mass media contact to explain the meaning of teen motherhood. The Canadian Press (1980a), for example, quoted Benjamin Schlesinger, a professor of social work at the University of Toronto, as saying, "It appears the wrong girl is keeping the baby. . . . It's babies having babies" (p. A17). Age is not the primary factor that makes these mothers wrong; the average age of the girls in Schlesinger's study was, after all, 19 years. What makes these the wrong girls is their family background, according to Schlesinger: "Teenage unwed mothers from broken homes are keeping their children while those from more stable backgrounds give theirs up for adoption" (p. A17).

In searching for solutions to the wrong-girl problem, bureaucratic experts, encouraged by theories produced within the academy, have identified adolescent emotional maladjustment as a root cause of early pregnancy and childbearing. Teen mothers must therefore receive constant help and therapy as well as monitoring. In advocating for an alternative school program for Victoria teen mothers, the school board chair argued:

> One reason we'd like a program where they could bring their babies and bring themselves when they're pregnant is so we can monitor them and help them with parenting skills. The statistics for child abuse show it is much more prevalent in teenage mothers because of all the frustrations they have and their inability to cope. (Canadian Press, 1980b, p. A19)

What distinguishes the bureaucratic experts from their conservative critics? Unlike conservatives, the experts frequently use theories and language that suggest teen mothers and their children are in need of protection—from themselves, from their families, from their male partners. Bureaucratic experts are, in general, strong proponents of sex education and birth control counseling as a means of preventing teen pregnancy. They rarely, however, view teen pregnancy and motherhood as positive. Yet because their premise is that many teen mothers are victims of abuse, they assert that society must address "the reality" and provide services to teen mothers (e.g., Rincover, 1991). Further, because their views are strongly contested by economic and social conservatives (discussed later in this chapter), experts—and the reporters who quote them—must frequently justify government intervention and spending by underscoring that its purpose is to "break the cycles of child abuse and welfare dependency." In short, this form of argument, although it destigmatizes extramarital, teenage sexual activity, it still stigmatizes a teenager's pregnancy and decision to keep her baby, albeit in an indirect way.

Reprivatization Groups: The Wrong-Family Frame

Economic, social, and religious conservatives, in contrast, are usually much more direct about what they think should be stigmatized or restigmatized. In a *Vancouver Sun* column, Les Bewley (1984), for example, pined for the days when

> any young, unmarried girl [who] allowed herself to become pregnant . . . was properly and publicly regarded as a fool, a tramp, or a slut . . . and she was ostracized by the community. If a young man knocked a girl up, he was expected to marry her and support her, even if it had to be at gunpoint, rather than leave her with a bastard child. (p. A11)

This approach, according to Bewley, accomplished three things: "girls had a powerful set of reasons for saying the simple word 'no,' young men had some powerful deterrents against knocking girls up, and the community was spared the very real threat of bankruptcy from social welfare programs."

Conservatives such as Bewley aim to exclude teen mothers from public places such as schools and return the responsibility for sex education to parents; they engage in what Fraser (1989) has termed "reprivatization discourse," that is, they seek "to repatriate newly problematized needs to their former domestic or official economic enclaves" (p. 157). Mass media stories about teen mothers do not usually build upon a conservative set of assumptions unless they appear in such right-wing publications as *Alberta Report* and *British Columbia Report* or on the editorial pages of mainstream newspapers. Yet reprivatization themes frequently provide the counterbalance to bureaucratic experts in mainstream news stories.

Teen mothers have become a touchstone for a number of reprivatization discourse themes. What unifies these themes is a concern over the fate of the traditional family—which conservatives define as a heterosexual, nuclear family made up of a sole breadwinner father, a homemaker mother, and children—as well as the changing relationship between families and the state. For conservatives, unmarried teen mothers not only symbolize the wrong family model, but through the government-funded services now provided for them and their children, they may pave the way toward official sanctioning of everything from universal child care to state-run adoptions.

More specifically: First, conservatives fear that public schools are taking away parents' rights to raise their children (Byfield, 1993) and they oppose liberal—or any—sex education in the schools. They would replace it with a program that promotes chastity. The conservative media present this as "an uphill fight" that parents face against the "liberal" public school system (Cunningham, 1992a, p. 28). These stories feature photos of teen mothers with such captions as "more teen pregnancies and more abortions" (Cunningham, 1992b).

Second, conservatives oppose teenagers' access to abortion and birth control. In the early 1980s in British Columbia, this became a point of contention between Health Minister Rafe Mair, who opposed abortion, and school officials who pointed out that "[Mair] is not prepared to put anything into prevention" (Canadian Press, 1980b, A19). A related and more recent example was conservative opposition to an amendment to the B.C. Infants Act that gave teens the right to obtain medical treatment (including an abortion) without parental consent (Brunet, 1992).

Third, conservatives oppose teen single motherhood. The editor of *British Columbia Report* (O'Neill, 1993) longs for the days

> when society wagged its collective finger at unmarried moms. It may have seemed cruel, but it served a greater usefulness (a recognition that a stable marriage was the best atmosphere in which to raise a family), and it certainly didn't preclude individual acts of compassion toward the unfortunate young women. (p. 2)

One underlying assumption of this analysis is that if these "unwed" mothers would only marry, then their husbands could assume financial responsibility for them and their children, thus sparing taxpayers the expense.

Fourth, conservatives oppose welfare for young people, believing it undermines the authority of parents and other adults and costs too much.[6] Teen parenthood is but the most striking example of how "children are choosing, or being pushed, into handling adult responsibilities." Citing leaders of teacher organizations, a writer for the *Ottawa Citizen* (Dube, 1993) argued that students who live on their own with the help of welfare dollars exist outside of "parental authority," which has "produced a big change": "Granted so much independence, it's hard to conform just because a teacher tells you to" (p. A4).

Fifth, conservatives often oppose regular school programs for teen mothers. Some object to any help at all because, they argue, this lets adolescents off the hook morally and financially and encourages promiscuity. Bewley (1984), for example, noted disapprovingly: "Pregnant children are beamed upon in the classroom, and at least one Vancouver high school publicly prides itself on its free day-care centre for the children of unmarried student mothers." Others "might not like the addition of another costly social program, but"—in a nod to bureaucratic expert discourse—"they generally recognize that if the young moms can lead productive lives by graduating, they are less likely to become a burden on society" (O'Neill, 1993, p. 2).

Still, they worry that babies are becoming "status symbols" among school children. Thus the editor of *British Columbia Report* (O'Neill, 1993) suggests "that it makes sense to at least ensure that teen parent programs are not located in regular high schools, but in separate facilities" (p. 2). Presumably these conservatives would favor the old model whereby pregnant and mothering girls stayed at home or went to homes for unwed mothers, perhaps receiving an education by correspondence.

Some pro-life conservatives, however, are more concerned that pregnant teenagers be supported in their decision not to abort. Ridiculing O'Neill's suggestion that teen mothers be "isolated," two pro-life women demanded, "[W]hy not put the fathers of the children of teen moms in separate facilities so they don't impregnate more girls?" (Green & Steel, 1993, p. 3).

Sixth, conservatives worry that school-based day care centers for the children of teen mothers will pave the way for universal, government-funded, group child care. The founder of the "pro-family" Citizen's Research Institute, for one, is concerned that when schools provide on-site child care, they send a message that "institutionalizing infants in day care is a normal and healthy measure" (Saenger, 1991, p. 23). A member of parliament, Bob Wenman, went even further, calling day care centers "little more than temporary orphanages" and a "misuse of taxpay-ers' money" (Cunningham, 1993, p. 10).

Finally, conservatives favor teen mothers giving their babies up for adoption and want to min-imize government regulation of private adoptions. During the House of Commons debate on Canada's abortion laws, pro-life conservatives began stressing adoption as the most sound choice a pregnant teenager could make (see Brodie, Gavigan, & Jenson, 1992, p. 65). Conservatives also worry that private adoptions be unfettered by government interference because, they argue, "many young mothers will choose to have an abortion rather than surrender their babies over to heart-less bureaucrats" (Kerby, 1993, p. 3).

To sum up, conservative groups seek to stigmatize abortion, and so some find strong moti-vation to destigmatize a teen's decision to carry her pregnancy to term. But in the contest over interpretations of teen mothers, "reprivatizers" employ heavy stigmas to enforce their idea of fam-ily: a family where sex occurs only after marriage; a family of two parents and a male breadwin-ner; a family independent of state aid. An unwed teen mother who relies on any government program and doesn't give her child up for adoption is, in this construct, the epitome of the wrong family.

Oppositional Movements: The Wrong-Society Frame

Several oppositional social movements, following on the achievements of the civil rights move-ment for racial equality, gained strength in the late 1960s and early 1970s. In particular, the Aboriginal people's rights movement, the anti-poverty movement, and the women's liberation movement each provided arguments that could be marshaled in support of teen parents and cre-ated space for an alternative discourse aimed at reducing the stigma of teen pregnancy. Such an alternative discourse, however, rarely informs, let alone frames, mass media stories about teen mothers.

An exception came during an interview with Nobel Prize-winning novelist Toni Morrison (in Angelo, 1989), who tapped into an oppositional discourse (feminist,[7] class-conscious, and anti-racist) to argue that teenage motherhood should be more accepted. She asserted that much of the reprivatization discourse is a subterfuge: "I don't think anybody cares about unwed mothers unless they're black—or poor. The question is not morality, the question is money. That's what we're upset about. We don't care whether they have babies or not." The interviewer followed up with a familiar question, "How do you break the cycle of poverty? You can't just hand out money." In response, Morrison demanded:

> Why not? Everybody else gets everything handed to them. The rich get it handed—they inherit it. I don't mean just inheritance of money. I mean what people take for granted among the middle and upper class-es, which is nepotism, the old-boy network. That's shared bounty of class. (p. 122)

Usually, to find views such as Morrison's, one must turn to the alternative media. But even there, liberal feminist versions of the bureaucratic expert discourse are heard (e.g., Billung-Meyer, 1982). This is so, I would argue, because mainstream feminists have often ignored social class, race, and age, key structures that contribute to the ongoing stigmatization of teen mothers (cf. O'Neill, 1998).

Scarce as it is, where the oppositional discourse is found, the following themes emerge. First, don't blame the poor for poverty and its consequences. Katha Pollitt (1992), a socialist feminist, wrote in her regular column for the *Nation:*

> When the poor are abandoned to their fates, when there are no jobs, people don't get to display "work ethic," don't feel good about themselves and don't marry or stay married. The girls don't have anything to postpone motherhood for; the boys have no economic prospects that would make them reasonable marriage partners. (p. 94)

Sometimes these and related views find their way into mainstream media accounts when a maverick bureaucratic expert or an advocate gets quoted. *Montreal Gazette* columnist Susan Schwartz (1991) approvingly cited a report that argued that teen mothers "need, among other things, a network to give them that voice, a revamped welfare system that takes into account their needs as young parents, organized community services to help young mothers to combat their isolation" (p. B4; see also, Bolan, 1993).

A second theme in oppositional discourse: Support "a woman's right to choose when, where, how, and with whom to give birth" (Maternal Health Society, 1982).[8] This means young women "need solid information and safe contraception that serves their needs," including safe, affordable, and legal abortions (Stevens, 1979, p. 11). Feminists have also stressed the need to change sex education. Susie Bright, for example, an important voice for the sexual-libertarian wing of the feminist movement (see Willis, 1996) and an on-line columnist for *Salon Magazine,* wishes she had "had someone mentor me about the absurd conflation of sex and love in young women's minds. . . . [Most young women] know how to say 'no' repetitively, but they're utterly at a loss as to what to say 'yes' to, or what form their own sexual initiative might take. Consequently, their refusals often wilt into guilty compromises and resentful ambivalence" (Bright, 1998).

The third theme of the oppositional discourse is respect and support for the diversity of family types. Feminists point out that there have long been moral attacks on single women with children, particularly those living in poverty. Given this historical context, it has been fairly easy to portray teen mothers as selfish, irresponsible, and so on, as is evident in the following *Newsweek* story (Ingrassia, 1993) about highly educated, single women with a fair income who decide to raise children on their own: "It's one thing to dismiss single parenthood as the act of petulant teenagers; it's another to ignore professionals having babies alone. But are these Murphy Browns any less self-absorbed than teens?" (p. 58). In this analysis, many feminists would see sexism: "There is an analytical link between moral attacks on single women on welfare and on women who achieved unusual degrees of educational success. In both cases, the women have displayed personal independence rather than dependence on individual men" (Wrigley, 1992, p. 13).

Critical feminists, among others, have stressed, instead, the notion of *interdependence*. Curiously, I have found that little of this analysis has filtered into the alternative press reportage on teen pregnancy and motherhood.

Teen Mothers' Self-Interpretations: The Stigma-Is-Wrong Frame

Teen mothers' self-interpretations draw from, resist, or transform the three major rival interpretations of their needs. Yet we rarely hear from teen mothers themselves in the mass media or, if we do, their remarks have been selected and edited in ways that can make them feel their main message has been distorted, as we saw in the case of Molly, the teen mother quoted at the start of this chapter. Recently, I have run across several first-hand personal accounts by young mothers or—more often—former young mothers (these accounts appear either as letters to the editor or op-ed pieces); they represent about 3% of the total articles about teen mothers (yielded in a search of the Canadian News Index, 1980–1992). In addition, a few articles quote young mothers extensively or report negative reactions of a group of young mothers to stereotypes about single teen mothers.

Based on this analysis (which was confirmed by subsequent interviews with teen mothers at City and Town Schools), I have found that some stress themes of empowerment and reject messages that portray them as victims, childlike, welfare abusers, or morally tainted. Often they claim the need to be seen positively as mothers and emphasize the following themes.

First, the right to choose, including motherhood and adoption, is essential. In an op-ed by Kim Anderson (1989) subtitled "Happy Teenage Mother Backs Right to Choose," a former teen mother, whose baby was then 7 years old, says: "We are especially lucky in Canada because we have programs that pay day-care fees, living expenses and even tuition for young mothers who want to complete high school." A direct beneficiary of such support, the author claims now to have a "well-paying, satisfying job." Pondering from a pregnant teenager's point of view the options of abortion, offering the baby up for adoption, or keeping it, Anderson concludes:

> Experts and well-intentioned outsiders on all sides of the issue should put themselves in her shoes. . . . The main conclusion is that a mother should have the right to choose her own destiny. She should know all the choices and all the problems associated with each of them. She should have time and space to think clearly about what she really wants to do. The parents of these girls should support their child's decision. (p. H2)

Second, choosing to keep one's baby should not be stigmatized. Millie Strom married the father of her baby and gave birth at 15. In an op-ed article appearing in the *Vancouver Sun* (Strom, 1993), she recounts how she escaped her battering husband by retreating to a mental hospital, the only refuge she could find. There, with a diagnosis of postpartum depression, she was labeled "unfit," and authorities coerced her to remove her son from his paternal grandparents, where he was happy. He was placed in foster care and, unknown to Strom, he lingered another 8 months before being placed with adoptive parents. This was contrary to the wishes of all family members, including Strom's ex-husband, the paternal grandparents, and Strom herself.

> I had been told that I would forget him. Since I would forget, I was not warned about the depressions around his birthday and on holidays such as Christmas. . . . Social workers often say adoption offers something to the new mother—a chance for a fresh start. However, this adoption ideology omits some important realities. Adoption does not obliterate the unplanned pregnancy. (p. A11)

Third, choosing to give one's baby up for adoption should not be stigmatized. Anouk Crawford, 20, and Christie Cooper, 22, are young women who founded Birth Mothers Coalition after they gave their babies up for adoption. They were profiled in a Vancouver *Province* article (Grindlay, 1993) headlined "Proud of Their Novel Conception." "'We're not supposed to be proud that we were young women and we had the courage to go through a pregnancy,' Crawford said. 'A birth mother is not supposed to be happy or proud of what we've done. We are'" (p. A23).

Fourth, high school programs dealing with sexuality as well as mothering should carry less stigma. Writing a letter to the editor in support of school-based infant day care, a teen mother ("Vancouver," 1981) argued, "If at the same time [as providing school-based day care] the School Board provided better sex education and the Health Department made birth control more available to teenagers then possibly, in the future this problem could be controlled" (p. 4).

Fifth, teen mothers are each other's best support system, which schools can encourage. Kathleen, age 16, told a writer for *BC Woman to Woman* (Rathie, 1989) that her school-based program for teen mothers kept her motivated to graduate:

> Just being together with 20 girls in one room who've had so many similar experiences. . . . There's times the teachers will look at you and say, "You know it's time to be quiet now," and you've been talking about your kids. You've been sharing what the problem was that week: the new tooth they just got or did your kid do this when he was that age . . . it's great! (p. 10)

Sixth, teen mothers have matured and taken responsibility; they deserve to be treated accordingly. As Molly complained to me about the "Children Who Are Having Children" article that omitted her views: "I don't see myself as a child—I am practically 18. I'm almost old enough to vote, and I'm old enough to drive." In this vein, teen mothers often represent themselves as emotionally mature enough to raise a child well, countering the discourse of the bureaucratic experts of the "abusive" teen mother.

Seventh, teen mothers not only recognize stigmas against them, they also fight back. A *Montreal Gazette* columnist (Schwartz, 1991) watched a National Film Board documentary about teen mothers with some young mothers and reported their reactions: "What angered me was that these three women were portrayed as so vulnerable," said Nina Sale, a single mother, age 22, "as being taken advantage of by the courts, by the welfare system, by social workers. There was no empowerment, no talk of anything to give them self-confidence or help them take control." A teen mother is quoted: "I love my daughter. Not once in that film did one woman say she loved her child. I can't imagine looking at that film and saying I ever wanted a kid" (p. B4).

A teen mother in New Brunswick expressed her opposition to official stigma by filing a complaint against the school board with the provincial Human Rights Commission (Sussel, 1989). Bobbi-Jo Hanson was not allowed to continue as student council president because she became pregnant. As one official at Saint John Vocational High School put it: "When I saw her my mouth dropped. . . . She was supposed to be a role model, a leader. We weren't going to put her out there and say 'this is a typical vocational girl'" (p. 2). Hanson won her complaint and the school board sent her a written apology.

The Usual Winners

When the various representers of teen motherhood wage their stigma contest in the media, an example of what usually results can be found in this passage from *Chatelaine* (Maynard, 1982):

> What's to be done about the problem of adolescent pregnancies? One extreme view, offered by a retired social worker who chooses to remain anonymous, is that both welfare support and abortions should be made less accessible. "Kids wouldn't get pregnant so easily if they knew *they'd* have to pay the piper." Another extreme is [psychiatrist] Dr. [Anne] Seiden's suggestion that instead of fighting them we might join them, "accept-

ing the legitimacy of adolescence as one part of a woman's life in which she might choose to bear her children," and offering full support. Most expert views fall somewhere in between. . . .

Of course society's best hope is not helping girls feel better about premature parenthood; it's prevention, making sure that those babies who are born are wanted and can be provided for. (p. 129)

In this morality play we find presented as "extreme" frames conservative and oppositional views, with decisive weight placed "somewhere in between," that is, with the bureaucratic experts. The reporter winds up with no call to destigmatize the decision to become a teen mother.

When presenting a public face, even advocates for teen mothers—advocates who are generally not interested in stigmatizing their constituency—find themselves compelled to pitch their message to skeptics, using the language of those less inclined to, say, vote for funds for their programs. Youth advocate Cat Adler (1982), in *Towards a Caring Community*—published by the Social Planning and Review Council of British Columbia—identifies three kinds of audiences: one is receptive to a humanitarian approach; one prefers a reasoned, factual approach; and one responds best to a "dollars-and-cents" approach. When it comes to convincing the latter to support "programs to prevent pregnancies and provide support to pregnant and parenting teenagers," Adler, in essence, recommends reinforcing the image of teen mothers as drains on welfare:

[I]t will be important to present teenage pregnancy statistics, the numbers of girls keeping babies, the many health and social services required, how much it costs to give public assistance, to say, an under-educated unwed mother, who may repeat pregnancy and become a dependent on the community. (p. 26)

One feminist I interviewed acknowledged that when she campaigns for public support for teen mother services, she drops the feminist discourse because it is too controversial. Were she advocating merely for herself, she would stick to her principles, even if that caused anti-feminists to label her "bitch or immoral," she said. But "if I'm trying to get a valuable service going [for others], I don't want to alienate."

Another factor in how the various representations of teen motherhood fare in the media is the storytelling framework that reporters and writers must work within. For example, reporters realize that if a story is to gain the interest of readers, it must affect them personally. Therefore, the liberal press often puts forward the message that teen pregnancy and motherhood could happen to anybody (e.g., Maynard, 1982, p. 91).

Although poverty has not been shown to cause teenage motherhood and having a child has not been proven to consign teen mothers to poverty, poorer teenagers are more likely to carry their pregnancies to term. Also, fertility rates are higher within certain ethnic and racial groups. Therefore, as Kristen Luker (1991, p. 81) has observed, the risk of teen pregnancy [and motherhood] does not occur with "equal frequency," and when people falsely universalize the issue, they mask and confuse disadvantages by class, race, and gender. When some attack teen mothers as a group, the class and racial bias in their argument is hidden; it appears on the surface that they are merely chastising irresponsible teenagers.

The media often build on the "it could happen to you" angle by telling an individual story full of personal choices and dramatic twists. Readers are invited to live vicariously the soap opera-like existence of a particular teen mother: We learn that fate caused her birth control to fail, we meet her dangerous boyfriend, we cry with her over dashed college hopes. Because the media like endings that affirm personal triumph, a few of the stories fall into a category I call the "Saga of the Teenage Supermother." Both *Jet* and *People* magazine, for instance, have carried stories about teen mothers who get straight A's and become valedictorians. Such Supermom storytelling, while compelling and even destigmatizing, plays down structural constraints and the benefits of institutional supports like day care and school services, sending instead a signal that young women, given enough individual mettle, can do it all.

The familiar flip side to the Teenage Supermom Saga is the media fascination with sex. Individualizing this theme often means casting the story as one of a personal form of moral deviance. Cultural studies theorist David Buckingham (1987) has noted that, "[W]hile on the one hand the press is concerned to define and to police the boundaries of 'respectable' conduct, it is also fascinated with behaviour which in various ways is seen to violate them" (p. 136). In reporting alarm over teen pregnancy in British Columbia, the *Province* ("Pregnancies," 1980) ended its story this way: "[T]he matter boils down to a single point: Who should teach morals, the family, the church or the school?" (p. A5). In other words, the matter boils down to the rights and wrongs of individual behavior, rather than more political issues such as sexism, racism, and unemployment. Readers are not encouraged to make links between individual lives and broader social forces.

Constrained by time and resources, reporters who tackle a complex issue such as teen motherhood must rely on a path prepared by others. It is common for a reporter to interview only a few people and label as "typical" the girl who fits the dominant frame of analysis. It is also the case, however, that the groups who might make available to the press other girls with more oppositional views have incentive to avoid doing so. The goal of an advocate for a funded program, for example, is to present a client to the public who sounds reasonable, grateful, and perhaps even repentant. Teen mothers, themselves not formally organized or in a position to create their own advocacy groups, rely on others with mixed agendas to speak on their behalf.

Those who work most directly with teen mothers are divided in their priorities and so do not speak with a unified voice in defining the needs of teen mothers. Some feminists worry that by disentangling teen pregnancy from other social problems related to poverty, broader material support for young mothers will disappear. As research challenges conventional wisdom about teen pregnancy and poverty, Luker (1991) is concerned that "the most subtle danger is that the new work on teen pregnancy will be used to argue that because teen pregnancy is not the linchpin that holds together myriad other social ills, it is not a problem at all" (p. 83).

Implications

The mass media largely attempt to reflect and construct dominant cultural values about teen mothers. The viewing, reading, and listening public looks there to see a "continuous performance morality play" (Golding & Middleton, 1983, p. 236). This morality play, with its attendant stereotyped images as well as its silences, then has repercussions. The morality play that the media conveys helps to (a) frame the public debate about teen mothers, (b) shape the implementation of public policy, and (c) influence the daily lives of young mothers and their children profoundly.

Politicians, particularly conservative ones, throughout North America have used allusions to irresponsible teen mothers to whip up public support for cutbacks in welfare payments and social services. In Alberta during the early 1980s, for example, the provincial government reduced welfare benefits to teen mothers. Even so, by the decade's end, Minister of Social Services Connie Osterman told an audience assembled in Edmonton for a conference on teen pregnancy that teens were getting pregnant because welfare was too easily available. Osterman neglected to mention that she herself had commissioned a study 2 years before that concluded the opposite: social assistance did not significantly encourage teens to become pregnant ("Study," 1989, p. B2). Teen mothers make such good political scapegoats partly because they are relatively isolated and powerless and partly because they have come to symbolize multiple meanings, often contradictory, related to sexuality, adulthood, attitudes toward work, and ideals of family. By engaging in such scapegoating, the state has reinforced and institutionalized the stigma attached to teen pregnancy and motherhood, especially in times of recession.

Negative stereotypes, so often publicly voiced, have permeated the institutions that control the fates of teen mothers. For example, in many districts of British Columbia—including those of Pacifica and Midland where City and Town Schools are located—the Ministry of Social Services now subsidizes day care for young mothers, regardless of whether they are on welfare. Although this is a valuable service for the mothers, the Ministry justifies this policy with the assumption that any child of a young mother is "at risk of neglect or abuse." Many teen mothers are poor and in need of material support, yet to receive it they get constructed as inadequate mothers. This occurs despite research suggesting that a mother's age is far less important than other factors in determining her parenting behavior, including potential abuse of her children.

In addressing the assumed inadequacies of teen mothers, special classes are offered; some of them, like "Parenting," are useful enough that every teenager might benefit from them. Others border on the absurd—even humiliating. At the Midland Maternity Home, I observed a workshop on "budgeting skills" in which a social worker read aloud from a typed list of money-saving tips, including: "Squash toilet paper rolls so the center is oval not round, the paper doesn't roll off 10 yards at a time! This will help to cut your toilet paper bill" (field notes, 5/11/92). This class did not much help the students cope with the contradictions and consequences of structural poverty.

The "cycles" that commonly come to mind when people speak of teen mothers are "cycle of poverty," "cycle of welfare dependency," and "cycle of child abuse." Perhaps it would be fruitful to bear in mind, instead, a "cycle of stigma"—a cycle helped along by experts and advocates who enforce negative stereotypes in order to attract funding and support; a cycle given a spin by politicians who ignore their own studies in seeking scapegoats; a cycle reinforced by a mainstream media that relays the stigmatized images it finds "somewhere in between" and largely ignores the discourses of opposition and of teen mothers themselves.

QUESTIONS TO CONSIDER

1. How does the author argue that the much of the media has mischaracterized discourse around teen pregnancy and motherhood? Did you share some of those views? Explain and give examples.

2. Kelly contends that the socio-economic effects of adolescent pregnancy and childbearing have been exaggerated. What is her argument for that claim? Do you agree? Why or why not?

3. The author views many "bureaucratic experts" and policymakers as playing into the stigmatization of teen mothers. Explain her argument, especially in light of the "wrong-girl" frame of reference.

4. Kelly criticizes conservative social and religious groups that have stigmatized adolescent mothers. What assumptions do they make, and what assumptions does Kelly make in her own critique? How valid is either perspective? Explain your response and provide examples.

5. How can teen mothers' self-interpretations reinforce or change the various frameworks that Kelly uses to analyze adolescent pregnancy and motherhood? Give examples.

6. How and why does mainstream public policy on these issues tend to follow a deficit model that highlights teen mothers' presumed deficiencies? Explain with examples.

Notes

This chapter originally appeared in Deirdre M. Kelly, *Pregnant with Meaning: Teen Mothers and the Politics of Inclusive Schooling* (New York: Peter Lang, 2000).

1. Molly is 1 of 12 teen mothers I interviewed formally as part of an ethnographic study of two public alternative high schools in California; La Fuente is a pseudonym of one of the schools (see Kelly, 1993a).
2. Statistics Canada reports that the teen pregnancy rate for Canada as a whole is lower than it was two decades ago, although it has increased a bit during 4 out of the past 5 years for which data are available (Wadhera & Millar, 1997). It remains too soon to tell whether these slight increases are just random variations in an overall downward trend or if they mark a new upward trend. In any case, the 1974 to 1994 period saw an overall drop in the pregnancy rate from 53.7 to 48.8 per 1,000 females aged 15 to 19 years (Wadhera & Millar, 1997, p. 11). In British Columbia the teen pregnancy rate per 1,000 declined from 70.3 in 1974 to 40.7 in 1994 (a 42.1% drop), including a 42.8% drop in live births and a 37.8% drop in hospital abortions (Wadhera & Millar, 1997, table 3). For the latest U.S. statistics on teen pregnancy and birth rates and a discussion of trends, see Henshaw, 1997.
3. The Alternative Press Index includes popular and scholarly magazines and journals and covers the following areas: African-American studies, anarchism, ecology, ethnic studies, feminism, gay-lesbian studies, international studies, labor, Marxism, radical democracy, and socialism.
4. Snowball sampling is a strategy in which a research participant suggests other potential participants, who then name or refer other participants, all of whom fit a particular profile established by the researcher.
5. Oppositional social movements include feminism, lesbian and gay liberation, Aboriginal rights, workers' rights, welfare rights, and other collective struggles of subordinated social groups.
6. In the late 1970s, for example, B.C. Human Resources Minister Bill Vander Zalm "overturned an arbitration board ruling that allowed two 17-year-old pregnant girls in Kelowna" to receive social assistance. Instead, he

offered that the ministry would "attempt to have the parents of the girls support their daughters" (Canadian Press, 1978, p. 4). Similar debates were occurring in the United States at this time. Liberals were arguing that pregnant and parenting teens were families in need of services; new conservatives, in contrast, wanted to strengthen the family that included the teenagers' parents "and to discourage measures that increased the autonomy of daughters" (Luker, 1996, p. 79).

7. There are a number of feminist lenses through which to view the subordination of women. It is beyond the scope of this chapter to distinguish them. My analysis of oppositional discourse about teen mothers, however, revealed that alternative press writers seemed most often to use a socialist feminist or multicultural feminist lens (see Jaggar & Rothenberg, 1993, for discussion of these and other feminist frameworks).

8. More recently, feminists have framed discussions of reproductive health issues in terms of rights rather than choices. According to Solinger (1998), this "reflects a growing recognition among advocates that 'choice' is the ultimate marketplace concept. When we construct the abortion arena on the marketplace model, we justify the fact that millions of women in the United States cannot afford to purchase adequate or necessary reproductive health services" (1998, p. 9; cf. Roberts, 1997). *Maternal Health News* is written and produced by volunteers in Vancouver, B.C. to provide a forum for ideas regarding controversial issues in maternal and child health care. It is informed by the feminist self-help movement, which encourages women to see reproductive functions as natural and normal.

References

Adler, C. (1982). *Towards a caring community.* Vancouver, BC: Social Planning and Review Council.

Anderson, K. (1989, December 2). Every girl's nightmare: Happy teenage mother backs right to choose. Calgary Herald, p. H2. (Reprinted from the Ottawa Citizen)

Angelo, B. (1989, May 22). Interview with Toni Morrison: The pain of being black. Time, pp. 120–122.

Arney, W., & Bergen, B. (1984). Power and visibility: The invention of teenage pregnancy. Social Science Medicine, 18 (1), 11–19.

Bewley, L. (1984, March 2). This is simply not done. Vancouver Sun, p. A11.

Billung-Meyer, J. (1982). Forsaken children. *Canadian Woman Studies, 4* (1), 27–30.

Binder, A. (1993). Constructing racial rhetoric: Media depictions of harm in heavy metal and rap music. *American Sociological Review, 58,* 753–767.

Bolan, K. (1993, August 21). Native leaders label custody ruling racist. *Vancouver Sun,* p. A1.

Boyer, D., & Fine, D. (1992). Sexual abuse as a factor in adolescent pregnancy and child maltreatment. *Family Planning Perspectives,* 24 (1), 4–11.

Brodie, J., Gavigan, S., & Jenson, J. (1992). *The politics of abortion.* Toronto: Oxford University Press.

Brunet, R. (1992, December 14). Parents fighting planned obsolescence. *British Columbia Report,* p. 23.

Buckingham, D. (1987). *Public secrets: Eastenders and its audience.* London: British Film Institute.

Byfield, T. (1993, May 10). Listen, Abbotsford, as Southams tell you how to raise your kids. *British Columbia Report,* p. 44.

Canadian Press. (1978, July 15). Pregnant girls off aid: Vander Zalm. *Province,* p. 4.

Canadian Press. (1980a, April 8). Wrong girls keep their babies, professor says. *Vancouver Sun,* p. A17.

Canadian Press. (1980b, October 18). Teen moms "must stay in school." *Vancouver Sun,* p. A19.

Canadian Press. (1990, July 27). Teenage parents emerging problem. *Winnipeg Free Press,* p. 12.

Clark, S. (1999). What do we know about unmarried mothers? In J. Wong & D. Checkland (Eds.), *Teenage pregnancy and parenting: Social and ethical issues* (pp. 10–24). Toronto: University of Toronto Press.

Clark, S., Dechman, M., French, F., & MacCallum, B. (1991). *Mothers and children, one decade later.* Halifax, NS: Nova Scotia Department of Community Services.

Cunningham, D. (1992a, October 12). Is virginity so bad? *British Columbia Report,* p. 28.

Cunningham, D. (1992b, December 14). Rediscovering chastity. *British Columbia Report,* pp. 18–21.

Cunningham, D. (1993, April 26). Institutionalizing infants. *British Columbia Report,* pp. 9–11.

Dube, F. (1993, April 22). Today's teens: It's payback time for rebellious children of the '60s. *Vancouver Sun*, p. A4. (Reprinted from the *Ottawa Citizen*)

Ericson, R. V., Baranek, P. M., & Chan, J. B. L. (1991). *Representing order: Crime, law, and justice in the news media.* Toronto: University of Toronto Press.

Fallon, C. (1979). *The rise in adolescent pregnancy and parenthood: Proposed intervention strategies for this population.* Unpublished paper, School of Social Work, University of British Columbia, Canada.

Fraser, N. (1989). *Unruly practices: Power, discourse, and gender in contemporary social theory.* Minneapolis: University of Minnesota Press.

Fraser, N. (1992). The uses and abuses of French discourse theories for feminist politics. In N. Fraser & S. L. Bartky (Eds.), *Revaluing French feminisms* (pp. 177–194). Bloomington: Indiana University Press.

Furstenberg, F. F., Jr. (1997). Foreword. In K. M. Harris, *Teen mothers and the revolving welfare door* (pp. i–xi). Philadelphia: Temple University Press.

Furstenberg, F. F., Jr., Brooks-Gunn, J., & Morgan, S. P. (1987). *Adolescent mothers in later life.* Cambridge: Cambridge University Press.

Geronimus, A. T. (1997). Teenage childbearing and personal responsibility: An alternative view. *Political Science Quarterly*, 112, 1–15.

Geronimus, A. T., & Korenman, S. (1992). The socioeconomic consequences of teen childbearing reconsidered. *Quarterly Journal of Economics*, 107, 1187–1214.

Golding, P., & Middleton, S. (1983). *Images of welfare: Press and public attitudes to poverty.* Oxford: Martin Robertson.

Gordon, D. E. (1990). Formal operational thinking: The role of cognitive-developmental processes in adolescent decision-making about pregnancy and contraception. *American Journal of Orthopsychiatry*, 60 (3), 346–356.

Green, T., & Steel, B. (1993, February 1). An isolated objection [Letter to the editor]. *British Columbia Report*, p. 3.

Griffith, A. I., & Smith, D. E. (1991). Constructing cultural knowledge: Mothering as discourse. In J. Gaskell & A. McLaren (Eds.), *Women and education* (2nd ed., pp. 81–97). Calgary, AB: Detselig Enterprises, Ltd.

Grindlay, L. (1993, September 5). Proud of their novel conception. *Province*, p. A23.

Grindstaff, C. F. (1988). Adolescent marriage and childbearing: The long-term economic outcome, Canada in the 1980s. *Adolescence*, 23 (89), 45–58.

Harris, K. M. (1997). *Teen mothers and the revolving welfare door.* Philadelphia: Temple University Press.

Hawkesworth, M. E. (1989). Knowers, knowing, known: Feminist theory and claims of truth. *Signs: Journal of Women in Culture and Society*, 14 (3), 533–557.

Henshaw, S. K. (1997). Teenage abortion and pregnancy statistics by state, 1992. *Family Planning Perspectives*, 29 (3), 115–122.

Hoffman, S. D. (1998). Comment: Teenage childbearing is not so bad after all . . . or is it? A review of the new literature. *Family Planning Perspectives*, 30 (5), 236–239, 243.

Hudson, F., & Ineichen, B. (1991). *Taking it lying down: Sexuality and teenage motherhood.* New York: New York University Press.

Ingrassia, M. (1993, August 2). Daughters of Murphy Brown. *Newsweek*, pp. 58–59.

Jaggar, A. M., & Rothenberg, P. S. (Eds.). (1993). *Feminist frameworks: Alternative theoretical accounts of the relations between women and men* (3rd ed.). New York: McGraw-Hill.

Jones, E. F., Forrest, J. D., Goldman, N., Henshaw, S., Lincoln, R., Rosoff, J.I., Westoff, C. F., & Wulf, D. (1986). *Teenage pregnancy in industrialized countries.* New Haven: Yale University Press.

Kelly, D. M. (1993a). *Last chance high: How girls and boys drop in and out of alternative schools.* New Haven: Yale University Press.

Kerby, W. (1993, May 3). Anti-choice and pro-abortion [Letter to the editor]. *British Columbia Report*, p. 3.

Krangle, K. (1980, March 1). Lure of teen motherhood is having someone to love. *Vancouver Sun*, pp. A1–2.

Luker, K. (1991, Spring). Dubious conceptions: The controversy over teen pregnancy. *The American Prospect* 5, 73–83.

Luker, K. (1996). *Dubious conceptions: The politics of teenage pregnancy.* Cambridge: Harvard University Press.

Maternal Health Society (Vancouver, BC). (1982). Maternal Health News.

Maynard, F. (1982, October). Teen-age mothers: A nationwide dilemma. *Chatelaine*, pp. 91, 126–132.

Miller, B. C., & Moore, K. A. (1990). Adolescent sexual behavior, pregnancy, and parenting: Research through the 1980s. *Journal of Marriage and the Family*, 52, 1025–1044.

Mitchell, A. (1993, November 9). Family thriving, study finds. *Globe and Mail*, pp. A1, A7.

O'Neill, K. (1998). No adults are pulling the strings and we like it that way. *Signs: Journal of Women in Culture and Society*, 23 (3), 611–618.

O'Neill, T. (1993, January 11). Message to trustees: Be careful with your new teen-parent programs [Editorial]. *British Columbia Report*, p. 2.

Phoenix, A. (1991a). Mothers under 20: Outsider and insider views. In A. Phoenix, A. Woollett, & E. Lloyd (Eds.), *Motherhood: Meanings, practices and ideologies* (pp. 86–102). London: Sage Publications.

Pollitt, K. (1992, July 20–27). Why I hate "family values" (Let me count the ways). *The Nation*, pp. 88–94.

Pozsonyi, J. (1973). *A longitudinal study of unmarried mothers who kept their first born children*. London, Ontario: Family and Children's Services of London and Middlesex.

Pregnancies in 14-year-old girls show alarming increase. (1980, October 15). *Province*, p. A5.

Rathie, E. (1989, November). Teen moms. *BC Woman to Woman*, pp. 8–13.

Rincover, A. (1991, December 10). Teenage mothers lacking resources needed to help raise their children. *Vancouver Sun*, p. C3.

Roberts, D. (1997). *Killing the Black body: Race, reproduction, and the meaning of liberty*. New York: Pantheon Books.

Saenger, E. (1991, December 9). Learning to accommodate teen moms. *British Columbia Report*, p. 23.

Schlesinger, B. (1982). Changing sexual mores: The student in the 80s. *School Guidance Worker*, 37 (5), 43-47.

Schur, E. M. (1980). *The politics of deviance: Stigma contests and the uses of power*. Englewood Cliffs, NJ: Prentice-Hall.

Schwartz, S. (1991, March 18). Teens live with joy, stigma of motherhood. *Montreal Gazette*, p. B4.

Solinger, R. (1998). Introduction: Abortion politics and history. In R. Solinger (Ed.), *Abortion wars: A half century of struggle, 1950–2000* (pp. 1–9). Berkeley: University of California Press.

Stevens, W. (1979, December). Teenage pregnancy: When they say chic I hear chick. *off our backs*, pp. 10–11.

Strom, M. (1993, August 26). Adoption: Mom's the word. *Vancouver Sun*, p. A11.

Study contradicts Osterman comments. (1989, March 18). *Calgary Herald*, p. B2.

Sussel, T. A. (1989, December 8). Pregnant student files human rights complaint. *Education Leader*, p. 2.

Vancouver: Would like high school daycare. (1981, Autumn). *News Bulletin of the Task Force on Teenage Pregnancy and Parenthood* (Social Planning and Review Council of British Columbia), p. 4. (Reprinted from the Vancouver Sun)

Wadhera, S., & Millar, W. J. (1997, Winter). Teenage pregnancies, 1974 to 1994. *Health Reports*, 9 (3), 9–17.

Willis, E. (1996). Villains and victims: "Sexual correctness" and the repression of feminism. In N. B. Maglin & D. Perry (Eds.), *"Bad girls" / "good girls" : Women, sex, and power in the nineties* (pp. 44–53). New Brunswick, NJ: Rutgers University Press.

Wrigley, J. (1992). Gender and education in the welfare state. In J. Wrigley (Ed.), *Education and gender equality* (pp. 1–23). London: Falmer Press.

CHAPTER THIRTEEN

What Does It Mean to Be in a Gang?

HAROON KHAREM

It became clear that school labeling practices and the exercise of rules operated as part of a hidden curriculum to marginalize and isolate Black male youth in disciplinary spaces and brand them as criminally inclined.

(ANN ARNETT FERGUSON, 2001)

True nerve exposes a lack of fear of dying. . . . the clear risk of violent death may be preferable to being "dissed" by another. . . . Not to be afraid . . . has made the concept of manhood a part of his very identity, he has difficulty manipulating it—it often controls him.

(ELIJAH ANDERSON, 1995)

For many teachers, gang life is a remote and terribly frightening concept. For many Americans, in general, few things scare them as much as the possibility of running into gangs. Many of us have watched the movie *Grand Canyon* and can relate to the fear that Kevin Kline's character experienced when his car broke down in Los Angeles on his way home from a Lakers game. He faces the scariest group in the United States—a group of young black men. He is saved from death only by the intervention of a "good" black man, portrayed by Danny Glover. Black men must always bear the consequences of such white fear. Indeed, one cannot understand American history without insight into the role that white fear of black men has played in shaping the nation's institutions and its consciousness.

Too infrequently do teachers and students in urban teacher education gain insight into what it means to be a black, Latino, or Asian gang member. Many of the programs purporting to educate teachers and other citizens about gangs have little to say about why young people feel the need to join them. Feelings of powerlessness, a lack of respect from others, and low self- esteem experienced by young black men and women and the relationship between these feelings and gang membership are not common insights among educators. So often the ostensibly "random acts of violence" committed by gang members are directly related to efforts to assert their self-worth, to demand respect, and to defend their dignity. In the twenty-first century the only solution to the problems presented by gangs in the cities involves building more prisons, installing metal detectors in schools, and treating children as adult offenders. Such policies, however, have not worked, as the number of black males in prison continues to increase. Incarceration rates for black males in the United States are five times higher than they were in South Africa at the height of apartheid.

From my vantage point as a black male who grew up as a gang member in Brooklyn, New York, I watch with amazement the ways that such policies are justified and implemented. Political and educational leaders often promote such policies with little effort to study and understand the experiences and perspectives of young people who grow up in urban poverty, with its attendant racism and class bias. Many of these policymakers have no experience working with or even talking to young people who face these realities on a daily basis. Without this knowledge, such policymakers make a career of responding to only the symptoms of urban social problems—not their causes. Urban schools spend millions of dollars developing more rules, hiring security personnel, buying metal detectors, constructing schools for at-risk children, and contracting antigang consultants. In these responses, students from gangs are viewed from outside the context of their lives and everyday experiences. Many of the answers provided to principals and teachers by antigang consultants never mention racism and poverty as factors that move young people to join gangs. They never ask what it might mean to be in a gang.

Such questions might produce information that could help political and educational leaders develop social and educational policies that actually work to solve the causes of gang-related problems. Students who are gang members many times speak with great insight about why gangs exist and often present very powerful suggestions about what schools can do to address the realities that create them. Such students are often far more helpful than paid consultants because they are not as concerned with telling school officials what they want to hear. Typically the only agenda such students are pursuing involves their struggle to be treated respectfully and with dignity. The knowledge they bring to school is the view from outside, the subjugated knowledge of institutions that is too often dismissed from our understanding of what really is going on in urban schools and the communities that surround them. A thirteen-year-old boy who is attacked daily on his way to school, for example, is a prime candidate for joining a gang. An antigang program that urges students to "say no" to gangs and study hard because it's the right thing to do has no meaning for the thirteen-year-old who is getting his teeth knocked out. The high moral tone of such programs can be offensive to those students who understand the complexity of moral choices involved in joining a gang.

To know the importance of listening to the voices of our urban students caught in the quagmire of poverty and racism is essential to being and becoming an urban teacher. Every urban teacher must understand the violence, fear, and sense of indignity that students bring to the classroom. Such understanding, I argue, cannot be separated from the curriculum of urban schools. While not all students experience these problems, those who don't have much to learn from those who do. New understandings of one another will emerge in the conversations that take place in this context. Teachers, principals, and educational policymakers who listen in to these conversations may learn more than they expected about the fabric of the society in which they live. We all have a story.

Returning to East New York and Ocean Hill-Brownsville for the first time in over 20 years brought strong emotional memories as I drove to an elementary school not far from where my sister used to live on Sutter Avenue and Barby Street. I was saddened that the building she lived in no longer existed, that there was no memory of the families, the kids, and the fire that claimed the life of my niece and nephew during the Christmas holidays of 1971. My memory of East New York and Brownsville is of vacant lots, the Pitkin Avenue shopping area, walking down Sutter Avenue hearing cuts from Curtis Mayfield's *Super Fly,* Isaac Hayes's *Theme from Shaft,* Earth Wind and Fire's "Power" from their album *Last Days and Time,* or the Dramatics' *Whatcha See Is Whatcha Get.* You could go from one end of Sutter Avenue to the other and see people you knew.

My other memories are of the street gangs that lived in the Brownsville-East New York section. One constant that has not changed is the level of poverty and the look of struggle and frustration on people's faces. The people are not mean or nasty, but as they go from childhood to adulthood in Brownsville-East New York, the daily struggles begin to etch lines in their faces. The other constant is that gangs still fight over the same turf over which those before them fought, turf that none of them ever legally owned. Yet many young black males fought and died over a cement block that they loved, and at the same time hated.

Street gangs have always existed for kids from poor, working- and middle-class families in New York City. The early 1970s were no different than the present, except for the names of the gangs that ran the streets back then: the Savage Skulls, the Savage Nomads, the Black Spades, and the Tomahawks. They owned the streets of Ocean Hill/Brownsville/East New York, as well as the South Bronx. They fought each other for control of turfs and no doubt supplied the precursors of those who fought the crack turf wars of the 1980s. There were no drive-by shootings back then, but gang battles were brutal, and anything that could maim or kill became a weapon. This was a time when a black teen had to know how to "use his hands," in close-quarter fights, because that was how you earned respect. Hollywood has created an image of gang members as karate and kickboxing experts. I never saw anyone use karate or kickboxing in a fight. The violence in gangs today differed from our lifestyle. We did not spray a rival gang member's house with automatic-weapons fire (such guns were not available on the streets yet). We did not threaten or hurt the family of a rival gang member. The killing has changed—not only is it more violent, but bystanders and family members are also injured and killed. Ocean Hill-Brownsville gang wars took a toll on black youth as the funerals mounted and prisons became full of gang members from the streets. Mike Tyson was from our neighborhood; he was a little too young to become a Tomahawk, but probably admired us as he watched us walking and sporting our colors without fear of the police.

Street gangs require only a few unspoken codes, the violation of any one of which can demand dire penalties. Allegiance/loyalty is the most important ingredient. If you grew up with most of the members, you had more than a mutual allegiance. There was a familial love—love that bound the members to each other—and an inner silent pledge to protect each other, your turf, and your community from all outsiders. There is this assumption (especially promoted by the movie industry) that gangs harass the community. However, I remember that many shopkeepers in black and Hispanic communities knew most gang members from childhood. If any harassment took place, it was usually the result of the shopkeeper's treatment of community members. The majority of the neighborhood people were not afraid to walk the streets, as everyone knew each other and the community was made up of extended family members and friends; in fact, many gang members kept the streets safe for the neighborhood. While the neighborhood had its collection of pimps and prostitutes, drug dealers, and other kinds of street entrepreneurs whom we knew on a first-name basis, we were not involved in those activities. In fact, some of the hustlers on the street were once in gangs themselves, and knew what lines not to cross. They were tolerated as long as their hustle did not harm any family members of gangs (mothers, fathers, brothers, sisters, even extended family).

While drugs were rampant in Brownsville and East New York, most gang members were not involved in selling drugs, as they are today—one could not be a viable Savage Skull, Savage Nomad, Black Spade, or Tomahawk and be on hardcore drugs. It is not to say that we did not consume drugs, but anyone becoming addicted to hardcore drugs lost any respect he ever had within the gangs.

As a young black kid in the Fort Greene section of Brooklyn, the first street gangs I remember were the Fort Greene Chaplains and the Mau Maus from the Marcy Projects on Flushing Avenue. As a kid in the first grade, we all looked up to these older gang members with awe—they seemed to sport their gang jackets (now called colors) without fear of the police. These were our heroes, the ones we wanted to be like, and we admired their stories, battle scars, their narrow escapes from the police, and their passage through the prison system. We wanted their approval and acceptance and waited for our turn to be able to join them and share our own stories of passage. Many of the older gang members were older brothers, cousins, or neighbors.

As I teach potential public school teachers, most seem to forget or not realize that when children leave the school premises, they have to survive in neighborhoods. They have to physically and verbally defend themselves and their family members. Some potential teachers believe, whether through societal beliefs or statistical data, that black children rarely make it into honors classes and should be relegated to compensatory or special education classes (Ferguson, 2001). I remember when we first moved into the Farragut Houses in Fort Greene, our building was right across the street from the Brooklyn Navy Yard. From my tenth-floor bedroom window I could see clear across Brooklyn. I can remember many nights when the gangs would fight the sailors and white workers from the Navy Yard. A sailor or worker verbally sexually harassing a teenager or young woman in the neighborhood drew immediate retaliation. This was always a major cause of the fights. My first trip to the store for my mother was an awakening experience that prepared me, as similar errands did for other kids, to know how to handle myself when I became older. I had to walk through the entire Farragut Houses projects to get to the store. This was a nightmare, as fear would grip me and many other kids, as we were always challenged by small roving bands of kids from the project. When I would reach the store, there were always older kids waiting for me to come out with change I supposedly did not have. Parents always sent their kids to the store to buy groceries or something they themselves forgot to purchase. To a kid in elementary school, it was either fun because you got to go outside (if you were being punished), or a nightmare if you ran into older kids waiting for you on the way to or from the store. Once confronted, you had two choices: You could give up the money and get slapped around a little or you could fight, and if you lost, you still lost the money. No matter what choice you made, you better not lose the money. If you did, you would have to face the wrath of an angry parent.

Some parents walked with you back to the store to confront the kids who took the money and beat you. It was common to see a mother standing there telling her child that he better get their money back. Readers may think that mothers were too harsh on the kid, but one could not grow up in the projects and have his or her self-respect questioned. (When my mother took my brother and me anywhere, we had to be on our best behavior so as not to embarrass her in front of white people.)

Young black males are perceived as behavior problems in schools because teachers and educators fail to understand their cultural norms, that self-respect is highly regarded, and for some it is the only thing they have. The idea of having "respect" has caused so much death among black males, and yet it is the least understood quality of being a black male. Growing up in the projects, this "respect" was crucial to survival and dignity. Having respect made others leave you alone. Such respect was earned by how well you could protect yourself from physical violence through the use of physical violence. While this respect may generate pride within the individual and respect from others, it is generated by a fear that emerges at an early age. Young black males are forced to make decisions while very young concerning their survival and well-being. I remember a fight I had with a bigger and older kid when I was in the second grade. All day in class and at lunch, my only concern was the fight. I did not pay attention to anything the teacher said all day. My greatest fear was what would happen if I ran away. I knew if I shied away from the fight, I would have no respect at all from my peers and I would be labeled a punk—a designation that would spread not only around the school but also throughout the projects.

Teachers need to understand that no child wants to be associated with being a goofy milquetoast, like Urkel in the TV sitcom *Family Matters* (a cartoon of a black intellectual). I remember that by fifth grade I was trying not to carry any books to school because when I got into fights I hated that my books were sprawled all over the sidewalk. More importantly, it was not cool or hip to carry books. While I enjoyed reading and read books voraciously—as did so many other kids—I did not want to be seen as not being cool. Gloria Ladson-Billings (2001) tells the story of a young black male who felt that his sense of respect among his peers in the community was more important than bringing his books home to do his homework. The teacher who saw that the student was clowning in class and not doing his homework could have punished him but instead struck a deal with him that allowed him to complete his homework and maintain his sense of respect with his peers in the community (pp. 77–8). Culture is more than historical heritage in this case; culture here is also defined as how young black males see themselves and the world. More importantly, the teacher was sensitive enough to see that the problem was not necessarily a behavior problem. Buoyed by this understanding, the teacher allowed the student to maintain his dignity and in the process empowered him to complete his homework.

I have observed many elementary school-aged black males struggling to holding back tears as teachers and other school administrators berate and scold them for minor infractions. Such students are attempting to maintain their sense of manhood and respect. What often happens is that tension builds up inside until something or someone causes them to become violent. They strike out sensing that they have no outlet, no alternative. Many young black males have a sense that no one cares for them, so why should they themselves care what happens? Nathan McCall (1994) makes an important observation: "For as long as I can remember, black folks have always had a serious thing about respect. I guess because white people disrespected them so blatantly for so long that blacks viciously protected what little morsels of self-respect they had left" (p. 55).

Last year I witnessed a third-grade teacher scream at one of the black males in her classroom to the point that he left his seat and walked out. The teacher continued to scream at him into the hallway. I followed the kid into the hallway and waited until he walked back down the hall toward me. When I asked him if he understood that if he maintained this path of just walking out of the classroom he would be sent to the principal's office, he replied that he knew it and did not care. I continued the dialogue and asked, "If you keep this up as you get older, you know where you are going to end up?" He replied, "Yes, prison." I was not only saddened but angered, wondering how schools became training grounds for the prison system, that this third-grade student already knew where he was headed because no one cared enough to detour him from the path he was traveling. I understood that this young black male felt that the only recourse he had was to leave the class to hold onto what little self-respect he had left.

When I entered the third grade, I did not realize that I was part of the experiment of desegregation. I was bused, without my mother's permission, to a predominantly white school in the Fort Hamilton section of Brooklyn. The policymakers who passed and implemented the desegregation never allowed us black kids to tell them what we thought about all of this busing. Why was I taken from a school just across the street from our apartment to a school all the way across Brooklyn? Why was I forced to be outside to catch the bus at 7:15 A.M. every morning until the sixth grade? (By the way, kids from the projects did not have school buses—we were required to use public transportation.) Also, why was this desegregation just a one-way street? No white kids were bused into the Fort Greene or Red Hook schools where some of the other black kids came from.

In the classes in the school to which we were bused, we were not allowed to talk because many of the teachers did not think we had any knowledge to contribute to the class. If one of us raised our hand, he/she was passed over. This made me mad and stopped me from even trying to participate in the class lessons. We were always placed in the back of the classroom and punished more harshly for behavior problems. If we got into a dispute with the white kids, it was always our fault. Many of the black kids had physical altercations with white kids over being called a "nigger," and we always ended up in the principal's office for starting the fight. Everett Dawson, a black teacher in North Carolina in the 1970s, said that he attended in-service seminars on how to deal with black students who were coming to the predominantly white schools. The "experts" on black students told a group of white teachers that the "black students weren't going to be polite [and] were not going to bring in all their homework every day, and [warned] the white teachers [about what they] were going to have to accept from the black students once the schools were integrated" (Foster, 1997, p 7). According to the narrative, the experts continued this for three days until a black teacher raised the question: "How are black teachers to get along with the white students?" Are potential teachers to assume that because a child is black, there will be problems? Are there workshops on what images and what societal beliefs a white teacher may bring to a classroom of black children? Does the term "at risk" (which really is a racial code word for a black or Hispanic child from a poor community) bring to the mind of the teacher an image of this child as one who cannot learn the same as any other child?

I remember vividly a geography lesson on the continents. When the teacher asked the class what kind of things would be found in Africa, all the students, even the black students, responded by saying jungles, elephants, gorillas, lions, and giraffes. There was no mention of people or cities, no mention of any civilization, because in their minds Africa was not a civilized place; it was the Dark Continent. I can remember most of us black students getting quiet in the class because Africa was not a place we wanted to be associated with, in comparison with what was discussed in class about the European and North American continents. We resisted participation in the lessons on Africa because we did not want to be people of African descent. To be called an African was an insult, even though the Black Power movement was just getting under way. Any reference to Africa throughout my school life was always that of the jungle, of wild animals or seminaked people who were in need of civilizing. As David Livingstone wrote in 1867: "We come among them as members of a superior race . . . that desires to elevate the more degraded portions of the human family" (Coupland, 1928, p. 107). Why would we want to associate with Africa or its cultural norms if all we were shown about the place we came from was primitive? As I write, the words of Carter G. Woodson come to mind, written back in 1933:

> The same educational process which inspires and stimulates the oppressor with the thought that he is everything and has accomplished everything worthwhile, depresses and crushes at the same time the spark of genius in the Negro by making him feel that his race does not amount to much and never will measure up to the standards of other peoples. (Woodson, 1990)

Our teachers never realized that our silence and resistance to their geography lessons had connections to a racist ideology that celebrated Eurocentric paradigms while it disparaged who we were as children of African descent. I can also remember a teacher telling one of the black students who had raised his hand and yelled out the answer to put his hand down, that we needed to learn how to be obedient to the rules so that we could learn "how to be taught." I never understood what she meant, until years later. She was telling us that we needed to learn complete obedience to the school rules, but more importantly she was telling us that we (and our culture) were deficient and in need of correction. The cultural orientation and ideological teacher preparation she had received in college had informed her that black children were all part of a deficient culture whose language skills needed *drilling* in the rules of "proper" English. The teacher had been abstractly trained against racism but had not been trained in how to translate the abstract into actual experience. Her pedagogy was still paternalistic and she delegitimatized our culture, history, and language.

Today, middle-class black teachers who refuse to identify with poor blacks have joined with those whites who believe that children from the projects are inadequate, pathological, and in need of civilizing. Recently, I was sitting in the office of a colleague when a former student came in to see the other professor. I asked her how teaching was and she responded with confidence, "They are animals!" I was surprised because within one year of teaching she had already come to believe that the kids in her elementary school were no better than animals that needed to be caged. When teachers can refer to young children and teenagers as animals, it is no surprise that within the course of the day there are many negative comments and few acts of encouragement. Many studies claim that the majority of the behavior problems in schools are caused by black males who need to be banished to the principal's office or expelled into the streets so that the other students can learn (Ferguson, 2001).

As I look back, I see bitterness among the black males who were bused to the white schools. By the time most of us were in the sixth grade, many hated going to the school. We had also become aware about race, and we knew we were not welcome in the white schools. Thus, we lived in a different world five days a week from 8 to 3. We were forced to live in a world where race was foremost in our consciousness, knowing as we did that the teachers thought we were unteachable. During lunchtime, when the white kids went to the store, we were not allowed to go, as the parents told the school they did not want us walking around their neighborhood. The other world was life in the projects, with its black and Puerto Rican families. Here we could be ourselves, as we were removed from the fearful microscope of white people.

By the time I reached the seventh grade, we were all in small gangs, or as they are called today, "crews." We were still being bused to the predominantly white schools in the Bay Ridge section of Brooklyn. Thus, we were still fighting white kids in school and on the way to the bus or train. Back in the projects, we mimicked the older gangs in our neighborhood. We would fight the gangs from Fort Greene over the smallest things just about every Friday night. However, these were only fistfights that were mostly caused by a kid from either project venturing into the other's project to see a girl, or as the result of an argument at a party. Most of us were still going to school, even though we were beginning to skip classes, being sent to the principal's office more often, becoming petty hustlers, and beginning to hang with the older gang members.

By the time I had reached the tenth grade, I was no longer going to school and was living with my older sister. I joined the Tomahawks, who were small when I joined in the beginning, but had the reputation as being one of the toughest gangs in New York City. As our reputation spread, we grew to over 500 members with chapters all over Brooklyn. The violence was constant, as we fought rival gangs from the South Bronx and other parts of Brooklyn. We periodically fought with a Crown Heights gang called the Jolly Stompers, who were kids from lower-middle-class/working-class black families. As I look back on all that we did as young black males, whether it was how we dressed, fought, or talked to girls, it always concerned our need for respect. The emphasis of the streets and our lives was rooted in respect. Some of the most brutal fights stemmed from petty incidents that embodied some affront to a person's respect.

The first part of my life having been spent on the streets of New York City, the second part has been spent correcting the consequences of the first part. As I attended college, I came to understand that many black males study for two degrees: One was earned in college; the other was earned as we studied who we were as black men, reading about African/African American history, sociology, psychology, and every other discipline to gain the knowledge we needed to appreciate who we were. Some might say I have arrived in society having received a doctorate degree. While I have crossed over the poverty line into a world of scholars and professionals, being a black man in American society has not changed much at all. I still get stopped by the police and questioned; I still get those looks from some whites as to why I am driving or walking through their neighborhood. I still receive looks from people that say I am intimidating to them, no matter how unaggressive and unthreatening I act without losing my "respect." It amazes me that some white people hate it when black males act aggressively on the job, but yet at the same time demand aggressive behavior as the ladder to upward mobility. They want passive young black males in the classroom, but then expect us, all of a sudden, to become aggressive as long as it does not threaten their position.

Negrophobia or the fear of the black man has a long history in the United States. It affects how black children are educated and prepared to become citizens in a country that consistently views them as a societal problem. For too long this negrophobia has caused the dominant society to tell us as black males that we are good for nothing, and we have internalized this and other opinions of the oppressor (our not being "capable of learning anything," our being "unproductive") to the point where we believe the lie ourselves. This negrophobia has caused a whole educational system to not expect much from black males. Instead, it has caused our society to construct and spend billions of dollars on massive prisons to house them, rather than educating them.

QUESTIONS TO CONSIDER

1. Kharem contents that young people often have "rational" reasons of their own for joining gangs. What are some of them, and why are they typically outside the mind sets of most educators and policymakers?

2. What does the author suggest that they do to learn more directly and concretely about the lives of teen gang members?

3. In reviewing his own experiences as a gang member, how does Kharem describe any changes that have occurred in gang life from the 1970s to the present? Give examples.

4. In what ways do some teachers lack understanding of the cultural norms and values of young African American makes? What is that the case? Explain.

5. How are Eurocentric ideas and models part and parcel of most American public schools? How can they by harmful? Give examples and elaborate.

6. What does Kharem mean by "negrophobia," and how is it central to his thesis? Explain. Do you agree with his overall argument? Why or why not?

Note

This chapter originally appeared in Shirley R. Steinberg and Joe L. Kincheloe (eds.), *19 Urban Questions: Teaching in the City* (New York: Peter Lang, 2007).

References

Anderson, Elijah (1995). The code of the streets. *Atlantic Monthly, 273,* 80 (94.

Coupland, Reginald (1928). *Kirk on the Zambesi: A chapter of African history.* Oxford: The Clarendon Press.

Ferguson, Ann Arnett (2001). *Bad boys: Public schools in the making of black masculinity.* Ann Arbor: University of Michigan Press.

Foster, Michele (Ed.) (1997). *Black teachers on teaching.* New York: The New Press.

Ladson-Billings, Gloria (2001). *Crossing over to Canaan: The journey of new teachers in diverse classrooms.* San Francisco: Jossey-Bass.

McCall, Nathan (1994). *Makes me wanna holler: A young black man in America.* New York: Random House.

Woodson, Carter G. (1990). *The miseducation of the Negro* [1933]. Trenton, NJ: Africa World Press.

CHAPTER FOURTEEN

Would You Like Values with That?

Chick-fil-A and Character Education

DERON BOYLES

"Character education" represents a long-standing staple of U.S. schools. From the "Old Deluder Satan" Law of 1647 to *The New England Primer* in the eighteenth century to McGuffey Readers from the late 1830s (and well into the 1920s), the idea of transmitting core values to the young is so deeply rooted in the history of schooling that "morals" is often assumed to be a "given."[1] Over time, various social and religious concerns melded into a taken-for-granted presupposition that schools should play a major role in transmitting "good character" and fostering character development. In contemporary schools, state curricula often include character education, and a series of organizations have been established to advance the idea that character education is fundamental to schools.

National programs that currently exist include, among others, "Character Counts!" from the Josephson Institute and "A 12-Point Comprehensive Approach to Character Education" from The Center for the 4th and 5th Rs (respect and responsibility). Other national and international organizations include the Character Education Partnership (CEP) and the Institute for Global Ethics.[2] These organizations proclaim themselves to be nonpartisan and each identifies universal values that should be adopted, though the number of values vary. Michael Josephson developed "Character Counts!," the most widely used character education program in the U.S. Josephson retired from careers in law, business, and education to run the Joseph and Edna Josephson Institute, named for his parents. He serves the organization without a salary and all proceeds from speaking engagements and written work are stated as going directly back into the nonprofit institute.[3] The Center for the 4th and 5th Rs is led by Thomas Lickona, a professor of educational psychology at the State University of New York-Cortland. The Center for the 4th and 5th Rs is a university bureau committed to "building a moral society and developing schools which are civil and caring communities."[4] Lickona is a widely published author who also serves on the board of the CEP. Josephson and Lickona, however, are not the only ones influencing character education programs. Truett Cathy also influences character education curriculum in the U.S.

Cathy is the founder and CEO of Chick-fil-A, the fast food restaurant headquartered in Georgia. Cathy is also an avowed Christian fundamentalist.[5] Accordingly, he donated an "age-appropriate" (Protestant) Bible to every school library in the state of Georgia in 2003. He is also the financial resource behind the national "Core Essentials" character education initiative based in Georgia, and through his financing, Chick-fil-A sponsors the teacher's guides sent to each school.[6] In addition, Cathy teamed with William Bennett to offer wristbands and cassettes as part of "kid's meals" at various Chick-fil-A stores. The wristbands and cassettes tout such values as "respect," "courage," and "honesty." This essay explores three main lines of inquiry: (1) the specifics of "Core Essentials" as a strategy for teaching character; (2) the role (and ironies) of private businesses influencing public school curricula; and (3) the assumptions inherent in the kind of teaching of character outlined by Core Essentials. Girding this inquiry is a concern about the problematic enterprise of teaching character itself as if it is an unquestionable domain. Further, the larger contexts of childhood obesity findings and Christian influences on and in public spheres will be considered along with Theodore Brameld's *Ends and Means in Education*, John Dewey's *Moral Principles in Education*, and Pierre Bourdieu's *Acts of Resistance* and *Firing Back*.[7] Ultimately, this article offers a critique and raises questions that may be helpful when considering character education and school-business partnerships.

Since Truett Cathy is a fundamentalist Christian as well as a private businessman, this chapter questions the understanding demonstrated by the Georgia state superintendent of schools, Kathy Cox, in a July 1, 2003, letter to Georgia school principals. She wrote that Truett Cathy is "a pioneering businessman" whose "generosity" allowed for an "age-appropriate Bible" to be placed in every school library in the state. She also wrote that Truett Cathy's "initiative has been completely funded by Mr. Cathy. No state funds have been used to supply this book to your school. Mr. Cathy has a passion for helping children, [sic] and he sees this as another way to encourage the youth of our great state."[8] What does the distinction between state and private funds for Bible purchases and placement mean? Does the fact that a Christian fundamentalist funded a character education program represent any challenges or concerns for, say, students who are Jewish or agnostic or Muslim? Is there any connection between Kathy Cox's endorsement, nay, praise of Truett Cathy and Cox's claim that the term "evolution" is a "buzzword" that should be replaced in the state curriculum of Georgia?[9] If Truett Cathy were actually interested in the welfare of children, why would he promote unhealthy fast food as part of a character education program that touts "honesty" as a virtue? Indeed, what assumptions are made by Truett Cathy, furthered by the state, and pushed into the hands of teachers by the private, nonprofit Core Essentials organization that Cathy's profits from Chick-fil-A support?

The Program Itself: An Overview of Various Aspects

A visit to the Chick-fil-A website reveals an interesting phenomenon. On the page displaying information regarding Chick-fil-A's support of "Core Essentials," the company also notes the following: "Amid our nation's growing concern for children's character development, Chick-fil-A has found a way to help. Since 2000 we've been a national sponsor of Core Essentials, an educational program that gives teachers and parents tools for imparting key values to elementary-age boys and girls. By teaching inner beliefs and attitudes such as honesty, patience, respect, orderliness and courage, Core Essentials helps children treat others right, make smart decisions, and maximize their potential. The entire program teaches 27 values over a three-year period. To learn more about Core Essentials, contact a Chick-fil-A franchise in your area."[10]

When you go to the website page and begin reading the paragraph just cited, you are interrupted by the cartoon image of the back of a cow's head. The image then scrawls "eat mor chikin'" across the screen, the very screen that includes the words "character development." It seems inconsistent, at least, to (1) have "more" and "chicken" spelled incorrectly on the page devoted to children's schooling, and (2) for those who would support the general notion of character education and the ensuing lists that accompany the phrase, where do "graffiti" and "interruption" appear on those lists?

Once past the website interruption, however, one can find more information about the program, and it does not take long to understand the underlying point. The website indicates that there is a booklet for teachers to help in the teaching of character. In *Core Essentials: A Strategy for Teaching Character*, the first page of the booklet *qua* teachers' guide outlines three main elements of the program: Identifying Basic Components, Preparation, and Establishing a Routine. Each of the three main elements has subheadings identifying key features indicative of the main elements as well as the overall intent of the larger program. Under "Identify the Basic Components" exists "teacher's guide, bookmarks/tablecards, value-able card, and posters." The teacher's guide is the booklet and tells teachers what to do, when to do it, and how to do it. The subsection that explains elements in the teacher's guide notes that "each month you have age-appropriate materials at two academic levels, K-2 and 3–5. Included in the guide are literature and video suggestions which may be displayed in the library by the media specialist."[11] For the bookmarks/tablecards, the booklet instructs that "the bookmark is perforated and should be separated from the tablecard, which is designed to be folded and placed in a convenient location at home (kitchen counter or table). The parents of each child may then use this tool to emphasize the value through family discussions and activities." For the value-able card, importantly, the booklet reveals that the " . . . card is a key component which leads to successful implementation of the program. It is designed as the incentive for children who are caught [sic] displaying the value. Each month you will see suggestions in the Teacher's Guide for 'Catching Kids.' Use these ideas to help you choose students who show they understand the value. The card rewards them with a FREE Chick-fil-A Kid's Meal. *Ideally, you should have enough cards to reward each student every month (if earned).*"[12]

Good, Old-Fashioned Character

With this overview, consider what happens to the students in classes that adopt the Core Essentials program. What I intend to do here is outline the specific instructions that are included in the teacher's guide and underscore the elements that make this character education plan a traditional, and thereby restrictive and troubling, approach to teaching children. One may argue that a traditional approach to character education is what is needed. Core Essentials relies heavily on the idea that values are to be "imparted," thus reinforcing a banking approach to teaching and learning whereby the teacher deposits data into the students' "empty vaults" (or minds).[13] This essay intends to problematize the banking approach and show that there are underlying ironies that make the program highly questionable. There are also elements of hypocrisy that make the entire enterprise suspect.

There is a different value for each month of the year represented by the guidelines in question. They include, beginning in September and ending in May: initiative, respect, uniqueness, peace, orderliness, kindness, courage, joy, and patience. For each month, the teacher's guide begins with the exact same formula: a definition of the term, a list of suggested books that represent the value, a list of quotes, a story about an animal that illustrates the value, and directions for teachers. Consider the directions for October. The value is "respect" and the teacher is given the definition: "responding with words and actions that show others they are important."[14] One of the "famous person" quotes given in the booklet is "Always respect your parents. . . . Do whatever your parents say. They are your best friends in life." Aside from the obvious parallel to one of the Ten Commandments (Honor thy father and mother), there is also an irony in having the quote signify "respect." The quote is attributed to George Steinbrenner, the notorious baseball owner whose fights with managers and team members are legendary.

For December, the value is peace and is defined as "proving that you care more about each other than winning an argument." The booklet also indicates that "the first step toward living peaceably is one made quietly inside ourselves. We must decide that other people are worth more to us than our own selfish desires, and that the value of agreement is greater than the satisfaction of defeating an opponent."[15] While the moralistic sentiment may sound nice, I wonder about a possible hidden agenda. Much like the "always respect your parents . . . do whatever they say" quote from the October lesson, I wonder about the degree to which students are actually being subjugated under a logic of hegemony. As though a sexually abusive parent's directions are always to be followed, the underbelly of universalism may reveal itself given careful analysis. That a corporate fast-food chain arguably interested in increasing market share via competition supports a program that appears to want to produce docile, unquestioning students goes to the heart of the school-business intersection as well. To wit, are schools about producing unquestioning consumers via a character education program that appears to elevate passivity and dogma? This concern does not only apply to the students subjected to the program, however. Teachers, too, are under a hegemonic rationale that subjugates and marginalizes their expertise and professionalism under pre-ordained scripts.

Each week in December, for example, has a corresponding paragraph that begins "Our value this month is peace. The definition of peace is 'proving that you care more about each other than winning an argument.'"[16] Forget that the vast majority of schools are not in session for a full four weeks in December; the four-week script nevertheless reflects a kind of proletarianization or de-skilling of teaching at the same time that it seems to mimic catechism-like recitations from Christian churches. For the "bulletin board" aspect of the teacher's guide for December, teachers are told to "design a bulletin board with a chimney made of craft paper. Give each child a stocking made out of construction paper. On the stocking, have the students write how they care for other people. The children may decorate their stockings afterwards. Hang their stockings on the chimney that you have made." The title given to the bulletin board assignment is "The Stockings Were Hung by the Chimney with Peace." Aside from the overly prescriptive directions that devalue teachers' autonomy and professionalism, stockings are typically hung by chimneys in Christian homes, not Jewish or Muslim homes. Furthermore, if stockings are hung in homes for the Christmas holidays, is the point of young children hanging the stockings to "care for other people" or to receive presents?

A Christian theme is able to be discerned in other parts of the Core Essentials handbook as well. For January, orderliness is the value, and while the paragraph begins with "a study of nature," the teacher is supposed to explain to the students that "the constellations are a beautiful example of the order which exists in the skies."[17] Given the recent controversy in Georgia concerning Kathy Cox and evolution, the "order in the skies" reference sounds eerily like creationist "grand design" assertions.[18] For February, the value is kindness, and the teacher is supposed to explain that a wise saying is "do to others as you would have them do to you."[19] Fine as far as it goes, the *un*hidden "Golden Rule" taken together with other religious themes raises concerns in my mind. Should elementary students hassle their parents into taking them to Chick-fil-A for their "free" meal during the month of *X*, they would receive a cassette and/or a bracelet/watch-type band that has a compartment to hold more information from the Core Essentials program. For "responsibility" the plastic holder on the wristband is a sheep dog and the insert of stickers includes statements like "guard sheep dogs are responsible for protecting sheep" and "shepherds trust their sheep dogs to do what is expected of them." While my intent is not to make too much of these points, it does seem to me to be another Christian theme. Sheep? Shepherds? Further, married with the religious and overwhelmingly Christian themes are themes about work and capitalism. For the month of April, for example, students read quotes from Dale Carnegie and Henry Ford. Carnegie's quote is "when fate hands you a lemon, make lemonade" and Ford's is "there is joy in work."[20]

What these and other quotes within the curriculum arguably indicate is the nexus of Christianity and capitalism. By weaving a language of accommodation with a language of economics, contrived optimism becomes an unquestioned foundation for docile, naïve workers. The nexus results in a kind of confused nationalist mythology that takes Christian values for granted while accommodating the lauding of individualism and pretenses of participating in a democracy. The mythology of "anyone can be anything they want" given "free markets," "hard work," and entrepreneurialism masks the reality faced by increasing numbers of workers. As Bourdieu points out,

> there are more and more low-level service jobs that are underpaid and low-productivity, unskilled or under-skilled (based on hasty on-the-job training), with no career prospects—in short, the *throwaway jobs* of what André Gorz calls a 'society of servants.' According to economist Jean Gadrey, quoting an American study, of the thirty jobs that will grow fastest in the next decade, seventeen require no skills and only eight require higher education and qualification. At the other end of social space, the *dominated dominant*, that is, the managers, are experiencing a new form of alienation. They occupy an ambiguous position, equivalent to that of the petty bourgeois at another historical stage in the structure, which leads to forms of organized self-exploitation.[21]

Part of the historical stage to which Bourdieu refers was outlined in 1926 by Richard Henry Tawney. In his classic text, *Religion and the Rise of Capitalism*, Tawney presaged that "rightly or wrongly, with wisdom or its opposite, not only in England but on the Continent and in America, not in one denomination but among Roman Catholics, Anglicans, and Nonconformists, an attempt is being made to restate the practical implications of the social ethics of the Christian faith, in a form sufficiently comprehensive to provide a standard by which to judge the collective actions and institutions of mankind [sic], in the sphere both of international politics and of social organizations."[22]

The scenario goes something like this: inculcate the youngest and most impressionable with externally contrived religious values and increasingly mold the docile congregation of followers into workers who honor authority. In the process, remove opportunities for critique and questioning by championing *a priori* notions of consensus and the status quo. According to Lindblom, corporations are intimately tied to this very process and set up the nexus of and integration between capitalism and Christian moral codes at the expense of public debate and authentic democratic governance. He notes the key features in business terms and calls them "the grand issues of politico-economic organization: private enterprise, a high degree of corporate autonomy, protection of the status quo on distribution of income and wealth, close consultation between business and government, and restriction of union demands to those consistent with business profitability. . . . They try, through indoctrination, to keep all these issues from coming to the agenda of government."[23] For the parallel to schools, I am reminded of Theodore Brameld's discussion of indoctrination when he was attempting to defend the notion of "partiality" in schools in his *Ends and Means in Education*.[24]

Brameld defined indoctrination as a "method of learning by communication which proceeds primarily in one direction . . . for the purpose of inculcating in the mind and behavior of the latter a firm acceptance of some one doctrine or systematic body of beliefs—a doctrine assumed in advance by its exponents to be so supremely true, so good, or so beautiful as to justify no need for critical, scrupulous, thoroughgoing comparison with alternative doctrines."[25] Brameld's concern was that schools practiced indoctrination at the expense of the society. For the purpose of this essay, however, he went even further. He indicted "the Church" for establishing the very conditions that promoted learning of the kind he deplored (and this essay challenges). "For many centuries," Brameld wrote, "the Church has deliberately and frankly inculcated its own doctrine as alone true and good, its chief indoctrinators being priests vested with authority to communicate its tenets to receptive minds. . . this kind of education flourishes oftener than not: inculcation of moral codes or social folklore, and especially of attitudes and programs identified with the traditional economic-political system, simply means that public schools, far more often than most of their personnel themselves realize, are under the heavy influence of the dominant ideology."[26]

When specifically looking carefully at the text of the Core Essentials teacher's guide, to link and illustrate Brameld's point, a series of questions comes to mind. When, in March, the theme is courage, teachers are told that "courage is the foundation of our democracy. Discover the courage of the young citizens in your class by using a few of these ideas: Watch for students who do the right thing even when it has consequences; observe students who stand up for their beliefs; notice those students who do not give in to peer pressure; and let students write or discuss what courage means to them. Allow them to make a pledge about their courage and watch to see who lives up to that pledge."[27] Given the preceding months that privileged meekness and obedience to authority, what should be "discovered" about the "young citizens" in the class? If citizenship has been crafted in a hierarchical and externally imposed fashion, with the teacher at the center—or more accurately, the Core Essentials program at the center—how serious are teachers supposed to take the task laid out for them? Further, in terms of power, if the teachers are the ones "allowing" students to make a pledge and "letting" students write and discuss what courage means to them, the idea of students as courageous citizens is further subjugated under the power and authority of the teacher via the Core Essentials curriculum.

Values and the Drive-Thru

Throughout the Core Essentials teacher's guide there are sections called "Catching Kids." These sections are ostensibly intended to "catch" children "doing good," so as to turn the idea of "catching" a student doing something into a positive rather than a negative action. Unique to the Core Essentials program, however, is that, because the program is underwritten by Truett Cathy and his Chick-fil-A fast-food chain, the "Catching Kids" sections have "value-able cards." These cards are considered "rewards" by the program and, when given out by the teacher to the student, enable the student to get a free "kid's meal" at Chick-fil-A. A couple of issues converge around this point. First, the students who "earn" the reward are specifically within grades K-2 and 3–5. What we have are the youngest and most impressionable students in schools being bribed to act in particular ways in order to get a meal that is unhealthy. As Carolyn Vander Schee has pointed out, childhood obesity is a concern that has direct links to schools and programs they sponsor (both via in-school food services and out-of-school connections like Core Essentials).[28] Other studies also conclude that fast-food intake among school children is part of a growing obesity epidemic.[29]

By using an unhealthy meal as a reward for complying with a "character education" program, one wonders about the hypocrisy. Where in the program, for example, are students instructed to demonstrate courage by questioning the corporate underwriting of the program itself? When are the students encouraged to consider the fact that, in order for them to redeem their "kid's meal" voucher, they will have to be accompanied by an adult who most likely will purchase food and provide profit for Chick-fil-A? Indeed, recall the direct quote from the teacher's guide noted toward the beginning of this chapter. The guide encourages teachers to "use these ideas to help . . . choose students who show they understand the value . . . *Ideally, you should have enough cards to reward each student every month (if earned)."* The point may not be to reward students for good character, even if we could agree on what good character means. The point is to get as many children from grades K-5 into a fast-food chain to eat greasy food with their parents. Can we imagine that the marketing department at Chick-fil-A has not surmised the amount of business they would generate over a three-year period of time? Differently, but related, when are students asked about honesty in disclosing complete calorie and fat content in the food that is being used to lure them to behave in particular ways? Chick-fil-A does have a section on its website where it lists the nutritional value of *items* on their menu.[30] But even the way the documentation is presented is misleading. To consider the amount of fat and calories in a "kid's meal," you have to know what actually comprises a "kid's meal." On the website, for example, both 4- and 6-ounce servings of chicken nuggets are provided on separate lines. A "kid's meal," however, includes more than just the chicken nuggets. The meal includes waffle fries and a drink. Why not be "honest" and include the combined caloric value of the entire meal (allowing for variants like whether the drink is a soda, lemonade, or water)? Is it easier to differentiate and parse the particulars so the whole is not easily discernible? Perhaps the most extreme evidence of Chick-fil-A's Janus-faced approach to the issue of caloric intake and nutrition is their stance that eating plenty of their fast food is not really the problem. The problem is lack of exercise. Indeed, and incredibly, Chick-fil-A offers a "Chick-fil-A 10-Second Tip" in the Children's Hospital's (Knoxville, TN) "Healthy Kids" newsletter. The tip is, "Rather than only focusing on decreasing a big eater's intake, try to increase activity and exercise."[31]

To illustrate the link between the previous claims concerning the problems with externally imposed ideology and health issues associated with fast-food intake, consider that students in the Core Essentials program are structurally inhibited from exploring the issue of healthy eating. The subject does not fall under any of the categories that are pre-ordained for and imposed on teachers. Furthermore, teachers are "sold" the idea that the program will "only take 15 minutes," so when would teachers find the time to go beyond the pre-packaged approach anyway? Missing is the kind of approach developed by Janet Cundiff. She suggests a general structure through which students can answer the question, "Can you 'eat healthy' by frequenting fast food restaurants?"[32] Her approach uses Web links and teams of students to investigate food pyramids and food facts. Teams are asked to learn more about various fast-food restaurants, including, among others, Taco Bell, Burger King, and Chick-fil-A. Teams search for healthy meals and individuals have roles regarding the various aspects of nutrition to be found on the various websites. Students then synthesize the information, present it to others, and reconsider, according to Cundiff, their own decisions, opinions, and arguments. Accordingly, the students are actively engaged in developing questions and critiques. The Core Essentials program does not foster these postures, as its primary concern is with external imposition of pre-ordained assumptions about character.

I wonder what it would be like if, during the month of October (when "respect" is the value of the month), students would be encouraged to ask whether they, as a group, are actually being shown "respect" via the very program touting the value. Said differently, when is respect for the children shown by the teachers, Core Essentials executives, and Truett Cathy? What role did they have in determining whether they should be subjected to the overtly Christian themes embedded in the program? I also wonder whether the lessons being taught—regardless of whether they are ultimately valid—are also being demonstrated by the people who are promoting the program? How patient would Truett Cathy be of students demonstrating against his company? How respectful of students would Kathy Cox be if they refused to engage in surveillance of one another as the "catching kids" section of the program encourages?

Implications and Further Considerations

One point, then, is to discern the ironies and to tease out the inconsistencies related to the Core Essentials program. We have, in short, a program funded by a fundamentalist Christian whose company uses "kid's meals" as a bribe for behaving in docile, disempowered, uncritical ways. Might this actually be the motive for the program? That is, might it be the case that imposing hierarchy, developing non-questioning students, and privileging Christian-corporate values are intentional acts perpetrated by those wishing to maintain and increase their power, even at the expense of the very students to which they preach equality and kindness? To have Core Essentials and Chick-fil-A work in tandem with William Bennett's *Book of Virtues* raises an obvious question about hypocrisy. Bennett, of course, was revealed to have gambled away millions of dollars at the same time he was loudly proclaiming the vital importance of teaching "virtues" in schools. Is this a "do as I say, not as I do" quagmire? What does it mean that universalists like Bennett actually represent particularist and contextual realities that are not easy to generalize? What does it mean when the Georgia State Superintendent of Schools, Kathy Cox, wishes to delete "evolution" from the curriculum, but applauds Truett Cathy's donation of Protestant versions of the Bible to all of the public schools in the state?

Beyond critique of those in power and control of the program, one has to consider the reality of classroom life. Teachers, in a perversely thankful way, simply do not have the time to spare to "add-on" the "curriculum" represented by Core Essentials. The state of Georgia already has a character education component. It also has a core curriculum that, given No Child Left Behind, is raising the degree to which teachers teach to end-of-year tests. Teachers simply do not have the time to alter their bulletin boards, monitor the Chick-fil-A vouchers, and "catch" students behaving in ways the authors of the program do not conduct themselves anyway. So, beyond exploiting the youngest students in schools, beyond the attempt to further proletarianize teaching, beyond attempting to mold obedient and subservient future workers, and beyond the irony and hypocrisy, is there anything valuable about the values valued by Core Essentials? Maybe.

If "Core Essentials" would be used as an object lesson itself, we might be able to reveal a kind of criticality that teaches about values while not externally imposing them without critique. Values exist in schools. Students bring values to the classroom just like their teachers. The question is whether those values are to be explored or whether they are to be assumed. Dewey makes it clear that "morals" are an important part of being a citizen (or any part of a group). He differs greatly from "Core Essentials," though, in that he is not interested in externally imposed, "specialist" developed terms and themes spread out over three years as part of a preparation plan for future work or future citizenship. In *Moral Principles in Education*, Dewey puts it this way: "We need to see that moral principles are not arbitrary, that they are not 'transcendental'; that the term 'moral' does not designate a special region or portion of life. We need to translate the moral into the conditions and forces of our community life, and into the impulses and habits of the individual. All the rest is mint, anise, and cumin."[33] In another passage, Dewey writes that "the emphasis then falls upon construction . . . rather than upon absorption and mere learning."[34] As though he is aware of Core Essentials and other such programs, Dewey argues that children are rarely emergent and constructive creatures in classroom settings. Their intellectual life is stunted by the proceduralism of traditional expectations and methods. So, too, says Dewey, of morals in schools:

> The child knows perfectly well that the teacher and all his fellow pupils have exactly the same facts and ideas before them that he [sic] has; he is not *giving* them anything at all. And it may be questioned whether the moral lack is not as great as the intellectual. The child is born with a natural desire to give out, to do, to serve. When this tendency is not used, when conditions are such that other motives are substituted, the accumulation of an influence working against the social spirit is much larger than we have any idea of—especially when the burden of work, week after week, and year after year, falls upon this side.[35]

Three years worth of value-able "kid's meal" cards externally dangled for Pavlovian results strikes me as the very thing Dewey would argue against. Importantly, Dewey is not arguing against morals. Instead, he is arguing against morals "in the air . . . something set off by themselves . . . [morals] that are so *very* 'moral' that they have no working contact with the average affairs of everyday life."[36] As a pragmatist and fallibilist, however, he argues that the utility that various values might have get their worth in their organic growth and development in context. Dewey again:

> Here, then, is the moral standard, by which to test the work of the school upon the side of what it does direct-ly for individuals. . . . Does the school as a system . . . attach sufficient importance to the spontaneous instincts and impulses? Does it afford sufficient opportunity for these to assert themselves and work out their own results? Can we even say that the school in principle attaches itself . . . to the active constructive powers rather than to processes of absorption and learning?[37]

I submit that the answers to Dewey's questions are "no," "no," and "no." Far too often in far too many schools, far too many teachers fall back on methods of teaching that are comfortable, traditional. Accordingly, students' natural tendencies to inquire become stifled in rooms that are organized (physically and in terms of curriculum) for convenience and platoon-style manage-ment.[38] While teachers are not primarily to blame for the external imposition of No Child Left Behind mandates and high-stakes testing that structure their lives, the very frustration they often feel with such external imposition is not recognized when they, in turn, impose upon their stu-dents. Core Essentials is simply another in a long line of impositions that teachers and students must navigate. The difference is the degree to which the program represents corporate infiltra-tion under the guide of character education and the universalism it entails.

Extending Dewey, Bourdieu challenges the rhetoric of universalism that sets up the struc-tures within which schools operate as stifling places for external imposition. For Bourdieu, "the effect of shared belief . . . removes from discussion ideas which are perfectly worth discussing."[39]

Indeed, Bourdieu envisions a kind of collective intellectualism that challenges deeply held beliefs. Long-standing assumptions become the focus of renewed critique and action. He is specifically interested in examining the major power brokers in modern society. As he puts it, "the power of the agents and mechanisms that dominate the economic and social world today rests on the extraordinary concentration of all the species of capital—economic, political, mili-tary, cultural, scientific, and technological—as the foundation of a symbolic domination with-out precedent. . . ."[40] This symbolic domination is difficult to critique, however, because of the power it has over members of society. For Bourdieu, students are also a direct target and engage in hegemonic practices that further subjugate them to the influence of the market. He claims, for example, "that the 'civilization' of jeans, Coca-Cola, and McDonald's [Chick-fil-A] has not only economic power on its side but also the symbolic power exerted through a seduction to which the victims themselves contribute. By taking as their chief targets children and adolescents, par-ticularly those most shorn of specific immune defenses, with the support of advertising and the media which are both constrained and complicit, the big cultural production and distribution companies gain an extraordinary, unprecedented hold over all contemporary societies—societies that, as a result, find themselves virtually infantilized."[41]

Recall that Core Essentials is imposed on students in grades K-5. Bourdieu's suggestion that the larger society is infantilized by the hold corporate interests have over it is even more striking when we consider that the project of disempowerment literally begins with infants. Organic growth of student interests, for Dewey, paired with sociological critique of business influences, for Bourdieu, make for heady prospects when envisioning what schools—and their curricula— might look like during reformation. It would take, however, a sober reconsideration of the roles of students and teachers in schools to engage in substantive reconstruction of schools. It would require a collective "intellectualization" of various roles and, in order to do so, a sloughing off of the dead skin of corporate- and fundamentalist-sponsored, universalist edicts in the form of, among others, character education programs like Core Essentials.

What is not being advocated is a substitution of one kind of pre-ordained morality for another. There should not exist, in other words, a revised script that suggests "The value of the month is criticality. Criticality is defined as. . . ." This sort of "bait and switch" game has been played for too long in the history of curriculum. The function of indoctrination is the same, even though the forms may morph. Instead, students and teachers should develop their own versions of criticality as those versions emerge (and change) through the natural curiosity of students in K-5. In this way, a singular (Christian) view of character education is replaced with a pluralistic understanding of character and students, taking a cue from Dewey, would utilize their instincts and impulses to explore that variety with one another. No fries are necessary.

QUESTIONS TO CONSIDER

1. The author argues that "Core Essentials" and the Chick-fil-A character education program espouse certain value assumptions. What are some of those assumed values, and do you basically agree with them? Why or why not?

2. With educational philosopher Theodore Brameld, Boyles contends that such programs Inculcate capitalistic and consumerist mind sets In youth. How does he argue that point? Again, do you agree or disagree? Why?

3. The author describes what he considers a hypocritical and unhealthy linkage between Chick-fil-A's "educational" programs and the diets they engender among young people. In light of a global child obesity epidemic, how would you assess such programs? Explain your response.

4. Is there also hypocrisy in the way religious and scientific issues are propagated in public schools? That is, are some such values celebrated while others are ignored or castigated? Give examples and elaborate.

5. What does Boyles mean by "universalism" in ethics, and how and why does he consider it a largely negative value? DO you agree? Why or why not?

NOTES

This chapter originally appeared in Deron Boyles (ed.), *The Corporate Assault on Youth: Commercialism, Exploitation, and the End of Innocence* (New York: Peter Lang, 2008).

1. See, for example, Richard Mosier, *Making the American Mind: Social and Moral Ideas in the McGuffey Readers* (New York: Russell & Russell, 1965); Carl F. Kaestle, *Pillars of the Republic: Common Schools and American Society, 1780–1860* (New York: Hill and Wang, 1983); Joel Spring, *The American School, 1642–2004* (Boston: McGraw-Hill, 2005), sixth edition; and Thomas Lickona, *Character Matters: How to Help Our Children Develop Good Judgement, Integrity, and Other Essential Virtues* (New York: Simon and Schuster, 2004); Ernest J. Zarra, "Pinning Down Character Education," *Kappa Delta Pi Record* 36, no. 4 (Summer 2000): 154–157; and Mary M. Williams, "Models of Character Education: Perspectives and Development Issues," *Journal of Humanistic Counseling, Education and Development* 39, no. 1 (September 2000): 32–40. See also Martin E. Marty and R. Scott Appleby, eds., *Fundamentalism and Society: Reclaiming the Science, the Family, and Education* (Chicago: The University of Chicago Press, 1997).
2. See, for example, http://www.character.org, http://www.charactercounts.org, and http://www.cortland.edu/c4n5rs/.
3. See http://www.charactercounts.org. See also Michael Josephson, "Character Education Is Back in Our Public Schools," *The State Education Standard* (Autumn 2002): 41–45.
4. See also Thomas Lickona, *Character Matters: How to Help Our Children Develop Good Judgment, Integrity, and Other Essential Virtues* (New York: Simon and Schuster, 2004).
5. See S. Truett Cathy, *Eat MOR Chikin: Inspire More People Doing Business the Chick-fil-A Way* (Nashville: Cumberland House Publishing, 2002); S. Truett Cathy, *It's Easier to Succeed Than Fail* (Nashville: Thomas Nelson Publishers, 1989); and Ken Blanchard and S. Truett Cathy, *The Generosity Factor* (Grand Rapids, MI: Zondervan, 2002). Both Thomas Nelson and Zondervan are Christian publishing houses.
6. Core Essentials, *Core Essentials: A Strategy for Teaching Character* (Alpharetta, GA: Core Essentials, Inc., 2001).
7. Theodore Brameld, *Means and Ends in Education: A Midcentury Appraisal* (New York: Harper and Row Publishers, 1950); John Dewey, *Moral Principles in Education* (Carbondale, IL: Southern Illinois University Press, 1909); Pierre Bourdieu, *Acts of Resistance: Against the Tyranny of the Market* (New York: The New Press, 1998), trans. Richard Nice; and Pierre Bourdieu, *Firing Back: Against the Tyranny of the Market 2* (New York: The New Press, 2003), trans., Loic Wacquant.
8. Kathy Cox, letter to school principals, July 1, 2003.
9. See Mary MacDonald, "Georgia May Shun 'Evolution' in Schools: Revised Curriculum Plan Outrages Science Teachers," *The Atlanta Journal-Constitution* (29 January 2004): A1.
10. See http://www.chick-fil-a.com/CoreEssentials.asp. Accessed 21 January 2004.
11. Core Essentials, p.1.
12. Ibid., italics in the original.
13. See Paulo Freire, *Pedagogy of the Oppressed* (New York: Continuum, 1970).
14. Core Essentials, 5.
15. Ibid., 11.
16. Ibid., 12.
17. Ibid., 14.
18. See Mary MacDonald, "Evolution Furor Heats Up," *The Atlanta Journal-Constitution* (31 January 2004): A1.
19. Core Essentials, 17.
20. Ibid., 23.
21. Bourdieu, *Firing Back*, 31. Italics in original.
22. Richard Henry Tawney, *Religion and the Rise of Capitalism* (New York: Harcourt, Brace, and Company, 1926), 5.
23. Charles E. Lindblom, *Politics and Markets: The World's Political-Economic Systems* (New York: Basic Books, 1977), 205.

24. Brameld, *Means and Ends in Education*, 65ff.
25. Ibid., 66.
26. Ibid., 67.
27. Core Essentials, 20.
28. See Carolyn Vander Schee, "Food Services and Schooling," in *Schools or Markets?: Commercialism, Privatization, and School-Business Partnerships*, ed. Deron Boyles (Mahwah, NJ: LEA, 2005), 1–30.
29. Shanthy A. Bowman, Steven L. Gortmaker, Cara B. Ebbeling, Mark A. Pereira, and David S. Ludwig, "Effects of Fast-Food Consumption on Energy Intake and Diet Quality Among Children in a National Household Survey," *Pediatrics* 113, no. 1 (January, 2004): 112–118; Richard J. Deckelbaum and Christine A. Williams, "Childhood Obesity: The Health Issue," *Obesity Research* 9, suppl. 4 (November, 2001): 239S-243S; David S. Ludwig, Karen E. Peterson, and Steven Gortmaker, "Relation between Consumption of Sugar-Sweetened Drinks and Childhood Obesity: A Prospective, Observational Analysis," *The Lancet* vol. 357 (17 February 2001): 505–508. See also Marion Nestle, *Food Politics: How the Food Industry Influences Nutrition and Health* (Berkeley, CA: University of California Press, 2003).
30. See http://www.chickfila.com/MenuTable.asp?Category=specialties. Accessed June 10, 2004.
31. "Chick-fil-A 10-Second Tip," *Children's Hospital's Healthy Kids: A Quarterly Publication for Parents Preschoolers* [sic] (Knoxville, TN), volume IX (Winter, 2003): 3. That the hospital condones (and promotes) this kind of logic is fodder for further investigation.
32. Janet Cundiff, "Living in the Fast (Food) Lane!" http://www.web-and-flow.com/members/jcundiff/fastfoods /webquest.htm. Accessed June 10, 2004. The movie *Supersize It!* also explores issues relating to and resulting from eating fast food.
33. Dewey, *Moral Principles in Education*, 58.
34. Ibid., 21.
35. Ibid., 22.
36. Ibid., 57.
37. Ibid., 53.
38. Herbert Kliebard, *The Struggle for the American Curriculum*, 1893–1958 (New York: Routledge, 1995), 84, 162.
39. Bourdieu, *Acts of Resistance*, 6.
40. Bourdieu, *Firing Back*, 39.
41. Ibid., 71.

Bibliography

Blanchard, Ken and S. Truett Cathy. 2002. *The Generosity Factor*. Grand Rapids, MI: Zondervan.

Bourdieu, Pierre. 1998. *Acts of Resistance: Against the Tyranny of the Market*. New York: The New Press. Trans. Richard Nice.

Bourdieu, Pierre. 2003. *Firing Back: Against the Tyranny of the Market 2*. New York: The New Press. Trans. Loïc Wacquant.

Bowman, Shanthy A., Steven L. Gortmaker, Cara B. Ebbeling, Mark A. Pereira, and David S. Ludwig. 2004. "Effects of Fast-Food Consumption on Energy Intake and Diet Quality Among Children in a National Household Survey." *Pediatrics* 113, no. 1, January.

Brameld, Theodore. 1950. *Ends and Means in Education: A Midcentury Appraisal*. New York: Harper and Row Publishers.

Cathy, S. Truett. 2002. *Eat MOR Chikin: Inspire More People Doing Business the Chick-fil-A Way*. Nashville: Cumberland House Publishing.

Cathy, S. Truett. 1989. *It's Easier to Succeed Than Fail*. Nashville: Thomas Nelson Publishers.

Chick-fil-A. 2003. "Chick-fil-A 10-Second Tip." *Children's Hospital's Healthy Kids: A Quarterly Publication for Parents Preschoolers* [sic]. IX. Knoxville, TN: Children's Hospital. Winter.

Core Essentials. 2001. *Core Essentials: A Strategy for Teaching Character*. Alpharetta, GA: Core Essentials, Inc.

Cundiff, Janet. 2004. "Living in the Fast (Food) Lane!" www.web-and-flow.com/members/jcundiff/fastfoods/webquest.htm.

Deckelbaum, Richard J., and Christine A. Williams. 2001. "Childhood Obesity: The Health Issue." *Obesity Research* 9, suppl. 4. November.

Dewey, John. 1909. *Moral Principles in Education*. Carbondale, IL: Southern Illinois University Press.

Freire, Paulo. 1970. *Pedagogy of the Oppressed*. New York: Continuum.

Josephson, Michael. 2002. "Character Education Is Back in Our Public Schools," *The State Education Standard*. Autumn.

Kaestle, Carl F. 1983. *Pillars of the Republic: Common Schools and American Society, 1780–1860*. New York: Hill and Wang.

Kliebard, Herbert. 1995. *The Struggle for the American Curriculum, 1893–1958*. New York: Routledge.

Lickona, Thomas. 2004. *Character Matters: How to Help Our Children Develop Good Judgment, Integrity, and Other Essential Virtues*. New York: Simon and Schuster.

Linblom, Charles E. 1977. *Politics and Markets: The World's Political-Economic Systems*. New York: Basic Books.

Ludwig, David S., Karen E. Peterson, and Steven Gortmaker. 2001. "Relation between Consumption of Sugar-Sweetened Drinks and Childhood Obesity: A Prospective, Observational Analysis." *The Lancet* 357. February 17.

MacDonald, Mary. 2004. "Evolution Furor Heats Up." *The Atlanta Journal-Constitution*. January 31. A1.

MacDonald, Mary. 2004. "Georgia May Shun 'Evolution' in Schools: Revised Curriculum Plan Outrages Science Teachers." *The Atlanta Journal-Constitution*. January 29. A1.

Marty, Martin E. and R. Scott Appleby. 1997. *Fundamentalism and Society: Reclaiming the Science, the Family, and Education*. Chicago: The University of Chicago Press.

Mosier, Richard. 1965. *Making the American Mind: Social and Moral Ideas in the McGuffey Readers*. New York: Russell & Russell.

Nestle, Marion. 2003. *Food Politics: How the Food Industry Influences Nutrition and Health*. Berkeley, CA: University of California Press.

Spring, Joel. 2005. *The American School, 1642–2004*. Boston: McGraw-Hill.

Tawney, Richard Henry. 1926. *Religion and the Rise of Capitalism*. New York: Harcourt, Brace, and Company.

Vander Schee, Carolyn. 2005. "Food Services and Schooling." *Schools or Markets?: Commercialism, Privatization, and School-Business Partnerships*. Ed. Deron Boyles. Mahwah, NJ: Lawrence Erlbaum.

Williams, Mary M. 2000. "Models of Character Education: Perspectives and Developmental Issues," *Journal of Humanistic Counseling, Education, and Development* 39, no. 1, September.

www.character.org

www.charactercounts.org

www.chickfila.com/CoreEssentials.asp

www.chickfila.com/MenuTable.asp?Category=specialties

www.cortland.edu/c4n5rs/

Zarra, Ernest J. 2000. "Pinning Down Character Education," *Kappa Delta Pi Record* 36, no. 4, Summer.

CHAPTER FIFTEEN

Implied Adolescents and Implied Teachers

A Generation Gap for New Times

CYNTHIA LEWIS & MARGARET FINDERS

On the surface, the emergence of new media and digital technologies seems to accentuate the generation gap between adolescent students and their teachers. This chapter argues, however, that the common meaning of "generation gap"—a gap caused by differences in age and interests—breaks down given that new teachers and their students are often close in age with common interests (especially related to popular culture). Instead, we argue that the "generation gap" that exists between these two groups is shaped by the fact that new teachers and adolescents are compelled to perform particular identities. We use the tropes of "implied adolescent" and "implied teacher" to show that what some may see as a generation gap, a simple case of divide between teachers and the "new media" adolescents they teach, is complicated by constructions of identity that come with material consequences related to access and authority.

The literary concept of the "implied reader" (Iser, 1978) provides a useful lens through which to view conceptions of adolescence in new times. Briefly, an implied reader of a text is the reader that is inscribed through the text's subject and style, the one that is positioned by the text to accept its ideology (McCallum, 1999; Nodelman, 1996). The text's ideological underpinnings are, in turn, constituted in the assumptions of the culture within which it was produced. Perry Nodelman (1996) provides a list of assumptions about children as the implied readers of children's literature that speak to commonplace contemporary constructions of childhood as a time of innocence and egocentricity. Pointing out that such constructions are historical, Nodelman proceeds to argue that one must understand something about views of childhood over time if one is to study and teach children's literature. Without such understanding, the ideology of the children's text will remain invisible to its readers.

We argue that this concept of the "implied reader/child" as it relates to children's texts maps onto a concept of the "implied adolescent" as it relates to youth culture. In fact, when Cynthia teaches a graduate course on ideology in adolescent fiction, she begins with Nodelman's list of assumptions about children and asks her students to brainstorm a similar list for adolescents. Inevitably, the students list such commonplace assumptions about adolescents as the following: rebellious, independent, peer-influenced, anti-adult, hormonal, and impulsive. Throughout the course, then, Cynthia and her students attend to the ways in which the textual features of particular works of adolescent fiction are inscribed with just such a notion of implied adolescence, thus reifying middle-class, white ideologies of youth culture.

We begin with this notion of "the implied adolescent" because we find it a fruitful trope as it relates to new literacies and adolescent learners. The ways that teachers envision their adolescent learners have everything to do with how they will teach these learners, especially given that most teacher education programs train teachers to focus on the needs of the learner. Interpreting a learner's needs, however, means that one must have a way of constructing the learner, a vision of who that learner is. Traditionally, this vision has come from developmental psychology which, along with cognitive psychology, has been the theoretical linchpin for most of teacher education. However, as the next section of this chapter makes clear, this process of constructing the "psyche" of the learner, and the life stage that we call "adolescence," occurs within a social, cultural, and historical context.

Related to new literacies, then, our conceptions of the "implied adolescent" are very important. Do we see adolescents as savvy users of new literacies (including popular technologies), perhaps savvier than we adults? Do we see them as mesmerized by new literacies and inattentive to more traditional forms of literacy? Are adolescents manipulated by new literacies and, therefore, lacking in analytical skills? And what conditions have led to these constructions of adolescent learners?

As important as it is to examine the "implied adolescent" as a social and historical construction, it is equally important to examine the "implied teacher" as the inscription of what a teacher is or should be. Just as our notion of who we believe adolescents to be is inscribed in our teaching practices, so too is our notion of who we believe a teacher should be in relation to adolescent learners. The latter is particularly important for pre-service and new teachers who often see themselves as barely beyond adolescence and therefore vulnerable about being or acting like the "implied adolescent." This vulnerability is reinforced by the discourse of teacher education with its emphasis on the "management" of children or adolescents. The "implied teacher," then, is one who is positioned by the text of teacher education (shaped, of course, by larger sociohistorical norms) to accept its ideology, an ideology that, as Allan Luke and Carmen Luke argue (2001), normalizes youth as the "uncivil, unruly techno-subject" (p. 8). In fact, engaging in new literacies makes adolescents all the more dangerous, according to Luke and Luke, because their knowledge and skills threaten adults who lack them, leading to the current panic for the good old days of print literacies. The real crisis, Luke and Luke claim, is "for the postwar trained, baby-boomer teaching, researching, and policy-making workforce entering the final decade of its productive leadership" (p. 12). Yet it is the postwar baby-boomer teacher who remains the "implied teacher" of our teacher education programs and the imagined self of our pre-service teachers.

In this chapter, we first consider historical shifts in conceptions of adolescence (the changing "implied adolescent") in the United States (and other Western nations). Following this discussion, we move to an illustration of particular adolescents' identity performances through digital literacies with a focus on how these performances are circumscribed by notions of implied adolescence. We move next to an example of a particular group of pre-service teachers struggling with normative concepts of what it means to be a teacher of adolescents in new times. Finally, we end by discussing adolescent and teacher identities as they are performed across social and institutional spaces that new media and technology have rendered less clearly demarcated.

Shifting Conceptions of the "Implied Adolescent"

Biological changes often characterize entry into adolescence and these changes have come to signify so much that we tend to describe adolescents in ways that reference their biological changes. We refer to "surging, quivering, quaking, raging hormones" as if to personify these famous biological changes and create a category we can all recognize. Yet the concept of adolescence did not exist before the last two decades of the 19th century (Klein, 1990). Gee describes the evolution of generations of adolescents called by many names (Generation Y, Generation XX, Echo Boom, Generation Next, the Bridger Generation, Generation 2K, Millennials) and characterized as shifting from the apolitical, cynical, detached genXers to the economically savvy shape-shifting portfolio adolescents of the fast-capital generation. Although we might tend to regard adolescence as a part of a "natural" life cycle that is biologically determined, adolescence as a life stage depends on the social and economic conditions of any particular historical period. Nancy Lesko (1996) argues that age is for the most part constructed as an orderly progression to a more rational and authoritative state. According to Lesko, adolescents occupy a border zone, a transitional state between "the mythic poles of adult/child, sexual/asexual, rational/emotional, civilized/savage and productive and unproductive" (p. 455).

What we call a "stage," then, must be situated within an ever-evolving complex sociopolitical climate. Klein succinctly describes the creation of adolescence based on social and economic factors:

> Basically, industrialization occurring during the later 1800s created the need for a stage of adolescence; the Depression created the legitimized opportunity for adolescence to become differentiated from childhood and adulthood; and the mass media influence/blitz of the 1950s crystallized this stage by giving it a reality all its own. (p. 456)

Adolescence as a life stage solidified largely due to economic conditions, specifically the Depression. Palladino (1996) explains that up until the 1930s most people in their teens worked for a living on farms, factories, and at home. They weren't teenagers or adolescents; they were adults. Palladino argues that it was this mass coming together in a school setting that solidified adolescence as a distinct age group. Thus, the emergence of adolescence as a life stage had more to do with economic conditions than it did with "raging hormones," the theory popularized by G. Stanley Hall.

In this country, G. Stanley Hall became known as the father of adolescence with the publication of his 1904 two volume-set *Adolescence*. Hall conceptualized the period of adolescence as biologically determined, with little consideration for any social or cultural influences (Santrock, 1993, p. 13). To Hall, adolescence was a period of "storm and stress" characterized as "a turbulent time charged with conflict and mood swings" (Santrock, 1993). According to Hall, hormonal factors account for the marked fluctuations in adolescent behaviors (Brooks-Gunn & Reiter,

1990). Coleman's (1961) landmark study in the 1950s grew out of this storm-and-stress model and led to a construction of adolescence as a subculture sharply distinct from adult culture. Coleman characterized the "adolescent culture" as hedonistic and centered on issues of popularity with peers rather than on academic achievement. Coleman's view of adolescence as a separate culture still persists, but unlike other "cultures," adolescence is denied diversity. Current assumptions about adolescence appear to homogenize the experience. Most often, the historical, economic, social, and cultural complexities that shape the lives of adolescents disappear as we hold tightly to a singular, biological view of the "normal" adolescent, which includes the following assumptions: (1) adolescents sever ties with adults; (2) peer groups become increasingly influential social networks; (3) resistance is a sign of normalcy for the adolescent; and (4) romance and sexual drive govern interests and relations (Finders, 1997, p. 28).

We now understand that class, race, gender, and individual life circumstances influence how one comes of age in this country. In cross-cultural anthropological studies, for example, Schlegel and Barry (1991) note that in middle-class homes where child labor is not needed, adolescents of both sexes are likely to spend a good deal of time with same-age peers. But girls in working-class homes or in families of Hispanic, Middle Eastern, or Asian extraction may be expected to spend their after-school time at home, while boys may be with peers or at work outside the home (p. 43). Likewise, Comer (1993) argues for the necessity of maintaining close ties among children and adults during this period. Similarly, Fine and Macpherson (1993) criticize studies of adolescence because often they do not take into account marked differences in terms of race, class, gender, or sexual orientation. In Cynthia's class on ideology in adolescent fiction, it becomes clear to students that some texts inscribe a different sort of "implied adolescent." Works by African American female authors, for instance, often center on young women who thrive in the midst of strong relationships among generations of women rather than adolescents who seek independence from their families. While recent research problematizes many commonly held assumptions about adolescence (e.g., Feldman & Elliott, 1990; Lesko, 2001; Takanishi, 1993), many educators and adolescents themselves continue to operate with the assumptions of "implied adolescence" in mind.

Performing the "Implied Adolescent" through Digital Literacy

We turn now to an illustration of particular adolescents' identity performances through digital literacies, intending to illustrate how two girls who engage in this extracurricular literacy practice do so within the boundaries of "implied adolescence." This section, based on research that Cynthia conducted with Bettina Fabos, discusses the social practices surrounding the use of a particular digital literacy, instant messaging (IM), which is short for online, real-time communication with peers. In many ways, the girls' use of IM was regulated by their sense of what it means to be a teenage girl, and they performed this identity very much as though they had invented it. That is, they took up identity stances relative to the normative roles in which they were cast. Nonetheless, the IM format did allow the girls to assume alternative identities that resulted in some movement and recasting of gender positions. Our analysis is informed by Judith Butler's (1993) argument that gender norms are reiterated through performances of identity that are already inscribed.

[P]erformativity must be understood not as a singular or deliberative 'act,' but, rather, as the reiterative and citational practice by which discourse produces the effect that it names. (p. 2)

However, because this reiterative process is not infallible, "sex is both produced and destabilized in the course of this reiteration" (p. 10). Thus, Butler's argument allows that through the repeated performance of gender, norms might be transgressed or reconfigured.

In previous research on IM interactions, Lewis and Fabos (2000) focused on the girls' creative and sometimes transgressive uses of IM. These two best friends negotiated the technology on three levels: language use, social practice, and surveillance. On the level of language use, the girls manipulated the tone, voice, word choice, and subject matter of their messages, facilitating multiple narratives in the process. On the level of social practice, they negotiated patterns of communication through IM to enhance social relationships and social standings in school. And on the level of surveillance, the girls were able to monitor the IM landscape for their own benefit, combat excessive or unwanted messages, assume alternative identities, and overcome parental restrictions on their online communication.

We think it is important to note these creative uses of digital literacies, particularly from the perspective of observing how youth, as participants in this new digital culture, shape and transform the culture. The girls who participated in this study used literacy for their own social and political purposes, performing multiple identities moment to moment for multiple audiences (especially when engaged in the common practice of Instant Messaging many buddies at once, and, therefore, negotiating multiple windows). Moreover, the girls' use of IM calls into question the deficit view of online activities that Allan Luke critiques in that language choices were self-consciously connected to purpose and audience indicating the girls' rhetorical acumen in peer-driven exchanges.

Despite these creative, and somewhat transgressive, uses of digital literacy, what we want to illustrate here, to advance our argument that the characteristic identity markers associated with the "implied adolescent" are normative, is the way in which the identities the girls perform through IM are already written into the discourses associated with being an adolescent female. To do so, we'll refer to two girls, Sam and Karrie (both age 13) who were the two best friends referred to earlier. Sam was from a working-class family, but she and Karrie interacted with friends across social class boundaries, underscoring Gee's point that social class today is often defined in terms of "affiliations with certain sorts of people, objects, technologies, and practices." Karrie makes the point succinctly: "I wouldn't be as cool to some friends if I didn't talk on the Internet."

One example of a scripted performance of identity related to gender roles was Sam's manipulation of attention, which contradicted in interesting ways Lankshear's and Knobel's argument that "people withhold attention if they have no interest in the exchange." Whereas several adolescents in the larger study discussed strategies they used to withhold attention from IM buddies who hold little status, Sam strategically withheld attention from boys from another school whom she wanted to get to know, hoping that making them wait longer for a response would attest to her own popularity. She reasoned that withholding attention would lead others to believe she was too busy with her many IM buddies to respond quickly to these high-status boys. One can say that in this case Sam was using the technology with rhetorical sophistication, allowing her to craft a desired identity. Another way to analyze this scenario, however, is to suggest that Sam performed an identity that was already scripted for her by her age and gender. She was cast in the role of "implied adolescent" female, and although she managed to wield some power in this role by withholding attention, she nonetheless enacts the norms expected of adolescent girls—attempting to impress boys and appear popular.

The girls do, indeed, try on other identities when they are online, but the identities they try on are, again, already scripted within normative gender constraints. Sam, for instance, "pretended" on occasion that she was "blond-haired, blue-eyed" because she believed having these particular media markers of beauty would extend conversations with boys she didn't know. As with the previous example, it is possible to view Sam as claiming power. Given a social sphere that excludes the body, she inserts one that will work for her. However, the fact that she does resort to traditional markers of white feminine beauty in the rare social sphere where it need not be central shows that normative gender and race positions are not so easily erased even in a space that is sometimes hailed as a new form of social existence (Jones, 1997) and multiple identities (Turkle, 1995).

Karrie also tried on alternative gender identities, playing the role of a male during occasional forays out of IM and into chat rooms. Her goal was to track her boyfriend into a chat room by assuming the "male" identity of "snowboarder911" because "that's sort of a typical kind of guy screen name," and try to find out what kind of conversations he was having. Since the physical body is not present in Internet interaction, Sam and Karrie did, indeed, have more space for play, parody, and performances that destabilized normative gender roles and gave the girls some control over their gendered positions. Yet, the girls clearly did not use online communication in ways that broke down gendered frames of reference.

The girls wanted to pose in ways that would increase their status as females. With Sam's help, Karrie was able to crack the block her parents had placed on her user profile so that she could include more information about her appearance and make herself sound more interesting and appealing to boys. On the other hand, when Sam and Karrie chose to enter chat rooms that were not age-specific, they made their user profiles more sketchy and lied about their age so as to pursue "adult" conversations with older people. This way, the girls felt they could control the rhetorical contexts of their interactions through careful consideration of issues related to status, age, and gender. These moves were very strategic, as is clear in Sam's comments:

> See if you tell someone you're 18, you sort of have to prepare ahead of time, 'cause they're going to ask what college you go to, what classes you take . . .

Despite this element of control, media attention to the dangers of Internet communication had convinced the girls that their parents had reasonable fears about the Internet and were right to block their access to chat rooms. (Karrie: "We've heard stories about kids where kids can get killed.") Indeed, Sam and Karrie's posing related to gender and age shows that the social and power relations that exist outside the Internet inhere within as well. As Butler suggests, those structures are at once solidified and destabilized in the repeated performances of everyday interaction.

New Literacies in Teacher Education: On Becoming the "Implied Teacher"

In order for adolescents like Sam and Karrie to begin to examine the social and power relations that implicate them, approaches that call for an expanded definition of literacy, which includes the ability to read and critique a wide range of media texts, are essential (Moje, Young, Readence, & Moore, 2000). If we are to support critical media literacy, we must prepare beginning teachers for such tasks. Carmen Luke (2000) notes, "What better site to begin developing new frameworks for knowledge and critical literacy than in teacher education?" (p. 425). What better site, we ask, than a high school English methods course in a conservative English Department in the rural Midwest? Margaret's English methods class provided just such a site.

While the parameters of the literacy program at Margaret's institution didn't allow for a full course in media and cultural studies, she set out to introduce pre-service teachers to the concept of multiliteracies and popular culture by selecting the text *Popular Culture in the Classroom: Teaching and Researching Critical Media Literacy* (Alvermann, Moon, & Hagood, 1999) as one of the required readings for the course. English education students at Margaret's institution come to this course with a fairly traditional literature background. Students in this program for the most part match the portrait of the typical student enrolled in teacher education:

> She is White and from a suburban or rural home town; monolingual in English; and selected her college for its proximity to home, its affordability and its accessibility. She has traveled little beyond her college's 100 mile or less radius from her home and prefers to teach in a community like the one in which she grew up. She hopes to teach middle-income, average (not handicapped nor gifted) children in traditional classroom settings. (Gomez, 1996, p. 112)

Carmen Luke (2000b) notes that those pre-service teachers growing up in a highly technological society may be more receptive to multimedia and multiliteracy approaches to teaching and learning. However, this characterization was contradicted by Margaret's students' resistance to taking new media and digital literacies into their classrooms. While all of these students were between the ages of 21–24 and most were quite savvy with technology and media, they were resistant to sharing what they considered to be their own "private pleasures." Perhaps this can best be understood in terms of the "implied adolescents" they have been and the "implied teachers" they are becoming. In discussing this study, we attempt to illustrate how pre-service teachers embraced the role of the implied teacher. In many ways their struggles with digital literacies were actually struggles with their sense of who they should be as teachers. In other words, their views of the implied teacher prevented them from fully realizing any potential that their own connection to new media may bring to the literacy classroom. Digital technologies did not allow this particular group of future teachers to assume alternative identities that may have resulted in some movement and recasting of their teaching positions. Instead, they clung tightly to their fledgling identities as "teachers," with all that the term implies. Just past adolescence themselves, these pre-service teachers thought of adolescence as a linear life stage that regulated their sense of what it means to be a teacher of adolescents.

Students enrolled in this course were able to examine their views, locate their pleasures, and begin to examine the ways in which social and economic ideologies may have shaped their interactions with particular forms of popular culture. For example, the pre-service teachers brought in CD covers, attempting to analyze how CD jackets get read from multiple perspectives. In attempting to understand the corporate construction of adolescent culture through the production and distribution of CDs, they examined naturalized conceptions of adolescence as a biological life stage. The students reflected on the pleasures people derive from various media forms and texts in an attempt to move toward an analysis of the politics of location. Margaret's aim was to provide students with the critical analytic tools to understand reader and viewer diversity of reading positions and the sociocultural locations that influence preferences.

During those class periods when the pre-service teachers felt freed from the role of "implied teacher," the conversations were animated and lively. Students laughed and shared and were able to read through and between the lines of the jackets. Ray was a class leader for the first time: For the first nine weeks of the semester, he had sat in the back of the room, often with his head down, never appearing to be engaged. However, when Margaret asked students to bring their favorite CDs to class, he volunteered to bring in his own CD player to ensure "better sound." He asked if there would be any "rules" about what lyrics would be considered out of bounds. After Margaret assured him that there were no such rules in their university classroom, he immediately began his list of what he would bring to class. During that next class period, Ray offered some of his collection to anyone who hadn't "remembered." And as you might guess, he volunteered to be first in leading a discussion of his CD selection. Another student asked if her country music would be booed out of the room before sharing the ways in which this music gave her pleasure. While the music shifted from country to techno to big bands, the class seemed to come together over their lively talk about how music fit into their lives and influenced their views of how to "be" an adolescent. They recognized that they may well have been positioned as a certain kind of target market, but as one student suggested, "When I was in high school, I didn't really care if they were trying to SELL me more than the CD. It's just a way to get into the whole image thing. I wanted to be part of the techno thing." Sure, there were groans and hoots over perceptions of "bad choices" but the atmosphere that day seemed filled with pleasure, respect, and the beginning of trying to understand how one's readings might be constructed by different audiences for different purposes. Ray, in his first attempts to examine notions of pleasure production, noted,

> I guess I always take a boys will be boys view. My music is probably what you might consider very masculine. How do I use it to construct my own notions of masculinity? I have no idea. It is just what I like. But I don't think that just because I watch AND LIKE videos of women in bondage that that makes me some kind of a chauvinist or pervert or something. But there is something that makes women in bondage pleasurable. And that's sort of creepy. And I have never thought about before. Do I need to look at how such images work on me? I guess so. I'm not saying that I think such images will lead to violence, but I guess I do need to think about why I am so comfortable with it. It's really the beat and not the video, I think.

All the while, there remained a sense of tameness to these discussions. The pre-service teachers readily selected CDs over other digital forms, perhaps because CDs are still perceived as "safer" or more appropriate for classroom discussions. While these pre-service teachers may have actually been much savvier than discussions revealed, the perception of a "generation gap" that exists between teacher and student (between classroom and living room) may have compelled them to hold to particular performances in a university classroom.

While pre-service teachers had worked with Margaret in previous teacher education courses and for the most part had established good working relationships, pre-service teachers may have sensed that this was uncharted territory for Margaret as well. Margaret came to this classroom with years of experience as a teacher educator, a repertoire of pedagogical approaches, and an interest in bringing popular culture into the classroom, but she was indeed a neophyte in terms of working with digital literacies. Yet, for Margaret and the pre-service teachers, interest and engagement with the content was highly animated. They were willing to speculate on how corporate culture shaped views of pleasure, on how they had embraced particular music lyrics and images to influence their adolescent identities.

However, when Margaret nudged the conversations to how these pre-service teachers' high school students might read such texts, conversations became less open, less speculative, more rigid, and more authoritative. Readings suddenly tended to be corrected. Laughter ceased and the pre-service teachers began to take up an authoritative discourse that may be all too familiar. They had willingly wrestled with multiple meanings during their own class discussions, but when asked to consider how a similar conversation might play out in a high school classroom, the students' tone changed. "Just another politically correct move," one said. Another argued, "They'll probably know more than me, I need to be in charge." Yet another insisted, "Parents won't like it."

In short, when pre-service teachers were cast as students of critical media studies, they found the cultural work valuable and engaging, but when they were asked to consider critical media studies from the perspective of a teacher, they found the work filled with controversies, inaccessible, and for the most part inappropriate. Attempts to shift the conversations into the middle or high school context were met with resistance: This material seemed "off limits." "I got my buddies and I've got my students. And I don't think I should mix the two," Ray explained. They saw themselves as holders of knowledge, the gatekeepers who control the "uncivil, unruly technosubject" (Luke & Luke, 2001, p. 8). Their conversations about teaching made it clear that they operated within the constraints of the "implied teacher" as regulator of the "implied adolescent," despite their own identifications with the pleasures commonly associated with adolescence.

In spite of their resistance, Margaret's students all complied with her directives to infuse media literacies into their literacy lessons. So what did their attempts look like? Where there was any attention to popular culture at all, it was in the form of teaching students to understand how media manipulate audiences, situating the teachers as liberatory guides and students as dupes. But for the most part CDs, Internet sites, and video clips were just more textual objects to be analyzed in a traditional literary manner. In fact, these lessons appeared to be much more traditional, closed to negotiations, and teacher-centered than those related to literary texts. Ray, who had been so vocal about his own musical pleasures and personal resistance to analyzing these pleasures, wrote the following:

> Use pop culture (specifically music) to define literary terms. My role as a teacher will be to determine the appropriateness of materials. I will choose the music shown for the most part. The students will be able to choose their own music to do outside projects. This gives them choice and choice is good. The unit will show students that some pop culture has merit and is valuable in the classroom. Students will learn definitions and real world applications for literary devices such as allusion, personification, connotation, denotation and various poetic terms.

Others in the course explained that they would tap digital literacies to "reproduce the different elements of narratives," "gain knowledge of different writing styles by examining popular culture," and "learn how to examine the credibility of the author." They envisioned using media in an attempt to make great literary works more accessible. For example, one wrote, "By using the *Raiders of the Lost Ark*, *Beowulf* will become more accessible to my students."

While many scholars warn that adolescents may resist teachers' attempts to have them talk about music, films, computer games, and other forms of popular culture in a school setting, these future teachers (just barely past adolescence themselves) were resistant to sharing their own pleasures in a school setting. They felt a need to create firm boundaries between their private pleasure and their professional authority as the "implied teacher" of their imaginations. One undergraduate said, "I want them to see me as their teacher, not just another kid." Another reported, "We shouldn't share our music because then it will make us seem too young. Too much like them. Not like teachers."

"Not like teachers" can perhaps best be understood as not like the implied teacher they were attempting to replicate. They spoke of their direct need as young teachers to widen, not bridge, the experiential and knowledge gap between themselves and their students. To widen the gap, they needed either to declare popular culture off limits or to force fit it into the traditional paradigm of English education. They felt compelled to take up the discourse of teaching with which they were most familiar. In Butler's terms, their teaching identities were already inscribed materially, reiterated through the discourses of schooling and teacher education as well as in the disciplining of their own bodies as students.

Asked to try on the role of teachers, they repeated the performances they knew. Asked to reflect, in journals, on their reasons for doing so, they resorted to the discourses of "implied adolescence" and "implied teacher" that would widen the generation gap that their own youth and interests narrowed. Taking up the position of the implied teacher, pre-service teachers in Margaret's class were primarily concerned with control, authority, and maintaining firm boundaries between their lives and their students. The implied teacher came already equipped with a normalizing discourse that served to regulate adolescent behavior. In their professional journals they wrote such things as "Kids can get way out of control," "You gotta keep 'em in line," and "I tried it and it didn't work. Kids get out of control." Embedded in the "implied teacher" is a need to be the expert. They feared, as one expressed, "Kids will know more than I do." Their pleasures with popular culture created roadblocks, not avenues. They didn't want to blur the boundaries between their own pleasures and their professional work: "My interests are none of their business."

Caught at the border between teacher and adolescent, young pre-service teachers struggle with knowledge, access, and authority. Boundaries between their teaching selves and their student selves, between their own private pleasures and their professional work, cause students to solidify the borders. Layered on to this struggle, pre-service teachers are faced with a struggle for what will count as official knowledge and competence in the world of school. The linear view of age development as an orderly progression to the more rational and authoritative state of mind creates a generation gap even for young "new media" teachers.

Ambivalent Identities across Social Spaces: Teaching Adolescents in New Times

Common sense suggests that those entering the teaching profession today nearer in age to their students and growing up with music videos, VCRs, and the Internet will perhaps be more receptive to new media and digital culture in their approaches to teaching and learning. Such views do not take into account the generation gap that is built into our conceptions of adolescence. This generation gap is constituted in policies and practices aimed to separate students and teachers: adult/child, civilized/savage, and productive/unproductive. Pre-service teachers seem to be caught at one historic moment between past youth and future teacher, the "implied adolescent" and the "implied teacher." Further complicating this generation gap is the fact that both the adolescents and their young teachers perform identities across social and institutional spaces that are shaped by conceptions of "implied adolescence."

Young people like Sam and Karrie write themselves, figuratively and literally—through digital literacy—within the bounds of the "normal" adolescent, seeking heterosexual affirmation, experimenting with identities that, while slightly transgressive, ultimately conform to normative gender categories. These digital literacies, although not yet part of their school's curriculum, do cross over into the social and institutional space of school. Online conversations are reported and discussed at school and, as Karrie pointed out, using IM is part of what it takes to be cool.

Like Sam and Karrie with their IM buddies, Ray, the pre-service teacher in Margaret's class, was attempting to cross over into a new social and institutional space of school, this time as a beginning teacher. He understood the terrain as two distinct spaces: "I got my buddies and I've got my students. And I don't think I should mix the two." What might happen when beginning teachers like Ray enter their classrooms filled with savvy adolescents like Sam and Karrie? Some educators see this as a hopeful time, a shrinking of the great divide between teachers now more media savvy and the new media adolescents they teach. However, if they accept the implied positions they are expected to occupy in a school space, Ray, Karrie, and Sam may enact the school's ideology, compliant in their relationships to knowledge, access, authority, and each other. Such ideologies circumscribe the performance of adolescent and teacher identities within a school culture. Left unexamined, these performances of "implied adolescents" and "implied teacher" may change little.

James Gee describes "enactive texts" as texts written by powerful people who in their very telling make such texts true. Notions of "the implied adolescent" and "the implied teacher" might be considered enactive texts, taken as true. We argue that one must understand something about the ways in which such identities relate to new literacies and adolescent learners. As we have shown, there are discourses and material conditions in place that compel adolescents and new teachers to perform these identities. Nonetheless, identities are not fixed. Considering identity to be "socially-situated" (Gee, 1999a, p. 13) allows for a way out of the quandary. Stuart Hall's (2000) description of identity is instructive here:

> [Identity] is situational—it shifts from context to context. The identity passionately espoused in one public scenario is more ambiguously and ambivalently "lived" in private. Its contradictions are negotiated, not "resolved." (p. xi)

Pre-service teachers often refer to their ambiguously lived identities when they enter classrooms as teachers, and they discuss as well the ambivalence, or downright discomfort, they feel about their teaching identities when they return to their social worlds outside the classroom. We know, of course, that many adolescents experience similar dissonant identities as they cross social spaces. Yet since new media and technology have begun to blur the social and institutional spaces in which adolescents and their teachers perform their identities, a new discursive space is possible—one where hybrid discourses enable students and teachers to borrow from the culture of classrooms as well as from youth culture, thus using linguistic constructions, textual designs, and interpretive norms appropriate to both spheres. Perhaps what is required of all of us—educators, researchers, and students alike—is to develop a bit more comfort with the ambiguous nature of identity so that more dynamic and multivoiced versions of what it means to be an adolescent and a teacher can flourish, "negotiated but not resolved."

QUESTIONS TO CONSIDER

1. What do the authors mean by the terms "implied adolescents" and "implied teachers"? What are some of the consequences of those constructions of youth culture and education, especially in the realm of digital literacy and technology?

2. In what ways does the wider use of technology de-privilege the role of the teacher? Give examples.

3. How can digital literacy influence gender identity In adolescence? Give reasons and examples.

4. The authors show that pre-service teacher education candidates as "critical media students" and as "actual teachers" can entertain different attitudes toward cultural controversies. Why is that the case? Explain your response.

5. How does Gee define "enactive texts"? How are they used in classroom practice? How might they be re-negotiated in the new world of technology and teaching? Give examples.

Note

This chapter originally appeared in Donna E. Alvermann (ed.), *Adolescents and Literacies in a Digital World* (New York: Peter Lang, 2002).

References

Alvermann, D. E., Moon, J. S., & Hagood, M.C. (1999). *Popular culture in the classroom: Teaching and researching critical media literacy.* Newark, DE: International Reading Association.

Brooks-Gunn, J., & Reiter, E. O. (1990). The role of pubertal processes. In S. S. Feldman & G. R. Elliott (Eds.), *At the threshold: The developing adolescent* (pp. 16–53). Cambridge: Harvard University Press.

Butler, J. (1993). *Bodies that matter*. New York: Routledge.

Coleman, J. S. (1961). *The adolescent society*. New York: Free Press.

Comer, J. P. (1993). The potential effects of community organizations on the future of our youth. In R. Takanishi (Ed.), *Adolescence in the 1990s* (pp. 203–206). New York: Teachers College Press.

Feldman, S., & Elliott, G. (1990). *At the threshold: The developing adolescent*. Cambridge: Harvard University Press.

Fine, M., Macpherson, K. (1993). Over dinner: Feminism and adolescent female bodies. In S. Biklen & D. Pollard (Eds.), *Gender and education: Ninety-second yearbook of the National Society for the Study of Education* (pp. 126–154). Chicago: University of Chicago Press.

Gee, J. P. (1999a). *An introduction to discourse analysis: Theory and method*. New York: Routledge.

Gomez, M. L. (1996). Prospective teachers' perspectives on teaching "other people's children." In K. Zeichner (Ed.), *Currents of reform in preservice teacher education*. New York: Teachers College Press.

Hall, S. (2000). Foreword. In D. A. Yon, *Elusive culture: Schooling, race, and identity in global times*. Albany: State University of New York Press.

Iser, W. (1978). *The act of reading: A theory of aesthetic response*. Baltimore: Johns Hopkins University Press.

Klein, H. (1990). Adolescence, youth and young adulthood: Rethinking current conceptualizations of life stage. *Youth and Society*, 21, 446–471.

Lesko, N. (1996). Past, present, and future conceptions of adolescence. *Educational Theory*, 46, 453–472.

Lewis, C., & Fabos, B. (2000). But will it work in the heartland? A response to new multiliteracies. *Journal of Adolescent & Adult Literacy*, 43, 462–469.

Luke, A., & Luke, C. (2001). Adolescence lost/childhood regained: On early intervention and the emergence of the techno-subject. *Journal of Early Childhood Literacy*, 1(2), 91–120.

Luke, C. (2000a). Cyber-schooling and technological change: Multiliteracies for new times. In B. Cope & M. Kalantzis (Eds.), *Multiliteracies: Literacy learning and the design of social futures* (pp. 69–91). Melbourne: Macmillan.

Luke, C. (2000b). New literacies in teacher education. Journal of Adolescent & Adult Literacy, 43, 424–435.

McCallum, R. (1999). *Ideologies of identity in adolescent fiction: The dialogic construction of subjectivity*. New York: Garland.

Moje, E. B., Young, J. P., Readence, J. E, & Moore, D. W. (2000). Reinventing adolescent literacy for new times: Perennial and millennial issues. *Journal of Adolescent & Adult Literacy*, 43, 398–410.

Nodelman, P. (1996). *The pleasures of children's literature* (2nd ed.) New York: Longman.

Palladino, G. (1996). *Teenagers: An American history. New York: Basic Books*.

Santrock, J. W. (1993). *Adolescence*. Dubuque, IA: Wm. C. Brown.

Schlegel, A., & Barry, H. III. (1991). *Adolescence: An anthropological inquiry*. New York: Free Press.

Takanishi, R. (1993). Changing views of adolescence in contemporary society. In R. Takanishi (Ed.), *Adolescence in the 1990s* (pp. 1–7). New York: Teachers College Press.

Turkle, S. (1995). *Life on the screen: Identity in the age of the Internet*. New York: Simon and Schuster.

CHAPTER SIXTEEN

Adolescent Engagement, Connectedness and *Dropping Out* of School

JOHN SMYTH

Introduction

The "old ways" of thinking and acting in respect of what is euphemistically (although quite misleadingly) labeled for shorthand reasons, "dropping out" of school, are clearly not working. Across almost all western countries at the moment the issue of young people, disconnecting, disengaging, opting out, drifting off, being excluded or pushed out of school, is becoming worse rather than better. We clearly need "new ways" of conceiving of, thinking about, and acting on this issue from a radically different point than the one we have been using up until now. How we frame problems and how we problematize them has a large effect on how we devise policies or solutions, and in respect of young people and the institution of schooling, herein lies a major part of the problem. Who or what gets to be labeled as the problem, and as a consequence, who or what is included as part of the solution, is not without profound consequences.

It hardly comes as a new revelation to say that adults have historically, or at least in recent times, regarded it their responsibility to nurture, enculturate, and educate the young, and as the period of formal schooling has been extended, so too has the length of the custodial period. Herein lies the rub—young people are maturing at a faster rate and at an earlier age than at any point in history, and they are taking on roles and responsibilities in the economy and their social behavior (some of them risk aversive like substance abuse and sexual activity), at the same time as social institutions like schools seem to be failing to keep pace with this kind of development.

Against this backdrop, this chapter seeks to pose and to worry some fundamental orienting questions, like (but not necessarily limited to or in this order):

- why are young people switching off school?
- why is school not working for increasing numbers of them?

- are some young people more susceptible to this phenomenon than others ?
- who is most affected by this apparent disconnect?
- what are the multiple dimensions of the problem?
- whose problem is this anyway?
- what are the challenges for schools in particular?
- why are old ways of thinking inadequate?
- what are the alternatives?
- what are the consequences of not acting differently?

To put it another way, what we need is some "re-framing" of the issue.

Shifting the Perspective

Dropping out is regarded by and large as a kind of youthful act of caring for the self, in the sense that young people construct their own identities without seeing school playing an active role in the construction of these identities. The essence of this behavior is captured in the archetypical young person's explanation for early school leaving: "I got a life!" The notion of getting a life (Holden, 1992) is presented as a kind of exercise in consumer sovereignty around the perceived irrelevance of the institution of schooling to young lives. In this respect, what is occurring is the individualization of education as an act of personal choice—replete with all of the consequences of risk, economic and otherwise, that accompany such pathway choices. As long as dropping out continues to be construed in these individually preferential ways, then it becomes difficult (if not impossible) from a policy point of view to advance a more sociological view of education as a public good that benefits the whole of society, not just a private benefit to those who are smart enough or who make wise choices. When conceived as an individual responsibility, dropping out is constructed as a discourse around maladaptive or aberrant young people who, either by dint of personal or group identity, are unwilling, incapable, or unable to take advantage of the cultural capital on offer by schools.

Elsewhere (Smyth & Hattam, 2004; Smyth, Hattam, Cannon, Edwards, Wilson, & Wurst, 2000) I have argued that the contemporary complexity and multi-dimensionality of young people's lives require that we analyze early school leaving in other than deficit-focused ways that blame young people. It no longer makes any policy sense to continue to focus on issues of personal responsibility and failure, when what is occurring is a failure of institutions to meet the needs, aspirations, hopes, and desires of young people. My argument, invoking Fine (1994) is that early school leaving is socially constructed—that is to say it is produced, sustained, and maintained by institutions, systems and cultures that stereotype young people as being a social problem in the minds of the general public. The effect of this is to banish many school leavers to the margins of society, from whence "they cohere momentarily around deficiencies, around who they are not" in ways in which they are "represented as unworthy, and immoral, or pitiable, victimized, and damaged" (Fine, 1994, p. 74).

MacPherson and Fine (1995) explain that we read the word and the world "through a set of assumptions, socially shared and often unconscious, that frame knowledge and our relationships to it" (p. 185). When applied to early school leaving, as Wyn, Stokes, Tyler (2004) note, what gets to be perpetuated as a result is the view that "it is the young person who is responsible for their plight rather than systemic or cultural influences. In other words, it is the young person who is in deficit, not the system" (p. 10). The effect then, of what is being constructed here are "moral boundaries of deservingness that thread research and policy, enabling researchers, policy makers, and the public to believe that we can distinguish (and serve) those who are 'deserving' and neglect honorably those who are 'undeserving' and poor" (Fine, 1994, p. 74).

We need to pursue this theoretical distinction a little further, because it is crucial in explaining what really occurs when young people terminate their schooling or drop out. When early school leaving is presented as if it were the result of individual deficits residing in young people themselves, then what gets masked or obscured are the workings of structural and institutional power—for example, when the values of the school are out of synch with the class, ethnic, or racial background of students and their families.

When categories like dropping out are portrayed in a partial way as if they were entirely brought on by the unmediated actions of young people, then the result is an entrapped way of thinking on the part of young people and society more generally. C. Wright Mills (1959/1974) argues that when people become induced or habituated into thinking and feeling "that their private lives are a series of traps," they have fallen into through actions of their own making, then they have diminished agency and feel even more trapped (p. 9). What he is saying is that we seldom define the troubles we endure in terms of "historical change and institutional contradictions" (p. 10). If this is the case, then we need to interrupt this shrouded and concealed way of thinking so as to reveal the patterns and interconnections embedded in what is really going on. It is not that we need more information, nor on their own, better skills of analysis, but rather as Mills argues, we need a "quality of mind that will help [us] use information and to develop reason in order to achieve lucid summations of what is going on in the world . . ." (p. 11). What we need is a way of interrupting introverted ways of thinking, with what Mills famously labeled "a sociological imagination."

What is significant about Mills's thesis for my present purpose is the crucial analytical and practical distinction he makes between "personal troubles" or private matters, and "public issues" that transcend local circumstances and that focus instead on social structures. The difficulty, Mills argues, is that "an issue often involves a crisis in institutional arrangements" (p. 15), which is to say, that it can be difficult to define and even more difficult to solve. In contrast, personal troubles are attributable to individuals as "biographical entities," and to that extent, the articulation of what is going on and "the resolution of troubles properly lies within the individual" (p. 15). Where the difficulty arises is in the mis-labeling of a public issue as a personal trouble. Mills gives the example of when a single person in a city is unemployed, then this is a personal trouble "and for its relief we properly look to the character of the man, his skills and his immediate opportunities" (p. 15). However, when unemployment occurs on a widespread, protracted, and exacerbated scale, then both the construction of the problem and the possibility of its solution lie beyond "the personal situation and character of a scatter of individuals"; rather, it may be that "the very structure of opportunities has collapsed" (p. 15).

The slide from the former to the latter is incredibly easy to do in a policy sense, and when it occurs, it leaves behind devastating consequences. The requirement to look in more complex ways at the workings of social and institutional structures, how they are organized, and for whose benefit they are organized the way they are is let entirely off the hook. Fine (1989) refers to this situation as "seeking private solutions to public problems" (p. 169) and likens it to the public sphere in effect packing up and walking away from its designated constitutional responsibility (Weis & Fine, 2001, p. 499). The substantive point is:

> The life of an individual cannot be adequately understood without references to the institutions within which his biography is enacted . . . To understand the biography of an individual, we must understand the significance and meaning of the roles he has played and does play; to understand these roles we must understand the institutions of which they are a part. (C. Wright Mills, 1959/1971, pp. 178–179).

Early School Leaving as a "Wicked Issue"

A "wicked problem" (Rittel & Webber, 1973) is not amenable to an easy definition or readily tamed in the sense of available workable solutions. Wicked problems are difficult to conceptualize, complicated, ambiguous, contradictory, intractable, unstable, and require quite idiosyncratic treatment. They are sometimes simply referred to as "social messes" (Horn & Weber, 2007). The Australian Public Service Commissioner (2007) summarized the features of "wicked problems" as being: "difficult to define . . . have many interdependencies [that] are often multi-causal . . . often lead to unforeseen consequences . . . not stable . . . have no clear solutions . . . are socially complex . . . hardly ever sit conveniently within the responsibility of any one organization . . . [and] involve changing behavior" (pp. 3–5).

The phenomenon labeled "dropping out" of school certainly fits the category of being a "wicked problem." While the label might have widespread and common parlance, it is ultimately a pejorative term that locates the problem squarely within the personages of young people—and to that extent, it may be unhelpful (even damaging) in framing up ways of analyzing what is occurring when young people leave school. It may even be a serious impediment in finding ways of better managing the issue. It is a bit like the phrase "disaffected youth" (Piper & Piper, 1998, p. 32), which is highly suggestive of an unwarranted portrayal of some kind of residualized, seething underclass, who are feral, indolent and hell bent on trouble-making.

A sense of the ambiguity and lack of clarity surrounding the issue is well captured in the titles of a small sample of some of the major research works on early school leaving: *Were They Pushed or Did They Jump? Individual Decision Mechanisms in Education* (Gambetta, 1987); *Culture, Politics, and Irish School Dropouts: Constructing Political Identities* (Fagan, 1995); *Last Chance High: How Girls and Boys Drop in and Out of Alternative Schools* (Kelly, 1995); *Debating Dropouts: Critical Policy and Research Perspectives on Leaving School* (Kelly & Gaskell, 1996); *Reconstructing 'Dropout': A Critical Ethnography of Black Students' Disengagement from School* (Dei, Mazzuca, McIsaac, & Zine, 1997); *Creating the Dropout: An Institutional and Social History of School Failure* (Dorn, 1996); *Subtractive Schooling: U. S.-Mexican Youth and the Politics of Caring* (Valenzuela, 1999); *Becoming Somebody: Toward a Social Psychology of School* (Wexler, 1992); *'Dropping Out,' Drifting Off, Being Excluded: Becoming Somebody Without School* (Smyth & Hattam, 2004).

Fine's (1991) *Framing Dropouts: Notes on the Politics of an Urban High School* is particularly informative of the complexity and contradictory nature of the problem. Fine admitted that too often, in the literatures the "image of the hopeless and helpless loser prevailed" (p. 4). In the absence of any other portrayals, it is not difficult to take Fine's category of "framing dropouts" to mean "a frame-up" in the sense of "a conspiracy to incriminate" (Smyth & Hattam, 2004, p. 14). What Fine (1991) does is draw attention to the way "dropouts" are often stereotypically represented as "depressed, helpless, and even without options . . . as losers" (pp. 4–5). She admits to asking herself the question" who is served by this seamless rhetoric of dropouts as losers?" (p. 5). If there is an unreasonable or unwarranted portrayal of individual inferiority here, "then the structures, ideologies and practices that exile them systematically are rendered invisible, and the critique [these young people] voice is institutionally silenced" (p. 5). Her study of a South Bronx high school caused Fine to conclude: "My naïve notions of what constituted a dropout and what made for educational persistence were uncomfortably disrupted" (p. 4. If we take the notion of wicked problems as a category or a lens, then it is appropriate to ask: in what sense is early school leaving an exemplar? Rittel & Webber (1973) explain that they use the term *wicked* as a label to distinguish it from problems that are *tame* or *benign*—ones that are usually tackled by scientists, mathematicians, or engineers in respect of which "the mission is clear [and] it is clear, in turn, whether or not the problems have been solved" (p. 160). By contrast, wicked problems are "malignant," "vicious," "tricky," or "aggressive" in that they are difficult to define and even more elusive in how, when, and by what means they might be resolved. Questions might include:

- When does early school leaving occur?
- What are its causes or contributing factors?
- What are its effects or consequences and on whom? (young people; peers; the school; neighborhoods; communities; society?)
- What treatments might be used to arrest it?
- Are some groups/individuals more vulnerable than others?
- How will we know if measures have been successful?

When Does Early School Leaving Occur?

Early school leaving is a process rather than an event, and it has a genesis that reaches a considerable way back into a young person's life, often to the early stages of primary or elementary schooling. Sometimes the process climaxes or culminates when a young person formally severs all connections with school. Conversely, it may more likely take the form of a young person gradually become disenchanted with school, slowly detaching himself or herself from school (or doing so only partially), and switching off, and gradually drifting off or fading away—in which case there is no cataclysmic or defining event.

This is what makes the issue of early school leaving so tricky—it is often hard to pinpoint the moment of leaving with any precision. It can be over an extended period of time, and possibly can only be definitely ascertained by looking backwards and seeing it with the clarity of hindsight—in which case it is impossible to treat the problem.

For example, it is possible for a young person to be physically in attendance at school while being in the throes of becoming disconnected. For all intent and purposes some students can be present but effectively switched off schooling and learning because there is little or no psychological or intellectual investment being made. To use an acronym, they are a RHINO—really here in name only! These young people can be attending school because it is a socially amenable place to be with friends, and in some instances a place that is safer than home or being on the streets. Minimal learning is occurring.

What Factors Contribute to Early School Leaving?

Offering general answers to this question is difficult because there are almost as many contributing factors as there are young people who fall within the category of early school leavers. It may make more sense to speak as we do (Smyth & Hattam, 2004) of "interferences" (Shor, 1980, p. 48) to completing schooling, which can include personal factors, but more importantly, systematic, structural, institutional, and ideological aspects as well. The latter reasons go beyond "personal problems" or "isolated pedagogical ones" to embrace interferences that are "social and pervasive" (p. 48). These issues need to be exposed in order to fully understand how and why young people become early school leavers. It makes more sense to talk about interferences than causes of non-completion.

The way to understanding school leaving is through the metaphor of young people "navigating a transition" (Smyth & Hattam, 2004, p. 37) to adulthood, or the process of "doing identity work" (Snow & Anderson, 1987). From this vantage point, young people are engaged as active players in a process of making choices, taking "consciously chosen action," and attempting to make sense of themselves and their contexts, as best they can, under "external constraints" (White & Wyn, 1998, p. 315) not of their own choosing. McLeod and Yates (2006) refer to this as the "making of the self" (p. 37), and it is multi-faceted, dynamic, relational, and neither simple nor unitary, embracing how "young people see themselves" (p. 37) as well as the full extent of "influences, practices, experiences and relations that combine to produce a young person" (p. 38). Identity is "fluid and multi-dimensional" (Wyn, 2009, p. 74).

As I have argued (Smyth & Hattam, 2004), interferences operate at the personal as well as the institutional and ideological levels, and a good example of this is how *power relations* operate to undermine school completion. Illustrative of this dynamic is how the "media saturated culture" in which young people live, provides "resources for identity formation" (p. 74). As we found in our research, for some young people, schooling simply "cannot compete with what media culture has to offer" (p. 75).

At a more personal level, power relations are played out on a daily basis in classrooms as young people contest authoritarian and autocratic relationships which they see as being out of kilter with contemporary life. This process of contestation and "speaking back" in the quest for a more democratic space, often leads to situations in which the burden of undemocratic school cultures is often borne by the students. The social conditions in many classrooms is such that the culture of fear acts to silence some students who respond by switching off, tuning out, and not learning. For others, the quest for voice and the attempt to alter power inequalities leads them into verbal and physical altercations and actions that amount to "running amuck" (p. 79) that amount to a stand-off between "uncooperative students and unyielding authorities" (p. 80) ending up with school policies being invoked in ways that propel these young people out of school. Behavioral confrontation can often combine with the emotional vulnerability that accompanies thoughts about suicide. Disciplinary strategies targeted at substance abusers in schools can often be used as a way of getting rid of "trouble makers"—suspension, stigmatization, and the difficulty of coping with catching up upon return to school, can often be enough to tip the balance for some young people who refuse to fit the norm of the conventional compliant student.

It is hard not to overstate the importance of friendships in the process of identity formation and how crucial the negotiation of relationships are in decisions to remain in school or to leave. Relationships with friends, for many young people, is the single most important reason for attending school. When relationships fail, or are not established for whatever reason, or alternative social spaces are not nurtured, then this can profoundly influence decisions to leave. A shorthand way of putting it is that "feelings matter." This concept can encompass a range of social and emotional ties including forms of harassment. Relationships and whether or not young people can effectively negotiate relationship troubles with one another are crucial elements in forming an attitude to school that is robust enough to ensure they remain there. An inability to form strong social ties or getting in with the "wrong company" can often mean doing hard emotional labor that runs counter to the kind of academic identity which is necessary, at least to some degree, in making school a viable option.

Economic independence looms large in the "self-making process" (Luttrell, 1996) of all young people. Some are able to defer gratification; others buy into it in a partial way through part-time employment, while for others paid employment is not an option in the survival of themselves and their families. In all cases young people have to read off in some way the rhetoric of what the school has to offer that will enable them to navigate a transition to economic independence. For those unwilling to buy the rhetoric that schooling will provide them with a passport to the labor market, or for those unwilling to delay the transition—in a word, for them, "school sucks!" (Smyth & Hattam, 2004, p. 93). They regard school as a "waste of time" and as having little of value to offer them. Schools can exacerbate this situation when they have unhelpful or poor strategies to enable such young people to make timely transitions into the labor market. For many, continuation with schooling gets in the way of their prospect of securing a job and they remain unconvinced of the rhetoric about a school credential providing them with economic security.

What we have been dealing with briefly so far are some of the personal interferences that make schooling unsustainable, particularly for young people from backgrounds that comprise cultural capital that are inconsistent with the middle-class norms of the social institution of schooling. As te Riele (2007) notes, often teachers attribute blame to students and their families when there is an inability to hang in with school. However, the marginalization and early school leaving, which accompanies the inability to stay in school, is more often in reality "a product of the institutions, systems and culture(s) we create and sustain" (Smyth et al., 2000, p. 4). Considering the institutional, ideological, and cultural interferences to schooling provides us with a much richer and more rounded way of thinking and talking about what militates against schooling. Put in these terms, doing identity work around schooling can be regarded as occurring in a context of the interacting constellation of class, race, and gender (Smyth & Hattam, 2004, p. 99).

Social class resonates strongly with decisions by young people regarding schooling. Often this is strongly framed by parental experiences of schooling, and the research clearly shows that "early school leaving is not a problem . . . for the well off" (Smyth & Hattam, 2004, p. 101). A lack of financial resources can be a partial explanation, and the struggle around material conditions, but family background and class location are far more salient. For young people living in poverty, schooling does not provide them with the space within which their voices can be heard or understood. Schools ride over or silence poverty. Schools act as an "organizational economy" (Wexler, 1992, p. 8) in the way they mediate "the flow of social and cultural resources" (Smyth & Hattam, 2004, p. 109) with which students construct an identity to succeed at school—a life space within which to concentrate on learning; a willingness to endure poor teaching; access to intellectual resources with which to complete tasks; IT facilities; an environment free from extenuating family circumstances; and, most of all, a background of literacy and numeracy skills with which to succeed. Students from poor backgrounds lack all or some of these resources and as a result find it tough going in school.

Gender provides a structural and cultural explanation for early school leaving that goes considerably beyond personal, material, positional, or relational explanations. In essence the argument, supported by evidence, is that schools often present a particular, invisible, and narrow identity that is often incongruent with the identity young people are trying to construct of themselves. The "trouble" arising from this exclusionary stereotypical activity can emanate from several sources, for example:

- curriculum, books, and learning materials/activities that fail to adequately portray the range of contributions of women and which by implication provide subtle stereotypical messages to girls about limited career prospects and horizons;
- a curriculum hierarchy which often operates to undermine girls' post-school options by, for example, reinforcing higher expectations for girls in non-scientific subjects;
- pedagogical practices that ignore girls in classrooms because they are less demanding and hence are made more invisible than boys, and because teachers respond to boys in different ways, for example, by giving them more air space in class;
- the perpetuation of male images as somehow being more important which has the effect of diminishing the spaces and places in which girls can flourish and experience success in schooling;
- similarly, when girls are constructed as having to engage in behaviors with male teachers that please them, then this promulgates an image of what is required by girls for academic success that can impede their pathways to successful schooling. (Smyth, 2007a, p. 391)

Not only girls may suffer, but boys, too, often have to struggle against a version of schooling that rests very uneasily with a hegemonic masculinity boys are constructing for themselves around "macho" images of what it means to be male. Under these circumstances gender results in some boys underperforming in school, engaging in aggressive behavior, and treating school with indifference that acts back against their own long-term self-interests. This assessment is not to suggest that some young people do not actively resist the gender stereotypes schools perpetuate, for they clearly do, but this resistance requires courage, persistence, and careful thought. It occurs, for example, when boys manage to live out an academic identity against the damaging influences of hegemonic masculinity. The issue is not whether schooling works universally in discriminatory ways for either gender (Teese et al., 1997). Rather the question is how gender inter-acts with issues of class. Harassment around gender can produce a situation for some young people that makes school a "living hell."

Continuing with McCarthy's (1988) argument that the effects of class, gender, and race on inequality are not discrete additives in the way they operate on non-completion of schooling, then race is the final element of this interactive constellation. Racism operates in systemic ways in schools that disenfranchises students, undermine opportunities, and further promotes inequal-ity through the ways student achievement is impacted by homelessness, substance abuse, crime, ill health, unemployment, and the "troubling inheritance" (Pearson, 1994) of race. As Moore (1993) put it, the process of racializing social formations occurs through the economy, the polit-ical system, and public institutions in ways that "impoverish, de-power, disenfranchise, divide, silence and exclude black people [by] ensur[ing] they receive minimal services" (pp. 5–6)—and resources of all kinds available in and through schooling, conspire to ensure that disadvantaged groups of color are significantly over-represented in the "dropping out" of school statistics in all western countries, a situation not improved by the humiliation that accompanies institutional-ly endorsed acts of racial harassment from students and teachers.

School culture features significantly and consistently in the reasons young people give for severing their connections with schooling. They describe a range of broadly related themes, including being treated in disrespectful and immature ways; having to endure a curriculum that is hierarchically determined and that they consider to be irrelevant; not having a space within school to give expression to their lives, family and community backgrounds, and future aspira-tions; teachers and school policies that are inflexible and out of touch with the context of their lives; forms of streaming and grouping that undermines their self-images and relationships to peers; a denial of the place of youths and popular culture in their lives outside of school; a school culture that treats them like children rather than young adults; behavior management approach-es that bear down on them harshly for infractions like the use of banned substances; a require-ment to be compliant or else be removed as a trouble maker; and, in general an approach that seems to be unsympathetic to young people's own sense of justice and that does not understand the wider changes occurring to their lives (for elaboration see: Smyth & Hattam, 2004, pp. 155–188; and Smyth, 2007b, pp. 635–658). While many of these aspects of school cultures are not immutable and are certainly constantly being contested and resisted by young people, and are not characteristic of all schools, they are nevertheless indicative of archetypes of school cul-tures that fail to foster empathy, understanding, connectedness, and engagement in the context of the educational complexities of young lives.

In the Interests of Pursuing Connectedness and Adolescent Engagement

If we return now to the notion of dropping out as a wicked problem in an educational policy sense, then moving beyond the difficulty of problem identification, causal connections, conse-quences, and effects on young lives, then it becomes clear that prescriptive solutions will be unworkable, and that any applications of treatments will have to be highly idiosyncratic and con-text sensitive. Whatever is tried will have to be done so in ways that are provisional and tenta-tive, and that are mindful of the need to continually monitor and re-focus in the light of experience. That having been said, there are some broad orienting ideas around which a new terrain might be constructed that re-frames the conditions that led to dropping out in the first place. We can lightly point to several important features (rather than laboring them prescriptively), that would involve:

- focusing on the disconnect between young lives and the institution of schooling;
- doing something radical to rectify the exclusion of student voice from conceptualizations of what schooling ought to embrace and what learning might be like;
- tackling how young people are being excluded and left out of the dialogue around their own learning;
- confronting the "silenced dialogue" (Delpit, 1988) by embracing issues of "power and pedagogy" (Delpit, 1995) in the education of "other people's children";
- reinserting context and connectedness back into learning for young people;
- having the courage to supplant what Kohl (2003) calls "tears of stupidity" with forms of educational creativity;
- creating what Perry, Steele, & Hilliard (2003) call "counter-hegemonic" communities (p. 93) that are "organized in opposition to the dominant ideology" (p. 91);
- modeling "imagined communities" (Holland et al., 1998, p. 49) that "inspire new actions" (p. 49);
- creating schools in the form of "as if" (Holland et al., 1998, p. 49) communities that are not locked into immutable or static past interpretations by vested power structures, but rather that emerge as ones capable of embracing the dynamic possibility that everybody can become a "somebody" (Perry et al., 2003, p. 92);
- acknowledging as Delpit (2003) does that "we *can* educate all children if we truly want to. To do so, we must first stop attempting to determine their capacity. We must be convinced of their inherent intellectual capability, humanity, and spiritual character. We must fight the foolishness proliferated by those who believe that one number can measure the worth and drive the education of human beings, or that predetermined scripts can make for good teaching. Finally, we must learn who our children are, their lived culture, their interests, and their intellectual, political, and historical legacies" (p. 20).
- pursuing the aspiration of "intentional communities" (Delpit, 2003, p. 19) that affirm counternarratives of those previously excluded by constructed stereotypes, and working them to develop "identities of achievement" (Perry, Steele, & Hilliard, 2003, p. 100) rather than identities of failure;
- genuinely differentiating between activities that educate in contrast to those that "imprison the spirit," or as Delpit & White-Bradley (2003) put it: "Teachers who choose to engage with the minds and the hearts of their students, to develop human beings rather than robots, must first be willing to develop a relationship with them individually and as a group" (p. 288);
- finally, publicly, and profoundly acknowledging in rhetoric as well as practice, Delpit's (2003) three touchstones of: first, believing in our children; second, fighting foolishness in the form of educational follies; and third, learning intimately who our young people are and the rich legacies they bring with them.

QUESTIONS TO CONSIDER

1. Why is it important to think about how we frame the issue of "dropping out" of school?

2. In what way is it problematic to speak of "dropping out" only in individualistic terms?

3. Whose problem is it when young people disconnect or disengage from schooling?

4. In what sense is "dropping out," or early school leaving, a "wicked issue"?

5. If you were a young person, what would be the basis of your argument that "dropping out" of school was not your personal problem?

6. What do we mean when we talk about "doing identity work around schooling"?

7. What, therefore, is wrong with the current policy approach that is aimed at fixing the problem of early school leaving, and what is the essence of an alternative approach?

Acknowledgment

The research reported on in this chapter has been supported by several grants from the Australian Research Council to whom appreciation is extended for the funding.

References

Australian Public Service Commissioner. (2007). *Tackling wicked problems: A public policy perspective*. Canberra: Australian Public Service Commission.

Dei, G., Mazzuca, J., McIsaac, E., & Zine, J. (1997). *Reconstructing 'dropout': A critical ethnography of Black students' disengagement from school*. Toronto: University of Toronto Press.

Delpit, L. (1988). The silenced dialogue: Power and pedagogy in educating other people's children. *Harvard Educational Review, 58*(3), 280–298.

Delpit, L. (1995). *Other people's children: Cultural conflict in the classroom*. New York: New Press.

Delpit, L. (2003). Educators as "seed people" growing a new future. *Educational Researcher, 32*(7), 14–21.

Delpit, L., & White-Bradley, P. (2003). Educating or imprisoning the spirit: lessons from Ancient Egypt. *Theory into Practice, 42*(4), 283–288.

Dorn, S. (1996). *Creating the Dropout: An Institutional and Social History of School Failure*. Westport, CT: Praeger.

Fagan, G. (1995). *Culture, Politics, and Irish School Dropouts: Constructing Political Identities*. Westport, CT: Bergin & Garvey.

Fine, M. (1989). Silencing and nurturing voice in an improbable context: urban adolescents in public school. In H. Giroux & P. McLaren (Eds.), *Critical Pedagogy, the State and Cultural Struggle* (pp. 152–173). Albany: State University of New York Press.

Fine, M. (1991). *Framing Dropouts: Notes on the Politics of an Urban Public High School*. Albany: State University of New York Press.

Fine, M. (1994). Working the hyphens: reinventing self and other in qualitative research. In N. Denzin & Y. Lincoln (Eds.), *Handbook of qualitative research* (pp. 70–82). Thousand Oaks, CA: Sage Publications.

Gambetta, D. (1987). *Were they pushed or did they jump? Individual decision mechanisms in education*. Cambridge: Cambridge University Press.

Holden, E. (1992). *Getting a life: Pathways and early school leavers* (Working Paper No.9 Melbourne Youth Research Centre): Melbourne University.

Holland, D., Lachicotte, W., Skinner, D., & Cain, W. (1998). *Identity and agency in cultural worlds*. Cambridge, MA: Harvard University Press.

Horn, R., & Weber, R. (2007). *New tools for resolving wicked problems: Mess mapping and resolution mapping processes*: Kinetics, L.L.C.

Kelly, D. (1995). *Last chance high: How girls and boys drop in and out of alternative schools*. New Haven, CT: Yale University Press.

Kelly, D., & Gaskell, J. (1996). *Debating dropouts: Critical policy and research perspectives on leaving school*. New York: Teachers College Press.

Kohl, H. (2003). *Tears and stupidity: Teaching and learning in troubled times*. New York: New Press.

Luttrell, W. (1996). Becoming somebody in and against school: Toward a psychocultural theory of gender and self-making. In B. Levinson, D. Foley, & D. Holland (Eds.), *The cultural production of the educated person: Critical ethnographies of schooling and local practice*. Albany, NY: State University of New York Press.

MacPherson, P., & Fine, M. (1995). Hungry for an us: Adolescent girls and adult women negotiating territories of race, gender, class and difference. *Feminism and Psychology, 5*(2), 181–200.

McCarthy, C. (1988). Rethinking liberal and radical perspectives on inequality in schooling: Making the case for non-synchrony. *Harvard Educational Review, 58*(3), 265–279.

McLeod, J., & Yates, L. (2006). *Making modern lives: Subjectivity, schooling, and social change*. Albany, NY: State University of New York Press.

Mills, C. (1971). *The sociological imagination*. Harmondsworth: Penguin. (Original work published 1959)

Moore, B. (1993). Anti-racist education: South Australian policy in black perspective. *South Australian Educational Leader, 4*(1), 1–12.

Pearson, N. (1994). A troubling inheritance. *Race and Class, 35*(4), 1–9.

Perry, T., Steele, C., & Hilliard, A. (2003). *Young, Gifted and Black: Promoting High Achievement Among African-American Students*. Boston, MA: Beacon Press.

Piper, H., & Piper, J. (1998). "Disaffected youth": A wicked issue. *Youth and Policy, 62*, 32–43.

Rittel, H., & Webber, M. (1973). Dilemmas in a general theory of planning. *Policy Sciences, 4*, 155–169.

Shor, I. (1980). *Critical Teaching and Everyday Life*. Chicago: University of Chicago Press.

Smyth, J. (2007a). Attrition from schools. In B. Bank (Ed.), *Gender and Education: An Encyclopedia* (Vol. 1, pp. 389–394). Westport, CT & London: Praeger.

Smyth, J. (2007b). Toward the Pedagogically Engaged School: Listening to student voice as a positive response to disengagement and "dropping out." In D. Thiessen & A. Cook-Sather (Eds.), *International handbook of student experience of elementary and secondary school* (pp. 635–658). Dordrecht, The Netherlands: Springer.

Smyth, J., Hattam, R., Cannon, J., Edwards, J., Wilson, N., & Wurst, S. (2000). *Listen to me, I'm leaving: Early school leaving in South Australian secondary schools*. Adelaide: Flinders Institute for the Study of Teaching; Department of Employment, Education and Training; and Senior Secondary Assessment Board of South Australia.

Smyth, J., Hattam, R., with Cannon, J., Edwards, J., Wilson, N., & Wurst, S. (2004). *"Dropping out," drifting off, being excluded: Becoming somebody without school*. New York: Peter Lang.

Snow, D., & Anderson, L. (1987). Identity work among the homeless: The verbal construction and avowal of personal identities. *American Journal of Sociology, 92*(6), 1336–1371.

te Riele, K. (2007). Educational alternatives for marginalized youth. *Australian Educational Researcher, 34*(3), 53–68.

Teese, R., Davies, B., Charlton, M., & Polesel, J. (1997). Who wins at school; which boys, which girls? In J. Kenway (Ed.), *Will boys be boys? Boys' education in the context of gender reform* (pp. 8–12). Deakin West, Australian Capital Territory: Australian Curriculum Studies Association.

Valenzuela, A. (1999). *Subtractive schooling: U. S.-Mexican youth and the politics of caring.* Albany, NY: State University of New York Press.

Weis, L., & Fine, M. (2001). Extraordinary conversations in public schools. *International Journal of Qualitative Studies in Education, 14*(4), 497–523.

Wexler, P. (1992). *Becoming Somebody: Toward a Social Psychology of School.* London: Falmer Press.

White, R., & Wyn, J. (1998). Youth agency and social context. *Journal of Sociology, 34*(3), 314–327.

Wyn, J. (2009). *Youth, health and welfare: Cultural politics of wellbeing.* South Melbourne: Oxford University Press.

Wyn, J., Stokes, H., & Tyler, D. (2004). *Stepping stones: TAFE and ACE program development for early school leavers.* Adelaide: National Council for Vocational Educational Research.

CHAPTER SEVENTEEN

Overcoming Negative School Experiences of African-American Adolescents

What School Counselors Can Do to Eradicate Ethnocentrism

DANA GRIFFIN & JULIA BRYAN

By 2020, the majority of the U.S. public school population will be classified as children of color (National Center for Education Statistics, 2006). That statistic is of grave importance because, nationwide, schools continue to face a persistent White-minority achievement gap and disproportionately high rates of suspension, expulsion, and referral to special education for children of color (Harry & Anderson, 1994; Monroe, 2005; Patton, 1998; Skiba, Peterson, & Williams, 1997). Just as alarming is the fact that Black, Hispanic, and American Indian students are less likely to pursue postsecondary education than White and Asian-American students (NCES, 2007). These data are alarming as school failure is related to poor social, economic, and health concerns. Students who fail out, drop out of school, or do not go on to postsecondary education are more likely to live below the poverty level, be incarcerated, or experience poor health (Bridgeland, Dilulio, & Morrison, 2006; Day-Vines & Day-Hairston, 2005; Stallings, 2007). Furthermore, the United States cannot retain economic viability among its global competitors if large numbers of its children continue to leave school ill prepared for the world of work.

While the U.S. student body is becoming increasingly diverse, the teaching body is increasingly White and middle class (NCES, 2006). Some researchers point to the differences between White-minority worldviews, cultural lens, communication styles, and socio-cultural-political experiences as major reasons for the negative school experiences and outcomes of students of color (i.e., Gay, 2000; Monroe, 2005; Nieto, 2000). These differences result in assumptions, communication gaps, misunderstandings, and decisions that may negatively impact students. Indeed, the phenomenon of having a positive bias toward one's own group and a negative bias toward other groups, known as ethnocentrism, leads individuals to perceive their own cultural values and worldviews as more legitimate than those in other cultures (Dana, 1998; Taylor & Jaggi, 1974; Vitaliti, 1998). Those with ethnocentric viewpoints tend to view their own culture as the standard to which to measure all other cultures. This attitude can be extremely damaging, especially to children of color, whose ethnic and cultural values and customs are often incongruent with mainstream America. To help facilitate positive school experiences and promote student academic achievement for American students, we present steps that school counselors can take to eradicate ethnocentrism in the school. We open with a discussion of African-American experiences in American society, followed by an overview of the disproportionality that occurs in the schools. We then describe three culture conflicts that occur in the school that lead to negative school experiences for African-American students. Finally, we present steps school counselors can take to address these conflicts which, in turn, can help eradicate ethnocentrism.

African-American Experiences in American Society

Numerous incidents in American history suggest that African Americans have worldviews and outlooks divergent from Whites. One recent social incident that has dominated national news highlights the cultural misunderstandings that arise as a result of these divergent worldviews. For example, take the incident involving Dr. Henry Louis Gates of Harvard University that occurred in July 2009 (Jan, 2009). The online edition of the reporting of this incident shows 2180 responses to the newspaper article. Comments range from support of Gates and cries of racism and racial profiling to support of the police officer. There have been comments from African Americans suggesting that Dr. Gates was being unjustly profiled because of his race, as well as from Whites claiming that he should have acted differently toward the police. A highly publicized photograph of Dr. Gates, handcuffed, and being escorted from his home by the police, demonstrates how worldviews interpret the actions that took place that day. Some Americans say that he was angry, combative, and aggressive, while others say he was just upset at the injustice of the entire incident and had a right to voice his opinion. Indeed, a multitude of recent situations such as these, where past experiences led African Americans to conclude that negative treatment occurred because of skin color, has occurred (e.g., Hurricane Katrina, Jena 6).

Historically, African-American experiences in this country have been negative (i.e., slavery, Jim Crow, lynching, segregation), and these experiences do influence perceptions of present-day happenings. Indeed, African Americans' past experiences of slavery, discrimination, and inequities perpetuated by government institutions, and present experiences of being stigmatized, will, more often than not, cause them to interpret events as race-related; conversely, those of the dominant culture often tend to see these experiences as occurring solely because of African Americans' *behavior*, exclusive of their race. Indisputably, one's experiences and worldviews influence the interpretations of events and behaviors, and given the socio-political dynamics of U.S. society and schools, the validity of that viewpoint will be determined by the dominant worldview (Wilson, 2005). Lack of understanding of cultural differences and the tendency to see behavior and actions through a dominant perspective can lead to discriminatory behavior (Vitaliti, 1998), which is often displayed in disproportionality in the U.S. school system.

Disproportionality in U.S. Schools

In addition to being plagued with low academic achievement, high drop-out rates, and low college application and college graduation rates (Ball, 2009), African-American students are often subjected to disproportionately high numbers in discipline referrals, suspensions, and expulsions, counseling referrals, special education placement, and disproportionately low numbers in gifted placement and placement in college preparatory courses such as Advanced Placement (AP) classes (Day-Vines & Day-Hairston, 2005; Patton, 1998). One reason given for disproportionality is a cultural disconnect between the students and their teachers (Ball, 2009; Gregory & Mosely, 2004; Monroe, 2005).

A huge body of research points to the fact that minority students are disproportionately referred for suspensions, disciplined for minor offenses, and referred to special education classes over their White counterparts. This fact is distressing in that suspensions from school have been linked to higher school drop-out, retention, and academic failure (Nichols, Ludwin, & Iadicola, 1999). Hosp and Reschly (2003) synthesized the results of numerous studies on referral rates. Choosing quantitative studies conducted in the United States after 1975 that explored differences across racial groups and school levels (elementary, middle, and high), they found 10 studies meeting the criteria that indicated that discipline referral rates for African Americans and Hispanics were greater than those for Caucasian students.

In a study analyzing the patterns of suspension in West Central Florida, Raffaele-Mendez & Knoff (2003) found that more males were suspended than females and Black students were found to be suspended most across all three school levels combined. Additionally, Black females were found to be suspended more than White and Hispanic males in all three school levels combined. Furthermore, almost half of Black males and a third of Black females were suspended at least once in a district consisting of only 13% Black students.

In their study on disproportionality, Skiba, Michael, Nardo, & Peterson (2002) found that, although White students were referred for discipline issues, they were referred for harsher offenses such as smoking and vandalism, while Black students were referred for minor offenses such as disrespect and excessive noise. They also found African-American students were referred at higher numbers than any other racial group. They studied the entire middle school population from a large school system with 56% African American students, 42% White students, and 1.2% Latino students. There were 51.8% male students and 48.2% female students. Through analyzing the school system's referral database, African Americans were found to receive higher numbers of referrals than students from any other ethnic background except Native Americans. Results also showed that the most common reasons for referral were minor offenses, such as lack of cooperation, insubordination, and inappropriate language.

Raffale-Mendez, Knoff, and Ferron (2002) conducted a study on out-of-school suspension rates. Results showed that middle school students had higher rates of out-of-school suspensions, followed by high school students, and elementary students. Additionally, they found that males accounted for over 70% of all suspensions, and Black males and females were suspended more frequently than other groups. White students were suspended the least. Disobedience was found to be the main reason students were suspended, followed by disruptive behavior and fighting, inappropriate behaviors, and non-compliance with assigned discipline.

In addition to race and gender, differences in suspension referrals have also been found along socioeconomic lines (Skiba et al., 2002). Brantlinger (1991) found that teachers would not only refer students of low socioeconomic status (SES) for suspensions, but also deliver harsher penalties, such as being sent out of the classroom, to students of low SES, while students of high SES would receive milder punishments, such as seat reassignment. Additionally, studies have shown that students receiving free lunches or lunches at a reduced rate were more likely to receive disciplinary referrals (Wu, Pink, Crain, & Moles, 1982; Skiba, Peterson, & Williams, 1997).

However, another factor that seems to be related to the disproportionality on referrals is teacher perception. Rong (1996) asserts that teachers' perceptions of appropriate behaviors are culturally defined, and Mehan, Hertweck, & Miehls (1986) found that teacher perceptions of students were a precursor of their referrals for discipline. Gregory and Mosely (2004) conducted a qualitative study in an urban high school with 3,300 students. There was an even number of African-American and White students at 37% each. The remaining population consisted of 11% Latino students, 9% Asian Students, 1% Filipino students, and .5% American Indian students. Although there was an even number of African American and White students, the teaching staff had only 15% African-American teachers, while there were 73% White teachers, 4% Asian teachers, and 6% Latino teachers. They found that teachers reported not considering issues of race in their disciplinary referrals, or as a factor in discipline. However, Gregory & Mosely (2004) assert that race was a factor in the way teachers discipline or refer students.

Negative labels have been shown to be a major factor in why minority students, and Black males in particular, are disproportionately referred, not only for discipline, but for special education placement. In addition to discipline referrals, African-American students are disproportionately referred for special education placement. "African American males have been disproportionately represented in special education since its inception" (Harry & Anderson, 1994, p. 603). Teacher perception has been linked to the high number of students referred for special education. It has been documented in the literature that White women have a fear of African-American males (Harry & Anderson, 1994). Additionally, African-American patterns of language and behavior can all be factors in teachers' negative perceptions of Black males (Harry & Anderson, 1994). This trend is distressing as student misbehavior is the most common reason teachers refer students to special education (Giesbrecht & Routh, 1979; Hutton, 1985). Teacher perception of those in low SES environments has also been labeled as problematic, as Ortiz and Yates (1984) assert that teachers may lower their expectations for students from poverty-stricken environments. Patton (1998) asserts that it is a serious problem that large numbers of African-American students are inappropriately labeled and placed in special education programs. In a review of literature, it is noted that this trend has not changed since 1975, when 38% of the African-American population was identified as mentally disabled, to now representing 35% of the special education population (Patton, 1998; Harry & Anderson, 1994). One reason for this trend could be in how schools define "normal" behavior, which may not include the behaviors of African-American students.

What Is Normal Behavior?

It is no secret that African Americans, as a group, are often misdiagnosed with severe psychopathological disorders (Solomon, 1992). As one progresses to pre-adolescence and adolescent age, that behavior can already be characterized by moodiness, aggressiveness, and defiance, which can be viewed in a more negative light for African-American adolescents. Although normal teen issues that arise during the adolescent stage include a search for identity that is often characterized by a need to redefine authority as teenagers struggle with new demands and deal with issues of sexuality and revision of rules and roles (Hines, Preto, McGoldrick, Almeida, & Weltman, 1999), the African-American search for identity also means searching for what it means to be Black (Tatum, 1997). As they are frequently confronted with negative stereotypes of Blackness, Black beauty, Black culture, or Black lifestyle, the quest for an identity can be even more difficult for African-American adolescents. African-American youths in our society are also challenged by sociocultural factors such as racial discrimination, institutionalized racism, and oppression, and community factors such as poverty, violence, crime, and drugs (Bemak, Chung, & Siroskey-Sabdo, 2005; Bryan, 2005; Locke, 2005; Schorr, 1997). Furthermore, African-American adolescents are vulnerable to media exploitation. Their values and beliefs about life, their views about gender relationships, the way they dress, talk and walk are all influenced by what they see on TV and in films and by the music they hear (Nasir, McLaughlin, & Jones, 2009; Walsh, 2003).

Defining normalcy is a difficult and highly judgmental process. Walsh (2003) studied normalcy with family therapists, and results showed that what is seen as healthy and normal varied due to the theoretical model to which they adhered. However, results also showed that the therapists' own beliefs and cultural background played a huge part in how they assessed normalcy because they brought their own beliefs about stereotypes and myths when working with families and in deciding what is normal and what is not normal. The worldview of African Americans is often pathologized by White Americans (Sue, 1994). For example, White Americans in dominant society may criticize African Americans for voicing their sense of being discriminated against, dismiss that viewpoint as invalid, and point to equal access and opportunity for success for everyone in the United States. For example, African-American students who say that the teacher does not like them or grades them more harshly because they are Black will more likely be told that they are imagining the treatment and that the teacher is not racist. Their claim will often not be investigated.

Just as therapists may have their own beliefs about normalcy that reflect their own values and beliefs, school staff may also hold ethnocentric viewpoints on normal behavior. They may over-pathologize students and families by identifying what is a normal pattern of behavior for students and their families as dysfunctional or abnormal (Walsh, 2003). There are many teachers who expect all students to perform and behave at a certain level, but they do not take into account the child's background. Black males most often receive the negative effects of ethnocentrism. Teachers and therapists often become intimidated by African-American males and begin to label them as aggressive, hyperactive, and failures as early as the fourth grade (Walsh, 2003). School personnel must be knowledgeable about different ethnic and cultural groups, and they must be aware of how their own worldview may conflict with the worldview of others, especially when defining normal and abnormal behavior. For example, in a review of the literature, Irvine and York (1995) have found that the culturally based traits and valued forms of nonverbal expressions of African Americans are physical movement, animation, spontaneity, and displays of emotions. Although African-American males may display these behaviors in the home, this behavior may be seen as aggressive or disrespectful in the schools. School personnel must continue to question themselves and ask how their beliefs are culturally based and be sure that they are not misinterpreting student behaviors that are incongruent with their expectations (Monroe, 2005).

However, it has been found that teachers who are assigned to work in diverse, urban environments feel unprepared to teach diverse students and interact with their parents, and have a general sense of low self-efficacy in working in that environment (Duhon & Manson, 2000; Hollins & Torres-Guzman, 2005). It is vital that those working in the schools have a deep understanding of the different cultural values and norms of their student population. We want to assert that all races can have an ethnocentric viewpoint, not just Whites. African-American teachers can also be punitive toward African-American adolescent behavior and speech, and label them as "abnormal." Although there are many cultural differences that occur in school, we believe the differences that can be most detrimental to African-American adolescents, especially those in middle school, are parenting practices, communication styles, and ethnic identity development.

Culture Conflict #1: Parenting Practices

African-American practices of parenting are often misunderstood by school personnel, especially when it comes to discipline. Although many African-American families use discipline known as "spare the rod, spoil the child," schools often misunderstand that the practice of spanking, or "whipping," is rooted in feelings of love and concern for their children's well-being (Walsh, 2003). While that form of discipline may be used in some African-American families, school personnel often see this as a form of child abuse, although the families may view it as a normal family value (Walsh, 2003). Viewing spanking as discipline or abuse depends on the lens through which we look. An African-American mother said, "Whipping my son lets him know who's boss. If I don't whip him, he will think he can run all over me and not listen to what I say. I got to teach him now while he's young, that he needs to respect me and all adults. If I don't do it now, he won't listen when he gets older and may end up on the streets. This is what's wrong with our children today. They don't know who's boss. They think they grown" (L. Williams, personal communication, February 26, 2009). On the other hand, a European-American school counselor had a different perception of spanking: "We are aware that many parents still believe in spanking as a form of discipline. However, there is a thin line between spanking and beating a child, and beating a child is wrong. A spank is a swat on the behind and more appropriate for younger kids and toddlers, not middle schoolers. We report all cases that have a mark—whether it be by a belt, switch, hand, or any other weapon" (C. Davis, personal communication, February 26, 2009). These interpretive differences are a huge problem in the school and represent a culture clash that often ends in negative repercussions for families because their point of view and cultural values are not seen as the norm and, more often than not, are not taken into consideration. Generations of African Americans have been raised with corporal punishment, and some may still disagree about the push against spanking and for a new type of punishment—"Time Outs." Indeed, John Rosemond, parent expert and nationally syndicated parenting columnist, wrote in a recent article, "If a consequence does not produce a permanent memory—and time-out most definitely does not—then it has been a waste of everyone's time" (Rosemond, 2009). One African-American mother lamented that the school took away her power as a mother to raise her kids, but then the schools wanted her to act when her child misbehaves: "What do you want me to do? On one hand, you tell me I can't spank my child, but now you call me telling me my child won't listen and you want me to do something about it. You can't have it both ways" (P. Jones, personal communication, February 26, 2009).

Culture Conflict #2: Communication Styles

Many may believe that only those whose first language is not English face a language barrier in the schools, but African Americans can also face that barrier. African Americans are at a distinct disadvantage when it comes to conformity in their communication styles. For example, some African Americans may exhibit a distinctive communication style that does not conform to the norms and expectations of school settings (Day-Vines & Day-Hairston, 2005). While Caucasians may be accustomed to more impersonal, emotionally restrained communication styles, the loud, intense, and confrontational styles of African Americans could be regarded as rude and inappropriate in the school setting (Day-Vines & Day-Hairston, 2005). I often find myself telling my own children to use their "inside" voices when I realize that we are speaking in tones louder than what is considered "normal." Then, more often than not, they will go into a whisper. To them, there are only two ways to communicate: loudly or, basically, not at all. When we are out in public, I can always find my two children because they have a loud, distinctive way of talking. This way of speaking has already gotten my oldest into trouble in school: I received a report from her teacher saying that she tends to be loud, and during reading group time, she can hear her talking across the room. However, is this abnormal? Not for us. Growing up in a family where you have to speak loudly to be heard, this way of speaking is completely normal, and to speak in the more acceptable quieter tones will be a behavioral change, which is not a quick fix. It is actually abnormal for the children in my family to be seen and not heard.

Not only is the loud way of speech a problem, but the African-American *way* of speaking is in conflict with the school culture. Ebonics, the form of African-American speech where grammar is not an issue, is a normal type of speech used by African Americans and especially African-American adolescents. Add to this the popular usage of computer networking devices such as Facebook and Twitter, and the ever popular text messaging, grammatically correct ways of speaking are quickly going by the wayside for most adolescents (and many adults as well). Nevertheless, Ebonics seems to occur in the speech of many African Americans as soon as they hit adolescence, regardless of how grammatically correct they can actually speak. It is almost as if it were a rite of passage. Ebonics, though, has been around for generations. Pick up any book of poetry written during the Harlem Renaissance, and you will find great poetry written in a way that incorporates the normal African-American way of speaking at that time. In any given family, Ebonics can be a normal way of speech, and some scholars argue that Ebonics should not be seen as a detriment to the African-American community, but more as an understanding of a way of speech (Kretzschmar, 2008). Others feel that it keeps African Americans from being successful in school and in the workforce. Again, this argument is a based on one's particular worldview. Outside of that argument, the fact is that African-American adolescents speak Ebonics, and those who use it frequently in school are often seen as less smart and less capable than those who use *correct* grammar. Just as with English-as-a-second-language speakers, African Americans are taught they must learn the "proper" way to speak and write English (Kretzschmar, 2008), which, more often than not, goes again their cultural norms.

Culture Conflict #3: Racial Identity Development

Another cultural conflict that occurs in the school concerns the effects of racial identity development. African-American culture takes pride in its music, hairstyles, clothing, and talk. To not understand that pride is to not understand African Americans. This lack of understanding invokes fear in others, especially the fear of the African-American male. Understanding the role of ethnic identity should be pivotal in helping school staff understand what is normal behavior for African-American adolescents.

Schools should begin to view the development of African-American adolescents through a racial identity development framework as a way to understand their behaviors (Tatum, 1997). As African-American youth reach adolescence and begin to explore their identity, they must often grapple with messages received from society about what it means to be Black, which often means trying to grapple with being a member of a group targeted by racism (Tatum, 1997). For example, African-American youth in the encounter stage (a period that causes them to recognize the significance of race and see the personal impact of racism) may develop an "oppositional" identity. This dynamic occurs when one seeks out racially homogenous peer support groups to maintain positive self-esteem, while keeping the dominant group at a distance. It is often within this phase that academic performance declines, especially if the support group does not value academic achievement (Day-Vines & Day-Hairston, 2005; Tatum, 1997). An example of adolescent behavior in this stage is when they begin to "segregate" themselves from others. They may often see the world through an ethnocentric viewpoint themselves and begin to see every other culture as inferior to theirs. This is a pivotal moment, and increased parental involvement is absolutely necessary. Indeed, a study with urban, high achieving African-American students found that parents who work to combat racism and discrimination experienced by their children by fostering positive racial socialization helped promote the academic success of their children (Sanders, 1997). The literature on ethnic identity development is extensive, and we highly recommend Beverly Tatum's "*Why Are All the Black Kids Sitting Together in the Cafeteria?*" as an excellent book for understanding ethnic identity development in African-American adolescents.

However, the research is conflicted about the role of identity development and academic success. Some researchers contend that high identity development is linked with low academic achievement (e.g., Fordham & Ogbu, 1986; Noguera, 2003), while others claim that having a strong African-American identity is a protective factor for education (Oyserman, Harrison, & Bybee, 2001), and has been shown to correlate with higher academic achievement (Spencer, Noll, Stolfus, & Harpalani, 2001). Regardless of the conflict, a high level of ethnic identity has been associated with positive psychosocial adjustment and positive feelings about oneself (Schwartz, Zamboanga, & Jarvis, 2007); and, among college students, high ethnic identity has been correlated with high grade point average (Sellers, Chavous, & Cooke, 1998).

The school system plays a huge role in the ethnic identity development of African-American adolescents (Shelton & Sellers, 2000). Schools can either foster ethnic identity development in the form of high expectations and a open line of communication and information sharing about college and other support (Mehan, Villanueva, Hubbard, & Lintz, 2004); or they can establish barriers to ethnic identity development through such tactics as academic tracking, low and negative expectations, and racially discriminatory practices (Davidson, 1996).

We previously mentioned three culture conflicts that often occur in schools, especially when school personnel view teenagers' cultural norms through an ethnocentric viewpoint. We believe that school counselors can help school staff understand how to work more effectively with African-American adolescents. Due to the nature of their profession, school counselors can play a huge role in creating change in the school system. The multicultural education received by school counseling professionals enables them to address the needs of their student population as well as help school staff offer effective, culturally responsive services to their students. Because school counselors are prepared to understand biases and barriers to school success, we present a list of four recommendations that can allow school counselors to take steps toward eradicating the ethnocentrism that is so prevalent in our schools.

Steps Toward Eradicating Ethnocentrism

1. Develop cultural awareness and knowledge.

Making schools free of ethnocentrism must first begin with individual cultural awareness and knowledge. School counselors can be proactive in helping the school staff develop cultural awareness and knowledge of the students with whom they work. They have the multicultural skills and knowledge that can enable them to be proactive in facilitating culturally responsive collaboration (Amatea & West-Olantunji, 2007). School counselors can help schools overcome a lack of cultural awareness and knowledge by helping the school develop a climate that is welcoming and open to all students, as well as affirming of different cultural norms. In order to this, school counselors can present workshops on cultural awareness and understanding, and help staff obtain cultural knowledge not only about the students and families with whom they work, but also about themselves (Bradley, Johnson, Rawls, & Dodson-Sims, 2005).

2. Establish trust with students.

The first step in establishing a trusting relationship is gaining an understanding and acceptance of the cultural norms and values of African Americans, and working with African-American students through accurate portrayals of the African-American life (Bradley, Johnson, Rawls, & Dodson-Sims, 2005). Therefore, school counselors must not be afraid to challenge existing school rules and policies that negatively affect students from diverse backgrounds. Indeed, they should advocate for new policies and procedures that are more advantageous for those from minority populations. They should also establish rapport with students before problems arise and develop groups that allow African-American adolescents to discuss their social, emotional, and educational concerns regarding experiences inside and outside of the school, such as college and career planning, what it is like for them to be an African American in the school, their hopes and dreams, and their aspirations for the future.

3. Develop an understanding of African-American communication styles.

School counselors can help school staff understand the many different nuances of communication styles as well as help students learn how to best communicate in the schools (Day-Vines &

Day-Hairston, 2005). Additionally, school counselors can play a critical role in facilitating better communication between home and the school. As personalized communication humanizes the school environment for students, it is crucial for counselors to make use of all communication channels. School counselors can begin to bridge the communication gap between schools and students by overcoming their fear of talking to and working directly with African-American students. They should commit to engaging with them on a regular basis. School counselors should function as learners in that situation. Just as one would ask what BFF (Best Friends Forever) means, one should also ask for clarification and understanding of communication patterns among African-American youths. The more often one practices such interaction habits, the easier it will become.

4. Advocate for new practices reflecting a new definition of "normalcy."

School counselors can be proactive in facilitating this process by conducting workshops with school staff, using open discussions regarding myriad cultural lenses and worldviews, cultural stereotypes and biases, and cultural communication styles. The workshop should include case studies, facilitation exercises, and reflections that integrate the following questions:

1. How do you define normal African-American adolescent behavior?
2. Which worldview are you using to answer that question?
3. How does your viewpoint disadvantage the students with whom you work?
4. What can you advocate for and change about yourself and in the school to ensure that African-American students are not disadvantaged and have equitable access to academic success?

Summary

As achievement and discipline gaps continue to remain between African-American students and White students, ethnocentrism is a phenomenon that needs to be addressed in order to truly have equitable practices in our schools. We have presented some ways in which school counselors can help facilitate change in schools that might move them toward a more culturally responsive approach to working with African-American adolescents. Schools and school staff have an ethical obligation to provide equitable and accessible education to all children, regardless of race, SES, and other cultural variables. However, barriers still exist that prevent African Americans and other children of color from succeeding at the same rate as their White counterparts. We propose that working through ethnocentric viewpoints actually perpetuates the gap that exists. Culturally responsive counseling can help facilitate the systemic change that needs to occur in schools in order to decrease those ethnocentric practices that impede access to an equitable education for African-American youth today and tomorrow.

QUESTIONS TO CONSIDER

1. Define ethnocentrism and explain how it can affect the development of children of color.

2. Describe the term "disproportionality" and how it affects the schooling of youths of color.

3. How can the concept of "normalcy" hinder student development? Explain your response and give examples to support your case.

4. Describe a "culture conflict" that can hamper student success and show how that conflict can be overcome.

5. What are some ways to ensure that ethnocentric views do not create barriers in your school? List and describe steps you would take to eradicate that ethnocentrism.

References

Amatea, E., & West-Olatunji, C. (2007). Joining the conversation about educating our poorest children: Emerging leadership roles for school counselors in high-poverty schools. *Professional School Counseling, 11*, 81–89.

Ball, A. F. (2009). Toward a theory of generative change in culturally and linguistically complex classrooms. *American Educational Research Journal, 46*, 45–72.

Bemak, F., Chung, R. C., & Siroskey-Sabdo, L. A. (2005). Empowerment groups for academic success: An innovative approach to prevent high school failure for at-risk urban African American students. *Professional School Counseling, 8*, 377–389.

Bradley, C., Johnson, P., Rawls, G., & Dodson-Sims, A. (2005). School counselors collaboration with African American parents. *Professional School Counseling, 8*(5), 424–427.

Brantlinger, E. (1991). Social class distinctions in adolescents' reports of problems and punishment in school. *Behavioral Disorders, 17*, 36–46.

Bridgeland, J. M., Dilulio, J. J., & Morrison, K. B. (2006, March). *The Silent Epidemic: Perspectives of High School Dropouts* (p. iv). Washington, DC: Civic Enterprises. Retrieved February 15, 2008, from http://www.civicenterprises.net/pdis/the silentepidemic3–06.pdf

Bryan J. (2005). Fostering educational resilience and academic achievement in urban schools through school-family-community partnerships. *Professional School Counseling, 8*, 219–227.

Dana, R. H. (1998). *Understanding cultural identity in intervention and assessment: Multicultural aspects of counseling, Series 9.* Thousand Oaks, CA: Sage.

Davidson, A. (1996). *Making and molding identities in schools: Student narratives on race, gender, and academic engagement.* Albany: State University of New York Press.

Day-Vines, N. L., & Day-Hairston, B. O. (2005). Culturally congruent strategies for addressing the behavioral needs of urban, African American male adolescents. *Professional School Counseling, 8*, 236–243.

Duhon, G., & Manson, T. (Eds.). (2000). *Implications for teacher education: Cross-ethnic and cross-racial dynamics of instruction.* Lewiston, NY: Mellen.

Fordham, S., & Ogbu, J. (1986). Black students' school success: Coping with the burden of "acting white." *The Urban Review, 18*, 176–206.

Gay, G. (2000). *Culturally responsive teaching: Theory, research, and practice.* New York: Teachers College Press.

Giesbrecht, M. L., & Routh, D. K. (1979). The influences of categories of cumulative folder information on teacher referrals of low-achieving children for special education services. *American Educational Research Journal, 16*, 181–187.

Gregory, A., & Mosely, P. M. (2004). The discipline gap: Teachers' views on the over-representation of African American students in the discipline system. *Equity & Excellence in Education, 37*, 18–30.

Harry, B., & Anderson, M. (1994). The disproportionate placement of African American males in special education programs: A critique of the process. *Journal of Negro Education, 63*, 602–619.

Hines, P. M., Preto, N. G., McGoldrick, M., Almeida, R., & Weltman, S. (1999). Culture and the family life cycle. In B. Carter & M. McGoldrick (Eds.), *The expanded family life cycle: Individual, family, and social perspectives* (pp. 69–87). Needham Heights, MA: Allyn & Bacon.

Hollins, E., & Torres-Guzman, M. E. (2005). The preparation of candidates for teaching diverse student populations. In M. Cochran-Smith & K. Zeichner (Eds.), *Studying teacher education: The report of the AERA panel on research and teacher education* (pp. 201–225). Mahwah, NJ: Lawrence Erlbaum.

Hosp, J. L., & Reschly, D. J. (2003). Referral rates for intervention or assessment: A meta-analysis of racial differences. *The Journal of Special Education, 37*, 67–80.

Hutton, J. B. (1985). What reasons are given by teachers who refer problem behavior students? *Psychology in the Schools, 22*, 79–82.

Irvine, J. J., & York, D. E. (1995). Learning styles and culturally diverse students: A literature review. In J. A. Banks & C. A. M. Banks (Eds.), *Handbook of research on multicultural education* (pp. 484–497). New York: Simon & Schuster/ Macmillan.

Jan, T. (2009, July 20). Harvard professor Gates arrested at Cambridge home. *The Boston Globe.* Retrieved September 5, 2009, from http://www.boston.com/news/local/breaking_news/2009/07/harvard.html

Kretzschmar, W. A., Jr. (2008). Public and academic understandings about language: The intellectual history of Ebonics. *English World-Wide, 29*, 70–95.

Locke, S. (2005). Institutional social and cultural influences on the multicultural perspectives of preservice teachers. *Multicultural Perspectives, 7*, 20–28.

Mehan, H., Hertweck, A., & Miehls, J. L. (1986). *Handicapping the handicapped.* Stanford, CA: Stanford University Press.

Mehan, H., Villanueva, I., Hubbard, L., & Lintz, A. (2004). *Constructing school success.* New York: Cambridge University Press.

Monroe, C. R. (2005). Understanding the discipline gap through a cultural lens: Implications for the education of African American students. *Intercultural Education, 16*, 317–330.

Nasir, N. S., McLaughlin, M. W., & Jones, A. (2009). What does it mean to be African American? Constructions of race and academic identity in an urban public high school. *American Educational Research Journal, 46*, 73–114.

National Center for Educational Statistics. (2006). *Characteristics of the 100 largest public elementary and secondary school districts in the United States: 2003–04 statistical analysis report.* Washington, DC: U.S. Department of Education.

National Center for Educational Statistics. (2007). *Status and trends in the education of racial and ethnic minorities: Percentage of 18–24 year olds enrolled in colleges and universities, by race/ethnicity: Selected years, 1980–2004.* Washington, DC: U.S. Department of Education.

Nichols, J. D., Ludwin, W. G., & Iadicola, P. (1999). A darker shade of gray: A year-end analysis of discipline and suspension data. *Equity & Excellence in Education, 32*, 43–55.

Nieto, S. (2000). *Affirming diversity: The sociopolitical context of multicultural education.* New York: Longman.

Noguera, P. (2003). The trouble with black boys: The role and influence of environmental and cultural factors on the academic performance of African American males. *Urban Review, 38*, 431–459.

Ortiz, A. A., & Yates, J. R. (1984). Linguistically and culturally diverse handicapped students. In R. S. Podemski, B. M. Price, T. E. C. Smith & G. E. Marsh II (Eds.), *Comprehensive administration of special education* (pp. 114–141). Rockville, MD: Aspen Publication.

Oyserman, D., Harrison, K., & Bybee, D. (2001). Can racial identity be promotive of academic efficacy? *International Journal of Behavioral Development, 25,* 379–385.

Patton, J. M. (1998). The disproportionate representation of African Americans in special education: Looking behind the curtain for understanding *and* solutions. *Journal of Special Education, 32,* 25–31.

Raffaele-Mendez, L. M., & Knoff, H. M. (2003). Who gets suspended from school and why: A demographic analysis of schools and disciplinary infractions in a large school district. *Education and Treatment of Children, 26,* 30–51.

Raffaele-Mendez, L. M., Knoff, H. M., & Ferron, J. M. (2002). School demographic variables and out-of-school suspension rates: A quantitative and qualitative analysis of a large, ethnically diverse school district. *Psychology in the Schools, 39,* 259–277.

Rong, X. L. (1996). Effects of race and gender on teachers' perceptions of the social behavior of elementary students. *Urban Education, 31,* 261–290.

Rosemond, J. (2009, September 29). Issuing consequences equals well-behaved children. *The News & Observer,* p. 2D.

Sanders, M. G. (1997). Overcoming obstacles: Academic achievement as a response to racism and discrimination. *Journal of Negro Education, 66,* 83–93.

Schorr, L. (1997). *Common purpose: Strengthening families and neighborhoods to rebuild America.* New York: Doubleday.

Schwartz, S. J., Zamboanga, B. L., & Jarvis, L. H. (2007). Ethnic identity and acculturation in Hispanic early adolescents: Mediated relationships to academic grades, prosocial behaviors, and externalizing symptoms. *Cultural Diversity and Ethnic Minority Psychology, 13,* 364–373.

Sellers, R., Chavous, T., & Cooke, D. (1998). Racial ideology and racial centrality as predictors of African American college students' academic performance. *Journal of Black Psychology, 24,* 8–27.

Shelton, J., & Sellers, R. (2000). Situational stability and variability in African American racial identity. *Journal of Black Psychology, 26,* 27–50.

Skiba, R. J., Michael, R. S., Nardo, A. C., & Peterson, R. L. (2002). The color of discipline: Sources of racial and gender disproportionality in school punishment. *The Urban Review, 34,* 317–342.

Skiba, R. J., Peterson, R. L., & Williams, T. (1997). Office referrals and suspension: Disciplinary intervention in middle schools. *Education and Treatment of Children, 20,* 295–315.

Solomon, A. (1992). Clinical diagnosis among diverse populations: A multicultural perspective. *Families in Society: The Journal of Contemporary Human Services, 73,* 371–377.

Spencer, M. B., Noll, E., Stolfus, J., & Harpalani, V. (2001). Identity and school adjustment: Revisiting the "acting white" assumption. *Educational Psychologist, 36,* 21–30.

Stallings, T. (2007). Missing persons: Understanding and addressing high school dropouts in North Carolina. *North Carolina Insight, 72–137.*

Sue, D. W. (1994). Whiteness and ethnocentric monoculturalism: Making the "invisible" visible. *American Psychologist, 59,* 761–769. Retrieved August 24, 2009, DOI: 10.1037/003–0664.59.8.761

Tatum, B. D. (1997). *"Why are all the black kids sitting together in the cafeteria?" and other conversations about race.* New York: Basic Books.

Taylor, D. M., & Jaggi, V. (1974). Ethnocentrism and causal attribution in a South Indian context. *Journal of Cross Cultural Psychology, 5,* 162–171.

Vitaliti, L. U. T. (1998). Rural Americans and persons with disabilities. In T. S. Smith (Ed.), *Rural rehabilitation: A modern perspective* (pp. 14–39). Arnaudville, LA: Bow River Publishing.

Walsh, F. (2003). *Normal family processes: Growing diversity and complexity* (3rd ed.). New York: Guilford Press.

Wilson, K. B. (2005). Cultural characteristics of the African American community. In D. A. Harley & J. M. Dillard (Eds.), *Contemporary mental health issues among African Americans* (pp. 149–162). Alexandria, VA: American Counseling Association.

Wu, S. C., Pink, W. T., Crain, R. L., & Moles, O. (1982). Student suspension: A critical reappraisal. *The Urban Review, 14,* 245–303.

CHAPTER EIGHTEEN

Why an Undemocratic Capitalism Has Brought Public Education to Its Knees

A Manifesto

RICHARD A. GIBBONEY

Freedom, if dangerous in the hands of the poor from ignorance . . . is . . . dangerous in the hands of the rich from influence.

— *THOMAS PAINE*, "A SERIOUS LETTER TO THE PEOPLE OF PENNSYLVANIA," 1778

It is wrong to say God made rich and poor. He made only male and female; and He gave them the earth for their inheritance.

—THOMAS PAINE

Unchecked capitalism is destroying our nation's public schools, and No Child Left Behind (NCLB) is the final nail in their coffin. Marching under the banner of "accountability," right-wing, pro-business forces are willfully undermining the democratic right of all children to a free, high-quality education.

Rather than support policies designed to reduce poverty and its toxic effects on the ability of children to succeed in school, our lawmakers are pursuing the misbegotten path of penalizing schools in poverty-stricken cities and rural areas for their failure to work educational miracles. In so doing, they are eroding the promise of our democracy.

Most children at the bottom of the economic ladder start their formal education years behind middle-class children in language development, social behavior, and general knowledge of the world. This self-evident fact, repeatedly confirmed in research studies, creates a learning gap of Grand Canyon proportions between the children of social privilege and those who grow up poor, who are disproportionately black and Hispanic.

No system of schools—public or private—has ever demonstrated that it can close this poverty-induced learning gap for most children. If policy makers know this—and they surely must—they ignore it. In fact, in the two decades preceding No Child Left Behind, a succession of presidents and Congresses gradually abandoned historically successful Great Society programs that had lifted many of the poor out of poverty. Today, more than one-quarter of American children live in poverty, more than in any other industrialized nation.[1]

At the same time, those in the corporate elite and their political allies have ratcheted up the pressure on schools with a harsh accountability system that they have consistently shunned for themselves. Can you imagine applying to Enron and the Wall Street financial manipulators who brought us the credit and home foreclosure crises the same punitive standards we now apply to the schools?

With No Child Left Behind, Congress ratified an upside-down education reform strategy: improve learning by feeding children less and testing them more. For those schools most affected by the false standards of NCLB—largely the ones in our poorest neighborhoods—all creativity, intelligence, and imagination have been sucked out of teaching and learning. The premise of the law—holding schools accountable for test results without any guarantees that students have received expert instruction in safe, well-equipped schools—contravenes science, flouts morality, and makes no economic sense.

And in what I believe to be a historic and an unconscionable failure, our nation's educators have stood by and let all this happen. Instead of relying on the energizing principles of democracy—equity, opportunity, and fairness—to fight this law and the mind-set it grows out of, educators have taken political and professional cover in technicalities.

Teacher unions and groups representing administrators and superintendents have protested No Child Left Behind only around the edges and primarily from a narrow and self-interested intellectual point of view. They have not engaged in meaningful policy debates about the relationship of poverty to educational achievement, the essential role public education plays in our democracy, the huge disparity in wealth between the "haves" and the "have-nots," or the role of schools in creating citizens/workers who can think. We educators cannot continue to act so thoughtlessly, or this nation will not survive as a democracy.

I am not saying, as knee-jerk critics of my viewpoint allege, that poor children cannot learn. Neither teachers nor policy makers should be allowed to hide behind this facile and insidious assumption. This Manifesto is not about the so-called soft bigotry of low expectations that denies poor children a path out of poverty.

Given all that we know from neuroscience about early brain development and the role of environment in nurturing aptitude, schools cannot be expected on their own to close the achievement gap between rich and poor. Yet teachers are pilloried and innocent children intellectually abused for failing to learn under the drill-for-skill, test-'em-often methods advocated by the Bush Administration, by both political parties, and by the biggest lobbying group in Washington, the U.S. Chamber of Commerce.[2] The leadership of the nation and of public education seems not to understand that an undemocratic capitalism wants to destroy public education in favor of a system of private and for-profit schools paid for with taxpayer money.

NCLB Threatens Public Schools

No Child Left Behind has made public education itself fair game for profiteers, and this can only mean two things: corruption and higher costs. This law turns over huge chunks of public education to those whose overriding goal is to make money, not educate children. Note the questionable tutoring industry that has materialized to provide "supplemental services" without solid evidence to date that it has helped poor children. And according to Jonathan Kozol, the test-prep and testing industry generated $2.8 billion in 2005.[3]

But those whose jobs are most threatened by the destruction of the public education system—teachers and administrators—have been unwilling to grasp the import of these developments. Their reaction confirms my thesis that our democracy is "tied and bound." Educators, too, are intellectual captives of the radical, undemocratic capitalism that has taken over our nation.

Unions Abandon the Fight

The best that the National Education Association has mustered in response to NCLB is the shrill complaint that Congress has declined to "fully fund" this disastrous law. The feeble response of the NEA is a sorry comedown for an organization that was once a vigorous defender of public education.

In *Whose America? Culture Wars in the Public Schools*, education historian Jonathan Zimmerman outlines how the radical Right in the 1940s and 1950s attacked public schools on several fronts: communism, internationalism (the United Nations), and "sexual depravity"(which it linked to race). Back then, however, these fearmongers had to face down an NEA that knew how to beat them at their own game.

In 1941, to counteract assaults on social studies textbooks, the NEA established the National Commission for the Defense of Democracy Through Education. In 1949, it teamed with the Rockefeller Foundation and the Carnegie Corporation to form the National Citizens Commission for the Public Schools, a body that included such distinguished citizens as Roy Larsen, president of Time, Inc. Both commissions used multimedia and advertisements to counter right-wing attacks.[4]

This advocacy touched me personally. When I was a teacher in a progressive school system in Ferndale, Michigan, during the height of Sen. Joseph McCarthy's Red-baiting, our staff was attacked by Allen Zoll. I remember his name as if it were yesterday. Zoll, the leader of a national right-wing organization with fascist connections, was an anti-Semite and a hater of public schools. His innuendo-ridden pamphlet was cleverly titled *How Red Is the Little Red School House?* The NEA was not timid then about using forceful public relations strategies to lash back at Zoll on behalf of both our district and public education in general.

But times have changed. Today, the NEA is quiet and is not engaged in defending public education directly through citizen involvement and headline-grabbing commissions, as it once did. Its blind acceptance of NCLB is akin to an innocent man's complaint on the way to the gallows that the hangman bought too cheap a rope.

Randi Weingarten, president of the American Federation of Teachers, also buys into what I call the child- and teacher-destructive essence of NCLB. In the October 2007 edition of her advertorial "What Matters Most," in the *New York Times*, Weingarten calls for changes to the test-based accountability system, not for its elimination. Like her colleagues at NEA, she prefers to ignore the role poverty plays in low student achievement and shows that she implicitly believes New York City schools can close the achievement gap between socially privileged students and those who are less privileged. This is nonsense.

Weingarten prefers to ignore data indicating that children in some of our most poverty-burdened schools post achievement test scores on a par with those of some Third World countries. In 2003, students in Washington, D.C., for instance, scored lower than those in 36 nations in mathematics, and 26 nations outscored Mississippi students in science.

But when one looks at average state scores in the 14 states where there is no massive urban poverty, we find that only one nation, Singapore, scored above those states in science.[5] Even if they teach test-prep and retest, NCLB-style, 35 hours a week, teachers and schools by themselves cannot reverse the crushing effects of poverty and unstable families on educational potential.

TABLE 1.

Eighth-Grade TIMSS Science and Math Scores by Degree of Poverty School Attended

Poverty Level	Score	
	Science	Math
Wealthy Communities	571	547
High-Poverty Communities	461	444
U.S. Average	527	504
International Average	473	466

Source: Data from Third International Mathematics and Science Study, 2003. Adapted from David C. Berliner, "Our Impoverished View of Educational Reform," *Teachers College Record*, August 2005, Table 2, p. 17.

Notice in Table 1 that both science and mathematics have a similar pattern: students in wealthy communities score about 100 points higher than students in high-poverty communities. Our socially privileged students are also nearly 100 points above the international average. This does not look like a failing school system to me. There is a huge political and democratic failure, however, in our toleration of poverty, but those among the elite don't want to talk about it. It's a safer "wealth protector" to deflect public attention to our "failing" public schools and to ignore the poor.

School superintendents are also misguided. As for school administrators, they are busy gaming the system by manipulating test-score results and subgroup sizes to make their schools look better rather than condemning NCLB itself as an attack on the oldest, most democratic system of public education in the world. In January 2004, I sent to 225 randomly chosen Pennsylvania superintendents (out of 501) a five-page abstract of "No Child Left Behind: Reform or Trojan Horse?"—an unpublished paper I had written. A short handwritten note from me invited their reaction. I received but 10 responses. One interested superintendent invited me to a discussion on NCLB with about 20 of his colleagues. That was it.

Even Phi Delta Kappa has succumbed. In 2006, its advocacy committee endorsed reauthorizing the law with amendments designed to "make it better." I hate to say it, but I think that, within the education profession today, numbers (i.e., test scores) are revered while ideas are suspect. The leadership of the teacher unions and the education professoriate are lost in a deceptively appealing array of disciplinary techniques typically devoid of democratic, theoretical, and historical content and, therefore, without practical democratic effect.

The superintendents and the PDK advocacy committee are examples of one reason why societies fail, according to Jared Diamond in his brilliant book, *Collapse*. That is, the leadership fails to identify a threat to society even though the cultural knowledge at the time is sufficient to recognize the threat. What the superintendents and PDK failed to see is that education is an idea game, not a technique game.[6]

Dewey Abandoned

As the practitioners and professors wander in this disciplinary thicket, they abandon the humanistic and generous philosophy of John Dewey. Dewey saw the sharing of ordinary experiences and interests as something to value; he described democracy as *life lived* (not just talked about) in a *community* "of varied and shared interests." Dewey feared, however, that without an intelligent vigilance, the few would take over from the many, the rich would dominate the poor, and the common good would be replaced by plutocratic corporate private interest.

Sadly, Dewey's fears are being realized. I can only conclude that educators have been seduced by the viewpoint that considers only the economic value of schooling as a training ground for workers and not the centrality of public education to the survival of democracy. In the endless parade of education "reforms," a focus on technical skills has replaced the pursuit of ideas, democratic ideals, and civic courage. My 1994 book, *The Stone Trumpet*, analyzed 34 reforms put forth by governments, foundations, researchers, and educators between 1960 and 1990. Only six fully cultivated democratic and intellectual values.[7]

By treating NCLB only as a technical and political problem rather than as a grave threat to democracy and to public education, our anti-intellectual unions and timid leaders undermine democracy itself. You may think that I am overstating the case. But all U.S. presidents, beginning with Ronald Reagan, along with a succession of Congresses, have favored the interests of corporations over the democratic and economic concerns of citizens. This pro-business bias has been hostile not just to public education, but to other social goods, including progressive tax policies and universal health care.

Structural changes in the economy—summarized in the term "globalization"—have opened new investment opportunities and sources of profit for such companies as Wal-Mart and have induced new stresses for their employees who work for "low pay and elusive benefits," as Robert Reich puts it.[8] Other economists such as John K. Galbraith, Paul Krugman, and Joseph Stiglitz acknowledge this fact as well.

Reich says that by 2007 corporations and wealthy individuals owned both the Democratic and Republican parties and the U.S. Congress. He outlines the threat to democracy posed by a voracious capitalism (although I don't think he discusses sufficiently the threat to our basic institutions, including public basic and higher education). While real wages for most workers have barely grown since the mid-1970s, executive compensation has soared to obscene levels, even for corporate leaders who have run their companies into the ground and brought disaster to our economy.

As a result of the administrations of the first President Bush and of President Clinton (who directed one of the most pro-business Democratic administrations ever), and in response to the destructive policies of the current President Bush, the undemocratic capitalist fox has been steadily devouring the public chickens. Medicare, Social Security, and any chance for widespread, publicly supported early childhood education have all been imperiled.

Democracy in Jeopardy

Next to go will be democracy itself. Think about it: What democratic civilization has ever thrived on the curious notion that its proper goal is making widgets for 50 cents and selling them for 100 cents *regardless of the human, environmental, and social cost*? Can such thinking ever lead to justice and domestic tranquility?

This obsession with profit-at-any-social-cost is inherent to capitalist philosophy. But most Americans are ill informed in this area or refuse to believe that the ax will ever fall on them.

Economist Duncan Foley, in *Adam's Fallacy: A Guide to Economic Theology*, explains how capitalism is good at doing some things well, like money accumulation for capital investment. On the other hand, he says, capitalism creates income inequality, tolerates poverty, and is hostile to the physical and democratic environment—including public schools. Foley speaks directly to my vision of "democracy tied and bound." He writes: "[Capitalism] creates new sources of wealth *and ways of life by destroying existing sources of wealth and community*" (emphasis added).[9]

Do not lightly pass over the italicized words in the preceding paragraph. You have just read the most socially radical words in the economic lexicon. Blue collar workers in Ohio and Pennsylvania may not know the words "[capitalism] destroys existing sources of wealth and community," but they feel the slashes an abstract economic idea can inflict.

But you will not find Foley's ideas in the incessant stock market reports and business commentary on TV, on radio, or in print. In these media, capitalism is implicitly characterized as a gift-giving Santa Claus, world without end. Few if any of the high social costs of unfettered capitalism get in the way of the 24/7 Good News.

At the same time, I've come to understand that the captivity of democracy by market forces is not the result of a corporate conspiracy. On the contrary, corporations are doing what they are "wired" to do: work fiercely for competitive advantage regardless of social or environmental considerations. Reich points out that "Wal-Mart executives are only doing what they are supposed to do: Make money for their investors and give customers low prices. Like players in any game, [Wal-Mart] executives are doing *whatever is necessary to win*" (emphasis added).[10]

We have gotten into the mess we're in today because the guardians of democracy—the leaders of our government and public institutions—have not been equally zealous in pursuing democratic goals. Instead, they have let themselves be seduced by the worst of capitalism's lures.

Capitalism Not Socially Neutral

Capitalism is never socially neutral; its effects ripple deep and broad. Take the development of the automobile and its radical effects on community life as a provocative example of technology's powerful influence on daily life in our democracy. In the short term, the auto industry made its creators and manufacturers rich and created a whole new market. But cars also made the sub-urbs possible, drained talent and money from cities, and stimulated massive highway building, which helped to create today's sprawl. At the same time, the automobile industry offered high-paid, if routinized, work that helped build the middle class after 1950. Today, automobiles con-tribute to global climate change, to our dependence on oil, and, it has been argued, to our ongoing engagement in Iraq.

Anyone who acts as if capitalism is socially neutral is not looking at the real world. The beast feeds itself by using its raw power to prosper. Our failure to hang onto our democratic ideals has permitted the social good brought on by innovation to morph into orgies of overindulgence by the privileged few.

And you know how this will always pan out. While families with incomes in the top 20% own about 90% of the nation's wealth, 80% of American households live on less than 10% of that wealth. It is clear that poor and working-class families are not receiving their fair share of the wealth they have helped to create by being good citizens, by working, and by raising their children.

From 1983 to 1998, the household gain in wealth for the bottom 80% of U.S. households—that is, most of us—was a mere 9%. For the next 19% of households, the figure was more than four times as much, 38%. What about the top 1%, you ask? Their wealth increased by a whop-ping 53%.[11] Such data make plain why schools alone, since school achievement is tied so close-ly to social class, will never be able to close the rich/poor, white/minority achievement gaps. But if we look at the net worth of white and black families in America, we can see in simple num-bers the huge disparity of wealth that reduces the achievement of poor minority and white youth in public schools, because school achievement is related to social class and class is related to wealth. Median net worth in 2004 for black families was less than $12,000; for white families, about $118,000.[12] These figures are less than democracy demands. Even the white family figure is low because it would pay for about three one-week hospital stays for a serious illness.

NCLB Undermines Public Trust in Schools

Facts about inequality haven't stopped the corporate elite that brought about this huge imbal-ance in wealth from blaming the public schools for the very low achievement of poverty's chil-dren. In No Child Left Behind, the full power of the federal government was mustered to implement a law that undermines the public's trust in education, needlessly requires the involve-ment of private corporations in the work of public schools, and imposes unscientific standards, punitive sanctions, and impossible deadlines for "results." All of this virtually ensures the fail-ure of most schools with high proportions of poor and minority students, while harassing teach-ers and students with needless and expensive testing.

For many critics, teachers have become the villains in the wealthy elite's panic over educa-tional accomplishment and foreign competition. But teachers don't cause financial meltdowns, home foreclosures, climate change, or hurricanes. And they don't invade countries or outsource jobs. Teachers don't cause mind-numbing conditions of poverty that limit children's ability to learn. However, teachers are the ones asked to cope with the poisonous effects of poverty. Why? Because most of society doesn't give a damn.

With our nation's demographics rapidly changing—black and Hispanic students now make up 42% of public school enrollment[13]—and the historically persistent correlation between minority status, poverty, and low achievement, one can imagine the results for public schools when the media give their usual shallow treatment to the predictably low achievement of these blameless children. More and more public schools will be dishonestly labeled "failures," and our democracy will be weakened and further imperiled.

Harvard sociologist Orlando Patterson begs us to understand and acknowledge our own history, recounting the "familial ethnocide" inflicted on African Americans by Southern slaveholders. In most cases, the post-slavery descendants of slaves have yet to recover fully from this assault on the black family. The result, Patterson writes, has been a lack of parental support and discipline, the absence of fathers from the lives of 70% of black children born to single mothers, and the recourse of young people to gangs as parental substitutes. "By whatever means . . . lower class Afro-Americans have got to recommit themselves . . . to stable [families] . . . and to raising their children," he writes.[14]

This bit of social science research reveals the false premises of NCLB and the absurdity of educators who did not apply the data of their ordinary school experience to understanding the law's hypocrisy. Until our supercapitalistic democracy recognizes the rights of the poor and moves to correct this shameful legacy, children, disproportionately black and increasingly Hispanic, will be needlessly denied the privileges of middle-class family membership, which motivates them to learn and to do well in school. Unless more families are helped to grow into the working and middle classes over several generations, their children will continue to achieve at Third World levels in New York, Philadelphia, Detroit, and Washington, D.C. And no fast-talking superintendent of schools—or even a CEO of schools—will make any difference for most children in poverty-stricken families.

In this presidential election year [2008], only former Sen. John Edwards spoke directly to the issues of poverty and class. Overlooking such an elephant in the living room is a measure of political neglect beyond reason. One would hope that our political leaders would act as if they understood that extreme inequality of wealth and child poverty are detrimental to a vital democracy.

Two Faces of Poverty

Before I go into my recommendations, let me try to put two faces on the seemingly unreal problem of child poverty and the unbelievable amount of learning and positive attitudes that socially privileged children acquire at home and bring to school. First, take my young friend Gabriella. Gabriella lives along Philadelphia's Main Line, a 30-mile stretch of affluent suburbs running along the old "main line" of the Pennsylvania Railroad.

To know Gabriella is to know how a rich and informal home learning environment can lead to phenomenal language and cultural learning by age 10. Her parents believe that the "cultivation of the mind and feelings is the best life and the best preparation for life" (interview with Gabriella's mother). Gabriella started improvising songs and dances with her mother when she was just 2, attended a high-quality preschool, has 300 books in her home, reads or is read to every night, has traveled to Italy and Hong Kong, regularly visits museums, and has attended Broadway shows. When she studied the Colonial period in school, Gabriella dressed herself and her dolls in Colonial clothes, and her parents helped her get library books on Colonial crafts and cooking. Her love of learning was fostered at home; her well-endowed school system can now build on her already solid knowledge and drive to learn.

Then consider Anthony, a young man I don't know personally, who lives in Newark, New Jersey. Anthony was abandoned as a toddler by his crack-addicted parents and grew up in a succession of unhappy foster homes. He was finally taken in by a hospital housekeeper who was a distant relative. But Anthony ran away when he thought he was being asked to do too many chores and now lives with an aunt. Once, he had a penchant for shoplifting, and he still tends to settle any disputes with his fist, a habit he is gradually breaking under the mentorship of Newark's mayor, Cory Booker, who took Anthony and two other boys under his wing.

Under No Child Left Behind, the same tests are administered to Gabriella and Anthony, and the same results expected. Their family lives and their school lives are in stark contrast. Gabriella's family is nurturing, and her school intellectually enriching. Anthony's family is dysfunctional, and his school overburdened.

Does this make any sense? No wonder our democracy is tied and bound.

The Doxology

The sun stands low on the democratic horizon. Where are the leaders we need? Who or what will break the eerie silence? With more than three million teachers and education professors, with two powerful unions, with enormous potential to raise many millions for a nationwide fight in the media against an adversary we've known since the 1950s, why have we chosen to play dead?

Isn't fighting for public education and democracy the worthiest of causes? How can you not join an army where no one is killed and everyone wins? Our enemies fight a ruthless fight, and if they win, everyone loses. Lies unchallenged are lies believed. Just ask John Kerry.

An enemy with a clear and firmly held set of beliefs, however destructive and unjust, has to love having wimpy opponents like us. We wilt at a frown. What, for God's sake, are we so afraid of? With leadership like this, World War II would have been a walkover for the Axis. Why do we line the darkening streets, silent before the march of the economic authoritarians?

Today, the voices of protest are weak and scattered. In the ordinariness of defeat, this day appears as any other in a century of days, and the ordinariness of this day mutes any instinct to cry out at the loss.

Why the silence? No one told the people. Sixty years of successful attacks have left public educators so addled that our leaders accept the corrupting ideas and values of those who would destroy us. We have adopted their false language of accountability, standards, profit, privatization, competition, and numbers. We then suffer the punitive and harsh demands of NCLB, the weapon designed to destroy us, inch by test score inch.

The "achievement gap" between the privileged and the poor will endure until the elite discard their damning "bigotry of low *social* expectations," expectations that have imprisoned generations in poverty and closed the door to their entry to the middle class.

Another decade of attacks in a procorporate federal administration of whatever party, and public education will be two heartbeats from death. The poor and the working class will suffer grievously.

Democracy is a verb, not a noun for a dead category.

Recommendations

1. Address the Problems of Poverty and Capitalism

If we as a society ever muster the courage to enact the two recommendations I am about to offer for dealing with the problems created by poverty, we are certain to close the achievement gap between socially privileged students, who are mostly white, and less socially privileged students, regardless of their ethnicity or color.

- *Long term.* Begin a systematic plan to bring at least half of the families living in poverty into the middle class in a generation. That is, by 2033. Bring the other half of families into the middle class by 2058.
- *Short term.* Establish excellent public prekindergarten programs for all 3- and 4-year-olds.

There is reason to believe we can reach all of these goals. Prekindergarten programs were part of Prime Minister Tony Blair's 1999 pledge "to end child poverty forever." By 2006, 700,000 kids—17%—were lifted out of poverty and found themselves within shouting range of Blair's short-term goal.[15]

Known as Sure Start, Britain's program looks a bit like a 1960s community action program in the U.S. But the British one is community action on steroids. The school becomes a center in which all social services combine to help the poor, working parents, and children of the middle class. A reporter for the *Guardian* describes the school/social centers this way:

> Every child from birth finds here everything necessary to thrive, especially for those who never see a book at home or learn to count, and barely talk. Here speech therapists, social workers, [home] health visitors, and high-calibre nursery teachers help all children reach primary school ready to learn. Here working mothers are guaranteed affordable child care, in a place where parents of all [social] classes create a hub for the local community. That's the dream and in some places it's all there.[16]

The U.S. has tackled major social problems before. In 1935, Congress created Social Security. At the time, older people were the largest poverty group in America. In about 65 years—slow and steady—90% of this group had climbed out of poverty. Today, children are the biggest poverty group in America.

Nobel prize-winning economist Joseph Stiglitz, in *The Roaring Nineties*, argues that the nation can afford to address poverty directly. "We could, if we wished," he writes, "end domestic poverty and malnutrition. We could, if we wished, ensure that everyone had a basic modicum of health care. . . . The United States chooses not to provide these basic services, because it chooses not to tax itself."[17]

Implementing my recommendations—moving poverty families to the working class and middle class in two generations and establishing excellent early childhood programs for all social classes—will truly leave no child behind. If we act on these two recommendations, the achievement level of public school students will slowly rise. Moreover, our national obsession with premature quantitative evaluations of new programs—a major error that Britain avoids—kills potentially successful programs before they can show their *social/democratic* worth.

2. Develop a Comprehensive and Democratic Theory of Education

We have lost our *idea* of the democratic purpose of public education, and that has infected our practice and policy making. NCLB is my evidence. We badly need to restore a comprehensive theory to undergird our policies. I believe John Dewey's theory of education is our best choice.

Dewey's theory of education is the only extant theory that is both *comprehensive and democratic*. It is compatible with scientific inquiry, the humanistic values of the democratic ethic, and the cultivation of the mind. Dewey's theory is humanistic, generous in spirit, yet suffused with the tough-mindedness of science.

The best source of a sound theory is philosophy, understood within the context of history and clearly linked to fundamental issues of practice. I believe that the history of educational research shows that no collection of theoretically unmoored research studies—often built on a false sense of precision through quantification—has ever led to a testable, comprehensive, democratic theory of education.

Psychological and sociological studies have not led to a comprehensive theory compatible with democratic and intellectual values. Many of these studies are useful, but they have not created a robust theory of education.

Broad social theories, such as Marxism, have not led to a comprehensive, democratic theory of education, though they have generated much writing on the subject.

Education is not primarily about technique. It's not about teaching technique, managerial technique, or research technique. These activities have value only insofar as they serve the essential purpose of education, which is the cultivation of democratic values and the cultivation of the mind. Absent the horizon-to-horizon reach of a comprehensive, democratic theory, technique wanders in a forest of incoherent empirical facts, no matter how many millions of dollars in grant money schools of education devour to raise their prestige ratings.

Today, these ancillary "fields" of teaching technique, managerial technique, and research technique dominate education in the universities. The democratic and intellectual ends of education are tragically ignored. How much—even in crude dollars—is this lack of a comprehensive theory costing us in lost brain power among the poor? Millions? Billions? More?

Schools of education should be teaching Deweyan theory, with the social sciences, humanities, and education serving as springboards for richer questions to explore and as critical frames for the theory itself. Let's scrap fragmented research programs in favor of pursuing theoretical and practical coherence.

I believe that too many public school leaders revert to technique rather than to ideas when they face a practical problem. This is the story of the profession's gutless, incoherent response to 60 years of planned attacks on all major social programs, including public basic and higher education. This cannot continue if we are to preserve our democracy.

Even Barack Obama gets an amnesia attack when education is the topic. In his great Philadelphia speech on race, he speaks against trivial distractions that obstruct serious political discourse and says, "Not this time. This time we want to talk about the crumbling schools that are stealing the future of black children and white children and Asian children and Hispanic children and Native American children. This time we want to reject the cynicism that tells us that these kids can't learn."

One would never know from Mr. Obama's statement that between 1820 and 1920 the children of more than 30 million Poles, Italians, Jews, and Germans learned English and democratic values in American public schools.[18] No expensive private school would dare tarnish its reputation by educating the ethnically blemished. Mr. Obama's education advisers are doing America harm by not educating him on the critical role public schools play in the democratization of immigrants to this day.

No private system of schools enrolls millions of poor children who speak little English. When will our governors, presidents, legislators—and public school teachers themselves—understand that the humble public school is one of the greatest democratic inventions in the world.

Henry Steele Commager, a great American historian, quotes Mary Antin, who arrived in America as a child. "Education was free," Antin writes, "the one thing [my father] was able to promise us . . . surer, safer than bread and shelter. . . . the freedom of the schools of Boston! No application to make, no questions asked, no examinations, rulings, exclusions; no machinations, no fees. The door stood open to every one of us."[19]

Not one idea in Mr. Obama's statement can withstand the academic scrutiny of mainstream social scientists or informed educators. Mr. Obama's statement might sound good to his education advisors who think that "multiculturalism" is a comprehensive education theory rather than a slogan (which fits nicely, by the way, under the more substantive category of democracy).

Mr. Obama's unfortunate statement is strong evidence of the effectiveness of 60 years of propaganda against public basic and higher education and the interests of the poor and working class. When a liberal presidential candidate mouths the attack ideas of the radical Right against public education, is this not reasonable proof that our "strategy" of being the quiet mice in this society has killed our voice even within the councils of the Democratic Party? Who speaks with political power and conviction for public education across the decades? No one.

3. Defend Public Schools

Teacher unions and organizations of professional educators—at both the national and state levels—must mount a vigorous and clear-headed campaign to defend a great American institution against the false charge that public schools are failing, leveled by those I refer to as the Mystic Monks of the Market. This charge is blatant propaganda pushed by the economic elite to discredit public investment that helps ordinary citizens. And teacher unions and the profession in general let it pass like any other casual remark. This is not prudent behavior.

The charge is nonsense, but it is clearly hurtful. The threat of school privatization hangs heavy in our political air like smog in Beijing. We already have Edison Schools and charter schools, some run by profit-making companies that take multimillion-dollar bites out of city education budgets.

Consider this possibility: imagine Wal-Mart or a billion-dollar hedge fund running a huge network of selective, undemocratic schools in America. Today, teachers are among the few middle-class toilers with decent jobs. When the Wal-Marters arrive, this private, cost-cutting money machine will have you, the teacher, working for $12 an hour with no benefits, a single-year contract, and no union representation.

It is imperative that the teacher unions initially organize an aggressive $50-million national and regional media campaign to tell the public and politicians the *democratic* success story of public education. The crudeness of that invidious media phrase, "our failing public schools," should be the first target of any such bold PR campaign.

If half the teachers in America contributed $20 each, a total war chest of more than $30 million would be available. Perhaps the Rockefeller or Carnegie foundations or Warren Buffett would throw in an additional $50 million. All it would take to get the ball rolling is a little out-of-the-box leadership.

You can be sure that the enemies of public education would not have sleepwalked through 60 years of ill-founded attacks. They would have fought like starving bears. Let's give public education the kind of warm and nurturing environment that the single-minded capitalists give themselves. Now *there* is a reform idea!

4. Defuse the Social Dynamite in Our Large Cities

In 1961 a conservative scientist and university president warned Americans of a danger more threatening to democracy than Iraq was when we invaded: "Social dynamite is building up in our . . . cities in the form of unemployed out-of-school youth, especially in the Negro slums. We need accurate and frank information [on this condition] neighborhood by neighborhood."

A page later James B. Conant speaks directly to this democratic failure when he says that he has "sought to create a sense of anxious thoughts" in the minds of good citizens who live in the suburbs but who work in the cities. Conant imparts this thought: "To improve the work of slum schools requires an improvement in the lives of families who inhabit the slums. . .but without a drastic change in the employment prospects for urban Negro youth, relatively little can be accomplished. . . . we need to know the facts, and when these facts indicate a dangerous social situation the American people should be prepared to take prompt action before it is too late."[20]

The school achievement of minority students, Conant says with uncommon sense, and their ability to work can come *only from the improvement of their family* and, I would add, their community lives. If, in 1961, we had started a two-generation "education for democratic citizenship" program to bring most of our poor families into the working and middle class, it is possible that by today, 50% to 70% of the children from formerly poor families would be achieving at or beyond grade level in our public schools, as middle-class children have always achieved in public schools. We chose instead to do nothing *significant* about family poverty and high minority dropout rates. By ignoring the morality of the democratic ethic, we chose to create an army of more than one million alienated youth annually, youth who are tenuously attached to school, work, family, and community.[21]

Is it sensible domestic or national security policy to dump one million undereducated and unemployed youth on the cold streets of our cities and towns every year? Does this human dumping accord with the morality of the democratic ethic?

A few years after Conant's warning about "social dynamite building in our cities," Los Angeles and Detroit were in flames. Must we wait for a second rebellion in these times of acute economic, political, and international stress—times that may mark the unraveling of American supremacy—before we discover the moral and social power of the democratic ethic, a power abused by both political parties since the 1980s?

QUESTIONS TO CONSIDER

1. Gibboney argues that "schools cannot be expected on their own to close the achievement gap between rich and poor." Which factors does he claim have been neglected in the dominant analysis of educational policy and practice, particularly in the No Child Left Behind (NCLB) legislation?

2. Do you agree or disagree with the author's statement that "leadership of the teacher unions and the education professoriate are lost in a deceptively appealing array of disciplinary techniques typically devoid of democratic, theoretical, and historical content, and therefore, without practical democratic effect"? What does Gibboney mean by that assertion?

3. The author contends that many public schools are "dishonestly labeled 'failures'" and that most of society "doesn't give a damn" about the root causes of poverty and inequality. Do you agree or disagree? Why?

4. What possible solutions does Gibboney offer in terms of righting the economy and education in the United States? How viable and realistic are his recommendations?

Notes

Richard A. Gibboney, "Why an Undemocratic Capitalism Has Brought Public Education to Its Knees: A Manifesto," *Phi Delta Kappan*, Vol. 90, No. 01, September 2008, pp. 21–31. Published here with permission of Phi Delta Kappa International.

1. *Democracy at Risk: The Need for a New Federal Policy in Education* (Washington, D.C.: Forum for Education and Democracy, April 2008), p. iii.
2. Robert B. Reich, *Supercapitalism: The Transformation of Business, Democracy, and Everyday Life* (New York: Borzoi Books, 2007), pp. 134
3. Jonathan Kozol, "The Big Enchilada," *Harper's Magazine*, August 2007.

4. Jonathan Zimmerman, *Whose America? Culture Wars in the Public Schools* (Cambridge, Mass.: Harvard University Press, 2002), p. 88–90, 97–98.

5. David Berliner, "If the Underlying Premise for No Child Left Behind Is False, How Can That Act Solve Our Problems" paper presented to the Iowa Academy of Education, Des Moines, 2004, pp. 7, 9.

6. Jared M. Diamond, *Collapse: How Societies Choose to Fail or Succeed* (New York: Viking, 2005).

7. Richard A. Gibboney, "Reforms's Green Fields," in idem, *The Stone Trumpet: A Story of Practical School Reform, 1960–1990* (Albany: State University Press of New York, 1994), p. 75.

8. Reich, p. 12.

9. Duncan K. Foley, *Adam's Fallacy: A Guide to Economic Theology* (Cambridge, Mass.: Belknap Press of Harvard University Press, 2006), p. 224.

10. Reich, p. 12.

11. Edward N. Wolff, *Top Heavy: A Study of Increasing Inequality of Wealth in the United States* (New York: Twentieth Century Fund, 2002), Figure 3.4, p. 14.

12. Henry Louis Gates, Jr., "Forty Acres and a Gap in Wealth," Op-ed, *New York Times*, 18 November 2007, p. 14.

13. "U.S. Data Show Rapid Minority Growth," *New York Times*, 1 June 2007, p. A-21.

14. Orlando Patterson, *The Ordeal of Integration: Progress and Resentment in America's "Racial" Crisis* (Washington, D.C.: Civitas/Counterpoint, 1998), pp. 186–87.

15. David L. Kirp, *The Sandbox Investment: The Preschool Movement and Kids-First Politics* (Cambridge, Mass.: Harvard University Press, 2007), pp. 228–31.

16. Ibid., pp. 231–33.

17. Joseph E. Stiglitz, *The Roaring Nineties* (New York: Norton, 2003), p. 317.

18. Robert L. Church and Michael W. Sedlak, *Education in the United States: An Interpretive History* (New York: Free Press, 1976).

19. Henry Steele Commager, "Our Schools Have Kept Us Free," *Life*, 16 October 1950, pp. 46–47.

20. James Bryant Conant, *Slums and Suburbs: A Commentary on Schools in Metropolitan Areas* (New York: McGraw-Hill, 1961), pp. 146–47.

21. Christopher B. Swanson, *Cities in Crisis: A Special Analytic Report on High School Graduation* (Bethesda, Md.: Editorial Projects in Education Research Center, 2008), Section 1.

My point of view in this Manifesto has been informed by John Dewey's philosophy, particularly his classic *Democracy and Education: An Introduction to the Philosophy of Education* (New York: Macmillan, 1916).

Democracy and Education is a book whose democratic spirit honors both intelligence and ordinary human experience. I regret that its power as a theory of education has been lost to generations of educators who have not the patience to deal with its brilliant ideas and its complex (if sometimes turgid) academic style.

In the spirit of practice and Dewey's respect for "ordinary experience," I want to list four books that speak more directly to the creative demands of "doing" progressive teaching than the Manifesto offered: Richard A. Gibboney with Clark Webb, *What Every Great Teacher Knows* (Brandon, Vt.: Holistic Education Press, 1998); Deborah Meier, *The Power of Their Ideas* (Boston: Beacon Press, 1995); Nel Noddings, *When School Reform Goes Wrong* (New York: Teachers College Press, 2007); and Laurel N. Tanner, *Dewey's Laboratory School: Lessons for Today* (New York: Teachers College Press, 1997).

PART THREE

Pedagogical Perspectives

CHAPTER NINETEEN

Deferred but Determined

A Middle School Manifesto

JOHN H. LOUNSBURY

Before embarking on this treatise that will provide a historical perspective on the middle level movement and examine its past successes and failings, and prospects for future improvements, I want to declare my great admiration for our public schools. Although I am indeed critical of certain recent developments, I believe that when historians look back on our civilization, they will point to our systems of public schools as America's greatest achievement. Today, in a climate of accountability, it is simply neither fair nor appropriate to label public schools in the United States as failures. Schools and teachers have been and still are America's greatest resource for what is good. What would we do without them?

Public schools in the United States evolved without benefit of a master plan. The elementary, secondary, and collegiate levels developed rather independently of one another. Elementary schools were not established first, and young men attended colleges such as Harvard long before we organized public secondary schools. America's school systems developed piecemeal over time and still are very much works in progress. By the late 1800s, however, many states had organized elementary schools and high schools in an 8–4 pattern that would become the standard as our country began to put its revolutionary vision of education for all American youths into being. The still relatively young middle school movement is part of the larger reorganization initiative that led to the creation of the junior high school in the first decade of the last century. The following four statements highlight relevant developments since then.

- Exactly 100 years have passed since the Indianola Junior High School, generally acknowledged as the first junior high school, was established in Columbus, Ohio, in 1909.
- In 1946, 37 years after the junior high school was introduced, the 6–3–3 pattern of school organization became the predominant pattern in the United States, replacing the 8–4 plan.

- In 1963, William Alexander speaking at Cornell University, first advanced the term "middle school." This event, just 17 years after the junior high school had become majority practice, is commonly used to mark the beginning of the middle school movement.
- By 1983, the new 5–3–4 plan of organization featuring a grades six to eight middle school had become the predominant pattern.

The movement to reorganize secondary education that began in 1909 might then be judged as highly successful, for it actually changed the face of American education twice in a century. The change to the 5–3–4 pattern is particularly remarkable. Just 20 years after entering the educational arena, the number of 6–8 middle schools exceeded the number 7–9 junior high schools. That success, however, has been more in the realm of school organization than in the more critical programmatic areas so central in the vision of both types of middle level organization. Although it is seldom acknowledged, it should be noted that the junior high school advocated by its founders was to be, using the contemporary term, a "developmentally responsive" institution.

However, by the mid-1960s the junior high school—as it had come to be in practice—was commonly viewed as failing. Captured by its parent, it had become what its ill-chosen name implied, a junior *high* school. Could a somewhat similar conclusion be made about the middle school today? Might it be said that the junior high school was the first middle school, or that the middle school is simply today's version of the junior high school? Or that the middle school movement is actually the rebirth of progressive education?

Like its predecessor, the middle school has come under heavy criticism. Because many students did not reach targeted academic goals it was labeled "the weak link in American education," primarily by those who believe the middle school's prime responsibility is to prepare students for advanced high school courses, and the presumption that the school's concern for students as persons was taking away from its academic responsibilities. The general public's perception, based largely on newspaper stories, that the middle school has been a failure is the result of the inability or unwillingness of critics to recognize the difference between the "middle school concept" and "the middle school" as it is commonly practiced. Because a school was newly labeled a middle school, observers assumed it was operating in ways that reflected the advocacy of its proponents, whereas this was seldom the case.

The middle school concept is a philosophy of education with a special spirit and deep theoretical roots, a set of beliefs about kids, education, and the human experience. Those who adhere to it are passionate and determined advocates. The concept's ideals and recommendations are direct reflections of its two prime foundations, the nature and needs of young adolescents and the accepted principles of learning, both undergirded by a commitment to our democratic way of life. The middle school concept is applicable wherever any 10- to 15-year-olds are enrolled.

Jackson and Davis (2000), authors of the influential *Turning Points 2000*, refuted the notion that the middle school has failed and instead optimistically claimed, "Far from having failed, middle grades education is ripe for a great leap forward" (p. 17). In this context, Dickinson (2001) has stated emphatically, "There is nothing wrong with the middle school concept. . . . The concept is as valid today as it was in either of its previous iterations at the turn of the 20th century or in the early 1960s." The problem, he said, is that the middle school itself is suffering from "arrested development" (pp. 3–4). He was correct; but now, since No Child Left Behind (NCLB) (2002) has been in force, mere arrested development has regrettably given way to regression.

The valid middle school concept, it should be recognized, has not been practiced and found wanting; rather, it has been found difficult to implement fully, and practiced then only partially. Putting it all into operation requires making changes that run counter to established school procedures; hence, the concept has not been practiced sufficiently or widely enough to be fairly assessed on a large scale basis. The obvious success of the middle school as an organizational pattern, however, led those who did not understand the difference between the middle school concept and the middle school as a grade organization pattern to the conclusion that the middle school concept was in force and was, therefore, the cause of the perceived failings.

Barriers to Implementation

A major barrier to more widespread implementation of the middle level philosophy is the lack of understanding among the general public about the period of early adolescence and an appreciation of its special importance. It has only been in recent decades that human development specialists have established a research base that informs educators and others about youth in this key transition period as childhood wanes and adolescence comes into its own, roughly between ages 10 to 15. Extensive research on the brain development of young adolescents has provided new insights that counter old assumptions and help us understand teens' behavior. Dr. Jay Giedd (n. d.), a neuroscientist at the National Institute of Mental Health, has conducted longitudinal studies that reveal extensive brain growth and changes occurring about the same time as puberty. The implications of these findings for educators and parents are significant. They provide scientific support for the beliefs about cognitive development upon which rest the foundation of the middle school concept. (See www.pbs.org/wgbh/pages/frontline/shows/teenbrain/interviews/giedd.html; Strauch, 2007)

Another barrier is the pervasive staying power of institutionalized schooling. Established bureaucracies in education perpetuate the status quo. The albatross of departmentalization, for instance, has been difficult to remove from the neck of middle level education, as it is supported by discipline-specific textbooks, tests, and teacher certification as well as long-standing tradition. The public as well holds to a perception of what schools should be like that is not receptive to new ideas. Tyack and Cuban's highly regarded book, *Tinkering Toward Utopia* (1995) offers valuable insights and a sound perspective on the whole process of school reform. They document the reality that reform is a slow and convoluted process at best.

A statement made by the economist John Maynard Keynes highlights a related barrier. "The real difficulty in changing the course of any enterprise," Keynes notes, "lies not in developing new ideas but in escaping from old ones." The soundness of that judgment was apparent in the 1930s and 1940s when neither progressive education nor the proposed junior high school was able to find wide acceptance. Those "new ideas," revived and reshaped by the middle school movement are still having trouble escaping established practices. In large part this is so because few educators have ever experienced schooling except in those old ways and therefore simply cannot envision how formal education could be conducted except via subjects, periods, and classes. Even so, the standard practices of grouping middle school students by chronological age, placing them in classes of 25, and scheduling them in 45–50 minute periods are bereft of any research to justify their unquestioned continuation as the "right" way to conduct an educational program for young adolescents. The stubborn facts of individual differences reach their peak in early adolescence as these young people, each at his or her own time and rate, mature physically, socially, emotionally, intellectually, and morally. Middle level schools, more than other levels, exist to serve diversity; and no scheme of school organization or federal mandate for uniform achievement can wash away human variability.

Positive Exceptions

There are, however, many examples of middle schools that have escaped old ways and implemented very successfully innovative ways of guiding the education of young adolescents. The Alpha team at Shelburne Community School in Vermont has been for 35 years an example of what can happen when educators break out of the conventional barriers (Kuntz, 2005). Putting aside existing practices, members of that multiage team created a highly successful educational program that has helped young adolescents become independent learners and democratic citizens as well as high achievers. The Watershed, Soundings, and Crossroads programs at Radnor Middle School, Wayne, Pennsylvania (Springer, 1994, 2006), are other impressive examples that exemplify how meaningful educational experiences can be when freed from the restrictions of classes, periods, and subjects. Students in these programs equal or exceed their peers in academic achievement, while gaining the skills and dispositions to be lifelong learners and responsible adults. These striking examples of highly successful middle school programs do not stand alone.

In hundreds of middle schools around the country, the middle school concept is practiced to a significant degree, and in those communities, parents are more than pleased with the education their children receive. For example, in 2009 there were more than 190 high performing middle schools in 18 states selected as Schools to Watch under the program sponsored by the National Forum to Accelerate Middle-Grades Reform (www.schoolstowatch.org/what.htm). These schools met the exacting nationally established criteria in the areas of academic excellence, developmental responsiveness, and social equity, with appropriate organizational structure and processes. Following their selection, they serve as mentors and models. Anyone who has spent time in one of the Schools to Watch knows how "right" it is for the students lucky enough to attend—and for the professional teachers who gladly give so much of themselves in guiding the learning and development of youngsters in true learning communities.

Major research studies including some involving networks of schools that have practiced the middle school tenets sufficiently have made it possible to claim with confidence: When the middle school concept is implemented substantially over time, student achievement, including measures by standardized tests, rises, and shows substantial improvement in fulfilling the other broader, more enduring goals of an education results (see *Research and Resources in Support of* This We Believe, NMSA, 2003b, and Felner et al., 1997).

Unfortunately however, the current state and national reform and accountability efforts, ignoring this body of research, continue to try to improve schools as they *currently* are organized, rather than breaking out of existing patterns and instituting changes that are more in harmony with the middle school concept. It is time for educators to end the charade of attempting to correct the acknowledged flaws of middle level schooling by making adjustments in the prevailing system, which is outdated, obsolete, and no longer subject to lasting improvement by cosmetic measures. Its curriculum and typical passive learning instructional approaches were designed for another era, a vastly different student body, and a society markedly unlike our current culture. This assessment was true even before technology expanded the ways students could learn and wrested from teachers considerable control over what students study. Technology, incidentally, has reinforced those elements that make the middle school concept special—collaborative learning, strong student voice, and students engaged with larger world issues.

The Narrowing of "Education"

Historically, public schools in America took responsibility for the social and character education of students just as much as they did for their skill and knowledge development—and parents wanted them to. Over time, however, the attention schools give to molding good citizens and good persons has diminished. The personal-social development of students has simply become less intentional on the part of teachers and schools—although not where the middle school concept is in force. This shift in the understanding of what an education entails was evident in the "back to the basics" years and in the days following *Sputnik* when science and mathematics took center stage. Then in 2002, NCLB with its fostering of an obsession with testing further eroded attention to anything that was not perceived as directly related to achieving acceptable test scores. Now it seems the public—and, indeed, much of the profession—is resigned to letting the temporary acquisition of information as measured by paper and pencil tests define an education.

This tendency to narrow what comprises an education comes at a time when our society is besieged with major problems, all of which result directly from the consciously chosen behaviors of individuals, ranging from unruly kids on the school bus and cyber-bullying to petty crimes, from random acts of violence on the street to high crimes in the corporate executive offices, from domestic violence, to teen pregnancy, to drug addiction, and on and on. It is imperative that youth receive guidance in the non-cognitive aspects of an education from those given the responsibility for providing a formal education. Middle level schools are the most appropriate places to influence students' personal-social behavior, for one's adult behavior runs in channels cut deep during early adolescence. Inescapably, middle school teaching is a moral enterprise, and an education in its fullest sense has to involve heart as well as head, attitude as well as information, spirit as well as scholarship, and conscience as well as competence.

The middle school is not just a physical place in which teachers teach about things needed in the future; it is an environment in which youth come of age, acting out new roles as maturing social beings. It is not a teaching factory, but a laboratory of living, not just a learning place, but also a growing place. In fact, what the process of education teaches young adolescents about themselves is likely to have more lasting impact than the content of the curriculum. If middle level schools do not fulfill their historic pastoral role and help develop ethical, responsible, self-reliant, and clear-thinking individuals, they will have failed at what ultimately is their most important responsibility.

A Broader View

Educators must help the public grasp a bigger and better vision of what constitutes an "education" with its many facets and understand the dynamics and intricacies of teaching, which is so much more than instructing, testing, and grading. Teachers shape lives less by direct instruction than by what I call "wayside teaching"—those small personal acts, probing questions, subtle reminders, earned commendations, and individual challenges. Their influence when on dress parade presenting information to a class is likely to pale in significance compared to the impact they may have in a 30-second up-close and personal conversation. Citizens all need to become fully aware of the importance of the teacher as a person and model, and appreciate the significance of the experiences youth undergo both in and out of school during these years when they are vulnerable and malleable. Early adolescence provides a window of opportunity to impact the lives of students in enduring ways, one that opens but once and is largely closed by the tenth grade.

The public also must come to recognize that success, both in future schooling and in life itself, will depend not so much on what courses have been passed, but rather on what skills, dispositions, and habits of mind have been developed. When the widely accepted goal of academic excellence is examined thoughtfully it really comes down to being more a matter of those skills and attitudes than the possession of certain bodies of knowledge. In addition, the overemphasis on improving test scores works against developing the very attributes needed to succeed in today's global society—initiative, effectiveness in working as a part of a team, and the ability to organize information, articulate ideas, and solve problems. Reports that cite the characteristics desired in employees all put teamwork at the top of the list of needed skills, along with problem solving and effective oral communication—behaviors not readily acquired under teaching procedures being used to prepare students for standardized tests.

America needs middle schools with missions big enough to help youngsters decide what to read as well as how to read and, for example, to ensure that their mastery of mathematics will not be applied in an embezzlement scheme. John Ruskin claimed: "Education does not mean teaching people to know what they do not know. It means teaching them to behave as they do not behave." In a similar vein, Teddy Roosevelt warned: "To educate a person in mind and not in morals is to educate a menace to society."

Mother Nature provides at this key transition time of life a golden opportunity for middle level educators to both influence the behavior of individuals and to take learning to a higher level, challenging students intellectually and engaging them actively in the teaching-learning enterprise. Sometime during the middle level years students reach a level of mental maturity that permits them to be analytical, to question, to hypothesize. They are ripe for being immersed in their education in new and more meaningful ways as they are capable of learning and achieving at levels seldom realized. Prescribing curriculum for young adolescents in an attempt to mass-produce a good education is counter-productive. However, educators continue to specify curricular content in the pious hope that enforced uniformity will produce excellence. The presentation of canned content, however, is not effective in advancing the *intellectual* development of students.

Future Prospects

Public education itself has been under attack in America, however quietly and slowly, for many years. The middle school movement, progressive as it is, has been a prime target for those forces that do not share the belief middle level advocates hold about the importance of a democratic, student-centered education. The future success of the middle school movement has implications that go far beyond what becomes of just those middle level grades, for the success of other theoretically sound reform efforts is closely tied to the middle school movement. Having almost weathered the storm—though sustaining considerable damage—of NCLB, can the middle school movement continue to be the green and growing edge of lasting reform? Can it lead the way to restoring pride in public education and its place of prominence in America?

What is past is prologue. Thus, I return to the Eight Year Study (Aikin, 1942) conducted in the late 1930s to find a perspective that fits what we should be about in the days ahead. The 30 experimental schools, some will recall, were free to establish their programs without concern for the college prep curriculum that hog-tied the secondary schools of that day. The work of these pioneer educators was guided by two major principles. The first was that "the general life of the school and methods of teaching should conform to what is now known about the ways in which human beings learn and grow" (p. 18). The second was "that the high school in the United States should re-discover its chief reason for existence" (p. 18). The 30 schools realized

> that the primary purpose of education is to lead our young people to understand, to appreciate, and to live the kind of life for which we as a people have been striving throughout our history. Other things are important, but only relatively so. It is necessary to teach the three 'R's,' science, language, history, mathematics, and arts, safety, vocations, and most of the other subjects that now crowd the curriculum of the schools; but unless our young people catch the vision which has led us on through all generations, we perish. Year after year the conviction became clearer and deeper that the school itself should become a demonstration of the kind of life in which this nation believes. (pp. 18–19)

Following these principles, the educators in those schools believed

> [t]hat the school should become a place in which young people work together at tasks which are clearly related to their purposes. No longer should teachers, students, or parents think of school simply as a place to do what was laid out to be done. The school should be a living social organism of which each student is a vital part. It should be a place to which one goes gladly because there he can engage in activities which satisfy his desires, work at the solution of problems which he faces in everyday living, and have opened to him new interests and wider horizons. (p. 17)

The middle school concept and those who seek to bring it to full life hold to these two principles and envision just such a school. There is a timelessness about these ideals. They may be deferred, but they won't be defeated. Contemporary leaders should take heart and be more determined than ever as they realize that common sense, the realities of human development, proven principles of pedagogy, substantial research, the consistency of recommendations by reputable associations, our national heritage, and our personal beliefs as humane educators all are aligned with the vision that National Middle School Association (2003a) has delineated in *This We Believe*. With such support, educators who see themselves as architects of change should be emboldened as they vigorously pursue the grand vision that is, and continues to be, the middle school concept.

QUESTIONS TO CONSIDER

1. The author raises the question, "Is the middle school movement the rebirth of progressive education?" He apparently believes that is the case. Consider that question further. Is there any basis for his claim? What specific examples exist to show that such a close relationship exists?

2. Related to the above question, if the middle school movement is indeed progressive education reborn, what are the implications of that rebirth? Is that a plus or minus relative to school improvement? Explain your response.

3. Do you accept the rather broad statement that there is no body of research to justify the unquestioning use of the basic organizational approaches that education has employed for so long? If not, what evidence can you offer to support their educational efficacy?

4. Do you agree or disagree with Lounsbury's belief that what constitutes a "good" education has been narrowed? Why or why not? When the general public speaks about the importance of a good education, what do they typically have in mind? What do you think are the essential components of a good education? And how are they best acquired?

5. Are the excerpts from the Eight-Year Study simply naïve philosophical thinking that is so removed from reality as to be meaningless? Have you ever known of, or seen, a school that fits its description? Is such a school really possible on a large scale? Explain your response.

6. Lounsbury claims that there are many positive factors and forces that support the benefits of the middle school concept. He also implies that such forces and factors are not usually welcome in present school practices and reform efforts. Why hasn't the middle school concept been more widely implemented? Is it likely to gain needed support in the near future? Why or why not?

References

Aikin, W. (1942). *The story of the Eight-Year Study.* New York: Harper and Brothers.
Dickinson, T. (Ed.) (2001). *Reinventing the middle school.* New York: RoutledgeFalmer.

Felner, R., Jackson, A., Kasak, D., Mulhall, P., Brand. S., & Flowers, N. (1997). The impact of school reform for the middle years: A longitudinal study of a network engaged in Turning Points-based comprehensive school transformation. *Phi Delta Kappan, 78,* 528–532, 541–550.

Inside the teenage brain: Transcript/PBS (n. d.). Interview with Dr. Jay Giedd. *Frontline:* WGBH Educational Foundation. Retrieved November 20, 2008 from www.pbs.org/wgbh/pages/frontline/shows/teenbrain/interviews/giedd.html.

Jackson, A., & Davis, G. (2000). *Turning points 2000: Educating adolescents in the 21st century:* New York: Teachers College Press.

Kuntz, S. (2005). *The story of Alpha: A multiage, student-centered team—33 years and counting.* Westerville, OH: National Middle School Association.

National Middle School Association. (2003a). *This we believe: Developmentally responsive middle level schools.* Westerville, OH: Author.

National Middle School Association (2003b). *Research and resources in support of* This We Believe. Westerville, OH: Author.

No Child Left Behind Act of 2001. Public Law 107–110, 2002.

Springer, M. (1994). *Watershed: A successful voyage into integrated learning.* Columbus, OH: National Middle School Association.

Springer, M. (2006). *Soundings: A democratic student-centered education.* Westerville, OH: National Middle School Association.

Strauch, B. (2007). *The primal teen: What new discoveries about the teenage brain tell us about our kids.* Palm Springs, CA: Anchor.

Tyack, D., & Cuban, L. (1995). *Tinkering Toward Utopia: A Century of Public School Reform.* Cambridge, MA: Harvard University Press

CHAPTER TWENTY

The Ideal High School for Future Adolescents

A Neo-Deweyan Perspective

DOUGLAS J. SIMPSON & MARGARET PRICE

Introduction

For many, our agreeing to write on the subject of the ideal high school for the future adolescent is prima facie evidence that we are not qualified to write on the topic. Questions such as the following immediately arise for the reflective person and could lead to the suggested authorial disqualification: Whose definition of ideal are you going to use as you answer the question? Do you really think you know enough about high schools and the enormous variety of students and their cultures in our world to even begin to address the question? If we have a difficult time saying which kinds of high schools we need today in just one country, why do you think you can identify what will be needed in the future by adolescents who will be characterized by a changing assortment of interests, developmental differences, vocational orientations, and national, ethnic, racial, cultural, and personal histories?

In the face of these and similar questions, we are happy to admit that we have no intention of answering the implied question—What is the ideal high school for the future adolescent?—in this chapter. In fact, we only intend to offer some tentative suppositions that need further examination by anyone interested in developing policies for, working with, or serving as an educator in high schools. These suppositions regard a limited number of the characteristics of high schools that may be advantageous for many adolescents in a number of future liberal and technological democracies. Ideally, these suppositions help surface an important set of considerations by those interested in high schools.

Beginning Suppositions Regarding Ideal High Schools

No doubt, the characteristics we offer for critique and reconstruction will be variously understood by educational experts, including those who staff our schools, study our institutions, and debate public educational policy issues. Even when—or if—we agree with a subset of the school features that are noted below, many of us will create unique configurations with these characteristics and, thereby, distinctive schools in locales that demand imaginative departures we may not envision and definitely do not mention. Hence, a beginning supposition is that

- there will be many different types of so-called "ideal" high schools in the future.

This supposition is rooted in part on the premise that current research (Eisner, 2005; Noddings, 2003, 2005; Sizer, 1992; Kohn, 1999, 2004; Goodlad, 1997, 2004) is only suggestive of ways to reconstruct high schools and does not offer definitive prescriptions for those who do the reconstruction work. In addition, the supposition is based in part on the claim that Dewey made regarding ideological dogma and sterility of educational thought. Dewey (1910) rightly claimed that a responsible freedom for experimentation and for creativity in schooling is necessary if legitimate learning and progress is to be made in the areas of education and schools. Moreover, he (1929) emphasized that we will never have a comprehensively well-informed theory of education unless we consistently and systematically study and learn from the experiential expertise that practicing educators have to offer. Myers and Simpson (1998), among others, have echoed this sentiment. Thus, a second supposition is that

- there will be a meaningful respect for the voices of educational practitioners in the construction and reconstruction of ideal high schools in the future.

These two initial suppositions indicate that our theorizing about ideal high schools is informed by the educational philosophy of Dewey. Admittedly, we have an affinity for his theory of education and draw on a number of his works, especially his lecture (1933) that has come to us under the heading of "Dewey Outlines Utopian Schools."[1] Of course, his ideas in this chapter are supplemented with, if not critiqued by other research and scholarly reflections. Hence, the subtitle—"A Neo-Deweyan Perspective"—suggests that we add to, subtract from, and otherwise modify Dewey's original vision of ideal or utopian schools if we wish to be open-minded about the ideas of other scholars.

In Dewey's lecture at Teachers College, Columbia University, he outlined his vision of utopian schools by making a series of claims. Initially, he asserted that "the most Utopian thing in Utopia is that there are no schools at all" (p. 137). Those familiar with Dewey's educational theory will immediately appreciate why he might want to abolish schools with learning environments that were steeped in the limitations of both the unreflective traditional and unthinking progressive schools of his time. For him (1916), schools were, relatively speaking, weak as educational environments but somewhat more powerful as cultural entities, e.g., institutions that pass on thoughtlessly and in traditional ways past and current values, mores and ideologies. Implying that many who heard him speak at the 1933 Conference on the Educational Status of Four- and Five-Year-Old Child might not be able to adequately conceive, much less appreciate the kind of de-schooled society he envisioned, he may have partially accommodated them by speaking of "assembly places" that are designated spaces for learning or, better, educative experiences.

Below we examine three general varieties of suppositions—regarding physical, human, and educative environments—that Dewey offered concerning schools of the future. Manifestly, these three varieties overlap, intertwine, and commingle at times. Our distinctions are exactly that: distinctions. These distinctions are not meant to create discrete categories of suppositions but instead to distinguish ideas that describe environments which constitute an ecological web of educational relationships. To us, these ideas are as pertinent to most ideal high schools as they are to most elementary and middle schools. Of course, our theorizing is shaped by our context and needs to be critiqued along with Dewey's philosophizing. We draw our suppositions from our own experiential knowledge and research of the current status of schools and schooling but also from researchers and academicians who spend a great deal of time and effort "looking" into classrooms. Their perspectives give us a platform as to why many current models of high school undermine what is best for students and how educative experiences might be reconfigured to give us the schools in the twenty-first century that our children need. Through their visions, ideas, and ideals we traverse and ultimately suggest a few ways in which the ideal high school might approach a dynamic state of educational equilibrium. This dynamic status we think is much preferred to schools continuing ad infinitum as fluctuating sociopolitical pawns of capitalist ideology and misguided pedagogical philosophy.

Physical Environment Suppositions of Utopian Schools

Imagine, if you dare, the physical space of a utopian high school, although the idea of a utopian situation is difficult to envision and very different from context to context for numerous reasons. We envision an environment whose physical space is aesthetically pleasing to the eye and stimulating to the imagination of students and staff as well as to other interested partners. The space is where students and teachers congregate in centers that encourage realistic curricular application and inspire creative abilities. The environment has non-institutional-like open space that invites collaborative inquiry and dialogue and continuous experimentation. Learners are not distinguished in this space by age or professional accomplishments, for everyone is both a learner and a teacher or contributor to the educative experience (Dewey, 1916).

Dewey (1933) went farther to suggest several additional ideas or suppositions about the physical environment of the places of learning that he visualized. His major suppositions concerning the physical environment in assembly places might be described as follows:

- there will be grounds and gardens that provide environments for growing, studying, and learning;
- there will be well-equipped and open-spaced buildings which are designed to promote intimate learning experiences in home-like atmospheres; and
- there will be laboratories, museums, libraries, and books that increase the learning of occupational and scientific opportunities.

In view of these suppositions, it seems relatively safe to conclude that Dewey visualized physical space that offered an environment which was an intrinsic source of learning, growth, pleasure, and pride; an intimate setting where teachers and students learn about and from one another; a relaxed atmosphere for important individual and group inquiry; and, a dynamic and rich facility that cultivated experimentation through occupational and scientific lenses into past, present, and future societies. While we could offer details to this skeletal image of many future high schools, Dewey himself might recommend, however, that groups of people—whether parents, policymakers, board members, administrators, teachers, students, or others (or, better, groups composed of representatives from all of these groups as well as other interested parties)— envision schools that considered these variables as they construct and reconstruct high schools.

Going beyond Dewey, yet affirming his mental picture of physical environments that are open, warm, welcoming, and attractive, Walden (2009) argues that schools need to be constructed in ways that students, staff, and visitors find them intellectually, emotionally, and personally satisfying. In essence, school facilities, structures, and activities ought to be informed by research in the field of psychology that indicates when and why students and educators are learning in ways that are enjoyable, rewarding, and fulfilling. Kohn (1999) goes so far as to outline for educators, parents, and visitors to schools what to look for in classrooms that offer students and teachers the idyllic but stimulating setting for meeting the individually unique psychological and altruistic needs of students. From how the furniture is arranged to the looks on children's faces, Kohn creates a vision of the effective classrooms and schools "our children deserve." This vision includes

- comfortable areas for learning, including multiple "activity centers";
- personal information, mementos of people who spend time together in the classroom;
- enthusiastic student faces that signify eagerness and engagement;
- exciting ideas that are being exchanged and analyzed;
- visitors who are both learning resources and transporters of what they learn;
- suitable rooms that overflow with "sense of purposeful clutter";
- creative students who contribute to and are involved in daily operations of the school (pp. 236–237).

Noddings (2005) adds to the picture of how the physical and psychological dimensions of a school environment may or should include the ethical, too, i.e., be permeated by an ethic of care. Her imagination leads her to conclude that the schools we need should address "the existential heart of life . . . drawing attention to passions, attitudes, connections, concerns and experienced responsibilities" (p. 47). Keeping in mind that different perspectives of interests, races, genders, socioeconomic classes, and religions are ever-present in our classrooms, schools should be centers of caring, organized around the mental and physical capacities of the students and common human tasks that enable them to be productive citizens. Eisner (2005), too, takes us beyond a minimalistic material environment when he suggests that schools and classrooms should reflect a "celebration" of diversity and thought. Through what he calls "forms of representation," Eisner suggests that when students and teachers are free to express ideas in multiple forms and improve on those ideas through experimentation and creativity, our students will be afforded "a decent conception of what our students are entitled to" (p. 211).

Of the many possible suppositions that could be suggested, we conclude that the following two suppositions about future high schools need examination, if not affirmation:

- there will be a recognition that the choices that influence the construction of the physical school environment are imbued with implicit decisions concerning many other dimensions of the school environment; and

- there will be an appreciation for and an educational response to the intersecting relationships of the physical, intellectual, emotional, and ethical in school environments.

These suppositions overlap with and lead us directly into what we labeled earlier the human environment suppositions.

Human Environment Suppositions of Utopian Schools

The human environment of schools has often been underappreciated by certain kinds of child development theoreticians and overemphasized by particular discipline-oriented curriculum philosophers. Hence, the problems that Dewey (1902) identified in *The Child and the Curriculum* continue to revisit us. Briefly but simplistically, some who emphasize the child via human development theories may also underemphasize the total human environment in schools, especially if they also have a romantic notion of human nature. Conversely, many of those who emphasize the curriculum via disciplinary studies may also overemphasize the adult human environment, especially if they also hold to the belief that teachers are unequivocally responsible for all educationally related school outcomes. However, cultural and school phenomena have in recent decades taken on new meaning in this either-or (child or curriculum) approach to teaching and learning, particularly to educators, parents, students, and researchers who have examined recent studies in developmental psychology, curriculum studies, teacher performance, high-stakes testing, and ethical expectations. The influences of gangs, school violence, illegal drugs, and school bullies have also precipitated interest in the anthropological dimensions of the school as a social, emotional, intellectual, and psychological entity.

Dewey's own view of desirable human environments in schools is rooted in a number of major suppositions concerning the assembly places he envisioned. Among his (1933) suppositions are the following:

- there will be student-student and teacher-student interactions that are indirectly directed by adults (teachers) who are experienced, mature, and knowledgeable;
- there will be staff members who have a knowledge of children that goes beyond the theoretical and includes an experiential understanding of and appreciation for children;
- there will be staff members who assist older children as they guide the educational activities of younger children;
- there will be older students who are self-identified as interested in becoming future teachers who develop their pedagogical skills in apprentice type situations;
- there will be small inquiry groups which are populated by both students and adult staff members who have similar interests and gifts; and
- there will be teachers and learners who place priority on learning attitudes rather than on developing minds that are dominated by educational and economic ideologies of competition, rewards, and punishments.

Obviously, Dewey has much more to say about the human environment, especially about students and teachers. Regarding students, he (1916) stressed that they need to be understood in terms of the developmental potential of their impulses, desires, and purposes as well as in terms of the curricular possibilities of their cultures, values, and beliefs. He happily identified the liberalizing influence of students learning from other students when he wrote: "The intermingling in the school of youth of different races, differing religions, and unlike customs creates for all a new and broader environment" (p. 21). So, from his standpoint, Dewey saw each student as an invaluable part of the complete school curricula. We are not caught unawares, therefore, to hear him claim that face-to-face interactions between students and between students and the teacher were indispensable. Diverse human personalities needed to be attached to cultures, religions, customs, mores, and nations if the richness of learning is to be experienced.

In addition to recognizing that the student is a tremendous curriculum for other students and teachers, Dewey underlined the importance of understanding that the teacher too is a critical part of the school curricula. In "The Educational Situation," he (1901) poignantly claimed:

> The real course of study must come to the child from the teacher. What gets to the child is dependent upon what is in the mind and consciousness of the teacher, and upon the way it is in his mind. It is through the teacher that the value even of what is contained in the text-book is brought home to the child; just in the degree in which the teacher's understanding of the material of the lessons is vital, adequate, and comprehensive, will that material come to the child in the same form; in the degree in which the teacher's understanding is mechanical, superficial, and restricted, the child's appreciation will be correspondingly limited and perverted. (pp. 273–274)

Needless to say, almost, Dewey highly valued teachers, teacher education, staff development, fields of inquiry and imagination, *and* students. We can add, therefore, other suppositions from Dewey's thinking, including the following:

- there will be an immense admiration for the academic preparation and pedagogical expertise of teachers and their abilities to development and utilize the human environment of their classrooms and schools, and
- there will be a widespread recognition of the importance of the diverse human curricula in schools.

Among many other proposals that merit attention by those who are examining the human environment for future schools is one that looks at schools through the lens of moral architecture. Wagner and Simpson (2009) invite policymakers, educational leaders, classroom teachers, and others to pay attention to what they term the moral dimensions of schools. They argue that local schools and districts should spend considerable time clarifying and building the kinds of moral architectures they consider justifiable in a liberal democracy. In doing so, they contend that school communities need to be able to distinguish between expedient policies and regulations, the implications of school law, and the implications of ethical principles. In addition, they argue in favor of distinguishing between three dimensions of a moral architecture: the foundation (virtues and ethical sympathies), the scaffolding (general ethical principles), and the aesthetic covering (prohibitions and prescriptions). They caution that the aesthetic covering is likely to expose the greatest degree of tension and disagreement and that returning to a school's moral foundation and scaffolding for further clarification is often necessary in order to reach some common ground. In particular, they emphasize constructing a moral ethos that is founded upon values such as tolerance, fairness, respectfulness, freedom, courage, and compassion. These ethical dimensions of the human curricula resonate easily with Dewey's (1916) emphasis on community, commonalities, and communication in democratically oriented schools. Many others (Apple & Beane, 1995; Conchas, 2006; Ginwright, Noguera, & Cammarota, 2006) stress the importance of democratic values and their connection to serving well all students. Appropriately, then, we can add another supposition about future high schools that are needed by youth and society:

- there will be a reflective cultivation of a democratic ethos and its implications for working and living together in schools.

Educative Experience Suppositions of Utopian Schools

Like many people who engage in normative inquiry about schools, their desirable aims and outcomes, and their facilities and environments, Dewey claimed that evaluative judgments are impossible to escape. Like Camus (1995), he claimed that there is no existential possibility of a school or society living with the notion that one judgment is ethically equivalent to all other options. One of the most informative ways he approached the questions of values was through his discussion of the nature of experience. In order to go straight to his value judgments, we note that he argued that all learning experience is not worthwhile much less of equal value to all other kinds of learning experiences. This rather jarring if not off-putting assertion to contemporary ears needs some explanation before we dismiss, accept, or revise it.

To begin with, it is important to recognize his distinction between educative and miseducative experience. In a few words, educative experiences are worthwhile, connected, produce personal growth, and lay a foundation for future personal and social development (Dewey, 1938). An example of this kind of experience might be polishing one's previously learned Spanish in high school, interacting regularly with Spanish speakers in one's local community, enrolling in a summer program in Guanajuato, Mexico, and reading from the writings of Latin Americans. Those high school students who have teachers—official and accidental—who create conditions and environments that lead to a reflective understanding of the Spanish language and related Latin American literature, history, music, religions, architecture, and traditions have the opportunity to enter into genuinely educative experiences, including the one Paz (1985, p. 46) understood so well when he wrote of the dehumanizing "person who creates Nobody, by denying Somebody's existence" and in the process changes her or himself into Nobody. In this kind of experience, we, like Onetti's (2000) character Risso, learn that the growth that comes with such experiences sometimes consummates in an understanding that appears to be free of volitional and intellectual involvement but not stress and anxiety. In reality, the whole person is involved in these educative experiences as they become more completely aesthetic in quality (Dewey, 1934).

Conversely, miseducative experiences (Dewey, 1938) are essentially defective, produce personal ungrowth, and lay a foundation for future social and individual malformation. Such experiences narrow our thinking, visions, appreciations, and lives. The overflow of these experiences impedes national and international growth, too. In *The Mis-Education of the Negro*, Woodson (1933) described the historical miseducation of many African Americans and European Americans in a country and world that was largely ruled and continues to be greatly influenced by racism. Imaginatively yet personally, Abse (1989) in "Case History" noted a similar kind of experience and its negative influence on a badly miseducated patient who calmly announced his prejudices to anyone who would listen. But Abse also offers a glimpse into the depth of the ethical educative experience of Abse's physician when he divulged that the physician prescribed for this ethnocentric and racist patient as if he were a member of his own family.

Noneducative experiences are probably the most questioned of Dewey's conceptual trio. We may want to ask: Are not all learning experiences either educative or miseducative? Dewey might respond that nearly any experience, if the term is used loosely, can be noneducative. Copying definitions, memorizing formula, and learning the rules of punctuation may lead nowhere. That is to say, these activities may lead to neither growth nor ungrowth. Poorly educated teachers, inadequately prepared classroom environments, unsatisfactorily designed materials, and largely passive students all have the potential of contributing significantly to noneducative experiences, not just to miseducative ones. Ridiculously obtuse pedagogy—e.g., mindless memorization and mechanical drills—is also an ally of the noneducative. Conjugating a verb—as helpful as it may be in language acquisition—may also be noneducative in the hands of a tedious and mind-numbing teacher who lacks a vision of what language fluency means. In his poem "But—," Dewey (1977a) may have hinted at this concept when he spoke of idle activities that fill the hours. In "To a Pedant," he (1977b) also spoke of outcomes that were probably both noneducative and miseducative as a pedant's mind is formed, including the deposits it received that are substitutes for reflective thinking.

In view of this triadic view of experience, Dewey's (1933) major suppositions concerning educational experiences in utopia might be as follows:

- there will be educative experiences that integrate forms of inquiry and creativity and students rather than segregating activities along disciplinary, age, and class lines;
- there will be many experiences which replace externally imposed school objectives and purposes with a discovered and developed understanding of students' own "aptitudes . . . tastes . . . abilities . . . and weaknesses";
- there will be emphases on natural learning experiences that include the learning of necessary information and attitudes of life as a normal part of living and inquiring rather than on artificial learning activities that are contrived so that students acquire and store information; and
- there will be an understanding that learning attitudes which are rooted in the practice of developing a faith in the "positive power" of eliminating trepidation, humiliation, restriction, and disappointment and a faith in the "human capacity" of creating self-confidence, pride, self-determination, and satisfaction is a crucial factor in ongoing or lifelong learning (pp. 137–140).

Within the last thirty years (or longer as some will quickly point out) the focus of educational reform has clearly been toward a public collective view of student academic success. The increased importance of assessment and achievement (of the student, the teacher, the school, and the district) that pervades the educational dialogue—or is it a monologue?—has driven a wedge between the goals of many educators and public policy makers. In effect, the student as individual learner has become a forgotten piece of the educational puzzle. Dewey's (1902) view of the student as learner and energizer of her or his guided educational journey has long been replaced by how and what can be registered on a standardized form of testing and/or standardized curriculum. Individual students and their needs as persons and societal needs for citizens who think and act in well informed ways are hardly the central focus of the learning experience. Rather, student scores on standardized tests and their preparation for economic competitiveness have become the norms for judging school success. Fenstermacher (2006) posits that the real result to this achievement-laden focus borders on students learning "the art of studenting"—becoming adept at negotiating around true learning and educative experiences and doing what it takes to be a student, jumping through hoops of sorts "wherein the learner is directed more to mastering the rules of the game of school than to the mastery of subjects that enhance his or her power to be and to act in the world" (p. 104). He further explains that this is a direct challenge to Dewey's idea that learners cannot be separated from their life experiences out of school: "the result is not authentic growth but some parody of growth" (p. 104). If these school norms continue and dominate the foreseeable future of high schools, they can hardly become ideal places for learning and education. Indeed, it may be that they will become classified by future educational historians as institutions for past ideals (Mamary, 2007).

Conclusion

In our brief discussion of a so-called ideal high school, we—with the help of many others, especially Dewey—have attempted to identify a set of suppositions that emphasize that there will be many different kinds of schools that will be designed and lead in part by utilizing the reflective and imaginative ideas of educational practitioners who want to break out of the current boxes that promote existing conditions and outcomes (Hayes, 2006). In these schools where environmental, physical, technological, and psychological considerations are of vital import, intimate learning environments facilitate interpersonal relationships among students, teachers, and others in numerous educational configurations. A joy of inquiry and growth will be furthered as various materials and methodologies are employed and as an understanding of the interrelationship of human intelligence and emotions is understood and valued (Goodlad, 1997). Learning how to learn and to identify and solve problems and think reflectively and democratically is valued above propagandizing and indoctrinating students (Noddings, 2006). A rich and diverse curriculum of teachers, students, and academic content will exist and facilitate overall student development in carefully planned interdisciplinary educational experiences. Learning experiences will be so much a part of ordinary interactions and so powerful that life and learning in school are highly valued. Consequently, a number of students will want to become teachers and be guided in their decisions by experienced mentors. Negative emotions and behaviors will be significantly diminished as students become members of small learning groups with teachers and guests and participate in larger groups that constitute the sub-communities and community of a school.

Of course, these schools will not automatically appear in the future (Eisner, 2005; Sizer, 2004a, 2004b). The suppositions that we have mentioned need to be collectively examined and reconstructed by interested parties into visions and goals which will not only be central to the concerns of the entire staff, but will be formulated in concert with students, parents, and others

(Coen & Scheer, 2003). The end result of such schools would be diverse but also, perhaps, predictable in that they will lead to higher achievement test scores. On the other hand, test scores will not be the criteria for success. Success would be measured in more imaginative and experiential ways, including, perhaps, by studying school attendance, retention, and graduation rates. Neo-psychometricians might also be interested in determining how many high school students enroll in dual credit programs and how many graduates complete some form of higher education program. Might they also look at the employment patterns of former school attendees and graduates? Dare they also look at current and former student arrest and incarceration rates to measure the success of schools?

In order for these schools to flourish, a range of collaboration is essential, involving at least those enveloped in the culture of the educative process, e.g., students, parents, teachers, administrators, community businesses, and social assistance programs. In our efforts to make schools truly responsive to both those who occupy them (e.g., students, teachers, staff, administrators, volunteers) and to those who are the recipients of their eventual expertise (e.g., families, businesses, government agencies, private entities, and society, in general), we envision educative spaces as being an ecological system composed of material and human resources that are engaged in educative processes. In essence, we need full-service institutions that incorporate the needs and desires of their inhabitants and the needs and desires of the community (Eisner, 1998; Goodlad, 2004). In order to be motivated to accomplish this goal, Dewey (1900/1976) claimed in *The School and Society* that "What the best and wisest parent [politician, educator, or business person] wants for his [or her] own child, that must the community want for all of its children. Any other ideal for our schools is narrow and unlovely; acted upon, it destroys our democracy" (p. 5).

QUESTIONS TO CONSIDER

1. How do the authors agree or disagree with the idea that schools should be designed to prepare students to live in a very different kind of world? Do you agree or disagree with their contentions? Why?

2. What are the obvious consequences of acting on the suppositions that the authors delineate? Does the adoption of these suppositions reflect a larger educational and societal and educational agenda? Explain your response.

3. What distinctions do you see between educative, miseducative, and noneducative experiences? Are the three concepts useful today? Give examples.

4. What assumptions—beyond the obvious suppositions provided—are manifested in the major emphases of this chapter? Do you agree or disagree with them? Why or why not?

5. Do the authors' explicit and implicit recommendations have a realistic chance of being acted upon today? Why or why not?

6. What societal and political conditions would best accommodate the ideas proposed by the authors? Which countries, if any, have these conditions today?

7. What alternatives to the authors' proposals do you think merit more attention than theirs? Explain your response.

Note

1. Although Dewey used the term *utopian* in this lecture, he was not a utopist in a traditional sense. He is better understood as a meliorist and a reflective progressivist who believed that schools could and should be improved but also thought that they would never be utopian in the sense of achieving an absolute perfection.

References

Abse, D. (1989). Case history. *White coat, purple coat: Collected poems 1948–1988*. London: Hutchinson Books Ltd.

Apple, M., & Beane, J. (Eds.). (1995). *Democratic schools*. Alexandria, VA: Association for Supervision and Curriculum Development.

Camus, A. (1995). *Resistance, rebellion, and death*. New York: Vintage International.

Coen, R., & Scheer, S. (2003). *Teacher-centered schools: Reimagining education reform in the twenty-first century*. Lanham, MD: The Scarecrow Press, Inc.

Conchas, A. (2006). *The color of success: Race and high-achieving urban youth*. New York: Teachers College Press.

Dewey, J. (1976). *The school and society*. In J. A. Boydston (Ed.), *The middle works* (Vol.1: 1899–1901, (pp. 1–110). Carbondale & Edwardsville, IL: Southern Illinois University Press. (Original work published 1900)

Dewey, J. (1976). The educational situation. In J. A. Boydston (Ed.), *The middle works* (Vol.1: 1899–1901, pp. 257–313). Carbondale & Edwardsville, IL: Southern Illinois University Press. (Original work published 1901)

Dewey, J. (1902). *The child and the curriculum*. Chicago: The University of Chicago Press.

Dewey, J. (1910). *How we think*. Boston: D. C. Heath & Co.

Dewey. J. (1916). *Democracy and education*. New York: The Free Press.

Dewey, J. (1929). General principles of educational articulation. In J. A. Boydston (Ed.), *The Latter Works* (Vol. 5: 1929–1930, pp. 299–310). Carbondale & Edwardsville, IL: Southern Illinois University Press.

Dewey, J. (1989). Dewey outlines utopian schools. In J. A. Boydston (Ed.), *The Latter Works* (Vol. 9: 1933–1934, pp.136–140). Carbondale & Edwardsville, IL: Southern Illinois University Press. (Original work published 1933)

Dewey, J. (1934). *Art as experience*. New York: A Perigee Book.

Dewey, J. (1938). *Experience and education*. New York: Collier Books.

Dewey, J. (1977a). But—. In J. A. Boydston (Ed.), *The poems of John Dewey* (pp. 50–51). Carbondale & Edwardsville, IL: Southern Illinois University Press.

Dewey, J. (1977b). To a pedant. In J. A. Boydston (Ed.), *The poems of John Dewey* (p. 78). Carbondale & Edwardsville, IL: Southern Illinois University Press.

Eisner, E. (1998). *The kind of schools we need: Personal essays*. Portsmouth, NH: Heinemann.

Eisner, E. (2005). *Reimagining schools: The selected works of Elliot W. Eisner*. London: Routledge.

Fenstermacher, G. (2006). Rediscovering the student in *Democracy and Education*. In D. T. Hansen (Ed.), *John Dewey and our educational prospect: A critical engagement with Dewey's Democracy and Education* (pp. 97–112). Albany, NY: State University of New York Press.

Ginwright, S., Noguera, P., & Cammarota, J. (Eds.). (2006). *Beyond resistance!: Youth activism and community change: New democratic possibilities for practice and policy for America's youth.* New York: Routledge.

Goodlad, J. (1997). *In praise of education.* New York: Teachers College Press.

Goodlad, J. (2004). *Romances with schools: A life education.* New York: McGraw-Hill.

Kohn, A. (1999). *The schools our children deserve: Moving beyond traditional classrooms and "tougher standards."* Boston, MA: Houghton Mifflin Company.

Kohn, A. (2004). *What does it mean to be well educated? And more essays on standards, grading, and other follies.* Boston, MA: Beacon Press.

Mamary, A. (2007). *Creating the ideal school: Where teachers want to teach and students want to learn.* Lanham, MD: Rowman & Littlefield Education.

Myers, C., & Simpson, D. (1998). *Re-creating schools: Places where everyone learns and likes it.* Thousand Oaks, CA: Corwin Press, Inc.

Noddings, N. (2003). *Happiness and education.* New York: Cambridge University Press.

Noddings, N. (2005). *The challenge to care in schools: An alternative approach to education* (2nd ed.). New York: Teachers College Press.

Noddings, N. (2006). *Critical lessons: What our schools should teach.* New York: Cambridge University Press.

Onetti, J. (2000). Hell most feared. In *The Vintage book of Latin American stories* edited by C. Fuentes & J. Ortega. New York: Vintage Books.

Paz, O. (1985). *The labyrinth of solitude* and *The other Mexico, Return to the labyrinth of solitude, Mexico and the United States, The philanthropic ogre.* Trans. by L. Kemp, Y. Milos, & E. Belash. New York: Grove Press.

Sizer, T. (1992). *Horace's school: Redesigning the American high school.* New York: Houghton Mifflin.

Sizer, T. (2004a). *Horace's compromise: The dilemma of the American high school.* New York: Houghton Mifflin.

Sizer, T. (2004b).The utopian high school in a democratic nation. *Independent School, 64* (4), 62–63.

Wagner, P., & Simpson, D. (2009). *Ethical decision making in school administration: Leadership as moral architecture.* Los Angeles: Sage Publications, Inc.

Walden, R. (Ed.). (2009). *Schools for the future: Design proposals from architectural psychology.* Ashland, OH: Hogrefe Publishing.

Woodson, C. (2000). *The mis-education of the Negro.* Chicago: African American Images. (Original work published 1933)

CHAPTER TWENTY-ONE

Beyond "Written Off"

Surviving and Thriving Through Adolescent Literacy

DAN BAUER, LINDA GOLSON BRADLEY, & LINDELL DILLON

Those of us who devote our lives to cultivating, augmenting, and nurturing habits of reading, writing, and thinking in the lives of adolescents do so with an understanding—and faith—that our efforts sustain and enrich the lives of youth in ways unequaled by potential alternatives. However, despite our best intentions, we know that some students get "written off"—by peers, by teachers, by each of us, and sadly, even by themselves. Given this milieu, in this chapter we propose a theoretical model for surviving and indeed thriving through adolescent literacy, which we call The Five R's. This framework emerges from a series of conversations, drafts, and reflections based on our own stories, our work with students, and our collaboration through the National Writing Project—a powerful network of exemplary teachers. The Five R's: Recognition, Rescue, Reaffirmation, Revolt, and Remembrance provide a roadmap for teachers who seek to reach all of their adolescent students in positive and productive ways, to move beyond being written off toward well-being and survival.

Recognition

How a teacher recognizes, or fails to recognize, the unique experiences and gifts that each student brings to the classroom has enduring ramifications. A story from one of our lives illustrates:

> Years of my schooling rolled by in a state of amorphousness. Teachers were absolutely puzzled in their attempts to "handle" me. As early as the first grade, I hid fictional books in my other subject books and read my time away. Every year I was sent to "reading lab" for diagnosis by a wonderful woman named Beverly Miller, my first truly positive human experience.
>
> "Your teachers tell me you can't read. Is that true?"

"I can read," I mumbled. A broad smile spread across her face.

"Okay . . . show me."

I would read stories on a timing machine and answer questions for a while.

"Wow! You CAN read . . . and quite well at that," she stated in the end. "Why don't you read your subject books?"

"They're not very interesting. They don't take me anywhere that I haven't already been."

"You know about other countries? Social Studies?"

"Through fairy tales . . . yes, ma'am."

"It isn't the same. Those are fantasy . . . not real."

Wow. Didn't she get it? Real life was what I wished to escape. She wasn't the son of a self-made miner who believed strongly in whipping a child for any transgression. She wasn't the son of a haunted, helpless, and hapless mother who gave out tongue lashings instead of hugs or kisses. She had friends . . . everyone loved her. She in no way understood the depths of the deviance that already coursed through me at such an early age . . . and if she would have . . . she would have hated me with the same passion that every other person in the world displayed.

My second grade teacher was Mrs. Brown. She hated my lack of involvement in schoolwork and eventually left me to my own devices when she couldn't get inside the impenetrable brick wall that stood between us. Yet, she gifted me with my first read-aloud . . . *Charlotte's Web* . . . and created a delusion so strong in me that I stopped loathing spiders and instead began to talk to them.

My third grade teacher was Mrs. Means . . . a feisty old lady who thought she could set me straight. She damaged me every chance she had in an effort to shame me to righteousness. She intercepted a love letter that I wrote to the smartest (but not prettiest) girl in class named Trudy Rader . . . except . . . I spelled her name as "Tudy." After reading my offering, Mrs. Means addressed its issues to me with the full attention of the rest of the class, including Trudy, listening: "How can you expect to garner a young woman's attention if you can't spell her name right?"

Mrs. Means's voice was the moniker of my father, who insisted I had only one chance to get something right, or I would reap the whirlwind, so I hated her from that moment forward. The other significant incident with Mrs. Means occurred after my mother had my father thrown in jail. Mom let him out in two days, and he came to visit me while I was out in the hall . . . not doing the Social Studies work my teacher set me to do in the absence of my classmates. Dad never did anything to me about being out there . . . but still . . . I couldn't get it right. Mrs. Means only affirmed the weakness sown by my father. I had had tools thrown into my chest before because I couldn't hand Dad the right one with perfect recall. From these repeated failures, I quickly learned to avoid doing anything at all as the only sure way to escape wrath.

My fourth-grade teachers were several. Beverly Miller from the "reading lab" took a few weeks and was pure heaven—the object of my affection. Then came a string of some teachers whom I can't even remember. Our last teacher was the principal's son . . . Mr. Applebee . . . who forced me to wear a dunce cap on a high stool in the classroom corner almost every day . . . because I refused to work for him. Tormenting him with my lack of humility became my chief chore . . . the more ridiculous the punishment . . . the more I enjoyed the torture. He never tried to understand me; he cared more about making a public example of me than he cared about "me." In the meantime, I consumed every book in each class library . . . especially stories of the fantastical. Like my father I was self-made: yet I survived and thrived only in this way . . . only through reading books and writing. I had begun writing poetry as early as the first grade . . . but my serious journaling began in Mr. Applebee's class . . . without his knowledge . . . or the knowledge of anyone else.

Enter, the fifth grade . . . and the meanest teacher ever . . . Mrs. Rivers. She never tried to bridge the gap between knowledge and me. She lived to embarrass me just like Mr. Applebee. However, she never used his trinkets of caps and titles about my neck with string . . . she used the coldest of words she could conjure from the deep well of her mouth. One day, after viewing my desk and calling it a "paper porcupine," she kicked my collage of waste from inside the desk and scattered it all over the room while yelling, "I don't even know why you bother coming here . . . you are the biggest waste of taxpayer money I've ever seen." That statement hurt . . . not because I wanted to let her hurt me . . . but because at that moment in life . . . a cold fear washed over me that perhaps what she said was the truth. Her words thus began the erosion of me from the inside.

The fictive paper world that I had built to inhabit began to flutter apart . . . and the naked world and its truth assaulted me with my guard down. Unfortunately, this new mindset reinforced one from my earliest school year. My peers began first grade a full two months before I did because I wasn't properly inoculated. They had time to form their peer circles and acclimate to each other. I became the live rabbit . . . thrown into a den of ravenous, starving lions. The boys filled my face with dirt and fists the second day at school. I didn't defend myself because I was not created in my father's image.

With no defense, thoughts of taking my life began in fifth grade. I shut down. Mrs. Rivers would get nothing from me. Neither would any teacher thereafter, or so I thought then. I had been written off so emphatically by others that I had also written myself off.

This story of Lindell's first five years of schooling demonstrates the power of recognition—and the lack thereof. Teacher after teacher failed to see Lindell, failed to understand who he was and where he was coming from, and failed to value the unique gifts he had to offer. Were these simply "bad" teachers who did not care, or do they reflect a deeper, more systematic flaw in the efficiency model of schooling where conformity and a single path to academic success trump the learning of individual students? Cuban (1993) argues that organizational and pedagogical practices of schools play a role in socializing students into categories within a larger socioeconomic system. On paper, this efficiency model of conformity in schools works beautifully—simply treat schools as a business to inspire competition and efficiency. However, Cuban (2007) recently proposed that this business model in schooling can lead to a range of problems including excessive standardization of both expectations for students as well as tests that determine their success.

Unfortunately, the efficiency model emphasizes disconnected content knowledge over relationships between individuals and concepts. We know that good teaching, especially in the field of literacy, depends on relationship building as much as any other element. Even so, the efficiency model often does significant and enduring harm through failing to recognize the importance of the idiosyncrasies that both teachers and students bring to learning processes. Lindell's frightfully few positive school experiences underscore the dangers inherent in this model. Multiple students like Lindell occupy our classrooms, written off by teachers, peers, and even themselves. We understand the harsh realities inherent in the transitions from childhood to adolescence to adulthood. Kunjufu (2005) describes the "Fourth Grade Failure Syndrome," as the point of no return, a point from which it becomes increasingly difficult for teachers to reach students (p. 33). While Mrs. York helped to rescue Lindell, too many of our students spiral downward until they are lost beyond rescue, thus becoming destined to drop out, land in jail, suffer in poverty, or cease to exist. Lindell, therefore, stands out as an anomaly, not in his marginalization, but rather in his sheer determination and persistence aided by a single perceptive teacher who recognized his many talents in the face of overwhelming adversity:

The sixth grade year began much the same as the others. By then, my soul had eroded to emptiness . . . and I was useless to the rest of the human race. My teacher, Mrs. York, regarded me from a distance . . . and became aggravated that her worthwhile efforts to reach me were futile. One day, while I was out on the playground, she rummaged through my belongings and found my journal. DAMN HER! My soul was imprinted on every page. The dark depths of grief were meticulously recorded in story and poem . . . and this mirror of me was not to be trespassed upon! Still, when the class returned . . . she began to read aloud a "neutral, trite" poem:

> Jaws of a dragon, flaming red
> He's the one that toasts my bread
> He hands them over one by one
> 'Till he gets them all done
> In the morning, as well as then
> He starts the process going again
> He hands me one, and then another
> Then he hands one to my mother
> My little toaster sits by the wall
> I think he is the greatest of all.

I sat, stunned at the invasion, frozen within and without. Even though she had chosen that particular poem to read . . . her act was unforgivable. How dare she?

The applause of my peers resuscitated me and prolonged my living. The validity shown from the same hands that beat me raw during every other week of six years of my life . . . were the same hands that gingerly lifted me up and gifted me with a renewed energy to want to live.

"That was a cool poem!"

"He ought to write in our school newspaper!"

"Who knew he could write like that?"

Everyone was gone from the room when I got the notebook back.

"How much did you read?" my voice quietly whispered.

"All of it . . ." her voice stammered as tears slid from the corner of her eyes and plopped loudly on my blue notebook. Those drops eventually faded the dark blue . . . and I carried them with me as eternal evidence that someone in the world finally knew who I was. I was no longer alone in the world. From that moment on, Mrs. York became my mother. She loved me when I needed it and chastised me when I tried to manipulate her trust. She bridged the gap between my ability to write and all the efferent text I had abhorred my entire life by asking me to pen poignant thoughts to read to classmates at the conclusion of every class:

"You have anything for us, Lindell?"

Sometimes I did . . . sometimes . . . nothing. She loved me whether I did or not. Mrs. York often read poetry aloud to the class. One particular poem, "Outwitted," by Edward Markham (1915) paralleled the journey of learning we shared together that year:

He drew a circle that shut me out—
Heretic, rebel, a thing to flout.
But love and I had the wit to win:
We drew a circle that took him in! (p. 1)

I blossomed under Mrs. York's wonderful tutelage and was preserved until core issues resurfaced at a later date.

Over three decades have passed since Mrs. York took a risk to recognize Lindell's unique gift with words. Nevertheless, her impact continues to mold and shape Lindell's personal and professional writing as well as his interactions with his own students. While Mrs. York's actions may seem consistent with a teacher's "ordinary" repertoire of strategies, upon closer look, she deftly used literacy to rescue Lindell from the realm of being written off. Her recognition led to recognition by peers and soon even self-recognition that Lindell had something valuable to say, a voice that had to be shared.

Mrs. York's actions reflect the process approach, as advocated by Donald Murray (2004), which suggests that we learn from our students as much as we offer to them. We learn from Murray that wisdom is not a limited commodity, but rather something that exists in abundance, thus forging our mission as writing teachers into that of wisdom workers, where we encourage students to learn about their own worlds what they did not recognize before, what they had not previously seen. This work does not require students to use only the language of school. If we really care to glimpse inside the parables that students offer, like Mrs. York, we must sometimes learn to use the language that is offered by students rather than only the one we demand. Both display "grammar," whether standard or not, and whether we recognize it or not. Rather than demand conformity at all costs, we must demonstrate a genuine desire to know, understand, and respect adolescent students.

Something universal exists in the desires of adolescents, desires that seem to surface somewhat capriciously. Adolescents want to find a place, some respect, and a way to fit in, if only for a moment. They simply seek recognition. However, their actions often baffle and sometimes frustrate those who are trying everything in their power to provide support. In essence, observable behavior simply does not always match the true feelings of an adolescent. This contradiction leaves teachers and parents wondering what in the world they should do next. Mrs. York's recognition of Lindell exemplifies an astute understanding that teachers must watch, wait, and listen to our students to truly recognize who they are and what they have to offer.

In thinking about how we might help students to feel more at "home" and more welcomed in our classrooms, where we teach writers rather than merely assign writing, we remember Kenneth Grahame's *The Wind in the Willows*. This classic adolescent novel celebrates the construct of home, a place parallel to the best classrooms, permeated by a welcoming sense of curiosity so essential to overall happiness and literacy development. Grahame elaborates on the character of Mole, who for years lives a life of joy in the humble abode of Water Rat. Upon Mole's return to his own home for a visit, Grahame (1908) tells us, "He saw clearly how plain and simple—how narrow, even—it all was; but clearly, too, how much it all meant to him, and the special value of some such anchorage in one's existence" (p. 87). Students who offer us authentic pieces of writing offer us gifts that are glimpses into their understanding and their most cherished identities. Hopefully, we will recognize these gifts and see with Mole's eyes as we look upon their efforts, thus offering them "anchorage" in their existence. Lucy Calkins (1994), Nancy Atwell (1998), and other important pioneers in the field of composition remind us that the environment one cultivates in one's classroom does more than anything else to determine how well students succeed in improving their writing. A recent study funded by the Carnegie Corporation reviewed hundreds of published research studies that yielded eleven common elements of successful writing instruction in grades 4–12. Not unlike the overall environmental factors that contributed so powerfully to Mole's well-being, these eleven elements collectively shape the classroom environment in significant ways, thus contributing to whether students are nudged toward success or failure (Graham & Perin, 2007). Luckily, increasingly large numbers of teachers accept the challenge to help students recognize who they are, how they "fit," what makes them unique, and how they might conceptualize and reveal their gifts. Research, theoretical models like the one offered here, and professional development networks like the National Writing Project provide vital support for teachers in this quest.

Rescue

Rescue, whether initiated by teachers or by students themselves, rejects failure and opens windows of opportunity for students to move beyond being written off. Mrs. York not only recognized the gifts inherent in Lindell, she also rescued him from years of being written off. She refused to take no for an answer. She continued trudging forward, never failing to explore opportunities for connection. Teachers engaging in rescue must first recognize who their students are, and this recognition must lead to action. Lindell became a teacher years after Mrs. York's rescue. During his first year of teaching, Lindell met a student named Lucas. Their relationship exemplifies how recognition leads to rescue:

> I knew the moment he came in, as he peered at me over the top of Hubble-filled glass frames and dropped himself in the front row with a solid frown. Before Lucas occupied that space, I was pre-loaded with generous advice from several teachers:

> "You got to watch out for Lucas. His momma carries his case file like a Holy Bible to every meeting with a teacher. If you go astray in the least . . . can you say "litigation?" Lucas cannot learn. He has a brother and sister whose futures are bright enough to inherit scholastic scholarships, but Lucas came out swimming from the low end of his parents' gene pool. Lucas uses his disability as an excuse to get out of work."

> What could a first-year teacher possibly do with such a daunting task?

> During the first class, I let the fact slip that we would do much reading and writing in our "grammar" class. After I dismissed the students, Lucas was there in two shakes of a lamb's tail:

> "You can't read my writing."

"Oh? Why not?"

"Terrible handwriting."

"Can you type?"

A deep sigh. "Yes, but it takes me forever. How long does it have to be?"

"As long as it takes for you to tell me what you want to tell me, as if I don't know a single thing about what you're telling me about."

"Come again?"

"Treat me like the world's biggest idiot, like I've never heard a story before."

"Ohhhhhh. . . . GOTCHA!" Lucas replied with an enormous thumbs up. "You won't like it, though."

"Why?"

"All my other teachers didn't like my writing. Some of them handed it back to me ungraded and said, 'Lucas, I'll grade this when I can read it.'"

"Just one time, bud . . . let's see what you've got. Try your best."

Lucas turned pale for a few seconds before nodding and trotting off to science class.

Conversations with Lucas continued. He invited me to lunch, and we sat at a table near the corner without other ears to hear. After talking about trivial matters for a brief moment, Lucas spilled his heart.

"I'll never be as good as my brother or sister. They make better grades; they have friends who like them; they have a future. I have nothing."

"Your mother loves you, Lucas." The effect of such a statement was like holy water splashed on a vampire.

"Whose mother doesn't?" he hissed as if I were as dense as a mahogany log. I couldn't tell him I didn't have that commodity at his age.

"Come on, Lucas. There's something you can do."

"What?" came his exasperated wail." Look at me . . . THIS (pointing to his ears and eyes) doesn't work. What can I do?"

"We'll find it, Lucas. We need time."

The words fell on deaf ears, as only words will often do. The weight of his soul was now on my heart like a heavy wet, thick towel over the nose and mouth of an immobile body. His horror was my horror . . . and at the moment, I didn't want to wear his shoes any more. I could get up and walk away intact . . . but Lucas had to sit there in a body that didn't offer him a similar option. My own pre-adolescent horrors flooded back at that moment. I wanted to tell him "this too shall pass," but those were only words. Words without hope or promise were weak indeed.

A short time passed, and Lucas wrote his first story about how his home was a dog magnet, where dogs broke into the yard instead of out of the fence. It was absolutely hilarious. My wife thought I had popped a cog and gone insane as I laughed on the couch opposite her while reading it. Tears rolled as I laughed.

"Lucas, this story is phenomenal. We need to read it to the rest of the class!"

"NOT a good IDEA! You know how I talk . . . they'll make fun of me like they always do."

"Do you mind if I read it?"

He shrugged his shoulders in skepticism. "If you think so."

The kids were pretty much in stitches, as I was the night before.

"So, who do you think wrote this story?" I asked the class

Guesses were made . . . all of the well-established writers in the class.

"Nope, it was Lucas."

Then . . . to my complete surprise . . . they whooped and clapped as if Hannah Montana had stepped into the classroom. Some of them actually patted him on the back and congratulated him.

Lucas's eyes extended the boundaries of saucers, and his mind whirled. He was basking in the sun and tasting the effect of his own unique talent and gift. From that moment in the fourth week of school, Lucas showed up in my room a half an hour before any other student made it to school. Sometimes we would just talk about whatever ran the gauntlet of his mind. Sometimes he would share something he wrote and we would work on making it better. Every story made it to the ears of his peers. He became famous in his class for writing the most humorous stories of any of his peers.

Failing to accept either the preconceived notions of other teachers or any other single measure of academic success made it possible for Lindell to rescue Lucas, just as Mrs. York had saved him so many years before. However, we recognize this process is far from easy; it requires ongoing reflection, dedication, the support of other teachers, and a willingness to take risks.

In other contexts, students can sometimes engage in the act of rescuing themselves from both the fear and reality of being written off, as we see in Dan's story:

Growing up in a tiny Iowa town during the 1970s, adolescence quickly became a time of deception and confusion. As a gay kid in a high school graduating class of just 59 students, I refused to be written off by anyone. Unfortunately, my small world included utterly no space to express my identity, so I quickly learned hypervigilance to subdue this forcefully emerging self, despite the fact that I fulfilled nearly every stereotype of the gay kid: scrawny and sassy, yet a wholly geeky teacher-pleaser. My peers could sustain and openly identify themselves by their heterosexual desires and affiliations, but I remained isolated yet insistent on not being victimized by the unwanted attention sure to accrue to one so longing for honest love and acceptance. Always the top student in every class, I despised PE classes because I was always the last chosen for team sports. Despite continual accolades and achievements outside of PE, I still feared exposure, and my only hope for athletic prowess lay in a sport that didn't require projectiles. So, I took up cross country and track where I finished last or nearly-last in every race in which I competed. Propelled on by the understanding that no one would suspect a standout athlete to be gay, by the time I finished high school I became a state champion long-distance runner. Through continued perseverance, I went on to become an NCAA national champ long-distance runner in college. While the world of literature offered a possible safe space, I searched in vain for any story—fiction or nonfiction—that made me feel less alone. No welcoming narrative emerged. Even so, in retrospect, the reaffirmation of one prized high school English teacher, Mr. Romine, sustained me for years: "In a whole class full of jocks, it amazes me that only the little skinny kid has a real story to tell."

Dan's rescue from the immediate tortures of adolescence involved a persistent determination to strive for excellence at all costs. He remained hidden through this rescue, except to the knowing eyes of Mr. Scott Romine, one of the nation's earliest participants in a National Writing Project site. Mr. Romine deftly planted the seeds of Dan's career in literacy education. While Dan largely rescued himself, his story reminds us that good teachers model recognition and rescue, whether they do so consciously or not.

Reaffirmation

All students need reaffirmation that they have an important voice to share. Furthermore, we must reaffirm students as they gain confidence in sharing this voice. Regardless of whether students have been ever been written off, all students deserve to be challenged and to build competence. We recognize that to this point, our examples have concentrated on extreme examples of being written off. However, we believe that this model also benefits students who have never been written off as well as those who may fall somewhere in between. Reaffirmation benefits every student, and this is most clearly evident through Linda's story of adolescence, as one who possessed positive advantages both at home and at school:

> When I consider the long and somewhat torturous days of adolescence, I think of Janell Cannon's (1993) famed picture book Stellaluna, that most adored story of a young bat accidentally separated from her mother and raised, for a short time, in a family of birds. Maybe I was a bit like Stellaluna, just a little bat in the big birds' world. Odd comes to mind as I reflect upon my identity throughout these years of tumult. Three different schools in three different towns thrust numerous challenges into the years between fifth and eleventh grade. Ughh . . . I landed in new schools about as gracefully as Stellaluna landed on a tree branch, "How embarrassing." Who knew that peers at my new school would resent me for getting good grades? My achievement threatened expectations for class valedictorian, salutatorian, and historian—all honors that were spoken for long before I arrived. Nevertheless, I had several great teachers who saw something unique in me and celebrated the gifts I sought to share. Mr. Moss, a stellar high school English teacher, bolstered my vocabulary, critical thinking, and my confidence as a writer. My teachers reassured and challenged me to continue to forge ahead in learning and relationship building at school and beyond.

> After much practice, I began to successfully learn how to blend in—just enough. But it certainly didn't feel natural and sometimes it tasted plain awful. To some degree, my lack of deep roots with a single group of peers or teachers provided me with power. Sure, moving always brought some sorrow, but I also had multiple chances to start all over and try things out. I had the luxury of regularly reinventing myself throughout adolescence. While not necessarily great at anything, I grew fairly adept at being okay and even pretty good at most things. I could fit into the mold wherever I went. The only problem was, somehow my unique identity seemed to get lost along the way. Some days I wanted to be just like the peers and adults who surrounded me, and other days I wanted to eschew everything about everyone else in a staunch effort to be true to the one and only me, whoever that was.

Linda's story represents a somewhat more typical adolescent transition. Despite moving to three schools, Linda profited from high-quality instruction provided by several outstanding classroom teachers. These teachers reaffirmed her through recognizing strengths, and they motivated her to learn content as well as the power of thinking and communicating through writing. Linda also had the luxury of reaffirmation from her family, a strong network who valued and cultivated critical thinking, communication, educational opportunity, and academic success. Nevertheless, like all adolescents, Linda needed reaffirmation through support with ongoing authentic challenges and opportunities to build competence with many chances to get it right. Exemplary teachers identify where students are, accelerate learning through meaningful instruction, student practice, and feedback. They challenge each student to move forward in learning.

Ladson-Billings (1994) endorses the concept of culturally relevant teaching in which teachers "see their teaching as an art rather than as a technical skill. They believe that all of their students can succeed rather than that failure is inevitable for some" (p. 25). Gay (2000) and Noddings (1998) similarly emphasize moral education and caring for students as fundamental to the developmental success of the whole student. This concept connects directly with rescuing and reaffirming students. It demands building relationships and using texts that reach out to all students, including those on the margins, to make them feel less alone and more empowered. Lindell's reflection on his relationship with Lucas attests to the difficulty of the work we face; our first response might be to walk away from the demands required in building relationships and connections. Thus, reaffirmation creates safe spaces for all students and teachers to engage in inquiry, regardless of race, gender, class, or sexual orientation.

Part of reaffirming involves understanding that we must not mandate "success" on every first draft. We must learn to measure the success of writers and thinkers by considering both process and product. "Many drafts are failures, but instructive failures . . . Each first draft is a new step into the unknown. It is by drafting (failing) that we uncover our true meaning" (Murray, 2007, p. 184). Teaching writing is not about sleuthing out and highlighting the "errors" in students' papers that somehow represent failure to produce a perfect product. Building the confidence of adolescent writers takes much more than one successfully published piece. We have to remind our students and ourselves repeatedly that we all have something important to say. "We must come to believe that our writing is worth reading by others" (Romano, 2007, p. 167). Building competence in adolescent writers is absolutely essential, but it takes time, recognition, connections through books and experiences, and action based on careful reflection.

As they discuss the importance of both challenging students and building competence, Wilhelm and Smith (2007) state, "even in areas where we have some expertise, we seek an appropriate challenge that shows us how we are expert and offers ways to display and extend this" (p. 239). Students need opportunities to really show us what they can do. Building competence often involves a rigorous and engaging challenge. When you finish, you know that you have really accomplished something. Our job as teachers of adolescent writers becomes to scaffold students as they discover competence through rigorous learning experiences with support.

Adolescents are trying on their identities, seeking out their place in the world as writers with both voice and choice. Growing up really means developing one's own story—we read, write, create, and reflect upon our own stories, our identities. Many scholars affirm the power of story within and beyond educational contexts (Bruner, 1996; Dyson & Genishi, 1994; Gay, 2000; King,

1993). In his epic ten-play cycle of African American life in the American 20ᵗʰ century, playwright August Wilson suggests that maturity and identity formation, which can happen in adolescence and extend into adulthood, are processes of "finding your song" (Wilson, 1988, p. 10). Wilson's notion of the transition from childhood to adulthood depends upon literate acts and lives—thus literacy becomes integral to surviving and thriving in adolescence and beyond.

Reaffirmation creates a window for students to develop competence in finding their own songs and living lives enriched by literacy. This conceptualization of literacy directly contrasts the current obsession with high-stakes testing and test preparation that have taken over too many reading and writing classrooms.

Revolt

As professionals, teachers can play an important role in resisting norms and traditions in education that lead to writing students off and accepting failure for some. We revolt against all practices and structures that threaten access to equitable, meaningful, and authentic learning opportunities for all students. We revolt in order to blend what we are required to do with what we know fosters student learning, based on both research and experience.

High stakes standardized tests too often simply reduce students to a score. These tests decontextualize and compartmentalize. They compact 180 days of school into a few hours. They reduce fiction, poetry, nonfiction, and drama into short passages and then reduce those snippets to a few questions. In the name of leaving no child behind, these tests reduce reading proficiency to four rigid responses, only one of which is "correct." Such measures offer little space—figuratively or literally—for the complexity inherent in full engagement with texts. Through the title, *Writing on Demand* (2000), Anne Ruggles Gere names the artificial, high-stakes conflation of the writing process with often-superficial prompts that allow perhaps thirty minutes for composing. These tests emphasize product over all other aspects of writing processes. We do our profession and our students a disservice to conceptualize writing only in this way. Cognition and complexity often demand collaboration and careful consideration. Revolt requires ensuring that these high-stakes tests do not displace the kind of wonder and inquisitiveness that we hope to inspire in the lives of our adolescent students.

Multiple external pressures create the need for revolt. Certainly, we cannot blame teachers, who, because of budget cuts that result in increased class sizes, may choose to assign fewer papers. We empathize with teachers who face immense pressure from administrators to raise test scores, and who try to foist exercises like daily grammar practice into classrooms as a means to that end. However, more than a hundred years of research document that this practice does not transfer to writing and often creates negativity toward writing, confusion, fear, and shame of one's home dialect (i.e., Braddock, Lloyd-Jones, & Schoer, 1963; Smith, 1986; Hillocks, 1987). In their meta-analysis, Graham and Perin (2007) found that traditional grammar instruction has an overall negative effect: "traditional grammar instruction is unlikely to help improve the quality of students' writing. Studies that specifically examined the impact of grammar instruction with low-achieving writers also yielded negative results" (Anderson, 1997; Saddler & Graham, 2005) (p. 21). Furthermore, too many writing classes serve thirty or more students. We know better. Governors and legislators should know better. NCTE reminds us unambiguously that classes should cap at twenty, with no more than fifteen for remedial classes. We revolt against busy work and repeated drills in arbitrary correctness, in order to teach writing as a thoughtful, generative process of discovery that recognizes research and that reaffirms and rescues students.

To fully embrace the kind of culture of writing and thinking that most enriches and inhabits an integral place in overall happiness and well-being, we must not only rebel against the testing mania and external pressures that have done so much to deaden teaching and learning. We must also restore the ownership of language to all students and teachers in order to encourage many forms of "correct" expression. This notion was best expressed in the National Council of Teachers of English's (NCTE) 1974 resolution affirming students' rights to their own language, thereby reinforcing the importance of honoring the 'home' language students bring to classrooms. Recent scholars further highlight the value of many forms of correctness (Scott, Straker, & Katz, 2008).

Remembrance

We must constantly remember the difference between merely assigning writing and actually *teaching* writers. While assigning writing focuses primarily on a task and a written product, teaching writers allows us to work with students on both process and product. These two distinct concepts represent a vast chasm yet too often get conflated. Many times student papers are examined for mechanical and grammatical errors prior to examination for originality and expression of ideas. When we teach writers rather than just assign writing, we learn to see the writer before the errors: we teach writers that they *can* write rather than that they can't.

When our town's most famous resident, Flannery O'Connor, tried for the first time to obtain a driver's license (at the age of 33), she failed the driving test miserably and likely did damage to the lawn on which her car finally stopped. Biographer Brad Gooch (2009) comments, "The attending state police officer advised, 'Younglady, I think you need sommo practice'" (p. 311), and eventually she later passed the exam. While Flannery clearly stood in need of remediation, could the same be said of the police officer? In some ways, it makes no more sense to "correct" English to eliminate "errors" in written prose than it does to "correct" a Southern drawl in speech. As Glenda Hull (1986) has shown, "errors" are driven by a deep logic and desire to figure things out. Furthermore, just as in the case of Ms. O'Connor's attending officer, what we often see as "error" arises out of divergences that result from respective cultural differences that shape dialects and each individual speaker's unique relationship with language—a phenomenon that linguists term an idiolect. All of these differences reflect the autonomy of language users who make language their own for particular purposes, parallel to the individualized trends in other areas, such as fashion trends like tight jeans, hobbies like drag racing, or social functions/rituals such as the sorority and fraternity rush. We do not usually greet such variations as something in need of remediation and standardization, but many teachers set out to control written language and confine it within very rigid parameters. In many classrooms, though, one set of variations get attacked as contrary to "Standard English," while other variations, like a drawl or idiosyncracies of teachers' speech, often garner little attention. Understanding and reinforcing a "master" system of conventions is supposedly the whole point of studying "grammar." However, the boundary between "error" and acceptability has an arbitrariness that defies any kind of systemic logic, as the evolution of language teaches us. In fact, linguists more frequently use the term "Standardized English" rather that "Standard English" to highlight and make visible the volatile social processes that sometimes unevenly shape notions of "correctness."

Teaching adolescent writers is a process of helping individual students in the midst of dramatic change find and express their voices in ways that help them to discover who they are, to play in the realm of thinking, to express ideas in ways that they had not previously considered, and to build community with and bridges to others. We should strive to equate writing with learning in the sense that we inspire students to synthesize what they do know with the unfamiliar. Good writing instruction asks students to grow beyond easy answers and to ask difficult questions. Through reflection, teachers and students learn how to write our lives onto paper rather than just go through the motions. In this sense, we help students to come to feel "at home" through literate acts—to survive and thrive through literacy.

The Five R model we advocate here welcomes students fully and unconditionally. It reminds us of the importance of a symbiotic relationship, the type of relationship that best honors what teachers and students both bring to the classroom. This environment differs dramatically from more competitive classrooms where students end up as winners or losers as they compete to become the best learner or simply fall to the bottom of the heap. In considering the purpose of literacy, we remember the words of Tom Romano (2007):

> Language is not just for expression and communication. Language is for discovery . . . Language is our canoe up the wilderness river, our bush plane, our space capsule, our magic. Instead of 'now you see it, now you don't,' using language works in reverse: 'now you don't see it, now you do' (p. 170).

Writing helps teachers and students learn to see not the obvious, but the sublime. The Five R's model of teaching writers helps move beyond "written off" toward more rewarding relationships between adolescents, texts, and teachers.

QUESTIONS TO CONSIDER

1. Describe the teacher who has done more than any other to empower you as a writer and thinker. What theory and beliefs seem to have fueled that teacher's work? How do that teacher's practices compare and/or contrast with notions of literacy instruction inherent in the Five R's model?

2. As a teacher, what strategies would you use to help advance the literacy and overall well-being of students like Lucas, Lindell, or Linda? What specific evidence would you seek to measure the success of your efforts and why?

3. Kevin Jennings (*Telling Tales Out of School*, 2000), C. J. Pascoe (*Dude, You're a Fag: Masculinity and Sexuality in High School*, 2007), Ritch C. Savin-Williams (*The New Gay Teenager*, 2006), and others document the virulent homophobia and heterosexism that

dominates schools and thus all too often leads to "writing off" students like Dan. While we have a concern for all students, sometimes that translates into the invisibility of some students. As a classroom teacher, how could you use the Five R's model to inform and enrich your pedagogy and your practice as they relate to teaching lesbian, gay, bisexual, and questioning adolescents?

4. Jawanza Kunjufu, Gloria Ladson-Billings, Lisa Delpit, Alfred Tatum, and others have documented and reflected on the ways that African American children especially get "written off." What modifications, if any, need to be made to the Five R's model to address the needs of African American adolescents? A powerful lesson from those four scholars reminds us to honor the individuality and diversity of every student. Therefore, think of specific teenagers with whom you have worked as you answer this question.

5. Some students find that their language is not accepted at school, and thus they lose part of their identity in trying to acculturate within school contexts. How might the Five R's model help teachers to honor the language students bring to school?

6. How do you want students to remember you as a teacher?

References

Atwell, N. (1998). *In the middle: New understandings about writing, reading, and learning* (2nd ed.). Portsmouth, NH: Heinemann.

Braddock, R., Lloyd-Jones, R., & Schoer, L. (1963). *Research in written composition.* (Report No. 142). Champaign, IL: National Council of Teachers of English.

Bruner, J. (1996). *The culture of education.* Cambridge, MA: Harvard University Press.

Calkins, L. M. (1994). *The art of teaching writing* (2nd ed.). Portsmouth, NH: Heinemann.

Cannon, J. (1993). *Stellaluna.* New York: Scholastic.

Cuban, L. (1993). *How teachers taught: Constancy and change in American classrooms 1890–1990.* (2nd ed.). New York: Teachers College Press.

Cuban, L. (2007). *The blackboard and the bottom line: Why schools can't be businesses.* Cambridge, MA: Harvard University Press.

Dyson, A. H., & Genishi, C. (Eds.). (1994). *The need for story: Cultural diversity in classroom and community.* Urbana, IL: National Council of Teachers of English.

Gay, G. (2000). *Culturally responsive teaching: Theory, research, & practice.* New York: Teachers College Press.

Gere, A. R. (2000). *Writing on demand: Best practices and strategies for success.* Portsmouth, NH: Heinemann.

Gooch, B. (2009). *Flannery: A life.* New York: Little, Brown.

Graham, S., & Perin, D. (2007). *Writing next: Effective strategies to improve writing of adolescents in middle and high schools—A report to the Carnegie Corporation of New York.* Washington, DC: Alliance for Excellent Education.

Grahame, K. (1908). *The wind in the willows.* New York: Charles Scribner's Sons.

Hillocks, G. (1986). *Research on written composition: New directions for teaching.* Urbana, Illinois: ERIC Clearinghouse on Reading and Communication Skills.

Hull, G. (1986). Acts of wonderment: Fixing mistakes and correcting errors. In D. Bartholomae & A. Petrosky (Eds.), *Facts, artifacts, and counterfacts: Theory and method for a reading and writing course.* Portsmouth, NH: Boynton/Cook.

King, N. (1993). *Storymaking and drama: An approach to teaching language and literature at the secondary and postsecondary levels.* Portsmouth, NH: Heinemann.

Kunjufu, J. (2005). *Countering the conspiracy to destroy black boys* (2nd ed.). Chicago: African American Images.

Ladson-Billings, G. (1994). *The dreamkeepers: Successful teachers of African American Children.* San Francisco, CA: Jossey-Bass.

Markham, E. (1915). Outwitted. In *The shoes of happiness and other poems.* Garden City, NJ: Doubleday.

Murray, D. (2004). *Write to learn.* New York: Harcourt.

Murray, D. (2007). Teaching writing your way. In K. Beers, R. E. Probst, & L. Rief (Eds.), *Adolescent literacy: Turning promise into practice* (pp. 179–188). Portsmouth, NH: Heinemann.

Noddings, N. (1998). *Philosophy of education.* Boulder, CO: Westview Press.

Romano, T. (2007). Teaching writing from the inside. In K. Beers, R. E. Probst, & L. Rief (Eds.), *Adolescent literacy: Turning promise into practice* (pp. 167–178). Portsmouth, NH: Heinemann.

Scott, J. C., Straker, D. Y., & Katz, L. (2008). *Affirming students' right to their own language: Bridging language policies and pedagogical practices.* Urbana, IL: National Council of Teachers of English.

Smith, F. (1986). *Insult to intelligence: The bureaucratic invasion of our classrooms.* Portsmouth, NH: Heinemann.

Wilhelm, J. D., & Smith, M. W. (2007). Making it matter through the power of inquiry. In K. Beers, R. E. Probst, & L. Rief (Eds.), *Adolescent literacy: Turning promise into practice* (pp. 231–242). Portsmouth, NH: Heinemann.

Wilson, A. (1988). *Joe Turner's come and gone.* New York: Plume/Penguin.

CHAPTER TWENTY-TWO

Urban Youth Engaging Poetry and Creating Learning Communities

KORINA M. JOCSON

Research shows that cultural relevance in the classroom is key to teaching and learning.[1] To improve the education of urban youth, critical educators not only recognize that students enter the classroom with loads of cultural knowledge, but also identify them as resources in the learning and teaching process.[2] In previous studies, the integration of students' culture(s) in the curriculum has had major implications on how teachers can scaffold students into understanding certain texts, or increase their fundamental interest in reading and writing. For example, it has been noted that students' cultural practices are valuable tools for learning and, in the case of African American students, how signifying and "speakerly" texts can incite fruitful discussions, assist in literary interpretations, as well as convey history, culture, and experience in the classroom.[3]

Increasing cultural and linguistic diversity looms large in many of today's classrooms. As educators, how do we (continue to) take on the challenge of seeking multicultural and anti-oppressive means to improve teaching and learning?[4] Indeed, there are myriad ways of valuing students' cultures and responding to students' needs in urban classrooms. One found to be effective is to devise a curriculum for high school English classes that incorporates the use of rap music and hip hop culture, aligning it with canonical texts such as novels and poetry, to promote academic literacy among urban youth.[5] Another is to mix genres of literature and film to engage students in thematic and structural development related to writing and popular culture.[6] Yet, despite these innovative practices and efforts to bridge school and home cultures, there still seems to be a kind of silencing that misses the expressive voices of youth, that is, the "brave new voices" in poetry.[7]

In recent years, despite cuts on arts education, I have seen youth increasingly participate in out-of-school activities that provide them opportunities to be creative and expressive.[8] Such activities have included poetry writing workshops and teen slam competitions, among others.

Certainly, poetry has become one of those critical spaces where urban youth can speak their minds while accessing an artistic, learning community. The (re)emerging cultural phenomenon in spoken word poetry as rooted in the African diasporic oral traditions of storytelling has also served as a site for uplifting marginalized voices and building a sense of community.[9] From my decade-long experience as a high school teacher in Los Angeles and researcher in the San Francisco Bay Area, I have come to understand the nature of writing instruction in many classrooms and, for the most part, the lack of opportunities for students to express themselves in more critical and profound ways, not to mention establish a sense of community. One exception is the work behind June Jordan's Poetry for the People program in Northern California.

Poetry for the People, or P4P as it is commonly known, is a UC Berkeley program that is in partnership with several organizations, including a high school, a church, and a prison. It is one in which a group of college student–teacher–poets (STPs) with the guidance of the late professor and poet June Jordan, collaborate with teachers, community members, and other artists to implement two significant objectives: (1) to create a safe medium for artistic and political empowerment, and (2) to democratize the medium of poetry to include "the people," or populations that have been historically denied equal access and representation.[10] Through my teaching and outreach work with P4P, I saw and imagined the potential of poetry in young people's lives. Hence, in my subsequent ethnographic study about urban youth poetry, I sought to investigate a number of high school students and their experiences in the context of P4P, and their poetry-related literacy practices both in and out of school. For the purposes of this chapter, I examine the experience of one male urban high school student named Naier to suggest how poetry can create learning communities, and facilitate the kinds of writing instruction that would further recognize the salience of urban youth culture in the classroom. In what follows, I represent his voice in selected quotations and include two of his poems. I begin with a brief description of Naier and his literate activities.

Writing Poems and Other Multi-Literate Activities

Nigerian American 16-year-old Naier attended Bellevue High School located in the San Francisco East Bay Area. He grew up with 10 other siblings in disparate cities and, at the time of the study, resided in a two-bedroom backhouse with his mother, stepfather, and seven-year-old brother Isa. Their home-centered between the 580 MacArthur and 880 Nimitz Freeways—was a place where, according to Naier, for "quiet time in this busy neighborhood." He carved his own space by "drowning" in literate activities such as listening to music, reading magazines, watching television, and writing poetry.

Naier started writing poems in the eighth grade when, in the process of repeating a previously "flunked" English class, his summer school teacher approached him and positively commented on what he recalled as "the very first piece" he ever wrote. Though that "(that poem) was really not that good," Naier recognized this experience as a critical moment that eventually led to his passion for poetry writing. Since then, he wrote "wherever and whenever, on the bus, BART [Bay Area Rapid Transit], waiting in line for something," in restaurants, in class, at home, or just "out and about everywhere." For Naier, these omnipresent literate episodes became a way of being that consisted of "reading his daily" (surroundings, that is) and jotting down words that "hit" him unexpectedly.[11] Not only did they reflect in writing what went through his mind between social encounters, but these episodes also shaped how he processed his realities and, consequently, how such realities shaped the way he responded to them. Furthermore, they were important in defining what was meaningful, in developing a particular kind of practice that was socioculturally embedded with, as well as situated in, his beliefs.[12]

In examining his poetry, I discovered Naier's ideological stance "about the world" as well as the political statements he made related to American society in concert with his personal values. Ironically, these statements were shaped *and* being shaped by the very thing that he wrote about. Like a critical ethnographer making observations, he recorded what he saw in relation to how he felt through his own/visceral reactions about power structures and social inequities.[13] He did so in the following poem, inspired by a "racial profiling" experience:

Hung on Past Ideas

Rage consumes me
as the noose of past generations
is tightened around my neck
Am I the southern Negro here to prance around
with a grin from ear to ear
like Amos & Andy
Yessa, ssorryssa, can I get that fo yasa
feeling like a boy
avoiding the whip of his father
Or am I the Negro with the caliber at my waist
protecting my 20-inch chain and my ounce of dope
because they mean more to me
than my 5-year-old son on welfare with my baby momma
Or am I just the Negro who knows to stay in place
pushing the envelope is impossible
Or if I ever get over
it's because I play football or act
I get thrown off the edge
10 years later my obituary says
Hung On Past Ideas

In his elaboration of why and how he wrote poetry, particularly the one above, Naier noted that he was often adamant about "not missing out on a thought, phrase, verse, line, stanza, rhyme, or just anything that comes to mind." He found any and every available writing tool—from his personal notebook to scratch paper, napkins, and/or old receipts—so that he could "capture the moment." In the classroom, such practices as in Naier's case can become relevant points of departure for writing instruction. The question is, what else should teachers know about their students' everyday experiences to innovate their practice and invigorate their curriculum? Here is one possibility and a closer look at Naier's life.

Like many of his high school peers, Naier was in school from 8:45 A.M. to 3:30 P.M. and enjoyed hanging out with friends in between. He stayed late after school to do homework to improve his overall 3.0 grade point average.[14] Whenever he arrived home around dinnertime exhausted from his day's activities, he either watched TV, read magazines, talked on the phone, played with his brother, or escaped the world through his headphones. He listened to various types of music from contemporary jazz to neo-soul, R&B, and Rap, and followed artists such as Najee, Jill Scott, Alicia Keyes, Case, Ginuwine, Beanie Sigel, and Talib Kweli.[15] In addition, Naier also watched music videos on BET or MTV, and sometimes engaged himself with the History or Discovery channels. While he kept up to date with "who's who" or "what's hot" by reading *Ebony, The Source,* and *Jet* magazines, he also maintained what he termed "cultural awareness" by reading African American texts such as the *Assassination of the Black Male Image* that his parents made available at home, or *Bearing the Cross* that his English teacher provided in the classroom. Considering his eclectic interests, it was evident that Naier's literacy practices were embedded and situated in his sociocultural environment, through interactions with music, magazines, books, etc. In short, he was shaped *and* being shaped by this outside world by popular media and their variegated cultural forms and icons, which have a degree of influence on one's literacy and can transfer into school literacy.[16] Thus, from the perspective of teaching and learning, it is important that such forms be considered and integrated in classroom curriculum and instruction. Asking students to bring physical samples of their interests could mark the beginning of insightful discussions, activities, and projects that make relevant subject matter content to their lives.

In many of his poems, Naier extracted from his everyday experiences as a young African American and remained conscious about identifying with those of others. He sought motivation from within himself and reached out to what he called the "likes of cultural renaissance makers" of his time. Upon blending various aspects of his environment in his poetry, Naier befittingly expanded the notion of literacy from being sociocultural, to that of being discursive at the same time. He did not only find himself situated within certain social and cultural spaces that he entered, exited, and navigated, but also used the discourses associated with them. One such example is a discourse community he participated in on a voluntary basis called Poetry for the People Too (P4P2), a name coined by members themselves. P4P2 was first initiated in 2001 when two sophomore high school students were invited to speak and discuss their poetry as well as writing processes at a conference sponsored by the National Council of Teachers of English held on the UC Berkeley campus. The duo gradually grew as six other students joined the group in later classroom talks held at several locations in the San Francisco Bay Area, including a city college and elementary school. Naier was one of P4P2's original members. For high school teachers, it is important to understand how and why he created and participated in this community.

Creating a Learning Community Youth Call Their Own

P4P2, a high school STP group, convened on certain occasions to present written poetry to different audiences. At the time of my study, it consisted of eight Bellevue high school students, all of whom were involved with the university–high school partnership aspect of the P4P program. P4P2 derived from P4P, a unique poetry program that, as described earlier, utilizes UC Berkeley college STPs to serve and work with high school students in their respective English classes. With their newly acquired and mediated knowledge about poetry, these eight members of P4P2 continued to follow P4P's writing guidelines and, in turn, took on the role of STPs themselves. Similar to the notion of an apprenticeship (i.e., master–student relationship), they were novices (beginner poets) who looked to college STPs (intermediate/advanced poets) as experts in and for their own construction of poetry—a situated learning activity that they as well as many of their peers experienced inside their English classes. For P4P2 members, however, what transpired as a result of this situated learning experience is a practice that began to extend *beyond* the classroom. Poetry writing as a learned activity gradually became an integral part of these students' lives, where "legitimate peripheral participation," that is, a generative social practice occurring over time, took place.[17] In other words, as the students' interest in poetry changed, so did the nature of their participation. Unlike the more consistent and structured schedule of P4P, P4P2 members met spontaneously by way of occasional "invitation-only" presentations in high school and college settings, and/or by swift exchanges during lunch or after school. Fellow English teachers and other Humanities or Social Science instructors interested in incorporating poetry and poetry writing in their own classes often were the ones who provided opportunities for such presentations.

P4P2 members as a whole, including Naier, wrote poems at their leisure. One stark difference between P4P and P4P2 writing activities was that students did not base what they wrote about on assigned prompts; rather, they chose their own topics or themes. Much like in P4P, however, students constructed poetic texts that reflected "truths" about their lived experiences and illustrated negotiations with their social worlds, which I found were often critical and ideological in nature. Everyday social realities were, according to Naier, "so forceful" and "so real" that making meaning was significant in the process of shaping how they saw themselves as urban youth and how such identities were shaped by external influences. Unfortunately, such realities were often not given priority in their social environments, particularly in school and inside classrooms. Hence, it is important for teachers to take the knowledge they have of students' experiences and utilize them critically to delve into issues that not only make them relevant, but also connect with them in ways that build more meaningful relationships. For Naier, "extreme emotions" like anger, joy, and love caused him to pick up his special blue ballpoint pen and poetry notebook, and started to write what naturally came to him. *Wastes Away,* a poem from January of 2000 when he was in the tenth grade, about his slain older brother, illustrates this type of negotiation and reality. Naier revealed that he began to write this poem exactly two days before his brother's death, a prophetic yet painful reality he was still living through and coming to accept every day:

Wastes Away

```
1    As he twists & turns through life
     His soul spins from divine to unkind
     Will he forever be punished
     For past sins of his lifetime
5    As he dies I see the whites of his eyes
     Burn red from greed
     He feels the need to lie, cheat and steal
     All to make that bill he thinks
     He needs so badly
```

10   But doesn't he see that while he's a G
       His gun is destroying equality for you and me?
       Doesn't he realize that he's erased the tracks
       Made by the broken backs
       Of his ancestors
15   But as he proceeds his family bleeds
       The pain which he causes
       And as time pauses
       He falls into a cycle of ill-begotten dreams
       That shatter like glass
20   That last for a lifetime
       He says he cherishes his life
       But cold enough to take another
       Demand his family to love each other
       But slap around his baby's mother
25   He's running for cover
       As the cold, hard wind of reality hits his face
       And the sun rises up, shines away
       The last strand of darkness
       He hides from the light
30   Afraid that his mask will decay
       And dare I say
       He wastes away

In the case of Naier and others, P4P2 as a discourse community provided youth some space to mediate their everyday realities through poetry. The production of poetic texts became one means of reifying the social meanings they made out of experiences from home, school, the streets, and places in between. In addition to social meanings, this community also engaged its members in the more rudimentary writing process that many teachers (continue to) emphasize in their writing instruction. According to Naier, the "raw, untouched, and unrevised" draft in his notebook turned into another draft by incorporating constructive comments from P4P2 peers. After subsequent workshops, he would then draft other versions on loose-leaf pages before "typing a decent one up." Understanding the complexity of the writing process, Naier stated that "a poem is never perfect" and recognized the importance of having poems workshopped or revised at least once, a stage of co-construction that allowed him to gain more confidence about his writing. Generally for him a poem could be cut short to be more precise in length and meaning or lengthened if/when it became necessary to expand on a point or "play up a metaphor" to build imagery, which to say are all choices in his discretion. Sometimes, he would change certain words for diction, others for rhythm and rhyme. Understanding the significance of language use, he noted that with P4P2, he was able to co-construct his poems with "stronger and more descriptive words" to make his writing more purposeful.

Through this process, Naier also exposed himself to a secondary "acquired" discourse (i.e., literary devices and language in poetry writing) that allowed him to participate more fluidly in constructing realities occurring in his primary "learned" discourse (i.e., everyday language use).[18] As his participation changed over time from periphery to center, he was both acquiring *and* learning at the same time. However, most interesting in all of Naier's writing was that he used this same arguable notion of a secondary discourse to critique happenstances within others' secondary discourses. For example, in *Hung on Past Ideas*, he challenged "blaxploitation Amos & Andy-type characters" (see lines 5–8), yet tied his critique to semantics adopted by descendants of African slaves as imaginatively illustrated in "Yessa, ssorryssa, can I get that fo yasa." Also and more broadly speaking, as seen in *Wastes Away*, he depicted his "brother's dim world through [his] own" understandings of American society, indicative in his question, "Doesn't he see that while he's a G/his gun is destroying equality for you and me?" (see lines 10–11).

Conclusion

For youth like Naier, literate practices, such as poetry writing, were shaped by multiple negotiations in his social practice. In P4P2 Naier created and sustained a discourse community set against a backdrop of larger communities of practice. The several talks of which he was a part demonstrated to others (i.e., the audience) the possibilities of poetry and related practices they could employ in their lives. What he learned in his own participation in P4P2 allowed him to actively exercise this access not only to influence others, but also to expand other present day communities of practice. His membership in P4P2 engaged him to further produce "meaning," mold "identity," sustain "practice," and define "community."[19] As I have illustrated here, P4P2 as a discourse *and* learning community, asserted these four key elements that, in turn, manifested in Naier's own poetry writing *and* actions as an STP in other classroom settings. For teachers who seek ways to improve student participation and social dynamics in the classroom, it is important to consider creating smaller communities of practice, in the form of teams or groups, that could potentially activate students' membership and learning processes.

Despite his high level of confidence and abilities as a student, Naier still felt disengaged "whenever and for whatever reason" in his own classes. So, instead of total disengagement, he would write poems to get him through the hour. He would jot down what came to him, smile at its potential, and simply keep it in his notebook. Perhaps rather than waiting to be read and shared at the next P4P2 presentation, these "hidden" poems consisting of "hidden" realities should be provided space *inside* classrooms, particularly in English/Language Arts classes. Perhaps then, a mere literacy episode such as a writing of a haiku on the bus or a "dope line" sparked by a rap song on a piece of scratch paper can serve as an impetus to innovate writing instruction, as well as a reason to expand more communities of practice that engage students in thinking about how their realities are relevant to teaching and learning. Ever since the eighth grade, Naier sought to grow and develop a more sophisticated way of expressing his "extreme emotions" through poetry. P4P2 as a discourse and learning community provided the critical space for this kind of expression that he had hoped soon his current classes would make available.

QUESTIONS TO CONSIDER:

1. Why does the author contend that poetry writing is so vital in youths' development? What does it do that other subject areas do not provide? Explain and elaborate.

2. How does Naier's growth illustrate Jocson's claim about the importance of poetry in his life? Give examples.

3. How did Poetry for the People Too (P4P2) transform itself from a relatively minor entity into one that became a social and cultural force? Explain and elaborate.

4. Explain how Naier changed his role from that of disengaged person to that of engaged student.

NOTES

This chapter originally appeared in Joe L. Kincheloe and kecia hayes (eds.), *Teaching City Kids: Understanding and Appreciating Them* (New York: Peter Lang, 2007).

1   G. Ladson-Billings, *The Dreamkeepers: Successful Teachers of African American Children* (San Francisco: Jossey-Bass, 1994); L. Delpit, *Other People's Children: Cultural Conflict in the Classroom* (New York: The New York Press, 1995); K. Gutiérrez, Baquedano-López and M. Turner, "Putting language back into Language Arts: When the radical middle meets the third space," *Language Arts 74(5)* (1997): 368–378.

2   L. Moll, "Mediating knowledge between homes and classrooms" in D. Keller-Cohen, ed. *Literacy: Interdisciplinary Conversations* (Cresskill, NJ: Hampton, 1994), pp. 385–401; C. Sleeter and C. Grant, "Mapping terrains of power: Student cultural knowledge versus classroom knowledge" in C. Sleeter, ed. *Empowerment through Multicultural Education* (Albany: SUNY, 1991), pp. 49–67; C. Lee, *Signifying as a Scaffold for Literary Interpretations: The Pedagogical Implications of an African American Discourse Genre* (Urbana, IL: NCTE, 1993); J. Mahiri and S. Sablo, "Writing for their lives: The non-school literacy of California's urban African American youth," *Journal of Negro Education, 65(2)* (1996): 164–180; E. Morrell and J. Duncan-Andrade, "Promoting academic literacy with urban youth through engaging Hip Hop culture," *English Journal, 91(6)* (2002): 88–92.

3   Lee, *Signifying as a Scaffold for Literary Interpretations.*

4   S. Nieto, *Language, Culture, and Teaching: Critical Perspectives for a New Century* (Mahwah, NJ: Lawrence Erlbaum, 2002).

5   E. Morrell and Duncan-Andrade, "Promoting academic literacy with urban youth through engaging Hip Hop culture."

6   D. Allender, "Popular culture in the classroom," *English Journal, 93(3)* (2004): 12–14. See also E. Morrell, *Linking Literacy and Popular Culture: Finding Connections for Lifelong Learning* (Norwood, MA: Christopher-Gordon, 2004).

7   J. Weiss and S. Herndon, *Brave New Voices: The Youth Speaks Guide to Teaching Spoken Word Poetry* (Portsmouth, NH: Heinemann, 2001). For a discussion on silencing, see M. Fine, *Framing dropouts: Notes on the politics of an Urban Public High School* (Albany: SUNY, 1991).

8   E. Soep, *"The Art of Critique: Learning from Youth Making Media,"* talk presented at the Graduate School of Education's Language and Literacy, Society and Culture colloquium series (University of California, Berkeley, CA, 2003); G. Hull and M. Katz, "Learning to tell a digital story: New literate spaces for crafting self," paper presented at the meeting of the *American Anthropological Association* (New Orleans, LA, 2002); S. Heath and Smith, *Art show: Youth and community development* [Documentary] (New York: Partners for Livable Communities, 1999); S. Meacham, "Reader writer freedom fighter:" Tupac Shakur and the struggle between liberatory litera-

cy and 'thug life' in Hip Hop music," talk presented at the meeting of the American Educational Research Association (Chicago, IL, 2003).

9   M. Fisher, "From the coffee house to the school house: The promise and potential of spoken world poetry in school contexts," *English Education 37(2)* (2005): 115–131. To clarify the term, "spoken word" is a type of poetry that centers on the oral form, or performance, of a written poem. Here I focus on poetry as a written form. For more on the history and present-day manifestations of the spoken word movement, see M. Algarin and B. Holman, *Aloud: Voices from the Nuyorican Poets Café* (New York: Henry Holt, 1994); Z. Anglesey, *Listen Up! Spoken Word Poetry* (New York: Ballantine, 1999); G. Glazner, *Poetry Slam: The Competitive Art of Performance Poetry* (San Francisco: Manic D, 2000).

10   L. Muller and the Poetry for the People Blueprint Collective, *June Jordan's Poetry for the People: A Revolutionary Blueprint* (New York: Routledge, 1995). Also see J. Jordan, *On call: Political essays* (Boston: South End. 1985).

11   S. Heath, "What no bedtime story means: Narrative skills at home and at school," *Language in Society 11(2)* (1982): 49–76; These literate episodes derive from what Heath calls "*literacy events,*" that is, any set of human interactions mediated by print/writing. Also see Gee (1996) for a discussion on literacy and Discourse, see J. Gee, *Social Linguistics and Literacies: Ideology in Discourses* (Bristol, PA: Taylor & Francis, 1996).

12   B. Street, *Literacy in Theory and Practice* (Cambridge: CUP, 1984).

13   Mahiri and Sablo, "Writing for their lives."

14   At the writing of these notes, Naier no longer had the time to do homework after school. He either went directly to work at a BioTech company or attended organizational group meetings held by Youth Together or the Black Student Union. He did his work when he got home.

15   At the writing of these notes, Naier listened more to artists such as Nas, Cee-Lo, 50 Cent, and Goapele than those previously named.

16   A. Dyson, *Writing Superheroes: Contemporary Childhood, Popular Culture, and Classroom Literacy* (New York: Teachers College, 1997).

17   J. Lave and E. Wenger, *Situated Learning: Legitimate Peripheral Participation* (Cambridge: CUP, 1991).

18   See Gee, *Social linguistics.* See also Delpit, *Other people's children.* This shift from one discourse to another implies that acquisition (not just learning) can also take place in one's primary discourse. Delpit argues that the separation between primary and secondary discourse, and/or other levels of discourse for that matter, is not as plainly rigid as Gee's theory explains it.

19   E. Wenger, *Communities of Practice: Learning, Meaning, and Identity* (Cambridge: CUP, 1998).

CHAPTER TWENTY-THREE

Teaching History to Adolescents

JOHN A. BEINEKE

Teaching adolescents and teaching history. There is no more important age group, and those who teach history would argue there is no more important subject. John Dewey made the case for teaching history when in his book *Experience and Education* he asked the question, "How shall the young become acquainted with the past in such a way that the acquaintance is a potent agent in appreciation of the living present."[1]

This chapter will look at the context of teaching history to middle school and high school students. The contribution will not be an attempt to encapsulate within these pages a course in pedagogy or provide an exhaustive review of the literature on the topic. It is more, to use an art metaphor, a palette that will include colors, hues, and shades by which to look at the teaching of history. The aim will be to examine ideas that will engage adolescents in twenty-first century America while at the same time combining ideas, research, and my own classroom experience.

Author and professor James W. Loewen has written that "Those who don't remember the past are condemned to repeat the eleventh grade." In a more serious vein, Loewen has noted that students "hate" history, find it "boring," frequently list it as the most irrelevant of twenty-one commonly taught subjects in school, and find it their least interesting subject at all grade levels. Most damaging might be from the rap group Jungle Brothers who declare: "Yeah, I cut class/ I got a D/ 'Cause history meant nothin' to me."[2]

Using the assumptions from three progressive educators, this essay will strive to suggest ways to make history "mean something" to adolescents through how it is taught. John Dewey spoke of "interest and effort"—if there was interest on the part of the student, then effort by the student would follow. William Heard Kilpatrick placed a variation of that thought in the phrase "activity leading to further activity." That was what teacher should seek in the classroom. And William Van Til spoke to what he viewed as the major goal of teaching in the title of one of his books *Curriculum: Quest for Relevance*. The intention of all three thinkers was to connect the learner to the subject at hand so that the motivation to learn would be, as much as possible, internal rather than external.

As educational researchers Johnson and Christensen have pointed out, the history of adolescence itself is both related and instructive to exploring the topic of teaching history. In the twentieth century several changes took place that had an impact on the stage of life known as adolescence. First, compulsory attendance laws increased school enrollment for 14- to 17-year-olds from 6 percent in the late 1800s to the significantly high levels we have today. Second, the juvenile justice system was formed making distinctions between adolescents and adults. Third, the 1938 Fair Labor Standards Act made many types of hazardous child labor illegal, making schooling rather than labor a preferable alternative for youths. Fourth, this age group became a unique field of study from 1890 to 1920, even being called the "Age of Adolescence" by historian David Tyack.[3] These examples demonstrate how history is about change, perspective, and the way in which cause and effect play on all aspects of life—even the adolescent.

The question of "why" should be answered when advocating the teaching of history to adolescence. B. L. Berg has identified five reasons for conducting historical research which apply to the teaching of history. They are:

- To uncover the unknown;
- To answer questions
- To identify the relationship that the past has to the present
- To record and evaluate the accomplishments of individuals, agencies, or institutions,
- To aid in our understanding of the culture in which we live.[4]

All of these elements are essential to teaching history to adolescents.

Before delving into the ideas and suggestions for teaching history to adolescents in the twenty-first century, there are three major trends that underpin and influence—some might even say control—the current educational milieu. These three elements are competing learning theories, the standards movement, and high stakes testing. In ways interrelated, all three have an impact on the teaching of history in today's schools.

Competing learning theories certainly have an effect on how we teach history. Possibly the phrase "the learning wars" might better capture the debates that surround current teaching and learning strategies. An incomplete list of theories includes the cognitive/developmentalist, the behaviorists, the followers of Howard Gardner and his theories of multiple intelligences, and the brain theorists. Some theories, such as the cognitive/developmentalist, have subsets such as constructivism and psychometrics. The disciples of these theories are devoted and committed.

Recently, in a large university bookstore, I perused several educational psychology textbooks. Each text had its own theoretical basis. Even so, I noted that the cognitive-based texts would neither reference behaviorist theory nor vice versa. They seemed to be two ships passing in the night failing to acknowledge that the other theory existed. A middle level methods text, in discussing learning, provides a paragraph on behaviorism citing Ivan Pavlov and B. F. Skinner and stressing rewards and punishment. The authors then state, "The idea that behavior indicates learning is unsatisfying for cognitive approaches to learning."[5] The "wars" proceed.

The reasons that various learning theories fail with adolescents vary. Some of the reasons include seemingly short attention spans, lack of motivation in the academic arena of adolescent lives, and competition with various media for a student's interest. Moreover, all too frequently, poor attendance and high mobility of students from school to school mean teaching opportunities are lost. For the purposes of this essay, an eclectic approach to learning theories will be the operating presupposition for the ideas and suggestions made in teaching of history to adolescents.

The standards movement is also a major reality to be dealt with when teaching history. Although arguably not taken to the extent of literacy and mathematics assessments, the history curriculum increasingly in the past quarter century has been codified and prescribed. The content of history now appears within most state standards sometimes referred to as frameworks or curriculum maps. From organizations such as the National Council for Social Studies to the Web sites of state departments of education, thematic outlines and specific content within the discipline of history are provided to teachers. History textbooks themselves could be viewed as a curricular map. The standardization of the history curriculum is now in place.

Closely aligned to the standards movement has been the rise of what has been familiarly termed "high stakes testing." Assessment and evaluation of what has been prescribed to learn has emerged as central to the teaching and learning process. As noted above, literacy and mathematics have been the major focus of high stakes testing. In a number of states, though, especially through the use of exit or graduation examinations, students face these tests. Support for high stakes testing can be witnessed in the expanding list of states that utilize them. In addition, thoughtful educators and historians have made the case both for and against their use by citing state examples and how policy is impacting testing and, and conversely, how testing is impacting policy.[6]

This chapter will not take further time to deliberate these current realities of teaching history to adolescents. However, the teaching of history cannot ignore learning theories, the standards movement, or high stakes testing. As a result direct instruction may be preferred over inquiry teaching, the repetition of a few historical topics are favored over examining a wider variety of topics in history, and an emphasis of learning for the sake of a test rather than what history can mean to a student on the personal and civic level may occur. These scholarly and policy debates should and will continue. The only fact that seems apparent at this point is that these three trends have resulted in the narrowing of instructional strategies and a limiting of the content examined in the process of teaching history.

One further assumption is made in this essay. The teaching of history is both an art and a science. Statistics have added a dimension to history not previously available. Ever-increasing demographic data on populations give historians more information with which to work and econometrics assist in better explaining economic downturns and expansions. Today's computers then allow historians to manage and manipulate such data bases, providing better explanations and context. Even so, history remains an art as well. It is a story that is told in different ways by different historians. Judgment, sequence, connections, and literary style must all come into play, especially in trade and textbooks, when illuminating the past for adolescents.

With these trends and assumptions in mind, we proceed to a number of suggestions that can be utilized to best engage the adolescent learner with history. The following can be categorized as methods, approaches, or strategies. These areas will only be successful, or partially successful, when they occur within a positive school climate that includes supportive and involved teachers, high expectations for students' conduct and achievement, and active student engagement.

The ideas will obviously work best when the student is active (working individually or within a group) rather than passive (listening or watching for an extended period of time with no direction).[7]

Textbooks

Many innovative teachers and pedagogues eschew the use of textbooks. Even so, they remain a major component of schooling that cannot be totally ignored. While some textbooks are both exhaustive (and at times exhausting) a recent move in the textbook industry has been the use of "brief" or "short" histories.[8] Although abbreviated they usually do not sacrifice accuracy. The downside is that they often must forego photographs and other visuals that make full-length textbook treatments preferable. They also lose the content that falls outside the political, military, and economic arenas such as the cultural, social, and literary components of our history—or at least offer them less space.

James W. Loewen's *Lies My Teacher Told Me: Everything Your American History Textbook Got Wrong*, setting aside its provocative title, does in a scholarly manner survey the failures and fallacies of current textbooks. Loewen does provide a number of germane points regarding textbooks that cannot be discounted. These include breadth and depth of content, organization of material, special features such as charts, photographs, maps, and summaries, and reference tools. He notes that textbooks can be terminology and information dense, user (student) unfriendly in terms of readability and interest, uneven in treatment of certain historical periods (especially recent times and events), and unfortunately factually incorrect.[9]

Providing adolescent readers with structure is critical when utilizing textbooks. The International Reading Association has published an expansive number of examples of what have previously been labeled "study guides" to assist in this undertaking. *Guiding Readers Through Text: Strategy Guides for New Times*, draws from research on effective reading practices and comprehension. This work includes interactive reading guides, profiler guides, inquiry guides, and listening/viewing guides to be used in conjunction with textbooks and audiovisual materials.[10]

Textbooks will be used in the teaching of history, although many teachers across the country are effective without them. The focus when using textbooks needs to be on the purposes for which they are employed. When used creatively, through several of the approaches that follow, they can give structure and information to students. When their purpose is neglected, they can add to the student belief that history lacks interest and relevance.

Primary Sources

The use of primary sources has been viewed as central to the teaching of history at all levels, but especially for adolescents. A primary source has been defined as any form of documentation that was created by a direct witness or in some other way directly involved or related to the event.[11] Examples of primary sources can include diaries, letters, memoirs, oral history interviews, government documents, film or photographs of an incident or event. A photograph, for example, of a young Civil War soldier—clearly too young to be fighting and looking none too happy about being in uniform—can lead to hypotheses and creative writing activities by students. Two outstanding locations to retrieve primary sources would be the National Archives and the National Council for the Social Studies' professional journal *Social Education* which publishes within its pages "Teaching with Documents."[12]

Although debated as to whether they are truly primary sources, newspapers and magazines provide a fairly uncomplicated way to incorporate primary sources in teaching history. Newspapers are accessible in microfilm form or on the Internet. Original editions of magazines, such as *Time* or *Newsweek* are often archived in university and public libraries. A primary source lesson that I have used asks students to find an article from the World War II era (1939–1945). They make a copy of the article they select from the microfilm if a newspaper or the actual magazine is available. Students are then to provide an overview of the article followed by an evaluation of their thoughts on the article in the context of today. Two global comments that students make are that newspapers of a prior era contain approximately five times the content per page as their counterparts do today and that the reading level is markedly higher.

For all the advocacy of primary sources, Keith Barton has challenged history teachers to be critical users of these materials. While labeling original sources as a "centerpiece of the history classroom," Barton points out that primary sources must be used selectively. As an example he points out that having students read the Northwest Ordinance solely to find out slaves had to be returned to their owners may not be as effective as just telling students this fact. In contrast, Barton has found that showing a photograph of coal miners in the 1920s is much more valuable in students' understanding of miners' strikes than laboriously describing or even reading about the event. Another example is having students read or view Martin Luther King, Jr.'s "I Have a Dream" speech rather than attempting to describe the importance of the March on Washington in 1963.[13]

Barton has a point on the use of primary sources. I once observed a lesson in a girls' high school in the midlands of England on Woodrow Wilson's Fourteen Points. While the term "torment" would be an exaggeration, the word "anguish" came to mind in what I saw. The teacher slogged through each point, most of which would be little remembered or even needed by the students to gain an adequate understanding of the World War I peace process. With the teacher literally sweating his way through the lesson, the young women with glazed eyes endured the lesson for an hour. It was painful to witness.

Shirley Engle in his classic look at using primary sources—and secondary as well—has suggested five questions students and teachers should pursue. First, when and why was it written? Second, whose viewpoint is presented? Third, is the account believable? Fourth, is the account supported by other sources? And fifth, after reading the document or viewing the image, how is one supposed to feel about the America that has been presented?[14] Asking and thinking about these questions can make the use of primary sources an indispensable tool in the teaching of history to adolescents.

The Internet

Adolescents live in the ubiquitous age of the Internet with its attendant texting, twittering, Googling, and blogging. It is therefore not surprising that the emergence of the Internet has added a new dimension and tool to the teaching of history. One survey found that 90% of American adolescents between the ages of 11 and 18 have access to the Internet and 80% percent have an Internet connection at home which most use daily.[15] A number of sites are most impressive. More importantly, some are highly useful to teachers as well as students. New sites that incorporate lectures and course outlines, lesson plans, readings, and audiovisual materials include TeacherTube, HippoCampus, and MIT's OpenCourseware.[16]

However, research by students may be the richest vein to be mined with this particular technology. Locating and evaluating online sources, managing data, and finally producing the results of the research are new skills that are indispensable in the Internet age. In fact, such resources to accomplish this process are increasingly available.[17] Students may not need technical assistance in working with the Internet, but as with any new instructional mode they may need guidance and even some monitoring (without censoring) of various sites on the Web.

There are, as would be expected with any learning tool like the Internet, potential drawbacks. These include excessive time in non-academic chat rooms, cyber experiences involving sexual predators, social isolation, and academic dishonesty. In this last category I have seen students use search engines to locate answers to low level identification questions and come up with wrong or even bizarre responses. When asked to identify Richard Nixon in the context of his role in the 1950s as communist-hunter and Vice-President, a student referenced Watergate: wrong decade, wrong significance. Another student looking for the *Lusitania* came up with the answer "an exotic flower." The significance of the sinking of the World War I-era passenger liner was lost on the student. The key, as will be seen during the discussion of critical thinking, is to limit such identification questions as much as possible.

The sheer size of Internet content can also be a drawback. A 2005 study on using the Internet for research provided an excellent example. In 1996 Franklin D. Roosevelt yielded fewer than 100 hits. In 2005, a decade later, the number was 150,000 and my own 2009 search yielded 2,100,000. Locating primary sources is no doubt the most useful tool the Internet now provides and as seen above many are quite strong. However, both valid and dubious sites need rigorous evaluation by students and teachers alike. It is not difficult to stumble onto sites that are sponsored by white supremacist groups who are debunkers of Martin Luther King, Jr. and deniers of the Holocaust. Obligatory questions that should be asked include: who created, hosted, and wrote the Web site? What is the Web site's domain? (e.g., .com, .org, .gov?) Are links provided? Finally, what are the purposes, points of view, and agendas of the Web site?[18]

Biography

History is about people and biography is the story of individuals. It has even been said that there is no proper history, only biography. Adolescents connect with people. The lives of women and men in American history can resonate with adolescents. The recipient of the prestigious Carter G. Woodson Book Award for elementary and secondary students is often a biography. While biographies of historical figures for adults have long been prize-winners and bestsellers—Jon Meacham's *American Lion: Andrew Jackson in the White House* and David McCulloch's *John Adams* have been recent Pulitzer Prize winners—young adult biographies for adolescents is a growing niche. The subjects run the gamut from the famous to the obscure, from the national to the local. *No Easy Answers: Bayard Rustin and the Civil Rights Movement* examines how a black leader on the national stage battled for social justice. At a community level, *Going over All the Hurdles: A Life of Oatess Archey*, explores how an African American from Indiana in the last half of the twentieth century overcame and prevailed against discrimination in the multiple fields of education, teaching, coaching, law enforcement, and politics. [19]

Cartoons

Who doesn't enjoy a cartoon? On opening a newspaper editorial page, our eyes often move first to the cartoon, usually placed near the top of the page. History textbooks frequently use cartoons. Assessments are increasingly using editorial cartoons within standardized tests to gauge analysis, application, and interpretation. One of the most frequently used cartoonists was Herblock—moniker for Herbert Block—editorial cartoonist for the *Washington Post* for 50 years covering the presidencies beginning with Franklin D. Roosevelt to George W. Bush. His autobiography is replete with a trove of cartoons excellent for classroom use. [20]

Before he was Dr. Seuss, Theodor Seuss Geisel was an extraordinary political editorial cartoonist. His work from the World War II era for the New York daily newspaper *PM* will immediately connect with adolescent students. The World War II related caricatures of people (Hitler and Tojo) and bizarre animals, drawn in the style of his children's literature books that began in the 1950s, are easily recognizable to today's students. This "early Seuss" made his political points in the 1940s as clearly as any of today's cartoonists. [21]

Higher Order Thinking

Whatever strategies are used with adolescents, activities to encourage and practice higher order thinking are an indispensable element. Discussion-based teaching that incorporates higher order thinking questions based on Bloom's Taxonomy which remains a solid model to learning theorists of all persuasions. Creating and guiding student discussions while maintaining a climate that supports student contributions are critical ingredients in teaching critical thinking. The art of asking questions and classroom questioning strategies, on the part of students and teachers, are an integral component in achieving higher order and critical thinking. As Neil Postman and Charles Weingartner wrote in their classic 1960s book *Teaching as Subversive Activity*, "Once you have learned how to ask questions—relevant and appropriate and substantial questions—you have learned how to learn and no one can ever stop you." [22]

John E. Henning has developed a critical thinking approach he calls the "bow tie." The teacher frames the discussion—the open end of the bow tie—narrows the discussion by shifting to a conceptual discussion and then widening the other side of the bow tie with applications generated by students. [23] The thoughtful selection of questions for inclusion in classroom discussions and assessments may be the most important act on the part of teachers in their daily decision-making.

Diversity: Gender, Race, and Social Class

History, as we teach it today, must contain the diversity that reflects the nation's population. The most obvious are gender and race. In terms of gender Nel Noddings has written that "If women's culture were taken more seriously in educational planning, social studies and history might have a very different emphasis. Instead of moving from war to war, ruler to ruler, one political campaign to the next, we would give far more attention to social issues."[24]

Cornel West has written on the primacy of race in American history and the need for all people—adolescents as well as adults—to gain a greater understanding of its impact on our everyday life. Since W.E.B. Du Bois wrote in *The Souls of Black Folk* that "The problem of the twentieth century is the problem of the color line" we have seen that American history cannot be taught or learned without addressing race. West has written that "From 1776 to 1964—188 years of our 218 year history—this racial divide would serve as a basic presupposition for the expansive functioning of American democracy."[25] It can be argued that race has been the defining and perennial issue in American history.

While the diversity of America cannot be ignored, its appropriate role in our schools has been disputed. Two examples of this debate have been Frances FitzGerald in the 1970s and Arthur M. Schlesinger, Jr., in the 1990s. Both pondered the potential divisiveness of focusing on our differences rather than our commonalities. FitzGerald, in her study of American history textbooks believed in the need to teach for tolerance and respect when looking at our differences. However, she also thought that the similarities between Americans that had bound us together as a nation were minimized. She saw a lack of integration of diversity in history textbooks, finding what she labeled a "patchwork." By "patchwork" she meant that texts often placed photos or would mention a minority such as Hispanic or Native American in an attempt to assure all races, ethnicities, and cultures were noted. Then, though, the textbooks would not adequately explain or integrate the material within the narrative. Schlesinger's similar thesis was that by emphasizing our differences in America we were in danger of forgetting what holds us together as a nation.[26]

Directly related to the teaching of history to adolescents is the work of the African American educator James Banks and his lifelong professional study of diversity and multicultural education. Always grounded in the assumption that education must be based on democratic values such as justice and equality, Banks calls for a "balance of diversity and unity." Examples are plentiful. Violent divisions based on culture or ethnicity can be seen in nations and regions throughout history, even in seemingly homogeneous countries such as Canada with its separatist elements in Quebec.

Banks also sees the need for balance in how black and white students look at history. Rather than exclusively emphasizing the victimization of the minority culture, multiple examples can and should be provided of whites fighting for oppressed groups in American history. These would include whites who were leading abolitionists and civil rights workers. For those groups that have been victimized and marginalized, Banks calls for a "transformative curriculum." An example that Banks provides is to select for inclusion in the mainstream curriculum ethnic heroes who challenged the existing social and political order such as Geronimo and Nat Turner. Another example is the courage of Mrs. Daisy Bates, local head of the NAACP in Little Rock, who suffered financial and personal turmoil for her stance in support of the Little Rock Nine.

A final example that Banks provides in teaching history from a diverse perspective is the need for what he calls viewing the United States from the concept of a "multidirectional" society. Often American history has been seen as an "east to west" phenomenon—the country moved from

Western Europe across the Atlantic Ocean then on to the Pacific. The familiar Manifest Destiny concept is a prime example. Banks suggests that insufficient attention has been paid to the north-easterly directional flow of culture from Africa, the northerly flow from Mexico and Latin America, and the easterly flow from Asia.[27]

Using the personal example of John Hope Franklin, the late black historian, adds to the discussion of diversity. He was influenced to choose a career in history rather than law by a white professor at the historically black Fisk University. Indeed, Franklin's contribution was two-fold: construct the history of African Americans while reconstructing mainstream American history.[28] Although produced in 1969, *Black History: Lost, Stolen, or Strayed* (available on DVD) examines how black history was either distorted or forgotten within mainstream treatments of American history. Hosted by a youthful Bill Cosby, the film is also an excellent artifact that documents the lack of status of black history fifty years ago and the resultant Black Power movement of the 1960s.

Along with gender and race, social class is a component of diversity that is critical in the teaching of history to adolescents. Jonathan Kozol, urban teacher during the 1960s, has long written about the link between school success and social class. His classic work, *Savage Inequalities*, exposed to the nation how social justice was a promise yet to be delivered on in American Society. In his most recent book, *The Shame of the Nation: The Restoration of Apartheid*, Kozol demonstrates how different academic and career goals are set for students in middle- and upper-class schools from goals for those students who attend schools in less affluent areas. To remedy this discrepancy, he calls for teaching students about social class and proposes a new civil rights movement.[29]

We also know that adolescents are best taught about diversity in history through real-life experiences. Most of all is the need for continuous and authentic interaction among cultural and ethnic groups. To this must be added community involvement and visits, guest speakers from various groups, and visual materials that make the experience of groups from the past real to the students of the present. Harvard's Henry Louis Gates, Jr., and his Du Bois Institute have begun to use genealogy with adolescent black students to both teach and personalize history. He has even provided DNA testing to enable the students to trace their ethnicity.[30] It is again the need when teaching history to adolescents to present an integrated, balanced, and accurate portrait of a diverse nation.

Movies, Movies, Movies

The media in general and film in particular are major components in the life of adolescents. A recent study found that the typical adolescent spends four hours a day listening to music and watching television. In addition, over 50% of adolescents, the largest film watching age group of the American population, views at least one film per month in a movie theater.[31]

A more in-depth analysis of this data has been undertaken by Sam Wineburg and his colleagues. Their research on the role of film in students' knowledge of history has shown that movies are what can be called "the cultural curriculum." In their study, the award-winning film *Forrest Gump* was found to be highly effective in teaching about the 1960s—from the Vietnam War to the hippie movement. The influence of the narratives from film that students bring to the classroom can be used by teachers to build deeper historical knowledge. Wineburg quotes the president of the Organization of American Historians as "begrudgingly recognizing films as the predominant influence on students' historical understanding."[32]

The amount of film that is available to teach the history of the twentieth century is remarkable. Documentaries to Hollywood productions provide history teachers a valuable venue to use to engage the adolescent learner. Popular movies about World War II such as *Schindler's List* and *Saving Private Ryan* combine compelling stories with outstanding filmmaking. One will never know the terror, brutality, and sacrifice of the Normandy invasion on D-Day. Even so, the first twenty minutes of *Saving Private Ryan* may come as vicariously close as one can to what that day was like. *The Holocaust and Concentration Camps: Jewish Life and Death in Nazi Camps* is the actual film footage of the liberation of the concentration camps. The scenes are graphic and the teacher will need to make a professional decision on what age is appropriate for viewing. However, pairing several minutes from Holocaust archives with the opening scenes from *Saving Private Ryan* explains better than any reading why World War II was called the "necessary war."

While again graphic, *Image of an Assassination: A New Look at the Zapruder Film*, the digitally enhanced version of the Kennedy assassination, is now available. Connecting it with ever-present conspiracy theories surrounding that November day in Dallas in 1963 can make for an absorbing lesson. A source of photographic documents that can be used in conjunction with movies is "Teaching with Historic Places" that can be found on the National Park Service Web site. In addition, there are several resource guides of movies to use to supplement and enrich history lessons.[33] Due to the normal limited attention spans of adolescents and classroom time considerations, the strategy of using excerpts rather than films in their entirety is advisable. To guide learners through the viewing experience, students should be required to respond to thoughtfully constructed questionnaires about the film that is watched.

Student Research

On occasion, a student research project can be a motivator for the adolescent. While the historical researching process is probably not applicable or appropriate for an entire class, using research as a motivator can be effective. For example, students could research the following historical questions: If the Declaration of Independence was signed on July 2, 1776, why do we celebrate the founding of our country on July 4? Who actually took the first machine powered flight? Was Charles Lindbergh the first person to cross the Atlantic by air? Discovering mistakes and errors in long-held and common historical beliefs can draw out the skeptical element within many adolescents.

One of the best structures in place to support student research is the National History Day project. Underwritten by educational and historical organizations each year it affords students the opportunity to research a selected aspect of history. Students then present their findings through a variety of venues that include performances, presentations, creating Web sites, and filmmaking in addition to traditional research formats. Each year a theme is provided, e.g, in 2009 it was the "Individual in History."[34]

Applied and Public History

There is a genuine need to connect adolescents with real-life applications in the study of history. Some have called this approach applied history or public history. William Hogeland has suggested that there has been a failing by those who work in the area of public history—museums, tourist attractions, state and national parks, and even popular historical works of fiction, nonfiction, and biography. Hogeland advocates for greater connection to the "non-specialist" (student) in our society through public history thereby inspiring the untapped imagination of the youth and citizenry.[35] It is the use of venues such as historic and preservation sites, archival work, museums, or learning firsthand what historians do that students relate to the field of history. There are now new degrees in fields such as heritage studies where students study the art, craft, science, and methodology of "doing history," not just reading it.[36]

History is often taught from a federal perspective through national events and issues—the election and lives of the presidents, the passage of laws by Congress, pivotal Supreme Court decision, and wars. To bring the relevancy of the national scene to adolescents, history should also be viewed through the lens of a state or community. An excellent model for applied history has emerged through public history projects. One of the best in this arena is the Marion, Indiana, Community History Project that was created and is maintained by high school students in that city.[37] Historians have found if they do not write for both the public and their fellow academics, they end up only talking to themselves. Public history is an anecdote to that challenge.

Controversial and Problematic Topics in History

The examination of controversial or problematic topics can be a highly motivational strategy in the teaching of history. It can also be one of the most treacherous and risky approaches when working with adolescents. Thus, it is with trepidation on my part and a word of caution to the teacher of adolescents that I offer up this section. Emblematic of the decade in the 1960s two social studies educators, Maurice Hunt and Lawrence Metcalf, wrote about "problematic" or "closed" areas of study. A controversial topic does need to contain some element of divisiveness, elicit strong opinions, possibly make students intellectually uncomfortable, and most critical— be boundary-pushing in some manner.[38] One study indicated that approximately 90% of teachers do not relish initiating controversial subjects or engaging in a class discussion when students raise them. Topics included the Vietnam War, politics, race relations, religion, or family problems.[39] One wonders how to teach history to students in the twenty-first century absent these vital topics and themes.

Conventional topics under the rubric of controversy within history have included: Should Thomas Jefferson have purchased the Louisiana Territory from France even though he believed in a limited federal government? Did Franklin Roosevelt have prior knowledge of the attack on Pearl Harbor? Or, should Harry Truman have dropped the atomic bombs on Japan? Whether any or all of these "controversial issues" are really that controversial or even of interest to adolescents is debatable.

It has been said that sex, religion, and social class are the troika of often taboo classroom topics. The prime example is probably sex. Recently, though, a textbook placed a sidebar or "box" providing a brief sketch of the sex research pioneer Alfred Kinsey. A deeper examination by high school students of this troubled and controversial man could lead to avenues of inquiry. His work was a precursor to what became known as the "radical sixties" in the area of social mores and practices. The novel *The Inner Circle* by T. C. Boyle, a film starring Liam Neeson as Kinsey, and a PBS American Experience video titled *Kinsey* all suggest the boundaries on previously closed topics may become more open.

I would add that for all our conversation on diversity that race is another arena of controversy that has never been fully recognized in our history. An example is the ongoing debate as to whether *The Adventures of Huckleberry Finn* is appropriate for adolescents in terms of its language (its use of the "n" word) or Mark Twain's views on race in the book. It is viewed by some as unrepresentative of modern-day African Americans, especially with the results of the 2008 election. Allison Samuels in a *Newsweek* article titled "Rethinking Race in the Classroom" has argued its necessity and quotes Duke University professor Mark Anthony Neal: "These stories let kids know just how amazing it is that this man (Barack Obama) is president right now."[40]

While topics can be controversial in the teaching of history, so too can how we interpret history. The "red/blue" political divide in our nation is represented not only on the presidential election maps and right-wing/left-wing talk radio, but in our history trade and textbooks. The title of Larry Schweikart's *48 Liberal Lies About American History: (That You Probably Learned in School)* is self-evident as to its point of view. Howard Zinn has had his *People's History of the United States* adapted for middle level students by Rebecca Stefoff with the title *A Young People's History of the United States: Class Struggle to the War on Terror*. Zinn serves up a number of varying interpretations of events in American history from the opposite end of the political spectrum. These include emphases on race relations, economic disparity among classes, questionable justifications for military involvements, and the venality of many politicians often viewed with great admiration by the public as a whole.[41]

Top Ten Lists

One must be careful to not too closely follow the trends of today's youth. A used and maybe over-used practice in many facets of everyday life is the employment of the "top ten list." Now in its second decade of use by late night talk show host David Letterman, the use of top ten lists seems to appear everywhere. Having my student years at Ball State University overlap slightly with those of Mr. Letterman's, I could claim that this strategy was found in the institution's curriculum. It was not. However, when used selectively and with a purpose, it can prove effective in capturing the attention of students.

The way I have used "top ten lists" has not been for humor, but as a means to allow students to gain basic factual information about individuals in history followed by employing comparisons and contrasts. Three examples I have used with modest success are the top ten differences between Thomas Jefferson and Alexander Hamilton, between W.E.B. Du Bois and Booker T. Washington, and between Martin Luther King, Jr. and Malcolm X. Students are provided the major ideas of these leaders and thinkers and also see how they differed and, at times, were similar. I have even been able to connect the four black leaders listed above by having students conjecture if Du Bois and Malcolm X or King and Washington were similar.

Using the Du Bois/Washington contrast also demonstrates how historiography can change our perspective. Conventional historical wisdom has viewed Du Bois as an advocate for blacks entering the professions and a challenger of the status quo for his fellow blacks. In contrast, Booker T. Washington has been characterized as more conciliatory in outlook and favoring blacks who use their vocational and economic tools for advancement rather than confront whites in the social and political worlds of his time. However, in a new book, *Up from History: The Life of Booker T. Washington*, Robert Norrell posits that Washington was much more of an activist than previously portrayed in textbooks. He vigorously opposed lynching, effectively garnered financial support from northern philanthropists, and spoke openly, albeit selectively, on issues of race in both the North and the South.[42]

Professional Development

A final aspect of teaching history to adolescents is the need for teachers constantly to be professionally "sharpening their saws" in both content and methodology. Loewen has reported that one survey of Indiana history teachers revealed that only one in five stayed current with their field of American history.[43] Professional development is essential for all teachers and is now built into school calendars, re-certification and licensure on the state and national levels, and in the work of teacher organizations such as the National Education Association and the American Federation of Teachers. The form professional development takes varies from the formal to the independent habits of growth practiced by teachers.

A week of professional development that is a week well spent is the training teachers receive at Advanced Placement Institutes. I know because I am an alumnus of the training. Advanced Placement (AP) has emerged over the past decade as a comprehensive approach to teaching gifted and high ability students. The forty-hour experience is content specific with American History and World History courses available. Teachers are specially trained with intensive class work led by master teachers in the methods and content of the discipline. When taken by high school students, AP courses carry college credit at most universities if a certain test score is achieved. One study has indicated that these more challenging AP classes cause greater engagement and greater intellectual satisfaction in the student than regular classes.[44] Moreover, anecdotal evidence appears to suggest that AP-equipped teachers transfer their expertise to non-AP classes.

One of the strongest professional development opportunities can be found each weekend on cable television. C-SPAN2 provides 60 hours of book talks, interviews, and panels with nonfiction authors. A majority of the book topics are historical, biographical, or political. Bookstores often host local authors in their establishments for readings and book signings. They are frequently related to local and state history or community figures of interest both past and present.

Educators (or students) should also not forget their local library. A recent visit I made to our city library offered up for me two books. Teachers can gain much from examining unique treatments of history such as Alan Axelrod's *The Real History of World War II: A New Look at the Past*. Axelrod has his text enriched with sections titled "Reality Check," "Links," "Takeaway," "Alternative Takes," "Details, Details," and "Numbers." In addition, there are quotes and photos with expanded narratives to accompany them. This approach provides the teacher with multiple discussion starters to expand on the usual material found in textbooks. One-page vignettes in Axelrod and Charles Phillips's *What Every American Should Know About American History: 225 Events That Shaped the Nation* provide solid, yet fresh insights and background on variety of familiar historical figures and episodes drawn from the worlds of sports, media, literature, medicine, and even gangsters.[45]

Conclusion

This chapter began with the question of the importance of history. While teachers and scholars will always defend and advocate for their disciplines, the study of history is indeed important. A recent episode of this fact is most telling. When President George W. Bush refused to let national security advisor Condoleezza Rice testify before the 9/11 Commission on the grounds of executive privilege, a historian came to the rescue. Philip Zelikow, a University of Virginia historian and executive director of the 9/11 Commission, found a November 22, 1945 *New York Times* front page photograph of Admiral William D. Leahy, chief of staff to Presidents Roosevelt and Truman, testifying before a congressional panel investigating the attack on Pearl Harbor. When the photo was faxed to a weekly news magazine, the president quickly allowed Rice to testify. History had made a difference.[46]

The suggestions in this chapter are by no means a comprehensive rendering of what motivated students and teachers can accomplish through the study of history. Maybe, though, no other approach to teaching history to adolescents is as effective as enthusiasm by the teacher. James A. Percoco in his *A Passion for the Past: Creative Teaching of U.S. History* has written that it may be a good idea to tell students, "Yes, class, I love history!"[47] As John Dewey's major disciple, William Heard Kilpatrick, once asked, "If students take a course in history and make the grade of 'A,' but end up hating history, have they really learned history?" Not all students will love history as much as Mr. Percoco and I. But no adolescent should leave a history classroom hating it.

QUESTIONS TO CONSIDER

1. In your experience, which teaching strategies and classroom practices seem to have contributed to history's reputation as dull, boring, and irrelevant?

2. What should be the balance for adolescents between standard reading assignments and the use of visual and Internet-related assignments?

3. What knowledge, skills, and dispositions does history provide that contribute to the cognitive growth of adolescents?

4. What professional development activities and resources, not mentioned in this chapter, are available to history teachers?

5. Are there diversity issues, in addition to gender, race, and social justice issues that need to be included in the adolescent history classroom? List and defend your suggestions.

6. How should teachers prepare for the potential reaction by parents and administrators to controversial topics and films in history classes?

7. Should teachers attempt to make all material in a history class relevant to adolescents? Is there some material, as E.D. Hirsch argues in *Cultural Literacy,* that educated individuals just "need to know"?

8. Beyond the use of Bloom's Taxonomy, how do teachers implement higher-order thinking in their classrooms?

Notes

1. John Dewey, *Experience and Education* (New York: Collier Books, 1938), 23.
2. James W. Loewen, *Lies My Teacher Told Me: Everything Your American History Book Got Wrong,* 2nd ed. (New York: Touchstone Simon & Schuster, 2007), 1, 330, 340.
3. Burke Johnson and Christensen, Larry, *Educational Research: Quantitative, Qualitative, and Mixed Approaches,* 3rd ed. (Boston: Allyn and Bacon, 2008), 422. See also David Tyack, *The One Best System: A History of American Urban Education* 1990 (Cambridge, MA: Harvard University Press)
4. B. L. Berg, *Quantitative Research Methods for the Social Sciences* (Boston: Allyn and Bacon, 1998).
5. Bruce E. Larson and Timothy A. Keiper, *Instructional Strategies for Middle and High School* (New York: Routledge, 2007), 6–7.
6. For a strong case against both the standards movement and the attendant testing milieu, see Sam Wineburg, "What Does NCATE Have to Say to Future History Teachers? Not Much," *Phi Delta Kappan* 86, no. 9 (May 2005): 658–55. Although beginning with O. L. Davis's statement, "The ideas of 'measuring history' can only be ludicrous (p. vii). See S. G. Grant, ed., *Measuring History: Cases of State Level Testing Across the United States* (Greenwich, CT: Information Age Publishing, 2006). See also Alfie Kohn, *The Case Against Standardized Testing: Raising the Scores and Ruining the Schools* (Portsmouth, NH: Heinemann, 2000).
7. Michael M. Rutter, "School Effects on Pupil Progress: Research Findings and Policy Implications," *Child Development* 54 (1983): 1–29; R. Sirin Selcuk, and Lauren,Rogers-Sirin, "Components of School Engagement among African-American Adolescents" *Applied Developmental Science* 9 (2005): 5–13; David J. Shernoff and Mihaly Csikszentmihalyi, "Student Engagement in High School Classrooms from the Perspective of Flow Theory," *School Psychology Quarterly* 18 (2003): 158–76.
8. For good examples of this type of textbook see Robert V. Remini *A Short History of the United States* (New York: HarperCollins Publishers, 2008).

9. Gene Wintner, *Texterpts: Mastering College Textbook Reading*, 2nd ed. (New York: Pearson Education, 2007), 3. See also Loewen, chapters 1 through 9.

10. Karen D. Wood, Diane Lapp, James Flood, D. Bruce Taylor, *Guiding Readers Through Text: Strategy Guides for New Times*, 2nd ed. (Newark, N.J.: International Reading Association, 2008).

11. Johnson and Christensen, 429.

12. For the National Archives see http://nara.gov.education and for the National Council for the Social Studies (NCSS) see http://socialstudies.org/resources/twd NCSS's journal, *Social Education* published a theme issue "Teaching U.S. History with Primary Sources," 67, no. 7 (November/December 2003). The example of the Civil War photograph is taken from Daniel C. King, "Drummer Boys: Creating Historical Fiction and Studying Historical Documents," *Middle Level Learning* 35 (May/June 2009): 10–12. This journal is published by the National Council for the Social Studies.

13. Keith C. Barton, "Primary Sources in History: Breaking Through the Myths," *Phi Delta Kappan* 86, no. 10 (June 2005): 745–53.

14. Shirley Engle, "Late Night Thoughts About the New Social Studies," *Social Education* 50, no. 1 (1986): 21.

15. Donald F. Roberts, Ulla G. Foehr, and Victoria Rideout, *Generation M: Media in the Lives of 8–18 Year-Olds* (Washington D.C.: The Henry J. Kaiser Family Foundation, 2005).

16. Award winning historical research site http://www.dohistory.org is excellent. C-SPAN has multiple Web sites that profile the presidents and other historical figures at http://www.C-SPAN.org. See the Public Broadcasting System at http://www.pbs.org; for TeacherTube see www.teachertube.com; for HippoCampus see www.hippocampus.org; for MIT's OpenCourseware Consortium see http://ocw.mit.edu.

17. Dave Munger and Shireen Campbell, *What Every Student Should Know About Researching Online* (New York: Pearson Longman, 2007).

18. Alan Gevinson, Kelly Shrum, and Roy Rosenzweig, *History Matters: A Student Guide to U.S. History Online* (Boston: Bedford/St. Martin's, 2005), v, 7–10. Google search of Franklin D. Roosevelt undertaken by the author on June 2, 2009.

19. Calvin C. Miller, *No Easy Answers: Bayard Rustin and the Civil Rights Movement* (Greensboro, NC: Morgan Reynolds Publishing, 2005); John A. Beineke, *Going over All the Hurdles: A Life of Oatess Archey* (Indianapolis: Indiana Historical Society Press, 2008).

20. Hebert Block, *Herblock: A Cartoonist Life* (New York: Times Books, 1998).

21. Richard H. Minear, *Dr. Seuss Goes to War: The World War II Editorial Cartoons of Theodor Geisel* (New York: The New Press, 1999).

22. Neil Postman and Charles Weingartner, *Teaching as a Subversive Activity* (New York: Delacorte, 1969), 23.

23. John E. Henning, *The Art of Discussion-Based Teaching: Opening up Conversation in the Classroom* (New York: Routledge, 2008), 14–31, 153–57.

24. Nel Noddings, "The Gender Issue," *Educational Leadership* 49 (1991–92): 65–70.

25. Cornel West, *Race Matters* (New York: Vintage Books, 1994), xiv, 157.

26. Frances FitzGerald, *America Revised* (Boston: Little Brown, 1979); Arthur M. Schlesinger, Jr., *The Disuniting of America: Reflections on a Multicultural Society* (New York: W.W. Norton and Co., 1994).

27. James A. Banks, *Cultural Diversity and Education: Foundations, Curriculum, and Teaching*, Fifth Edition, 2006 (Boston: Allyn and Bacon), 23, 143, 209, 213–14, 332–33.

28. John Hope Franklin, *From Slavery to Freedom: A History of Negro Americans*, 3rd ed. (New York: Knopf, 1967).

29. Jonathan Kozol, *The Shame of the Nation: The Restoration of Apartheid* (New York: Three Rivers Press, 2006).

30. See the Du Bois Institute at http://dubois.fas.harvard.edu for the African American Lives, Genealogy, and Genetics Curriculum and the African American National Biography Project. Also the PBS series *African American Lives*.

31. Edward Palmer, "Schools, Advertising, and Marketing," in *Encyclopedia of Children, Adolescents, and the Media* Arnett, ed. J. Jeffery (Thousand Oaks, CA: Sage, 2006); Jane D. Brown, Jeanne R. Steele, and Kim Walsh-Childers, eds., introduction and overview to *Sexual Teens, Sexual Media: Investigating Media's Influence on Adolescent Sexuality* (Mahwah, NJ: Erlbaum, 2002).

32. Sam Wineburg, Susan Mosbog, Dan Porat, and Ariel Duncan, "Common Belief and the Cultural Curriculum: An Intergenerational Study of Historical Consciousness" *American Educational Research Journal* 44, no. 1 (March 2007): 40, 67–68.

33. See the National Park Service's Teaching with Historic Places at www.nps.gov Two somewhat dated but excellent resource books on historical movies are Wendy S. Wilson, and Gerald H. Herman, *American History on Screen: Teachers' Resource Book on Film and Video* (Portland, OR: J. Weston Walch, 1994) and Mark C. Carnes, ed., *Past Imperfect: History According to the Movies* (New York: Henry Holt, 1995).

34. "The Individual in History: National History Day 2009." For more information see www.nhd.org.

35. William Hogeland, *Inventing American History* (Cambridge, MA: MIT Press, 2009), xiii-xiv.

36. James A. Percoco, *A Passion for the Past: Creative Teaching of U.S. History* (Portsmouth, NH: Heinemann, 1998), 12–16.

37. See http://wikimarion.org/Marion_High_School.

38. Maurice P. Hunt, and Lawrence Metcalf, *Teaching High School Social Studies* (New York: Harper and Row Publishers, 1968), 292–94.

39. Allison Samuels, "Rethinking Race in the Classroom" *Newsweek* March 9, 2009, 52–53.

40. Loewen, 327.

41. Larry Schweikart, *48 Liberal Lies about American History: (That You Probably Learned in School)* (New York: Sentinel, 2008); and Howard Zinn, (adapted by Rebecca Stefoff) *A Young People's History of the United States: Class Struggle to the War on Terror* (New York: Seven Stories Press, 2007). See also Ed Welchel, *Reading, Learning, Teaching Howard Zinn* (New York: Peter Lang, 2009).

42. Robert J. Norrell, *Up from History: The Life of Booker T. Washington* (Cambridge, MA: The Belknap Press of Harvard University, 2009).

43. Loewen, 327

44. April Blescke-Rechek, David Lubinski, and Camilla P. Benbow, "Meeting the Education Needs of Special Populations: Advanced Placement's Role in Developing Exceptional Human Capital," *Psychological Science* 15 (2004): 217–24.

45. Alan Axelrod, *The Real History of World War II: A New Look at the Past* (New York: Sterling Publishing, 2008); Alan Axelrod, and Charles Phillips, *What Every American Should Know about American History: 225 Events That Shaped the Nation*, 3rd ed. (Avon, MA: Adams Media, 2008).

46. James A. Bryant, "The Fax About History," *Phi Delta Kappan* 86, no. 10 (June 2005): 754–56.

47. Percoco, 5.

CHAPTER TWENTY-FOUR

Critical Civic Literacy in Schools

Adolescents Seeking to Understand and Improve The(ir) World

KENNETH TEITELBAUM

I still have materials I used when I taught high school United States history classes many years ago, including a supplemental "textbook" I developed that included brief historical narratives that I wrote, copied portions of publications, and class activities and exams. Although the use of this more progressive textbook was compromised by the state Regents exam that was required in New York State at the time (that counted for 20% of the total grade for each student), which meant considerable pressure to "cover" material that would be on the exam, I did feel that I managed to present students with materials that were more engaging than the assigned textbook, as well as more honest and socially critical (Apple & Teitelbaum, 1986). What I notice as well when I go back and review these materials are my attempts to bring the study of the past into the present. To be sure, my teaching included the dusty (and numerous) facts of history that I felt needed to be presented and discussed, which I must admit I had a passion for (having at one time planned to go on for a doctoral degree in the field). However, it was often linked to my efforts to convince the many recalcitrant students in this largely working-class community that the policies, practices, events, and people that existed before they were born have relevance to their understanding of the current issues about which they were (or should be) concerned. Years later I read a passage that resonated with my thinking at this earlier time: "I would wonder what kind of present you could possibly have without knowing the stories of your past" (Mendelsohn, 2006, p. 162)—which I interpreted broadly in terms of a shared sense of humanity, or at least national identity.

During my master's degree program, I had a well-known historian as an instructor who paraphrased the famous quote by George Santayana thusly: "Those who cannot remember the past are condemned to repeat it; and those who do remember the past are condemned to repeat it." I understood and to some extent shared his cynicism, this during the time when our country was extricating itself from the War in Vietnam. However, I generally remained hopeful that I could play a role in enhancing the civic literacy of my students by providing them with opportunities not just to learn about our nation's history and its relevance to current affairs but also to critically reflect on that past and the present. (I adopted a similar approach in the sociology elective classes I taught, in which we addressed issues of race prejudice, economic inequality, women's rights, and the like.) I realized that, while we must not "suppress the nature of the danger" (Williams 1989, p. 322), hope is crucial if we are to make any progress in righting wrongs and in imagining and building alternatives worth pursuing (Apple, 2006).

I loved high school teaching. I left it because I became too interested in it—and wanted to learn more about what was taking place in schools, especially what was being taught and why, and the consequences of the choices that were made. Since then I've traveled a circuitous route in a way, but my work in teacher education and curriculum studies has always been in large part about the same thing, related to the extension and enhancement of critical civic literacy among the students with whom I am in contact, as well as among my professional colleagues, broadly speaking. It seems more important than ever to keep this goal in the forefront of public schooling.

Critical Civic Literacy

If literacy generally connotes having the ability to read, write, speak and listen in meaningful ways, then civic literacy means being well-versed in social and political knowledge, understandings, dispositions, and skills. It means not only being able to essentially de-code and make meaning of the world around us but also to employ information and abilities for active engagement with and within civic relationships and institutions. In other words, if literacy education seeks to have people not just master but also use their skills—that is, to be literate is to read, not just know how to read—then likewise, civic literacy in our country is not just focused on learning about political structures and associations but becoming/being active democratic citizens.

Adopting a critical stance means not taking for granted what is known and in place, instead rigorously and wholeheartedly questioning the assumptions that undergird current ideas, practices, policies, and structures. It suggests a level of reflective inquiry that goes beyond techniques and strategies, beyond a consideration of doing of X better, to the ethics and goals that drive one's practices, in essence to the choice of doing X (rather than Y or Z) in the first place. As Michael Apple, Wayne Au, and Luis Armando Gandin (2009) suggest, it involves "fundamental transformations of the underlying epistemological and ideological assumptions that are made about what counts as 'official' or legitimate knowledge and who holds it" (p. 3). In addition, although not all observers might agree, I share their view that "being critical" in a democratic society includes social commitments as well, specifically "toward social transformation and a break with the comforting illusions that the ways in which our societies and their educational apparatuses are organized currently can lead to social justice" (p. 3). Critical civic literacy, then, entails more than becoming knowledgeable, skilled, and engaged in citizenship issues in the usual ways, e.g., knowing how a bill becomes a law and participating in local volunteer activities, and oftentimes including mindless rule-following (Westheimer, 2009), a kind of blind patriotism (Hamot, 2008; Kahne & Middaugh, 2006), and becoming "unquestioning followers of the capitalist system" (Lefrançois, Éthier, & Demers, 2008, p. 72). It involves interrogating the basic assumptions we have about social science knowledge and democratic citizenship, including critical inquiry of differing accounts of historical events and current affairs and the extent to which democratic participation actually exists; focusing in active ways on concerns and problems that are meaningful to students; and linking ideas, policies, and practices to larger issues of social justice.

Every period of one's life can be viewed as in some way involved with issues of civic literacy and critical reflection, from the early experiences of the pre-school age to the later senior citizen years. Indeed, a good argument can be made that unless critical literacy starts in the earliest grades (e.g., James & McVay, 2009; O'Mahony, 2009) and is consistently addressed throughout schooling, it will continue to be viewed as an afterthought or add-on to what is "really" important in the curriculum and thus what is really valued in life. Still, drawing on the work of Erik Erikson and others, many educators consider adolescence to be a prime period of life in which we are exposed to and are able to formulate conceptions of what we believe and what we can and should do with regard to social and political commitments and engagements, and it thus deserves a special place in the fostering of civic literacy (Jones, 2009). It is a crucial time in our development, or maturation, when we are better able to take account of the world beyond our immediate self and family. For many, it sets us on our path to seeking to better understand and improve our/the larger world, or, alternately, to feeling disinterested and disempowered to play any role at all in social and political change. Surely, we all agree about the crucial responsibility that schools have in promoting the former of these results. Or do we?

The Need for Civic Literacy in Our Schools

The United States was founded on the democratic ideal, what Abraham Lincoln famously described in his Gettysburg Address as a "government of the people, by the people, for the people." While since its inception this ideal has meant multiple things to different people, and while there have been notable accomplishments and notorious failures in our country's 200+ year history to live up to this ideal, one thing has been certain since the time of Thomas Jefferson, which is that education is assumed to play a crucial role in the definition, re-definition, and revitalization of democratic life. As Jefferson put it in his letters, "If a nation expects to be ignorant and free, in a state of civilization, it expects what never was and never will be. . . . Whenever the people are well-informed, they can be trusted with their own government." He considered the future of republican government in part to be "absolutely hanging on the hook [of] public education" (Coates, 1995). It is clear that for a very long time our schools have been entrusted with much of the education for democratic citizenship that is expected and considered essential for the young. As Benjamin Barber (1997) puts it, "public education . . . [is] the very foundation of our democratic civic culture. Public schools are not merely schools for the public, but schools of publicness: institutions where we learn what it means to be a public and start down the road toward common national and civic identity. They are the forges of our citizenship and the bedrock of our democracy" (p. 22). Simply put, one of the primary aims of education in the United States, seemingly as much agreed upon as any social goal, is "to prepare youth to contribute to civic life in a democracy" (Rubin, Hayes, & Benson, 2009, p. 3). Conceptualized broadly, such civic education would incorporate knowledge of politics, history, government, and current events; skills that enable communication, analysis, deliberation and action; dispositions that lead to a concern with and belief in the need for social and political change; and behaviors that involve being actively engaged in civic affairs (Levinson, 2010). It would include but go beyond a focus on how the government works, voting for political candidates to represent our individual interests, and engaging in charitable or public service projects.

How best to educate for democratic citizenship, as well as what democratic citizenship specifically means, has been a matter of debate for a long time among educators, government and business leaders, media pundits, and others. This is not the place to delve into the varied definitions, goals, and approaches, which need to be contextualized temporally as well as in terms of the varied experiences of different racial, ethnic and other groups, except to suggest that as we move into the second decade of the twenty-first century, it is clear that we need to take a closer look at current efforts to provide a meaningful and effective education for (not just about) democracy. At least three related factors can be identified that bear on this need.

First, it is important to consider where we find ourselves today with regard to civic engagement, particularly among the young. The following exchange is simply all too common:

Interviewer:	What are your feelings about government and politics?
Boy's voice:	It's boring.
Interviewer:	When you say it's boring, what's boring about it?
Boy's Voice:	The subject matter.
Girl's Voice:	Yes, very true.
Boy's Voice:	It's not just the work. It's what the work is about. We don't care about it.

(Kahne, Chi, & Middaugh, 2006, p. 388)

While certainly not all indices of civic competency and activism can or should be viewed as the result of the role of schools—that is, any suggested failure is one that many aspects of our culture can share—they do indicate a need for schools to re-think whether or not they are doing all they can to promote civic understandings and participation, especially given the historic role schools have been assumed to play in this area and particularly following the September 11, 2001, terrorist attacks (Shreiner, 2009). What we find today is that a large majority of young people are unlikely to vote, believe government can affect their lives, or even pay attention to politics at all; indeed, it appears that "American youth civic and political participation are at historic lows" (Kahne & Westheimer, 2006; Jacobsen, Frankenberg, & Winchell, 2009, p. 1). While some researchers point to an increase in voting for the 2008 presidential election and a possible increase in interest in volunteerism and service learning experiences, they still conclude that "political engagement is at an all-time low" (Jones, 2009; James & Iverson, 2009, p. 3). Former Supreme Court Justice Sandra Day O'Connor, for one, is quoted as saying that "[m]ost young people today simply do not have an adequate understanding of how our government and political system work, and they are thus not well prepared to participate as citizens" (Shreiner, 2009, p. 9). One study by the National Constitution Center found that only 38% of respondents could name the three branches of government, and yet another poll conducted two years earlier found that 59% of all Americans could name the Three Stooges (Kahne & Westheimer, 2003, p. 35). Particularly disconcerting is the seeming lack of interest among those pursuing education as a career; in one survey, 11.9% of them reported discussing politics on a regular basis, well below the already low national average of 20% (James & Iverson, 2009).

This lack of involvement is especially the case for graduates from urban schools. No doubt this gap is at least in part the result of a "civic opportunity gap," in which those who are more academically successful, White, or have parents of higher socioeconomic status receive more classroom-based civic learning opportunities and the actual knowledge, skills, and participatory experiences to become civically literate (Marri, 2009). Similarly, another researcher refers to "a profound *civic empowerment gap* between poor, some minority, and immigrant youth and adults, on the one hand, and middle-class or wealthy, white, and native-born youth and adults, on the other" (Levinson, 2010). As she notes, such a gap serves to "diminish the democratic character and quality of the United States" (p. 26). It also prevents urban students from gaining the kinds of social capital that would enhance their chances for academic success and future social mobility (Taines 2009; Jones, 2009; Jacobsen, Frankenberg, & Winchell, 2009). Just as importantly, it can lead to political identities that are based on a mistrust of "the government," which in turn reinforces a sense of powerlessness that leads to a lack of hope for a better future (Nygreen, 2008).

Clearly, there is increasing concern expressed about the level of civic knowledge and participation in our country. A good deal of this concern, however, especially from conservative groups, primarily laments "our fading heritage" and links it strictly to the inability of students to identify the three branches of the federal government, the nature of the Bill of Rights, the language of the Gettysburg Address, and so forth (Intercollegiate Studies Institute, 2008). While certainly knowledge of history and politics is crucial for young people to attain, simply adding more courses and multiple-choice assessments will do little to address the larger and more significant issue of not just the prevalent disinterest in significant historical events and important aspects of government but also the current apathy toward engaging in substantive civic activities. It is in this realm in particular that one can ask whether or not schools are doing all that they can and should. It is a vital question because meaningful participation in democratic life, not just in government per se but in what John Dewey (1916/1944) referred to as an inclusive "mode of associated living, of conjoint communicative experience" (p. 87) requires understandings, skills, and dispositions that can perhaps only be systematically developed in formal educational settings.

This general situation has not been helped any during the last decade by the second factor, which involves recent educational developments like the No Child Left Behind (NCLB) Act of 2001. I refer in particular to the legislation's strong (some might say heavy-handed) focus on reading, language arts, and mathematics, including frequent high-stakes standardized assessments of learning in those subject areas that hold directly accountable the teachers and schools involved. A related trend is the continuing overemphasis in American secondary schools on preparation for the workplace (Kliebard, 1999). Current Secretary of Education Arne Duncan is clearly not alone in suggesting that schools need to help in the effort "to educate our way [to] a better economy" (National Public Radio, 2009). Such educational policies and pronouncements serve to draw considerable attention and time (and other resources) away from social studies education in general (Au, 2009), despite the occasionally overheated rhetoric of various political and business leaders and media pundits about the need to "protect" our country's democratic heritage.

As I write this chapter, it is uncertain whether or not NCLB will be reauthorized, and if so in what form. However, it clearly has already had a substantial effect on what is taught in schools and how this teaching takes place. For many in the classroom it is the case that "real world experiences and meaningful curriculum projects are obsolete because their format does not support the test preparation regimen mandated by their school districts" (Ponder & Veldt, 2009, p.

4). Social studies education in general has become "the disappearing subject"; in a study done by the Center for Education Policy, one teacher no doubt speaks for many by stating that "[NCLB] has torn apart our social studies curriculum" (Au, 2009, p. 47). Civic education in particular gets less than half of one percent of the overall budget of the Department of Education and is increasingly "pushed to the margins of education efforts that challenge students to grapple with tough questions about society and the world" (Kahne & Westheimer, 2003, p. 35; Westheimer, 2009, p. 261). An account of one teacher educator working to address the situation in Florida notes that "civics education is being crowded out of the curriculum in many schools" (University of Florida College of Education, 2008). There is evidence as well that supplementary projects involving middle school students in activities focused on global issues have been curtailed (Teitelbaum & Brodsky, 2008). Indeed, due to NCLB and policies and legislation like it, "While we say we value a democratic society, the very institutions expected to prepare democratic citizens—our schools—have moved far from this central mission" (Kahne & Westheimer, 2003, p. 34).

The notion that schools are helping to "create a public" with a strong foundation of civic knowledge, skills and dispositions has withered in the midst of the panic for increasing reading and mathematics test scores and preparation for the workplace. Reports on education with titles that suggest a general focus on educational issues, such as recent ones from Advance Illinois (2009), The Brookings Institution (2006), and the Center on Education Policy (2009), often focus almost entirely on the teaching and learning of reading and mathematics. The increasing emphasis on high-stakes standardized tests with their expectation of "right answers," has eroded appreciation for the kinds of unsettling questions that drive critical civic literacy and the more difficult to measure results of activities to encourage civic participation.

Nevertheless, we know that our democratic way of life cannot be taken for granted or assumed to perpetuate itself without any effort on our part. Indeed, this is where the public school can play a crucial role, if it is defined as such. Perhaps it would be helpful to learn from the strategies of the proponents of the managerial new middle class (Apple, 2006) and advocate for standardized testing of youth's civic development. Indeed, several researchers have noted attempts to do so in a way that would take into account the actual participatory outcomes associated with civic education, although participation is often narrowly defined (Rubin, 2007; Jones, 2009).

Finally, the need for greater attention to civic literacy in schools comes from a consideration of the world that our young people are facing in the twenty-first century. The intensification of globalization in its many forms is transforming nation-states and local communities in significant and complicated ways (Singh, Kenway, & Apple, 2005). The most recent financial crisis has made clear what many already knew that economies are at the same time increasingly interlocked and competitive and jobs that seem to be taking place in one country can actually exist, rather easily and more cheaply, elsewhere. Climates are so intertwined that the effects of environmental despoliation in one area can have literally rippling effects across the planet. Infectious diseases and other health concerns start one place in the world and travel rapidly to continents far away. Technologies and media are ubiquitous, having the effect of bringing peoples of the world closer together on a daily basis and at the same time providing increased opportunities for privatized (and corporate) ventures. We are witnessing an unprecedented worldwide flow of immigration, in essence moving in all directions at once, which has the effect of providing greater opportunities for cross-cultural learning at the same time as exacerbating ethnic and religious conflicts. These and other complications of globalization will more than ever require an educated citizenry that can critically evaluate the complexities and defend the common good against the rapacious interests of wealthy and powerful individuals and transnational corporations. More than ever adolescent students, about to enter not just the workplace but also adult citizenship, will need to learn and embrace the kinds of critical civic understandings and skills that can help to protect and enhance the democratic ideal and cultivate the kind of caring inclusive community that supports it. Strengthening democracy takes on added urgency during such unsettling and even volatile times when problem solvers, critical thinkers, and imaginative and innovative citizens will be needed more than ever.

In sum, we need to reverse the general erosion of civic engagement in our society and seek to encourage more direct and substantive participation in social institutions like schools. We need to contest aspects of NCLB and similar policies when they serve to seriously weaken possibilities for enhanced civic knowledge, skills, and commitments among our young people. We need to become more aware of the nature of the increasingly globalized world and how more sophisticated understandings and activism will be needed to extend democratic citizenship and social justice. Moreover, we need to develop viable curricula and instructional strategies that can be used in the classroom, to give adolescent students meaningful opportunities not just to learn about democracy but to experience for themselves the value of civic literacy and participation.

Kinds of Citizenship

The processes by which individuals come to see themselves as democratic citizens are varied, and the conceptions of democratic citizenship that guide them are different as well. This is not necessarily a bad thing; indeed, "multiple perspectives are an asset—not a hindrance— to democratic thinking, participation, and governance" (Hess, 2009, p. 77). Discussed openly and honestly, they can serve to enhance rather than weaken democratic life. What is particularly important here is a recognition that young people come to identify themselves as political subjects in wideranging (and rather messy) ways. In other words, a "one size fits all" approach will not adequately address the needs and interests of the diversity of students in our schools primarily because of the civic opportunity and civic empowerment gaps mentioned earlier. Given the different experiences, interests, cultural backgrounds, senses of efficacy, and other factors that exist among adolescents in our country, pedagogical strategies that "work" for one group of students will not necessarily be the case for another. As in all matters educational, there are complications and contradictions to consider. The worst approach would be to pretend that such complexity does not exist. Better to take account of this complexity to the extent possible as we seek to provide opportunities for young people to become more knowledgeable, skilled, engaged, and hopeful about the nature of our democracy, rather than feeling limited and relatively powerless to participate in political relationships and institutions.

The actual processes of determining one's political identity involve many different aspects of society; here we are concerned in particular with what happens in schools, which one could argue are "uniquely positioned to help cultivate the cognitive components that will help people solve the problems and make the decisions necessary for such democratic citizenship" (Shreiner,

2009, p. 333). What is needed first, perhaps, is to identify the conceptions of citizenship that can guide this work. Realizing that any such categorization can conceal significant differences as much as clarify similarities, the work of Joel Westheimer and Joseph Kahne (2004) is helpful in distinguishing three types of citizenship to promote critical civic literacy.

The first ideal type is the *Personally Responsible Citizen*. These are individuals who regularly vote, pay taxes on time, obey laws, give to charities, and follow current events. They may also help during times of serious need (storms and floods), contribute to clothing and food drives, give blood, and pick up litter and recycle. This kind of citizenship has a lot to do with actions at the individual level and includes primarily limited involvement in the needs of the local community, with little focus on the larger social structures and institutions of which the local is ostensibly a part. Such a conception can function comfortably within pervasive neoliberal ideology, which "prizes individual accomplishment, distrusts government, and disparages the need to work across political, ethnic, and religious differences" (Eisenhart, 2009, pp. 1–2).

The second kind of political identity is the *Participatory Citizen*. In this case, individuals are more actively involved in civic affairs, which could take place at the local, state and/or national levels. They do not just vote but they also campaign for chosen political candidates; do not just contribute to clothing and food drives but help to organize them; do not just give to charitable agencies but become actively involved on advisory boards; and do not just recycle at home but participate in neighborhood clean-up campaigns. This kind of citizenship includes greater engagement with collective efforts, joining with others in political and related activities to help shape the world in which we live.

The third category of citizenship referred to by Westheimer and Kahne is the *Justice Oriented Citizen*. These individuals are particularly concerned with addressing systems of privilege and oppression and the root causes of social problems. They actively participate in collective strategies for change that challenge inequities related to issues of race, class, gender, and the like. While such individuals may be engaged in charity work and may volunteer for community-based organizations, they also identify with and advocate for larger social movements that seek to effect systemic change in support of the democratic ideal. They do not just help to organize clothing and food drives but also seek to address issues of hunger and homelessness in society; do not just engage in recycling but also organize with others to address the causes of environmental despoliation and climate change; and do not just vote or campaign for political candidates but actively work (and demonstrate) on behalf of policy and legislative changes that will insure the enhancement of democratic values and more equitable social conditions.

No doubt one must consider the local context when deciding what conception of citizenship is realistic to adopt in the classroom. This context will be influenced by, for example, school administrators, parents, students, and community members; local elected officials and state policies and mandates; resources available for certain educational materials and activities; and so forth. Nevertheless, an argument can be made that the first kind of citizenship, which no doubt is most prevalent, represents a welcomed but quite limited form of civic participation. Given the factors discussed earlier, as well as the disparities and divisions of our country, a more ambitious goal would seem worthwhile, one that promotes more critical civic understandings and more active support of and participation in democratic life. As such, it is the second and third categories described above that seem especially important to guide the work of schools today.

How can our schools help adolescent students, especially those from low-income and immigrant backgrounds, to feel included and empowered in areas of citizenship, rather than disengaged and passive, as seems so common today? How can we best prepare them to be participatory and justice-oriented in their role as active global citizens in the twenty-first century? It is to these questions that we now turn.

Teaching for Critical Civic Literacy

As Deborah Meier (2008) suggests, parents seem to be particularly concerned with their children being well behaved in school, learning to read, and getting high test scores. Of course, these are all important ingredients of and for academic success. However, what seems to be increasingly ignored is the school's role in sustaining our democratic way of life, an effort that needs to be re-born and re-vitalized with each new generation in relation to broad social changes that occur. Indeed, as Meier states, "It is in schools that we learn the art of living together and where we are compelled to defend the idea of a public, not private, interest for the common good of our children." Nevertheless, "oddly enough, we have created a system for growing up in which no one takes responsibility for democracy." The result is that local citizens hardly get involved in decision making, and it is considered a significant achievement when a majority of those eligible to vote do so. Meier asks, "Can we educate children and adults for democracy if they have never experienced it? . . . Where is the time and space to make room for democracy?" (p. 23).

The most thorough approach would be for schools to become communities of learning in which the value of civic participation is made public and accessible and is realized as an integral and regular part of daily school life. In such educational settings, civic education would not be a topic but part of the very definition of the school experience; not a subject to be covered but one of the primary aims of educational practice; not a project but a curriculum theme that helps to guide teaching and learning in all grades. Schools would be less about educating "for" democracy and more about educating "through" democracy, with attention given to both the creation of "structures and processes by which life in the school is carried out" and the "curriculum that will give young people democratic experiences" (Apple & Beane, 2007, pp. 9–10). Rather than essentially ghettoizing the preparation of democratic citizens into, at best, one-hour time blocks during the afternoons in senior year Government classes, it would be viewed as an essential and fundamental part of the mission-in-use of the school. Rather than an emphasis on the accumulation of factual knowledge and some future participation in civic affairs, the educational environment would be geared to engendering democratic subjectivity, with students being provided with authentic opportunities to take initiative and to be engaged (Biesta, 2007).

I am suggesting that such a holistic, integrated, and wholehearted approach to critical civic literacy is the ideal to undertake. However, of course it will not be adopted any time soon in most public schools. What are needed, then, are projects and other activities that in more limited but still significant ways can help schools to encourage adolescents to work together and to become more critically reflective and knowledgeable about and participatory in civic affairs. We need concrete curriculum materials and instructional strategies that will help to move civic education beyond a narrow focus on the different branches of government and the act of voting—and a reliance on lectures, textbook readings, and worksheets—to give students real opportunities to address social issues and problems that are consequential to them, whether in the school, local community, or at the state or national level. In essence, they need experiences in learning more about and improving the(ir) world, typically in social studies courses but quite possibly in other subject areas as well, usually in the classroom but perhaps also in after-school activities.

There are many related challenges to such a re-direction, besides those that pertain to the particularities of the local context. One challenge concerns being able to offset the initial feeling of discouragement and apathy among young people toward history, politics, government, and public service; many are consumed instead with "managing daily life, finishing school, earning money, having fun, etc." and, if involved in community service at all, do so primarily to pad their college resumes (Eisenhart, 2009, p. 1). This phenomenon is completely understandable, of course, given current economic pressures, media, and commercial constructions of youth culture, and the mistrust of our political institutions especially among traditionally marginalized groups. Indeed, this is the problem in a nutshell. Another challenge involves the development of meaningful activities that take seriously adolescents' own lived experiences, skills, and interests and that do not simply privilege "the teacher's agenda" (Gustavson & Applebaum, 2005). There are many intellectual, cultural, and other differences within any class of students, as well as between schools, which include different experiences with, for example, political leaders and the police. Being aware of and sensitive to these differences when planning curricula can be a daunting task. It also means teachers willing to give over some "control" of the curriculum to students; and at the same time students departing from their typical "teacher as expert" assumptions and being willing and able (prepared) to take on more of such responsibilities. In addition, assuring the physical and emotional safety of students, that is, being sure that projects and activities engaged in are "safe" for students to pursue, must be of paramount concern. If, for example, gang-related drug use is a serious community issue (Rubin & Hayes, 2009), to what extent should students be encouraged to study and attempt to resolve the problem as part of a school-based civic learning experience? Another concern relates to the importance of political efficacy among young people and specifically the sense of hopelessness that can occur if students' efforts at civic activism are not deemed "successful." An argument can be made that feelings of efficacy are in fact crucial for later civic participation. However, at the same time, should one avoid potentially controversial issues in fear of instilling feelings of despair (Levinson, 2009; Kahne & Westheimer, 2006)? Finally, where in the curriculum is there space to pursue critical civic literacy, given the increased emphasis on reading and mathematics? This issue goes beyond standardized testing to the very courses required for graduation. For example, during the last five years in Illinois, high school graduation requirements have gone from including three years of language arts, two years of mathematics, one year of science, and two years of social studies, to four years of language arts, three years of mathematics, two years of science, and two years of social studies (Illinois General Assembly, 2009). The result is less opportunity for students to enroll in social studies and related elective courses.

Such difficulties are very real and need to be considered when seeking to introduce critical civic literacy efforts in the classroom. Depending on the context, and the extent of each of these challenges, efforts may need to be more or less limited in terms of "encouraging students to move toward human agency . . . by exercising agency through critical thinking, individual social action, and group social action" (Marri, 2009, p. 31). Still, there are many good stories to share of projects taking place in (and out of) the classroom that include rigorous study and purposeful action. Here, briefly, are a dozen of them:

- Fifth-graders who live in or near a Chicago housing project conduct research on improving conditions in their own neighborhood, specifically with regard to replacing their dilapidated and dangerous school building (Schultz, 2007).
- Students in a high school in southeastern Ohio participate as a team to interview and deliberate with teachers and others to help determine the hiring of new teachers for the school (Wood, 1998).
- High school students in a Northeastern community, in which 50% of the youths live below the poverty line, compile a scrapbook to document the ways in which their lives have been impacted by murder and drugs, to share with school, community, and state officials (Rubin, Hayes, & Benson, 2009).
- Students in a "last chance" public high school in New York City engage in an examination of Supreme Court cases dealing with issues of injustice and participate in mock re-trials of these cases (Marri, 2009).
- Students in a high-poverty, urban, continuation high school in California organize a Participatory Action Research Team for Youth that establishes a vigorous political discourse among them and eventually leads them to teach a social justice class at their own school (Nygreen, 2008).
- An after-school club of 11 to 17-year-olds in a low-income Midwestern city conducts an oral history project with community elders to critically examine the recent history of their own community (Jones, 2009).
- An environmental justice class is developed by a science teacher at a high school in Boston, with students researching the problem of air quality and rising asthma rates in the surrounding neighborhood, and then organizing rallies, writing press releases, and testifying before the city council (Smith, 2008).
- A community-based youth organization in a Midwestern state provides opportunities for urban high school students to plan a Youth Summit to lobby for school funding reform, which includes having to secure school backing for the event (Taines, 2009).
- Tenth graders in an after-school engineering program for girls with strong academic records at three urban high schools in Colorado help in the construction of a playground for disabled children (Eisenhart, 2009).
- High school government students in a suburban, white, East Coast community investigate the feasibility of curbside recycling by conducting phone interviews, examining maps of population density, and analyzing projected housing growth and environmental impacts, eventually writing editorials and making public presentations on the issue (Kahne & Westheimer, 2003; Kahne & Westheimer, 2006).
- As part of a "Taking Action" curriculum design in mathematics classes, 7th graders share their analysis of data on the local costs of the U.S. war in Iraq and demonstrate to city council members that the city could channel money away from war-based efforts toward programs for the homeless and for improved park services (Applebaum, 2009).
- In an action project focusing on waste management, 7th grade students in Ontario

examine hazardous wastes and their labels and then seek to change where their personal and home waste is being directed, encourage their neighbors to be mindful of littering, and reduce their own water usage (Sperling & Bencze, 2009).

These 12 examples can perhaps help us to envision what critical civic literacy projects can look like in our schools. (The publication *Rethinking Schools* is an excellent resource for other examples.) They might initially be more modest than one would like; they might not be easy to sustain; and they might not always be successful. However, without such opportunities to experience (practice) substantive research and authentic civic participation, students will know very little about what it means to be democratic in a robust way. Whether focused on school or community concerns, such projects can help students to see a purpose in what they are being taught and to experience the active role in civic affairs they can pursue after they graduate. Such curricula can include not just acquiring pertinent knowledge and participating in relevant activities but also asking basic, crucial questions concerning "what is [and is not] democratic about our . . . current state of 'democracy'?" (Tupper, 2009, p. 77). Such learning opportunities, as George Wood (1992) puts it, are guided by a vision that "is not limited to what kids learn about academics *in* school, but designed to encompass what sort of people they will be when they *leave* school" (p. 234).

Conclusion

"Democracy is not a spectator sport." Try Googling that sentence and, at least on the day that I did so, within a second you will get more than 900,000 hits. However, one should not let the overuse of this sentence obscure its central insight. Democracy requires not just a well-informed citizenry but an actively involved one as well.

I have argued in this chapter that, first, renewed efforts to promote civic literacy in schools are very much needed, given circumstances related to current levels of civic understanding and participation, educational policies that have narrowly focused attention elsewhere, and the changing, globalizing nature of the world; second, attempts to promote civic literacy should incorporate substantial components of knowledge, skills, dispositions, and experiences, as well as a sense of criticality, both in the reflective/analytical sense and the profound commitment to social justice; third, civic literacy projects should be guided by a conception of citizenship that is participatory and justice-oriented, and encourage a more collective and comprehensive approach to civic activism than the typical personally responsible forms; fourth, schools should be re-cultured to deal with issues of democratic citizenship as an integral part of school life; until that occurs, substantive and consequential critical civic literacy projects and activities of different kinds should be developed for and with students; fifth, these curricula should take as their starting (though not necessarily ending) point the varied experiences, skills, and interests of students, to engage adolescents in concerns and problems that are personally meaningful to them, so they can develop their own sense of civic identity. We need to inspire adolescents to become fully realized democratic citizens; we need to give them hope that their engagement in critical analysis and civic participation can lead to an improvement of the(ir) world, even if in small ways; and we need to provide them with opportunities to experience for themselves the significant personal and social advantages to becoming more involved in the public (political) sphere. Students need practice in becoming the kind of citizens who are not content simply to vote, or to give to charity, or to know how a bill becomes a law, but who seek the skills and understandings, and the courage, to actively engage in the continuous re-construction of democratic life. We cannot maintain a functioning democracy without such citizens, and schools can and should play a significant role in fostering them.

At the same time, although there are good examples of educational practice to share, schools alone cannot take on the responsibility for civic literacy and for building a more just and humane world. As Gert Biesta (2007) points out, "schools can neither create nor save democracy—they can only support societies in which action and subjectivity are real possibilities" (p. 470). The larger society needs to become more committed to, and one might even say obsessed with, an enhanced, thick version of democracy whereby people go beyond a mild interest in electing politicians to represent and secure their rights and instead are passionate and active in support of the dignity and rights of all individuals. Without advocacy and energy from the larger society, in multiple forms and with sufficient resources dedicated to these efforts, schools will continue to find it difficult to sustain civic education programs that substantially depart from repetition of "the dusty (and numerous) facts" of social science, the approach that leads students to announce, with a sense of resignation in their voices, that it is simply "boring" and they just "don't care about it." As such, schools will remain an untapped resource to help cultivate the informed and active citizenry that every democracy needs to survive.

QUESTIONS TO CONSIDER

1. What does the author mean by a "critical" approach to civic literacy? How might it differ from an approach that does not place an emphasis on "being critical"?

2. Why does Teitelbaum call for renewed efforts to promote civic literacy in schools? Do you agree that such efforts are needed? Why?

3. Teitelbaum describes three conceptions of citizenship that can guide work in civic literacy. Explain each of them. Which of the three (or some other one) would you most favor, and why?

4. What are the possibilities for critical civic literacy in schools today? Are there examples included in this chapter that you particularly appreciate? Why? Describe any other projects or activities that you have observed or experienced that could be included.

5. Teitelbaum concludes by emphasizing that "schools alone cannot take on the responsibility for civic literacy and for building a more just and humane world." Share your reactions to his concluding paragraph.

References

Advance Illinois. (2009). *We can do better: Advancing public education in Illinois*. Chicago: Advance Illinois.

Apple, M. W. (2006). *Educating the "right" way: Markets, standards, God and inequality*. New York: Routledge.

Apple, M. W., Au, W., & Gandin, L. A. (2009). Mapping critical education. In M. Apple, W. Au, & L. A. Gandin (Eds.), *The Routledge international handbook of critical education* (pp. 3–19). New York: Routledge.

Apple, M. W., & Beane, J. A. (2007). The case for democratic schools. In M. W. Apple & J. A. Beane (Eds.), *Democratic schools: Lessons in powerful education* (pp. 1–29). Portsmouth, NH: Heinemann.

Apple, M. W., & Teitelbaum, K. (1986). Are teachers losing control of their skills and curriculum? *Journal of Curriculum Studies, 18*(2), 177–184.

Applebaum, P. (2009). "Taking action"–mathematics curricular organization for effective teaching and learning. *For the Learning of Mathematics, 29*(2), 39–44.

Au, W. (2009). Social studies, social justice: W(h)ither the social studies in high-stakes testing? *Teacher Education Quarterly, 36*(1), 43–58.

Barber, B. (1997). Public schooling: Education for democracy. In J. I. Goodlad & T. J. McMannon (Eds.), *The public purpose of education and schooling* (pp. 21–32). San Francisco: Jossey-Bass.

Biesta, G. (2007). Education and the democratic person: Towards a political conception of democratic education. *Teachers College Record, 109*(3), 740–769. Retrieved August 15, 2009 from http://www.tcrecord.org/PrintContent. asp?ContentID=12830

Brookings Institution, The. (2006). *How well are American students learning?* Washington, DC: The Brookings Institution.

Center on Education Policy. (2009). *Is the emphasis on "proficiency" shortchanging higher- and lower-achieving students?* Washington, DC: Center on Education Policy.

Coates, E. R. (1995). Thomas Jefferson on politics and government. In *University of Virginia Library Thomas Jefferson digital archive*. Retrieved September 19, 2009, from http://etext.virginia.edu/jefferson

Dewey, J. (1944). *Democracy and education. An introduction to the philosophy of education*. New York: Free Press. (Original work published 1916)

Eisenhart, M. (2009). Civic engagement as history in person in the lives of high school girls. Paper presented at the annual meeting of the American Educational Research Association, San Diego, CA.

Gustavson, L., & Applebaum, P. (2005). Youth cultural practices, popular culture, and classroom teaching. In J. L. Kincheloe (Ed.), *Classroom teaching: An introduction* (pp. 281–298). New York: Peter Lang.

Hamot, G. (2008). Citizenship education. In S. Mathison and E. W. Ross (Eds.), *Battleground schools* (101–110). Westport, CT: Greenwood.

Hess, D. (2009). *Controversy in the classroom: The democratic power of discussion*. New York: Routledge.

Illinois General Assembly (2009). Illinois Compiled Statutes. Retrieved April 10, 2009, from http://www.ilga.gov/legislation/ilcs/fulltext.asp?DocName=010500050K27–22

Intercollegiate Studies Institute (2008). *Our fading heritage: Americans fail a basic test on their history and institutions*. Retrieved September 13, 2009, from http://www.americancivicliteracy.org

Jacobsen, R., Frankenberg, E., & Winchell, S. (2009). Civic engagement and school racial context: How changing student demographics affect civic engagement outcomes. Paper presented at the annual meeting of the American Educational Research Association, San Diego, CA.

James J. H., & Iverson S. V. (2009). Civic actors, civic educators: Justice-oriented service in a pre-service teacher education program. Paper presented at the annual meeting of the American Educational Research Association, San Diego, CA.

James, J. H., & McVay, M. (2009). Critical literacy for young citizens: First graders investigate the First Thanksgiving. *Early Childhood Education Journal, 36*(4), 347–354.

Jones, D. (2009). From receivers of service to givers of service: Promoting civic engagement in youth from disadvantaged circumstances. Paper presented at the annual meeting of the American Educational Research Association, San Diego, CA.

Kahne, J., Chi, B, & Middaugh, E. (2006). Building social capital for civic and political engagement: The potential of high-school civics courses. *Canadian Journal of Education, 29*(2), 387–409.

Kahne, J., & Middaugh, E. (2006). Is patriotism good for democracy? A study of high school seniors' patriotic commitments. *Phi Delta Kappan, 87*(8), 600–607.

Kahne, J., & Westheimer, J. (2006). The limits of political efficacy: Educating citizens for a democratic society. *PS: Political Science & Politics 39*(2), 289–206.

Kahne, J., & Westheimer, J. (2003). Teaching democracy: What schools need to do. *Phi Delta Kappan, 85*(1), 34–40, 57–66.

Kliebard, H. M. (1999). *Schooled to work: Vocationalism and the American curriculum 1876-1946.* New York: Teachers College Press.

Lefrançois, D., Éthier, M. A., & Demers, S. (2008). Justice sociale et réforme scolaire au Québec: le cas du programme d'Histoire et éducation à la citoyenneté [Social justice and curricular reform in Quebec: Exploring the case of the History and Citizenship Education program]. *Revue International d'Éthique Sociétale et Gouvernementale, 11*(1), 72–85.

Levinson, M. (2009). "You have the right to struggle": The construction of historical counternarrative as a tool for civic empowerment. Paper presented at the annual meeting of the American Educational Research Association, San Diego, CA.

Levinson, M. (2010). The civic empowerment gap: Defining the problem. In L. R. Sherrod, J. Torney-Purta, & C. A. Flanagan (Eds.), *Handbook of research and policy on civic engagement in youth.* New York: Wiley.

Marri, A. R. (2009). Closing the civic opportunity gap: Engaging urban youth in civic education. Paper presented at the annual meeting of the American Educational Research Association, San Diego, CA.

Meier, D. (2008). Educating for what? The struggle for democracy in education. *PowerPlay: A Journal of Educational Justice, 1*(1), 20–27.

Mendelsohn, D. (2006). *The lost: A search for six of six million.* New York: Harper Perennial.

National Public Radio (2009). Duncan: "Educate our way to a better economy." Retrieved August 15, 2009 from http://www.npr.org/templates/transcript/transcript.php?storyId=100249947

Nygreen, K. (2008). Urban youth and the construction of racialized and classed political identities. In J. S. Bixby & J. L. Pace (Eds.), *Educating democratic citizens in troubled times: Qualitative studies of current efforts* (pp. 81–106). Albany, NY: SUNY Press.

O'Mahony, C. (2009). Core democratic values: Children's growth in understanding from grades three through five. Paper presented at annual meeting of the American Educational Research Association, San Diego, CA.

Ponder, J., & Veldt, M. V. (2009). Closing the loop in civic education: From teacher education, to professional development, to student learning in the elementary classroom. Paper presented at the annual meeting of the American Educational Research Association, San Diego, CA.

Rubin, B. (2007). "There's still no justice": Youth civic identity development amid distinct school and community contexts. *Teachers College Record, 109*(2), 449–481.

Rubin, B., & Hayes, B. (2009). From "no backpacks" to "murder": Studying civic problems Across diverse contexts. Paper presented at the annual meeting of the American Educational Research Association, San Diego, CA.

Rubin, B., Hayes, B. & Benson, K. (2009). "It's the worst place to live": Urban youth and the challenge of school-based civic learning. *Theory Into Practice, 48*(3), 213–221.

Schultz, B. (2007). "Feelin' what they feelin'": Democracy and curriculum in Cabrini Green. In M. W. Apple & J. A. Beane (Eds.), *Democratic schools: Lessons in powerful education* (pp. 62–82). Portsmouth, NH: Heinemann.

Shreiner, T. L. (2009). Framing a model of democratic thinking to inform teaching and learning in civic education. Unpublished doctoral dissertation, University of Michigan.

Singh, M., Kenway, J., & Apple, M. W. (2005). Globalizing education: Perspectives from above and below. In Apple, M. W., Kenway, J. & Singh, M. (Eds.). *Globalizing education: Policies, pedagogies, & politics* (pp. 1–9). New York: Peter Lang.

Smith, G. (2008). Letter to President-elect Obama. In Cookson, P. & Welner, K. (Eds.), *Fellows' education letters to the President* (n.p.). Boulder, CO: Education and the Public Interest Center, University of Colorado. Retrieved July 12, 2009 from http://epicpolicy.org/publication/Letters-to-Obama

Sperling, E., & Bencze, J. L. (2009). "Particle theory isn't everything": Engaging students in action-oriented citizenship through science education. Paper presented at the annual meeting of the American Educational Research Association, San Diego, CA.

Taines, C. (2009). Urban students' activism for educational reform and their development of social capital. Paper presented at the annual meeting of the American Educational Research Association, San Diego, CA.

Teitelbaum, K., & Brodsky, J. (2008). Teaching and learning in the age of accountability: One experience with the not-so-hidden costs. *Journal of Curriculum and Pedagogy, 5*(1), 100–110.

Tupper, J. (2009). Unsafe waters, stolen sisters, and social studies: Troubling democracy and the meta-narrative of universal citizenship. *Teacher Education Quarterly, 36*(1), 77–94.

University of Florida College of Education (2008). Professor heads effort to bring civics back to middle school. *Education Times*, Fall/Winter, 7.

Westheimer, J. (2009). No child left thinking: Democracy at risk in American schools and what we need to do about it. In H. S. Shapiro (Ed.), *Education and hope in troubled times: Visions of change for our children's world* (pp. 259–271). New York: Routledge.

Westheimer, J., & Kahne, J. (2004). What kind of citizen? The politics of educating for democracy. *American Educational Research Journal, 41*(2), 237–269.

Williams, R. (1989). *Resources of hope*. London: Verso.

Wood, G. H. (1992). *Schools that work: America's most innovative public education programs*. New York: Plume.

Wood, G. H. (1998). *A time to learn: The story of one high school's remarkable transformation and the people who made it happen*. New York: Plume.

CHAPTER TWENTY-FIVE

Teaching Students How to Think Critically

The Confederate Flag Controversy
in the High School Social Studies Curriculum

SUSAN L. SCHRAMM-PATE & RICHARD LUSSIER

Introduction

Critical pedagogy has developed out of the critical theory of the early Frankfurt School in Germany and has evolved though the influences of the emancipatory work of Paulo Freire and the influences of postmodern theories. Critical pedagogy has expanded from a focus mainly on class issues to a broader theory encompassing issues such as race, gender, ability, age, sexual preferences, religion, ethnicity, and language.

Concerned with the elimination of oppression and the resurgence of hope and possibility, critical pedagogues analyze the effects of the changes on individuals and various groups while simultaneously seeking areas for opposition and opportunities for change. Their goal is a just world free from oppression and suffering and the achievement of a democratic society in which all individuals have a voice. They seek to contribute to the development of a more vibrant democracy by empowering students to become active creators and promoters of a better society though the elimination of social inequalities.[1] As Ira Shor has observed, the methods of critical pedagogy are hopeful avenues for teachers working in privileged communities as well as underprivileged communities because they involve a variety of small and large intellectual exercises that offer students some immediate context in which to understand feelings of lesser status, Inferiority, anger, and alienation.[2]

In this article, a social studies unit titled, "Confederate Heritage," is described. The Confederate flag controversy provided the organizing theme of the unit that was taught in a working-class poor, majority White, and rural high school in upstate South Carolina from a popular cultural issues-oriented perspective using critical pedagogical techniques.[3] This perspective and approach offered ways for these students to grasp the critical understandings within current events and democratic models of social change. Following Henry Giroux who noted,

"Pedagogy in the critical sense [illuminates] the relationship among knowledge, authority, and power,"[4] we aimed to design and implement a social studies curriculum that was situated in the real issues of our students' lives. We used language as a vehicle for opening up different spaces for our students to speak to and to be aware of multiple voices and existing power relations.[5]

We found that critical pedagogical approaches to learning and democratic models of social change offered strategies that helped scaffold our students into ongoing discussions and debates around the complex historical, economic, political, sociocultural, and contemporary issues surrounding Confederate symbols. We invited and challenged our students to imagine, to raise issues, and to see that although they may not necessarily agree with the conclusions that others drew, it was still vitally important to address complex issues within the flag debates such as diversity, discrimination, racism, sexism, violence, and prejudice.

The article begins with a framework for the unit by examining ways in which the Confederate flag controversy was presented in the popular press and next presents ways in which ambiguities inherent in Confederate symbols can be integrated into critical classroom discussions. The article culminates with practical suggestions for teaching the unit including fostering democratic dialogue in the classroom, situating the curriculum within the learner's reality, and enhancing participatory teaching formats and critical literacy.

The Popular Press as Instructional Text

By using material from sources other than the traditional and conservative views often presented in state-mandated textbooks, social studies teachers can generate themes to promote critical consciousness in their classrooms. For our unit, "Confederate Heritage," we found the school's textbook, U.S. Constitutionalism,[6] to be detached from the real issues of student life and of the critical curriculum issues we aimed to explore. To supplement their textbook, our students read from publications such as, *The National Review, The New Republic, The Nation, Mother Jones*, newspapers such as, *The New York Times, The State, The Greenville News*, and *The Charlotte Observer*, and websites such as the American Civil Liberties Union (ACLU) and the National Association for the Advancement of Colored People (NAACP). Student journal entries suggested that the alternative views presented in these texts enabled them to sharpen their own opinions and determine what others believed.

They read articles that detailed the highly publicized affair in August of 2000 in which the Confederate battle flag was removed from atop the state house dome to its present location on a flag pole behind a statue of a uniformed Confederate soldier in front of the massive stairway leading up to the front of the state house. This action that positioned the Confederate flag on the South Carolina State house grounds as part of a Civil War monument may be understood as a temporary "settlement"[7] or "accord"[8] in this ongoing battle over the representation of southern heritage. Apple observed that capital's strategic agenda is advanced only with the cooperation of other groups whose own needs are met as well.[9] Following Apple, we designed discussions on holders of technical/administrative knowledge who have autonomous interests and whose support signifies a settlement or compromise with the dominant fractions of capital.

During the Confederate flag controversy in South Carolina, "us versus them" themes emerged in the popular press. For example, stories of proponents wrapping themselves in the Confederate flag during the debates to remove it from the state house dome indicated that many

Whites felt that issues of "honor," "courage," "duty" and "respect" for their Confederate ancestors were at the root of the flag issue.[10] Articles and editorials by opponents of the flag were also included with Blacks accusing Whites of "living in the past," and of celebrating the legacy of "racist slave masters."[11] Exploring themes such as these enabled us to conduct our class in a democratic fashion by probing through critical inquiry and discovery-learning rather than merely serving as mechanical answer-givers within preset lesson plans.

To emphasize the importance that rhetoric plays in debates over "heritage," vis-à-vis the Confederate flag controversy, students analyzed the popular press as a depository and resource of rhetoric. For instance, students spent considerable time on the idea of representation in understanding symbols and used the tools of literary criticism (e.g., identifying rhetorical devices such as metaphors, plot structures, roles, imagery, ideographs, and types of narratives) as well as, the tools of social science analysis (e.g., identifying ideology, values, and whose interests are served) to deconstruct popular press texts and situate them within wider social and historical contexts.

Popular press articles and editorials about political symbols such as Confederate flags and the controversy surrounding re-enactment of Civil War battles enabled our students to consider the flag compromise as a settlement and to evaluate its staying power. Our goal was to enable our students to see that the flag is a political symbol with multiple meanings-not simply those described by one group or the other and that this recognition would have consequences for whatever compromise was worked out.

The students debated one another, read things that are not always palatable, engaged in role playing, performances, journaling, and essay writing. They begin to see, feel, and understand what "dialoguing across differences"[12] is like. In their journal free-writes, they reflected upon their citizenship and how the values that inform it are transmitted through their "reading" of popular press texts. We reminded our students that in an academic setting, such as a school classroom, it is not enough to simply make claims in a oracular fashion, but that their claims needed to be buttressed with grounds (or evidence) to support their claims.

Our students not only deconstructed the meaning of Confederate symbols such as the flag and other Confederate monuments, but also Civil War re-enactments and the concept of "heritage." Throughout the unit, our students read articles and editorials from *The State* newspaper[13] that described certain pro-flag "heritage" groups who had begun organizing and raising money both to persuade legislators to stand firm on keeping the flag flying over the state house dome as well as articles detailing the activities of anti-flag marchers who surged through Columbia. Our students also analyzed visual texts from the popular press.[14] One particularly powerful photograph of 6,000 pro-flag marchers, many in Confederate regalia waving Confederate battle flags in front of the state house, elicited considerable response from our students in class discussions and journal free-writes.

Student debates often drew from readings within the popular press and included taking sides with particular issues that were presented (e.g., whether or not President Clinton should have weighed in on the Confederate flag controversy in South Carolina; Governor Jim Hodge's proposed "compromise" of moving the flag to the Civil War monument; the NAACP's tourism boycott of South Carolina; and whether or not NAACP president, Kweisi Mfume, was using the South Carolina Confederate flag controversy to promote his own political agenda.[15]

To prepare for debates, students read various historical accounts of the American Civil War and noted how historians differ in their opinions, just as editorial writers and reporters in the media do. For example, they were exposed to historians who argued that slavery was the issue of the American Civil War. They compared and contrasted that view with historians who argued that there were multiple issues besides slavery involved in the Civil War including states' rights, Christianity, and King Cotton. As a result, the student debates were lively and clearly demonstrated their engagement in the narratives that circulated in the media. They began to understand the subjectivity involved in the writing of history as well as the popular press.

We enabled our students to understand how the Confederate battle flag controversy is dichotomously coded in the popular press as a symbol for some who argue that the flag has less to do with slavery than it does states' rights, southern pride, and constitutional government and for some who argue that the flag is a reminder of the historic struggle of African Americans for social justice vis-à-vis Jim Crow, segregation, persecution, injustice, and slavery.

After watching a History Channel video on Civil War re-enactments and Confederate symbols, our students read an article by Governor Hodges[16] about the controversy and the compromise and began a wide ranging discussion that touched upon the issues of representation, interpretation, social class, race, gender, and stereotyping. We found Michael Apple's concept of "settlements"[17] or compromises within hegemonic political discourses to be a useful critical pedagogical tool to enable our students to consider the struggle over the Confederate flag. In other words, while the compromise did not satisfy everyone, some people in the popular press argued that it at least restored a measure of peace, if not closure.[18] In the aftermath of the compromise, our students reflected in their journals prompts such as: What is in the best interest of power brokers in the State?; How has the struggle over where to put the flag become institutionalized?; How do struggles over the flag affect the State's image?; Threaten social peace?; Have a negative impact on businesses?; and Will the compromise hold? After the journal free-writes, our students debated the various issues and then worked in small groups to come to a "compromise" among themselves.

Multiple Readings of Signs and Symbols

An attempt to avoid some a priori standards that declare all Confederate flags as offensive, evil, and oppressive, is necessary if there are to be multiple readings of these poly-vocal symbols as a visual and social text. The Confederate flag has spawned much controversy in recent years because of ambiguities inherent in the symbol itself and because of contradictory readings of southern history in general, and the Confederacy in particular.[19] These ambiguities present a great impetus for classroom discussion. For example, our students learned that symbols are inclined to multiple interpretations because they are abstract, often nonverbal expressions of ideas that depend on a complex interrelationship among and between human cognitive processes and the ability to use and understand language.

They also learned that what we often call a "symbol" actually is a sign-that is, a tangible, physical representation of a symbol which conveys an idea separate and apart from the sign.[20] For example, while they accepted that the Confederate flag symbol does not hold the same meaning for all audiences, our students struggled with the notion that the problem of interpreting the flag lies not so much with the flag itself, but with the underlying symbolism. Consistent with critical pedagogical practices,[21] we spent considerable time enabling our students to understand that in the case of the Confederacy, with its deplorable and dubious legacy, the problem of interpreting the symbolic meaning of the flag has led to a conflict between groups of people.

A debate forum helped our students play out the conflict between those that pay homage to the sign and those that take offense to the sign. One side represented the flag protagonists and the other side represented the flag antagonists. The protagonists argued that we must remember and respect history, traditions, and culture of the South, while the antagonists argued that it is the worst reminder of African Americans as an inferior people and a belief that slavery was necessary to the economic and cultural interests of the antebellum South.

In another debate, our students deliberated how those on the political "right" struggled to challenge the negative representations of the Confederate battle flag and defended the symbol as representative of "southern culture and heritage" and organized around "family values" and patriarchal, White, middle-class forms of identity, while those on the political "left" saw the flag as representative of discrimination, oppression, and intolerance. Within each debate, both sides posed arguments around pressures that they felt needed to be exerted on the public institutions for either the removal from the state house grounds altogether or a compromise somewhere in between.

Guest speakers were also brought into our classroom during the implementation of the unit. For example, a local Civil War re-enactor talked to the students about using the Confederate battle flag as in re-enactments of battles, parades and "living histories."[22] According to him, the Civil War re-enactors he knows tend to view the Confederate flag as a historical artifact associated with the particular soldiers of a particular battle. He said that just because re-enactors are interested in "living history," that it does not necessarily mean that they wish to promote racism or that they wish to return to the days of that "peculiar institution" known as slavery. He also argued that many re-enactors he knew did not want the flag over the state house dome, although he did say that most did not have a problem with its display at memorials to Confederate soldiers. His presentation in class helped our students to begin to see that neither the acknowledgement of these multiple interpretations means that there is no right or wrong way to interpret the flag nor that one interpretation is more valuable than another.

Implications for Social Studies Curriculum and Pedagogy

If we think of schooling as one of the many powerful social systems that quietly orders us about, normalizes us, and makes us function, it is also necessary to look at the interests of particular classes or groups of citizens. Dennis Carlson's action toward critical literacy[23] requires moving social studies education from discourses that merely include mythic heroes such as Sojourner Truth and Rosa Parks to questioning whose interests are served in relation to specific historical struggles. Within the tradition of critical pedagogy, Pepi Leistyna's call for a critical multiculturalism[24] and Peter McLaren's call for a revolutionary multiculturalism[25] are also useful to social studies educators who aim to provide their students with the opportunity to actively engage in truly critical and difficult multicultural problems within current events.

By pointing to the tensions and possibilities inherent in the Confederate flag debates; we aimed to affirm all of our students and their families while at the same time confronting difficult and troubling questions of structural inequality and deep-seated biases. Following Giroux's notion[26] that cultural struggles are increasingly over representation, and thus over symbols, narratives, and myths, we recognize current events such as the Confederate flag controversy as a fundamental way to reframe social studies curriculum through critical pedagogy.

Critical pedagogists illustrate that the rhetoric of images is very similar to that of the word and that both the word and the image use rhetorical devices such as argument, imagery, genre, and ideographs. Critical pedagogy needs a language that allows for competing solidarities and political vocabularies that do not reduce the issues of power, justice, and struggle, and the inequality to masternarratives that suppress the contingent, historical and the everyday as a serious object of study.[27] This suggests that curriculum knowledge be developed as part of an ongoing engagement with a variety of narratives and traditions that can be re-read and re-formulated in politically different terms.

Teaching critical literacy empowers individuals to become more autonomous agents who are able to recognize hegemonic forces and become citizens who enthusiastically and competently engage in processes of social transformation. Giroux argues that in both political and pedagogical terms, the category of difference must be central to the notion of democratic community.[28] Following Giroux, we agree that as part of a language of possibility, educators can investigate opportunities to construct knowledge/power relations in which multiple narratives and social practices are constructed around politics and a pedagogy of difference. We enabled our students to read the world differently, analyze power and privilege, and construct an alternative democratic community. By studying the Confederate flag controversy, they learned that differences can be affirmed and articulated within categories central to public life (i.e., democracy, citizenship, and public spheres).

Teachers have a larger responsibility beyond the formal curriculum; the responsibility to assist in preparing students to function effectively in a society rife with peril, temptations, confusion and bewildering choices. As Paul Theobald states:

> What [students] deserve and must receive through schooling is an education conducive to the development of a sense of political efficacy and, coupled with this, a program of concerted community enculturation in the ethic of shouldering a responsible measure of civic virtue.[29]

What Theobald refers to as "civic virtue" is what Amy Gutmann, writing in the tradition of John Dewey, refers to as "democratic character,"[30] the development of which is essential to any society that claims to derive its authority from the consent of the governed. Political education is, therefore, valued by a democratic state in order to predispose young people to behave democratically and thereby, strengthen the substantive elements within our procedurally democratic government.

In our view, in order to maintain and deepen our political heritage as a representative republic, teaching civic virtue is essential. The practical questions for us became—How?; And with what materials?; And under what circumstances? In the process of asking these questions we interrogated the concept of "civic virtue" as a social text laden with contradictory values. To paraphrase Apple, we also asked, whose concept of civic virtue will be taught?[31] Since schools are places where meaning is constructed and teachers are responsible for enabling students to become critical thinkers, we aimed to enable our students to participate actively and confidently in the political process.

Apple also described how easily social studies curriculum can become the locus of struggle between competing groups of various political and religious orientations, each seeking to influence, if not to indoctrinate, the nation's youth. Within the social studies classroom setting, our students critically evaluated history and governmental institutions as a prelude to a wider understanding of the social and economic dysfunctions of the Confederate flag controversy.

As Theobald observed, "It is a sure bet that if strengthening communities is indeed part of the antidote to our most serious social problems, creating schools dedicated to this goal is a step in the right direction."[32] To this end it is necessary to focus upon the categories of social construction, identified by critical theory as gender, race, and social class, as a matrix within which to analyze and evaluate the impact of social problems upon our formal, procedural institutions of society and state. Giroux advocates assisting students in developing a "power-sensitive discourse" that helps those who have been traditionally marginalized in our culture to "find their voices."[33] At stake he says, "is the rewriting of history within a politics of difference; from one metanarrative to many local ones."[34] From the cultural transmission of the traditional view of what it means to be "an American," to the exploration of the many ways our citizenship can be expressed within a political theory built on negotiating diversity rather than squashing it.

Traditionally, the social studies narrative presented in American history and government books, is one of progress, peace, freedom, democracy, and prosperity with things just getting better all the time. This is remarkable in view of the fact that a cursory glance at the history of the nation's expansion both here on this continent and abroad is a litany of unremitting warfare, conquest, colonialism, subjugation, and economic imperialism. The parents and guardians of our students expect their children to be socialized to accept and support the socioeconomic and political status quo, not critique it. Embedded within the curriculum of U.S. government and civics classes at our school is a broad syllabus of topics that teachers are expected to "cover" if their students are to have any chance of "passing" state mandated standardized proficiency tests. As Giroux has memorably observed, "a critical pedagogy for democracy does not begin with test scores but with questions."[35]

Among the topics that loom in the traditional advanced social studies curriculum at the high school level in South Carolina, for example, are federalism, civil liberties and rights, church-state relations, judicial history, classical republican theory, the nature of modern political science, elections, and the relations between the President and Congress. Virtually every one of these topics lends itself to challenging the masternarratives of a patriarchal, Eurocentric view of constitutional development as essentially the product of farsighted White forefathers who very wisely wrought upon this continent a new nation conceived in liberty. There was liberty, of course, but for whom and to what purpose?

Teaching a Unit on "Confederate Heritage"

Burbules and Rice's concept of "dialogue across Differences"[36] is integral to the challenge of enabling diverse groups of high school students, who often lack prior training in discussion and conference techniques from earlier grades, to discuss their differences in a civil tone with one another. One of the critical educator's tasks, therefore, is to enable students to cope with a discussion-oriented course where differing opinions are openly expressed and where talking reasonably with one another is essential.

Moving the dialogue along and keeping the potential conflict manageable in the classroom is part of the critical pedagogue's role as facilitator. Dialogue depends upon the virtues of reasonableness, acknowledgment, and patience. It also depends on the postmodern notion of curriculum as a collection of multiple truths and topics to be discussed and debated rather than universal truths to be advanced through rote memorization and lecture.

By following Peter McLaren's notion of "decentering Whiteness"[37] and by taking an Afrocentric and feminist approach to teaching,[38] we aimed to make our classroom a "safe" space where all of our students' voices were heard and where our students learned to "dialogue across differences." We explained to our students how the evocative power of the phrase, "dialogue across differences," wraps up a panoply of ideas and attitudes: broadmindedness, mutual respect, and an awareness that understanding, not conversion, is the goal of conversation and the real hope of compromise, accommodation, and renewed community through the process of common intellectual struggle.

We found that our students also needed an adequate grounding in their own traditions before they could engage in a fruitful dialogue. At the beginning, they simply traded uninformed opinions which made us realize the necessity of explaining to them that a politics of difference does not require a monolithic resolution to a problem, but rather the democratic virtues of open-minded deliberation and compromise. We also found that our students needed practice in discussing controversial issues with one another. Enabling them to discuss Confederate symbols, civil rights, Civil War re-enactments, and federalism from a critical perspective was much different than the ways in which the U.S. History narrative has typically been presented to them. In other words, our students were used to traditional classes where teachers relied solely on uncritical American history and government textbooks.

In terms of what was substantively done in our classroom for our "Confederate Heritage" unit, the overarching objectives included: 1) substantive vs. procedural democracy: what is the impact of the Confederate flag debate on either or both?; 2) dual vs. national federalism: where does sovereignty reside in determining questions surrounding the Confederate flag?; and 3) what does it mean to be an American: how does the Confederate flag debate illuminate this question? We implemented our unit in an Advanced Placement Government and Politics course at the high school and merged the insights of critical literacy (i.e., developing competencies in decoding, deconstructing, and demystifying the dominant narratives in various types of texts) within our school's traditional college preparatory curriculum (i.e., lesson plans that are filled with factoids and uncritical and unreflective exercises). Moreover, our school setting was staunchly traditionalist (i.e., heterosexual view of the relations between men and women and an attitude of racial marginalization in the curriculum for people of color).

At the beginning of our unit, students viewed video-taped programs dealing with Civil War re-enactments, and the South Carolina Confederate flag controversy. The viewings were broken into two segments to facilitate discussion and note taking over several class periods. During the course of the presentations, our students were asked to think about the various meanings that the flag represents to various constituencies and to write reflective essays. Journal prompts were also used for free-writing exercises. For example, we asked them if they believed the various meanings that the flag represents were reconcilable and, if not, did the flag belong in a position of sovereignty over the state house dome? Or was it better at the Confederate Soldiers monument?

After each presentation of material, our goal was to promote discussion and facilitate via open-ended questions. Our students were encouraged to think both as "political scientists" and as "politically informed citizens." They spent considerable time decoding and deconstructing hidden meanings in the various texts they read. For example, they identified metaphors, plot structures, roles, and multiple layers of conflicting meaning within a variety of political symbols and Confederate symbols. By the end of the unit, both the African American students and the White students began to see the Confederate flag as a symbol that has multiple meanings. This was reflected in both their journals and in their classroom discussions.

As they reflected upon their citizenship (i.e., their responsibility as a citizen in our representative republic) specific values were transmitted. However, from our normative position, we believe that this is a step in the right direction since educated persons should be concerned with American democracy, sovereignty, identity, and citizenship. By exposing our students to a wide range of discussions that touched upon the issues of representation, interpretation, social class, race, gender, stereotyping, and settlement, we enabled them to do counter hegemonic work. For example, our class discussions brought to light the power brokers in the State and revealed how their institutionalized struggles over the flag affected the State's image, threatened social peace, and had a negative impact on local businesses. They also discussed the role of the NAACP and whether it contributed to or inflamed the issue. Students noted how the "compromise" did little to change the substance of South Carolina politics and that while it did not satisfy everyone, it at least restored a measure of peace, if not closure.

Conclusion

Opening a can of worms with a whole range of unsolved socio-political problems is not how we typically teach American history. Interpreting the flag as a "text" to be "read" in terms of race, class, and gender, however, can be fruitful in bringing students to an awareness of how meanings are determined and what affiliation means for one's identity. For example, if one sees the flag as representative of the values of action-oriented, competitive, young, White heterosexual males who drive pick-up trucks and display Confederate symbols intended to glorify hostility and racism, it is also very much a reflection of the way our society constructs masculinity as competitive, pack-oriented, and reflexively supportive of the home team. Gendered and racial values as well as social class are implicit in the Confederate flag controversy and compromise.

An awareness of the discursive practices that traditionally shape our existence is crucial to individuals and collective empowerment for people from socially marginalized groups. Simply repeating and amplifying the "knowledge" outlines in the state approved text book reinforces the impression that there is only one discourse that matters and it happens to be White, male, capitalist, competitive, highly individualistic, and ever-dominant. As Carlson states:

> The discourses of Afrocentrism and feminism have been important in their recognition that epistemologies are culturally and historically specific, that oppositional epistemologies always exist, and that we can

and must move beyond patriarchal, Eurocentric, and capitalist mindsets in order to empower marginalized students.[39] And it is that empowerment of marginalized groups of people of color and women to which we oriented our unit on "Confederate Heritage" and which we believe will ultimately lead to the rethinking of master narratives within social studies curriculum that are essentially Eurocentric, White, competitive, patriarchal, heteronormative, objectivist, modernist, foundational, and totalizing. The critical study of history according to Greene, is a place for "speculative audacity"[40] as students learn to interrogate the values and beliefs that serve as the basis for choosing what events to include in the unfolding drama of human existence on this planet and as they learn to hear the voices of those traditionally marginalized by the typical school reading of the subject.

The role of language in the production of "historical truths" also needs critical consideration: historians traditionally view the narratives they produce as fundamentally different from literature. The later is fictional whereas the former is somehow as real as our lived experiences. It is the task of teachers and students collectively to disrupt master narratives by interrogating their philosophical foundations and this cannot happen if master narratives continue to be uncritically accepted in classrooms where assimilation and reproduction of facts on standardized tests is the order of the day. Objectivist, factoid-driven curriculum is conducive to socially-conservative worldviews that often serve to marginalize people of color and women and misappropriate power constructs.

Both the theme of the "Confederate Heritage" unit and the pedagogical practices helped engage our students and open them up to the possibility that the world may not work the way they believe it does. They were required to think for themselves and to find their own voices within the public discourse over the flag. Students were asked to participate as informed citizens in a democratic society that encourages the option of dissent rather than the silence and security of the status quo.

Although formal segregation has been abolished and Jim Crow laws repealed, the mindset of conscious citizenship transmission to support the existing social order still pervades social studies instruction in secondary schools not only in the South, but across America. Critically understanding the past of a country that has historically shut women and people of color out of its curricular master narratives that model the American experience is imperative for the creation of a more egalitarian democratic republic and all the more necessary in a nation with many people who simply do not wish to hear voices other than their own.

QUESTIONS TO CONSIDER

1. How do the authors define "critical pedagogy," and how is it used in their social studies unit?

2. What artifacts, sources, and other resources are utilized in exploring the Confederate flag controversy?

3. What methods and strategies do the authors use to augment critical understanding of the complex issues involved? Give examples.

4. How do they employ multicultural concepts and ideas to generate "dialogue across differences"? Give reasons and examples.

5. How can the unit be described as a lesson in democracy? Elaborate and explain.

Notes

This chapter originally appeared in *The High School Journal*, Vol. 87, No. 3 (December, 2003/January 2004): 56–65. Published here with permission of University of North Carolina Press.

1. See, for example, Douglas Kellner, *Critical Pedagogy, Cultural Studies, and Radical Democracy at the Turn of the Millennium: Reflections on the Work of Henry Giroux* http://www.gseis.ucla.edu/faculty/kellner/kellner.html (Retrieved July 13, 2003).

2. Ira Shor, ed. *Freire for the Classroom: a Sourcebook for Liberatory Teaching* (Portsmouth, NH: Boynton/Cook Publishers, 1987).

3. See, for example, Dennis Carlson, "The Life of a Myth: Of Rosa Parks, Cultural Studies, and Multicultural Education." Paper presented at the annual conference of the American Educational Research Association (AERA) in New Orleans, April 2000 in a symposium on "Cultural Studies and the Curriculum; and Dennis Carlson and Michael Apple, eds. *Power/ Knowledge/Pedagogy: The Meaning of Democratic Education in Unsettling Times*. (Boulder, CO: Westview Press, 1998); and *Henry A. Giroux, Pedagogy and the Politics of Hope: Theory, Culture, and Schooling* (Boulder, CO: Westview Press, 1997); and C. Lankshear and Peter McLaren, eds. *Critical Literacy: Politics, Praxis, and the Postmodern* (New York: State University of New York Press, 1993); and L. M. Semali and A. W. Pailliotet, eds. (1999). *Intermediality: The Teacher's Handbook of Critical Media Literacy*. Boulder, CO: Westview Press, 1999); and Ira Shor, ed. *Freire for the Classroom*.

4. Henry A. Giroux, *Disturbing Pleasures: Learning Culture* (New York: Routledge, 1994), 30.

5. Nicholas Burbules and Suzanne Rice, "Dialogue Across Differences: Continuing the Conversation" *Harvard Education Review*, 61 (1991), 393–415.

6. The adopted social studies textbook, *US Constitutionalism*, for this high school is written by John Dilulio of the University of Pennsylvania who is a member of the George W. Bush administration.

7. Carlson, *Making Progress*.

8. Apple, *Official Knowledge*.

9. Apple, *Official Knowledge*.

10. Brad Warthen, "Hodges Steps Out as Leader with Well-Thought-Out Flag Plan" *The State* (February 20, 2000): D2); and Armstrong Williams, "NAACP Extension of Boycott of South Carolina Brutally Sad" *The Greenville News* (May 19, 2000): 15A.

11. See, for example, B. Willingham, "Community Reactions Divided on Decision" *The Greenville News* (May 19, 2000): 10A); and J. Stroud, "As Legislators Return S.C. Senator's 'Insult' Hardens Flag Debate *The State* (January 11, 2000): A1-A10.

12. Burbules and Rice, "Dialogue Across Differences," 393–415.

13. See, for example, Warthen, "Hodges Steps Out as Leader" D2; and Williams, "NAACP Extension of Boycott" 15A; Willingham, Community Reactions Divided on Decision 10A; and Stroud, "As Legislators Return" A1-A10; and John Monk, "The War Over the Flag: Strife Ripples from Grass-Roots Level" *The State* (March 19, 2000): B1-B9; and John Monk, "God, Barbecue, Slavery Mix at Maurice's" *The State* (October 1, 2000): B1-B5.

14. See, for example, D. Firestone, "South Carolina Clings to Dixie: Unfurling a Battle Cry and its Last Hurrah" *The New York Times* (January 23, 2000): 5; and K. Avin, "Letters to the Editor" *The State* (February 20, 2000).

D2; and B. D. Ayres, B. D. "NAACP Opposes Compromise on Flag" *The New York Times* (February 20, 2000): 13.

15. NAACP President Mfume and the NAACP were also involved in the debates over the Confederate flag in locations of sovereignty in other southern states such as Georgia, Mississippi, and Alabama.

16. James Hodges, "Those Who Want to End Confederate Flag Debate Can Do So" *The State* (February 20, 2000): D3.

17. Michael W. Apple, *Official Knowledge: Democratic Education in a Conservative Age* (New York: Routledge, 1993).

18. See, for example, Ayres, "NAACP Opposes Compromise":13; and J. Day, "In Confederate Flag's Shadow, Festival Fights to Find the Light" *The State* (May 21, 2000): F1; and Firestone, "South Carolina Clings to Dixie": 5.

19. John Coski, "The Confederate Battle Flag in Historical Perspective," in *Confederate Symbols in the Contemporary South*, Michael Martinez, William D. Richardson, and Ron McNinch-Su, eds. (Gainesville, FL: University of Florida Press, 2000), 89–129).; and Robert Jeffrey, "Southern Political Thought and the Southern Political Tradition," in *Confederate Symbols in the Contemporary South*, Michael Martinez, William D. Richardson, and Ron McNinch-Su, eds. (Gainesville, FL: University of Florida Press, 2000), 25–47.

20. Ludwig Wittgenstein, *Tractatus Logico-Philosophicus* (London: Routledge and Kegan Paul, 1961).

21. C. Lankshear and Peter McLaren, eds. *Critical literacy: Politics, Praxis, and the Postmodern* (New York: State University of New York Press, 1993).

22. For commentary on American Civil War re-enacting, see, for example, Tony Horwitz, *Confederates in the Attic* (New York: Vintage Books, 1998); and David Goldfield, *Still Fighting the Civil War: The American South and Southern History* (Baton Rouge, LA: Louisiana State University Press, 2002.

23. Carlson, "The Life of a Myth: Of Rosa Parks"

24. Pepi Leistyna, *Defining and Designing Multiculturalism: One School System's Efforts* (New York: State University of New York Press, 2002).

25. Peter McLaren, "White Terror and Oppositional Agency: Towards a Critical Multiculturalism" in *Multiculturalism: A Critical Reader*, David Goldberg, ed., (Cambridge, MA: Blackwell, 1994).

26. Henry A. Giroux, "Doing Cultural Studies: Youth and the Challenge of Pedagogy" *Harvard Education Review*, 64 (1994), 393–415.

27. See, for example, Lankshear and McLaren, *Critical Literacy: Politics, Praxis, and the Postmodern*; and L. M. Semali and A. W. Pailliotet, eds., *Intermediality: The Teacher's Handbook of Critical Media Literacy* (Boulder, CO: Westview Press, 1999).

28. Giroux, "Doing Cultural Studies."

29. Paul Theobald, *Teaching the Commons* (Boulder, CO: Westview Press, 1997), 133.

30. Amy Gutmann, *Democratic Education* (Princeton, NJ: Princeton University Press, 1999), 51–52.

31. Apple, *Official Knowledge*.

32. Theobald, *Teaching the Commons*, 159.

33. Henry A. Giroux, *Border Crossings*. (New York: Routledge, 1993), 56.

34. Giroux, *Border Crossings*, 56.

35. Giroux, *Border Crossings*, 74

36. Burbules and Rice, "Dialogue across differences," 393–415.

37. Peter McLaren, "Decentering Whiteness: In Search of a Revolutionary Multiculturalism" *Multicultural Education*, 50 (1997), 4–11.

38. Carlson, *Making Progress*.

39. Carlson, *Making Progress*, 69.

40. Maxine Greene, *The Dialectic of Freedom* (New York: Teachers College Press, 1988), 128.

CHAPTER TWENTY-SIX

Urban Success

A Multidimensional Mathematics Approach with Equitable Outcomes

JO BOALER

The poor performance of students in America's urban high schools, both in absolute terms and in comparison with their more economically secure counterparts in suburban schools, is a critical issue for the country, and the opportunity for all students to learn mathematics has been heralded as the new "civil right."[1] In a recent study of mathematics teaching in different schools, I and a group of graduate students at Stanford[2] found that students at Railside High School (a pseudonym), an urban school in California nestled within a few feet of the train tracks, performed better in mathematics than students at other schools and that differences in achievement among Railside students of different cultural groups were reduced in all cases and eliminated in some.

Railside was one of three schools in which we spent four years following cohorts of students from their freshman to their senior years as they experienced different approaches to mathematics instruction. As part of our study, we documented the teaching practices of the Railside mathematics department—practices focused upon equity.[3] I will consider here some of the most important aspects of the Railside approach—an approach that transformed students' lives by helping them to see mathematics as a part of their future and by providing them with the quantitative reasoning capabilities needed to function in an increasingly technological and global economy.

Railside used a reform-oriented approach to mathematics instruction, with groups of students working together on complex conceptual problems. Students in the other two schools in our study were taught using traditional methods of demonstration and practice, with students working individually on short, closed questions. The study included more than 700 students, and we employed a range of qualitative and quantitative research methods to investigate the effectiveness of each instructional approach. Our research consisted of 600 hours of classroom observations, assessments and questionnaires given to all students in each of the first three years of the study, and interviews with approximately 160 students.

At Railside, students learned more, enjoyed mathematics more, and progressed to higher levels of mathematics than students in the other two schools. Students in Railside's mathematics classes had a very high work rate and developed a lot of respect for one another, regardless of differences in ethnicity, culture, gender, social class, or attainment level. The ethnic cliques so evident in many schools were rare or absent in these classes. What made these results more striking was the fact that Railside is an urban school that serves students from homes with limited financial resources, many of them English-language learners from a culturally and linguistically diverse community. Upon entering high school, the Railside students were achieving at significantly lower levels than the students at the other two, more suburban, more affluent schools in our study. Within two years, the Railside students were significantly outperforming the students at the other schools. By their senior year, some 41% of Railside students were taking advanced classes of precalculus or calculus, while approximately 27% of the students in the other two schools were doing so.

The important achievements demonstrated by the Railside students can be attributed to the unusual approach to mathematics at the school.

Heterogeneous Classes

At Railside High, students were not tracked into different mathematics classes, and the teachers had developed an effective approach for teaching the heterogeneous classes. The other two schools in our study placed freshman students into algebra, lower-level versions of algebra, or geometry, whereas Railside placed all incoming freshmen into heterogeneous algebra classes.

Mathematics at Railside was taught in groups, and teachers utilized an approach called "complex instruction" that was designed to counter differences of social and academic status.[4] A key aspect of the complex instructional approach is the creation of multidimensional classrooms. Typical mathematics classrooms could be described as one-dimensional because in them a single practice is valued above all others—executing procedures correctly. At Railside the teachers created multidimensional classes by valuing many aspects of mathematical work. When we interviewed students at the school about what it took to be successful in mathematics class, they described a variety of practices, such as asking good questions, helping others, using different representations, rephrasing problems, explaining ideas, being logical, justifying methods, or bringing a different perspective to a problem. Teachers acknowledged the value of these various practices in their interactions with students and in the grades they assigned.

When we asked students from traditional classes how to be successful in mathematics classes, most of them described one practice—paying careful attention. The students in traditional classes regarded mathematics as a set of procedures, and they believed that their role in class was to pay careful attention to the teacher's presentation of procedures so that they could memorize them for later use.[5] The primary focus of traditional mathematics classes on one form of mathematical work often means that only a narrow range of students, those for whom this kind of work is appealing, are successful.[6]

At Railside, because there were many more ways to be successful in math class, many more students were successful. The success that students experienced in mathematics class meant that they worked harder, felt more positive about mathematics, and ultimately developed higher levels of understanding.

Group-Worthy Problems

The mathematics department at Railside designed its own curriculum, drawing from different reform curricula like the College Preparatory Mathematics Curriculum (CPM) and the Interactive Mathematics Program (IMP).[7] The curriculum units were organized around unifying themes, such as "What is a linear function?" Students were organized into groups to learn math, and the mathematics teachers spent many hours choosing and designing problems that they regarded as "group-worthy." These were problems whose solutions required the perspectives of different students, that could be solved using different methods, and that emphasized important mathematical concepts and principles.

I observed a class in which the students were working on an interesting and typically difficult problem. They were using their "math tools"—t-tables and graphs—to produce an equation in the form $y = mx + b$ that would help them determine the length of shoelaces needed for different shoes. The teacher encouraged the groups to work with a real shoe contributed by a group member. She introduced the problem by telling the students that there were lots of ways to approach it and that achieving a solution would require the team members to communicate effectively—i.e., listen to one another and give one another a chance to think through their work. The teacher also explained that the grade on the assignment would be based in part on the students' use of multiple methods to show and explain their work.

As with many mathematics questions, the most difficult aspect of the problem for many of the students was figuring out where to start. They had been given the fairly open instruction to form an equation that would help them buy shoelaces. The students had to discover that certain variables—the number of lace holes on the shoe and the length of lace needed to tie a bow—could be represented in their equation. They also needed to determine what "y" should represent in the equation—the length of shoelaces needed for their shoe.

As I watched the class work, I noticed that many of the groups struggled with getting started. In one group, a boy quickly announced to his group that he didn't "get it," and one of his groupmates agreed, saying, "I don't understand the question." At that point, one of the girls in the group suggested that they reread the question out loud. As they read, one of the boys asked, "How is this shoe connected to that equation?" Another boy suggested that they figure out the length of the lace on the shoe. The group set to work measuring the lace, at which point one of the boys said that they would need to take into account the number of lace holes on the shoe. The group continued working, with different students posing questions for the group to consider.

Before long all of the groups in the class were engaged in solving the problem. Their engagement was due partly to the work of the teacher, who had carefully set up the problem and had circulated around the room asking questions. But it was also because of the "group-worthiness" of the task, which was sufficiently challenging and open to allow different students to contribute their ideas; the multidimensionality of the class, in which students and teachers valued different ways of doing mathematical work, such as asking questions, drawing diagrams, and making conjectures; and the high levels of communication between students who had learned to support one another.

The students at Railside typically worked on problems that could be solved and represented in different ways. They had been encouraged to read problems out loud and to ask one another questions when they were stuck—e.g., What is the problem asking us? How could we rephrase this question? What are the key parts of the problem? The teachers asked students these kinds of questions, and the students, in turn, learned to ask one another the same sorts of helpful questions. Such practices contributed to the high levels of persistence we observed in the classrooms. Many mathematics departments employ group work, but they do not experience the high rates of success from students and the impressive work rate that we witnessed at Railside.

Shared Responsibility

The students at Railside almost always worked in groups and spent a lot of time discussing mathematical ideas and learning to help one another. The teachers were very careful to emphasize that students were responsible for the learning of their peers. They reinforced this message in many ways, including requiring that all group members understood something before the group moved on and giving grades to group discussions. The teachers graded the work of groups by circulating around the room on designated days and recording on an overhead projector notes regarding the quality of group conversations. This sent a clear message to students that mathematical communication—including conjecturing, questioning, voicing, and revising ideas—was important and valued.

Early in our study we interviewed students in their freshman year, and some of the high achievers in the school complained that they were required to spend too much time helping others. In later years, these students had changed their minds, as they learned to appreciate that the act of explaining their work helped deepen their own understanding. As one of the senior girls taking calculus explained:

> I think people look at it as a responsibility. I think it's something they've grown to do, since we've taken so many math classes. So maybe in ninth grade it's like, "Oh my God, I don't feel like helping them; I just want to get my work done. Why do we have to take a group test?" But once you get to AP Calc, you're like, "Ooh, I need a group test before I take a test." So the more math you take and the more you learn, you grow to appreciate it—like, "Oh, thank God I'm in a group!"—*Imelda*

The students also changed their minds about working together because they had developed a greater appreciation of the value different students bring to tasks and had come to realize that all students could offer something in the solving of problems. As the approach to learning became more multidimensional, the students came to regard one another in more multidimensional ways, valuing their peers' different ways of seeing and understanding mathematics. When asked, "What do you think it takes to be successful in math?" Ayana and Estelle, two fourth-year students, replied:

Ayana:	Being able to work with other people.
Estelle:	Being open minded, listening to everybody's ideas.
Ayana:	You have to hear other people's opinions because you might be wrong.
Estelle:	You might be wrong because there's lots of different ways to work everything out.

The students also told to us that through the mathematics approach used at Railside they learned to value all students, regardless of culture, economic class, or gender. Robert and Jon, fourth-year students, made the following observations.

Robert:	I love this school, you know. There are schools that are within a mile of us that are completely different—they're broken up into their race cliques and things like that. And at this school everyone's accepted as a person, and they're not looked at by the color of their skin.
Interviewer:	Does the math approach help that, or is it a whole school influence?
Jon:	The groups in math help to bring kids together.
Robert:	Yeah. When you switch groups that helps you to mingle with more people than if you're just sitting in a set seating chart where you're only exposed to the people that are sitting around you, and you don't know the people on the other side of the room. In math you have to talk, you have to voice if you don't know or voice what you're learning.

The mathematics teachers at Railside valued the principle of equity very highly, but they did not use curriculum materials that were designed specifically to address issues of gender, culture, or class, as some have recommended.[8] Instead, the math teachers taught students to appreciate the different ways that each of them saw mathematics problems, and, as the classrooms became more multidimensional, students learned to appreciate the insights of their peers from different cultures and circumstances.

Block Scheduling

Railside High followed a practice of block scheduling with lessons lasting 90 minutes and courses being taught in half a school year, rather than over a full academic year. An exception was made in order to prioritize the introductory algebra curriculum; it was taught over an entire year—the equivalent of two ordinary courses at Railside. The teachers chose to spread the introductory content over a longer period of time to ensure that the foundational mathematical ideas were taught carefully and that particular norms, such as discussing ideas, exploring different methods, and taking responsibility for others, could be established.

The fact that mathematics courses were only half a year long at Railside may appear unimportant, but that organizational decision had a profound impact on the opportunities for students to take higher-level mathematics classes. In most high schools, mathematics courses are taught over one year, beginning with algebra. This means that students cannot take calculus unless they are advanced, as the typical sequence of courses is algebra, geometry, advanced algebra, and then precalculus. If a student fails a course at any time, he or she is knocked out of that sequence and will have to retake the course, further limiting the level of content that student can reach.

At Railside, the students could take two mathematics courses each year, so even if they failed classes, started at lower levels, or chose not to take mathematics for a particular semester, they could still reach calculus. This scheduling decision, along with the exceptionally high standard of teaching across the department, was one of the reasons that significantly more students at Railside enrolled in advanced classes than did students in the other two schools in our study.

Departmental Collaboration

Railside's mathematics department was highly collaborative, and the teachers reported that the collaboration was critical to their students' high level of achievement.[9] The mathematics teachers at Railside spent many hundreds of hours together planning curriculum, deciding upon group-worthy questions, and sharing pedagogical methods. They met in course teams weekly throughout the school year to share good teaching ideas, and, over several summers, they met as a department for a week of planning.

The collaboration within the Railside mathematics department was critical to the teachers' morale and work. I have often been asked whether individual teachers could use the Railside approach to mathematics with similar success. This is an important and difficult question. I do believe that individual teachers could bring about higher and more equitable achievement with the Railside approach, but the departmental collaboration at Railside was extremely important and enhanced the achievements of the teachers and students.

During the last six years, Railside has had five different principals and has been labeled an underperforming school by the state. The school's scores on the California state tests remained lower than those of the wealthier school in the district, despite Railside students' scoring significantly higher on a districtwide test and on the various assessments we administered as part of our study. There was considerable evidence that the reason the students did not do as well on the state tests was the complex language used on those tests, which erected barriers for the school's English-language learners.[10] The state tests did not do a good job of measuring the mathematical understanding that Railside students had demonstrated on all other tests. The demoralizing label attached to the school because of the state test results did not reflect the positive achievements of the teachers, and it severely threatened their professional morale.

Conclusion

This short article has been able to give no more than a taste of the amazing work of the teachers at Railside.[11] I have not, for example, mentioned the hours that teachers made themselves available to help students, the high expectations they held for all students, and the ways in which they respected the students' personal lives. The features I have highlighted—departmental collaboration, heterogeneous grouping, group-worthy problems, block scheduling, and student responsibility—are those that emerged from our four-year study as critical to the success of the students.

The work of the mathematics teachers at Railside school was important not only because the students achieved good grades, took more mathematics courses, and learned to respect others from different circumstances, but also because they underwent transformative experiences that gave them access to mathematical careers, higher-level jobs, and a more secure financial future. We are now developing video case studies that show the Railside classrooms so that other teachers may learn from the school's success.[12] But I fear that the important lessons that may be learned from Railside school will be too expensive for U.S. policy makers to adopt for widespread use. Moving away from tracked classes and rote procedural approaches will require a long-term, sustained investment in teacher learning, but, if we care about the future of students in urban, multicultural classes, it is an investment that we need to make.[13]

QUESTIONS TO CONSIDER

1. What factors made Railside High School such a success in mathematics instruction? Give examples.

2. What is meant by the concept "complex instruction"? Explain and elaborate.

3. What is meant by "group-worthiness" of the task in teaching and learning? Explain and elaborate.

4. Why and how was "shared responsibility" such an important element in the efficacy of mathematics education at Railside? Give reasons and examples.

5. What do you see as the advantages and disadvantages of "block scheduling," especially in mathematics instruction?

6. Why and how was faculty collaboration so vital to students' achievement at Railside? Explain and elaborate.

Notes

This chapter originally appeared in *Phi Delta Kappan*, Vo. 87, No. 5(January 2006): 364–369.

1. Robert P. Moses and Charles E. Cobb, Jr., *Radical Equations: Math, Literacy, and Civil Rights* (Boston: Beacon Press, 2001).
2. Working with me on the study were Karin Brodie, Jennifer DiBrienza, Nick Fiori, Melissa Gresalfi, Emily Shahan, Megan Staples, and Toby White.
3. Jo Boaler and Megan Staples, "Creating Mathematical Futures Through an Equitable Teaching Approach: The Case of Railside School," *Teachers College Record*, in press. Available at www.stanford.edu/~joboaler.
4. Elizabeth G. Cohen, *Designing Groupwork: Strategies for the Heterogeneous Classroom* (New York: Teachers College Press, 1994); and Elizabeth G. Cohen and Rachel A. Lotan, eds., *Working for Equity in Heterogeneous Classrooms: Sociological Theory in Practice* (New York: Teachers College Press, 1997).

5. Jo Boaler, *Experiencing School Mathematics: Traditional and Reform Approaches to Teaching and Their Impact on Student Learning*, revised and expanded edition (Mahwah, N.J.: Erlbaum, 2002).

6. Jo Boaler and James G. Greeno, "Identity, Agency and Knowing in Mathematics Worlds," in Jo Boaler, ed., *Multiple Perspectives on Mathematics Teaching and Learning* (Westport, Conn.: Ablex Publishing, 2000), pp. 171–200.

7. Tom Sallee et al., *College Preparatory Mathematics* (Sacramento, Calif.: CPM Educational Program, 2000); and Dan Fendel et al., *Interactive Mathematics Program: Integrated High School Mathematics* (Berkeley, Calif.: Key Curriculum Press, 2003).

8. Eric Gutstein et al., "Culturally Relevant Mathematics Teaching in a Mexican American Context," *Journal for Research in Mathematics Education*, December 1997, pp. 709–37.

9. Ilana Seidel Horn, "Learning on the Job: A Situated Account of Teacher Learning in High School Mathematics Departments," *Cognition & Instruction*, vol. 23, 2005, pp. 207–36.

10. Jo Boaler, "When Learning No Longer Matters: Standardized Testing and the Creation of Inequality," *Phi Delta Kappan*, March 2003, pp. 502–6.

11. For a more comprehensive article, see Boaler and Staples, op. cit.

12. Jo Boaler and Cathy Humphreys, *Connecting Mathematical Ideas: Middle School Video Cases to Support Teaching and Learning* (Portsmouth, N.H.: Heinemann, 2005).

13. Deborah Loewenberg Ball and David K. Cohen, "Developing Practice, Developing Practitioners: Toward a Practice-Based Theory of Professional Education," in Gary Sykes and Linda Darling-Hammond, eds., *Teaching as the Learning Profession: Handbook on Policy and Practice* (San Francisco: Jossey-Bass, 1999), pp. 3–32.

CHAPTER TWENTY-SEVEN

Making High School Science Instruction Effective

THOMAS R. KOBALLA, JR. & ABDULKADIR DEMIR

Effective science instruction is not an educational trend. However, the evolution of what is considered to be effective science instruction has benefited from a number of educational trends over the years. Educational trends indicate directions of change and bring focus to what the future may hold for science instruction. Educational trends that have recently and will likely continue to affect the nature of science instruction in American high schools center on what is known about how students learn, the pedagogical and technological innovations that promote student learning, and the changing demographics of the school age population.

In this chapter, we discuss effective science instruction by highlighting the influence of these trends on characteristics of instruction that research indicates play a role in making science instruction effective. Here we use the term *effective science instruction* to mean deliberate teacher actions and interactions that lead to students learning science as a body of knowledge, but more importantly as ways of thinking and investigating. An important goal of effective science instruction is the development of scientifically literate citizens, persons able to use their understandings of science to make informed personal decisions, participate actively in a science-based society, be economically productive, and who pursue a better understanding of science throughout their lives (American Association for the Advancement of Science [AAAS], 1989; National Research Council [NRC], 1996).

The characteristics of effective science instruction that have been and continue to be influenced by educational trends (e.g., NRC, 2000) and, with no claim of completeness, will be the focus of our discussion and include

- motivation
- use of prior knowledge
- intellectual engagement

- use of evidence
- sense-making.

These characteristics of instruction have been identified as linchpins of teacher practice that promote students' science learning (Banilower, Cohen, Parley, & Weiss, 2008). We use a running vignette of a science classroom to provide glimpses of how the characteristics reveal themselves in practice. The focus of the running vignette is Mr. Buford and his high school chemistry students while addressing a section of a unit on the states of matter that highlights behavior of gases. Mr. Buford believes that his students should develop understandings of chemistry that will enable them to be successful in the future, whether the future for them involves further education or not. He is committed to helping his students see chemistry as more than facts and theories, but as a body of knowledge useful to them in their daily lives and as decision makers in a democratic society.

Motivation

Students' learning achievement is influenced by their motivation to engage in the learning task. While student motivation to learn science may be extrinsic, prompted by separate, external outcomes such as grades or the threat of punishment, more desirable is motivation that results from students' inherent interest or enjoyment in the learning task (Koballa & Glynn, 2007). Effective science instruction is organized to enhance students' enthusiasm by means of intrinsic motivational strategies of contextualization, choice, challenge and curiosity. Let's peer into Mr. Buford's chemistry classroom to see what he does to motivate his students.

Mr. Buford began the section of his unit on the states of matter that focuses on gas behavior by showing students copies of a brochure that he obtained from a local car dealership. The brochure makes the claim that "All Drivers Should be Riding on Nitrogen Filled Tires" and includes a number of arguments to support the claim. He told the students that the cost of filling four car tires with nitrogen gas is $29.95. Among the arguments presented in the brochure are the following:

1. Why nitrogen is better than compressed air.
   - Nitrogen is a dry gas free of moisture.
   - Nitrogen doesn't deteriorate rubber like the "wet oxygen" in compressed air does.
   - Nitrogen has a larger molecular structure and won't leak like oxygen.
   - Nitrogen makes tires less susceptible to air loss with temperature change.

2. Why "wet oxygen" in compressed air is harmful.
   - The "wet oxygen" found in compressed air contains moisture.
   - Over time oxidation breaks down tire rubber.
   - Oxygen molecules are smaller than nitrogen and leak 3 to 4 times faster.
   - After rubber is broken down, it loses elasticity, strength, and leaks even more.

(KRESKA TECHNOLOGIES, 2005)

After allowing the students to organize themselves into groups and to study the brochure, he challenged each group to choose one or two arguments to investigate. Mr. Buford recommended that groups investigate certain arguments based on his knowledge of the abilities and talents of group members. He instructed the groups to generate a paragraph for each argument they chose before beginning their investigations using the Internet and other resources available in the classroom. Mr. Buford told his students to include in their paragraphs details about their experiences and understanding related to the arguments presented in the brochure to support the claim.

After giving their paragraphs to Mr. Buford, the students begin talking vigorously about the claim and arguments, conducting Internet searches, and requesting to use lab equipment to test their hunches. Most of the students had recently obtained their driver's license and were solely or partially responsible for the maintenance of the cars they drove.

With 10 minutes left in the class period, Mr. Buford called for the groups to stop their work. Several students responded to his call by saying that that the class period had gone by too quickly and asked if they could continue their investigations of the arguments on their own after school.

Mr. Buford told his students that their study about the behavior of gases over the next several days would help them better understand the arguments offered in the brochure to support the claim and prepare them to make a decision about whether or not to pay to have their car tires filled with nitrogen gas. He also told the students that he would return their paragraphs after they studied about the behavior of gases and allow them to amend their paragraphs before discussing the validity of the arguments in support of the claim as a class.

Mr. Buford's instruction incorporates several intrinsic motivational strategies described in the research literature (Cordova & Lepper, 1996; Malone & Lepper, 1987). The first strategy involves contextualization of the learning task. Rather than presenting the new materials about gas behavior in an abstract and decontextualized form, Mr. Buford chose to couch students' learning about gas behavior in an everyday experience that has practical utility for his students. Investigating gas behavior in the context of the claim and the arguments presented in the brochure created an instructional setting that seemed to appeal to Mr. Buford's students.

Also evident in Mr. Buford's lesson is planning to incorporate the motivational strategy of providing students with a challenge that is closely coordinated with their content understandings and skills. Generating evidence or locating sources of evidence on the Internet that support or refute the arguments found in the brochure can be a daunting task, particularly within 45 minutes. However, when such a challenge is coordinated with students' understandings and skills, as was the case in Mr. Buford's lesson, they may become so involved in the learning task that they lose track of time and become oblivious to other things going on around them. Students' experiences of success when working on a challenging learning task can lead them to try even more challenging tasks and to sustain their intrinsic motivation (Pintrich & Schunk, 1996).

The lesson's context also fed into Mr. Buford's approach for arousing student curiosity. Rather than arousing students' "sensory curiosity" by means of animation and sound effects as often used in computer games and simulations, Mr. Buford set his sights on arousing their "cognitive curiosity" (Malone & Lepper, 1987). He attempted to do this by encouraging students to decide whether they would choose to pay to have their tires filled with nitrogen based on their understandings of gas behavior developed over several days of study.

A fourth intrinsic motivational strategy present in Mr. Buford's lesson is learner choice. He allowed students to form their own working groups, rather than assigning students to groups, and to select the arguments presented in the brochure to investigate. By providing his students with a measure of choice over two aspects of the lesson, Mr. Buford likely contributed to the students' sense of control over their learning. The provision of choice has been shown to contribute to learner enjoyment, persistence, and enhanced performance (Malone & Lepper, 1987). Providing students with choices about their learning, as done by Mr. Buford, can be applied regardless of lesson context to enhance motivation.

Students' intrinsic motivation for school learning is near its lowest point during the high school years (Lepper, Sethi, Dialdin, & Drake, 1997). For this reason motivation should be an important consideration for high school science instruction. The intrinsic motivational strategies of contextualization, choice, challenge, and curiosity should be an integral part of science lesson design and implementation. As Mr. Buford's lesson reveals, incorporating any of these strategies requires considerable thought and prowess as well as knowledge of students and their everyday experiences. Students who are not new drivers with responsibilities for maintaining their vehicles would likely find Mr. Buford's lesson less motivating than his class did. For students without an interest in vehicles and their maintenance, another context for framing their learning about gas behavior would seem appropriate.

Learning environments are being developed and tested that incorporate the intrinsic motivational strategies of contextualization, choice, curiosity, and challenge. More and more of these learning environments are making use of computer technology that incorporates branching options that vary context and challenge and promote cognitive curiosity in order to appeal to diverse[1] student audiences. Investigations of these learning environments indicate that motivating high school students is not easy but offer hope for the design and use of science learning experiences that motivate students and that produce cognitive gains.

Prior Knowledge

While motivation affects students' engagement in a learning task, what students learn from engaging in the task is greatly affected by what they already know (Ausubel, 1960). Research is clear that students come to science class with understandings about most topics studied, and their understandings, whether based on scientific evidence or everyday experience, may enable or impede their learning (Scott, Asoko, & Leach, 2007). For this reason, science teachers need to gather information about students' prior knowledge and use the information to design instruction that builds on this knowledge. The need to gather and use this information is particularly acute for high school, where the difference between school science and everyday explanations of science-related phenomena can be great.

Let's check in on Mr. Buford's chemistry class to learn how he elicits students' prior knowledge and makes use of this information.

> Recall that soon after challenging his students to choose one or two arguments presented in the brochure to investigate, Mr. Buford instructed them to write paragraphs that detailed their personal experiences and understandings related to the arguments. He also told his students that he would return their paragraphs after they studied about the behavior of gases and allow them to amend them.

> That evening Mr. Buford read his students' paragraphs. He knew he would be amused by what some of the students wrote, but his reading was prompted by his interest in discovering their understandings about filling tires with nitrogen gas and using this information to plan lessons to guide their learning about the behavior of gases. Here is one paragraph written by Mr. Buford's students that he found very informative.

The argument our group chose to investigate is "Nitrogen makes tires less susceptible to air loss with temperature change." The argument seems to make sense to us, but we're not totally sure why. On a cold day a tire appears flatter than on a very hot day, according to Ramona. She said she saw this happen with her bicycle tires. We think this is why Joey's dad tells him to check the air in his car tires before they heat up from driving. But we are not sure what causes this to happen, and we are not sure how nitrogen gas is different from air. All this did not make much sense to Alvaro, who recently moved here from South America, as he never had such experiences with bicycle or car tires.

The paragraphs that Mr. Buford collected from his students reveal their ideas and beliefs about the behavior of gases. From the group's paragraph presented in the vignette, we might surmise that Mr. Buford believes that his students would benefit from a review of kinetic theory before engaging in a demonstration that involves immersing an inflated tire tube in buckets of ice water and hot water. This demonstration would allow students to visualize the direct relationship between pressure and temperature at a constant volume, as predicted by Gay-Lussac's Law. To help the students link their developing understanding of Gay-Lussac's Law to the argument, Mr. Buford might also plan to have students in this group use the Internet to learn more about the gases that make up the air and the relative sizes of the gas molecules. He would likely provide differentiated instruction for the other groups to help them develop understandings about gas pressure.

Gathering information about students' personal experiences and understandings related to a science phenomenon at the beginning of a unit is a practice that more and more science teachers are adopting. This practice is based on a growing body of research about students' science-related conceptions that are at odds with those held by members of the scientific community (Bransford, Brown, & Cocking, 1999; Scott et al., 2007). Similar in purpose to a medical examination in determining appropriate treatment, gathering information about students' personal experiences and understandings enables the teacher to effectively design instruction to meet their learning needs.

The recognition that students' conceptions can influence their science learning has led to the use of a number of strategies for gathering this information. For instance, the strategy used by Mr. Buford to reveal his students' prior learning experiences and understandings about the behavior of gases is called memoir writing (Abell & Volkmann, 2006). Other strategies that can be used to gather information about students' ideas and beliefs at the beginning of a unit include concept mapping, brainstorming, interviewing, questionnaires, and card sorting tasks, where students are asked to sort multiple cards with written or pictorial information about confusing science concepts and then describe the reasoning for sorting the cards as they did (Abell & Volkmann, 2006).

A recent U.S. Census Bureau report revealed that 44% of children under the age of 18 and 47% of children under the age of five are now from minority families (CNN Money, 2009). As our school age population becomes more diverse, the job of teaching science so that all students develop meaningful science understandings is indeed a challenging one. To be successful, teachers must recognize how students' backgrounds and needs affect their learning. Recall the memoir written by the group of students and how it revealed that Alvaro's conception of cold and hot temperature was different from that of other group members. Alvero is from Ecuador and lived his entire life in the city of Salina before immigrating to the United States with his family. The city, located on the Santa Elma peninsula, has an average temperature of 23 degrees C or 75 degrees F that fluctuates little during the year. This information about Alvero's background helped Mr. Buford situate this student's prior knowledge of gas behavior.

In this regard, research guided by the science conceptual change tradition has informed the practice of differentiating science instruction to serve the needs of diverse learners. We see evidence of differentiated instruction in Mr. Buford's effort to help the group link their developing understandings of Gay-Lussac's Law to the argument they chose to investigate. Carol Tomlinson and Jay McTighe (2006) identify the elements of time, space, resources, student grouping, instructional strategies, learning strategies, and teacher partnerships as classroom variables that teachers can manipulate on a daily basis. Using information about students' prior knowledge, these classroom variables can be manipulated to achieve desired student learning outcomes. Enabling the practice of differentiating science instruction based on students' ideas and beliefs are the science literacy maps created by the National Science Digital Library (NSDL) (http://strandmaps.nsdl.org). Based on strand maps published in the *Atlas of Science Literacy*, volumes 1 and 2 (AAAS, 2001; 2007), these online resources can be used by teachers to consider how a unit's learning goals are related to students' prior and future learning experiences.

Destined to sharpen the practice of using students' prior knowledge to plan instruction are investigations of science learning progressions. "Learning progressions are descriptions of the successively more sophisticated ways of thinking about a topic that can follow one another as children learn about and investigate a topic over a broad span of time" (Duschl, Schweingruber, & Shouse, 2007, p. 219). As a result of the generation of models of learning progression around such core ideas of modern science as atomic-molecular theory and evolution, teachers of the future will be better able to make use of available instructional resources to guide the development of students' science understandings.

Intellectual Engagement

Intellectual engagement is more than students being on-task or attentive to the actions of the teacher. When intellectually engaged, students are interested in the topic under study and intentionally strive to learn (Banilower et al., 2008). Students need to be intellectually engaged in order to learn science with understanding (Anderson & Lee, 1997). The understandings that students construct or reconstruct when intellectually engaged enable them to do something with the knowledge they possess. They can solve problems, recognize relationships between what they are learning and already know, share their knowledge with others, and even create new understandings for themselves (Killen, 2003). Intellectual engagement in science activities may also lead to students wanting to learn more science.

Teachers are key to the intellectual engagement of their students. They must consider the intellectual demands and goals of the learning task as well as the instructional strategies and teaching techniques that they use to promote students' science learning. Let's see how Mr. Buford facilitates the intellectual engagement of students in his chemistry class.

Mr. Buford started the lesson by reminding students of the tire store advertisement and that today's lesson would bring them closer to deciding if inflating tires with nitrogen was worth the cost. He then showed them a tire tube from a wheelbarrow and two buckets of water—one at 10 degrees C and the other at 30 degrees C. He instructed students to use a tire pressure gauge to measure the pressure exerted by the air inside the tire and to verify the temperature of the water inside the buckets using thermometers.

Mr. Buford then asked his students, "What will happen to the pressure inside the tire tube when it is placed in the two buckets of water? And, how will you know?" He waited for students to write down their predictions before continuing.

After seeing and touching the tire tube when it was removed from the two buckets of water and measuring the pressure with the tire pressure gauge, the students began to talk among themselves and to Mr. Buford.

Mike addressed the class first, "The tube seemed to get smaller when it was put in the cold water, and got bigger when put in the hot water. That's what I predicted."

Jennifer added, "Yea, there seems to be a relationship between temperature and pressure. When the temperature was lower, the pressure got lower; but when the temperature was higher, the pressure got higher."

Other students began to offer related comments, with some referencing their tire pressure gauge measurements and linking their observations to kinetic theory. One student showed a chart that she created comparing tire pressure at different temperatures.

"OK," said Mr. Buford, "How can we describe what Mike, Jennifer, and others have talked about mathematically? Think about Charles's Law and how it provides us with an expression of the relationship between gas volume and temperature."

Mr. Buford walked about the room listening in on students' conversations. As their discussions warranted, he encouraged groups to read sections in their textbook about Gay-Lussac's Law and the Combined Gas Law. After about 15 minutes, Mr. Buford asked students to write the mathematical relationships for Gay-Lussac's Law ($P1/T1 = P2/T2$) and the Combined Gas Law ($P1 \times V1/T1 = P2 \times V2/T2$) on the whiteboard, to calculate an unknown pressure or temperature when other variables are given, and to explain their answers.

Mr. Buford concluded the day's lesson by telling students that the tire inflation values that are printed in vehicle glove boxes and door panels are industrial standards called "Cold Inflation Pressures"(CIP) that are measured at 18 degrees C (65 degrees F). He gave students an article that describes sensors placed inside truck tires to monitor both tire pressure and temperature and to provide temperature compensated pressure values, calculated based on CIP. Mr. Buford asked students to read the article for homework and to come to the next day's class prepared to discuss the value of the device to long-haul trucking companies that frequently suffered losses due to blow-outs and tire fire as a result of improper tire inflation.

Mr. Buford's lesson incorporates several of the instructional strategies and teaching techniques that research suggests promote students' intellectual engagement. First, Mr. Buford engaged his students with real science content, not just materials (Banilower et al., 2008). He provided his students with a reason for immersing the tire tube in the buckets of water and collecting measurements of tire pressure and water temperature. The demonstration served to provide his students with physical experiences around which to build understandings about the relationship between gas pressure and temperature.

Second, Mr. Buford prompted students to think carefully about the demonstration through the conceptually challenging questions he asked. His initial questions encouraged students to make predictions and to consider the understandings on which their predictions were based, while questions he asked later in the lesson encouraged students to express the relationship between gas pressure and temperature mathematically. His questioning approach prompted students to work collaboratively, question one another's thinking, and to build consensus around plausible answers. These are student interaction patterns that research suggestions facilitate learning (Prather, Slater, Adams, Bailey, Jones, & Dostal, 2004).

Third, Mr. Buford made explicit the purpose of the lesson and its link to learning goals. Specifically, he talked to his students about the potential of the day's lesson to aid their quest to address arguments related to the claim made in the brochure that drivers should be riding on nitrogen-filled tires. Supporting this learning goal, his instruction led students to construct understandings about the relationships between gas pressure, volume, and temperature, as hypothesized by Lussac's Law and the Combined Gas Law. Mr. Buford's homework assignment functioned to extend students' understandings about the behavior of gases to the practical application of sensors placed inside truck tires to monitor tire pressure and temperature.

As an alternative or follow-up to the demonstration, Mr. Buford could have presented them with a series of drawings that show a tire tube being immersed in water of different temperatures and asked them to order the drawings from highest to lowest pressure. Ranking tasks of this kind, that present slightly different variations of a physical system, have been found to enhance students' intellectual engagement (Hudgins, Prather, Grayson, & Smits, 2006).

In his lesson, Mr. Buford sought to promote a learner-centered environment by having students and their thinking become the centerpiece of the learning experience. It is clear that his students are not passive recipients of knowledge but engaged in purposeful intellectual work that centers on important science content. Mr. Buford structured his lesson to enable his students to learn how to think about the behavior of gases as a community of scientists might do, using Gay-Lussac's Law and the Combined Gas Law, and to apply their understandings to the practical concerns of vehicle maintenance, thus bridging the cultures of science and everyday experience.

Use of Evidence

Evidence lies at the heart of all sciences. It is the reliance on evidence that serves to distinguish science from pseudoscience, dogma, popular opinion, and tradition (Popper, 1963). Science as the evidence-based pursuit of knowledge is rooted in the work of Aristotle (Arya, Wolford, & Harken, 2002). Arya et al. argue that Aristotle was the first who "created the discipline of science by insisting on a rigorous delineation of evidence and logic for the use of evidence to create theory" (p. 1302). Since the time of Aristotle, scientists have actively sought confirmation of their ideas via evidence. They do this through the use of tests, observations, and discourse with peers, which lead to the development of mechanistic explanations for phenomena.

There is much that science teachers can do to help their students develop an understanding of science as a series of conceptual structures that should be constantly revised in the light of new information or evidence (Schwab, 1966). Central to students developing this understanding is their seeing science as a social process of knowledge construction, rather than a rhetoric of conclusions (Atkins, 2008). In classrooms that emphasize the social processes of science, evidence serves as the grounds on which scientific claims are endorsed or rejected. Let's glance into Mr. Buford's classroom to see how evidence is used to support his students' science learning.

To further his students' understanding about the behavior of gases, Mr. Buford engaged them with a computer simulation. The simulation presented a cylindrical container fitted with a frictionless, weightless piston with a burner positioned below the container, allowing for the manipulation of volume, pressure, and temperature. For today's class, Mr. Buford wanted his students to explore the relationship between gas temperature and pressure, while keeping volume constant.

After allowing the students to familiarize themselves with the functions of the simulation working in groups of three for several minutes, he posed a problem for them to investigate.

The gas left in a spent hair spray can is at a pressure of 100 kPa at 20 degrees C. If the can is placed in the following conditions, what is the pressure of the gas inside the can?

Conditions	Pressures
Freezer at ⁻10 degree C	
Oven at 100 degrees C	
Incinerator at 1000 degrees C	

Mr. Buford then instructed his students to use the simulation to replicate the conditions of the spent hair spray can, determining the actual pressures and considering the condition of the can at the new pressures. He reminded his students to remember to express temperatures using the Kelvin scale.

With 30 minutes left in the period, Mr. Buford called on groups to report their results. Not all the groups reported the same results, leading to some students becoming frustrated and one group saying that they failed to meet Mr. Buford's expectations. Jason expressed his frustration by yelling at his classmates, while Carry asked Mr. Buford if her group could rerun the simulation for the three conditions. Carry's group reported a higher pressure for the freezer condition than for the incinerator.

Mr. Buford assured his class that it was OK that all groups didn't end up with the same results. He encouraged them to examine the evidence of their work available through the tracking function of the computer simulation. Mr. Buford asked the students to examine every step they had taken while working on the problem, recording the values and units entered for each of the conditions investigated. "You always have results. They may not be the ones you wanted and they may not make sense to you at the time, but they are still your results," he stated.

As discussion of the results continued, group members conjectured as to what may have led to their results being different from results reported by other groups. In addition, classmates used the evidence of their own work to ask questions and discuss the condition of the spent hair spray can under the three conditions presented in the problem and other conditions. Students became very animated when the discussion turned to the conditions under which a spent hair spray can would explode. Mr. Buford was particularly pleased by the question asked by Alvaro toward the end of the discussion, "How hot might a car tire have to get before it will explode if the tire's Cold Inflation Pressure is 32 PSI?" He recognized his question as providing a bridge between the classes' discussion and the arguments about filling tires with nitrogen presented in the brochure.

With evidence as the centerpiece of the learning experience, students can engage in sophisticated scientific practices and develop deep understandings of appropriate science concepts (Metz, 1995; Lehrer, Carpenter, Schauble, & Putz, 2000). This emphasis on evidence can be distilled throughout the *essential features* of inquiry (NRC, 2000): asking and answering scientific questions, constructing explanations using evidence to support claims, and communicating and justifying findings. According to Minstrell (2000), an inquiry is complete when "we should know something we did not know before we started. Even when our investigation fails to find the answer, at least the inquiry should have yielded a greater understanding of factors that are involved in the solution" (p. 473). Mr. Buford's classroom was a place where students can use mistakes as learning tools as opposed to constantly regarding mistakes as "bad." This perspective of teaching prompts a higher degree of trust between students and teacher. This rapport encouraged his students to do more exploring and questioning. What Minstrell considered as inquiry was the case in Mr. Buford's classroom. The students were not deterred by results not considered correct. They continued to question, request, and seek additional evidence, and develop new understandings.

Issues of diversity are oftentimes unacknowledged in science classes. However, Mr. Buford adopted a pedagogy that welcomes diversity by promoting a trusting and respectful learning environment where all kinds of evidence are considered and their value assessed. Students in Mr. Buford's class were given the opportunity to interact with data and to determine if the data could serve as evidence in support of their developing science understandings. Through his efforts, Mr. Buford's students developed a new view of science learning in which asking questions and figuring out ways to find answers are more important than knowing the right answers. Students learned as much from their mistakes as from anything else during this experience. They became more attentive to the value of evidence to endorse and refute claims and the implications that evidence might have for further studies. It allowed them to view exploration and scientific knowledge as a process rather than an end result.

Sense Making

Sense making is a process by which people use their understandings to explain surprises in their environment (Lewis, 1980). According to Karl Weick (1995), sense making is triggered by noticing discrepant cues in light of past experiences and results in plausible speculation about cues and their rarity. More specifically, scientific sense making highlights real world observations and measurements and the theories and models used to explain them (Newman, Crowder, & Torzs, 1993). Because sense making is a social activity, classroom talk reveals much about students' sense making in science. Studies of students' scientific sense making makes clear that context and past experiences affect what students extract as cues from lessons and the understandings they construct (Warren, Puttick, Conant, & Rosebery, 1992). Let's see how Mr. Buford promotes scientific sense making with his class.

> To conclude the segment of his unit on the states of matter that focused on gas behavior, Mr. Buford chose to return to the claim about filling tires with nitrogen, as he promised his students. Mr. Buford handed back to students the paragraphs that they had written immediately after examining copies of the brochure he had

obtained from the car dealership. He was very aware that the lessons in which he engaged his students about the behavior of gases would enable them respond to some, but not all, of the arguments included in the brochure. Mr. Buford wanted to see if and how his students would apply their new knowledge to address the arguments.

After allowing students 15 minutes to reread the paragraphs and discuss with classmates about what they had written, Mr. Buford asked for volunteers to talk about how what they had learned about the behavior of gases was helpful in moving them closer to making a scientifically informed decision about purchasing nitrogen for their car tires.

Michelle initiated the class discussion, "Steve, Bev, and I looked into the argument that nitrogen makes tires less susceptible to air loss when the temperature changes. From learning about the Ideal Gas Law and the other gas laws, we now know that temperature and pressure are related. When temperature goes up, pressure also goes up."

Bev added, "So, the argument seems misleading. We wondered if what is being called air loss is really something having to do with lower pressure due to colder temperatures.

"Bev is right," interjected Michelle, "We need to know more about the situation, you know, temperature and pressure in the tire, and maybe how nitrogen compares with air before we are convinced by this argument to fill our tires with nitrogen."

Other students began to speak up about how their new knowledge about the behavior of gases served to inform their thinking about the claim that all drivers should be riding on nitrogen-filled tires. For example, Jeff, Jamie, and Sam talked about how articles they found on the Internet did not answer their questions about the size of nitrogen and oxygen molecules and which would leak faster, but led them to conduct an experiment that they hoped would. Their experiment involved filling balloons with nitrogen, oxygen, and compressed air, obtained from a commercial gas supplier, and weighing the balloons every day for two weeks. Another group conducted the same experiment, but with contradictory results. This prompted the two groups, and other students, to ask questions about their experimental methods.

Internet exploration and telephone interviews of area garage owners by Ramona's group promoted her to confidently proclaim to the class, "Hey y'all, air is about 80 percent nitrogen. So, when you put air in your tires, you're putting in mostly nitrogen, anyway. I think I'll hold on to my money!"

As Mr. Buford encouraged more students to share their thoughts, he captured the highpoints of the discussion in his notebook. He wanted to use the students' developing understandings as building blocks in future chemistry lessons.

There is much that teachers can do to promote students' scientific sense making. Primary to their actions is establishing a classroom environment that encourages students to engage in sense-making conversations about scientific phenomena and science-related issues, in ways characteristic of a community of scientists. Students' sense-making conversations may include such moves as reframing a question, offering an explanation, rebuffing an explanation by presenting disconfirming data, or arguing that measurements are flawed (Newman et al., 1993). We see evidence of some of these sense-making moves in Mr. Buford's class.

Facilitating sense-making moves of these kinds by students are teachers' questions and the discourse patterns that they encourage in their classrooms (Michaels, Shouse, & Schweingruber, 2008). Mr. Buford asked his students to apply their developing understandings of the behavior of gases to arguments presented in the brochure about filling tires with nitrogen. The classroom environment that Mr. Buford established for his students also encouraged students to make predictions, draw relationships, relate cause and effect, and draw conclusions. For example, when reading their earlier written paragraphs and talking with classmates about what they wrote, students recognized that they had developed understandings about the behavior of gases that could help address some arguments in the brochure, but that there was also more that they needed to know. The students' conversations indicate that they were reflecting on and, in cases, applying their new knowledge to a situation about which they earlier had little understanding. Providing students with novel situations and encouraging them to apply ideas with which they have been engaged is a hallmark of teacher practice shown to promote sense making (Banilower et al., 2008).

Recent research highlights the need for science teachers to recognize that sense making is heavily dependent on students' culture and socialization (Barton, 2007). Rather than viewing the social, cognitive, and language practices of linguistic and ethnic minority groups as barriers to scientific sense making, emerging thinking suggests that there is considerable continuity between everyday and scientific ways of dialog and understanding that should be leveraged in the course of science instruction (Warren, Ballenger, Ogonowski, Rosebery, & Hudicourt-Barnes, 2001). In response to changing demographics of the school age population, science teachers must strive to better understand the diversity of students' sense making practices, particularly the practices of students from traditionally marginalized groups. Improved understandings will enable teachers to establish classroom learning communities that build on students' everyday modes of communication to support their learning "to explain the world around them scientifically" (Warren et al., 2001, p. 548).

Conclusion

What is considered effective science instruction is constantly changing. Emerging understandings about how students learn, innovations, especially those involving technology that promote student learning, and the changing demographics of the school age population have been and will continue to influence the nature of science instruction. In this chapter, we discussed five characteristics of science instruction that support student learning. Our discussion of these characteristics is based on findings and practices primarily associated with two research traditions.

The first is the conceptual change tradition, where learners are portrayed as naïve thinkers and learning as conceptual change. We see evidence of this tradition in the practice of eliciting students' misconceptions, tools used to gather this information, and the strategies used to differentiate instruction based on students' science understandings. These practices continue to hold great promise for helping students develop understandings of science that reflect those of scientists.

The second is the sociocultural tradition; it brings attention to the culture and language of learners interacting as members of a community of practice. We see evidence of this tradition in the emphasis given to students' language and group participation in scientific sense making, as well as in students' use of tools familiar to scientific communities to promote their intellectual engagement in science learning experiences. Linking this tradition to effective science instruction are the teacher's ever-improving instructional practices that promote student intellectual engagement and sense making as well as students' capacity to obtain and appraise scientific evidence in the context of social norms of language and cultural values (Moje, Collazo, Carillo, & Marx, 2001).

What is considered effective science instruction has been least influenced by the critical research tradition. The focus of this research tradition is on how students who are not members of dominant cultural groups have been disadvantaged or marginalized in the current system of science education (Anderson, 2007). The influence of this tradition on science instruction is beginning to be seen in the increasing attention given to students' everyday sense making as a bridge to scientific sense making as well as in the enhanced awareness given to evidence provided by multiple data sources, which can empower students to distinguish "fair-minded" knowledge from that which is not (Barton & Yang, 2000). The critical research tradition seems to have great potential to inform how science instruction will serve the needs of diverse student populations in the future.

Like these traditions, recent research on learner motivation has benefited from a constructivist view of learning. The research makes clear that students' motivation should be taken into account in explanations of science learning and that there are a number of means available to science teachers to pique students' intrinsic motivation for learning science (Koballa & Glynn, 2007).

New understandings emerging from these research arenas will further change what is considered effective science instruction. As educators, we must be attuned to the influences that affect the instructional process and consider how emerging understandings can be applied to ensure that all students have access to a quality science education.

QUESTIONS TO CONSIDER

1. Motivation
   Determine whether science instruction is organized to enhance students' enthusiasm by means of intrinsic motivational strategies.
   a. Is the context of a science lesson used to focus student attention on what needs to be learned?
   b. Are students ready to learn the material being studied?
   c. Are there any incentives that are likely to motivate students?
   d. Does the science lesson provide a context that would cultivate student curiosity?

2. Use of prior knowledge
   Determine whether a set of assessment techniques can be used to gather information about students' ideas and beliefs about the topic at the beginning of a science lesson, e.g., concept mapping, brainstorming, interviewing, memoir writing, etc.
   a. What do the students already know or think they know about a science topic?
   b. What essential information or skills do students need before they engage in a science lesson?

    c.   What misconceptions might students have about a science topic?

3. Intellectual engagement
Determine whether there is a hook for the science lesson that encourages students to take responsibility for their own learning.
    a.   Are students being encouraged to raise questions about the material being studied?
    b.   Are questions posed in the science lesson relevant to students?
    c.   Does the science lesson provide students with a context to generate, refine, and focus questions for investigation?

4. Use of evidence
Determine whether students are giving priority to evidence in responding to questions raised during the science lesson.
    a.   Are students encouraged to use their senses and instruments to collect evidence?
    b.   Do students have opportunities to decide what data to collect or how to collect it?

5. Sense-making
Determine whether students are bridging context and past experiences as they construct explanations using evidence as the basis for their explanations.
    a.   Are students encouraged to generate explanations from evidence?
    b.   Are students asked to explain their reasoning?
    c.   Do students compare explanations based on how well they account for the evidence?
    d.   Are students encouraged and asked to revise their explanations in light of evidence?

Note

Throughout this chapter, the terms *diverse* and *diversity* are used with reference to students who are from different race/ethnic, language, culture, divergent perspectives and socioeconomic status, including girls and students with special needs.

References

Abell, S. K., & Volkmann, M. J. (2006). *Seamless assessment in science: A guide for elementary and middle school teachers.* Portsmouth, NH: Heinemann.

American Association for the Advancement of Science. (1989). *Science for all Americans.* Washington, DC: Author.

American Association for the Advancement of Science. (2001). *Atlas of scientific literacy.* Washington, DC: Author.

American Association for the Advancement of Science. (2007). *Atlas of scientific literacy,* Volume 2. Washington, DC: Author.

Anderson, C. W. (2007). Perspectives on science learning. In S. K. Abell & N. Lederman (Eds.), *Handbook for research in science education* (pp. 3–30). Mahwah, NJ: Erlbaum.

Anderson, C. W., & Lee, O. (1997). Will students take advantage of opportunities for meaningful learning? *Phi Delta Kappan, 78,* 720–724.

Arya, J., Wolford, H., & Harken, A. H. (2002). Evidence-based science: A worthwhile mode of surgical inquiry. *Archive of Surgery, 137,* 1301–1303.

Atkins, L. J. (2008). *The role of evidence in scientific argument*. In C. Henderson, M. Sabella, & L. Hsu (Eds.), Physics education research conference. College Park, MD: American Physics Institute.

Ausubel, D. P. (1960). The use of advance organizers in the learning and retention of meaningful verbal materials. *Journal of Educational Psychology, 51*, 267–272.

Banilower, E. Cohen, K., Parley, J., & Weiss, I. (2008). *Effective science instruction: What does research tell us?* Portsmouth, NH: RMC Research Corporation, Center on Instruction.

Barton, A. C. (2007). Science learning in urban settings. In S. K. Abell and N. Lederman (Eds.), *Handbook for research in science education* (pp. 319–343). Mahwah, NJ: Erlbaum.

Barton, A. C., & Yang, K. (2000). The culture of power and science education: Learning from Miguel. *Journal of Research in Science Teaching, 37*, 871–889.

Bransford, J. D., Brown, A. L., & Cocking, R. R. (Eds.) (1999). *How people learn: Brain, mind, experience, and school*. Washington, DC: National Academy Press.

CNN Money. (2009). Census: U. S. becoming more diverse. Retrieved May 19, 2009 from http://cnnmoney.mobi/money/archieve/archive/detail/146012/full:isessionid=6EA657BA498D144AE090FD2638FB1AA8.

Cordova, D. I., & Lepper, M. R. (1996). Intrinsic motivation and the process of learning: Beneficial effects on contextualization, personalization, and choice. *Journal of Educational Psychology, 88*, 715–730.

Duschl, R. A., Schweingruber, H. A., & Shouse, A. W. (2007). *Taking science to school: Learning and teaching science in grades K-8*. Washington, DC: National Research Council.

Hudgins, D. W., Prather, E. E. Grayson, D. J., & Smits, D. P. (2006). The effectiveness of collaborative ranking tasks on student understanding of key astronomy concepts. *Astronomy Education Review, 5*, 1–22.

Killen. R. (2003). *Effective teaching strategies: Lessons from research and practice* (3rd ed.). Tuggerah, Australia: Social Science Press.

Koballa, T. R., & Glynn, S. M. (2007). Attitudinal and motivational constructs in science learning. In S. K. Abell & N. Lederman (Eds.), *Handbook for research in science education* (pp. 75–102). Mahwah, NJ: Erlbaum.

Kreska Technologies. (2005). *NitroFill: What NitroFill could save you is tough to put a price on*. Pompano Beach, FL: Author.

Lehrer, R., Carpenter, S., Schauble, L., & Putz, A. (2000). Designing classrooms that support inquiry. In J. Minstrell & E. Van Zee (Eds.), *Inquiring into inquiry learning and teaching in science*. Washington, DC: American Association for the Advancement of Science.

Lepper, M. R., Sethi, S., Dialdin, D., & Drake, M. (1997). Intrinsic and extrinsic motivation: A developmental perspective. In S. S. Luthar, J. Burack, D. Cicchetti, & J. Weisz (Eds.), *Developmental psychopathology: Perspectives on adjustment risk and disorder* (pp. 23–50). New York: Cambridge University Press.

Lewis, M. R. (1980). Surprise and sense making: What newcomers experience in entering unfamiliar organizational settings. *Administrative Science Quarterly, 25*, 226–251.

Malone, T. W., & Lepper, M. R. (1987). Making learning fun. In R. E. Snow & J. F. Marshall (Eds.), *Aptitude, learning and instruction, Vol. 4: Conative and affective process analysis* (pp. 223–253). Hillsdale, NJ: Erlbaum.

Metz, K. (1995). Reassessment of developmental constraints on children's science instruction. *Review of Educational Research, 65*(2), 93–127.

Michaels, S., Shouse, A. W., & Schweingruber, H. A. (2008). *Ready, set, science!* Washington, DC: National Academy Press.

Minstrell, J. (2000). Implications for teaching and learning inquiry: A summary. In J. Minstrell & E. van Zee (Eds.), *Inquiring into inquiry learning and teaching in science* (pp. 471–496). Washington, DC: American Association for the Advancement of Science.

Moje, E., Collazo, T., Carillo, R., & Marx, R. W. (2001). "Maestro, what is quality?" Examining competing discourses in project-based science. *Journal of Research in Science Teaching, 38*, 469–495.

National Research Council. (1996). *National science education standards*. Washington, DC: National Academy Press.

National Research Council. (2000). *Inquiry and the national science education standards*. Washington, DC: National Academy Press.

Newman, D., Crowder, E. M., & Torzs, F. (1993). The world in the classroom: Sense-making and seasonal change. *Interactive Learning Environments, 3*, 1–16.

Pintrich, P. R., & Schunk, D. H. (1996). *Motivation in education: Theory, research, and applications.* Columbus, OH: Merrill.

Popper, K. (1963). *Conjectures and refutations.* London: Routledge and Kegan Paul.

Prather, E. E., Slater, T. F., Adams, J. P., Bailey, J. M., Jones, L. V., & Dostal, J. A. (2004). Research on a lecture-tutorial approach to teaching introductory astronomy non-science majors. *Astronomy Education Review, 3*(2), 122–136.

Schwab, J. (1966). *The teaching of science.* Cambridge, MA: Harvard University Press.

Scott, P., Asoko, H., & Leach, J. (2007). Student conceptions and conceptual learning in science. In S. K. Abell & N. G. Lederman (Eds.), *Handbook of research in science education* (pp. 31–56). Mahwah, NJ: Erlbaum.

Tomlinson, C., & McTighe, J. (2006). *Integrating differentiated instruction and understanding by design.* Alexandria, VA: Association for Supervision and Curriculum Development.

Warren, B., Ballenger, C., Ogonowski, M., Rosebery, A., & Hudicourt-Barnes, J. (2001). Rethinking diversity in learning science: the logic of everyday sense making. *Journal of Research in Science Teaching, 38*, 529–552.

Warren, E. A. Puttick, G., Conant, F., & Rosebery, A. (1992). Sense-making practices in science: Case study of an ESL teacher. *Hands On! 15*(2), 4–19.

Weick, K. (1995). *Sensemaking in organizations.* Thousand Oaks, CA: Sage.

CHAPTER TWENTY-EIGHT

Teaching About Global Warming in Truck Country

JANA DEAN

"**M**s. Dean, are you trying to tell me I can't drive a truck?"

Alex,[1] an eighth grader, leaned back until he was perched on two chair legs, his arms crossed defiantly. It was the end of a class period, the second day of our class's study of climate change. I knew Alex expected he'd someday drive a big truck like his father.

"Not necessarily," I answered, "but together we are going learn enough science to understand global warming. Then we'll do something about it."

Global warming is a subject most of us don't like to think about. Worst case scenario: Ocean currents come to a rolling stop, resulting in a domino effect of chain reactions and a climate unlike anything in the collective memory of humanity. In other words, the ecosystem as we know it is a goner, and it isn't going to be pretty. Among the predictions are wars over water and total economic and social collapse.

What's creating this change? Measurable increases in gases such as methane and carbon dioxide that absorb and hold heat radiating from the surface of the earth. What's worse, the global thermal balance that drives ocean currents reacts gradually. We've only begun to see the impact of changes that occurred in the atmosphere years ago. We may not feel the real global impact of atmospheric change until it's too late.

In the unit I taught, I wanted my students to understand the physics and chemistry that explain the anthropogenic (human-produced) causes of climate change. I also hoped my students would reflect on their own lives and consider how their own behavior could change to become more "climate friendly." I entertained the possibility of a broader political response, but accepted at the outset that I might not have time to build enough background in global economics and trade to expose the politics behind global inaction as the earth heats up. As a science teacher operating within the constraints of a bell schedule, I decided to prioritize the science.

And I had another motive, which was embedded in my answer to Alex's challenge two days into our study: Together we would do something about global warming. I wanted my students to join together to create change. For them, uniting across socioeconomic, racial, and political differences can be uncomfortable territory. Yet that's just what needs to happen as humanity faces a global environmental crisis.

I teach in a public middle school on the edge of Washington State's capital city. While mostly white, my students are socioeconomically diverse. To the north, Tumwater's middle- and working-class neighborhoods of houses and apartments merge with the city of Olympia. To the south, junkyards and machine shops set among small industry and warehouses gradually fade into a rural mix of wood lots, farms, subdivisions, and trailer parks. Many students spend an hour on the bus getting to school in the morning. The homes they leave behind range from upscale new houses to trailer parks in some of the most under-served neighborhoods in the county. Our community offers few private schools, and the district has only two middle schools, both of which serve a similar mix of suburban and rural areas: We get the wealthy students along with the poor.

When I first moved here in 1989, logging trucks still rumbled in from the surrounding forests to dump logs by the millions at our port. Many of those trees were hauled out of the woods by the relatives of my students. Even though the economy has changed, a rural cultural relationship to the land remains intact. Most families still have plenty of practical uses for a truck. They cut and haul firewood. They pull stumps. They keep livestock. Even many families that don't actively use a truck for work choose to drive one because on weekends they haul and hunt. I teach in truck country. As the daughter of a gas station owner, I have many stories about trucks and a father who always smelled of grease and gasoline. I learned to drive my father's Ford when I was still too small to shift it without using both hands. Many of my students and I have truck culture in common.

Jimmy comes to school a few times a month hobbled after trying to lift "a tranny with guts in it." Kylie drives her quad ATV into ditches. Justin stays home some school days to help his dad with the fifth-wheel trailer. I figured our knowledge of fossil-fuel-powered internal combustion engines would support us in understanding the causes of global warming.

But when Alex first crossed his arms, I began to realize that indicting our beloved motors for global warming before building a ton of background would be like petting a cat in the wrong direction. At the same time, it was a sign that I was going in the right direction: Change doesn't happen without resistance. As auto-dependent rural people, we love the ease, convenience, and speed of the open road. My up-front commitment to action had activated in my students a fear of losing a way of life they'd been raised to inherit. Alex's statement, echoed by many of his classmates—yeah, what about my quad, my motorcycle?—worried me, and I had to talk myself into pushing past the resistance. But I would have to proceed carefully since fearful people have a hard time thinking critically.

Carbon Dioxide Would Have to Wait

I decided to carefully sidestep any mention of the causes of global warming until we thoroughly understood the effects.

To get a handle on the effects, we did two projects using a curriculum developed by the Union of Concerned Scientists. (See Resources.) The first involved following links on a world map to learn about scientifically proven signs of rising temperatures. The map is based on measurable data and climate models that predict increased flooding, drought, heat waves, and wild fires, along with more catastrophic weather events. The second had students studying the transmission cycle of tropical diseases and their vectors.

We learned that changes in climate are severely affecting the polar regions. In many parts of the Arctic, sea ice has decreased by 50 percent or more. For the first time, scientists have observed open water at the North Pole. The population of penguins in the Antarctic has declined by one third. Large sinkholes have developed in Alaska as permafrost melts and the ground collapses. Glacial ice in Olympic National Park will be gone by 2070 if it continues to melt at the current rate. In tropical Africa, rising temperatures and rainfall have both increased the range, severity, and frequency of tropical diseases such as malaria and schistosomiasis.

I asked students to write about what concerned them most about global warming. As they shared aloud, I wrote down their worries on poster paper hung at the front of the class. The mood was somber. My students sat so still and silent we could hear each other swallow.

I learned that Ryan, who lives for hunting season, worried about elk that will suffer from diminishing alpine environments. Brandon loves penguins and lamented the loss of sea ice. Other students cited enormous wild fires attributable to warmer and drier trends in some parts of the world. Many of them felt deep concern about the spread of malaria and other tropical diseases.

Whenever I bring my students' awareness to big problems, I worry I will overwhelm them and short-circuit their potential for critical thinking. I knew that we'd be more likely to be able to push through to more learning if we took the time to talk about how we feel: Acknowledging feelings opens the way for clear thinking. Otherwise emotions and thoughts get muddled up in each other. But in my experience, asking eighth graders to name their feelings can be like trying to get a stone to talk.

I asked the class, "How many of you have ever had a time when things were going wrong and you felt there was nothing you could do about it?" Nearly every hand went up. "Turn to your partner and tell them the story you're thinking of. If you don't have one yet, go second." The room hummed with the noise of storytelling.

After five minutes of talking, I directed everyone to write down the incidents they had shared, and then we read to the class what we had written. Jimmy wrote, "On Sunday night I was walking a friend home. Right as we walked in her driveway the cops had their spotlight on us. I got a ride back to my cousin's house in a cop car. It sucked." Kylie described being stuck in a ditch on her quad and not being able to get out. Julie read about being lost on a city bus. Warren read about moving: "I feel overwhelmed every time I have to move from house to house." Our stories helped us to see that when faced with an out of control situation—like global warming—we will feel angry, overwhelmed, stuck, confused, trapped, and scared.

I told my students, "As we continue to learn about global warming, expect to feel all of those feelings. We'll be learning and feeling together. In many of your stories you were alone. In the global warming story, we'll have each other."

Arctic Meltdown

I thought that by then we might have been ready to look again at the causes of climate change. *Arctic Meltdown, Rising Seas* (See Resources.) features stories and interviews of indigenous people in Alaska and in the Marshall Islands who are suffering as ice melts and sea levels rise.

Before showing the video, I asked students to listen carefully to the narrative for "Changes on the Ice" and "Changes on the Beach" and to take notes.

The video opens with footage of people in Alaska meeting with a scientist: "Polar bears are thin and hungry. Walruses are fewer and fewer every year, and we depend on them for our food."

The video continues with interviews of a family from the Marshall Islands who almost lost a baby in a rogue wave that swept in at high tide. With that story, feelings ran high. The class was silent. Interviews with Marshallese scientists reveal that erosion due to higher sea levels is taking away their land and their way of life. The film then bombards us with a message about our cars, our trucks, our factories, our consumption.

As he put his notebook away, Ron slammed it shut and said: "I don't get it. What are we gonna do? Stop driving?" Consternation ran through the class. "What about my quad . . . my motorcycle . . . how will we get to school . . . too far to ride my bike." I had no answer.

Even though I had previewed the film, and knew it would challenge their assumptions, I wasn't ready for the strength of their opposition. Students' responses reminded me of how much harder it is to imagine change when it disrupts your sense of identity. My students have grown up with the expectation that they will have the privilege of driving. They weren't ready to give up their dreams of the open road.

How could I teach about the fossil fuel causes of global warming and at the same time respect local identity? I knew from the outset that in proposing change I'd meet with resistance. I would have to proceed very carefully to build science background in a non-politicized manner. I decided to wait to thoroughly teach the causes of global warming until I could figure out how to do it effectively. At this point in our learning, the film was too confrontational for these heirs of truck culture.

During the next class I acknowledged that the film had made some students feel uncomfortable, and that some of them felt angry. I explained that understanding the message of the film would take more science background, and that I was ready to teach them that background so they could form a powerful reasoned opinion about the film's message.

We spent the next two weeks building science background. I demonstrated the expansion of water as it heats by placing a flask with a stopper and a pipette over a candle. With a five-degree rise in temperature, the water in the pipette rose more than one inch. The molecules in a warm fluid move more energetically and therefore occupy more space if they can. This is a factor in rising sea levels. Warm water takes up more space than cold water.

I created convection currents with smoke in a fish tank. Following the directions in the sourcebook *Physics Is Fun* (See Resources.) I cut holes at either end of a plywood lid, filled the tank with smoke and then started the current by placing a lit candle under one hole.

On a global scale, such rising and falling air and water currents are responsible for our climate as we know it. We then modeled the greenhouse effect with plastic bottles set on a sunny windowsill. One bottle had large holes cut in the side and the other had small ones. The second bottle simulated an atmosphere with more heat-trapping gases.

Charting Our Stuff

Finally, I felt we had enough background to learn about the anthropogenic sources of greenhouse gases. One of the problems with greenhouse gases is that they are invisible. Unlike the particles in the wood smoke that wafts through our neighborhoods all winter, the gases can't be seen. I wanted my students to connect these unseen gases to things they could see.

I told students they now had enough background to understand the science behind some of the causes of global warming that the film had quickly introduced. I told them we'd be starting with things they knew well: everyday items. They would find out what it took to make them. "For example," I said, "the materials to create one piece of paper weigh 98 times the paper itself, and 95 percent of the energy to make an aluminum can is expended before the metal reaches the plant that makes the container."

I explained the assignment: "Pick a product and place it on the end of your roll of adding machine tape [that I'd distributed]. Then work together to brain-storm everything everyone in your group knows about what it takes to make that product. For each thing you can think of, make a labeled drawing. Trace what it takes for as long as you can, drawing arrows between each step." Justin, Sarah and Angel worked on a poster together. Angel was bursting with questions.

"Ms. Dean, what does it take to make cans?" she asked.

"Electricity."

"Ms. Dean, where does electricity come from?"

"A dam, or a steam plant powered by coal."

"Okay. A dam," she simplified. "What does it take to make a dam?"

"Concrete."

"What does it take to make concrete?"

"It comes from rock, which is mined."

She rushed back to her group, eager to have them include what she'd just learned on their chart. As soon as she got them going, she was back at me, ready to take it further.

"What does it take to make a mine?"

"An excavator."

"What does it take to make an excavator?"

I don't like to spoon-feed students, even when they are excited about pursuing a topic. I realized that with this one, Justin probably knew more about excavators than I did. Justin's got a lot of big equipment in his life. He's quiet and often lets other people do the talking. Until then he'd been relying on Angel for the answers, so I told Angel, "Ask Justin. He knows better than I do."

Before they had finished, their chart included three different kinds of metal, hydraulic fluid, oil, and diesel. As they ran out of time, they'd moved on to the road it would take to drive the excavator to the mine and Justin was working on describing a grader to his group so they could figure out what it took to make one of those.

By the end of the day, the charts stretched for up to 20 feet around the room. They demonstrated how much we knew about the world around us and made visible a lot of the process behind manufacturing products. I told my students, "I think you now have enough background to really understand the sources of greenhouse gases that the video introduced."

I was right. They were ready. Students listened and took notes attentively as I gave a half-hour lecture on the sources of the most common greenhouse gases. I provided for students 15 anthropogenic sources of these gases, including the extraction and production of fossil fuels, deforestation, hydropower, and livestock digestion. Also included on the chart were landfills, which account for 10 percent of anthropogenic methane, and fossil-fuel combustion, which accounts for 75 percent of anthropogenic CO^2.

Together students brainstormed a list of every fossil fuel they could think of. By the end of the period they saw greenhouse gases everywhere—in tailpipes of tractors, in stockyards, in the power behind the pump, in oil wells, in the manufacturing of hydraulic fluid, in the coal that powered the cement kiln.

I wanted to see if my students could apply what they finally seemed so eager to learn. The next day, I challenged them: "Show me how much you understand about the causes of global warming by making one more poster. Pick any product you want and show at least three ways CO^2 or methane results from its production." I can rarely claim universal success, but this time, every student in my class was able to make the connections I was looking for.

Taking Action

I polled my students on what action they wanted to take to combat global warming. I had them consider five levels of action by finishing sentence stems that read: "I can. . . . My family can . . . . Our school can. . . . Our country can. . . . The world can. . . ." At the individual level, most of them said something about walking or riding their bikes. They suggested their families could turn off the lights. A few brought up the possibility of shorter showers. Many of them suggested re-using products and not buying anything they didn't need. A few mentioned looking for local producers to limit the transportation of goods to market. At the national level, they named efforts to support alternative fuels. Internationally, they wrote of treaties and a united global agenda to decrease dependence on fossil fuels. At the level of "our school" almost all of them named recycling as a way to make a difference.

This may have been the result of conventional and simplistic environmentalism that most students are exposed to. It's easy to believe that recycling is an easy way to solve environmental ills—sort paper, plastic, and aluminum and you feel like you've done something without changing the underlying patterns of consumption that create so much waste in the first place. But I had four reasons to pursue recycling as a collective action:

- I teach eighth graders, many of whom are at their best when they are moving.
- Our school didn't recycle at all.
- A push to have the school recycle on the basis of global warming would give my students a chance to teach others about what they had learned, and teaching concepts goes a long way in strengthening them.
- Landfills and the transportation of waste *are* a significant part of the problem.

I told the students they needed to find out exactly how recycling could reduce our contribution to global warming and how to set up a program in our school. They prepared questions and I invited the recycling coordinator from our local disposal company along with an educator from the county solid waste department to tell us what we needed to know.

Together, my students and I learned that our school currently produces two 10-yard dumpsters a week, most of which is paper. We learned that every resident of our county generates on average five pounds of waste per day, and that amount has increased by more than 15 percent over the past three years. The reasons? Increased packaging and consumption and reduced recycling. People are buying more stuff and throwing more of it away. We also learned that our waste goes from a local collection site into rail containers that make their way south to the Columbia River, then up the Gorge to Roosevelt Landfill. The trains depart daily and are just about half a mile long. Almost all of Western Washington's waste crosses the mountains for burial in the desert.

While my students asked their questions, I asked my own. "How does transporting waste create greenhouse gases?"

John asked, "What powers trains?"

"Diesel," I answered. "What gas will result?"

"Carbon dioxide."

Someone added, "Methane too when it's extracted."

We learned that the monstrous regional landfill is capped and lined with a thick rubber sheet that keeps the "garbage juice" from entering the ground water.

"Anaerobic decomposition," I said. "What gas comes from that?"

"Methane."

It turns out that over the course of 20 years methane is 62 times more powerful a greenhouse gas than CO_2 because it traps more heat radiated from the Earth's surface. Landfill operators have to do something with it, and usually, they burn it off. This environmental compromise results in more CO_2.

My students then took what they had learned and launched an incrementally growing schoolwide recycling effort. First they perfected a paper recycling system for our classroom and took responsibility for maintaining it. Students then set out to teach every seventh grader and the rest of the eighth graders in our building about the connection between waste and global warming. We visited seventh-grade science classes and the rest of the eighth-grade science classes and delivered recycling bins donated by the disposal company and posters depicting the connection between atmospheric gases and the catastrophes that so worried us when we first learned about the effects of global warming.

Students emphasized to others how important it was that everyone work together, and that we could only keep the support of our custodian if we stuck with it and emptied the bins every single day. Our effort is slowly expanding to recycle all the waste our school produces in the classrooms. The lunchroom is next.

Looking Back

Thinking over what my students learned, I wonder how it might have played out differently if I hadn't made the commitment to action so early. The student resistance that resulted may have cost us valuable learning and time.

On the other hand, that activated resistance may have created in my students a powerful need to know that kept them engaged until we decided on action. But early on, I gave up on indicting auto emissions as a key greenhouse gas contributor—unfortunate, because the statistics are so impressive. According to Dauncey (See Resources) an average SUV emits about 13 tons of CO_2 per year, while more efficient hybrid cars reduce that to 3 tons. If I had built more background before introducing fossil fuel emissions at all, there's a chance we could have gone further.

Also we started our recycling effort too late in the school year. Because the year was wearing on and we needed to take action before summer break, I took on some of the tasks students would have completed if we'd had more time. I identified teacher captains in each of the four wings of the building and garnered administrative and custodial support for our efforts. If the students had done this work, they might have learned more about how to create institutional change.

But the recycling project helped my middle school students see with their own eyes how the actions we take collectively speak much louder than words. And I want my students to see themselves as agents in our world, rather than subject to it. They made a change in their school that will last much longer than their short stay in eighth grade. And they've established a climate of concern in their school that I can take further next year.

The Future

A few weeks ago, Alex popped a piece of gum into his mouth. When he got to the garbage with his wrapper, he stopped. He looked at it. He looked at me.

"Ms. Dean, what am I supposed to do with this?"

"I don't know, Alex."

"I have aluminum and paper here right?"

"Yes."

He didn't say anything more. He stuck around after the bell to separate the foil from the paper so neither would end up in the landfill. Maybe when the time comes for Alex to buy his first truck, he'll stop and remember what he learned in eighth grade about global warming.

QUESTIONS TO CONSIDER

1. What objectives did Ms. Dean have for her class on global warming?

2. What problems did she face in attempting to teach lessons in environmental science, especially in her region and community?

3. What strategies, methods, and resources did Ms. Dean use to motivate critical thinking? Give examples.

4. What kinds of social-action projects did her students undertake to reinforce their environmental awareness?

Note

A version of this chapter originally appeared in *Rethinking Schools*, Vol. 20, No. 1(Fall 2005). Published here with permission of Rethinking Schools.
1. All students' names have been changed.

Resources

Arctic Meltdown/Rising Seas

Video produced by Greenpeace, 2001, 32 min. Distributor: www.videoproject.org. The Video Project, 200 Estates Drive, Ben Lomond, CA 95005. 800–4-PLANET.

Early Warning Signs: Global Warming Curriculum

Union of Concerned Scientists (www.climatehotmap.org/curriculum/) The curriculum is downloadable as a PDF file and the map is an interactive student resource.

Physics Is Fun

(Octavo Editions, 1995) Order at www.awsna.org/catalog/. This book is filled with easy-to-make and inexpensive demonstrations that show the beauty of the laws of physics.

Stormy Weather: 101 Solutions to Global Climate Change

By Guy Dauncey (New Society Publishers, 2001) This is an especially helpful teacher resource.

CHAPTER TWENTY-NINE

"If You're Good at Nothin', What Are Ya Good for?"

Disability and Identity

MELISSA M. JONES

Everyone reading this page has intimately known adolescence. We have lived through the exploration, self-doubt, excitement, disappointment, and angst associated with that turbulent period of development. We screamed, wept, and giggled alongside peers who were negotiating the same territory, vying for independence and positioning ourselves in the social hierarchy, while simultaneously resisting constraints conferred by the adults around us. We know what it is like to be first picked and to be left out. We remember (even though we may try hard to forget) the inner turmoil as we tested the ground, sometimes in triumph and sometimes in defeat.

However, even with the most personal knowledge of adolescence, students of this age continue to confound us. To reach and to teach adolescents, we first need to get in touch with our own adolescent histories and appreciate the experiences as part of the necessary process for becoming who we are today. The antics of adolescence are not a choice, nor are they purposeful attempts to undermine our wisdom. Adolescence is a right of passage that is more easily negotiated with support.

I teach a class that focuses on secondary special education programs to both graduate and undergraduate teacher education majors in special education. Each semester, I begin the class by asking students to describe the characteristics typically associated with adolescence. The students in the class predictably begin with adjectives that have negative connotations: egocentric, rebellious, risk-taking, opinionated. . . . As the list develops, eventually someone in the class recognizes the negative slant to the list and offers a more positive view of adolescents. The very traits previously considered a detriment in one setting undergo a metamorphosis, becoming positive traits from a different perspective. Egocentric turns into reflective; rebellious becomes creative, independent, and self-reliant. Other attributes, such as risk-taking, initially viewed as a concern if adolescents take chances that put them or others in harm's way, become valued when it means that an individual is willing to explore and try new things. Opinionated is suddenly viewed as committed to an ideal. Through this exercise, the teachers and pre-service teachers in the class begin to focus their view of adolescence on the positive attributes these young people possess. Understanding what an adolescent brings to the table, and recognizing the trials and triumphs associated with that developmental period are essential when setting out to teach this group of students. For adolescents with disabilities, however, the equation becomes even more complicated, and even more important to decipher.

Recognizing the Person First

Caught in the in-between world of childhood and adulthood, adolescents in general struggle with the dichotomies they are confronted with and attempt to reconcile. The characteristics of adolescents belong to all young people in the teenage range, regardless of their perceived academic, physical, or social abilities. Adolescents with disabilities are as fairly typical in their worldview as their peers without disabilities and are no less immune to the need for exploration and independence. They too, are subject to self-examination, comparisons, questioning, and rebellion. Like their more abled peers, adolescents with disabilities want to belong, to fit in, to be successful. They also have the same fears, anxieties, anger, and depression as their counterparts without disabilities. This period of negotiation is difficult for anyone, but when you already know that you "don't get it" when others do, when peers call you "retard" or "spaz-boy," when you are always in the lowest group or, worse yet, in the "special" room down the hall, when you spend more time in the principal's office than in the classroom, when you cannot communicate your wants and needs, or when you simply see the world differently from others, the negotiation of life's right of passage becomes a treacherous minefield.

Adolescents with disabilities are often noticed for their disabilities and not recognized as adolescents first. The student with significant cognitive differences who is said to "function" at a five-year-old level, is still going through the same biological changes of her same-age peers. Hormones rage, and the innate desire to be independent and a sexual being does not disappear just because the individual lacks the skills for independence. Students with an emotional and/or behavioral disorder, who act out as a means for expressing their wants and needs, are first seen as students with a disability, with little recognition that some of these characteristics may be more closely tied to adolescence. The label of disability overshadows the traits related to individual personality, and those marking the developmental period of adolescence, limiting the individual student's choice of identity, solidifying the identity of inability. Instead of the jokester, the song-writer, the socialite, or the jock, students with disabilities suddenly become anonymous, labeled "the special education student," "the LD kid," or "the three IEPs in my room." Without the recognition of who each is as a unique individual, educators are blinded to teaching and learning approaches that might actually enhance academic growth and independence in adolescents with disabilities.

Disability and Social Isolation

For students with learning disabilities, the processing differences that cause them to struggle with reading, writing, calculating, memorizing, or organizing, may also impact their ability to maintain friendships and solve problems in life situations. Their ability to negotiate the world may be as compromised as their ability to negotiate academics in the classroom. If a student has difficulty with the psychological processes of perception, this deficit may manifest itself as a difficulty with recognizing letters and words on a page, negatively impacting the student's ability to read. However, perception encompasses more than reading because difficulties with perception can also affect how an individual perceives a situation, the choices available for responding to that situation, and the resulting consequences. Social situations can become hotbeds of confusion and misunderstanding for students with disabilities, complicating the already difficult social terrain of adolescence. Verbal and nonverbal cues are misread, impulsive responses ensue, and conflict emerges. The psychological, cognitive, and physical forces at work that hinder a student's ability to master academics often have an impact on how students problem solve social situations, which in turn can lead to social isolation.

In a comprehensive review of literature, Yosinski and Firmin (2008) found resounding evidence that rejection by one's peers, particularly during adolescence, can leave devastating psychological scars, contributing to school drop-out (French & Conrad, 2001), suicide, self-harm, and suicidal ideations (Bearman & Moody, 2004; Rutter & Behrendt, 2004), depression (Nolan, Flynn, & Garber, 2003), eating disorders (Mangweth et al., 2005), and low self-esteem (Sommer, Williams, Ciarocco, & Baumeister, 2001). The risk of these devastating outcomes increases for students who do not have the skills needed to navigate the social terrain.

"The Retard Room"

Aside from the obvious social isolation that can result, there exists another form of isolation with which adolescents with disabilities are often confronted. This form of isolation is perhaps even more powerful and detrimental than the naturally occurring social isolation and is the isolation created through groupings of students based on perceived ability. Through special education practices, students with disabilities have been systematically abandoned by their general education teachers and removed from the social milieu of schools. Allocated to segregated spaces, students with disabilities are forced into artificial social groups that may not have otherwise been formed (Jones, 2004). Other than disability (and there are vast differences within this category), many of these students have nothing in common, with dissimilar interests, talents, and strengths. In my pre-service teacher programs and graduate programs, I still hear today the misperception that "those kids would feel more comfortable with others like them." The common belief is that students with disabilities find comfort being surrounded by others who share similar experiences with disability, feeling power in numbers. However, many students with disabilities do not readily share their experiences of disability with anyone, even others who also have a disability. Oliver Queen (2001) described his adolescent experience in a segregated group in this way:

> Despite sharing the pain of alienation and ridicule that went with being LD, we were not drawn together and made stronger—quite the opposite was the case. No one reached out and dared to speak of the pain that went with being LD. No one opened the debate on how it felt being the objects of scorn and jest. No one . . . dared to show how deep their scars ran. (p. 11)

The assumption that students would rather be with others "like themselves" is a misperception with devastating consequences.

As Mara Sapon-Shevin notes, "Exclusion is not about difference; it is about our responses to difference" (2003, p. 26). Why is it we feel compelled to categorize and separate students who learn differently? Is it for the students' benefit, or ours? These questions are only the tip of the iceberg. If we were to look more deeply into the practices in which educators are entrenched, we would find multiple layers of misperception at the foundation of those practices.

Isolation, Labels, and Identity

As mentioned earlier, adolescents with disabilities are often viewed through the lens of disability, with little regard to the adolescent within. The labels derived in special education perpetuate the stigma of disability, adding another layer to the cloak under which adolescents typically hide. For any adolescent, the innate drive toward autonomy is overwhelming, as budding adults are compelled to try on various identities like a multi-colored robe. Adolescence involves a profound desire to make a mark, to be noticed for something. Students position themselves in various groups based on how they perceive themselves, how they feel they are perceived by others, and how they hope to be perceived. Some gravitate to athletics, others to the fine arts. Some students excel in technology, others in creative writing or leadership. Each student creates an identity based on the group to which he or she strives to belong.

However, what are the options of students with disabilities, particularly those who do not achieve in any of the above areas? In the face of failure or ridicule, students with disabilities are often inclined to embrace the identity of a "troublemaker." As my colleague Stephen Walker explains, "it is better to be a bad ass than a dumb ass." Oftentimes, students use this identity to save face when confronted with no other alternatives.

Velvet Cunningham (2001), who describes her high school experience as an educational outsider with dyslexia, wrote:

> . . . I started to prepare myself to fight the elements of reality. This was not an easy task. I felt like I could truly say that I know the hell the medieval knights went through preparing for a battle. Armor is not an easy thing to put on, especially by yourself. First, the clothes. Tattered jeans? No. Stretched pants? Oh, what's this? An old black plastic bag. I can just cut it here and put it on like this and tie it off here, a mini skirt. Great, now what shirt? This one looks good (faded black and ripped across the back). . . . I headed into the bathroom where my altar of hair spray and makeup awaited me.
>
> No need for a shower. My Mohawk is still in pretty good shape. Just a few teases and a splash of Mop an' Glow. Perfect! It will stay up all day. Now the face plate. This part was easy. I just held the black eyeliner up to my eye and drew a straight line from the bridge of my nose to the middle of my temple. That was it for the left eye. The right eye was a little trickier: four straight lines that connected my eyelids to my eyebrows, giving the effect that the eye was behind prison bars. . . . (p. 87)

This suite of armor, as Cunningham describes it, was necessary to protect her from the identity of "stupid" because she could not read. It kept everyone at bay, allowing her to save face in the classroom.

Rose-Colored Glasses (or Black or Gray?)

Recently, I witnessed an unveiling of sorts, as middle school students in a special education resource classroom were asked to describe themselves through poetry. As a culminating activity on descriptive words and poetry, students were given a prompt to complete:

If I were to introduce myself as a color, I would be . . .

As I watched the students bow their heads toward their papers, busy at work on the assignment, my mind swirled with the colors I thought I would use to describe myself. Blues for calm, green for nature, yellow for a positive attitude. I eagerly anticipated the outcomes of the creative forces at work. I scanned the room to see who would choose violet or ebony, or chartreuse.

Pen in hand, foreheads wrinkled in thought, heads lowered close to their papers, I watched patiently. Although several of the small pack needed prompting to begin, once started, the students appeared to be thoughtfully engaged in the assignment. I tried to unobtrusively spy over the students' shoulders, but most protected their work with fortitude. Respecting the personal nature of the assignment, I stepped away and once again waited for the final products to be shared. As students finished their work, my first observation was of the limited number of colors the students chose to describe themselves. Absent were the scarlets, bronzes, mosses, and sky blues I remember from the Crayola box of my youth. Instead, these students chose red, gray, and black. That's it—only three colors among the seven students.

Initially disappointed, I took a closer look at what was written on their pages. Although concise, the poetry that unfolded touched at the core of what occupied the thoughts of this band of adolescents, encompassing both themselves and the reality of the world around them. Each poet exposed a piece of himself or herself through the color choices, demonstrating how narrowly each defined his or her identity. Black signified the fear experienced at night as visions of intruders infiltrated their dreams. Red was either reminiscent of love lost or of a bloody end to anyone who dared to cross the student's path. Gray represented a sense of loss and resulting isolation and sadness. No one wrote of the sun. No one described joy or playfulness. No one wrote of intrigue or adventure. Just how are these students seeing themselves? How has the educational system, created to support them, contributed to their sense of self? If this is how these students define themselves as adolescents, what can we hope for them as adults?

Rodis (2001) theorizes that disability is determined by culture, so any negative mental health consequences related to a disability are the result of "inappropriately narrow and prejudicial cultural notions of what constitutes intelligence, social attractiveness, and academic excellence" (p. 208). He goes on to explain:

> The essence of this position is that there is nothing inherently wrong or deficient or disabled about persons with different cognitive processing styles, but that mainstream culture—especially mainstream educational culture—does a startlingly good job of making such persons feel like damaged goods. (p. 209)

At the heart of this theory is the impact the culture of school has on the formation of an adolescent's identity, particularly when the student has an identified disability. If we are to reach children deemed unreachable, then we must first consider the impact the current structures and processes inherent in the culture of schools have on individual students.

Stages of Identity Formation for Persons with Learning Disabilities

While there are noted stages of identity formation during typical adolescent development (if there truly is such a thing as a "typical" adolescent), one cannot remove the added impact the process for special education eligibility must have on a student's sense of self. Rodis (2001, pp. 213–222) provides us with seven plausible developmental stages related to this process, with several of them directly related to identity formation during adolescence.

1. The Problem-without-a-Name Stage: The student knows there is something wrong, but does not really understand why she/he is different or struggling. The success of one's peers is in stark contrast to the student's personal academic struggles.

2. Diagnosis: The problem is given a name and initiates a revision of one's sense of self and identity. There have been meetings about the young student, resulting in a label of disability. The student now has a reason for her/his difficulties. However, many times the student remains in the dark about what the label actually means.

3. The Alienation Stage: This stage often occurs in early adolescence, depending on the age at which the student was identified as having a disability. The student feels alone and isolated from peers and family, resenting the disability as the cause of her/his troubles.

4. The "Passing" Stage: Typically occurring in early to middle adolescence, the student tries to ignore her/his disability and even deny its existence, attempting to pass as a more abled student. For some students, this behavior results in embracing an alternative persona that detracts from the stigma of disability, including such identities as class clown, hippie, tough guy, or wild woman.

5. The Crisis and Reconfrontation Stage: This stage usually occurs during late adolescence or early adulthood. Attempting to *pass* often complicates matters, and can sometimes lead to a more devastating form of denial involving high-risk behaviors, including alcohol and drug use and abuse, which are quite common among adolescents with learning disabilities and behavior disorders. However, living through such crises can also provide an opportunity for individuals to "reopen important questions regarding their self-identifies" (p. 219). This process of self-questioning and reflection often promotes a reclamation of previously disregarded components of one's identity.

6. The "Owning" and "Outing" Stage: Again, late adolescence and early adulthood can be the setting for the next stage of identity formation for individuals with disabilities. It is at this time that a person with a disability might begin to wear the disability badge, recognizing it as a central part of who they are. The learning disability becomes a personal marker of empowerment and a source of motivation.

7. Transcendence: During Transcendence, individuals with disabilities will embrace their disability, recognizing how living with a disability has enabled them to learn, grow, and become a stronger and better persons.

Stages 3, 4, 5, and 6 are the stages that educators should most understand since they more than likely occur during adolescence for many students. Recognizing the need of students during the teenage years to search for an identity that "fits," educators can actively support students by helping them to recognize the characteristics of a disability each might possess, and understand how that characteristic plays a role (or not) in their sense of self. In special education, this is called *self-determination.*

Student Empowerment in the Classroom

Self-determination implies an understanding of one's own personal attributes and making decisions that affect one's own life. When students are self-determined, the knowledge one has about personal strengths and difficulties contributes to the development of a positive self-image (Deci, Vallerand, Pelletier, & Ryan, 1991; Zionts, Hoza, & Banks, 2004). Students who are considered to have self-determination skills are those who can self-advocate because they understand what they need to succeed, taking pride in their accomplishments and asserting themselves when necessary (Jones, 2006; Zionts, Hoza, & Banks, 2004). Self-determination leads to student empowerment as students become aware of the personal authority each has to control their own lives, making decisions that affect their own destiny, and choosing the paths that they wish to go down through the course of a lifetime (Jones, 2006). The development of skills related to a self-determination curriculum should be the ultimate goal of any educational program. By supporting adolescents to become self-determined individuals, educators can contribute to the development of a positive self-image and identity choices that are fulfilling, both personally and socially.

One criticism of the idea to overtly teach self-determination is that teachers are often already under intense pressure to cover the curriculum, leaving little room for "fluff." My question to naysayers is, at what cost do we forgo teaching adolescents about their personal needs and learning styles? How can we afford not to prioritize that goal in our curriculum? If a student were to become more aware of how she learns, would she not be better prepared for required standardized assessments? Would she not be better able to handle the rigors of classroom assignments and evaluations? Would she not have a greater chance of actually learning the content of the curriculum?

Empowering students with knowledge about how they learn best does not need to detract from the core content of the general education curriculum (Jones, 2006). In fact, it can be embedded in the daily activities of any classroom. One middle school of which I am aware actually spends the first few weeks of school helping students discover their individual learning styles, recognizing each other as resources for various tasks throughout the school year. With that knowledge, students are better able to choose appropriate roles during group work and offer valuable contributions to the class. In addition, students with disabilities are suddenly recognized as having something to offer to peers without disabilities.

Abandoning the Notion of "Broken"

Too often, the focus of special education has been to remediate a problem or fix something (or someone) deemed broken. The answer, however, is not to fix someone with a disability, as traditional medical notions of special education would promote, but rather to help reframe what it means to be *abled* and *[dis]abled.* The current deficit-driven models of special education are based on assumptions that only do damage to an adolescent's identity formation. We must begin to deconstruct how our current practices affect one's sense of personhood and "no longer think of disability as a medical condition but as a human condition" (Charlton, 2000, p. 115).

While each disability carries with it its own historical context and stereotypes, none remains more injurious than the label of mental retardation. In the not too distant past, individuals with mental retardation were referred to as idiots, feebleminded, morons, and imbeciles. Although the terms used to describe individuals with cognitive differences have changed over the years, the stereotypes and preconceived notions about the identity of individuals have failed to evolve, remaining negative, enabling, and even self-fulfilling. While a debate ensues about the use of disability labels, perhaps, as J. David Smith suggests (2007), what we should be focusing our attention on is changing the way people think about disability and the people who live with a disability.

In McIntosh's (2008) article on white privilege, she writes about the need to acknowledge the "unseen dimensions" of social systems in order to redesign them. The problem, she contends, is that too often those in power seem oblivious to the inequalities and injustices that exist, "protecting unearned advantage and conferred dominance" (p. 57). The same can be said for our current educational practices of segregating students based on academic prowess. Those who are educated and academically capable have a stake in maintaining academic privilege. If access to knowledge and educational opportunities remains limited, then those who have access remain in power, perpetuating a social hierarchy of privilege and ability. The notion that individuals with disabilities are less valuable is a false consciousness collectively supported by dominant groups. Educators need to defy the dominant images of disability through raised consciousness, disregarding the fallacies of that antiquated ideology (Charlton, 2000). Then, adolescents with disabilities would be recognized as adolescents first, with their unique quirks and emotions as well as the personal attributes each possesses. Disability simply becomes another form of difference in the classroom.

Students want to be successful, to be respected, and to have choices (Jones, 2004). To meet these goals, schools would need to begin to embrace a philosophy of support for student strengths, abandoning the deficit-driven models of intervention that have permeated our school cultures. When students struggle, our prioritized efforts should not be on discovering what is wrong with a student and classifying it but rather gaining an understanding of what the student's interests and skills are and building on those special abilities (Jones, 2004). Schools should focus on becoming places where students can feel connected, have a sense of well-being, realize a sense of academic initiative, and develop a sense of knowing (Maeroff, 1998).

In a safe environment, students are not judged by their family history or medical diagnosis, but rather by their character and skills. Perhaps, most importantly, in a safe environment students are nurtured to recognize their own strengths and areas for potential growth. Instead of admonishing, controlling, and segregating the forces of adolescence and difference, we should enjoy, embrace, and nurture the unique characteristics of this developmental period and all it entails. As Gill (1994) envisioned,

> . . . in the ideal world, my differences, though noted, would not be devalued. Nor would I . . . There would be respectful curiosity about what I have learned from my differences that I could teach society. In such a world, no one would mind being called Disabled. (pp. 44–45)

I would take that one step further. In such a world, no one would need to be called [Dis]abled.

QUESTIONS TO CONSIDER

1. In what processes and practices do educators participate that might perpetuate the medical model of disability? What can educators do to decrease their harmful effects? Are there ways to restructure schools to remove the need for such processes and practices? Explain.

2. What structures, traditions, and expectations exist in public middle and high schools today that promote the segregation of students with disabilities from academics? From social activities? What are the underlying purposes of those structures, traditions, and expectations?

3. How are they propagated and maintained? What can be done to enhance both academic quality and social justice within those constraints? Explain.

4. What are the reasons for labels in education? Are there ways for students who struggle or learn differently to receive support and services without the use of labels? What would need to change in today's schools in order for such transformation to occur?

References

Bearman, P. S., & Moody, J. (2004). Suicide and friendships among American adolescents. *American Journal of Public Health, 94,* 89–95.

Charlton, J. I. (2000). *Nothing about us without us: Disability oppression and empowerment.* Berkeley, CA: University of California Press.

Cunningham, V. (2001). Lovelvet. In P. Rodis, A. Garrod, & M.L. Boscardin (Eds.), *Learning Disabilities & Life Stories* (pp. 82–96). Needham Heights, MA: Allyn & Bacon.

Deci, E. L., Vallerand, R. J., Pelletier, L. G., & Ryan, R .M. (1991). Motivation and education: The self-determination perspective. *Educational Psychologist, 26* (3 & 4), 325–346.

French, D.C., & Conrad, J. (2001). School dropout as predicted by peer rejection and antisocial behavior. *Journal of Research on Adolescence, 11,* 225–244.

Gill, C. (1994). Questioning continuum. In B. Shaw (Ed.), *The Ragged Edge: The Disability Experience from the Pages of the First Fifteen Years of the Disability Rag* (pp. 44–45). Louisville, KY: Avocado Press.

Jones, M. M. (2004). *Whisper writing: Teenage girls talk about ableism and sexism in school.* New York: Peter Lang.

Jones, M. M. (2006). Teaching self-determination: Empowered teachers, empowered students. *Teaching Exceptional Children, 39*(1), 12–17.

Maeroff, G. I. (1998, February).Altered destinies: Making life better for schoolchildren in need. *Phi Delta Kappan,* 425–432.

Mangweth, B., Hausmann,A., Danzl, C., Walch, T., Rupp, C., Biebl, W., et al. (2005). Childhood body-focused behaviors and social behaviors as risk factors of eating disorders. *Psychotherapy and Psychosomatics, 74,* 247–253.

McIntosh, P. (2008). White privilege: Unpacking the invisible knapsack. In J. Noel (Ed.). *Multicultural education* (2nd ed.) (pp. 55–57). Columbus: McGraw-Hill.

Nolan, S.A., Flynn, C., & Garber, J. (2003). Prospective relations between rejection and depression in young adolescents. *Journal of Personality and Social Psychology, 85*, 745–755.

Queen, O. (2001). Blake Academy and the green arrow. In P. Rodis, A. Garrod, & M. L. Boscardin (Eds.), *Learning Disabilities & Life Stories* (pp. 3–16). Needham Heights, MA: Allyn & Bacon.

Rodis, P. (2001). Forging identities, tackling problems, and arguing with culture: Psychotherapy with persons who have learning disabilities. In P. Rodis, A. Garrod, & M. L. Boscardin (Eds.), *Learning Disabilities & Life Stories* (pp. 205–230). Needham Heights, MA: Allyn & Bacon.

Rutter, P.A., & Behrendt, E. (2004). Adolescent suicide risk: Four psychosocial factors. *Adolescence, 39*, 295–302.

Sapon-Shevin, M. (2003). Inclusion: A matter of social justice. *Educational Leadership, 61(2)*, 25–28.

Smith, J. D. (2007). Mental retardation and the problem of "normality": Self-determination and identity choice. *Education and Training in Developmental Disabilities, 42(4)*, 410–417.

Sommer, K. L., Williams, K. D., Ciarocco, N. J., Baumeister, R. F. (2001). When silence speaks louder than words: Explorations into the intraspsychic and interpersonal consequences of social ostracism. *Basic and Applied Social Psychology, 23*, 225–243.

Yosinski, K. J., & Firmin, M. W. (2008). Adolescent awareness of isolation's consequences. *Journal of Ethnographic & Qualitative Research, 2(2)*, 145–152.

Zionts, L. T., Hoza, T. E., & Banks, T. I. (2004). Self-advocacy, self-determination, and adolescent brain research: What are the implications for youth with EBD? *Beyond Behavior, 13(3)*, 9–11.

CHAPTER THIRTY

How Important Is Technology in Urban Education?

VANESSA DOMINE

Most respond to the question of technology in urban education with the complaint that "poor" schools don't have sufficient access to computers. Given the current digital age and the tumultuous history between technology and public schooling in the United States, the misguided definitions of technology as only computers and of urban communities as merely "poor" are not surprising. What is particularly problematic is the overarching assumption that computer access alone can address the challenges (overcrowding, high dropout rates, low test scores, inadequacies in teacher preparation) and opportunities (racial, ethnic, cultural, and linguistic diversity) within urban settings. While the use of computers can address some of these challenges on some level, their haphazard presence in the classroom more often than not indicates a dysfunction in the ideal of technology as consisting exclusively of computers and the Internet, and the lack of attention to the real needs of urban school teachers.

Thus, my answer to the question, How important is technology in urban education?, has to do with renewing our commitment to urban education while downplaying the technologies. I do not wish to diminish the importance of technological proficiency, as it plays a significant role in achieving educational innovation. However, success within urban education requires an authentic and ecological approach to schooling. In the context of student learning, urban schools are merely one component within a larger system that includes family, community, and government. In the context of teaching, technology is merely one component within a larger system that involves professional development, leadership, communication, assessment, and ongoing support. From this perspective, the excessive pursuit of computers and Internet access is another attempt to find a technological panacea for perceived "ills" of education, while shifting the attention away from the political, economic, and social motivators that compel urban education.

Moving Beyond Access

Over the past ten years, the United States has spent more than $40 billion to place computers in schools and connect classrooms to the Internet. In 1997 the government subsidized a $2 billion program called Educational Rate (E-rate) to help schools and libraries obtain Internet wiring and services. E-rate provided up to a 90 percent discount to schools with the largest number of poor children. The goal of E-rate was to increase equity of access or bridge the "digital divide" across poor and wealthy communities within the United States. Amidst controversy over widespread "fraud and abuse" within the administration of the E-rate program (Reuters, 2003), approximately 99 percent of schools (not classrooms) in the United States have access to the Internet. While nearly all schools have some level of Internet access, the digital divide remains a reality in the homes of many students within urban communities. Only 25 percent of the nation's poorest homes have Internet access, compared with 80 percent of homes with annual incomes above $75,000 (Dickard, 2003). The double-edged sword of E-rate is that the poorer school districts that obtain subsidized access without the funding support for professional development or technical support also have increased access to failure. The emergent inefficacies of technology in the classroom perpetuate myths of the teacher as Luddite and of low-performing students as inherently inferior. The lessons of E-rate teach us that urban education in the United States is still very much a complicated issue, despite federal efforts to operationally define educational success as access to computers and wiring. Widespread lack of professional development poses a serious risk to the nation's investment in educational technology, as many teachers have neither the experience nor the skills in using technology in meaningful ways that support, rather than detract from, their curricula. The federal government only recently realized that equipment and wiring are not enough for the successful integration of technology within schools.

Access to information is inarguably the first step toward knowledge. However, as humans, we need to do more than just access information. Any teacher who has received a cut-and-paste essay from students who conducted "research" on the World Wide Web realizes that students need a framework for understanding information. Such a framework extends beyond the practical skills of technological literacy and encompasses *media literacy,* the ability to access, analyze, evaluate, produce, and communicate information using a variety of technologies (Aufderheide, 1992). Cultivating media literacy among students requires acknowledging the constructed nature of information. It also requires an awareness of ownership in the sense that those who control our technologies influence the information we have access to and therefore determine social, political, and economic power. Conversations at the policy level about technological literacy therefore need to move beyond student acquisition of a set of technical skills to include habits of mind that allow students to thoughtfully navigate the mediated world in which they live. Given this broad view of literacy, access to the technology is important—but only the first step.

The Myth of Technology

Addressing the importance of technology within urban education requires us to establish a shared understanding of the word *technology* and its relationships to urban education. Not until the Great

Exhibition of 1851, in the Crystal Palace in London, did technology become associated exclusively with machines. Beyond the technical lies a philosophical dimension that denotes a methodology, or a process of doing things, that lends itself to a particular way of thinking (Ellul, 1980; Finn, 1972; Winner, 1986). Technology is therefore ideology and a way of looking at the world. From this perspective, it cannot be limited to one specific machine or discipline of study or even a course subject area. Rather, it embodies political, social, and cultural ideologies that are woven throughout all bodies of knowledge, throughout all of education, and even throughout our daily lives (Downing, Mohammadi, & Sreberny-Mohammadi, 1995). Thus, conversations about technology cannot be separated from conversations about curriculum, teaching, learning, or the purposes of education. Do our attitudes about computers within urban schools assume that if students can just get access to information, they will learn and excel? Do teaching and learning occur through the mere delivery and reception of information through value-free tools?

It is not until a specific technology is employed within a particular context, such as classroom instruction, that it serves as a medium for communication. Books, television, and computers are more than just tools for delivering information. They are mediators of information that influence students' lives both inside and outside the classroom in ways that are commercial, cultural, political, and social. The experiences of urban youth are commodified and commercialized through the cultural capital of clothing, video games, compact discs, cell phones, and pagers. In one sense, these technologies provide students with a common culture. In another sense, the languages of these technologies are, to a certain extent, constraints that create distinctions or divisions across youth. Stereotyping is one example of a shortcut to meaning that is inherent within the conventions of television, film, and the Internet. How then do we reconcile using these technologies in meaningful ways that value diversity in urban education? To address this, we need to look not just at tools or machines, but more broadly at the wider mediated environment of teaching and learning.

Reframing technology as ideology calls for intellectually rigorous conversations about the ways in which technologies-as-media shape information and alter the ways in which individual students learn and individual teachers teach. Using technology in educationally significant ways requires teachers and educators to transcend the technical into a realm that, although mediated through technology, is driven by social and political consciousness. This paradigm shift renders obsolete the traditional role of the computer teacher and instead positions all teachers as educational leaders who orchestrate a variety of technologies to support personal, professional, and pedagogical goals. This view of technology empowers teachers to select what media will shape the classroom environment and how they will impact individual students beyond the four walls of the classroom. Authentic technology integration in the classroom calls for an abandonment of the technological elitism associated with computers in the classroom and an understanding that higher-level thinking skills can and should occur across older print and video as well as newer digital technologies. In this sense, student empowerment has little to do with the mobility associated with laptops and wireless networks, and everything to do with social and political mobility into a world of the student's own creation.

Given this rigorous definition of the role of technology within urban education, it is not surprising that conversations about ideology are few and far between. It is much easier (although equally problematic) to talk about the tangible equipment than to articulate and then examine our ways of seeing education, technology, and the world around us. Despite its arduousness, questioning the impact of technology on our lives is essential to our survival as humans and relegates conversations about computer and wiring to the back burner—if only temporarily.

An Ecological Approach

The continuous pressure for educators and administrators to keep an eye on the moving target of technological innovation distracts us from what should be of paramount importance to education—the students themselves. The pendulum of history has swung from individualized student learning back to subject-matter emphasis. The inability to reconcile the two is illustrated in the current achievement gap that dangerously isolates the student in terms of individual achievement, race, and ethnicity. The gap refers to the disparity in school performance (e.g., grades, test scores, course selection, college completion) according to racial and ethnic differences. In 1996, several national tests found African American and Hispanic twelfth graders scoring at roughly the same levels in reading and math as white eighth graders (Johnston & Viadero, 2003). The designation of this disparity as an *achievement* gap implies inherent deficiencies in student performance and simultaneously ignores as possibilities the failures of teachers, educators, and leaders charged with supporting student achievement. In addition, aggregating testing scores in this manner perpetuates the stigma that race and ethnicity are valid determinants of success or failure. Yet, the achievement gap is not exclusive to urban education. Reported "gaps" exist in cities, suburbs, and rural school districts alike, suggesting that disparity of student achievement is symptomatic of a more serious condition within the larger system of public education in the United States.

In an effort to bridge the achievement gap, the federal government enacted the No Child Left Behind (NCLB) Act. Enacted in 2002, NCLB requires every identified racial and ethnic group to perform at grade level or make "adequate yearly progress" toward that end. If schools or districts are unable to prove successful performance or progress, they are threatened with mandatory tutoring and even privatization (U.S. Department of Education, 2002). The NCLB legislation mandates that every student in the United States be "technology literate" by the eighth grade. The U.S. Department of Education through NCLB funds the costs of standardized testing while cutting funds to the preexisting Technology Innovation Challenge Grants and the Technology Literacy Challenge—both national funding streams that support thoughtful and integrative uses of technology in schools and communities. NCLB and the achievement gap hauntingly echo E-rate and the digital divide in ignoring the fundamental principle that increased access to and accountability for student achievement and basic technological proficiency require *systemic* support, and cannot be accurately measured in terms of standardized test scores and quantities of computers.

Educational policy avoids the commitment to use technology in the service of urban education. Ironically such a policy stance does not directly support the belief in diversity of race, ethnicity, culture, and language as the greatest asset as well as challenge to urban education. For a teacher, generating and coordinating multiple thinking styles and ways of seeing the world is central to achieving pedagogical excellence and student achievement within the four walls of the classroom. The greatest potential source of strength for accomplishing this lies in the insight and commitment of educators to see the bigger picture of schooling as one component of a larger system that includes families, housing developments, community centers, schools, religious organizations, libraries, universities, and business professionals. After all, urban communities face challenges associated with conflicting cultural identities, poverty, drug abuse, and disease before some children ever enter the classroom. The goal is not to derive a formulaic vision or template for technology to then apply to all urban settings or even urban education. Rather, the value of technology is in facilitating and supporting a shared purpose within the larger urban community and a felt pedagogical need within the school classrooms.

Herein lies the value of computers and the Internet for urban education: strengthening localized communities through a strategic use of communication technologies, such as e-mail, discussion boards, and/or live chat. One urban high school principal in Detroit was inspired by the technological savvy of her college-age children and chose to acquire computers and Internet access specifically for increasing parental involvement in schools within the district (Means, Penuel, & Padilla, 2001). The principal creatively assembled Title I funding and business partnerships to build electronic networks between district schools and neighborhood housing developments. This orchestration of funding included monies for a technology coordinator and two computer labs—both in schools and within housing developments. The principal supported community professional development in which parents, teachers, and families collaborated on webpages for their classrooms and schools. The webpages announced school activities and hosted discussion threads for interaction among teachers, students, and parents. What is particularly powerful about this systemic approach to technology integration is its insight into the importance of parental and even whole-family support in student achievement. Also insightful is the reframing of professional development as a communal activity that includes parents, teachers, and students.

Another powerful example of using technology in the service of urban education is the Bilingual Excel Grant at McKinley High School in Buffalo, New York. Teachers faced the challenges of linguistic diversity among students as well as lack of student knowledge and awareness of their larger community and its cultural agencies:

> Students planned a tour of their community using a variety of modes of transportation. Through field trips in which students visited the public libraries, the art and historical museums, horticultural gardens, and a butterfly conservatory, they learned to describe and differentiate among the functions of each of these agencies and sites while improving their effective social communication in English. They gained an understanding of the social, historical, and cultural diversities within their communities by using various print and technology resources. Students applied learned technological knowledge and skills to design a Web page with the assistance of a consultant. As a result of working cooperatively with other students throughout this project, they developed cross-cultural skills and an understanding as well as an appreciation of one another. (Kearney, 2000, p. 153)

Although many urban schools do not have the funding for student transportation and technology consultants, similar efforts can be replicated by bringing cultural institutions to the school setting through volunteers, guest speakers, and Internet websites. Whether these connections happen through face-to-face communication or digital communication (or both) is secondary to the larger goal of building bridges between students and the communities in which they live.

Given this emphasis on technology in the service of urban education, the more fruitful questions to ask are: What are the authentic educational needs of the school community? How might teachers marshal the available print, video, and digital resources within the schools and the surrounding community to support such needs? Privileging the diversity of media forms afforded through technology is key when thinking about ways to support classroom curriculum. Although sometimes painful, critical conversations about technology are the only means by which an educational community can establish a common purpose for education and technology. Community-based decision making invites members to determine which technologies are appropriate, empower, and represent an urban community. Whose stories are told and whose stories are left untold by history textbooks, live and online museum exhibits, or instructional films? What publishers, producers, and corporations are most likely to support the goals and interests of this particular urban community, and less likely to commercially exploit it? Within urban communities, it is incumbent upon school leaders to elicit from teachers, students, parents, and community leaders expectations for teaching and learning, to more thoughtfully guide the uses of technology within the classroom.

Redefining Pedagogy in the Context of Technology

Just as schools are one component within a larger community system, so teachers are one component within the larger school organization. Unfortunately, too many of these teachers are compartmentalized by the bureaucratic characteristics of attendance, discipline, testing, grading, and class schedules. A more holistic approach to classroom teaching situates the teacher as an empowered orchestra leader who uses a variety of resources to create a classroom environment that supports a consistent vision for teaching and learning. Among the sources of support are school leadership, communication, professional development, standards and assessment, and technology resources. In the context of technology, the educational commitment lies not just with the equipment, but also in building and sustaining a network of direct support for the pedagogical goals of the classroom teacher.

For urban schools that have existing imbalances within their educational communities (e.g., high dropout rates, low parental involvement, discipline problems), adding technology haphazardly runs the risk of perpetuating the cycle of putting blame on teachers and students for the lack of technology skills or performance. Technology integration is more complex than simply using technology in the classroom. It's about having the widest possible repertoire of instructional media and technologies available and selecting the most appropriate for use depending upon goals for students and pedagogical preferences. This approach does not pressure teachers new to either curriculum or technologies (or both) to immediately change their teaching philosophy. Instead of thinking up ways to blame teachers for the lack of technology integration, we need to ask, How can we support teachers in their felt need for technology within their classrooms?

Teacher professional development and technology integration need to be reframed in terms of how technology directly supports teaching and learning by its variety, not just in the form of computers. Just as the uses of technology should privilege diversity within communities and among students, they should also privilege diversity of technologies and teaching styles.

In the context of the classroom, privileging diversity requires intervening among individual students' understandings and the texts and technologies of instruction. For example, a teacher may require students to read an essay, visit a website, or view a documentary about the Civil War. Regardless of the medium, the teacher should ask students to consider: Whose story is being told? Whose story is being left out? To what extent is this information representative of your own experiences? Specific to the medium, students should also ask: Who is the author and what is his/her motive for telling this story? Why did the author use print/digital/video format? How did the author construct this essay/website/film? Who has access to this essay/website/film? The culminating pedagogical act is to then ask students to express alternative views of Civil War history choosing the content and medium for their (re)production. On a more grassroots level, students might access and analyze crime statistics within their neighborhood and look at news media portrayals of crime within the larger community. What information about the community is *not* reported? How do these representations compare with those of other communities? Are such portrayals accurate? Are they fair? It is within this progression of access, analysis, evaluation, and communication that the uses of technology can meaningfully support both media literacy and cultural diversity.

Using technologies in the context of student-produced media requires reconfiguring time and space in relation to pedagogy. Many urban schools have neither computer labs nor computers in the classroom and therefore struggle with equitable access and technological literacy for all students. Hands-on production work requires students to immerse themselves in the content and to experiment with the technology. Therefore, such teaching and learning demands extended blocks of time—not the 40-minute standard during the school day. Since many students within urban communities do not have access to these technologies at home, the opposition to such project-based work is almost insurmountable. The question arises, What is the most valuable use of classroom time? From a technological standpoint, the classroom is biased toward community. That is, there is great potential for student interaction, group discussions, and collaboration—despite traditional alignment of desks in rows. Although overcrowding is prevalent, a source of strength for student learning can be the classroom community. From this perspective, it does not make much pedagogical sense to use face-to-face classroom time for students to sit behind a computer, other than for live technical demonstrations or a formal class presentation. If students have neither school nor home access to computers, then how will such technological proficiencies be achieved in urban communities? What other technological resources can students and teachers draw from within the community? Can public libraries, community centers, and nonprofit organizations collaborate with teachers to compensate for the lack of equipment? If such partnerships can be forged and equity of access to computers and the Internet can be accomplished by combined efforts and technologies within homes, libraries, churches, and community centers, then the possibilities and resources for classroom teaching and learning with technology are virtually limitless.

Professional development is not training, but rather a transformative process that begins with experimentation at a basic level and grows as teachers gain experience with using technology with students in enacting curriculum in the classroom. Teachers need time and the freedom to experiment with a variety of technologies to discover authentic pedagogical strategies that are grounded within the real needs of the classroom and curriculum—that are linked to communities outside the classroom. Thus professional development must entail thinking about curriculum and the technologies that can (and cannot) successfully support it.

Rethinking professional development calls into question the value of one-day district workshops in which teachers are "released" to address issues pertaining to teaching, learning, and administration. Yet such a model is punitive, as it decontextualizes teaching. A new model for professional development involves continual practice, experimentation, and ongoing support in the uses of technology. Off-campus technology training sessions should be community based, where teachers can forge connections and cohorts within the surrounding community. Cohorts of curriculum design teams can meet on regular bases as a companion to ongoing (individual or group) uses of technology within the classroom. Such conversations are grounded in the reality of daily teaching experiences and allow for immediate transformation of what happens in the classroom. Fostering experimentation allows for daily occurrences of planning, design, integration, assessment, and redesign. In sum, the theory and practice of technology integration need to be inextricably connected to the processes and products of curriculum development.

To view the challenge of technology within urban education as merely one of access to computers and the Internet is to dangerously view the issues as involving technological uses of education, rather than authentic educational uses for technology. Ultimately, the focus must shift away from merely accessing computer equipment to embrace a more holistic and humanistic framework that privileges diversity of all kinds—including technological diversity. The successes and failures of technology within urban education will be measured by the (in)ability of educational leaders to forge connections between schools and their communities. Ultimately, the school principal is responsible for bringing together all the elements within the educational community to support schooling. This leadership role requires the vision of education as a social, political, and economic responsibility that is enacted locally through the integration of families, schools, and community institutions. It is incumbent upon teachers and teacher educators to set their sights on developing authentic models of teaching and learning using a variety of technologies that support a shared, communal purpose instead of surfing the next technological wave.

QUESTIONS TO CONSIDER

1. What does the author envision as the Ideal role for technology in urban education? Do you agree or disagree with her analysis? Why?

2. Why does she argue that technological literacy needs "to move beyond student acquisition of technical skills"?

3. What does the author mean by "authentic technology integration," and why does she claim it is so important?

4. What would be included in Domine's vision of an "ecological" system of technological education?

5. In the author's pedagogical framework, how would the use of technology need to be transformed to make it an authentic, critical tool for classroom teachers?

Note

This chapter originally appeared in Shirley R. Steinberg and Joe L. Kincheloe (eds.), *19 Urban Questions: Teaching in the City* (New York: Peter Lang, 2007).

References

Aufderheide, Patricia (1992). *Proceedings from the National Leadership Conference on Media Literacy.* Washington, DC: Aspen Institute.

Dickard, Norris (Ed.) (2003). *The sustainability challenge: Taking edtech to the next level.* Washington, DC: The Benton Foundation.

Downing, John; Mohammadi, Ali; & Sreberny-Mohammadi, Annabelle (Eds.) (1995). *Questioning the media: A critical introduction* (2nd ed.). Thousand Oaks, CA: Sage.

Ellul, Jacques (1980). *The technological system.* Trans. from French by Joachim Neugroschel. New York: Continuum.

Finn, James D. (1972). Automation and education: Technology and the instructional process. In R. J. McBeath (Ed.), *Extending education through technology: Selected writings by James D. Finn on instructional technology* (pp. 141–160). Washington, DC: Association for Educational Communications and Technology.

Johnston, Robert C., & Viadero, Debra (2003). Unmet promise: Raising minority achievement. *Education Week, 19,* 1, 18 (19.

Kearney, Carol A. (2000). *Curriculum partner: Redefining the role of the library media specialist.* Westport, CT: Greenwood Press.

Means, Barbara; Penuel, William R.; & Padilla, Christine (2001). *The connected school: Technology and learning in high school.* San Francisco: Jossey-Bass.

Reuters (2003). *House panel expands probe into E-rate program.* March 13. Washington, DC: Reuters News Service.

U.S. Department of Education (2002). *No Child Left Behind.* Website: http://www.nochildleftbehind.gov. Accessed November 8, 2003.

Winner, Langdon (1986). *The whale and the reactor: A search for limits in an age of high technology.* University of Chicago Press.

CHAPTER THIRTY-ONE

The New Vocationalism

What It Is, What It Could Be

W. NORTON GRUBB

Vocationalism is rampant once again. The claims that schooling ought to better prepare workers for the 21st century have become increasingly strident since the publication of A Nation at Risk more than a decade ago. Various practices to incorporate work-related skills into the curriculum have been proposed, and the most recent initiative of the Clinton Administration—the School-to-Work Opportunities Act of 1994—has attracted an amazing amount of attention for what is, after all, a piddling program. No one is proposing to resurrect conventional vocational education, but the notion that public education should be more "relevant" to our country's economic future is widespread.

How should education respond? The movements within the "new vocationalism" include many odd partners with wildly differing ideas of how to respond to economic imperatives. Some are atavistic; others claim to have discovered such new directions as the shift to a "high-skills economy"; still others have rediscovered practices with long and checkered histories in our schools, such as work-based learning. Many of these reforms have the potential to improve teaching and learning. But the nature of these reforms, their links to vocational purposes, and the specific ways in which they might improve learning remain murky. Moreover, many forms of the "new vocationalism" are only barely emerging.

In this article I disentangle the strands of renewed interest in the occupational purposes of schooling, concentrating on the high school—the institution that seems both the least successful and the most resistant to change. After describing five different versions of the "new vocationalism," I interpret these changes through a matrix of approaches to pedagogy and to academic and vocational content.

The penultimate section examines the economic context of the "new vocationalism," and the final section examines the prospects for reform. There are strong reasons to think that enduring reforms are possible, but there are equally powerful forces that might sweep away the most innovative aspects of the "new vocationalism." Our tasks are to identify those elements that merit widespread adoption and to institutionalize them so that they are not blown away by the first winds of pedagogical conservatism.

Practices of the 'New Vocationalism'

A Nation at Risk, generally conceded to be the spark that ignited the current reform movement, epitomizes the first strand of the new vocationalism. The great threat to our country's future was "a rising tide of mediocrity" in the schools, which was causing a decline in competitiveness with the Japanese, the South Koreans, and the Germans. Subsequent commission reports picked up the economic rationale for education reform, with such titles as *Higher Education and the American Resurgence*. To be sure, the emphasis on economic roles for schooling was leavened with a nod to the importance of preparing a well-informed citizenry: both *A Nation at Risk* and *Higher Education and the American Resurgence* approvingly quoted Thomas Jefferson on this subject. But the connection between education and democracy came off as an afterthought. The dominant rationale given for schooling—indeed, the only apparent rationale in the more utilitarian reports, such as the report of the Secretary [of Labor]'s Commission on Achieving Necessary Skills (SCANS), *What Work Requires of Schools*—was the preparation of future workers.

But the content of schooling was not to change. *A Nation at Risk* recommended the "New Basics": English, math, science, social studies, and (the only novelty) half a year of computer science. The states took up the charge and imposed higher academic standards in the form of new graduation and testing requirements and new content standards for teachers. As many commentators noted, the dominant response was "more of the same": the same academic curriculum that has dominated the high school since the 19th century, taught in roughly the same ways, though with a new sense of urgency. The only condition that changed was that enrollments in conventional academic subjects increased at the expense of enrollments in vocational and remedial subjects.[1]

Of course, ever since Horace Mann the academic orthodoxy has had its economic underpinnings; the only thing different about *A Nation at Risk* was that the political, intellectual, and intrinsic arguments for the standard curriculum—knowledge as its own reward, the "beauty, pleasure, surprise, personal enlightenment and enrichment at the heart of the classic liberal-arts ideal"[2]—had been completely displaced by an economic argument. In vain might one argue that combining an occupational rationale for schooling with a conventional academic curriculum could only exacerbate a disjunction in the American high school: the high school is an inescapably vocational institution, critical to students' employment futures, while the dominant courses are those of the academic track, whose connection to later employment is obscure.[3]

As noted, the first round of school reform did change course-taking patterns, but otherwise mediocre performance seemed to drag on. One of many responses was the emergence of a second strand of the "new vocationalism": the argument that the changing economy requires new skills of its workers and therefore new approaches to teaching. In the widely read *SCANS* report, the high-skills workplace requires a range not only of basic skills (e.g., reading, writing, math, listening, speaking) but also of thinking skills (e.g., decision making, problem solving, knowing how to learn), as well as such personal qualities as responsibility, sociability, self-management, integrity, and honesty.

But these SCANS skills—or "workplace basics"—are not well taught through conventional didactic instruction with its emphasis on individualized rather than cooperative learning, on abstract principles and decontextualized context, and on fact acquisition rather than problem solving.[4] Thus SCANS and others have called for changing instruction through more experiential learning outside of classrooms and more contextualized teaching:

SCANS believes that teachers and schools must begin early to help students see the relationship between what they study and its applications in real-world contexts. . . . We believe, after examining the findings of cognitive science, that the most effective way of teaching skills is "in context." Placing learning objectives within real environments is better than insisting that students first learn in the abstract what they will then be expected to apply. . . . Reading and mathematics become less abstract and more concrete when they are embedded in one or more of the competencies; that is, when the learning is "situated" in a system or a technological problem.

By referring to the work of cognitive scientists, the *SCANS* report explicitly linked the demands of employers to the claims of education reformers. The metaphor of "cognitive apprenticeship" captures this approach. Just as apprentices learn their tasks in the context of ongoing work, so too the student-as-apprentice-learner would learn academic competencies in some meaningful context. Simpler components would be mastered before moving to more difficult tasks; the master or teacher would provide guidance ("scaffolding") at early stages and then allow the apprentice/student to do more ("fading"). The teaching would include not only a complete range of technical skills but also the interpersonal skills, the customs, and the culture of the craft.[5] As a model of teaching, this is quite different from the standard didactic approach in which learning lacks any context and the ultimate goal of instruction is either unclear or abstract.

However, while the methods of instruction may have to change according to this second strand, the content of formal education could stay the same. The *SCANS* report suggested ways to teach various SCANS skills (e.g., interpersonal skills, systems thinking, and knowledge of technology) in such core curricular areas as English, math, and science. Recommendations for the "forgotten half" also preserved the conventional curriculum of the high school, while adding to it various forms of community-based learning.

In particular, it has been clear that the skills "employers want" are not those of conventional vocational education. The Committee for Economic Development declared that "business, in general, is not interested in narrow vocationalism. It prefers a curriculum that stresses literacy and mathematical and problem-solving skills." Similarly, the National Academy of Sciences Panel on Secondary School Education for the Changing Workplace concluded:

The education needed for the workplace does not differ in its essentials from that needed for college or advanced technical training. The central recommendation of this study is that all young Americans, regardless of their career goals, achieve mastery of this core of competencies up to their abilities.[6]

Thus the second strand of the "new vocationalism" has continued the economic and utilitarian emphasis of *A Nation at Risk*, giving top priority to employers and the skills they profess to need and retaining the conventional academic subjects, though with a transformed pedagogy.

The third strand of the "new vocationalism" has more directly addressed the deficiencies of the "old vocationalism"—traditional vocational education dating from the turn of the century, generally focusing on specific skill training for entry-level jobs. Many critics of conventional vocational education have called for occupational preparation to become broader, better connected to academic content, more accommodating of goals other than immediate employment (e.g., postsecondary education), and more critical of the current system of employment than is conventionally the case.[7] Such efforts calling for a more general form of vocational education have a long history that is linked to the deficiencies of specific vocational training on the one hand and to problems with the "irrelevance" of academic instruction on the other.[8]

Such improvements in vocational education have been given a substantial boost by the 1990 Amendments to the Carl Perkins Act, which funds vocational education. The amendments require that every program supported by federal funds "integrate academic and vocational education . . . through coherent sequences of courses so that students achieve both academic and occupational competencies." Other sections of the amendments support tech-prep programs that combine high school and postsecondary education (usually in community colleges) and clarify that vocational education is not a terminal program for those not destined for college. Still another provision promotes teaching students about "all aspects of the industry" they might enter, again an effort to broaden content beyond job-specific preparation.

In response, a large number of secondary schools have experimented with various forms of curriculum integration, and tech-prep programs—sometimes interpreted simply as curriculum integration—have proliferated. Several networks of schools have developed, including one instituted by the National Center for Research in Vocational Education and one organized by the Southern Regional Education Board. In large measure, the forms of integration adopted so far have been the simplest ones: the incorporation of more academic skills into vocational courses and the development of "applied academics" curricula that present the applications of math or writing or other "communications skills" in employment.[9] In many cases, the kinds of higher-order skills advocated by SCANS and other champions of the high-skill workplace are also included.

This strand of the "new vocationalism" represents a reform of vocational education by broadening its content. Unlike the more thorough forms of integrating academic and vocational education that I describe below, these practices typically focus on self-selected vocational students and continue the separation of "vocational" and "academic" tracks. By grafting academic content onto existing vocational programs, they continue the emphasis on preparation for relatively unskilled entry-level jobs right after high school.

A fourth strand of the "new vocationalism" has emerged from the new interest in school-to-work programs. Initially, such programs looked more like the German apprenticeship programs on which they were modeled.[10] That is, they were work-based programs lasting for relatively long periods of time and yielding some sort of portable credential or certificate. As this conception developed into the School-to-Work Opportunities Act of 1994, it changed into a tripartite program incorporating school-based learning (in which academic and vocational education would be integrated within "career majors" and linked to at least one year of postsecondary education); a work-based component; and "connecting activities" to make school-based learning consistent with work-based learning. The school-to-work legislation also contains hints of pedagogical reform in its calls for "the use of applied teaching methods and team-teaching strategies." Thus school-to-work programs might be more contextualized and constructivist, and they can be seen to extend the reforms of the third strand of the "new vocationalism" by reemphasizing the integration of academic and vocational education while adding a work component to provide a different form of learning.

It is too early to tell what school-to-work programs will become, since the legislation is too new, most states are still in early planning stages, and Congress will probably consolidate funding with other vocational education and job training programs. It is possible that school-to-work programs will be used as levers to shape high school reform, constructing "career majors" or clusters such as those described below.

But two other limited outcomes are possible and, in historical terms, seem more realistic. One is that school-to-work programs will create "work experience" programs in which some high school students—especially those considered "at risk"—spend some time in work placements of varying quality, but without changing the structure, the content, or the pedagogy of the high school one whit.[11] This approach would replicate the work experience programs that were widely supported during the 1970s without ever making much difference to high schools. Over time, we could expect such efforts to wither, as did the reforms of the 1970s. A brighter possibility is that high-quality school-to-work programs will be created for small numbers of students, leaving the college-prep track and the general track largely unchanged.[12]

A cynical (but realistic) view of the school-to-work legislation is that it is an example of "piddle politics."[13] It has captured the attention of educators and business leaders not normally interested in occupationally oriented education, and it presents an image of a federal initiative devoted to building education "systems" instead of creating trifling programs that leave basic institutions unchanged. But the amounts of money—an authorization of up to $300 million a year, vanishing at the end of five years, with only $115 million appropriated for 1995—seem piddling when compared to federal vocational education funds (about $1.3 billion), federal job training funds (about $5.8 billion), total public spending for secondary education (around $85 to $90 billion), or total spending for secondary vocational education (perhaps $15 to $20 billion). Unless the federal government can promote a clear vision of school-to-work programs that will galvanize others into action with state and local resources, the school-to-work legislation seems more of a symbolic gesture than a commitment to any form of the "new vocationalism."

In looking across these four stands of the "new vocationalism," the differences are striking. The first has been conservative in every sense of the term, while the other three are reformist in different ways. The first two emphasize academic subjects without any incorporation of vocational content, while the third and fourth incorporate vocational content as well. They vary in their emphasis on reforming pedagogy, with the second most insistent on changing teaching methods. The fourth incorporates employment-based learning activities outside the school walls, though the second and third incorporate some of this expansiveness as well. All agree, however, in making the skills required in employment first among the goals of formal schooling, and they all continue a separation between academic programs and vocational programs.

Using Occupations To Contextualize Instruction

Like the third and fourth strands, a fifth strand of the "new vocationalism" has attempted to integrate academic and vocational education. But it has done so by restructuring high schools so that the opportunities for integration are more consistent. These efforts have taken three principal forms, varying in their scale.

1. Career academies. Career academies operate as schools-within-schools. Typically, four teachers collaborate: one each in math, English, science, and the occupational area that defines the academy (health, electronics, finance, tourism, and so on). Each class of students takes all four subjects from these teachers, and they stay with the same teachers for two or three years. Students take other subjects outside the academy in the "regular" high school.

One essential element of this approach is that a group of teachers works with a group of students over a period of years. The opportunities for coordinating their courses, including special projects that cut across three or four subjects, are substantial. And because each academy is focused on a cluster of occupations, it becomes relatively natural to integrate occupational applications into academic courses.

A second essential element is a relationship with firms operating in the occupational area of an academy. These firms typically provide mentors for all students, send individuals to talk about particular aspects of their operations, give tours of their facilities, and offer summer internships for students. These opportunities represent other sources of instruction and motivation (cognitive, behavioral, and financial) in addition to those provided by teachers.[14]

Because of their small scale, academies also create communities of both students and teachers. The existence of a community of students is important to teaching methods that involve work in cooperative groups, and a community of teachers helps with curriculum integration and with identifying the problems of individual students. Since academy teachers come to know their students much better than most high school teachers can, it is less likely that their students will feel "lost."

2. Clusters. In some schools, students choose a cluster (or career path or "major"), often at the beginning or end of 10th grade. Like academies, clusters are usually broad occupational or industry-based groupings that reflect local labor markets and structure the curriculum of the remaining two or three years of high school accordingly. In some schools students take some coursework in the occupational area of the cluster—usually a two-period class over the entire two- or three-year period—while other subjects are taken in regular classes outside the cluster. In other schools students take some academic courses within the cluster, and a few schools have replaced conventional discipline-based departments with departments organized along occupational lines.

The cluster organization provides focus for each student, and the required course sequence reduces the "milling around" so common in high schools.[15] Except that every student elects a cluster, clusters are much like academies. They have all the potential of academies to create a focus within which curriculum integration can take place and to develop communities of students and teachers. In addition, choosing a cluster requires an active decision on the student's part, with all the benefits associated with choice.

While there still aren't many schools that use clusters, the concept has been widely promoted at both federal and state levels. The School-to-Work Opportunities Act requires students to choose "career majors" no later than the beginning of the 10th grade. In California, the High

School Task Force recommended "curricular paths" for all students; in its Educational Act for the 21st Century, Oregon defined six clusters or "focus areas" for non-college-bound young people; and a task force in New York recommended the creation of career pathways for youths not headed for college.

3. Occupational high schools and magnet schools. These programs emphasize preparation for vocations in a particular area. Some of these schools—such as Aviation High School, the High School of Fashion Industries, and the Murry Bergtraum High School for Business Careers in New York—have been established for a long time; others are magnet schools that were developed as mechanisms for racial desegregation, many of which have an occupational focus. Every student within an occupational school is enrolled in a curriculum incorporating courses related to the magnet's focus, though the number of these courses ranges from a trivial two or three courses in a four-year sequence to a substantial commitment of time.

Occupational high schools are similar to academies and clusters, except that the scale is schoolwide. This offers obvious advantages for curriculum integration. The incentives to incorporate applications from the school's occupational focus are strong, and the resources to do so are at hand. Occupational high schools are also excellent examples of "focus schools" - schools with clear missions, organized to pursue their educational goals, and operating with explicit social contracts that establish responsibilities for teachers, students, and parents.(16) Similar strengths are emerging in the current movement for charter schools.

Academies, schools offering clusters, and occupationally oriented high schools share certain distinctive features. They impose some coherence on the "shopping mall high school," and they increase opportunities for cooperation and integration across the disciplines. Moreover, the combination of academic and vocational content allows students to plan for postsecondary education, for employment, or for a combination of the two. Students in magnet schools often consciously follow such a "two-track strategy." As one senior in a magnet school commented, "This is my last year, and I'm going to get my cosmetology license. After I get my license, I'll just go to college for business. If the one doesn't work out, I'll go to the other."[17]

In general, students must choose academies or clusters, and in some cities they can choose among magnet schools as well. This requires students to think, early in their high school careers, about their occupational futures. Typically, schools that have adopted one of these ways of educating through occupations have ended up strengthening or developing more active forms of guidance and counseling.

In theory, these practices allow for the integration of occupational content not only with the academic subjects considered utilitarian—math, science, and communication skills—but also with such subjects as literature, history, and social studies. Indeed, an occupational focus may be a way to engage students in subjects that they generally dislike. For example, students might explore the history of technology and economic development or the politics surrounding employment and technological change or the themes of meaning and alienation in work.[18] (Unfortunately, I have seen very few examples of such practices in high schools.)

Most occupationally focused high schools have used broad clusters of related occupations rather than the occupation-specific focus of traditional vocational education—transportation rather than automotive repair or business rather than secretarial and clerical occupations, for example. This approach provides opportunities to explore a wider variety of academic topics and avoids the problem of having modestly skilled jobs dictate the teaching of relatively low-level academic content. It also allows students to explore a wider variety of careers and to understand how occupations are related to one another. If broadly structured, clusters can reduce the class, racial, and gender segregation common in high schools, as students from different backgrounds with varied ambitions come together. For example, health clusters would include both would-be doctors and those who aspire to become practical nurses.

Finally, the use of occupational clusters provides a natural opportunity for building links with employers and with appropriate postsecondary institutions through tech-prep programs. These links need not be contrived, as they often are in comprehensive high schools, since academies, clusters, and magnet programs have already focused the curriculum on occupations of interest to postsecondary institutions and to particular employers.

In addition to these strengths, the movement to develop occupationally focused high schools is consistent with other strands of education reform.[19] In line with current efforts to profession-alize teaching, these programs require teachers to be able to develop their own curricula, to collaborate with teachers from other disciplines, and even to work with employers. Under the best conditions, occupationally focused schools foster more student-centered, project-based, and meaning-centered instruction, partly because of their connection to traditions of vocational education that have used such methods and partly because of the interdisciplinary nature of integrated instruction. In most cases, these innovations introduce student and parental choice and encourage the development of smaller units. And these ways of shaping high schools give restructuring and local control a definition and a purpose.

Of course, academies, clusters, and magnet schools could have nonoccupational themes, too—e.g., the environment, math and science, or the problems of cities. Thus the advantages of academies, clusters, and magnet schools come at least partly from their focus, smaller size, and the communities of students and teachers they create—not just from the specific subjects that form their core.

However, there are good reasons for choosing broadly defined occupations for such a focus. John Dewey articulated several of them 80 years ago in Democracy and Education, when he argued that "education through occupations consequently combines within itself more of the factors conducive to learning than any other method."[20] In modern parlance, we would call such an education contextualized, and it would treat the learner as a social being rather than an isolated individual.

Dewey also feared that conventional vocational education would narrow the education of those preparing for lower-skilled jobs and deny them the opportunities for developing their full range of capacities. Such "trade education" would "defeat its own purpose" as changes in industry took place and narrowly trained individuals were unable to adjust. But the broader conception of "education through occupations" would avoid these limitations. Indeed, Dewey offered examples of such a program that sound remarkably like an academy or cluster school.

Thus we can interpret the fifth strand of the new vocationalism as following a path articulated by Dewey 80 years ago. It was abandoned when the "old vocationalism"—a highly utilitarian and job-specific form of preparation for entry-level work—won the battle for federal funds and for a place in the high school. To be sure, the fifth strand incorporates many elements of the other four, including the stress on higher-order skills, the efforts to integrate academic and vocational education and to connect secondary and postsecondary education, and the potential link with employers through work-based learning. But using occupations to focus instruction—rather than maintaining the distinction between academic education and vocational education—seeks to minimize differences between the college-bound and the non-college-bound. Thus in its broadest and most Deweyan form, "education through occupations" can incorporate the entire range of political and moral purposes, rather than simply assume that the needs of employers are paramount.

The Dimensions of Pedagogy and Content

Of course, the reforms proposed as part of the "new vocationalism" are even more varied than I have described, because each strand has many versions determined by local preferences, resources, and labor market conditions. Indeed, the hallmark of many current reforms is that they replace a unitary conception of the high school with a kind of "principled heterogeneity" that is suited to the variety of student interests and the diversity of student backgrounds. Given this bewildering variety, it is useful to develop a schematic to understand the changes of the "new vocationalism." At the risk of oversimplification, Figure 1 presents a way of understanding recent changes, displayed by variations in pedagogy and in content.[21]

Pedagogy. Approaches to teaching generally fall into one of two long-standing traditions. The dominant approach in virtually all educational institutions in this country (save perhaps early childhood programs) is what I call "skills and drills." It answers to a variety of other names, including didactic or teacher-centered instruction, behaviorist teaching, skills development, and conventional wisdom. The alternative tradition is one that I call "meaning-making" and that others have called student-centered, constructivist, or holistic instruction, or simply the alternative to conventional wisdom.[22]

Each approach to teaching is founded on many assumptions—about dominant forms of learning, about appropriate roles for teachers and students, about the nature and variety of intelligence, and so on—and within each tradition the different elements are consistent with one another. Of course, there are also eclectic or hybrid approaches to teaching that draw on elements from both of these traditions, which are often difficult to recognize precisely because these approaches blend inconsistent elements. In some cases hybrid teaching looks like a step toward innovation, while in other cases practices from meaning-making traditions are simply tossed into a conventional classroom, often without much impact.

Within the two principal pedagogic traditions, there may be academic content only or vocational content only or a mixture of the two. Secondary schools in this country rarely provide vocational content only; this is reserved for short-term training programs outside the schools and for industry-based training. The practices of most high schools differ by whether they offer academic subjects only or a mix of academic and vocational content.

Content. While academic content is defined by academic disciplines of relatively long standing, the conception of vocational content is less well-developed. There are at least five useful conceptions of vocational content.

1. The issues that arise in vocations are used in academic subjects, such as history and social studies. For example, the causes and effects of technological developments, the meaning of work, and public policies toward technology and employment are topics that can be analyzed within conventional academic disciplines. Those who call for a critical approach to work and economic systems also tend to promote this approach to occupational issues. This kind of content fits comfortably within the academic tradition, though material drawn from economic issues has been relatively uncommon in many high school courses.

2. Teaching about occupations familiarizes students with the variety of occupations, the demands they place on individuals, their rewards and liabilities, and the like. This was the dominant content of career education in the 1970s, and it continues to be proposed as a vehicle for career-oriented guidance. While this kind of content is not "academic," it is also not vocational in the sense of preparing individuals for success on the job; instead, it represents the kind of information necessary to make decisions about vocations.

3. The content applicable to broad groupings of related occupations can be taught. This might include, for example, general knowledge of electronics or of business procedures or the reading of blueprints and other kinds of diagrams. Particular applications of academic subjects—the kinds of algebra and trigonometry used in electronics, for example, or the biology and chemistry that are important to health occupations—could also be included. This kind of content is definitely not "academic," though it is unlikely to be job-specific; we can consider this to be general vocational content.

4. Job-specific skills include instruction with the machines and the procedures used in particular jobs. Such instruction is intended to prepare individuals for success in performing those jobs. This has been the content of traditional vocational education, which has usually included "hands-on"—sometimes to the exclusion of classroom instruction. There is a real question whether school-based programs can adequately teach truly job-specific skills; the skills employers look for are often so specific and the machines and procedures so characteristic of a given firm that there is no way job-specific instruction can be delivered except on the job.[23]

5. The most specific form of vocational content involves practice in repetitive movements and procedures to gain speed and automaticity in job tasks. This kind of vocational content is rarely included in programs considered "education," though it does appear in job training programs; indeed, repetition and practice could be used to distinguish "training" from "education."

The various combinations of pedagogy and content yield the approaches shown in Figure 1. The traditional college-prep curriculum falls in cell number 1, as does the "New Basics" approach outlined in *A Nation at Risk*.

The recommendations of SCANS and other advocates of preparation for the high-skills workplace shift education in the direction of meaning-making because of their emphasis on "higher-order thinking skills," problem solving, contextualized instruction, and the like—but they have not abandoned academic content.

Older forms of "progressive" education are the closest historical examples we have of meaning-making (except in early childhood education). Currently, a variety of pedagogical reforms—including contextualized instruction, cognitive apprenticeships, cooperative learning, the process approach to writing, problem-solving approaches in mathematics, and alternative assessment—also fall into cell 7, though each of these reforms typically focuses on a few elements of meaning-making or on a particular academic subject rather than on the entire range of practices.

Conventional vocational education falls somewhere between cell 2 and cell 5. Certainly there are "skills and drills" versions of vocational education: the method of sloyd, for example, used by the manual training movement, took students through a graduated series of woodworking exercises. This approach was also continued in woodshops and metal shops and in competency-based vocational education, with its long lists of competencies to master. The tendency to sort students according to their probable occupational futures and to use vocational education as a "dumping ground," appropriate for the "manually minded" and the non-college-bound, is another reflection of the fragmentation typical of the "skills and drills" tradition.

To be sure, traditional vocational education has also made use of project-based instruction and small-group work. It has been somewhat more student-centered than the academic track, and students in vocational programs have reported that they feel more supported by their instructors than they do in academic classes.[24] In these ways vocational education is more of a hybrid, incorporating some elements from the meaning-making tradition of teaching. Efforts to broaden vocational education by integrating academic and vocational education push vocational education further in this direction.

The organization of high schools into career academies, clusters, and occupational high schools has moved vocational education furthest in this direction, incorporating instructional methods from meaning-making as well as broadening the goals of secondary education, integrating students from different tracks, and weakening the division between academic and vocational education.

The third column of Figure 1—vocational skills only—has typically been the responsibility of job training programs. Most of these programs fall squarely in cell 3, with highly routine instruction following the approach of "skills and drills." To be sure, Ira Shot has articulated a Freirean conception of job training, falling in cell 5, in which clients would be more broadly educated with academic and vocational competencies and a more critical approach to work.[25] In addition, the School-to-Work Opportunities Act can be interpreted as implying a model of job training that fits in cell 5, in which both academic and vocational competencies would be taught, more active pedagogies would be used, and programs would be linked to those of higher skills.[26] And the idealized craft apprenticeships described by the supporters of cognitive apprenticeships might fall into cell 6 because they emphasize the teaching of job-related skills within an instructional mode associated with meaning-making.

The most important question for educational institutions is not what job training should look like, but what the work-based component of school-to-work programs might be. The purpose of work-based learning is presumably to teach those competencies that cannot be taught in school settings. Some of them—including discipline, punctuality, and teamwork—have general applications, while others are likely to be quite specific to a particular firm. In addition, the teaching methods in work settings are not particularly different from those in schools: bosses can instruct by command, threat, and humiliation or by example, encouragement, and the bestowal of increasing amounts of responsibility.[27]

In the best examples of work placements, such as those found in good co-op programs, employers take pains to provide a variety of job opportunities and a broad view of production rather than view their "student workers" as sources of cheap labor for routine tasks. If work placements are confined largely to vocational skills, then those programs that emphasize firm-specific rather than general skills, those with authoritarian supervision, and those with an exploitive rather than a developmental purpose fall into cell 3. On the other hand, work placements that teach more general competencies (or a greater variety of skills), with more supportive supervision, and in a greater variety of settings would fall into cell 6.

Thus an ideal school-to-work program might combine a school-based component in cell 8 and a work-based component in cell 6, A more traditional program might combine a conventional vocational program from cell 2 and the kinds of routine work-experience programs that developed during the 1970s (in cell 3). But such an approach would maintain the sharp divisions between academic and vocational education, between school and nonschool settings, and between college-bound and non-college-bound students.

With the help of Figure 1, then, we can see that the "new vocationalism" represents two kinds of changes: a shift away from the conventional academic programs of cell 1 and toward the second column, and a shift away from "skills and drills" approaches to instruction and toward hybrid instruction and the meaning-making approach. Moreover, these shifts do not take place in a vacuum; thus the shift to more interdisciplinary, contextualized, and project-oriented instruction leads to high school curricula that are friendlier to occupational content, even if there is no such content within a particular program. Or the adoption of applied academic courses can be a precursor to the more thorough reforms of academies and clusters, which are in turn more receptive to incorporating work-based components in school-to-work programs.

It is valuable to interpret intermediate changes as linked to more thorough reforms because both the integration of academic and vocational education and the shift toward new pedagogies upset educational practices of long standing. The difficulty of undertaking these reforms should not be underestimated. But, as I will argue below, the prospects for reform are bright.

The Labor Market Context

In the development of vocational education, there has been a long history of misconstruing the nature of employment. At the turn of the century, the movement for vocational education became caught up in celebrating preparation for "careers"—for sequences of jobs of ever-increasing skill, responsibility, and pay. This image of careers was appropriate for the emerging professions of medicine, law, engineering, and the professoriate, for example. But it did not apply to the semiskilled jobs for which vocational education prepared students. While some workers might become foremen and others might become owners of small businesses, there were few chances of upward mobility for most workers.[28]

Ever since then, the image of "career" has been repeated, despite its uncertain applicability. For example, career education of the 1970s continued to use the term at precisely the time when union-based careers were beginning to disappear. It's important, then, to be careful about changes in employment, lest we recapitulate overly romantic notions.

The past decade's interest in preparing workers for the 21st century has rested on a consensus about changes in employment. As suggested by the title *America's Choice: High Skills or Low Wages!* our economic system has been moving away from an old Taylorist system of employment, in which most workers were only moderately skilled, work was finely divided, and layers of supervisors provided direction, made decisions, and communicated with others inside and outside of the firm. We are moving toward a system in which hierarchies are flatter and frontline workers are more broadly responsible. Thus they require decision-making, problem-solving, and communication skills that they didn't previously need.

Early guesses of the magnitude of new forms of high-skill employment have been imprecise. *America's Choice*, for example, stated without a shred of evidence that about 5% of employees were in firms using high-skill approaches. But a new conventional wisdom about the direction of the economy has developed, and it underlies all aspects of the "new vocationalism." Paul Osterman has suggested that revised employment practices are much more widespread: only 22% of employers have failed to adopt any of the practices associated with workplace transformation, two-thirds have adopted at least one practice relatively thoroughly, and 35% have made substantial use of flexible work organization.[29] Based on this evidence, there is some reason to think that there's a new day dawning.

But two other scenarios about the direction of employment are plausible. One is based on the observation that a great deal of unskilled employment persists. Even though the rate of increase of such relatively skilled jobs as systems analyst, medical technician, and computer programmer is projected to be high, the greatest numbers of new jobs will be in such conventional, low-skilled positions as retail sales, cashiers, office clerks, and truck drivers. This version of the old argument that the economy will continue to need garbage collectors is also consistent with the view that both upskilling (creating new jobs with greater skill demands and educational levels) and de-skilling (creating jobs of lower skill levels) are taking place simultaneously.[30]

The other plausible scenario, not yet completely developed, points to the recent growth of contingent or temporary employment. Indeed, some firms have operated with a substantial fraction of their workers—perhaps 30% to 40%—hired from "temporary" job agencies. One plausible development is that firms will retain a core of permanent employees who will direct a substantial number of temporary or contingent workers, ranging from the moderately skilled, such as secretaries and assemblers, to the more highly skilled, such as accountants, drafters, and engineers. While some higher-order competencies may be required of contingent workers—communications skills, independence, initiative, and motivation are particularly crucial—others, such as problem solving and initiative in the pursuit of the firm's best interests, may rest largely with the core of permanent employees.

And with limited prospects for mobility among contingent workers, older notions of career, defined by increasing responsibility within a firm, may be even less applicable. Instead, individuals may be forced to cobble together "careers" by moving to unrelated jobs as openings occur and by moving among firms. Current discussions about the "virtual firm" and the "demise of the job" may be alarmist, but they contain the germ of substantial changes in employment.

The most likely future is one in which all three kinds of employment persist. For educators, the implication is that schools should not buy wholeheartedly into any single vision of the future, since any such vision is likely to be incomplete. This suggests that changes in schools should rest in part on educational principles and not entirely on occupational imperatives—not only because occupational goals are only some of the purposes of education, but also because those imperatives cannot be precisely known. The forms of the new vocationalism that require education to be driven solely by the requirements of employers and the demands of the 21st-century labor force should be particularly suspect: no one can forecast what these demands will be, and those who pretend to do so impose an overly narrow conception of education on the schools.

Prospects for Reform

What are the chances that the current forms of the "new vocationalism" will have any enduring effects and not succumb to another round of curricular conservatism within the decade? While there are many reform movements, there are contrary tendencies: efforts to establish competency-based instruction, the presence of curricular movements to reinstate the classics or to return to the "essentials" of education, the various projects to develop curriculum standards for specific subjects. And of course the elections of November 1994, with their substantial shift to the right, could also usher in a new round of educational conservatism.

One reason to hope that the schools can avoid the prospect of "reforming again and again and again" is that the demands from outside the schools have changed. The division of labor and the advent of Taylorism around the turn of the century reinforced the separation of management and execution, of the academic and the vocational. But current trends in employment seek to undo this pattern. For example, the growth of more integrated production and the development of flatter hierarchies with more responsibilities for production-level workers have reduced the traditional divisions. As a result, the business community has spent the past decade decrying "narrow vocationalism" and calling for workers with higher-order thinking skills, communication skills, problem-solving abilities, and greater independence.

But demands from outside the schools have never been especially effective. So a second reason for optimism is that external pressures for reform are consistent with internal motivation—with the desires of teachers themselves to be professionalized. Unlike other reforms—e.g., the accountability movements of the 1980s—some current efforts to reconfigure curriculum and instruction (including "education through occupations") return power to teachers. Reforms that give more responsibility to teachers are likely to have more impact than are reforms imposed on unwilling teachers.

Still another reason for optimism about integrated instruction, including the efforts to integrate academic and vocational education, is that such instruction offers a way of addressing another urgent problem that educators and those outside the schools want to resolve: improving the quality of education for low-income and other at-risk students. Critics of conventional education have long pointed out its inequities, and these criticisms have been louder in the current period because of increases in the numbers of low-income, minority, and non-English-speaking students. Standard decontextualized approaches to teaching present motivational problems for all students, but the children of well-educated, middle-class parents are better able to cope. Those who are left behind tend to be students without their own sources of motivation, without role models in their families or communities—that is, the children of the poor, whose parents are poorly educated or have jobs for which formal schooling is irrelevant.

Various strategies have tried to influence parents or compensate for their deficiencies—e.g., parent education and parent involvement. But the success of such efforts has been limited. The alternative—changing teaching so that intrinsic motivation is improved by providing meaningful contexts for students themselves—has rarely been proposed. However, a recent analysis of teaching and learning for disadvantaged children has concluded that more active, student-centered approaches are the most promising ways of teaching such students. And these methods are consistent with contextualized and integrated teaching.[31]

More generally, the efforts to create contextualized instruction provide a way of creating heterogeneous but egalitarian schools as a response to the diversity of race, class, language, and culture. The past solutions to the challenges of diversity have been inadequate. One approach—the development of the common school with a unitary curriculum, the "one best system"[32] with its institutional and instructional rigidities—has been a failure because the inequalities of motivation and preparation associated with students' diverse backgrounds have been magnified within the seemingly egalitarian schools. The alternative approach—the development of differentiated schooling, with different tracks based on differences in ability, motivation, and interest—is an inherently inegalitarian solution because the different types of schooling have always led to futures of considerably different status and power.

But the development of integrated instruction organized around broadly defined occupations—or a combination of occupations, social problems, and other engaging topics—provides the opportunity to create heterogeneous forms of schooling that are "separate but equal." Such a principled heterogeneity represents a relatively egalitarian way to respond to diversity in all its forms, including the diversity of interests now stifled in the college-prep curriculum.

A fourth reason for optimism is the confluence of several reform movements, all roughly consistent with one another. Efforts to "restructure," to return greater control to the school level, are consistent with the fact that contextualized and integrated teaching must be locally developed and implemented. "Authentic assessment," the movement to replace intrinsically meaningless measures of learning (e.g., multiple-choice exams) with more intrinsically valuable indicators (e.g., exhibitions, portfolios of accomplishments) is also more consistent with contextualized teaching, the use of projects, and the like. And the movement to give students and parents "school choice" can be fulfilled by offering alternative occupational clusters or magnet schools.

Finally, several ways of institutionalizing changes provide some hope that current reforms might not be blown away by the next cycle of revisions. In the past, changes in teaching methods have often been idiosyncratic—limited to particular teachers and vulnerable to their personal commitment. Interdisciplinary courses have also been fragile, readily replaced by conventional disciplinary courses once a few teachers lost interest. The alternative schools created in the 1960s were marginal to the mainstream schools that defined them as "alternative," and they were all too readily abandoned under the fiscal pressures and the conservative curricula of the late 1970s and 1980s.

But the institutional structures developed in the past decade—academies and other schools-within-schools, magnet schools with particular themes or teaching approaches, charter schools with distinctive identities, and occupational clusters or majors within a high school—are potentially more enduring ways of changing instruction. These structures include larger numbers of teachers and administrators and are not dependent on a crucial one or two. They can develop identities and cultures of their own, which are then useful in recruiting students and socializing new teachers; they can therefore perpetuate themselves in ways that individual teachers or courses could not. They also provide a social setting within which a community of teachers can improve its teaching, thereby removing some of the isolation that many teachers experience.

These changes, difficult though they may be, have enormous potential, They provide a very different image of what a high school should look like, but it is an image potentially strong enough to replace the fragmented "shopping mall high school" and to institutionalize changes in curriculum and pedagogy. And they promise a new approach to vocationalism, one that recognizes the inescapable occupational purposes of high schools without eliminating the political and moral purposes that have always been at the heart of public education.

QUESTIONS TO CONSIDER

1. Grubb describes and interprets five different versions of what he calls the "new vocationalism" in U.S. high school. Which version(s) makes the most sense to you? Why?

2. The author examines diverse ways to integrate academic and vocational education: career academies, cluster organizations, occupational high schools, and magnet schools. What are the advantages and disadvantages in each of those structures? Which do you prefer? Why?

3. That did John Dewey mean by "education through occupations"? What were his worries about conventional vocational schools? Which view(s) of restructured vocational education would he likely advocate? Why?

4. Of the five conceptions of vocational content that Grubb presents, which do you find to be most sound? Why?

5. Why does the author argue against adopting a vocational path "driven solely by the requirements of employers and the demands of the 21st-century labor force"? Do you agree or disagree? Why?

6. What kind of reform does Grubb proffer? What are its possibilities for fulfillment? Why?

Notes

The chapter originally appeared in *Phi Delta Kappan*, Vol. 77, No. 8 (April 1996): 535–546. Published here with permission of Phi Delta Kappa International.

1. Richard Coley, *What Americans Study Revisited* (Princeton, N.J.: Educational Testing Service, 1994).
2. Patricia Kean, "Building a Better Beowulf: The New Assault on the Liberal Arts," Lingua Franca, *The Review of Academic Life*, May/June 1993, pp. 1–28.
3. High school students rank vocational goals higher than intellectual, personal, or social goals. However, both parents and teachers rate intellectual goals highest. See John I. Goodlad, *A Place Called School: Prospects for the Future* (New York: McGraw-Hill, 1984), chap. 2.
4. *What Work Requires of Schools* (Washington, D.C.: Secretary's Commission on Achieving Necessary Skills, 1991). See also Cathy Stasz et al., "Teaching Generic Skills," in W. Norton Grubb, ed., *Education Through Occupations in American High Schools, Volume 1: Approaches to Integrating Academic and Vocational Education* (New York: Teachers College Press, 1995).
5. Alan Collins, John Seeley Brown, and Susan Newman. "Cognitive Apprenticeship: Teaching the Craft of Reading, Writing, and Mathematics," in Lauren Resnick, ed., *Knowing, Learning, and Instruction: Essays in Honor of Robert Glaser* (Hillsdale, N.J.: Erlbaum, 1989), pp. 453–94.
6. See *Investing in Our Children: Business and the Public Schools* (New York: Committee for Economic Development, 1985), p. 15; and National Academy of Sciences Panel on Secondary School Education for the Changing Workplace, *High Schools arid the Changing Workplace: The Employers' View* (Washington, D.C.: National Academy Press, 1984), p. 13.
7. See, for example, Charles Benson and Harold Silver, "Vocationalism in the United Kingdom and the United States," Working Paper No. 16, Institute of Education, University of London, 1991: David Spence, "Rethinking the Role of Vocational Education," *Educational Horizons*, Fall 1986, pp. 20–23; Kenneth Gray, "Vocational Education in High School: A Modern Phoenix?," *Phi Delta Kappan*, February 1991, pp. 437–45; John F. Claus, "Renegotiating Vocational Instruction," *Urban Review*, vol. 21, 1989, pp. 193–207: Roger Simon, Don Dippo, and Arleen Schenke, *Learning Work: A Critical Pedagogy of Work Education* (New York: Bergin and Garvey, 1991); Theodore Lewis, "Difficulties Attending the New Vocationalism in the USA," *Journal of Philosophy of Education*, vol. 25, 1991, pp. 95–108; Marsha Rehm, "Emancipatory Vocational Education: Pedagogy for the Work of Individuals and Society," *Journal of Education*, vol. 171, 1989, pp. 109–23; and Leonard Cantor, "The Re-Visioning of Vocational Education in the American High School." *Comparative Education*, vol. 25, 1989, pp. 125–32.
8. W. Norton Grubb, "'The Cunning Hand, the Cultured Mind': Sources of Support for Curriculum Integration," in idem, *Education Through Occupations*, Volume I, pp. 11–25.
9. W. Norton Grubb and Cathy Stasz, *Integrating Academic and Vocational Education: Progress Under the Carl Perkins Amendments of 1990* (Berkeley: National Center for Research in Vocational Education, University of California, 1993).
10. See, for example, Stephen Hamilton, *Apprenticeship for Adulthood: Preparing Youth for the Future* (New York: Free Press, 1990).
11. Harvey Kantor, "Managing the Transition from School to Work: The False Promises of Youth Apprenticeship," *Teachers College Record*, Summer 1994, pp. 442–61; and W. Norton Grubb, "True Reform or Tired Retread? Seven Questions to Ask About School-to-Work Programs," *Education Week*, 3 August 1994, p. 68.
12. The "triple track" approach has emerged most conspicuously in the academic, vocational, and general tracks that persist (in practice, if not in name) and in the life adjustment movement, with its program of life adjustment education for the 50% of students for whom neither academic preparation for college nor vocational education is appropriate.
13. My thanks to Lorraine McDonnell for this apt phrase.
14. See David Stern, Marilyn Ruby, and Charles Dayton, *Career Academies: Partnerships for Reconstructing American High Schools* (San Francisco: Jossey-Bass, 1992); and Marilyn Ruby, "The Career Academies," in Grubb, *Education Through Occupations*, Volume 1, pp. 82–96.

15. For a variety of ways in which clusters and majors have been adopted. see W. Norton Grubb, "Coherence for All Students: High Schools with Career Clusters and Majors," in idem, *Education Through Occupations*, Volume 1, pp. 97–113.

16. On focus schools see Paul Hill, Gail Foster, and Tamar Gendler, *High Schools with Character* (Santa Monica, Calif: RAND Corporation, 1990).

17. Amy Heebner, "The Voices of Students," in Grubb, *Education Through Occupations*, Volume 1, pp. 148–66.

18. Ken Koziol and W. Norton Grubb, "Paths Not Taken: Curriculum Integration and the Political and Moral Purposes of Education," in W. Norton Grubb, ed., *Education Through Occupations, Volume 2: The Challenges of Implementing Curriculum Integration* (New York: Teachers College Press, 1995), pp. 115–41).

19. Erika Neilsen Andrew and W. Norton Grubb, "The Power of Curricular Integration: Its Relationship to Other School Reforms," in Grubb, *Education Through Occupations*, Volume 1, pp. 39–56.

20. John Dewey, *Democracy and Education: An Introduction to the Philosophy of Education* (New York: Macmillan, 1916), p. 309.

21. I developed this interpretation in the summer of 1994, in the glorious setting of the Radcliffe Camera in Oxford. I then discovered a strikingly similar analysis of the British changes in Philip Hodkinson, "Liberal Education and the New Vocationalism: A Progressive Partnership?," *Oxford Review of Education*, vol. 17, 1991, pp. 73–88. His is a 2 x 2 matrix in which "traditional" and "progressive" pedagogy are distinguished on one dimension and academic and vocational content on the other.

22. W. Norton Grubb and Judy Kalman, "Relearning to Earn: The Role of Remediation in Vocational Education and Job Training," *American Journal of Education*, November 1994, pp. 54–93.

23. See W. Norton Grubb, *Working in the Middle: Strengthening Education and Training for the Mid-skilled Labor Force* (San Francisco: Jossey-Bass, 1996).

24. Penelope Eckart, *Jocks and Burnouts: Social Categories and Identity in the High School* (New York: Teachers College Press, 1989); and John Claus, "Opportunity or Inequality in Vocational Education? A Qualitative Investigation," *Curriculum Inquiry*, vol. 20, 1990, pp. 7–39.

25. Ira Shor, "Working Hands and Critical Minds: A Paulo Freire Model for Job Training," *Journal of Education*, vol. 170, 1988, pp. 102–21.

26. See the conclusion to W. Norton Grubb, *Learning to Work: The Case for Reintegrating Education and Job Training* (New York: Russell Sage Foundation, 1996).

27. See Sue Berryman, "Apprenticeship as a Paradigm of Learning," in Grubb, *Education Through Occupations*. Volume 1, pp. 192–214.

28. Joseph Kett, "The Adolescence of Vocational Education," in Harvey Kantor and David Tyack, eds., *Work, Youth, and Schooling: Historical Perspectives on Vocationalism in American Education* (Palo Alto, Calif.: Stanford University Press, 1982), pp. 79–109.

29. Paul Osterman, "How Common Is Workplace Trans formation and Who Adopts It?," *Industrial and Labor Relations Review*, vol. 47, 1994, pp. 173–88.

30. This view is often associated with Henry Levin and Russell Rumberger. See, for example, Russell Rumberger, "The Potential Impact of Technology on the Skill Requirements of Future Jobs in the United States," in Gerald Burke and Russell Rumberger, eds., *The Future Impact of Technology on Work and Education* (Philadelphia: Falmer Press, 1987), pp. 74–95. For the most recent occupational projections, see George Silvestri and John Lukasiewicz, "Outlook: 1990–2005: Occupational Employment Projections," *Monthly Labor Review*, November 1991, pp. 64–94. For a review indicating that both upskilling and downskilling are taking place, see Kenneth Spenner, "Upgrading and Downgrading of Occupations," *Review of Educational Research*, vol. 55, 1985, pp. 125–54.

31. See W. Norton Grubb, "The Old Problem of 'New Students': Purpose, Content, and Pedagogy," in Erwin Flaxman and Harry Passow, eds., *Changing Populations/Changing Schools: 94th NSSE Yearbook, Part II* (Chicago: National Society for the Study of Education, University of Chicago Press, 1995). The empirical evidence that methods derived from meaning-making are more effective for low-income students is presented in Michael Knapp et al., *Teaching for Meaning in High-Poverty Classrooms* (New York: Teachers College Press, 1995).

32. David Tyack, *The One Best System* (Cambridge, Mass.: Harvard University Press, 1974).

CHAPTER THIRTY-TWO

Character Education for Adolescents

Pedagogy of Control

TIANLONG YU

Character Education: A National Movement

It is important to define the term *character education* from the outset. Even if character education, past and present, has been diverse and multifaceted in both theory and practice, its core is still unique and identifiable. Both proponents and critics of character education have defined it as virtue-centered moral education (Lickona, 1999; McClellan, 1999; Noddings, 2002). For example, according to Thomas Lickona (1999), one of the most noted theorists of character education, "Character education is the deliberate effort to cultivate virtue. Virtues are objectively good human qualities" (p. 23). The Character Education Partnership (CEP), the largest organization that promotes character education in the United States, defines character education in a similar way:

> Character education is a national movement encouraging schools to create environments that foster ethical, responsible, and caring young people. It is the intentional, proactive effort by schools, districts, and states to instill in their students important core, ethical values that we all share, such as caring, honesty, fairness, responsibility, and respect for self and others. (CEP, 2009)

In schools, this emphasis on the inculcation of virtues in students is often carried out through curricular and extracurricular activities focusing on identified virtues, which, in schools, are often called "core values," "character traits," or "life skills." *Eleven Principles of Effective Character Education,* authored by Lickona and his associates (1995) and widely distributed by the CEP, has become a staple for many schools in developing character education programs. These principles highlight a "comprehensive" approach to promoting core ethical values in students.

Character education, as defined above, enjoyed a prominent place in the educational agenda of the eight-year Bush administration. Although the character education movement had already begun to gain momentum before the Clinton era, it received unprecedented support from President George W. Bush. During the Bush years, federal support of character education came in the form of substantial legislation and grants. The No Child Left Behind Act, the education centerpiece of the Bush administration, not only authorizes the Secretary of Education to award grants to state and local educational agencies for the design and implementation of character education programs, but also outlines directives for such design and implementation. For example, it requires the selection of "elements of character" (such as caring, civic virtue, and respect) to be taught under the program for which the grant was awarded. It also suggests factors that may be considered in evaluating the success of programs funded (which include discipline issues and student academic achievement). As Glanzer and Milson (2006) note, at no other time in history have Americans attempted to legislate such a specific vision of character education.

As President Bush declared during the 2005 National Character Counts! Week, under his watch, over 60 state and local education agencies had received funding from the Department of Education to provide programs in character education. According to Josephson Institute's national office of Character Counts!, in August 2007, there was $400 billion available in federal grants designated for character education. Complying with NCLB, 80% of 50 states have now passed legislation to mandate character education in their public schools (Nucci & Narvaez, 2008). This high level of both legislative and financial support from the federal and state governments for an education initiative focusing on students' values, morality, and character is historically unparalleled in the United States. Largely due to this powerful governmental support, the character education movement is thriving across school districts in the nation.

Character Education in the Past: Sociopolitical Orientation

Character education is not today's invention. It has a long and contested history in American schools. A careful look into this history will help us understand the current movement. As William J. Reese (1999) states: "History has a tremendous role to play in explaining the fate of teaching of moral, ethical, and religious values in the schools" (in McClellan, 1999, p. vii). The common school movement of the mid-nineteenth century made state-funded public schools the most important educational institutions in the United States. Moral education, in general, was seen as a necessary means to achieve a common culture. Horace Mann, the champion of the common school movement, argued for a central place for moral education in the new public school. Moral education was integrated into the entire life of the school, especially in elementary schools. For example, moral lessons were diffused through textbooks—readers, spellers, and even arithmetic books. Famous spellers and readers, such as the *McGuffey Readers*, expressed a pronounced moral emphasis. The moral values taught were a blend of traditional Protestant morality and nineteenth-century conceptions of good citizenship. Educators believed in absolute rules in moral training and left little room for interpretation and flexibility. As an integral part of the common school agenda, moral education was emphasized to help maintain a common culture and solidify the established economic and political order. The sociopolitical orientation of moral education was evident at the very beginning of American public schooling.

The dawn of the twentieth century was a time of turbulence in American society. The fast-paced technological advances, increasing urbanization, industrialization, and immigration dramatically transformed society and people's lives. The schools responded to social changes by shifting their attitudes toward, and practices of, moral education. Educators began to give far more attention to academic and social competence to meet the increasing demands of a modern industrial economy. Religious-based traditional moral training promoted in the common school movement declined in the increasingly secular schools. Conversely, the call for character education was still heard. This call was commonly justified by a perceived moral decline in society. Dramatic social changes at the turn of the century brought about break-ups in the home, rampant individualism in the workplace, negativity in the media, political corruption, shifting cultural values, rising crime rates, and the decline of religion. A moral, or character, breakdown was thought to be behind all of these trends and renewed moral education was expected to solve social problems (McKown, 1935). Some influential organizations, such as the National Education Association, joined the choir to call for the building of children's character as the central aim of schools. Recognizing the inadequacy of the old-fashioned moral training scheme, advocates hoped that a newly defined program of character education would operate effectively under the altered modern circumstances.

Responding to the rising new faith in science and the secularization of morality, advocates of character education accepted the State in general and the school in particular as the new bearers of morality (Yulish, 1980). They also tied moral education more closely to a growing modern society. Character building was thought to be crucial for an individual's life adjustment, citizenship, vocational efficiency, and worthy use of leisure time. The call for character education was also greatly reinforced by World War I, which not only cemented the need for character training, but also provided it with a particular emphasis. The nationalistic, jingoistic fervor in America during the war pushed the schools to place a stronger emphasis on patriotism, duty, and civic training. Morality largely became civic responsibility. The concept of the good person was redefined to become synonymous with that of the good citizen. This trend of integrating character education with citizenship training would continue well into the modern time.

A virtue-centered approach characterized character education in schools. The virtues were often called character traits or conduct codes. One of the first character education programs was developed in Toledo, Ohio, in 1901. It consisted of a five-minute talk each morning on such traits as obedience, kindness, and honesty. One topic was scheduled for each month (McKown, 1935). This was probably the earliest form of the one-virtue-per-month approach, which is extremely popular in today's character education movement. In 1909, the Character Development League of New York City initiated a plan of using the biographies of great men for character education. James Terry White's book on character education in the school and home (1909) was especially written for this purpose. In White's book, the series of "character lessons" subdivides good character into thirty-one traits, including obedience, honesty, perseverance, purity, self-control, and patriotism. The author suggested that several traits be taught in each grade. As a whole, the character lessons were to be taught systematically throughout each year of the school course. Pupils were not only expected to understand these lessons but also to practice the virtues. All subject teachers were required to combine moral lessons with their class instruction. Schools across the country quickly adopted similar character traits or codes as a focus of their programs in character education. Educators attempted to integrate character traits or morality codes into all aspects of school life. The codes provided themes for both formal instruction and extracurricular activities. Curricular and extracurricular activities aiming to promote virtues are common in today's character education schools.

Character education was pervasive in American schools in the first three decades of the twentieth century, but its influence began to decline in early 1930s when "economic and social dislocations seemed to call for a more critical approach to moral education" (McClellan, 1999, p. 55). Progressive educators, led by John Dewey, best voiced that call. The progressives' concerted attack on character education not only declared the end of its dominance but also started a new era of more humanistic and constructivist approaches to moral education. In the subsequent half century, traditional virtue-centered character education never played a central role in American schools, while moral education in general waned in its influence. The mid-1960s started a slow revival of interest in new forms of moral education, including Values Clarification and the cognitive-developmental approach to moral development. Reflecting the post-World War II social and cultural shifts in America, those two approaches rejected the overemphasis on social stability, political stasis, and cultural preservation that traditional character education so strongly promoted and instead attempted to elevate individual freedom and cultural diversity. By the early 1980s, that progressive vision of moral education began to fall into a defensive position.

Character Education in New Times: Moral Decline and Character Building

The resurgence of character education began in the early 1980s, with popularity unseen for a long time. As McClellan (1999) comments: "[Proponents of character education] mounted the strongest campaign for virtue-centered education the nation has witnessed since the early twentieth century" (p. 89). Not surprisingly, the modern character education crusaders used a very similar rationale to push for the new movement, a rationale widely and successfully utilized to launch character education in the early twentieth century.

To support their call for traditional character education, the proponents construct a seemingly logical rationale. They systematically describe a serious moral decline in the society, claiming that the overall moral, sociocultural, and behavioral conditions of American society are troubling as indicated by widespread problems such as crime, violence, drug abuse, sexual promiscuity, and other deviant behaviors, especially among young people. They argue that these problems are either moral problems themselves or problems caused by moral decline. Based on these allegations, they conclude that only a virtue-centered moral education could solve these problems.

One of the most influential early leaders of modern character education is William Bennett, one of the most outspoken cultural and political conservative pundits in America. Bennett served as Secretary of Education for the Reagan administration and the "Drug Czar" under George H. W. Bush. In his 1994 book on "cultural indicators," Bennett emphasizes the "troubling" condition of American society and provides statistical and numerical breakdowns, charts, graphs, and analyses of the data on crime, family and children, youth pathologies and behavior, education, popular culture, and religion. According to him, total crimes, violent crimes, and juvenile violent crimes all have increased. Meanwhile, the conditions of the family and children have deteriorated while illegitimate births, single-parent families, and divorce rates have increased. His comments on those problems are straightforward and problematic. For example, he views illegitimate birth as "the single most important social problem of our time" (p. 48). In addition, the picture of American youth is particularly dark with increasing problems of teen pregnancy and illegitimate births. He bemoans dropping SAT scores and the rising disciplinary problems in schools. His statistics show that American children watch too much TV and that sex and violence are too pervasive on the media. He also complains that religion is losing its believers.

Based on the above claims, Bennett draws his conclusion: "Over the past three decades we have experienced substantial social regression. . . . Unless these exploding social pathologies are reversed, they will lead to the decline and perhaps even the fall of the American republic" (p. 8). Obviously he refers to crime, illegitimate births, children living in single-parent homes, divorce, and the decline in SAT scores as "social pathologies." Furthermore, for him, those social pathologies clearly reflect moral decay. When addressing the lack of moral education in society as the cause of these problems, it is clear that he emphasizes the linkage between these problems and individual morality.

Bennett is not alone. Another character education leader, Thomas Lickona, also makes sweeping claims of moral decline. Lickona routinely opens his call for character education by claiming that the United States is in "deep moral trouble." In his widely publicized (often through his own character education training programs) 1991 book, *Educating for Character: How Our Schools Can Teach Respect and Responsibility*, Lickona justifies his case for character education with "accumulating evidence of a moral decline, first in society at large and then among the young" (p. 12). While Bennett prefers the use of statistics and focuses on larger "social pathologies" and attention-getting issues such as violent crime and drug abuse, Lickona favors informal surveys, personal stories, and casual anecdotes to show that moral slippage is everywhere in our society. His signs of moral decline include employee theft, phony resumes, drunkenness, and people who deceive their best friends and cheat on their marriage partners as well as on their tax returns (p. 13). Furthermore, moral decline is best shown in youth trends, argues Lickona (1991, 1993, 1996). He repeatedly remarks on "ten troubling trends in youth character" to show that "the general youth trends present a dark picture" (Lickona, 1991, p. 13). Those trends include rising youth violence, increasing dishonesty (lying, cheating, and stealing), growing disrespect for authority, peer cruelty, a resurgence of bigotry on school campuses from preschool to higher education, a decline in the work ethic, sexual precocity, a growing self-centeredness and declining civic responsibility, an increase in self-destructive behavior, and ethical illiteracy.

Along with the aforementioned claims of moral decline, character education leaders emphasize that moral poverty has caused social pathologies such as crime and drug abuse. In Bennett's (1994) opinion, even if we face a serious "social regression," the overall political and economic systems are fine: "The United States has the strongest economy in the world, a healthy entrepreneurial spirit, a still-healthy work ethic, and a generous attitude—good signs all" (p. 8). For him, the capitalist economic production machine still runs well; the social resources are fairly distributed; and the political system is just and effective. In a word, the social structure has few consequential problems. However, the general picture of the social and cultural conditions of the United States is still dim, and we still suffer severe social pathologies and behavioral problems. Why has this happened and how can we deal with it? As Bennett (1994) answers: "The social regression of the last 30 years is due in large part to the enfeebled state of our social institutions and their failure to carry out a critical time-honored task: the moral education of the young" (p. 12). He is clear about this: Loss of morality matters most; failure in moral education results in social regression.

In their book, *Body Count: Moral Poverty . . . and How to Win America's War against Crime and drugs*, Bennett, Dilulio, and Walters (1996) go one step further and emphasize "moral poverty" as the root cause of problems such as crime and drugs. Their portrait of juvenile crime is eye-catching and very scary:

> America is now home to thickening ranks of juvenile 'super-predators'—radically impulsive, brutally remorseless youngsters, including evermore pre-teenage boys, who murder, assault, rape, rob, burglarize, and deal deadly drugs, join gun-toting gangs, and create serious communal disorders. (p. 27)

It is hard to find more extreme cases of the demonization of young people. However, this kind of reasoning reflects a deeply held belief about what has caused crime and drug abuse. "The nation's drug and crime problem is fueled largely by moral poverty" (p. 14). Bennett and his associates have determined that "today's lack of self-restraint and social norms, the breakdown of civil society, the attenuation of individual responsibility and commitments, and the importance of religious faith" are at the root of problems of crime and drugs (pp. 14–15). If problems such as crime and drugs have resulted from moral poverty, moral education presumably becomes the solution to the problems. As Bennett (1994) claims, "We desperately need to recover a sense of the fundamental purpose of education, which is to engage in the architecture of souls" (p. 12).

Lickona agrees with Bennett that moral education is the only answer. Lickona (1993) believes that "troubling" youth behavioral trends offer convincing evidence that we are largely failing to transmit our most basic moral values to the next generation. Then, he blames schools for not doing a good job in moral education. He nostalgically recalls the old days when "schools tackled character education head on"—through discipline, the teacher's example, the daily curriculum, the Bible as sourcebook, *McGuffey Readers*, and lessons about honesty, hard work, thriftiness, patriotism, and courage. Even if he never explicitly calls for bringing the Bible back to the classroom, he praises old character education practices, which were grounded in religious traditions.

Like Bennett and Lickona, other character education leaders frequently address similar concerns about the so-called moral decline in society and the failure of moral education in schools (Kilpatrick, 1992; Ryan, 1989; Wynne, 1989a, 1989b). Together, these influential political and educational figures successfully launched a public moral crusade. Their reasoning about moral decline served as tone setter for the national character education movement.

Deconstructing the Myth of Moral Decline

Character education leaders' claims about moral decline need to be critically examined. They may provide some important information about the conditions of American society and raise some concerns about certain social problems. However, the sweeping rendition of social problems as or caused by moral problems is largely unfounded. Though crime, drug abuse, sexual misconduct, and violence do exist, the claim that they are widespread and out of control is exaggerated. Exaggeration of the seriousness of the problems does not help solve them. We need to clearly define the nature and the scope of the problems in order to find effective solutions. Spina (2000) warns about misconceptions of school violence and notes that we do not intend to downplay the tragedy of school shootings or minimize the expectation that schools should be absolutely safe, but we must also understand the level of fear surrounding the so-called epidemic of school violence.

More importantly, the cause-effect relationship character educators often draw between moral decline and social problems is troublesome. Again, we must fully realize that there are indeed crimes in our society and behavioral problems among young people. There are even indications that over the past generation or two some crimes have become more egregious, particularly in school settings. However, we must carefully look at the context of the formation and development of those problems. We cannot view violence and drug abuse simply as individual behavioral problems caused by a lack of personal morality, even though the moral implications cannot be overlooked. These problems do not represent solely an individual moral decay; rather they reflect flaws in the larger society or culture. These problems have fundamental social, political, cultural, and economic causes.

The problem with character educators' logic is that they focus on the question of personal character when addressing those social problems and even magnify it while simultaneously casting a blind eye on the social and cultural roots of the problems. It is not an issue of deciding whether violence or drug abuse is a social problem or an individual problem but about understanding how the broader economic and social structure affects individual behavior and morality. It is not a matter of assigning a percentage of blame—for example, 35 percent individual and 65 percent social. The personified, individually located problems are predominantly and fundamentally rooted in sociocultural and economic causes. In the case of poor minority youth, whom character educators often target, moral poverty results from the lack of power—political, economic, and cultural power. Being marginalized, being victims of economic displacement and institutional racism, seriously damages personal development and well-being. How can moral life flourish amid the chemical refuse of corporate capitalism in East St. Louis? The hopelessness is rooted in powerlessness.

Such structural analysis of social problems is rarely found in the writings of character education leaders. Character educators do not attempt to conduct an in-depth analysis of why young people commit violence and what has caused them to kill or deal drugs. They do not look deeply into youths' inner world, nor do they extensively check the external environment children live within. That there is something wrong with their morality becomes a convenient explanation. That may be true. However, morality does not develop in a vacuum. Obviously, the moral deterioration identified by character educators results from something other than children's lack of character. The real causes may lie in the exploitation and oppression in their lives and the resulting alienation from self and others.

Targeting the Youth: Blaming and Scapegoating

Character educators have largely targeted youths as scapegoats for social problems. Their critique is an integral part of a popular culture and public discourse that degrades youth. Henry Giroux

(2000) argues that popular culture, represented by Hollywood films and other mainstream media, presents youth as a social disorder and a menace. In films and other media images, "Youth [*sic*] are increasingly defined through the lens of contempt of criminality" (p. 94). For example, in many Hollywood films, such as *Dumb and Dumber* (1994) and *Kids* (1996), teenagers are portrayed as vulgar, disengaged pleasure-seekers, and over-the-edge violent sociopaths. They are decadent, drug-crazed, pathological, and criminal. In a word, youth are demonized. On the other hand, youth are commodified or constructed as consuming subjects. Advertising targets youth as commodities. In these popular narratives, "One dimensional and ahistorical representations of youth erase the complexities and contradictions of place, style, language, and individual histories" (Giroux, 1997, p. 24). Missing from this media discourse is any mention of power, ideology, and human rights. Also absent is any challenge to the exploitation and domination youth suffer today.

Going along with the popular narrative, politicians and some intellectuals use the popular cultural image to wage more assaults against youth. In their view, youth become symbols of aberrant promiscuity, social degeneracy, and moral decay. Youth are accused of leading the country into moral decline and tearing the fabric of the nation asunder. We have witnessed this demonization approach in Bennett, Lickona, and other character education leaders' writings. Their sweeping views have fooled the uncritical public, including many teachers, into believing in the dark view of youth. Setting up youth as scapegoats resonates with political and economic policymakers who make policies that harm youth. Giroux (1997) points out:

> As the discourse on youth shifts from an emphasis on social failing in the society to questions of individual character, social policy moves from the language of social investment—creating safety nets for children—to the language of containment and blame. (p. 170)

Bennett (1994) actually argues that social investment is not needed. Instead of talking about eradicating poverty, building decent schools, and creating viable jobs, Bennett and other conservative commentators either invoke the punitive demand for more prisons or emphasize Victorian morality.

In character educators' portraits, young people are no longer seen as a symptom of a wider social dilemma; they are the problem. For example, character educators always criticize the sexualization of youth in Hollywood movies, but they simply blame youth for sexual acts. By such criticism, they send the simplistic and misleading message that sex is bad. Abstinence-based sex education has been integrated into the character education movement (Lickona, 1993). Many such programs spread fear and misinformation with grotesque and terrifying imagery, portraying teenage sexuality as decadent and predatory and urging youth to simply say no to sex. These strategies do not prepare teens to deal with their emerging sexuality. They lack a genuine respect for, and understanding of, young people and fail to establish a connection between youth and their social context. The effectiveness of these programs is of course limited.

Character educators portray kids as if they live in a historical, political, and cultural vacuum without memory or history. They provide no context for understanding the cultural, social, and institutional forces in their lives. They treat violence, drugs, and sex as personal choices. In reality, however, violence, drugs, and sex may constitute the daily experience of young people who live in places and situations that foster suffering and oppression. Violence, drugs, and sex may be part of their everyday struggle. Even in affluent communities, many children of the rich, the powerful, and the famous, are left free to experiment. They have more than they need or want and resort to seeking pleasure in alienated lives. Like the poor kids, they are also culturally and socially impoverished.

Character Education for Social Control

Defining youth as behaviorally deviant and morally corrupt naturally leads to character educators' next claim: Children and youth need to be socialized to the established rules and standards of society. The socialization, or rather social control, of youth, is thus legitimated as the central goal of character education.

Politicians, such as American presidents, have always seen schools as the moral underpinning of the nation. Theodore Roosevelt's statement, "To educate a person in mind and not in morals is to educate a menace to society," has become one of the most popular slogans in the current character education movement. The 2002 White House conference on character education strongly stressed the link between character education and national service, recommending both military service and civil service. At the conference, Secretary of State Colin Powell emphasized character education as the means of transmitting the values of the United States as a nation. Another keynote speaker, William Damon, urged educators to embrace the "transcendent purpose" of character education—patriotism.

The implication of these slogans, claims, or arguments is this: Via moral/character education, schools become society's policing agents. Schools must transmit the values that are reproduced by, and support, the established society and its existing political and economic systems. Education becomes socialization. Educators seek to socialize children and youth to be productive, yet obedient, members of society. This ideology stems from a long tradition of schooling, which has philosophical support from theorists such as Aristotle and Emile Durkheim and the contemporary endorsement of social elites, such as William Bennett, who benefit from established power and economic relations and, therefore, defend the status quo.

That tradition expects schools to enforce a moral code and act as an agent of stability to prevent delinquency (Tyack, 1974; Tyack & Cuban, 1995). This expectation has been well integrated into education policy-making throughout the history of American education. As we have seen, the nineteenth-century Common School was charged with the duty of assimilating poor immigrants (who were viewed as wild, prone to violence, and antisocial) into the American social order. During the Johnson administration, the Commission of Law Enforcement and Administration of Justice stated that the school, "unlike the family, is a public instrument for training young people. . . it is the principal public institution for development of basic commitment by young people to the goals and values of our society" (Anderson, 1998, p. 318). Obviously, today's politicians such as President Bush and educators such as Lickona have wholeheartedly embraced this long-standing tradition and worked to strengthen the expectation that schools will maintain the established social order by socializing youth.

In the character education movement, social control is achieved mainly through an overemphasis on social values and a narrow definition of citizenship. Again, this has a historical precedent. The growth of character education in the 1920s was largely the State's response, via schools, to the declining ability of the church and family to maintain the social order. The character education program represented a State-sanctioned moral system. Worthy character was seen as the basis of good citizenship, and the school, through character education, had to produce good citizens for the State. The goal of an ideal society was ever present in character education programs. In the character traits or morality codes developed by character educators, social values took precedence over other values.

Similar social orientation is emphasized in today's character education. While bemoaning the so-called moral decay in society and troubling youth behavior, the leaders of character education seem to be more worried about the possible decline of the republic and the fall of American civilization than the well-being of children and youth. They put the nation's political and economic interests before the individual. The overwhelming emphasis of character education objectives is placed on socially oriented values which are expected to make students strong citizens.

A revealing example in this regard is found in a problematic schema of patriotic education prevailing in many character education schools. After the attacks of September 11, 2001, American schools were increasingly directed to step up patriotic rhetoric. The federal role in encouraging this trend has been significant. On October 12, 2001, the White House called on the nation's 52 million schoolchildren to take part in a mass recitation of the Pledge of Allegiance. Four days later, the U.S. House of Representatives passed a resolution (404–0) urging schools to display the words "God Bless America" to reinforce national pride. In 2002, several months before the U.S. invasion of Iraq, the federal government announced a new set of history and civic education initiatives aiming directly at building national identity, pride, and a strong sense of patriotism in young Americans. President Bush declared, for the purpose of patriotic education, that we must teach youngsters "America is a force for good in the world, bringing hope and freedom to other people" (qtd. in Westheimer, 2007, p. 172). Echoing or answering the federal call, numerous states introduced legislation to either encourage or mandate patriotic exercises for all students in schools. By 2007, according to Westheimer (2007), twenty-five states required the Pledge of Allegiance to be recited daily during the school day and thirty-five required time to be set aside in school for the pledge.

The patriotic fervor has been naturally infused into the character education movement, which enjoyed unparalleled momentum with the signing of the No Child Left Behind bill into law by President Bush in 2002. In many schools, patriotism is a core value being taught along with other "universal virtues" or "character traits." Schools organize events and activities with an emphasis on patriotic citizenship education and character building. For example, many schools have events to honor soldiers back from Iraq or Afghanistan. The soldiers are hailed as patriotic heroes who fought for their country. They are portrayed as role models who demonstrated a strong character of selflessness, discipline, courage, and above all, love and sacrifice for the country.

Many have challenged this form of patriotic education. Deborah Meier (2007) simply puts it: "In the name of the War on terror or the War on Iraq, we have experienced the narrowing of our national understanding of patriotism" (p. 52). Westheimer (2007) observes that "the form of patriotism being pursued by many school boards, city and state legislatures, and the federal government is often monolithic, reflecting an 'America-right-or-wrong' stance—what philosopher Martha Nussbaum warns is 'perilously close to jingoism'" (p. 172). In schools and classrooms, this narrow and jingoistic patriotism shunned any controversy and reinforced the America-is-righteous-in-her-cause message. Such patriotism rejects teaching for democratic citizenship, "the kind of citizenship that recognizes ambiguity and conflict, that sees human conditions and aspirations as complex and contested, and that embraces debate and deliberation as a cornerstone of patriotism and civic education" (Westheimer, 2007, p. 173).

What is missing from the popular "salute to the troops" scenario, or any other character education activities, is critical examination of the controversial war itself. While adopting an unquestioning stance toward citizenship during wartime and instilling loyal obedience in students to the government, little room is left for dissent or debate about U.S. foreign policy and especially questions surrounding the legitimacy of the wars. Pedro Noguera and Robby Cohen (2007) argue, "A nation with so strong a military and so vast a military presence must have an education system that is equally strong in teaching its future citizens to think critically and independently about the uses of American power and about the role of the American military in the world" (p. 28). They call on school educators to take the responsibility to ensure that students today acquire an intellectual grounding in history, civics, and culture that will enable them to develop informed opinions about the current wars, about U.S. foreign policy toward the Middle East, and about the implications of the wars for civil liberties in American society. To the dismay of many, however, such a call is not taken seriously in our schools, which are now open to military recruiters, mandated by NCLB, but often opposed to antiwar protests.

Bush era patriotism was really a form of "authoritarian patriotism," which demanded allegiance to the government, not to the principles underlying democracy. Under such authoritarian patriotism and narrow citizenship training, character education becomes mere socialization or control. The role of the individual as an active participant in the general polity is typically overlooked or ignored. Society and its government are promoted as having absolute authority and without being subject to significant critique or challenge. This political inactivity is certainly what the Bush administration and politically conservative pundits wanted.

Uncritical social education by character educators must be challenged. It is of course important to locate the individual's moral life within social life and to uplift the school's responsibility to advance the welfare of society. However, education, and moral education in particular, must move beyond socialization. A return to John Dewey is warranted here. Dewey (1897/1974) argues that children must be educated for democratic citizenship. The child must be educated so that "he may take charge of himself; may not only adapt himself to the changes which are going on, but have power to shape and direct those changes" (p. 114).

This is certainly the empowerment we owe to youth today.

QUESTIONS TO CONSIDER

1. What role has the government played in the character education movement? Why is it important to critically analyze the politics of character education?

2. What are the similarities and differences between character education in the past and character education today?

3. What are the sociopolitical forces driving the modern character education movement?

4. What social interests and political ideologies are present-day character education meant to serve?

5. What is the underlying view of children and youth held by many character education advocates? How do blaming and scapegoating youth lead to social control in character education?

6. How does today's character education promote a narrow, authoritarian citizenship and patriotism? How can civic and patriotic education be defined and approached differently?

7. How can educators take up the challenge to resist social control and promote education for self-empowerment and social change?

References

Anderson, D. (1998). Curriculum, culture, and community: The challenge of school violence. In M. Tonry & M. Moore (Eds.), *Youth violence* (pp. 317–364). Chicago: The University of Chicago Press.

Bennett, W. J. (1994). *The index of leading cultural indicators: Facts and figures on the state of American society.* New York: Simon & Schuster.

Bennett, W. J., Dilulio, J. J. Jr., & Walters, J. P. (1996). *Body count: Moral poverty . . . and how to win America's war against crime and drugs.* New York: Simon & Schuster.

Character Education Partnership. (2009). What is character education? Retrieved April 21, 2009 from http://www.character.org.

Dewey, J. (1974). Ethical principles underlying education. In R. D. Archambault (Ed.), *John Dewey on education* (pp. 108–138). Chicago: The University of Chicago Press. (Original work published 1897)

Giroux, H. (1997). *Channel surfing: Racism, the media, and the destruction of today's youth.* New York: St. Martin's Griffin.

Giroux, H. (2000). Representations of violence, popular culture, and demonization of youth. In Spina (Ed.), *Smoke and mirrors: The hidden context of violence in schools and society* (pp. 93–105). Lanham, MD: Rowman & Littlefield.

Glanzer, P. L., & Milson, A. J. (2006). Legislating the good: A survey and evaluation of character education laws in the United States. *Educational Policy, 20*(3), 525–550.

Kilpatrick, W. K. (1992). *Why Johnny can't tell right from wrong.* New York: Simon & Schuster.

Lickona, T. (1991). *Educating for character: How our schools can teach respect and responsibility.* New York: Bantam Books.

Lickona, T. (1993). The return of character education. *Educational Leadership, 51*(3), 6–11.

Lickona, T. (1996). The decline and fall of American civilization: Can character education reverse the slide? *Currents in Modern Thoughts, June 1996,* 285–307.

Lickona, T. (1999). Religion and character education. *Phi Delta Kappan, 81*(1), 21–27.

Lickona, T., Schaps, E., & Lewis, C. (1995). *Eleven principles of effective character education.* Washington, DC: Character Education Partnership.

McClellan, B. E. (1999). *Moral education in America: Schools and the shaping of character from colonial times to the present*. New York: Teachers College Press.

McKown, H. C. (1935). *Character education*. New York: McGraw-hill.

Meier, D. (2007). On patriotism and the Yankees: lessons learned from being a fan. In J. Westheimer (Ed.), *Pledging allegiance: The politics of patriotism in America's schools* (pp. 49–60). New York: Teachers College Press.

No Child Left Behind Act of 2001. Public Law 107–110, 2002.

Noddings, N. (2002). *Educating moral people: A caring alternative to character education*. New York: Teachers College Press.

Noguera, P., & Cohen, R. (2007). Educators in the war on terrorism. In In J. Westheimer (Ed.), *Pledging allegiance: The politics of patriotism in America's schools* (pp. 25–34). New York: Teachers College Press.

Nucci, L. P., & Narvaez, D. (Eds.). (2008). *Handbook of moral and character education*. New York: Routledge.

Ryan, K. (1989). In defense of character education. In L. Nucci (Ed.), *Moral development and character education* (pp.3–17). Berkeley, CA: McCutchan.

Spina, S. U. (2000). Introduction: Violence in schools: Expanding the dialogue. In S. U. Spina (Ed.), *Smoke and mirrors: The hidden context of violence in schools and society* (pp. 1–39). Lanham, MD: Rowman & Littlefield.

Tyack, D. B. (1974). *The one best system: A history of American urban education*. Cambridge, MA: Harvard University Press.

Tyack, D. B., & Cuban, L. (1995). *Tinkering toward utopia: A century of public school reform*. Cambridge, MA: Harvard University Press.

Westheimer, J. (2007). Politics and patriotism in education. In J. Westheimer (Ed.), *Pledging allegiance: The politics of patriotism in America's schools* (pp. 171–188.) New York: Teachers College Press.

White, J. T. (1909). *Character lessons in American biography for public schools and home instruction*. New York: The Character Development League.

Wynne, E. A. (1989a). Transmitting traditional value sin contemporary schools. In L. Nucci (Ed.), *Moral development and character education* (pp. 19–36). Berkeley, CA: McCutchan.

Wynne, E. A. (1989b). Managing effective schools: The moral element. In M. Holmes, K. Leithword, & D. Musella (Eds.), *Educational policy for effective schools* (pp. 128–142). Toronto: OISE Press.

Yulish, S. M. (1980). *The search for a civic religion: The history of the character education movement in America, 1890–1935*. Washington, DC: University Press of America.

CHAPTER THIRTY-THREE

An Empowering, Transformative Approach to Service

JEFF CLAUS & CURTIS OGDEN

> To become an integrated person is not only to understand the world in which we live and work, but to become the kind of person who will take part in shaping and reshaping those worlds. This emphasis on critique of current realities, and on participating in the re-creation of our worlds, is a central part of democratic life.
>
> —LANDON BEYER, *CREATING DEMOCRATIC CLASSROOMS*

As the idea of service learning gains momentum and becomes more integrated into the life of schools and communities, we think it is important to continue thinking about what we hope to accomplish through service and what kinds of programs are most likely to help us achieve these goals. In a recent article, Stan Karp (1997) worries that the service-learning movement may become yet another "anemic" application of a potentially powerful idea. Similarly, Kahne and Westheimer (1996), Boyte (1991), and others (e.g., Jones, Maloy, and Steen, 1996; Lakes, 1996; Youniss and Yates, 1997) have cautioned us against adopting a "weak," "feel good," or "superficial" version of service. We share these concerns. Behind the belief that service work is a powerful pedagogical tool lurks the risk of rendering a complex activity banal through efforts to standardize and spread the service-learning movement. Service learning is not simply a pedagogical innovation rooted in the principles of experiential education and an interest in helping people and organizations in need. It also has the potential to become a transformative social movement, but this will only be realized if we view it as such.

Since 1992 the Learning Web, a community-based, youth-service agency in Ithaca, New York, has been the recipient of state and federal funds to run community-service programs for seventh through tenth graders in schools throughout its county. Both authors of this chapter have directed and been responsible for developing these programs.[1] During this time our thinking and program design have evolved toward an approach to service learning we think of as both empowering and transformative—empowering of youth and transformative of both youth and the society in which we live. We have worked to create circumstances in which youth are intrinsically motivated to reflect critically and to work together to improve their communities and the lives of people in them. In the process, youth appear to develop a wide array of skills and perspectives important both for living effectively in the world as it is currently constructed and for transforming the world into a better place. This, we feel, is an experience with implications not only for the individual development of participating youth but for the future of our society and world. From the perspective of our approach, individual development occurs as a consequence and within a framework of working to create a better world. It is closely linked to "the dream of changing the world, rather than adapting to it" (Freire, 1992, back cover).[2]

In this chapter we discuss some of what we think can and should be guiding principles for an empowering, transformative approach to service learning, and we describe a program we have developed for high school students in accordance with these ideas. By doing this we hope to encourage those involved in creating, running, and funding service programs to embrace the notion that service learning will be most motivating, meaningful, and effective for young people when it provides them with opportunities (i.e., when it empowers them) to define, investigate, think critically about, participate in, and act to improve the communities in which they live. We believe service learning has an extraordinary potential to engage young people in experiences involving explorations of community and self, critical thinking, democratic activism, and the pursuit of a more just and humane world. At its best, service learning can create circumstances in which young people develop a deeper understanding of their world and themselves and an improved sense of purpose, justice, agency, and optimism. It also provides them with tools for acting upon this understanding. Service-learning programs cannot achieve all of this, though, unless they are designed and carried out with these goals in mind.

The Principles of Empowering Education

Building on the ideas of Paulo Freire, John Dewey, and many others involved in the work of democratic, transformative education, Ira Shor, in his book *Empowering Education: Critical Teaching for Social Change* (1992), sets out a number of interwoven ideas we feel are particularly relevant to the task of developing an empowering, transformative approach to service learning. We would like to discuss five, of these briefly here to create a framework for better understanding the design and philosophy of our program. These five concepts are *situated learning*, *dialogic discourse*, *teachers as problem posers*, *critical thought and consciousness*, and *activist learning*.

Situated learning means learning rooted in the lives, interests, themes, and concerns of the students. This approach to instruction makes the learning experience more personally meaningful and motivating than the traditional teacher-centered model, in which educators often "download" a predetermined curriculum. Shor describes this approach as fundamentally democratic. "To be democratic implies orienting subject matter to student culture—their interests, needs, speech and perceptions—while creating a negotiable openness in class where the students' input jointly creates the learning process" (Shor, 1992, 16). This, we think, is critical to achieving empowering service learning and is a key starting point and building block in the program we run. As we will discuss in detail below, our program allows students to determine their own group service projects on the basis of their evolving definitions of service, their interests, and an assessment of community needs. This helps develop a strong sense of ownership, motivation, and involvement in the varied work required to carry out a substantial service project.

Consistent with this idea is the concept of *dialogic discourse*, which means engaging students in a democratic, participatory process in which dialogue and group discussion are central to defining and negotiating the direction and progress of the learning experience. When applied to service learning this means participants work as a group and take an active role in discussing and deciding on the nature and path of the service activity. In the process they employ and develop democratic, group-process skills, which are fundamental to democratic decision making and success in the work of social reform.

The concept of *teachers as problem posers* encourages educators to generate critical, relevant, motivating questions, with and for students, and to use these questions to lead and frame the learning experience. In some cases these are the product of teacher-student dialogue and collaboration; in other instances they are provided by the teacher with an interest in helping students to become more aware of and to critically reflect on and question the world around them. When employed in service learning, this concept leads to a sequence of generating, investigating, and trying to answer critical questions that address issues and problems of interest to the participants and that are of significance to society. It means raising questions with young people about their community, for the purpose of generating and guiding investigation, reflection, dialogue, planning, and action. Through problem posing, service learning can become an experience of conducting critically reflective research which leads to community action.

Related to this idea is the concept of *critical thought and consciousness*. Without a critical, questioning perspective, Shor and many others argue, education supports the status quo and thus cannot be transformative As a result, Shor encourages teachers to engage students openly and explicitly in analyzing, questioning, and rethinking important societal arrangements and structures, noting that without a critical perspective and awareness students will not be able to identify those aspects of society and their lives that will benefit from constructive change. He sees problem posing, dialogue, and critical thought or awareness as working together not only to raise important questions but to illuminate a path toward transformative action.

> Problem posing offers all subject matter as historical products to be questioned rather than as universal wisdom to be accepted. . . . In this democratic pedagogy, the teacher is not filling empty minds with official or unofficial knowledge but is posing knowledge in any form as a problem for mutual inquiry. (Shor, 1992, 32–33)

> When educators offer problem-posing, democratic dialogue in the classroom, they challenge socialization into the myths, values and relations of the dominant culture. . . . Critical teachers provide a social experience in education that questions previous experiences in school and society and that models new values, relationships, discourse, knowledge, and versions of authority. (Shor, 1992. 117–118)

> The basic process of dialogue—problem-posing—actively questions schooling, society, teacher-talk, and existing knowledge. It democratically invites students to make their education, to examine critically their experience and social conditions, and to consider acting in society from the knowledge they gain. (Shor, 1992, 188)

In service learning, critical consciousness or awareness is important because it informs and guides service in a way that the service can be transformative of the world rather than simply adaptive. Critical awareness takes students beyond the act of feeding those who are hungry to questioning why people are hungry and working to help the hungry feed themselves. This constitutes development of an analytical, reflective perspective that helps service participants better understand their world, with an eye for improving it.

Finally, *activist learning* means not just guiding students to question the past and present for the purpose of envisioning an improved future but actively pursuing reform on the basis of the knowledge gained through research and reflection. It means helping youth connect a critical perspective to social action in order to become agents of constructive change. Shor continues: "Activist learning is oriented to change-agency. Change-agency in this pedagogy means learning and acting for the democratic transformation of self and society. . . . [It means] actively studying life to change it" (Shor, 1992, 190–192). Or, as Sorensen (1996) writes, "Decision making, critical thinking, reflection, and recognizing multiple viewpoints are all part of the process of empowerment. However, empowerment cannot be achieved without action. . . . Empowerment involves action; action involves change. Empowered individuals work to make meaningful changes to benefit their community" (91).

What this means for service learning is that it should be centered, from the outset, around the pursuit of constructive change. Questioning, dialogue, planning, reflection, and action should all be framed by the purpose of achieving meaningful reform. This is at the heart of the potential power in service, as youth can be given an opportunity to critique, plan, and act in personally relevant ways to improve their communities and world. Thus, what otherwise might be viewed as an adaptive ad of service becomes a transformative step in community development. In the process, young people often develop a sense of agency and optimism, a hopefulness, about their capacity to realize their own visions for a better world.

Taken together these concepts suggest an approach to service learning that begins with student-derived interests and perspectives; proceeds with dialogue, research, and critical thought; and leads to social action and ongoing reflection.[3] This, we think, is what empowering, transformative service learning is all about. Ultimately, it is this guided: process that creates for youth a view that change is possible and that they can play an important role in achieving it.

ImPACT: The Learning Web Approach

During the past five years, the Learning Web has developed and run an extracurricular community service program that it offers on a rotating basis to the county's middle and high schools. At the high school level the program is called ImPACT, which stands for the Importance of Participating, Acting, and Coming Together. Initially focused on small schools in rural communities, the program has recently expanded to include a larger city high school as well. Each project ultimately consists of a Learning Web staff person, one or two college interns, about 8–12 student volunteers, and a handful of teachers and school staff who come together to create a service initiative that we hope will lead to self-sustained service activity in the future.

In all of its programs the Learning Web works closely with schools to provide interested youth with experiential learning opportunities. A central objective of the organization is to help youth develop the skills necessary to be more self-directed in their learning and lives. As Learning Web founder Michelle Whitham wrote in 1976, the organization "attempts to facilitate the decisions that its clients make about what they want to take place . . . rather then requiring each student to participate in a pre-designed curriculum. . . . In other words, the students direct their own experiences" (21).

In accordance with this philosophy, the Learning Web gives young people in its community-service programs the opportunity to determine what their projects will be and how they will be carried out. We begin this process as we recruit volunteer after-school groups, presenting information, generating discussion, and soliciting participation in high school classrooms. From the outset, including during the recruitment phase, we engage young people in reflecting on and discussing their lives, communities, and views of service. We feel these discussions allow young people to construct personally meaningful definitions of service and community, and they motivate youth to get and stay involved and to pursue action of significance to them. This approach also introduces potential volunteers to the youth-centered, participatory nature of the program and helps guide eventual project planning.

Initial Steps in the Youth-Centered Approach

One of the main questions we pose and pursue in the recruitment and initial phases of the program is, "What is community service?" The ensuing discussions and comments usually reveal a range of experiences with and perceptions of service, from the sophisticated and enthusiastic to the limited and negative. On the negative end, for example, we sometimes hear comments such as these: "Community service is usually just picking up garbage. That's so boring." "Community service is for kids who've gotten in trouble."

At this stage we acknowledge all relevant feelings and reactions and encourage a discussion of what community service could and should be. In association with negative views, a question often raised is, "*Why* should I get involved in community service?" Rather than answering this for young people, we let dialogue be our guide. We make clear that the program is an opportunity for young people to define community service in ways they find meaningful and to pursue community action they feel is valuable. If we simply refuted negative perceptions of service, we feel we would risk invalidating real experiences that can be fertile ground for reflection and, ultimately, committed participation. Some very lively conversations about what community service should be have grown out of recruiting sessions, and we think these are productive. In this way we try to go where young people are rather than ask them to come to us.

As part of this process of situating community service in the experiences of young people, we often use an exercise in which we ask students to study a list of about a dozen activities that could be defined as community service, then to rank them in terms of their own ideals. There are always differences in response, even in the smallest group, and these are an excellent source of discussion and reflection. Some people, for example, choose "talking with a friend" as their ideal, while others may put this last. Some people pick "riding your bike to work and leaving the car at home," while others roll their eyes. Many choose "cooking a meal for the homeless," while "joining the armed forces" is often a controversial choice. Differences in experience and values quickly become apparent, and discussion of these differences generally leads to a broader understanding and definition of community service, reflective of social and cultural aspects of the students' lives and their views of community need. When we ask young people to boil all of this down to a basic definition, it generally reveals that everyone thinks that community service should be about helping others or contributing to the common good, including striving for positive change. This, in turn, opens up conversation about what they, as young people, would like to see done in their communities.

During recruitment, we have also made it a practice to bring along former youth program participants to share some of their experiences with the program and the service projects they have done. This peer-to-peer sharing often proves to be a powerful motivational tool and a further contribution to the pool of project possibilities. At this point we attempt to elicit some concrete examples of activities we might undertake, and we distribute a sign-up list for those who are interested in taking the next step.

The next step is an after-school meeting during which we show and discuss a video about young people throughout the United States taking the initiative to get involved in their communities.[4] This video was produced by, with, and for teens and young adults, a fact that always catches the attention of our youth audience. It is common for viewers, after watching the film, to comment that although they like the video it has little to do with issues in their community. This too, then, becomes a launching point for critical group reflection and discussion about their communities, issues that are important to them, and ways in which they might address some of these issues.

Students generally respond positively to these sessions. We think this is because they are given an opportunity to reflect critically in a way that validates and shows respect for the knowledge and insight they bring to the project. As one young woman commented in a final evaluation of the program, "One big reason I joined ImPACT was that you began by asking me my opinion. You really showed us that this was *our* project." Thus, before they have done anything project-oriented, students in the program engage in fundamental reflection that requires them to think about and define community service so it is meaningful to them and consistent with their experience, ideals, and concerns. In this way we attempt to both orient young people to service and orient service to the lives of young people. This, we believe, situates the work of the program in the culture of youth participants and sets the stage for meaningful action and learning.

Developing Deeper Connections to Service

We form/select a volunteer group that usually consists of 8–12 young people and is established to work together for about four to six months. In accordance with grant specifications, at least half of each group is made up of students who are identified as "at-risk" using criteria provided in the grant. Meetings are held twice a week after school for a total of about five hours of activity a week. We begin each group with discussions and exercises that focus on self-concept and are geared toward developing self-esteem and strengthening personal connections to the program's themes.

One of the first conversations we have with a new group centers around each individual's motivation and goals for joining the program. In each group young people articulate a variety of reasons for getting involved, including altruism, an interest in doing something about some aspect of their community or society they feel needs attention, boredom, a desire for community and to be with peers after school, a desire to have a new experience, and resume building. Some youth have very specific goals and ideas from the outset, while others have trouble explaining why they have decided to join. At this point, we are most interested in maintaining dialogue as a guide and motivational tool.

Participants definitely learn about and influence each other constructively as they discuss why they have volunteered. We have also found that participants' goals change over the course of a project, and we want them to be aware of this evolution. Quite often they go from being interested primarily because they want to do something after school other than go home to watch television, to being genuinely concerned and reflective—sometimes passionate—about a social issue and/or an aspect of their community they want to address. We think helping youth become self-reflective about this kind of development can be an important part of developing critical awareness and a socially conscious sense of identity.

Another exercise we use early on with each group is to develop a skill or talent inventory of its members. This gives participants an opportunity to identify and share their individual strengths and interests and a chance to connect these to the future work of the project. Once we have generated a list of talents—"a group resume"—we ask how some of these talents might be applied to community service activity. For example, if someone in the group states that he or she is musically inclined, we ask how that skill might be used in a project. The same goes for those who say they are skilled in fixing cars or computers, working with people, gardening, writing, and so on. The idea we want to convey at this point is that service is not simply about joining conventional responses to perceived problems but can be more meaningful when people use their talents and creativity to dream up new approaches.

We also engage groups in exercises geared toward clarifying values and then follow up with discussions about how these values might affect their choice of projects. For example, having young people prioritize values at play in their own lives (financial security, love, personal safety, etc.) can help guide them in the selection of certain themes or issues they hope to address. This can raise awareness of the bigger picture behind service work. At times, these exercises will reveal contradictions between aspirations for one's self, such as wealth, and those for society at large, such as equity. Addressing these contradictions is a way to get young people to think critically, to reconcile individual and social goals, and to clarify visions for meaningful change. Another exercise we often use is called "Roles We Play." In it, members are asked to think about the roles they play in a given week (student, daughter, sister, friend, congregation member, Girl Scout). This helps explore individual connections to community and ways in which these relationships might lead to service options. It enlivens and expands a group's outlook, and it has proven especially useful and motivational in smaller communities where conventional service activities (often through institutional linkages) may not be so readily apparent or available. It is also important to mention that in addition to holding group meetings, we often arrange an initial one-time or short-term service project for each new group to undertake after its first couple of weeks together. We have a connection with a local volunteer coordination service that organizes college students to do renovation work in the low-income and not-for-profit housing sector. Through them we set something up. This gives our group a real experience with volunteer service upon which we can reflect. *What did you think? Did you enjoy this project? Why or why not? Was it valuable, and, if so, in what ways? What community needs did the work address? Why do these needs exist? How else might you address these needs? What lessons can we take from this experience and apply to our own service work?* In this way, participants continue to develop a sense of their own visions of community service and to engage in discussions of how they would like to define and address their community's needs. These are, we think, important first steps in the process of pursuing empowering and transformative service and action.

The Value of Working in Groups

While we support the idea of having young people personalize the concept of service, we also want to be sure not to make it a selfish undertaking. In initial brainstorming sessions we sometimes hear suggestions of projects that are essentially self-serving ("let's organize a party") or lack meaning outside of the immediate group. This is when we move our focus from individual interests to community building. This can be achieved through questioning—"How will throwing a party contribute to the community's well being? Who will it help? How will it help them? What issues will it address?"—or the use of certain discussion tools, including quotes and poems.[5] It is important to situate service in the lives of young people, and it is equally vital to encourage work that is socially meaningful. Striking this balance is what our approach is all about, bringing together the processes of individual growth and community development.

Thus the fact that we work with *groups* of young people is very significant. Each group consists of a mix of students with regard to academic performance, social class, gender, ethnicity, and personality. Bringing together multiple outlooks and aspirations requires shared leadership and negotiation. This means that participants have to learn how to communicate, understand, respect, and get along with each other to carry out their service projects. Developing these skills is an integral part of Learning Web community service. As we say to each group, "If you want to help build community *out there*, you might as well begin *right here*."

Interpersonal issues often arise as part of this group-building process, and we make sure to engage young people in discussion about these issues and the differences in their lives. Issues of social class and school and community social structure, for example, must often be addressed before we can proceed in our work together. These issues thus become teachable moments that sometimes seem to take us far beyond the details of the task at hand, but not in an irrelevant way. They introduce some young people to issues of social justice they had not been objective about, even though the issues are a central part of their lives. Some groups have even decided to address these issues in their project work.

As the group settles into its routine, we engage participants in moving beyond individual identity to think about group identity. How do they want to function as a group? How will they make decisions? Where do they want to meet? How will meetings be facilitated? What is their agenda? How do they want to present themselves to the wider community? Answers to these questions develop over time and with practice as youth experiment with leadership and decision making. In the initial stages of each project, Learning Web staff play more of a facilitation role, but as time passes the young people generally become more active and take more responsibility as they learn appropriate skills and gain experience and confidence.

In addition to discussion and the practice of group facilitation, we introduce various exercises and activities designed to build trust within the group, to illustrate the importance of cooperation, and to train participants in the process of developing consensus. Cooperative problem-solving games emphasize the importance of listening, focus, synthesis, prioritization, and clear communication in successful group work. The next step is to take these skills out into the field, with the reminder that just as we must work cooperatively and respectfully within the group, we must apply these practices to the wider community of which we are all a part.

Community Investigation

Community investigation is another activity fundamental to our model for service learning. As already noted, we believe that giving young people the opportunity to identify and pursue their own projects helps them develop the tools to take initiative in the future. As the Zimbabwean proverb goes, "Spoonfeeding teaches one nothing but the shape of the spoon." Or, as Jerome Bruner writes, "Acquired knowledge is most useful to a learner . . . when it is discovered through the learner's own cognitive efforts, for it is then related to and used in reference to what one has known before" (1996, xii). A next important step in the process, then, is for the group to engage in community investigation and research that will help them make decisions about which service projects to pursue and how. This, too, encourages participants to move beyond their own immediate frames of reference to consider the needs of others and issues in the wider community and society.

When we speak of *community* for the purposes of our projects, we generally begin with the geographic school district in which we are operating, though this can be subdivided into neighborhoods or expanded to the county level. This exploration period allows participants to develop a meaningful context for any service project they carry out and deepens their understanding of possibilities for action. The group is ultimately guided by its collective interests and problem-posing techniques. It all begins with the questions "What are the components of a community and this community in particular?" and "How can we gather information that will help us pursue meaningful, effective action here?"

To begin to focus more intensely on the actual community, we use an exercise that asks participants to make lists of the five characteristics they think best describe their community, the five things they like most about their community, and the five things they like least about their community. Using these lists as a starting point, we brainstorm and discuss changes they would like to see made in their community, being sure to guide the group to identify both community assets and areas for improvement. This information becomes critical as the group progresses toward choosing issues to address. It also sets the stage for deeper investigation.

For purposes of gathering community information, we employ a variety of investigative techniques, with some suggested by the young people and others proposed by Learning Web staff. One thing we always do is introduce participants to anthropological perspective and method. Anthropology, and in particular the ethnographic method, does not seem to make its way into many middle and high school classrooms, although it is very useful in helping young people understand their communities and different people's experiences in them. A discussion of culture and social structure, and the ways in which they affect individual outlook and social interaction, can point to the importance of trying to see life through the eyes and experiences of others. This is helpful in developing both compassion and critical thought as young people learn to consider multiple perspectives and to raise questions about social problems as seen by others.[6]

The next component of the investigative stage is consideration of the community resources participants will tap to learn more about what is going on and what might be done in the future. This is most often done simply by asking youth to identify institutions, facilities, and people that exist in the community. Sometimes we break down the community into areas such as economy, politics, education, religion, culture and recreation, health, and social services to help guide young people's thinking. We also discuss power relationships within the community. *What is power? Who has power? What kind of power f do they have? Who lacks power? What are the implications of power relationships for the way things are in their community and for how things get done?* Investigation is not just a question of discovering who lives in the community but of how these people relate to and interact with each other and where the young people themselves fit in.

Community investigations have taken many different forms. These include conducting observational walking tours in certain parts of the community; studying a map of the area and identifying key geographic features; gathering information through surveys and inventories; interviewing members of the community (both peers and adults) about social issues, history and project ideas; soliciting input from the community by putting notices about the group in local newsletters and newspapers; meeting with representatives of appropriate organizations and local government; and scanning local publications. In one community, group members came up with the idea of convening a forum of community leaders, during which they asked the leaders about pressing community issues and the potential role they saw young people playing to address them. In another community; the group handed out cookies at lunchtime in the school cafeteria in return for project ideas.

Something else that often happens at this stage is that we offer to take participants to visit a local service clearinghouse, Cornell University's Public Service Center (in Ithaca, where we are based), which publicizes local, national, and international volunteer opportunities. This trip to Cornell allows group members to ask a lot of questions, to learn about what makes a project successful and satisfying, and to look at concrete examples of initiatives taking place in other communities that they might want to adapt to their own surroundings.

Throughout this process participants are encouraged to determine the direction of the investigation, to make calls and arrangements, and to design and conduct interviews and other information-gathering activities. They work as a group to identify questions they would like to ask and have answered, and they conduct research. In addition, we engage participants in discussions of what they are experiencing and learning as they think about the future direction of the project(s). The guiding questions for this phase are, "What needs are there in the community?" "Whose needs are these?" "What are the sources or causes of these needs?" "How might we contribute to and help improve the community, by addressing some of these needs?" "What resources might we use/are available?" And, "What do we want to do as a group to act on answers to these questions?"

In postprogram evaluations, students generally comment on how much they enjoy this stage. They particularly like interviewing community members on subjects of interest to the group. These activities also tend to raise important social issues for discussion and debate, including hunger and homelessness, local and national health issues, funding for social programs, educational philosophy and practice, limited roles for young people, zoning practices, issues of race and class, and so on. We find that young people very much like thinking about and discussing major issues such as these when their views and ideas are taken seriously and have a purpose.

Decision Making

The community exploration phase of each project continues through the end of our time together as we keep our eyes and ears open to ongoing developments and opportunities; nevertheless, its primary purpose is to help the group select a project or projects to pursue. For this we use a democratic approach that centers around group discussion, reflection, and consensus. Not everyone has the same interests, but we try to prioritize, to focus on feasibility, and, if we decide to take on a number of projects, to address topics of interest to most members of the group.

In one community, for example, after interviewing teachers, parents, friends, and others and after much discussion, the group narrowed their project ideas to two. The group then visited the two possible sites to investigate further. First they went to a senior citizens' residence to talk to the manager and some of the residents about what the group might do there. On the basis of this visit and substantial discussion afterward, the group decided that opportunities for significant and satisfying contribution did not seem as promising there as they had hoped. They then visited a small, rundown park they were considering rehabilitating. While there they conducted a thorough inventory of what they thought needed repair. Next, after a discussion of what they might do in the park and how this would contribute to the community, they decided to put together a questionnaire and canvas the neighborhood near the park to find out how people used it and what they would like to see done to improve it. Then the students arranged a meeting with some members of the local government on a committee overseeing parks to discuss what permission they might need to go ahead with the project and how local officials might help the students accomplish their goals. Finally, after a good deal of reflection about service, the community, and what they hoped to accomplish in the group, the students decided democratically to undertake the park project.

In the process of community exploration, this group learned a great deal about their community and its issues, government, and citizens. They learned about their town's governmental structure, who occupied key positions in it, and how to engage these people. They also gained confidence in their ability to accomplish community service goals, coming to a new understanding of their power to work for change.

The projects we have completed over the years have varied greatly depending on the youth and community involved. Some groups have chosen long-term commitments, others a series of shorter projects. Some have decided to help existing initiatives, others have decided to start their own. To name a few of the projects worked on during our five years: groups have assisted with housing renovations for low-income families and nonprofit agencies; renovated rundown parks in neighborhoods with limited resources; helped nonprofit agencies with office work and fundraising; painted play equipment at a child care center; worked with senior citizens living in a retirement home; painted buildings at a community-owned fairground; planted trees in public settings with little landscaping; made and distributed food for a food pantry; worked with animals at the SPCA; picked up trash in yards and along roadways; contributed artwork to a community festival; reviewed youth grant proposals; produced a magazine about increasing youth participation in the community; organized a community concert with five bands to bring youth together, combat youth idleness, and raise funds for an organization supporting poor families; lobbied local government to create more avenues for input from young people; and drawn up a proposal for a youth center.

While some of these projects do not look much different from those of many other service groups, what is different is the process. In other words, while these may be conventional on the surface, they are more unconventional in substance, especially from the participants' point of view. For example, one group of youth began by expressing disdain for any project that might require them to pick up garbage. After a month of youth-led investigation, however, the first project the group selected was a clean-up of a local park. In the end, it was not a question of the activity itself but the meaning behind it. The group had time to discover connections between their own values and community needs and, therefore, did not see themselves as merely picking up garbage but as beautifying a place that was important to many people in the community and (in their words) "setting an example" for their peers. We feel this illustrates the importance of an empowering process, one that allows time for exploration and real decision making. As Bruner (1996) writes, "Educational encounters, to begin with, should result in understanding, not mere performance. Understanding consists in grasping the place of an idea or fact in some more general structure of knowledge" (xi, xii).

Purposeful Reflection

As we have written elsewhere (Ogden and Claus, 1997), we feel strongly that reflection is a critical part of substantive service learning. Without reflection there is little meaningful learning. We also believe that reflection is richer and more engaging for adolescents when it plays a functional, contributing role in the development and implementation of a community service project or work related to it—that is, when it is I an integral, necessary part of the service process, as opposed to something that occurs somewhat artificially apart from service. This is what we call purposeful reflection, and it is our sense that this approach is more intrinsically motivating for young people and contributes to deeper critical awareness and concern.

Thus, as projects progress, we continue to engage participants in reflecting on their communities, lives, and service goals, paying close attention to opportunities to raise issues of social justice along the way. This helps participants find and create relevance in their work and to think critically about various aspects of their community and society as they work to improve them. The work of carrying out the project(s) can be a very powerful source of emotion and discussion, especially when it involves working with and for other people. As a result, we make sure to discuss what group members are doing and feeling as they perform their service work, whatever it may be. We do this both formally, as part of the ongoing planning and revising process, and informally, on trips to and from the service sites, and, when appropriate, during our work time together. This becomes a key way for group members to process their emotions and to contribute to the functioning and direction of the group.

During a project at a low-income senior citizens' home, for example, a couple of youth, on the trip home one day, commented that they had worked with a woman who seemed crabby and not appreciative of their presence and desire to help. The group immediately struggled to make sense of this. This provoked a discussion about how older people are viewed and treated in our society. For an hour we discussed how being treated as needy, because of your age and finances, might anger people who have been able-bodied and independent most of their lives. We talked about pride, respect, and what it means to grow old. We also discussed the limited finances of the people the students were working with and how-this might affect their attitude toward society and the students themselves. This conversation welled up naturally from the emotions of the participants who have been moved by the experience, and then it was nurtured by Learning Web staff. Ultimately, it led to a more compassionate approach to their work with seniors, and it generated a broader interest in and awareness of issues of ageism and social policy for seniors.

Service can and should be used as a powerful vehicle for achieving a deeper kind of learning about and from others—others who may often be thought, by youth or in our society, not to have significant or important knowledge. This requires keeping an eye on possibilities for genuine two-way exchange between students and the people they interact with while providing service. With reflection, youth often come to the conclusion that they are receiving more than they are giving, and they develop a new understanding of and respect for those being served. An example of this is a small project in a rural community in which a group set out to help a visually impaired senior citizen save an old tree in her yard. In return for their efforts, the senior shared her jam-making skills with the young people, and, in turn, they produced a batch of strawberry jam, which they donated to the local food giveaway. In reflective discussion during this interaction and afterward, many young people in the group came to the conclusion that the relationship between the server and the served is a complex, ambiguous, and ever-changing one that must be closely attended in order to achieve and maintain balance and a sense of pride for both. This experience truly played on everyone's strengths, leaving no one in the singular role of service provider or recipient.

We also encourage participants to keep written accounts of their service experience as part of the task of remembering and noting things the group may want to include in their own write-ups of their work or to communicate to the press. Writing often proves to be very functional in the life of a project as it finds its way into press releases, proposals, volunteer recruitment, and editorials. Related to this activity, we generally try to enlist local television and newspapers in reporting on a group's work as it is occurring. This allows us to engage group members in preparing to be covered by the media, which means having them think about what they would like to show and tell the journalists, what questions they think would be interesting questions to answer, and how they might answer likely questions. We also tell participants that expressing their views can be a form of service itself when it motivates others to take action or consider something from a new or different point of view.

It is part of the Learning Web's mission to build bridges between young people's work in the community and school by working with teachers to get participants credit or to create opportunities for class projects related to their experiences. This can be an empowering process in and of itself when young people have the courage to approach their teachers and suggest projects that they see as relating to a given subject matter. In the past, participants have been awarded credit for articles by English teachers, for creative reflection by art teachers, and for surveys and questionnaires by social studies and careers teachers Creating these opportunities for credit can go a long way in motivating young people to reflect on their community service experiences and help them understand the connections between school and "the real world."

Another way of motivating young people to reflect is through written materials and speakers that address issues that crop up in the course of each project. These might include editorials, newspaper clippings, books, activists, and so forth. We encourage young people to bring in relevant resources as they come across them, and Learning Web staff occasionally distribute handouts or invite presenters with the blessing of group members. This can deepen our appreciation of certain issues at the local level or broaden and connect them to national and global happenings.

For example, in one rural school district, participants discovered that their town did not have much coherence or community spirit. As they interviewed residents about community issues and asked for suggestions on possible projects, they encountered considerable apathy and complaints that people did not really seem to care very much for the town. Part of the reason for this is that the town has no recognizable center. As one community member said, "This is like a rural residential strip mall. There really isn't any place to gather." This tended to carry over into most people's lack of enthusiasm about community service. The group elected to do a few small beautification projects and then heard about a local landscape architect who was interested in creating a town center by designing a town green. We Invited her to talk with us about town planning and community development and about ways in which the group might contribute to creating more community spirit. Our session ended with the architect asking group members for ideas on the town center.

There are indeed many opportunities to weave reflection into the entire process of carrying out a project, and we view each of these as essential to helping young people deepen their awareness, widen their outlook, consider and respect other perspectives, inform their decisions, question their world, and develop a sense of agency.

Closure and Continuity

An important part of concluding a Learning Web service project is to have the group identify things they feel they have learned—about themselves, others, their service, and their community—and to have them communicate this both within and beyond the group. This work involves both evaluative reflection and the defining of possible future action. By the end of a project, many participants develop insights into the workings and needs of their community that they want to share with others. Groups often, for example, create a list of tasks or activities that they had hoped to complete but must leave unfinished, and they identify additional community needs they would like to see addressed. Participants also often want to encourage members of their community to volunteer service time and effort as they themselves have done. These ideas are then presented to appropriate officials and community members, sometimes in the form of written lists and proposals, sometimes in the form of newspaper articles or letters to the editor. As mentioned earlier, participants in past projects have actually assisted with the recruitment phase at other schools by sharing their experiences and opinions and encouraging their peers to get involved. Some participants have also been involved in giving presentations at youth leadership conferences, to local youth commissions, and in college education classes.

Additionally, we ask participants at the end of a project to help us improve our running of the program by filling out an evaluation form. Here, too, we are able to engage the group in thinking and talking about their experience, this time as they work to help us do a better job in the future. We ask them questions about the quality of the program and about their experience and sense of growth in it. We also ask them to help us develop more ideas for making the program appealing to other youth, and we ask them to tell us what we should say to potential participants to help them understand what they might get out of the experience.

We also work as a group to plan a celebration of what has been accomplished and experienced. We allow the group to plan their own celebration, with the stipulation that the event somehow be related to their service efforts and not just be a self-serving party. The group that rehabilitated the park, for example, had a picnic at the park to which they invited local officials, some people from the neighborhood, and a few friends. At this gathering the group reviewed and showed what they had done and presented to local officials a list of things they had not had time or resources to complete. They secured a promise that the work would continue. They also hung a sign with the name of the park, having the mayor hammer in the last nail, and they had pizza, chicken, cake, and soda, some of which had been solicited from and donated by local businesses. In addition, they were presented with individual awards of recognition from the local government.

In all of the programs we have facilitated, at least some of the students in each group conclude they want to continue being involved in community service work. In three instances this has meant that students, with our help, have worked to create a service group that would live beyond the term of the Learning Web program. To accomplish this, the students had to seek out resources and support from their schools or appropriate youth programs, and they did their own recruiting. Much of this desire to continue in service work can be credited to the youth themselves, though we also see the process of tool building and self-direction employed throughout our program as a vital impetus for sustained activity. We have found that young people in our programs have a heightened awareness of where to turn to keep things going and the confidence to get some of this done themselves. A number of times a group of young people we recruited has turned around at the end of our time together and recruited their own adult advisor (whether a teacher, youth worker, or parent).

Throughout the past few years we have also held numerous reunions and retreats, which bring members of these older and still-functioning groups together with our students in current programs to discuss issues and take on big projects. This has forged a countywide network of youth who support and inspire one another across community boundaries through shared stories and collaboration. Furthermore, many of these young people have had opportunities to attend state and national conferences on service learning and community building, where they meet their peers and observe both the diversity and the common themes in this youth movement. In the process, their developing excitement for acting on the world in critically reflective ways is supported and reinforced.

Conclusion

Having witnessed the richness of service that aims to empower young people, we are concerned that service learning may become "just another graduation requirement," often failing to engage youth fully in a mix of critical reflection and democratic action. To counter this possibility, we encourage use of a student-centered, activist approach, which, we feel, makes service more motivating, meaningful, and substantive for youth and promises fuller and more truly democratic participation in the pursuit of constructive social change. We embrace the view that "schools and classrooms"—and, we add, communities—"should be laboratories for a more just society than the one we now live in. Unfortunately, too many schools [and communities] are training grounds for boredom, alienation, and pessimism. . . . Classrooms [and communities] can be places of hope, where students and teachers gain glimpses of the kind of society we could live in and where students learn the academic and critical skills needed to make it a reality" (Bigelow et al., 1994, 4).

This view sometimes takes us into risky territory, because it makes a clear choice concerning the role of education in our society. It acknowledges, in fact embraces, the reality that all education is political activity—that there is no neutral or apolitical education—and it argues for viewing schools and educational programs as agents of change and social justice rather than instruments of social control and the status quo. This opens the door to conflict, but in this risky zone lie the promise and optimism of youth and adults engaged in, not alienated from, society as they pursue the improvement of their communities and issues of social justice. As Bruner (1996) writes, "Education is risky, for it fuels the sense of possibility. But a failure to equip minds with skills for understanding and feeling and acting in the cultural world is not simply scoring a pedagogical zero. It risks creating alienation, defiance, and practical incompetence. And all of these undermine the viability of a culture" (42–43).

Thus, a strong, democratic version of service learning is, we think, the best choice for the development of youth, our communities, and society. It promises engagement over alienation, and it places at least one element of education in the position of being the head of the societal dog instead of the tail.

We would also like to draw attention to what we think is the value of community-based organizations in providing this kind of service learning. Community-based organizations often occupy positions in their communities that allow them a unique perspective and capacity for guiding youth in community exploration, critical reflection, and the pursuit of community/social change. Community-based organizations can develop programs and provide services that are particularly capable of bridging school and community and of raising and addressing issues relevant to both. Recently, for example, the Learning Web was invited to offer ImPACT as part of a special program for "at-risk" youth in a local high school. Under this arrangement, Learning Web staff teach ImPACT as a class two days a week and work with a team of teachers to integrate reflection into other subject areas. As we move through the school year, we identify themes common to the students' ImPACT projects and their other classroom activities. In this way, community-based organizations can be vehicles for both community activism and constructive school reform.

In closing, we want to stress that it is not enough in service programs to acknowledge that social problems exist. We need to go further to reflect on the sources of these problems and to build the skills and perspectives required for engaging in reform. There is value to service learning as a process that addresses needs and builds community, and there is another level on which the service experience can raise critical questions and open the door to social change. As Martin Luther King, Jr., observed, "Education without social action is a one-sided value because it has no potential; social action without education is a weak expression of energy." We think service learning provides an opportunity to integrate education and social action into a reciprocally intertwined, broad, and powerful whole. In this view service is not only a vehicle for substantive individual development and curricular enhancement; it is also an important foundation and springboard for social reform.

QUESTIONS TO CONSIDER

1. What are the crucial concepts that drive the authors' approach to service learning? Would you agree that they are all critical? Do you have any disagreements with their argument? Explain your response.

2. What do Claus and Ogden mean by "youth-centered" service learning? What do you regard as the advantages in that approach? Do you see any possible problems with it? Give reasons and examples in your response.

3. How and why do the authors emphasize the importance of group work in their Learning Web? Do you agree or disagree with that methodology? Why or why not?

4. What are the purposes and benefits of community investigation in service learning? Give reasons and examples to support your case.

5. According to Claus and Ogden, how can service learning empower youth to be more effective decision-makers and reflective participants in efforts to change their communities? Give examples.

6. In the authors' view, what kinds of pedagogical tools and resources can assist the service-learning experience?

Notes

This chapter originally appeared in Jeff Claus and Curtis Ogden (eds.), *Service Learning for Youth Empowerment and Social Change* (New York: Peter Lang, 1999).

1. Jeff Claus was the initial director and Curtis Ogden is current director of the Leaning Web community service program. The Learning Web is a community agency that works closely with schools, other agencies, businesses, and adult volunteers to provide youth in the county, between the ages of 12 and 21, with program opportunities for individualized apprenticeships, group community service, and entrepreneurial experience. For more about the Learning Web, see Claus, 1994, and Hamilton, 1981.

2. Freire's view of the ideal developmental state is expressed in his concept of "integration," which, he explains, "results from the capacity to adapt oneself to reality *plus* the critical capacity to make choices and to transform that reality (1973, 4).

3. We encourage readers to consult the work of Shor (1992) and Freire (1970, 1973) directly for detailed and substantive discussion of these ideas and much more. Also recommended is Bigelow et al. (1994).

4. *Get It Together*, produced by John L. Jackson, Jr., and Melissa Brockett, 1993, available from The Video Project, 5332 College Avenue, Suite 101, Oakland, CA, 94618.

5. Two quotes we often use to generate discussion/reflection here are: "We make a living by what we get, but we make a life by what we give" (Winston Churchill) and "Life's. most persistent and urgent question is what are you doing for others" (Martin Luther King. Jr.).

6. Books that are helpful in understanding and teaching the perspective and methods of anthropological/ethnographic research include James Spradley and David McCurdy's *The Cultural Experience: Ethnography in Complex Society*, 1972 (first edition) and 1996 (second edition), published by Science Research Associates; David Fetterman's *Ethnography: Step by Step*, 1989, published by Sage; and Ernest Stringer's *Community-Based Ethnography: Breaking Traditional Boundaries of Research, Teaching, and Learning*, 1997, published by Lawrence Erlbaum.

References

Banks, J. 1991. A curriculum for empowerment, action, and change. In C. Sleeter (Ed.), *Empowerment through multicultural education*. Albany, N.Y.: SUNY Press.

Beyer, L. 1996. Introduction: The meanings of critical teacher preparation. In L. Beyer (Ed.), *Creating democratic classrooms: The struggle to integrate theory and practice*. New York: Teachers College Press.

Bigelow, B., L. Christensen, S. Karp, B. Miner, and B. Peterson. 1994. Creating classrooms for equity and social justice in B. Bigelow, L. Christensen, S. Karp, B. Miner, and B. Peterson (Eds.), *Rethinking our classrooms: Teaching for equity and justice*. Milwaukee, Wis.: Rethinking Our Schools.

Boyte, H. 1991. Community service and civic education. *Phi Delta Kappan*, 72: 765–767.

Bruner, J. 1996. *The culture of education*. Cambridge, Mass.: Harvard University Press.

Claus, J. 1994. The Learning Web: A grassroots, community-based model for youth apprenticeship. Paper presented at the annual meeting of the American Educational Research Association, New Orleans.

Freire. P. 1970. *Pedagogy of the oppressed*. New York: Seabury.

———. 1973. *Education for critical consciousness*. New York: Seabury.

———. 1992. Book jacket, back cover. In I. Shor, *Empowering education: Critical teaching for social change*. Chicago: University of Chicago Press.

Hamilton, S. 1981. The Learning Web: The structure of freedom. *Phi Delta Kappan*, 62, 600–601.

Jones, B., R. Maloy, and C. Steen. 1996. Learning through community service is political. *Equity and Excellence in Education*, 29(2): 37–45.

Kahne, J., and J. Westheimer. 1996. In the service of what? The politics of service learning. *Phi Delta Kappan*, 77: 593–599.

Karp, S. 1997. *Educating for a civil society: The core issue is inequality. Educational Leadership*, 54: 40–43.

Lakes, R. 1996. *Youth development and critical education: The promise of democratic action*. Albany, N.Y.: SUNY Press.

Ogden, C., and J. Claus. 1997. Reflection as a natural element of service: Service learning for youth empowerment. *Equity and Excellence in Education*, 30(1): 72–81.

Schor, I. 1992. *Empowering education: Critical teaching for social change*. Chicago: University of Chicago Press.

Sorensen, K. 1996. Creating a democratic classroom. Empowering students within and outside school walls. In L. Beyer (Ed.), *Creating democratic classrooms: The struggle to integrate theory and practice*. New York: Teachers College Press.

Youniss, J., and M. Yates. 1997. *Community service and social responsibility in youth*. Chicago: University of Chicago Press.

CHAPTER THIRTY-FOUR

The Early College Concept

Building Hope for Students, Parents, Professionals and Community

CAMILLE DANIEL-TYSON & LIANNA NIX

When I first opened the door at Georgia College Early College (GCEC), I had 55 students, 55 sets of pioneering parents, three staff members, and one secretary. I was in the process of trying to find furniture for the classroom (desks for students) when Abraham walked through the door with his father, George. Abraham was our newest addition because another student from the county had changed locations.

"Excuse me for appearing so nasty, but I had to close the tire store to be here," explained George as he stood before me in greasy mechanic blue.

"You could have come after you closed the store this evening," I patiently explained.

"No … this is way too important to miss. I was actually afraid you would call someone else if I waited too long."

They both took time to fill out the paperwork, and I asked them if they wanted to sightsee anything on campus.

"No," was the quick answer from Abraham, but his father interrupted.

"Actually, he would like to see the campus library."

I thought that a simple trip to the library would consume only a small portion of my afternoon, so we began walking across campus. As we entered the library, George wandered through every floor of the library, found the plate glass window that overlooked the North section of campus and would point to Peabody Hall and motion excitedly to his son, "That's where you will be going to school, son!"

With the library tour complete, we started back toward his truck. I was anxious to get back to school to move furniture in my shorts and white tee, but George wasn't quite finished with me yet. He drew a photograph from his wallet and said, "I want to show you my family." The photo contained five children and two adults. Obviously, he wanted to share the multi-racial family with me and was expecting the standard southern appraisal and judgment.

"What a beautiful family!" I stated excitedly.

"Did you really see it? My family is different."

"My family is different, too," I concluded . . . and we walked on.

With the meeting over, we strolled toward his truck, and he stopped me again.

"Hey, miss . . ." he called. I turned to face him. "I need to ask you one more question."

He looked at me intently for a moment before asking, "Is this really a promise?"

"Yes, it is," I replied. At that moment I realized we were not building just a simple school. We were building a legacy of hope in the lives of the most underserved, misrepresented, and fearful contingency of parents and students in our immediate area. My job at GCEC was not to change the present stories of the lives of these students. Whatever past and prejudices that filled their lives up to this point was immutable. Our ultimate goal consists of educating these students to the extent that **their** children would not perpetuate generations of hardship and pain. Someone has to be brave enough to break that cycle.

Georgia College Early College is a part of a fairly recent movement in education: that of "early college high schools," which are small, non-traditional schools of choice within the public system that target populations who are statistically at risk to miss out on access to postsecondary education—clearly an indicator for social and economic empowerment (Goldberger & Bayerl, 2008; Wick, 2006; Hoffman & Bayerl, 2005). An "early college" is a program that is assisting high school students who are often underrepresented in postsecondary institutions, especially those who would be first-generation college attendees. Many are labeled at-risk, i.e., they might well drop out of high school or, at least, not pursue a college education. The first such program opened in 2002, and there are presently over 150 early college high school programs across the nation aiming to serve tens of thousands of students by offering them access to postsecondary options. The endeavor is supported by the Early College High School Initiative, funded by the Bill & Melinda Gates Foundation and others (Hoffman & Bayerl, 2005). Chad Wick (2006), of Knowledge Works Foundation, summarizes the early work of these model schools and speaks to the "battle for change" subsequent to their emergence:

> While this movement is still new . . . early results show that these students—most of whom are the first in the families to attend college—are more likely to stay in school and earn higher grades in college. Even so, we recognize that change on this scale is hard won. On the front lines, where teachers, students and those who support them struggle to create new ways of learning, the battle for change is fierce. Some of the obstacles they face are always moving—the constant shifting of funding priorities, legislative mandates, public support and societal needs. Others may seem immoveable—the brick wall of entrenched habits, values and expectations. It is a battle against almost insurmountable odds. (p. 2)

Georgia's Early College Initiative holds to the ideals articulated above, and seeks to bolster high school graduation rates and support college readiness and bachelor's degree acquisition rates among Georgia students, including those from majority and minority populations, the gamut of income groups, and urban and rural regions in the state ("Jobs for the Future," 2006).

Opening its doors for its inaugural year of 2006–2007, Georgia College Early College (GCEC) launched a middle Georgia version of the EC initiative situated in Milledgeville, Georgia. GCEC is the product of a cooperative effort among the Baldwin County School System, Putnam County School System, Georgia College, and State University, Oconee RESA (Regional Educational Services Agency), Georgia's Board of Regents, and such philanthropic organizations as the Bill & Melinda Gates Foundation, and the Woodruff Foundation. The first group of students is part of a six-year cycle, beginning with seventh grade, aimed at working with students from families who have no college graduates, and who fall in the third lowest quartile of academic achievement as measured by their performance on the Iowa Test of Basic Skills. These learners represented middle Georgia's ethnic spectrum: the inaugural class was comprised of a mix of 60% African Americans, 34% Caucasian, 4% Mexican Americans, and 2% Asian Americans, heterogenously grouped (Newton, 2008).

> Most individuals begin a new enterprise with a sense of hope, but our students broke the mold by beginning early college very guardedly and skeptical of the principles upon which GCEC was founded: respect, caring, integrity, and personal responsibility. Interactions within their communities had somehow swallowed whole their belief in any principle or mantra and left no room for hope. However, the patience, love, and consistency of college and EC staff members, principal, and parents began to change student perspectives . . . and dim futures began to glow with promise:

- Gabrielle, who entered the seventh grade obese, possessing a dark personality, and practicing self-mutilation, has become a poised and prideful 15-year-old with a promising future.
- Stephanie, who was abused by her grandfather at 12 years of age, struggled academically in her initial year, but she is now on the verge of successfully completing an honors program.
- Jacinta refused to speak during her inaugural year, but she has become a campus ambassador and spokeswoman for GCEC.
- Marcus was born addicted to crack and abandoned in the hospital (his foster mom was told he would never crawl, walk, or talk). He now has continually kept his eye focused on getting into Georgia Tech.
- Jerome was once a front man of a gang, but now he is a top leader in the classroom, a football star and vocal about not being in a gang. He is adamant about the fact that his strength is a gift that should only be used for good.
- Starlene's mother was married seven times, and Starlene was conditioned to believe that promises were meant to be broken; however, she has found her voice through powerful writing and realizes that promises are meant to be kept.

> It is our job to be the promise keepers in the lives of these students because they have had plenty of promise breakers.

After the completion of its inaugural year, GCEC had already obtained a reputation as a successful model for small-school reform efforts in preparation for postsecondary achievement. According to a recent report from Jobs for the Future, GCEC made "dramatic" gains in math achievement after just one year, in spite of the fact that mathematics was, for its participants and constituent systems, the area of greatest need, and the fact that it serves "a more academically challenged group of students" (Goldberger & Bayerl, 2008, p. 8).

The participating population of 54 seventh-grade students drawn from rural Baldwin and Putman Counties represents the state's first middle school cohort of early college attendees. These students were, and are, confronted with an expectation of proactive participation in their academic attainment, i.e., that they will become successful college graduates. At its very heart, the Early College Program is instilling motivation for self-efficacy in a population statistically at risk to have low personal and collective self-efficacy. One of the most significant challenges is the daily encouragement of a disposition toward learning and toward life in general that is proactive rather than passive—a stance focusing on problem-solving rather than reinforcing perceived helplessness or apathy. That is, GCEC is a fundamentally *agenting* institution.

It is certainly noteworthy that of the 54 "at-risk" learners with whom the program began, scholastic achievement (as measured by the Georgia Criterion Referenced Competency Test, 2006–07) demonstrated significant success for those students in most core subjects. Several students had come to GCEC falling in a range from one to five years below grade level in reading. Of those 54 students, 100% met or exceeded state expectations in language arts, and 98% did the same in reading. Notably, 89% met or exceeded standards in mathematics. The program began with only 40% who had previously met or exceeded state standards (Newton, 2008). Several GCEC students *exceeded* state mathematics standards for the year, even though the state of Georgia had implemented a new, more challenging, curriculum (Georgia Performance Standards).

Perhaps the most definitive dynamic of GCEC is that its culture truly is that of a *co-constructed learning community*. Lambert (2002) posits that in creating such communities that "function as ecological social systems" (p. 50), members of such communities must work together in mutually meaningful, interdependent, and trusting ways. The goal of such an organic orientation is evolution toward self-sustaining and long-term entities, "since it takes time to deepen the spiral of meaning-making, seek shared purpose, and develop interdependent professional cultures" (p. 50). The GCEC faculty and students are in a unique position to cultivate such a shared culture as the cohort of a modestly unique educational experiment. That organic systemic approach lends itself to a wholesome, naturalistic, interconnected community of relationships; it involves a rich contextual soil of sense-making, learning, teaching, and ongoing personal growth and development for all its constituents (Lambert, 2002). It seems that GCEC is ideally "primed," as it were, to fulfill such a vision for a community committed to sustainability of growth, both for its professional faculty, its supporting institutions, and its participants and their families.

> For a very long time in our educational system, our communities have held an amorphous and vague meaning where parents are concerned. What exactly do we mean by parental involvement? At GCEC, parental involvement begins instantly. Parents have to be so vested in their children's lives that they have to be willing to go through the tedious process of applying. They also understand that attendance at all student/parent events are non-negotiable—and that they will show up. We expect them to be present for convocations, chili cook-offs, award nights, readings, art shows, or whatever event is scheduled. We understand that we can't educate their children without them. They need to be involved. One statistic that proves we have been vastly successful in accomplishing that goal is that, out of 220 student-families, 96 parents have gone back to further their education since their child was inducted into the school.
>
> The dynamics of changing parental perspectives is evident when comparing former staff/parent relations to current GCEC staff/parent relations:

- Her name is Rhea and as she sat in the chair across from my desk, I realized that education had not been kind to her. Her principal had known her name, but not because she had any value or a voice. They had known her because she didn't matter. As we dissected the problems with Tony, she could not forget the fact that her principal knew her son's name. She explained that the problem was that his name was known because he was trouble . . . just like at all the other schools he had gone to before. She thought he was known by reputation . . . not because he was a student. I was caught off-guard and had to explain that I knew every child's name. Rhea asked me why I knew all those names. I simply responded that there is power in a name. It is our identity. It is who we are. Every child in the school had an identity and a purpose. I called him by his name because of his purpose; this is who he is.

- Ben's mom called me back to let me know that Ben's medicine would arrive on Thursday. She told me she hadn't known that anything was wrong with him. I responded, "It's okay, Ben is brilliant. He's gonna make it." I was surprised when she began to cry over the phone. Then I heard her response: "Thank you, Mrs. Tyson, you are the only person in any school who has ever told me that my boy is good and is gonna make it. Everyone else told me he wouldn't make it."

- I was called over to Georgia Military College because of a paper written by Lisa, Alfred's mom. The topic had been "What was the most life-changing event in your life?" Her answer had been that Alfred's admission into GCEC changed her life. No one had ever encouraged her to go to college, but she knew that he wouldn't risk going to GCEC if she weren't willing to take a risk as well.

- Parents give GCEC its strength, and GCEC gives parents their strength. Early College parents give their children two things that they have never had before: a college education and a voice in society. GCEC gives parents comfort while learning to navigate a culture that they do not understand and weren't invited to. When one of our parents came to the initial college campus tour she questioned, "You mean they get to cross the street into the gates?" This parent lived within walking distance to the college, but she had never been on the campus.

What does it look like in the halls and classes at GCEC? Like all organic entities, it can be messy some days. Students struggle, teachers struggle, and the whole body of learners is continually undergoing a systemic, ongoing evolution as it adjusts each year to the new group of incoming seventh graders and as each class moves up in the social structure that is Early College. Human business is like that. However, without question, the overwhelming reality is that this community is becoming a collective movement toward a future of promise for its participants.

GCEC is a place of ongoing mutual learning. A frequently heard mantra on campus is, "We're all learners and we're all teachers." That stance toward learning as a joint venture of all stakeholders enables students to become vested owners, as it were, in the corporate learning machine; it is the "family business." This is demonstrated frequently in classrooms where kids offer themselves one to another as they question, deliberate, challenge, and argue during whole group and small group instruction. It is also evidenced in the ongoing professional development model adopted by the faculty at GCEC: the "rounds" model. Teachers routinely sit in on one another's classroom and later debrief in mutually respectful ways—supporting, encouraging, and questioning each other about instructional practices and student responses and behaviors.

We have tremendously dedicated faculty members, who not only work as a team of educators, but as a community of learners as well. For the most part, those teachers are modeling a life of continuous education, not just preaching it. A tradition of excellence has continued in that the teachers are involved in personnel searches (as are select students). Most of our employees work long hours, tutoring after school to make sure students understand concepts. It affords teachers opportunities to be very creative and to not be afraid to dream outside the box. Our professionals allow students to write rap songs, author a math book, and start their own school newspaper—all impossible without the leadership of faculty. Faculty members are willing to transfer the ownership of their children's education into their own hands. They believe in the strength of their students, which gives students their own voice. Teachers are willing to share their classrooms with Georgia College MAT students, and they guide those college students in caring, challenging ways.

Of course, I need to speak about our legacy class teachers—those teachers who "built the plane while in flight." One of those original teachers was Ed Averett, who comments on the concept of building our very first classrooms at GCEC: "We had decided that the most important thing in our school was to establish a culture of community, a culture of respect. And, ironically, when we took our eye off the ball of instruction in the classroom to deal with all the little things, I think we realized that we never really took our eye off the ball. It's the little things that make up a community. What are we allowed to wear? What are we allowed to eat? When can we go to the bathroom? How do we get home? How do we get books to the students? When do we change classes? To what forms of technology do we have access? And then came the deeper questions. Why are we here? Who are we right now? Who do we want to be? Why do we not always get along? What does this work, this mathematical problem, this literature, this other culture on the other side of the world ... mean to me? To us? And so, we had to find a real connection to this stuff. We had to not only try to understand it, but we had to be understanding about it. We had to recognize that this was our curriculum, and we had to make the most of it—just in the way we had to make the most of each other."

The physical structure of GCEC, sitting on the campus of Georgia College and State University, is another factor that indubitably supports the organic learning culture. GCEC has grown up from its initial location in GCSU's John H. Lounsbury College of Education and has expanded across the small university environs to classes in three other buildings. Students are fully immersed in a very real and thriving college community; it is, no doubt, that ethos that makes higher education more of an everyday norm to them. In addition, the university's staff supports the work and vision of GCEC. Members of GCSU's College of Education faculty were intrinsically involved in the birth of the program and continue to exercise significant influence in the evolution of GCEC. Almost every GCEC class has a preservice teacher placed within it while he or she works toward satisfying field requirements of GCSU's well-respected educational programs; that symbiotic relationship has served to advance both GCEC and the College of Education. The infusion of preservice teachers into the learning community also provides a connection to students' own learning futures.

Georgia College & State University has embraced the same vision of hope as GCEC itself. First generation college faculty members have been most instrumental because someone in their life had given them hope. Each year as we grow, our college partnership grows. Someone always steps up to fill our needs, which are progressively greater each year. They published our first book, hosted our first art show, and allowed us access to their university library. This year, they installed several Promethean boards that cost several thousands of dollars for all of our 7th- and 8th-grade classrooms. The university constantly gives us the ability to go far beyond the parameters of a traditional school. Being able to work in a society of friends, who are able to sit down and find solutions for the common good, has been an invaluable asset. That vital partnership has changed the mindset of many educators because it has taken the pages out of the book and turned the written word into reality.

I would be remiss if I did not include the collaborative partnership we share with two counties that rarely work on anything collectively, yet have united to combine two school districts for the benefit of students who attend GCEC. We have been blessed by superintendents who are not afraid to go against the grain to address issues of a high-risk population of students.

All those who have a vested interest in GCEC understand a fundamental reality of teaching and learning: it is contextualized most powerfully in relationships. Learning is dialogic, dialectic, and socially constructed. Safe relationships serve adolescent developmental needs in countless ways, not the least of which is their provision of a risk-free environment for exploration and sense-making. Student relationships among their cohorts are expected to evidence the core values of GCEC: respect, caring, integrity, and personal responsibility. Relationships among teachers, teenagers, principal, college professors, preservice teachers, and all other partners are the seedbed for the construction of both personal identity and robust learning; and the *esprit de corps* is evident all over campus.

Other than the students themselves, perhaps the most influential element of the learning community is the faculty. According to a number of recent studies, teachers account for the greatest influence on student achievement outside of those uncontrollable external factors of home, socioeconomic status (SES), and culture. High quality teachers are incontrovertibly important to higher quality education for students, especially for those with low SES (Nye, Konstantopoulos, & Hedges, 2003). In fact, recent studies cited by the Center for Public Education (2006) suggest that student achievement is more heavily related to teacher quality than race, class, academic record, or particular school of placement, especially for low SES and African American students. Fortunately, Georgia College Early College is staffed by teachers who are highly qualified, content-rich, and committed to doing what works for their students, most of whom qualify in both of the above categories.

Teachers *do* care about those with whom they work and invest deeply in their efforts. It seems important to teachers to know that their colleagues are caring, committed, like-minded in their aspirations for student success, and driven to reach for the best for their students and their profession (Amrein-Beardsley, 2009). From its inception, GCEC faculty cultivated a shared investment in the lives and learning of students. They themselves built relationships founded on mutual trust and high expectations, and their shared passions are infectious among each other, their students and to visitors. "Half-hearted" is not in their vocabularies; and they send two powerful messages to students: *you* are worth the effort, and *learning* is worth the effort. After all, actions speak much more eloquently than words.

Teachers are consistently supportive of the development of self-efficacy, consistently offering choices and voice, consistently giving feedback with opportunities for ongoing development. One way they achieve the desired end of cultivating learner empowerment is by repeating the aforementioned mantra, "We are all learners, and we are all teachers." Another key strategy of EC teachers is the enculturation of an inquisitive posture. Questions must be formulated, questions must be honored, and questions must be refined in a rather Socratic fashion. That goal of refinement of articulation is part of the ongoing work of teachers to create and sustain a holistic literacy across curriculum and instructional styles. Processing and perspective taking are modeled and expected; and higher order thinking prompts and responses flow richly in all classes. Indeed, literacy events are prevalent across the curriculum.

A principal also has to be deeply involved in students' lives, in their concerns, and in soliciting stakeholder investment for GCEC's aims and outcomes. She needs to be a risk-taker, and one who is willing to change course when something does not work out for the good of the whole. She needs to be impassioned about empowering GCEC students toward goal setting and achievement. She needs to be their advocate. That posture toward students sends them the same message as teachers' passions: *you are worth it.*

The ascription of value and significance to our children cannot be overstated. As they internalize the value being ascribed, their dispositions toward active learning and toward success begin to evolve in positive ways. Evidence to that effect is rampant: student work is displayed; active, rich discussions are taking place in many classes; decisions are challenged in proactive, healthy ways; risks are taken; university campus involvement occurs; and expectations for the future are becoming bolder and continuously aligned with the goals of lifelong learning.

How could I possibly conclude this vision of hope offered by GCEC without talking about Ladario's wish? Ladario was already having a bad day, beginning with a conversation at home about his future. His mother had basically told him that he would never amount to anything and that he would probably just end up in jail like his father. I told him to expect a walk in the afternoon to the college bookstore to get some candy, and we could talk. On the way, he saw the college fountain, and his eyes lit up for a second.

"Is that **a real** wishing well, Mrs. Tyson?"

"I guess it can be."

"You think I could make a wish here?"

"Sure . . . we can do it on the way back."

We finished our trip to the bookstore, and he requested to see some of the on-campus classrooms where some of our GCEC students were already attending classes, so I took him to the classrooms and introduced him to the teachers and students. We were close to returning to Peabody Hall when he stopped me.

"Mrs. Tyson, you promised me I could make a wish."

I nodded, and we walked back to the fountain. I searched for a penny, but couldn't find one. I produced a quarter instead.

"This has to be a powerful wish, if we're using a quarter," I said quietly.

He grasped that coin like it was treasure that one could only hold once in a lifetime. He closed his eyes and intently focused hard on whatever wish ran the corridors of his mind . . . opened his eyes and tossed the quarter in with a splash. He watched it twitch and tumble to the bottom before looking at me again, full of questions.

"You reckon my wish will come true?"

"I don't know, Ladario. Did you wish to graduate from college?

"No."

"Did you wish to graduate from Early College?"

"No."

"Then what did you wish for?"

He studied me for a moment before responding, "If I tell you, it might not come true."

"We can do it, together, Ladario. I'll help you as much as I can. Now, what was your wish?"

"I just wish I can make it through the seventh grade," he stated with an exasperated look.

"Well, will you do something for me, next time you make a wish?"

"What's that, Mrs. Tyson?"

"The next time, wish for something bigger."

Given the path of his life and the influences that direct him, I understand why such a small wish meant so much to him. What happens here at Early College is just a repetition of Ladario's wish … with different faces and different dreams. The common thread is that our students go from classroom to classroom, from year to year … and from small dreams to larger dreams. May our Early College always be a fount of hope!

QUESTIONS TO CONSIDER

1. What do the authors suggest are the overriding components of a "learning community," and how are their characteristics exemplified at Georgia College Early College?

2. What are some often unacknowledged preconceptions one might need to confront in order to improve instruction for an at-risk population?

3. What educator dispositions are particularly important to a successful school model for at-risk students?

4. How is the concept of a "school as organic system" manifested at Georgia College Early College?

5. Discuss how that model might be conceptualized in other school scenarios.

6. How transferable is the Georgia College Early College model? What are its essential elements?

7. How could a group of educators at other schools attempt to replicate the model while holding true to their own institutions' identity and individuality?

References

Amrein-Beardsley, A. (2009, November 5). Recruiting expert teachers into hard-to-staff schools. *Phi Delta Kappan.* Retrieved from the Internet.

Covington, M. (1992). *Making the grade: A self-worth perspective on motivation and school reform.* New York: Cambridge University Press.

Goldberger, S., & Bayerl, K. (2008). *Beating the odds: The real challenges behind the math achievement gap—and what high-achieving schools can teach us about how to close it.* Report prepared for the Carnegie-IAS Commission on Mathematics and Science Education. Boston, MA: JFF.

Hoffman, N., & Bayerl, K. (2005). *Early college high school initiative: Accelerated learning for all.* Retrieved from the Internet on January 30, 2007.

Jobs for the future. (2007). *Occupational outlook handbook. Washington, DC: U.S. Department of Labor.*

Lambert, L. (2002). Towards a deepened theory of constructivist leadership, in L. Lambert, et al, *The constructivist leader* (pp. 34–62). New York: Teachers College Press.

Newton, A. (2008). Empowering students for success: How Georgia College Early College changes student aspirations. Published for Jobs for the Future.

Nye, B., Konstantopoulos, S., & Hedges, L. V. (2003, December). Institute for the Study of Labor (IZA) http://hub.mspnet.org/entry.cfm/13947

Nye, B., Konstantopoulos, S., & Hedges, L. V. (2004). How large are teacher effects? *Educational Evaluation and Policy Analysis,* Winter 2004, pp. 237–257.

Teacher quality and student achievement: Things to consider as you move from research to practice. (2006). Center for Public Education. Retrieved from Education.com. at http://www.education.com/reference/article/Ref_Research_Q_consider/?page=4

Wick, C. (2006). Learning by degree: Real-life stories from three early college high schools. KnowledgeWorks Foundation. Retrieved from the Internet on February 20, 2007 at http://www.kwfdn.org

CHAPTER THIRTY-FIVE

How Can Caring Help?

A Personalized Cross-Generational Examination of Violent Adolescent Experiences in Schools

BARBARA J. THAYER-BACON

Adolescents in the United States are growing up surrounded by violent acts of aggression. We can read about attempts to injure or harm others in the news, see examples in the movies and television shows, and hear violence in teenager's music and on MTV. We come face to face with the violence our children grow up with when researchers tell us the three most frequent causes of death for adolescents are accidents, murder, and suicide.[1] It is not surprising to find that children's lives are affected when they grow up with violence all around them, and they potentially become violent themselves, even to the point of owning guns and killing each other. What can schools do, particularly teachers and students, to help curb the violence we live around? How can we help to create safe, peaceful environments in our schools in which adolescents can learn to be peaceful themselves? These are the questions to be explored in this article.

Before we can explore these questions, however, we must define what we mean by violence and peace. If we define violence in terms of the use of extreme physical force, as in war situations, then peace is defined simply as "the absence of extreme physical force (war)." However, if we define peace to include "the presence of social justice" then we expand what we mean by violence.[2] In this article I embrace a "positive peace" definition to include issues of social justice. I wish to distinguish violence in terms of levels and degrees, so that acts of aggression that are physical (e.g., assaults, rapes) are considered overt forms of violence, and acts of aggression that violate individuals' dignity (e.g., verbal harassment, belittlement, and threats) are viewed as covert forms of violence. In this way, violence is "a behavior that violates other individuals" and that violation can by physical (overt violence) or mental, emotional, even spiritual violence (covert violence).[3]

Now that we are able to talk about violence in terms of levels and degrees, let us move to place schools within their larger social context. Schools are just one social institution among many that affect the qualities of our lives. Other social institutions include the government, the economy, families, religions, cultural communities, the expressive arts, and the media. Schools fulfill many purposes for society, too. Traditionally we have asked schools to pass on the knowledge of our society and to help inculcate our young so they will be prepared to participate and contribute to our society as adults. In a democratic society such as the United States, we ask our schools to prepare democratic citizens for the future of our country.

As other institutions struggle with changing roles due to events and changing factors in our lives, so too do our schools. In the twentieth century we have asked our schools to take on roles that have historically been the responsibility of other institutions. For example, in the past, our churches and families have mainly taught children about

right behavior, and how to live a moral life. Now changes in economic institutions, as well as in cultural communities have caused families and churches to change their roles in our lives. Schools are called on to fill a gap in teaching morality that families and churches traditionally filled. Schools are also called on to assume parental roles in actual physical care of children, including making sure our children are fed, clothed, rested, and protected from physical harm.

Because our schools are one among many social institutions in our society, they reflect whatever conditions the larger society is experiencing. When our society feels tensions due to racial or sexual discrimination, these same tensions are experienced in our schools. When our society struggles with economic loss, due to changing economic conditions and the loss of jobs which results in the lowering of income levels, our schools show the wear and tear signs of a society in economic decline. When adults in our society cope with their problems by using drugs and alcohol, our youth model their behavior, and drugs and alcohol are then found in our schools. And when our society experiences an increase in violence, as can be seen by an increase in crimes and the purchasing of arms, for example, then these same conditions are reflected in our schools. Racism, sexism, and poverty manifest themselves in overt forms of violence such as gang fights, and in covert forms such as sexual harassment.

In order to consider how teachers and community leaders can help our schools be peaceful environments in which adolescents can learn to be nonviolent, peaceloving, and peacebuilding individuals, it will be fruitful to consider what are necessary qualities of peace. This is a philosophical question, and as a philosopher of education, this is what I hope to contribute to the larger discussion on peacebuilding for adolescents. While schools clearly cannot eradicate violence, they can foster a more peaceful environment. If we can better understand the essential ingredients for peace to occur, then we can explore ways to ensure these ingredients are present and thriving in our schools. It is my contention that one vital quality of a peaceful environment is that it is a *caring* environment. When we examine examples of overt and covert violence in any setting, we always find that the setting lacks genuine forms of caring. In order to defend this contention, I must thoroughly explore what caring means, how it relates to other qualities, and how it effects all of us.

I use my own experiences as an adolescent and as a teacher, as well as my three teenage children's experiences, as autobiographical and biographical narrative to help us look at caring in our schools. I do not wish to imply by the use of this personal data that my family's experiences are representative of others' experiences, or even that they are more significant in terms of the covert violence they describe: they are not. Rather, I tell our stories as a way of contextualizing myself as a writer, by exposing my subjective voice. I want the reader/hearer to know who I am. 1 am a unique, qualitative being. I am not an abstract, third-person, objective, neutral, anonymous philosopher. I speak from the first-person perspective to remind you (and myself) that ideas do not have a life of their own. They do not sprout out of the ground drawing nourishment from the soil, water, air, and sunlight. Ideas are *peoples'* ideas, and that means they are influenced by such contextual variables as social, political, psychological, economic, and historical forces. Theory that is estranged from the empirical world and social contexts runs the risk of being universalist or dogmatic. I also hope that these particular stories will serve as metaphors to the reader's own stories, for all of us have experienced covert violence in school, with a teacher toward a student, and between students.

I tell a story from my teenage years and one from my daughter's adolescence in order to help us make a cross-generational, personalized examination of adolescent experiences. This autobiographical and biographical narrative approach makes it possible to contextualize schools within our larger society, as well as compare how things have changed over the past thirty years. By drawing on real peoples' experiences, I will also be able to speak philosophically about what happens in our schools in terms of *caring* in a concrete fashion that teachers, guidance counselors, and school administrators will be able to understand. It is important to remember, though, that the data I present through these stories are unique, as with any qualitative study, and are not generalizable to all people. Still, they should bring out some general points about caring and how it relates to peacebuilding that are applicable to all of us in our own unique situations.

These stories will serve as examples of a lack of caring and they will help us understand how lack of caring results in covert and/or overt violence. I then describe how caring could have helped, or did help. It is my hope that through an examination of caring we can look at ways schools already care for their students, examine structures and factors that get in the way of schools doing a better job of caring for students, and make suggestions for ways in which schools can improve their caring capabilities. Schools can be more caring places, and they can teach people to be more caring of each other. Understanding *caring*, teaching people the value of *caring*, and helping people experience *caring* and its effects will go a long way toward lessening the violence we currently experience in our society at large.

What is Caring[4]

What is caring and how does it function as an emotional feeling that helps us in our efforts to inquire? Maxine Greene presents the case that caring involves a form of "attachment to those one is serving or working with."[5] It is possible, however, for people to form attachments in ways that are not caring, as we will find later. Jane Roland Martin looks to the home and parenting to help define caring and Sara Ruddick defines caring in terms of "mothering" in *Maternal Thinking*.[6] However, placing caring in a domestic domain, even a redescribed domestic domain, risks reinscribing a false dichotomy between private and public domains. Thus, caring is allowed to remain hidden from public sight, and caring remains devalued as private and personal. Carol Gilligan and Belenky et al. describe caring as being a feminine ethical orientation that is relational, based on a concept of self that is rooted in a sense of connection and relatedness to others. Nel Noddings describes caring in terms of feminine qualities.[7] These ways of defining caring leave us vulnerable to the false conclusion that caring is feminine, and therefore, gender-specific. Feminist scholars such as Jean Grimshaw, as well as the above-named authors, have warned us *not* to link caring to only girls and women.[8]

Milton Mayeroff describes caring as "recognizing the intrinsic worth of the 'other' and being committed to promoting its growth for its own sake."[9] Nel Noddings also describes caring as always being relational, between the carer and the one cared-for. Caring involves a "feeling with" the other (other people, other life forms, or even inanimate objects), and it stresses attending to the other. All caring involves presence (being present), generosity, and acquaintance. Noddings does not describe caring in terms of "empathy," for empathy can be taken to mean a projecting of oneself onto others. For her, caring is a move away from the self toward being receptive of the other. We will find that this relational quality of caring is very important for it helps us identify and understand false forms of caring.

Joan Tronto[10] agrees with Noddings that caring is necessarily relational, it must have an object. In her earlier work, however, she disagrees that the object of caring occurs with abstract ideas as well as with living beings. Tronto distinguishes between "caring about" and "caring for" based on the objects of care, arguing the "caring about" refers to "a specific, particular object that is the focus of caring. Caring for involves responding to the particular, concrete, physical, spiritual, intellectual, psychic, and emotional needs of others." Tronto presents the case that "traditional gender roles in our society imply that men care about but women care for."[11] In making this distinction Tronto reveals more about caring and traditional assumptions of gender difference. Like Jane Roland Martin's analysis of domesticity, Tronto points to political issues involved with caring in her discussions.[12] Unfortunately, by distinguishing "caring for" from "caring about," Tronto reinscribes a traditional philosophical assumption about people and ideas being separable. Let me explain.

From an epistemological standpoint, emotional feelings like caring affect us, as inquirers, because our emotional feelings help us choose what questions we want to address and try to understand. They also affect how we address the questions on which we choose to focus. Emotional feelings such as caring are what motivate us and inspire us. They are what make us feel unsettled and troubled about issues and problems. They are what make us feel excited and give us the desire to carry on with our efforts to understand. When we attempt to divorce reasoning and critical thinking from emotional feelings, we make the mistake of separating ideas from people. This is the mistake Tronto makes in distinguishing between "caring about" and "caring for." Just as violence is not just an idea, but an action done by people which affects other *people*. When I care about ideas such as peacebuilding, I do so because I understand the abstract concept of peacebuilding in relation to real peoples' lives for whom I care. An important necessary ingredient toward helping us change violent situations into peaceful ones is learning how to care for and about, to attend to and value peoples' problems in relation to ideas that help give meaning to peoples' experiences.

People do not have to lie or love each other in order to care. People do need to develop the ability to be receptive and open to other people and their ideas, willing to attend to them, to listen and consider their possibilities. Care does *not* entail that people agree with each other. Care does mean people are open to possibly hearing others' voices more completely and fairly. Caring about other people (and in agreement with Noddings, other people's ideas, other life forms, or even inanimate objects) requires respecting others as separate, autonomous people, worthy of caring. It is an attitude that gives value to others by denoting that others are worth attending to in a serious or close manner. Attitudes of acceptance and trust, inclusion and openness are important in all caring relationships.[13] My position is that without caring, one cannot hope to understand the violence in our society, let alone change it. Let's begin to explore caring for people in our schools.

Teachers and Students in the 1960s

When I think back on all the *crap* I learned in high school,
It's a wonder I can think at all

PAUL SIMON, *KODACHROME*

Now as a teacher and mother of three teenage children, I look back on my high school years as violent times. The civil rights movement was in full force and I watched rioting on my television screen and experienced racial strife in my school. Black, white, and Hispanic students struggled to understand each other and appreciate each other's anger, fears, and hopes for a better life. At the same time that racial tensions were high, so was the fear of war, and I spent my teenage years watching daily body counts on the television news concerning the Vietnam War. This war kept escalating while I was in high school, and my friends had to face the reality of potentially dying in a war we did not understand. The Vietnam War affected me at a personal, family level for my father was a career officer in the Air Force, a refueling pilot who spent two tours of duty in Vietnam and the surrounding regions. On top of all this confusion, anger, and frustration, we were also part of the sexual revolution. We expressed our feelings and coped through drugs, alcohol, and rock 'n roll. I know what it is like to be a teenager living in violent times.

Let me share a story that illustrates a lack of caring between teachers and students, resulting in covert violence. I tell this story from my perspective as a teenager. My story is not one of verified overt violence, physical acts of aggression intended to injure or harm others physically, but rather covert violence, in terms of verbal harassment, belittlement, and threats which harm others' self-esteem and self-dignity. Most children and teachers in schools, past or present, do not regularly experience physical threats to injure or harm them, but implied threats such as I will describe are common occurrences. If we can explore the lack of caring demonstrated in this story, and describe how caring could have helped, then perhaps we will have a clearer understanding of ways we can help build peace in our schools.

When I was a senior in high school I made the cheerleading squad along with six other girls. Seven of us were required to spell out "BOMBERS," our school team's name. We lived at Ramey Air Force Base in Puerto Rico, where our fathers worked as career officers or enlisted men. This was the only Department of Defense (DOD) school I ever attended, and it represents an example of one kind of implied threat with which students live. Our schools, and societies at large, threaten adolescents by insinuating that they need to follow the rules or they will bring dishonor and disgrace to their families. Their parents' jobs could be jeopardized, depending on how the students conducted themselves. In my case, this was literally true. I learned there was a double meaning to DOD schools, for if students made mistakes or caused problems in school their actions could be written up in their father's annual reviews, as the school board was comprised of the base commander and his senior staff of officers. Everyone knew that a bad or even a luke-warm review in the military meant no more promotions and an end to a parent's career. We were dependents being defended by the Department of Defense, and we were on the defensive.

The seven of us fortunate enough to be chosen for the cheerleading squad began to experience another form of covert violence many students experience on a regular basis, in the form of bullying behavior from teachers. Many students experience teachers who intimidate, frighten, and/or attempt to manipulate them on a regular basis, for the teaching role is one that involves power. Our cheerleading sponsor, Miss Taylor, was an unusual person.[14] As a cheerleading sponsor she looked unusual because she was overweight and not very physically attractive. She lived with another teacher, a frail, delicate, quiet woman, Miss Snyder, and together they were partners in love and work, traveling and teaching for DOD schools. What makes Miss Taylor an example of covert violence in our schools is not her appearance or love life. It is the manner with which she coached us, her pedagogical style, which was covertly violent. She had a way of addressing us that was more typical of a sadistic football coach or drill sergeant than a cheerleading sponsor.

As I remember, things pretty quickly began to unravel for our cheerleading squad. At first we were bribed to put up with Miss Taylor's overbearing, demeaning approach by promises of beautiful uniforms and state-of-the-art equipment. This is not an uncommon tactic bullying teachers, or students, use. We practiced two-three hours, five days a week, all summer long with a sponsor who screamed at us, belittled us, or locked us in our practice room when she was not there "to make sure the boys wouldn't bother us." When Miss Taylor was not there we complained bitterly about her and plotted her demise. The first girl to quit the squad was Chris, one of the returning seniors. Chris had put up with Miss Taylor as a sophomore but did not try out as a junior because of her abusive pedagogical style. She was talked into trying out for her senior year with the promise that things would be different with Miss Taylor. When she discovered that this was not true, she quit in August before school even started. An alternate replaced her, a sophomore named Cindy.

Miss Taylor's bribery lost its impact when the uniforms and equipment arrived and we discovered that our uniforms were handmade in Aguadilla, Puerto Rico, not what we had chosen from the catalogs we had pored over. We also found out that the school was not paying for our equipment, we were. This ushered in Miss Taylor's second set of tactics to keep us in line, also commonly used by bullies, overt threats and covert subterfuge. Two of the seniors on the cheerleading squad were Puerto Ricans, Maria and Roberta, whose fathers were enlisted men. They could not afford to pay for their uniforms and equipment. Miss Taylor paid for their bills with the understanding "they owed her." This exchange meant she could ask them to do favors such as run errands or wash her car, and treat them however she wanted. She harassed and bullied them mercilessly. Rumor had it she was sexually involved with Maria, but that was never confirmed. It was confirmed, however, that Miss Taylor expected Maria to spy on us and give regular reports back to her. We began to mistrust each other and be careful about what we said. Our misery increased as the football season progressed.

Then came the final tactic Miss Taylor used on me, to try to keep me quiet and in line. I was someone she did not harass very much, but my best friend, Vanessa, was one of her main targets of verbal abuse. I went to talk to Miss Taylor about her treatment of Vani, and her response was to tell me that Vani had not legitimately qualified with the judges to make the cheerleading squad, but that Taylor had made an "executive decision" and placed her on the squad anyway. This was our little secret and in her mind it gave her the right to treat Vani however she wanted. She threatened to tell Vani of her status as a team member and remove her from the squad if I complained to higher authorities. Miss Taylor was counting on our dreams to be cheerleaders and on our friendships to conceal her antics.

Miss Taylor represents a dangerous, violent form of false caring that is found in our schools, as well as our homes and other social settings. It is an infantile, hedonistic form of false caring that I call "mirror caring," in which people act as though they care for another, only as long as the cared-for person fulfills a need of the one caring. We see this false form of caring in schools with teachers who attempt to see themselves through their students' eyes. They want their students to mirror their own image back as a way of reaffirming the value of who they are. Mirror caring is an infantile demand for more love, in which teachers call to their students for needed attention. This demand for love from students is a way of seeking confirmation of our wholeness. The issue is one of identity, and teachers are in a position to require students to affirm their own identity by demanding and insisting students reflect what teachers want to see. As Jo Anne Pagano has perceptively noted, talented students "reflect us back to ourselves as twice our size by seeming to become us or like us."[15] Without that affirmation, the hedonistic desire to have students be mirrors can turn sadistic, as it did with Miss Taylor when the girls who were not willing or able to reflect her identity back to her became the targets of her wrath.

Scholars such as Jo Anne Pagano are concerned about caring as "love" and describe a hedonistic, indoctrinating side to teachers who love their students too much. The erotic side of teachers' loving their students is a danger no matter what sexual orientation the teachers or students have. Pagano worries about the dangers of coercions that act upon the bodies of students as teachers perceive themselves as loving their students as disembodied minds. This is an illusion of innocence because in fact students are embodied, sensual beings, as are their teachers. Pagano notes that teachers' desire to be loved "seems too large for the student-teacher relationship to bear. Certainly too large for any student to bear."[16] The dangers of teachers desiring to be loved by their students were apparent on Miss Taylor's cheerleading squad. We suffered the kinds of consequences students suffer in violent situations (whether they be covert or overt): loss of physical and mental health, lowered self-esteem and depression, loss of friendships, and isolation from our peers.

Did Miss Taylor really care for us? If caring means one tries to apprehend the reality of the person cared for, and support that person by being receptive to his or her needs, then certainly Miss Taylor failed to care for Vani, Roberta, Maria, Chris, Cindy, Susie, Tara, or me. I am sure Miss Taylor perceived herself as caring in her relationship with her cheerleaders, because she was willing to be the sponsor and devote a great deal of her time to make sure we did a good job and represented the school well. However, Taylor's acts of care were not perceived as such by us, because she was manipulating and using us for her own needs, and she was unable to develop a reciprocal relationship with us at any level. It is important to remember that while we as teachers may perceive ourselves as caring, that unless that caring is perceived as caring by our students, it is not caring.

What happened with the Ramey Bomber cheerleaders? When Miss Taylor told me that she did not intend to change her violent style of teaching, I turned to my fellow cheerleading friends to try to solve our situation. At this point I organized my first rebellion. We met and decided to resign in mass. We figured that if we all resigned the adults would have to realize there was a problem and the problem did not rest with us, but rather with our cheerleading sponsor. We were hoping to get Miss Taylor replaced by anyone else. It is interesting to note we did not turn to other adults for help. In the middle of football season I turned in a letter of resignation and went home, announcing to my parents I had resigned. I waited to see what would happen.

What happened? Nothing. No one else turned in a letter of resignation. Miss Taylor remained the cheerleading sponsor and the cheerleading squad went on without me. Vani resigned at the end of football season when her nerves could not take it anymore and she became physically ill. Roberta resigned in the middle of basketball season, having a nervous breakdown. However, it was too little, too late. All pictures of Chris, Roberta, Vani, and myself were removed from the school yearbook when they were mailed to the publisher, and all records of us as cheerleaders are gone.

My parents tell me I never told them what was going on. I do not remember. They say that I just came home one day and announced I had resigned. They knew something was terribly wrong because they knew how much I had wanted to be a cheerleader. My parents went to the school superintendent and requested an investigation. Because my father was a lieutenant colonel, the school administration moved to comply with their request. They called us into the superintendent's office in pairs to ask what was going on, a younger girl with an older girl, a Puerto Rican girl with a White girl. Nobody said anything, except me. I watched in amazement as my friends remained silent in intimidation and my career as a cheerleader came to an end. My parents tried unsuccessfully to get Miss Taylor fired; they were only able to have an incident letter placed in her file. At the end of the year she transferred to another DOD school to continue her teaching career.

What was hardest for me to understand, and therefore forgive, at the time of this experience was how my own friends responded to our cheerleading sponsor dilemma. Why were we unable to help each other? Why were they unable to stand beside me, rather than capitulating and leaving me hanging there alone? Is it because they did not care? They never offered me their reasons for changing their minds. Because they were not able to be open and honest with me, their actions betrayed my trust, and I perceived them as falsely caring. Now I realize that most of them probably did care about me to some level or degree, but their kind of caring was weak and ineffectual, a kind of "timid caring." We were teenagers with very little political sway in a scary situation, and it would have taken all of us standing together to solve the problem of our cheerleading sponsor. My friends' fears outweighed the courage they needed to be able to show they cared for me. While it is not always necessary, courage can play a very important role in acts of care. To different levels and degrees, we all lacked self-confidence, which affected our courage. (How many teenagers really do feel good about themselves?) We also lacked self-awareness and an understanding of how our society's rules shaped our lives. We were acculturated to be respectful of adults, and as girls, to be quiet and not complain. For my friends to be able to speak up meant going against their cultural beliefs which had surrounded them since birth. This is extremely difficult for anyone to do, especially people who are not yet adults, still trying to develop their voices.

This story represents many forms of covert violence, with overt violence possibly mixed in (if Miss Taylor was in fact having sex with a minor). It also is a story that helps us understand how caring plays an important role in eliminating violence and building peace. The Ramey Bomber cheerleaders needed some teachers (and more parents) who were able to be receptive to our situation and generous in their efforts to try to understand and believe us. We needed teachers who cared about us and had the courage to act on our behalf. We also needed to be brave, ourselves, and act together.

Why did we feel we only had each other to turn to as a way of solving our problem? What about the other adults in the cheerleading story, the students' parents and other teachers? As the mother of three teenagers, I know it is hard to have a caring relationship with teenagers. They strive to break free from their parents and be autonomous and independent. Often they experience problems in their lives of which parents are not even aware. Apparently, we did not talk to our parents about what was going on with Miss Taylor, so they were removed from being able to help us. As for the other teachers at the high school, I cannot imagine that they were not aware of problems with Miss Taylor, but maybe I am wrong. Maybe they really did not know. Still, I think there were missed opportunities and a failure occurred for the adults, both parents and teachers, with whom we spent so much time.

Teenagers do talk, mostly to each other. We talked to each other continually about what we were experiencing. Were the adults just not listening carefully to what we were saying? I suspect more adult effort to attend to our situation and be receptive to what *was* being communicated would have given us a sense of being cared for and would have encouraged us to open up and seek more help. Why seek help from adults who will not believe your word over another adult's, and who make you feel devalued, immature, and deceitful?

As it was, when I did talk to my parents, they were not able to help me solve my problems. This is a hard lesson for any child to learn. However, I remember feeling tremendous relief when my parents finally knew what was going on, and I greatly appreciated their efforts to help remove Miss Taylor as our sponsor. I knew that they believed me and they supported my efforts, unlike many parents and teachers who doubt children's words. I felt validated and strengthened in my resolve to not just let things be. Their caring had a powerful effect on me.

The Ramey Bomber cheerleaders needed the adults in our lives to help us solve our problem, especially the teachers who worked on a daily basis with Miss Taylor and knew what she was like with her students. Most of our teachers maintained an uninvolved, neutral stance throughout the year. Some of them actually began to intimidate us in their interactions with us as a way of helping Miss Taylor and further harming our resolve. I was president of the Honor Society that year, and Miss Snyder, Miss Taylor's roommate, was the sponsor of that organization. My ability to serve as president came into question after I resigned from the cheerleading squad. I was also in the honors senior English class with a teacher who had taught with Miss Taylor at her previous DOD school assignment, as well as in Puerto Rico, and I began to be belittled in his class, and received the first C I ever received in high school that next grading period. The guidance counselor called me into his office and advised me not to go to college as I would probably not have the resolve to complete it. When I applied to college and saw that I had to have letters of recommendations from my guidance counselor and senior English teacher,

I remember a sinking, panicky feeling that I was in serious trouble, and might not get admitted into college, even though I had a GPA of around 3.8 and I graduated fourth in my class. My teachers' protection and support for their colleague were terrifying to me!

What does this story teach us about caring and peacebuilding? As adults, we have opportunities to teach children how to communicate and relate to each other, and to us. We have chances to set up environments in ways that encourage interaction and responses from others. However, we must be careful to not abuse our powerful roles as authority figures. We have responsibilities to ensure that environments are safe, so that immature, fragile, and contrary voices are heard. We must try to protect those who have less power and authority (e.g., children, students), and we must commit ourselves to genuinely caring about them. This means we must really try to listen, and hear what they have to say. And when there are acts of violence, we must be stirred to action, to try to help them. As Paulo Freire points out in *Pedagogy of the Oppressed*,[17] there cannot be a neutral stance in oppressive situations. If a person is involved in an oppressive, dehumanizing condition, either that person is working to help transform the situation or she or he is supporting the efforts of the oppressor, even if she or he is doing nothing. Freire warns teachers:

> The educator does not have the right to be silent just because he or she has to respect the culture. If he or she does not have the right to impose his or her voice on the people, he or she does not have the right to be silent. It has to do precisely with the duty of intervening, which the educator has to assume without becoming afraid. There is no reason for an educator to be ashamed of this.[18]

I hope you are beginning to understand the power of caring and the destruction or ineffectuality that comes from false forms of caring or lack of caring. Genuine caring is necessary to help prevent or end harmful, oppressive behavior. I move on to story .two and concerns about peacebuilding in relation to caring in our schools today.

Teachers and Students in the 1990s

Here we are now, entertain us!
I feel stupid and contagious!

KURT COBAIN OF NIRVANA, *SMELLS LIKE TEEN SPIRIT*

My children attend high school during another violent time in our society. I teach in these current times of fear for one's safety and well-being, with students coming to school with knives and guns and becoming members in gangs as ways to protect themselves and help them feel like they have some control over their lives. In the 1990s, we still live with discriminatory tensions related to racism, sexism, and poverty, and the expressive release of those tensions through crime, drugs, alcohol, rock 'n roll, and new forms of music such as rap. While my children say they have never been in a fight, or experienced direct physical harm, they have seen fights, and have had times when someone verbally or physically threatened them, and they were afraid. They consider these experiences routine, however, and typical behavior of adolescents who are trying everything out for the first time. They have found their friends to be their best sources of help in times of need, not their teachers or other adults. When adults are the aggressors, students may need other adults to help them solve their problems, but when the aggressors are peers, students can help each other pretty effectively, though not without some false starts or mistakes along the way.

I am in the unique position of being able to affirm my children's claims, for I was a teacher for two of my children at different times in their school careers, and my daughter experienced an unusually aggressive and hostile school year while she was a student in my class. This was my most volatile teaching experience, and it occurred in an exclusive resort town on the coast of California, not in an inner city, and not with the lower-income, minority children often portrayed in the media as instigators of violence. The children I taught that year were from wealthy or middle-income families, the class size was small (nineteen students), and there were sixteen white students in the class. In my daughter's situation she had two teachers in the classroom who both cared a great deal about her, and were well aware of the aggressive, intimidating behavior she was being confronted with on a daily basis, and still we were not able to help her or her colleagues in the room. I learned a lot that year, and found it a very humbling experience. I worried all year about its affects on my daughter, but she brushes it off as not being that significant of an experience.

I tell my daughter's story as I remember it, for it represents a lack of caring between students, and the overt and covert violence that was the result. It also will help us understand how caring can help build peace in our schools, for in this story the students were able to end the violence and be successful peacebuilders. They used their ability to care for my daughter as a way of helping them understand how she might be feeling, and therefore move to end their aggressive, harmful behavior.

What happened? My daughter was new to this school, as I had just accepted a teaching position. As an attractive girl, she was the center of the boys' attention. She enjoyed their attention and did not want to hurt any of their feelings, so she tried to be friends and flirt with all of them. This was a mistake. There was one particular male in the class who already had a girlfriend, and often she would do things with Thad, his girlfriend Sara, and one of the other boys. Halfway through the year Sara moved away and Thad was alone. There was a turning point when Thad seemed to feel left out and excluded from my daughter's attentions, and the other boys seemed to tire of her trying to be friends with all of them. Their caring for her was another false form of caring, "amorphous caring," one that changes as peoples' needs dictate. Thad rallied the other boys to join him in excluding my daughter and harassing her. She began to experience sexual harassment that became more aggressive and intimidating as the year progressed and her teachers continued to try to resolve the problem.

The boys began by teasing and belittling my daughter verbally and gossiping about her. This is a kind of harmful behavior that adolescents experience as well as participate in on a daily basis. She did what most teenagers do to cope; she ignored them and spent her time with the girls in the class. My co-teacher and I ignored them as well, knowing that often the best course of action is no action that draws attention to their behavior, since attention is what they are seeking. Indirectly, though, we talked to the whole class about "caring community" kinds of issues and ways to model this. We also talked privately to my daughter, so she knew we were aware of what was going on. We gave her advice on how her friendly flirting had probably caused jealous feelings to be aroused, and what she could do to prevent this from occurring in the future. We also offered advice on how to handle the situation she was now in, and we offered emotional support. If I had not been her parent, we would have also called her parents at that point so they were aware of the situation and would be able to offer their daughter support at home as well.

Because I was the parent, as well as teacher, my co-teacher and I shifted responsibilities so that I was not directly teaching my daughter in case that was exacerbating the situation for her. The boys became more aggressive and intimidating, and scared the other girls in the class into avoiding my daughter, with threats of reprisals to them if they did not. The girls stopped being my daughter's friends in class, although some of them would occasionally call her at home. This action on the girls' part hurt my daughter a great deal, as she lost the protection of her peers. She also lost respect for the girls and their apparent lack of courage and concern for her well-being. Again, as I had at her age, she found that it is very difficult for teenagers (especially girls who have been acculturated to be submissive) to stand up and offer help under potentially violent, abusive conditions. They have not had the opportunity to develop their self-esteem, as well as make decisions concerning their values and beliefs, to the point that they can express their voice and act in times of fear and distress. We see them again representing timid caring, which can be found in adult relationships as well. The girls' withdrawal and decision to not act in support of my daughter added to the power of the impact of the boys' threatening behavior. It also seemed to open the door on the boys' aggressive behavior, because they shifted from verbal harassment to more physical harassment.

The boys began to knock my daughter's books off her desk when they would walk by, or pinch her or jab her with their elbows. They were physically attempting to intimidate her. My daughter held her ground and continued to ignore them, refusing to let them know that they were getting to her. Most often she would not show that she was upset with what was going on until she got home, where she would cry. Occasionally she would confront them when they did something to her. My co-teacher and I stepped up our surveillance of the room, and began punishing the boys for what they were doing. This created a backlash effect. The boys seemed to gather strength from knowing their actions were causing a rise, and they became more subversive but also more threatening with their tactics. When our punishing did not stop matters, we turned to our administration for assistance, and were advised to call the parents of the boys who were doing the harassing, to enlist their support by talking to their children about their behavior. This created an even bigger backlash effect. After calling parents, my co-teacher and I walked into a classroom that we could see was excited to know they were creating enough concern to have their parents called. Thad pulled a knife on my daughter outside of the classroom within a week of our seeking parental support. She war terrified. He was suspended, but when he returned to school he proceeded to do the same thing to her again. Neither the school, teachers, nor parents were able to end this violent behavior.

In the end, the students themselves solved the problem and came to my daughter's aid. When Thad's behavior became so extreme that even they could see it was dangerous and scary, they started to step in, speak on her behalf, and offer her protection. The support came first from one of the boys who had participated in the sexual harassment. He was one of the minority students in the class, and he was finally able to empathize with how my daughter might be feeling when he started to experience exclusion himself by the other boys. José spoke up to the whole class at a class meeting and told them that what they were doing was wrong and shared how painful it felt to be excluded. This brave action seemed to break the resolve of the group and open up space for others to begin to show my daughter that they cared. They began to see that while my daughter might have made a mistake in terms of flirting with the boys, what Thad was doing was violent and an extreme overreaction. They stopped trying to hurt her emotionally or physically, apologized to her, and began to try to win back her friendship. My daughter struggled to trust those students again. She was leery of their offers of friendship, but she kept that to herself, and tried to act like she was willing to be friends. They all began the painful process of forgiving.

Once my co-teacher and I knew we had the aggressive behavior of the group under control, we were better able to focus on Thad's needs and try to find out what else might be going on in his life to cause him to act violently. We found out that Thad's parents had gone through a bitter divorce, and that his father, who was apparently very wealthy, had moved away. Thad rarely saw him at a time in his life when he may have really needed him. We also found out that the parents had a serious drug problem and, as Thad was old enough to know what was going on with his parents, it is possible he was using drugs as well. Overall, Thad seemed to have parents who were struggling to cope with their own problems and were unable to attend to Thad's needs as they should.

Thad's story is typical of the aggressive, violent students I have taught. Children learn how to be aggressive because their social institutions. (including their families, extended families, and friends, their neighborhoods and larger communities, their expressive arts and media, and their schools) teach them how to be violent. If we want to help our children be able to live in peace with their environment and each other, we have to teach them about peace, and treat them in a peaceful manner. Caring is an important and necessary ingredient for peacebuilding, for caring is what helps us understand others' perspectives. Our ability to care is also what moves us to action. If we can show our students that we genuinely care about the situations in their lives, and that we genuinely care for them as people living in these situations, we will empower them to help find solutions to their problems.

We also need to take responsibility for the way things are, even as we recognize that institutions that shape and affect our lives are ones we have socially constructed.[19] Once we are able to recognize and begin to understand our own responsibilities for current conditions, we can stop blaming others and work together to change things in a more peaceful direction. It takes a lot of courage, as we saw with José in story two, and myself in story one, to claim responsibility and move to act in ways that change things in positive directions. There is no guarantee that our actions will be successful; in story one, mine were not, but in story two José's were. Not to act in a caring manner, however, does guarantee that violence will continue to prosper.

What does story two teach us about how caring can help build peace? We learned in this second story that students are abler to help each other against aggressive peers, although not without some mishaps along the way. Adults can certainly help adolescents gain the skills they need to be successful builders of peace by helping adolescents develop their abilities to communicate and relate to each other. Students also need chances to develop their abilities to constructively think about ways to creatively solve their problems. Tools that all people have available to help them constructively think are reason, intuition, imagination, and emotional feelings like caring.[20] As Maxine Greene reminds us in *Releasing the Imagination*:

All we can do is to speak with others as passionately and eloquently as we can; all we can do is to look into each other's eye and urge each other on to new beginnings. Our classrooms ought to be nurturing and thoughtful and just all at once; they ought to pulsate with multiple conceptions of what it is to be human and alive. They ought to resound with the voices of articulate young people in dialogues always incomplete because there is always more to be discovered and more to be said. We must want our students to achieve friendship as each one stirs to wide-awakeness, to imaginative action, and to renewed consciousness of possibility.[21]

Conclusion

We learned that violence is reflected in our social institutions: abuse in our homes, crime in our neighborhoods, physically and verbally damaging behavior on our televisions, distrust for our public officials, and disrespect for our school personnel. Schools are only one of many social institutions. They cannot solve all the problems of our society. These problems are much too complex and interrelated to be taken care of by one institution. However, schools can be a site where people can come together to study and learn about our problems, attempt to generate possible solutions to our problems, and model for our larger society and our other social institutions ways to solve our problems.

We can begin to build peace through acts of genuine caring. We found through the stories shared that there are many forms of false caring, such as mirror caring, timid caring, and amorphous caring. Genuine caring involves an attitude of respect and trust; it is a receptive valuing of others in a generous manner. I have made the case here that caring is vital to help us turn acts of aggression into peaceful acts, for without a caring attitude we cannot hope to understand others and what they are experiencing. It is only through their willingness to tell us that we can hope to enlarge our own views and gain more insight. We can hope to have others open up to us and share their lives with us when we show them we care. Caring is *not* a panacea—it will not solve all of our problems. But caring is a starting place. Without it we cannot even begin to lessen the violence we currently experience in our schools, homes, places of work, communities and neighborhoods, on our televisions and radios, all around us.

QUESTIONS TO CONSIDER

1. What does Thayer-Bacon mean by "positive peace"? How does she define "overt" and "covert" violence? How are those terms played out in her essay?

2. Compare the cross-generational story of her own teenage years and that of her daughter. In what ways are they similar and different?

3. Thayer-Bacon employs various uses of the concept of "caring." Which usage makes the most sense to you in (a) everyday life and (b) teaching? Explain why.

4. How does the author explain the root causes of aggression and violence in youth? What are her remedies for such behavior?

Notes

This chapter originally appeared in Linda Rennie Forcey and Ian Murray Harris (eds.), *Peacebuilding for Adolescents: Strategies for Educators and Community Leaders* (New York: Peter Lang, 1999).

1. Compiled by John McIntosh for the American Association of Suicidology: National Center for Health Statistics, Washington, DC (1996).

2. Scholars in the field of Peace Studies debate how to define peace. Kenneth Boulding represents a narrow definition of peace, which Johan Galtung labeled "negative peace" in contrast to his broader definition of peace that includes social justice, which Galtung called "positive peace." See Linda Rennie Forcey, "Peace Studies," in *Protest, Power, and Change: An Encyclopedia of Nonviolent Action from ACT-UP to Women's Suffrage*, ed. Roger S. Powers and William B. Vogele (New York: Garland Press, 1997).

3. Ian M. Harris, "From World Peace to Peace in the 'Hood: Peace Education in a Postmodern World," *Journal for a Just and Caring Education* 2 no. 4, pp. 378–95, 381 (October 1996).

4. This section overlaps with my paper "The Power of Caring," *Philosophical Studies in Education* (1997): 1–32.

5. Maxine Greene, "The Tensions and Passions of Caring," in *The Caring Imperative in Education*, ed. M. Leininger and J. Watson (New York: National League for Nursing, 1990): 29–44.

6. Jane Roland Martin, *The Schoolhome* (Cambridge, MA: Harvard University Press, 1992); Sara Ruddick, *Maternal Thinking: Toward a Politics of Peace* (Boston: Beacon Press, 1989).

7. Carol Gilligan, *In a Different Voice* (Cambridge: Harvard University Press, 1982); Mary Field Belenky, Blythe McVicker Clinchy, Nancy Rule Goldberger, and Jill Mattuck Tarule, *Women's Ways of Knowing* (New York: Basic Books, Harper Collins Publisher, 1986); Nel Noddings, *Caring* (Berkeley: University of California Press. 1986). See also Nel Noddings, *The Challenge to Care in Schools: An Alternative Approach to Education* (New York: Teachers College Press, 1992).

8. Jean Grimshaw, *Philosophy and Feminist Thinking* (Minneapolis. MN: University of Minnesota Press, 1986).

9. Milton Mayeroff, *On Caring* (New York: Harper and Row, 1971).

10. Joan C. Tronto, "Women and Caring: What Can Feminists Learn about Morality from Caring?" in *Gender/Body/Knowledge*, ed. Alison M. Jaggar and Susan R. Bordo (New Brunswick, NJ: Rutgers University Press): 172–187. See also Joan C. Tronto, *Moral Boundaries: A Political Argument for an Ethic of Core* (New York: Routledge, 1993).

11. Tronto, "Women and Caring," 174.

12. Toronto, "Women and Caring."

13. Barbara Thayer-Bacon, "Caring and Its Relationship to Critical Thinking," *Educational Theory* 43, no. 3 (summer 1993): 325.

14. All names are changed to protect the anonymity of the people involved in the stories.

15. Jo Anne Pagano, "Taking our Places," Keynote Address, Ohio Valley Philosophy of Education Society, Indianapolis, IN, 1994, 18.

16. Ibid., 11.

17. Paulo Freire, *Pedagogy of the Oppressed* (New York: The Seabury Press, 1968). See chapter one.

18. Paulo Freire and Myles Horton, *We Make the Road by Walking*, ed. Brenda Bell, John Gaventa, and John Peters (Philadelphia: Temple University Press, 1990), 138.

19. Peter L. Berger and Thomas Luckmann, *The Social Construction of Reality: A Treatise in the Sociology of Knowledge* (Garden City, NY: Anchor Books, 1996).

20. Barbara Thayer-Bacon, with Charles Bacon, *Philosophy Applied to Education: Nurturing a Democratic Community in the Classroom* (Columbus, OH: Prentice-Hall, 1997). See chapter four.

21. Maxine Greene, *Relating the Imagination* (San Francisco: Jossey-Bass, 1995), 43.

CHAPTER THIRTY-SIX

"I'm a Person; I'm Not Dirt!"

The Impact of Power Relationships on Perceptions of Caring in a Secondary Classroom

MARCIA PECK

Ms. Jones, an 8th-grade math teacher, slid into an orange metal chair in the faculty lunch room with a heavy sigh. Another teacher looked up from her reheated noodle casserole and asked, "What's wrong this time?"

"It's those same three kids in third period," Ms. Jones stated. "Jeffrey is the ring leader. No matter what I do, they won't do any of the work and just sit there and talk to each other across the room! It's so disruptive; I can't teach. Those kids just don't care about anything, not the other students, or me, or their education! I don't know why they even come to class. I wish they just stayed home!"

Out in the cafeteria, Jeffrey slouched into a seat at the long, brown, laminated table and slammed down his books. "I hate that math class!" he loudly proclaimed. "It sucks so bad! All the teacher ever does is tell us to get to work. She never explains anything and won't help anyone. She just walks around the room yelling at us. Today she said, 'Jeffrey, how come you don't do your work? You'll never be able to support yourself if you don't do your school work.' She obviously doesn't care about us or teaching us anything. She just wants us to sit there and not bother her. I wish they fired her!"

Anyone who spends time within a secondary school will, sooner than later, hear conversations similar to those detailed above. It seems both students and teachers feel justified in claiming the other demonstrates, on a daily basis, a general lack of caring, about education, about other people, or about themselves. While Jeffrey's outburst or the sentiments expressed by Ms. Jones may elicit a smile or a shrug because, "That's just the way it is in school," the anger and frustration resulting from perceptions of lack of caring are deeply felt and have profound and lasting effects on students' educational engagement and attainment as well as teacher satisfaction, retention, and engagement in their work. For example, Ms. Jones is unlikely to continue to put effort into her classroom instruction if her perception is students don't care. The same could be said of Jeffrey and his classmates. Students are unlikely to engage on more than a perfunctory level in the classroom, if at all, if they perceive their teacher as not caring about them or their education. Despite the fact that students are mandated to attend school in order to have their academic needs met, meeting their emotional needs can not be ignored in this process.

Such statements and beliefs regarding caring in schools as those voiced by Ms. Jones and Jeffrey have been documented for many years. Indeed, much research has been conducted and philosophical positions asserted in an effort to improve caring in schools (Beck, 1995; Garza, 2009; Kohn, 1991; Mayeroff, 1971; Noddings, 2002, 1998, 1992, 1984; Valenzuela, 1999; Watras, 2004).

Noddings's (2002, 1998, 1992,1984) research on caring is perhaps the best known. Noddings advocates that the aim of education should be the nurturance of an ethical ideal with this ideal having its foundation in the recognition and longing for relatedness. She claims that the role of the teacher is to act as a model of "one-caring," in which the teacher pays close attention to the student. Teachers are to accept student opinions, no matter how controversial they may be, participate with students in service activities, and attribute the best possible motives to students, a practice she terms "confirmation." Noddings also highlights the importance of reciprocity within in a caring relationship. Such reciprocity entails a recognition and acceptance of the care being offered to the "cared-for." Noddings (1992) states that "no matter how hard teachers try to care, if the caring is not received by students, the claim 'they don't care' has some validity. It suggests strongly that something is very wrong" (p. 15).

More recent research (Rolón-Dow, 2005; Sidorkin, 2002; Todd, 2003) has expanded Noddings's definition somewhat, but still maintains to a large degree her basic premise that teachers should engage in an ethic of care with their students by exhibiting compassion, attentiveness, and consideration towards their students' personal and educational well-being. The underlying notion behind much of this work focusing on caring is the conviction that students who feel cared for will be more likely to participate in their own education in positive and productive ways.

Up until 2008, I too embraced a view that defined a caring teacher as one who demonstrated consideration and kindness for her students by asking about their lives, sharing appropriate vignettes from her own experiences when appropriate, and offering help or a listening ear when needed. Additionally, my definition of caring also encompassed caring about the students' education by providing appropriate learning opportunities to help students master the required knowledge and skills to be successful in and outside of school. Both of my definitions of caring are fairly standard in the research literature and in the education of pre-service and in-service teachers (Alder, 2002; Cothran & Ennis, 2000; Goldstein & Freedman, 2003; Mihalas, Morse, Allsopp, & McHatton, 2009; Noddings, 1992).

Such a definition of caring, or in other words attending to the emotional and academic needs of students, was called into question for me by my accidental involvement with three 8th-grade students. This experience caused me to question whether such a characterization of caring was too limited in scope. After talking with these students, I began to wonder if my definition of caring in schools should be widened to include not only teacher behaviors and dispositions, but also how the relations of power engaged in both within and without the classroom were recognized and negotiated within the space of a school.

The genesis of this hypothesis about caring was a conversation I had in 2008 with a 13-year-old male student. This particular morning, I was checking in with one of the new teachers I had been assigned to mentor, Ms. Williams. She had been having difficulties with student behavior, and I wanted to let her know I was there as a resource if she needed me. As I was leaving she asked me to escort one of her students to the office. She wanted the student out of the room due to his confrontational behavior. I waited at the door while this young man and Ms. Williams argued about his impending exit from the class. Eventually, he angrily slammed out of the room. As we walked away, I heard a student yell out, "How come you sent him to the office? He didn't do anything!"

The young man's face was red and his teeth clenched as he stalked furiously down the hall beside me. In order to ease the situation as we walked to the office, I asked him what his name was. "Matt," he stated abruptly.

"Okay, Matt," I said. "What's going on?"

Matt replied, "I've got to get out of that class! My I.Q. is dropping by the minute!"

Frankly, I was taken back by his remark. I had expected one of the usual comments I hear uttered by students in this situation such as, "I didn't do anything; she just hates me," or "She's always picking on me!" Never in my 22 years of teaching had I heard a student on his way to the office for discipline state that his main complaint was that the teacher couldn't or wouldn't teach him what he needed to know. From my experience, what and how a teacher instructed her class was so low on the radar of what is important to a middle school student that it receives little if any notice. You just don't often hear a 13-year-old say to the principal, "Well, I was angry because she didn't teach me the Pythagorean Theorem, and so I called her a *#!!"

Matt's comment so surprised me, I thought about it for several days. I knew some students believed that how a teacher instructed them was an illustration of caring, but usually students stated they didn't like a teacher because she was unfair or mean, not because she didn't teach them well. Based on Matt's comments, I decided I wanted to find out what students perceived to be going on in that particular class. I knew from talking with Ms. Williams that she did care about the students and although she tried repeatedly to implement new teaching strategies to increase student learning, student behavior made even basic teaching strategies nearly impossible to execute. In fact, during one observation I made to one of her 7th-grade classes, students continuously talked in a loud voice to each other while totally ignoring anything Ms. Williams tried to say or do. They would not even look at her. Once when the volume lowered for a short time, one student yelled out, "We're too quiet!" and the noise level rose again.

I invited Matt and two other students from his math class to come to my classroom during my consultation period and participate in a focus group interview discussing the topic of caring from a student's perspective. Like Matt, the other two students were sent out of the classroom often because of their poor behavior. All the students were in the 8th grade and could be said to come from working class socio-economic backgrounds. Besides Matt, a 13-year-old Caucasian, the other two students were Alicia, a 14-year-old Latina, and Luis, a 13-year-old Latino. I had met Matt only briefly on our walk and had not known the other young man at all before the interview. I had taught Alicia for ten weeks before she moved to a different school.

The focus group interview was unstructured and lasted approximately 75 minutes. Student responses were recorded on audiotape. The students knew they were there to talk about what had gone on in math with regard to caring teacher behaviors. There were no pre-determined questions or format because I did not want to decide what information was shared. I wanted them to feel free to say what they wanted about their experience and not be directed by my questions to particular areas. I informed the students that anything they said would be private and would not be shared with anyone else within the school. I also told them I would not identify them or the school by name in any work resulting from the interview. They all expressed disappointment in this fact as they wanted their names used. The only question that I posed was, "How do you define a caring teacher?" After that initial question, the students talked freely.

After the interview, the tape was transcribed. Excerpts from the interview are included in this document. It should be noted that Ms. Williams had already left the school by the time the interview was conducted and a long-term substitute had taken her place.

Caring About Me as a Person

In an initial analysis of the transcript, one definition of caring voiced by all the students entailed teacher behaviors that demonstrated concern and empathy for the students. Such a response was not unexpected because generally that is one way most students and teachers define caring (Alder, 2002; Garza, 2009). For example, below is an excerpt from the interview where all three students are talking about caring behaviors they appreciate in their teachers.

Alicia: A caring teacher will listen to you; they explain things, greet you when you come in. They're in a good mood most of the time and don't take things out on people, like if they're having a bad day. You (the teacher) have to be respectful, have a positive attitude, or it just doesn't work out.

Matt: Teachers are supposed to be encouraging. Tell you to get your grades up, come on let's do it; you're going to get through school.

Luis: A caring teacher acts like they are glad you are there. They ask you about your day, like how things are going for you. Like last year, Mr. Robins always asked me what was going on.

Caring About Me as a Student

The students also discussed the importance of a teacher demonstrating that she cared about them as students by providing them with appropriate instruction and tools for learning the material including maintaining classroom control. Such statements reminded me of my initial conversation with Matt on the way to the principal's office and, like the conversation I had with him, surprised me to some extent. Although other researchers have also documented such a definition of caring (Alder & Moulton, 1998; Cothran & Ennis, 2000), my experience as a teacher seemed to suggest that students were often eager to get out of school work and would prefer to "party" whenever possible. However, the comments these students made seemed to suggest the opposite. Not only did they care about their learning, they expected their teachers to care about it just as much as demonstrated by this excerpt from the interview. The students are talking about Ms. Williams.

Luis: So pretty much it was like, "Here's your work; do it; it's due by this time.

Alicia: She gave us a little amount of time (to do it) also. She didn't know how to teach right, and I used to be good; I used to have an A (last year), and now it's like an F. And sometimes she lost our work. I just had a lot of problems with her.

Peck: Last year you had an A and now you're hanging around an F; why is that?

Alicia: She didn't teach me . . . . I gave up because she didn't teach me.

Matt: That's the thing with me. My parents are, "Matt, how come you are missing so many assignments?" Because I gave up. It came down to where I turned in the same paper seven times to be graded. I finally had to start getting papers with her signature saying she put in the score. I got an offer to go to a specialized math program in 9th grade and for that to go on my college application would be so like amazing. Ms. Williams had ruined my math so bad, I couldn't go. If you want to go to college, math is a big thing, and she just ruined that for me.

Caring About Me as a Powerful Person

These two ways of demonstrating caring, being considerate, and teaching appropriately seemed on the surface to dominate the conversation and substantiate the commonly held view of what constitutes caring in school. However, as I analyzed the transcript, I kept getting glimpses that something else was going on in this situation based on comments made by the students. Repeatedly, students referred to instances where teachers, particularly Ms. Williams, treated them as less than human beings, referring to being treated as a "dog," a "wolf," and "dirt." They point- ed out times when a teacher took advantage of a privilege that was not afforded to a student and how they felt that was unfair. They also pointed to times when they were belittled for a choice as when Alicia stated to Ms. Williams that she wanted to be a hairdresser and was ridiculed for doing so because according to Ms. Williams, "You can't support yourself on a hairdresser's salary." These instances of mistreatment were perceived by students as something more than a teacher just not being "nice." They saw these actions as attacks on their actual "personhood."

What I began to see illustrated in these students' comments, then, was their unhappiness, and at times anger, when they were not treated as powerful people in their own right who deserved to have this power recognized and honored by the teacher. It appeared from what they were saying that for these students, this issue of recognizing student power, more than any other, defined a caring teacher. This notion was particularly true for Luis.

Such a view of caring has its genesis in the power relations that exist within the space of a classroom and can be divided into two themes. The first focuses on the power relations taking place within the context of the classroom, and the second centers on the power relations among students outside the classroom that they bring with them when they enter it.

When I use the terms *power relations* or *relations of power*, I am referring to a particular view of power (Foucault, 1990; McWhorter, 2005) that stipulates that power is not held or wielded or shared but that it is co-constructed and exercised by the participants within a relational dynam- ic (Margonis, 2006).

For example, in all social interactions, individuals engage in relations of power no matter their age, gender, socioeconomic status, race, or ethnicity. Power relations are characterized by the social construction of one's role within a specific relationship. For example, the flashing red lights of a police car behind another vehicle indicate that the driver is ordered to pull over to the curb, thus reflecting a relation of power and subordination between the police officer and the stopped driver. In other words, the supposedly delinquent driver and the authoritative police officer writing the ticket are constructed in a relation of power with the driver being in a less powerful position than the person with the badge. Later that day when that same driver, now the customer in a nice restaurant, wishes to complain about the food to the waiter, he or she is constructed within this relationship as a person to be reckoned with, and the server is the individual in a secondary position of power in relation to the paying customer.

Teachers and students engage in relations of power every day within the walls of a school. Generally, in such a relationship, a teacher is constituted as a powerful person who provides instruction, maintains discipline, and distributes grades. Teachers quite often expect their students to respect them as the teacher and do as they are told because of the teacher's age, advanced training and skills, and the authority conferred upon them in such an educational affiliation.

On the other hand, whether educators wish to acknowledge it or not, due to the relational nature of the educational interaction, students, too, are constituted within it as powerful people. Although students do not hand out detentions or determine grades, within the classroom relationship students exercise their "studenthood" power in a variety of ways such as working with the teacher to accomplish learning goals or, as was the case with the 8th-grade math class previously mentioned, creating chaos.

When teachers fail to acknowledge the nature of the student/teacher relationship and prefer to construct their students as the aforementioned motorist and themselves as the police officer, it is my contention that some students will engage in behaviors calculated to demonstrate the power they believe is or should be afforded them due to the relational nature of the classroom interactions. Consequently, in such a classroom students may engage in behavior such as disrupting or failing to complete work as a means of restoring a power relationship they understand to be out of balance.

As teachers, we all certainly want our students to engage in positive ways in the classroom. However, when students feel uncared for that is not likely to happen, and for the students in this interview being cared for involved the teacher recognizing and honoring that they too were constructed as powerful people within the relational space of the classroom. Some of this power resulted from engaging in power relations with the teacher, and some came about from the relations of power outside school.

Power Relations Within the Classroom

First and foremost for these students, a caring teacher demonstrated the same respect for her students that she would afford another adult, in other words, to treat them like people.

For example, in this excerpt all three students were discussing their math teacher's lack of caring about their power. She expected them to respect her power, but from their perspective, she did not recognize that they should be afforded respect as well.

Luis: You got to give respect to get it. Show respect. Like, "Hi take a seat," instead of, "Go do this; do your bell ringers." She just told us what to do like we're dogs;

Matt: Like wolves!
Luis: She never said please. She'd tell us to sit like a dog, she'd tell us to raise our hand like a dog;
            she'd never say please.

Such a sentiment was not so much an illustration that these students considered themselves on equal footing with adults, but that they had experienced that children in a classroom received little respect and felt that was wrong. They each sensed that within the dynamic of a teacher/student relationship they as students had a certain amount of power and felt that should be taken into account, just as it is in adult relationships. An example of this notion is illustrated when Matt discusses participating in relations of power in a classroom. His comments clearly suggest that he has a certain amount of power conferred on him based on his role as a student.

Matt: Well, I wait a while before I start giving a teacher attitude. Kind of depends on the teacher.
            If they have an attitude, I'll give them a week, cause everyone has a bad day, but then that's
            it.

Additionally, the students indicated that their presence in the classroom should be valued just as much as that of an honored guest or high status official such as the principal, a sentiment that also illustrates that they understand that the role of student is a powerful one and they believe that role should be given respect despite their youth.

Matt: You need to make students feel like they're welcome. Like if you go to a party or to a friend's
            house, they welcome you in, ask how you doing; they want you to be there.
Luis: Exactly! Like sometimes Mr. Tanner will meet you and shake your hand and say, "How are
            you?" All the good teachers know that.

Later in the interview, Matt stated a similar sentiment when he voiced the following:

Matt: The teacher should treat you right when you come into the room, like how they would treat
            the principal when she walked in, like you are someone special. Cause you know, I'm a per-
            son; I'm not dirt!

On another note, I found it interesting that these students viewed the classroom relationship as a reciprocal one based on the give and take of two powerful entities, in this case the teacher and the student. Such a sentiment extended not only to their behavior in class but also to how they viewed their labor within the classroom.

For example, these students did not view their academic labors as only their responsibility or solely for their benefit. It was as if they perceived their efforts in the classroom as a reward they bestowed on their teacher, but only if she was worthy, and that worth was determined by how caring she was toward them.

Matt: If the teacher wants me to do crap for them they need to show me respect.
Alicia: Well, Mr. Lewis sent me out into the hall and later came and sat down by me and he said,
            "I just really want you to try." It seemed like he cared, so I got my positive attitude back and
            did my work and got my grade to a C. If they try, I'll try and show them respect.
Luis: If a teacher gives me respect, I give them respect back. Well, I'd still probably goof around,
            but when they'd ask me what I'm doing, I'd kind of be nice. But with Ms. Williams, I'd answer

> her in a tone that would freeze, because she lost my respect. She doesn't want to do anything to make the kids satisfied; it's either her way or no way.

Indeed, the students seemed to be saying, "This is a relationship and like in any relationship there is a give and take involved."

Power Relations Outside of School

Besides the relations of power inherent in the social interaction within the classroom environment, some students engage in particular relations of power in their homes and communities that place them in positions of authority such as contributing to the financial security of their family or acting in a caretaker role with younger siblings and relatives. Such a scenario is more often evident for students of color or those coming from a low socioeconomic background, two groups already disenfranchised by the larger society and often the school.

Such a situation was evident particularly with Luis. In his life outside of school, he was afforded, and felt he was entitled to, quasi-adult power and status because of his paid employment. He worked in construction with his father and brothers on the weekends and sometimes after school, labor that he was paid for. He felt justifiably proud of this work and willingly told anyone who would listen that he made $200 a week working in construction. In his home and community, Luis was a quasi-adult because he assumed an adult role by becoming an apprentice in a skilled profession as well as earning wages while helping to support himself and his family.

When Luis arrived in a classroom, though, he encountered two situations which effectively altered the status and power he was afforded at home due the adult roles he engaged in. In the first instance he was a student and therefore considered a child and often treated with less respect than an adult, a situation previously discussed. In the second instance, he found his position of power as skilled wage earner and provider either not recognized or worse, dishonored or belittled. Being constituted as a powerless child within the classroom dynamic on Monday when just the night before he was constructed as an adult worker and provider was somewhat galling for Luis. It is little wonder that he identified such behavior as demonstrating a lack of care for him as a person. Luis spoke of this situation when he talked about his math teacher, Ms. Williams.

Luis: I disliked everything about her. She was a . . . witch with a B. Like one time she tried to talk to me about what my life was going to be like if I didn't do my work in her class. She talked to me about it in front of the whole class. She told me I wasn't going to be able to support myself. I told her I already had a job working construction and made $200 a week. She just laughed at me. She said, "You can't support children on $200 a week!" I told her I wasn't going to have any kids. I don't want a kid!

In this excerpt, it appeared that Luis was not only angry about being singled out for ridicule in front of the class and being treated as if he were an immature child who didn't understand economic realities, but he was also infuriated that the very thing he took pride in and provided him status in his "real" life, as opposed to his school life, was being denigrated and treated as a thing of very little value. When a person perceives he is being constructed as less powerful than he thinks he is, it is natural to want to remind others of the power inherent in the classroom relationship. It is little wonder, then, that when speaking of his behavior in some of his classes, Luis stated the following:

> A teacher tells me to do something; I'll do the exact opposite. Depends on how much they respect me. If they respect me a lot, I'll do it. They don't respect me at all, I'll do the opposite. (Pause) I'd rather have people fear me than respect me.

Whether it should or not, often engendering fear in a relationship provides an individual with more power than gaining another's respect. Perhaps that is why Luis made that statement. (Re)gaining power through engaging in a relationship that produces fear may also be why his behavior in some classes was so oppositional and confrontational. By his own admission, if he felt cared for, he would often comply or at least "be nice"; when he didn't feel cared for, he reacted in ways that could promote fear as when he would answer his math teacher in "a tone that would freeze."

How much more respectful toward his teachers would Luis be willing to be if he did not only feel cared for as a person but if his power as a wage earner and provider were included in the relational definition of Luis as a student?

An Improved Definition of Caring

It seems evident based on these students' responses that when students enter a classroom environment where the authority produced within their teacher/student relationship is not addressed, they do not feel "cared" for. These feelings of being uncared for often lead to interruptions or even chaos in the learning environment, resulting in a negative experience for all involved. This dynamic is particularly true for students who operate from powerful positions in their home environment and find on entering the classroom this authority is unrecognized or belittled as was the case with Luis.

For the remainder of this chapter, I wish to return to my earlier supposition that while the traditional definitions of caring in school are certainly valid and worthwhile, this definition should be widened to include acknowledging and attending to the power relations in the classroom. It appears that when an educator demonstrates caring by attending to the relationships of power from which students operate both in and outside the classroom, students are more likely to engage in positive ways within the classroom as opposed to displaying oppositional and resistant behaviors.

For example, the following excerpt from the transcript illustrates how these students characterize their teachers. The ones they want to "hang out with" could be said to be teachers who do not seem to mind hanging out with them. It appears these teachers recognize that the students are people, maybe young people, but people just the same, who are endowed with power and therefore have a legitimate claim to being treated with respect. These teachers realize that the educational process comprises reciprocal relationships, power relationships, and that caring for students means recognizing this fact.

Matt:	You have basically three ranks of teachers. You have your top level ones. The ones that are awesome. They know how to teach the kids. They're fun to talk to . . .
Luis:	They're fun to hang out with. They want to know what's going on with you . . . talk to you like you're a person, like they talk to another teacher.
Alicia:	Like Ms. Smith, she's always interested in what is going on in my life. I told her my mom had a baby and a couple of days later she asked if my mom would like some of the baby clothes she didn't need anymore.
Luis:	They are respectful.
Matt:	Yeah, respectful. Meet you at the door with a smile on their face. They don't have BO. (Laughter) They shower, you know, stuff like that. Hygiene is good. That's your top ranked teacher.
Luis:	Yeah, like Mr. Renquist. He's cool.
Matt:	Then you have your middle rank of teacher and that's the one that knows what they're doing, knows their lessons fine.
Luis:	They're not boring.
Matt:	Yeah, they're not too boring to hang out with.
Alicia:	They're not too boring; they're not too cool.
Matt:	Yeah, they're like right in the middle.
Matt:	Then you have your bottom rank teachers. They don't know what they're doing—at all. They don't care about the kids. They can't teach their class. They can't get the kids under control. They let the kids do whatever they want.
Alicia:	And then punish them for doing it.
Matt:	Yeah, and punish them for doing it. And, you know, that's not cool. Those are the teachers who should be in the lowest schools, should be getting the lowest pay and everything.

Where Should We Go from Here?

Based on this supposition that attending to caring within a school should not only entail gestures of compassion and proper academic instruction, but also encompass attending to power relations, it would seem prudent to implement certain ways of relating to students both in terms of those relationships that occur within the classroom and those that take place outside of it but still impact the classroom.

Attending to Power Relations in the Classroom

An expanded view of caring implemented within a classroom, in my opinion, would entail the recognition and respect of the fact that students are endowed with power because of the relational dynamic of teacher and student. Such recognition is not based on the premise of a teacher condescending to share her power with the students, but on the reality that power is inherent in the exercise of one's studenthood. Consequently, education needs to be viewed as a negotiation between two powerful entities.

While relationships between students and teachers have always operated within such parameters, it appears students today, for whatever reason, are more aware of it, on some level, and are therefore unwilling to conduct themselves in a particular manner just because a teacher told them to do so. Having just finished a teaching career that spanned over two decades, this one characteristic, more than any other, seems to me to encompass how students are different today from how they were twenty or even ten years ago.

A teacher who displays a "my-way-or-the-highway" attitude will most likely find herself engaging in a battle every day with her students. She will be perceived as uncaring and disrespectful when it comes to dealing with students as fellow human beings. Although they may not articulate such a notion in exactly this manner, when analyzing what the students in this study have said, it is clear that is what they mean. Luis illustrated this concept well when he stated, "A teacher tells me to do something; I'll do the exact opposite. Depends on how much they respect me."

The negotiation of power relationships within a classroom does not mean that a teacher should not conduct her classroom as she sees fit; after all, she is the adult and has been equipped with unique skills and knowledge that can benefit the students. What such a supposition does mean, though, is that she needs to keep in mind that the students, in most cases, can be her allies in the educational endeavor as they pursue the same goals she does.

For example, as noted in the student comments included in this chapter as well as being documented by other researchers (Alder & Moulton, 1998; Cothran & Ennis, 2000; Garza, 2009), students expect their teacher to provide appropriate instruction so that students can master the material as well as maintain classroom control so that everyone has the opportunity to learn. Such a sentiment was voiced by all three students when they talked about the "top rank" teachers who knew how to teach compared to the "bottom rank" teachers who did not know what they were doing and could not control the class. Students interpret proper educational techniques as indicting that the teacher cares about them as students. While it is not surprising that teachers want a classroom climate conducive to learning, often teachers are surprised when they learn that students have the same desire.

A favorable learning environment seems to be the goal of both teachers and students. The trick, then, would be to negotiate the power relations in the classroom to facilitate reaching this objective. Academic and classroom research detailing work with democratic education in classrooms appears to offer useful guidance in such an endeavor (Fraser, 1997; hooks, 1994; Kohn, 1999; Koshewa, 1999). A good place to start an investigation into the topic is *Democratic Schools* by Apple and Beane (1995). In this accessible and teacher-friendly book, the authors devote the first chapter to introducing the concept of a democratic school. Subsequent chapters, authored by the teachers who applied democratic principles within their classrooms, provide illustrations of the powerful learning and sense of community that results when democratic education is implemented. For example, chapter four describes the positive outcomes when a group of middle school students and their teachers worked *together* to create a curriculum based on questions students had about themselves and their world. Implementing principles of democratic education within the relational dynamic of a classroom has the potential to create a caring connection between teachers and students wherein teacher and student needs are negotiated and realized as both work *together* to design and implement meaningful learning experiences.

Additionally, both teachers and students want to feel valued and appreciated for the work they do. As mentioned above, students often viewed their labor as a way to reward the teacher. Jessica stated that Mr. Lewis seemed to have a positive attitude toward her, so she felt the need to reciprocate with one of her own. Admittedly, such a notion is an unusual way of thinking about student work as from a teacher's perspective a student's work is actually of little direct benefit to the teacher. Most teachers want their students to do their work so that they will be successful learners, but they would probably meet a student assertion that "I won't work for you because you're mean!" with a slight shrug. On the other hand, it is important to note that such a theme is running through the statements made by these students as illustrated by Matt's comment, "If the teacher wants me to do crap for them they need to show me respect."

Perhaps not all students, or even the majority fall into the group that views student work in this manner, but it would seem some do. Consequently, a caring teacher who recognizes student power should place an emphasis on recognizing and honoring student efforts to be successful instead of assuming that such behavior is just the norm. Just as a teacher appreciates student comments recognizing her labors, the same is true of students. The reality is that successful classrooms are the result of collaborative efforts on the part of all participants.

Attending to Power Relations Outside the Classroom

Dealing with relations of power taking place outside of the classroom involves not only a negotiation but also recognition. If a student works in the family business in order to help support his family or is in charge of the caretaking of younger siblings, the reality is they are engaging in particular ways in what society generally considers to be adult roles; consequently, *some* students may feel justified in exhibiting defiance in situations in which they perceive they are being treated or regarded as immature children. One second-year math teacher, Mr. Branch, who works in a high-poverty school in the southern United States, explained this situation to me in the following manner,

> You can hold a 13-year-old after class and talk to him about his poor behavior or missing work, and he just gives you this look that says, "Why are you talking to me about this kid stuff? Last night, I picked my little sisters up from school, fed them, helped them do their homework, put them to bed and did the dishes because my mom was working late. This morning I got them up, made sure they had breakfast, got them dressed and off to school. And today, I'm going to do that again. You can't talk to me like I'm a kid because I sure don't live a kid's life." You know . . . that kid has a point.

Teachers need to recognize that having an adolescent in their class who must take on an adult role in a particular area has the potential to create a different dynamic in the classroom between the teacher and the student. As expressed by Mr. Branch, such a student may feel mistreated or belittled if his "adulthood" is not reconciled with his "studenthood" within the classroom relationship.

A disconnect between a student's sense of self as a powerful person outside of school and the manner in which he is viewed within the classroom is further complicated when the student also comes from a group that has been traditionally disparaged in American society such as students of color, non-English speakers, or poor students. Such students already feel disenfranchised when they enter the school where they often encounter a culture composed of white, middle-class teachers and white, middle-class standards and values that may be foreign to them. Such students are already aware that they are constituted by the larger society as well as the school as somehow less than their white, middle-class peers (Popkewitz, 1998). They often feel invisible and their culture misunderstood or even maligned—a painful proposition (Valenzuela, 1999).

How much more painful then is it for such students to feel that the very thing they take pride in, supporting their family or taking care of siblings is either ignored, or if it is acknowledged that it is designated as either a harmful burden to the student or nothing of import. Such actions and attitudes are certainly not caring. Therefore, the adults within a school should not be surprised when such students react negatively to what is going on within the school and within the classroom.

Manuel, a 15-year-old Latino voiced his thoughts on this type of situation to me one day after school. He stated,

> You white teachers just don't understand. You don't know what it's like to be Mexican. Like, if my mom hits me to punish me, you would all be like, "That's bad. Your mom shouldn't hit you." But that's part of who we are. That's what we all do. I don't see it as a bad thing for me. And that's just one example. There's lots of stuff you teachers just don't get about us. You don't care that things are different for us than for the white kids. Like my citizenship grade was automatically dropped because I missed four times last term. But what was I supposed to do? Three of those times my mom needed me to stay home and look after my little brother so she could go to work. The babysitter was sick. So, what am I supposed to do? Leave my brother alone? I told my counselor about it but she said these were the rules and I have to follow them. This school sucks!

Manuel appeared in his statement to be saying that as a teen from a background different from his teachers, he often felt constituted as deviant or inferior resulting in him feeling less powerful than the "normal" students and therefore not cared for. On top of this situation, he also expressed anger that his caretaking role went unnoticed and unappreciated by the school and instead resulted in a punishment for him.

Even an even-tempered, mature student when faced with similar circumstances as Manuel would be prone to acting out in some fashion in order to illustrate his unhappiness with being constituted within the classroom relationship as "less than." Such a supposition was demonstrated by Luis's self-reported behavior in classes where he was treated poorly and his powerful role as student and worker dismissed.

Unfortunately, adolescents are seldom even-tempered or mature; their temperament often seems to depend on whether there was a full moon the night before or if it snowed that morning. Thus, because of their status in the larger society, students such as Manuel, Luis, and Alicia often find themselves more inclined to disengage from school and resort to inappropriate behavior as a way to express their anger and resentment at what they perceive to be the uncaring environment of the school that constructs them as less than the white, middle-class students in the classroom.

In dealing with these particular students, a teacher should first determine if she is caring for them as students in her classroom by showing compassion, teaching appropriately, and attending to the power relations inherent in the association between a teacher and her students.

Additionally, students who summon adult power through their activities outside of school need to have that power and those activities recognized in a genuinely positive manner. As teachers, we need to acknowledge that how we see the world is not the only or correct way to view it. Although we may want to gossip and wag our heads about Jorge's mother who does not seem to value education as we do since she allows him to work with his uncle laying brick all weekend, we need to take a step back and acknowledge that although bricklaying may not meet *our* definition of appropriate educational activities, to someone else it does. After all, Jorge is learning a marketable skill, is spending time with a strong male role model, and is helping pay some of the family's financial obligations, thereby developing an attitude of responsibility and unselfishness that will most likely serve him well in the future.

It would also prove advantageous for all students, not just those engaging in adult roles outside of the school, to weave into the curriculum, whenever possible, the various characteristics of these adult roles. For example, Gonzalez, Moll, and Amanti (2005) described an elementary school curriculum unit that a group of teachers created to tie into a Latino student's involvement in his family's business selling candy. Such a curriculum affirmed the student's place of power both within and without the classroom, while also educating the other students about what went into managing a business. Although this example took place in an elementary classroom, similar experiences can certainly be implemented in secondary schools as well.

Such a stance on the part of a teacher does not mean she stops providing quality lessons or encouraging students, such as Jorge, to achieve in school or take advantage of college or other postsecondary educational opportunities. Instead, what such an attitude indicates is an acceptance that her cultural realities, or, in other words, her own set of lived and learned experiences, are only one way of understanding the world and that others who are different from her, have the legitimate right to claim a different interpretation. The belief that something is wrong with students, families, and cultures, who view the world differently from a white, middle-class perspective is the utmost indication of a lack of care.

Conclusion

In a text intended for the training of school leaders the authors stated the following, "It takes a courageous leader to be able to change the focus from 'What is wrong with the student?' to 'What is it we need to do differently to meet students' needs?'" (Terrell & Lindsey, 2009, p. 15). In a manner of speaking, this chapter has addressed this second question by focusing attention on expanding the definition of what should constitute caring relationships within the classroom. By attending not only to our treatment of students and our teaching methodologies, but also focusing on the way power relations are enacted and negotiated within the classroom, teachers can become better equipped to create *with* their students collaborative learning communities where both may have their need to be cared for met within reciprocal relationships of respect. Instead of asking what is wrong with Luis, or Matt or Alicia, it is time to look instead at altering our faulty perceptions of power in the classroom, which place students in subordinate roles for as Matt so eloquently stated, "I'm a person! I'm not dirt!"

QUESTIONS TO CONSIDER

1. Why do you think caring is so important in schools?

2. What is your definition of caring in schools?

3. In what ways do students participate in relations of power within a classroom?

4. Why do you think students today are more aware of their position of power within the relational dynamic of the classroom?

5. What are some things teachers should be aware of if they are attending to power relations in a classroom?

6. In what specific ways can a teacher recognize and respectfully honor students who participate in quasi-adult roles outside of school?

References

Alder, N. (2002). Interpretations of the meaning of care: Creating caring relationships in urban middle school classrooms. *Urban Education, 37*(2), 241–266.

Alder, N., & Moulton, M. (1998). Interpretations of the meaning of care: Creating caring relationships in a middle school classroom. *Research in Middle Level Education Quarterly, 21*(3), 15–32.

Apple, M., & Beane, J. (1995). *Democratic schools*. Alexandria, VA: ASCD.

Beck, L. G. (1994). *Reclaiming educational administration as a caring profession*. New York: Teachers College Press.

Bosworth, K. (1995). Caring for others and being cared for: Students talk caring in school. *Phi Delta Kappan, 76*, pp. 686–693.

Cothran, D. J., & Ennis, C. D. (2000). Building bridges to student engagement: Communicating respect and care for students in urban high schools. *Journal of Research and Development in Education, 33*(2), 106–117.

Foucault, M. (1990). *The history of sexuality: Vol. 1*. R. Hurley (Trans.). New York: Vintage.

Fraser, J. (1997). *Reading, writing and justice: School reform as if democracy matters*. Albany, NY: State University of New York Press.

Garza, R. (2009). Latino and white high school students' perceptions of caring behaviors: Are we culturally responsive to our students? *Urban Education, 44*(3), 297–321.

Goldstein, L., & Freedman, D. (2003). Challenges enacting caring teacher education. *Journal of Teacher Education, 54*(5), 441–454.

Gonzalez, N., Moll, L., & Amanti, C. (2005). *Funds of knowledge: Theorizing practices in households and classrooms*. Mahwah, NJ: Lawrence Erlbaum.

hooks, b. (1994). *Teaching to transgress: Education as the practice of freedom*. New York: Routledge.

Kohn, A. (1991). Caring kids: The role of the schools. *Phi Delta Kappan, 72*(7), 496–506.

Kohn, A. (1999). *The schools our children deserve*. New York: Houghton Mifflin.

Koshewa, A. (1999). *Discipline and democracy: Teachers on trial*. Portsmouth, NH: Heinemann.

Margonis, F. (2006). Seeking openings of already closed student-teacher relationships. In D. Vokey (Ed.), *Philosophy of Education* (pp. 176–184). Urbana, NY: Philosophy of Education Society.

Mayeroff, M. (1971). *On caring*. New York: Harper & Row.

McWhorter, L. (2005). Where do white people come from? A Foucaultian critique of whiteness studies. *Philosophy and Social Criticism, 31*(5–6), 533–556.

Mihalas, S., Morse, W., Allsopp, D., & McHatton, P. (2009). Cultivating caring relationships between teachers and secondary students with emotional and behavioral disorders: Implications for research and practice. *Remedial and Special Education, 30*(2), 108–125.

Noddings, N. (1984). *Caring: A feminine approach to ethics and moral education.* Berkeley: University of California Press.

Noddings, N. (1992). *The challenge to care in schools.* New York: Teachers College Press.

Noddings, N. (1998). Philosophy of education. Boulder, CO: Westview Press.

Noddings, N. (2002). *Educating moral people: A caring alternative to character education.* New York: Teachers College Press.

Popkewitz, T. (1998). *Struggling for the soul: The politics of schooling and the construction of the teacher.* New York: Teachers College Press.

Rolón-Dow, R. (2005). Critical care: A color(full) analysis of care narratives in the schooling experiences of Puerto Rican girls. *American Educational Research Journal, 42*(1), 77–111.

Sidorkin, A. (2002). *Learning relations: Impure education, deschooled schools, & dialogue with evil.* New York: Peter Lang.

Terrell, R., & Lindsey, R. (2009). *Culturally proficient leadership.* Thousand Oaks, CA: Corwin.

Todd, S. (2003). *Learning from the other.* Albany, NY: State University of New York Press.

Valenzuela, A. (1999). *Subtractive schooling.* Albany, NY: State University of New York Press.

Watras, (2004). What does caring share with doing? *Philosophical Studies in Education, 35*, 101–110.

CHAPTER THIRTY-SEVEN

Talks with Teenagers and Teachers

NEL NODDINGS

Talks with Teenagers: Message One

A few years ago, I was asked to speak to a large group of fourth graders about bullying and cruel behavior. The school experiencing problems was a wealthy school, and its teachers were trying to figure out why their mostly privileged children were so often behaving cruelly toward one another. I was not interested in lecturing or threatening the kids, and their teachers did not advocate such an approach. Instead, I opened the dialogue by asking, "Could *you* ever be a bully?"

I was astonished by the flood of remarks that followed. One boy said, "Sometimes I am so mad at my father that I'd like to kick him! I can't do that, so I pick on the first person I see at school." Others admitted that, although they did not act as bullies themselves, they sometimes stood by silently while others bullied their classmates. This comment, made several times, evoked a related concern. Some kids were afraid that they *might* join in the bullying. They were afraid of becoming victims, but they were also afraid of becoming perpetrators. Why? They feared being ostracized by a powerful group, or becoming the next victim, or being ridiculed as too weak and sissy-like.

Why didn't they report these episodes to their teachers? What! And be branded as a snitch? They would prefer to suffer victimization, loneliness, guilt, and the agonies of indecision to being labeled a snitch. Did the kids think they could handle the situation without the intervention of adults? No, they just didn't know what to do. Not one student said that he or she had ever attempted to stop an incident of bullying, although they felt bad about it. Talking about the problem without mentioning names or referring to particular incidents seemed to help. At least, the kids seemed to be relieved that they were not alone in what they were going through.

Now I'd like to ask you, teenagers, the same question: Could you ever deliberately do something cruel to another person? Why might you do such a thing? To whom? My guess is that, in discussing these questions, you will discover that you have much in common with the younger students—similar provocations, similar fears, similar feelings of guilt. Getting all of that out into the open is a good start.

It is common knowledge that many pre-teens and young teenagers are afraid to go to school. Cruel behavior seems to hit a peak in the middle school years, and students become afraid of their peers and how they will be treated by them. Bodies are changing rapidly, and all differences are keenly noted. But think about it. Should we make fun of people who seem to us to be too fat, too skinny, have too many zits, knobby knees, bad hair, or other physical traits we would hate to have ourselves? We all know the answer to that, and yet we often poke fun anyway. Why?

Psychologists and other scientists have shown convincingly that cruelty committed is almost always a product of cruelty suffered. A. S. Neill, a psychologist and educator, wrote, "Every little bully has had his life warped in some way. Often he is simply doing to others what has been literally done to him."[1] But we have to remember here that people differ greatly in their sensitivities. Some people are easily hurt by remarks that wouldn't bother others at all. That suggests the need for human understanding, for empathy. We must learn to listen to what each particular person needs and to respond in sympathy. Some people enjoy being joshed a bit; others dread it. It is more important to learn how to tell the difference—to develop empathic accuracy—than it is to learn algebra, and this is an old math teacher talking to you.

Learning something about human nature is a crucial educational task. The great philosopher, Socrates, told us that self-knowledge is the foundation of all knowledge. Thus, the first task is to study yourself and try to answer the questions I asked earlier. If you are treating others badly because, like the little boy who wanted to kick his father, you have been hurt, consider that one hurt is likely to provoke another, whereas kindness may invite kindness.

Keep in mind also that bullies as well as victims may need help—perhaps even more so. If Neill was right (and I think he was), the bully has been hurt. Punishing him will probably not make his behavior better. What he (or she) needs is a friendly intervention, an invitation to quit harassing someone and join you in a healthier activity. Without condemning Bill when he is cruel, you might say, "C'mon, Bill, let's play ball (or take a walk, have a coke, complain about the math teacher. . ."). I'll say more about what else you might do in my next message on friendship.

One common source of student cruelty is forced competition. When you choose a sport or club, you often enter a friendly competition. Certainly, not all competition is bad. However, when the school or its teachers force you to compete for grades, there is something nasty about the situation. Learning should be a joyful quest; it should not be competitive.

You may already have read John Knowles's book, *A Separate Peace*. If not, I urge you to do so. In that book, Gene—the narrator—looks back on his teen years when he placed himself in a competitive drive to do better academically than his classmates. He worked for grades, not for learning, and he misunderstood the behavior of his best friend, Phineas, thinking that "Finny" was also fiercely competitive. At the end of the book, Gene mourns his own lack of understanding and the human tragedies resulting from such ignorance of the human heart:

All of them, all except Phineas, constructed at infinite cost to themselves these Maginot Lines against this enemy they thought they saw across the frontier; this enemy who never attacked that way—if he attacked at all; if he was indeed the enemy.[2]

In my next message, I'll talk about friendship, a relationship that, properly developed, provides a bulwark against cruelty—against becoming either a victim or a perpetrator.

Thoughts for Teachers

We teachers often suppose that our first duty in the matter of bullying is to protect the victim. That means to stop the bullying. However, the worst such incidents do not happen where we can see them. Often, then, because we have been unable to stop a bullying event, our next option, upon learning of it, is to punish the bully. That'll teach him, we think. By doing this, we hope to prevent future incidents. Alas, as A. S. Neill has pointed out, punishment may well make things worse. Our real job as teachers is to help kids understand why they engage in cruelty or fail to stop it in others. The first step here is dialogue. Without threats or veiled censure, we talk and listen; we try to understand ourselves and others. When we know a child fairly well, we should be able to detect a *better self* beneath the bullying exterior. I have called the detection and encouragement of this better self "confirmation."[3] For caring teachers, confirmation is a beautiful response to the needs of an erring cared-for.

Teachers can also help students to understand that bullying and cruelty have a long history in student life. Bullying appears in stories of medieval school days, and biographies from the twentieth century tell many tales of cruelty. It would be useful to discuss with teenagers George Orwell's "Such, such were the joys," an essay on his miserable school days.[4] Reading the Orwell essay reminds us that teachers are themselves sometimes the agents of cruelty. If adults who are assigned the duty of educating the young act like bullies, what can we expect students to learn from them? Many teachers today violate a sacred trust when they use sarcasm, public ridicule, or even thoughtless repartee with students. In the last case—one of supposedly friendly banter—some students join in the fun while others are hurt and shrink from classroom interactions. Humor should have a place in the classroom, but it should be carefully controlled and never used at the expense of those present.

I mentioned in my message to students that forced competition is sometimes a cause of cruelty. Teachers can do a lot to reduce this kind of competition. We would be dishonest to do this by giving everyone an 'A'. However, we can reject formulas like the bell curve that pre-determine how many As, Bs, and Fs will be assigned. We can make it possible for all students who have the ability and are willing to work conscientiously to earn decent grades. We can also help students to understand that many fine, adequately intelligent people have a hard time with some subjects—math is a familiar example. It should be all right not to like math, and good teachers urge students to find something in which they *are* interested. A student's self-worth should not be dependent on high grades in any one particular subject.

Message Two to Students

In my first message, I said that a good friendship serves to protect us from becoming either a victim or a perpetrator of cruelty. However, what is a good friendship? The Greek philosopher, Aristotle, wrote eloquently about friendship. He said that the most important characteristic of friendship is that friends wish the best for their friends for their own sake; that is, friends act to promote the well-being of their friends, not merely to further their own interests. He then went on to describe different types of friendships. For example, we often form friendships with people who share our business or recreational interests. You might, for instance, have friends with whom you play tennis or chess. If either of you loses interest in that activity, the friendship might naturally fade away. Still, while it lasts, it is a real friendship so long as you both wish and act on the best for each other.

The highest form of friendship—a "complete friendship"—according to Aristotle, is one in which friends share moral attributes and admire the finest moral characteristics in one another. Such friends learn from and encourage each other to grow as thoughtful moral people. If we take Aristotle's description seriously (and I think we should), it becomes our duty—a duty of friendship—to intervene when a friend is doing something clearly wrong. As I suggested in my first message, you might distract a friend who is teasing or bullying someone. However, you should do more. Suppose Bill, the boy who was acting as a bully, is your friend. When you get him alone, you might try to find out why he was behaving that way. "What's wrong?" you might ask. "It isn't like you to be mean. . . ." In asking these questions, you give Bill support and also let him know that you expect better of him. You point your friend upward.

Now, of course, if you can't honestly say that a friend's mean behavior is "not like" him, if he is regularly mean and cruel, why do you think of him as a friend? When we care, as we must for a friend, we continually support the quest for a better self—that of the friend and that of our own self. If associating with a person makes you a worse person, you should consider finding other friends. That possibility—that you might become a worse person—is the main reason that parents are so concerned about the people with whom their children associate.

Aristotle also pointed out that young people usually form friendships in search of pleasure, and this is to be expected; we all seek pleasure. However, as we mature, we refine our concepts of pleasure, the good, and happiness. We come closer to Aristotle's definition of complete friendship, a friendship based on admirable, shared moral attributes. As we practice helping our friends to do generous and friendly things, we get better at it.

In one of my books, I discuss friendship at some length.[5] In it, I discuss a story from a collection of adolescent biographies.[6] One night, a group of girls got together for an evening's fun. They decided to make a phone call to another girl and give her a hard time for making one of them angry. The comments got out of hand, very nasty. The girl telling the story became more and more upset by what her companions were doing. Finally, completely disgusted, she told her friends that what they were doing was wrong, and she left. After leaving, she feared that she might become their next victim or, at least, that she would lose their friendship. The next day, though, the other girls, regretting their meanness, admitted that they respected her for leaving, and they were glad that she had inspired them to halt their harassment. This is a good example of a friend acting to protect both the victim and the perpetrators.

We can agree with Aristotle that a complete friendship must have a strong moral base and still acknowledge that we seek pleasure in our friendships. Another great philosopher, David Hume, pointed out that certain traits of personality contribute to the pleasure of friendship. We naturally prefer to be with people who are amiable, sympathetic, considerate, interesting, and attractive. Moreover, it is easier to behave morally with people who are pleasant than with people who are disagreeable. Part of attracting and keeping friends is to cultivate an agreeable personality but, as I've noted, that does not mean to "go along" with things that are wrong. However, if you are usually agreeable and pleasant, your friends may listen to you when you frown at their behavior, and you may sometimes have to frown.

Thoughts for Teachers

Dialogue is once again the key. Talking about friendship, conflicts of loyalty, and how to support one another in a mutual quest for moral goodness should at least persuade students that their teachers regard healthy relationships as important.

Teachers should also model the behavior they advocate. I think it was Aristotle (again) who said that teaching does whatever it does "as to a friend." Although teachers and students are not often friends in the usual sense, teachers rightly want the best for their students, and they surely have an obligation to encourage the potential goodness in their students, to confirm them. Behavior that would kill a friendship will also damage the teacher-student relation—put-downs, ridicule, anything that humiliates or embarrasses. On the positive side, it helps to recognize small kindnesses and pro-social behaviors. This can be done quietly—"that was a nice thing you did"—no need for M&Ms, gold stars, or lavish praise. Indeed, as Alfie Kohn has suggested, rewards for either good behavior or academic success often backfire.[7]

In my first message, I warned students that coerced competition often encourages unfriendly, sometimes cruel, behavior. Some highly successful students (like Gene in *A Separate Peace*) think that "the whole point is to 'beat each other and rise above.'"[8] The outstanding student, Eve, who admitted this to a researcher, also confessed that, to win an advantage, she sometimes hid certain information even from her close friends. She took the "survival of the fittest" seriously and did not seem to understand that there is more to a fully human life than "beating" others at the game of scholarship.

How much responsibility do teachers bear for such student attitudes? We could argue that the system is at fault here, and teachers are themselves a product of it. Teachers, though, can do a lot to reduce unhealthy competition. They should certainly abandon grading on a curve which inevitably generates competition. As a math teacher, I allowed students to take tests over again to improve their grades and to ensure that they would be ready for the next unit of study. As a university professor, I abandoned grades entirely and instead asked students to revise and resubmit papers until the results satisfied both of us. Teacher and student can and should work together toward a mutually satisfying and satisfactory product.

Somehow—through dialogue, story-telling, and consonant teaching strategies—we should encourage students to understand that there is more to a good life than success in high school, admission to a top-flight college, securing a well-paid job, and having lots of money to spend. These things are not unimportant, but developing satisfying human relations is more important to achieving a fully human life.

Message Three to Students

So far, I've been trying to assure you that the key to human flourishing and happiness is to be found in generous, caring relationships, not merely in "beating" others literally or figuratively at the grade game. That said, I hope you can find some genuine interests in schoolwork—that you will be fortunate enough to discover the joy of learning. Throughout a long career in education, I have never lost the joy of learning. I like teaching, but I love learning even more.

Not everyone is so lucky. To get the most from your schooling, it makes sense to study yourself and your habits. When do you do your best work—morning or evening? With music or with complete quiet? With or without food and drink at hand? Before or after exercise? As you study your own habits, you may be able to convince your parents that you have learned how to manage your own workload.

Here are some ideas to consider. Keep a monthly or weekly to-do list. You might even devise categories and label each of them. For example, my own categories (column heads) are *students*, *writing*, *speaking*, *professional activities*, and *correspondence*. (I keep a separate to-do list for household tasks.) Look at the master list often, and make a manageable daily list from it. Then start your work with the tasks that appeal to you least. I hope that there will be at least one assignment each day that you will enjoy; that task will serve as something to look forward to—a motivator or reward of sorts.

Some adults may have told you, "Always do your best in everything." I think that is bad advice. If you follow that advice, you may have little energy left to do those things about which you are passionate. We live in a world where there are many tasks to complete, and they are not always of our own choosing. One of the hardest things to learn—some people never learn it— is to do an adequate job on the things you are forced to do, and save some energy for your central, continuing interests. Again, you can learn an important lesson from Gene in *A Separate Peace*. Gene wasn't really interested in learning at all—just in getting good grades. He spotted his main rival, Chet, and saw how to beat him:

> . . . I began to see that Chet was weakened by the very genuineness of his interest in learning. . . . When we read *Candide* it opened up a new way of looking at the world to Chet, and he continued hungrily reading Voltaire, in French, while the class went on to other people. He was vulnerable there, because to me they were all pretty much alike—Voltaire and Molière and the laws of motion and the Magna Carta and the Pathetic Fallacy and *Tess of the D'Urbervilles*—and I worked indiscriminately on all of them.[9]

Would you rather be like Gene or like Chet? Who enjoyed school more? Unfortunately, many students never find something in school that they study "hungrily," but I hope you will stay open to the possibility. It is truly wonderful to find a subject or occupation that you can engage with some joy. I'll talk to you again about this possibility in a discussion of occupations.

Before leaving this discussion of analyzing your habits and interests in schoolwork, I want to say a bit more about structure and organization. They really are important, and they are the keys to time management and efficiency. Quite a few people think mistakenly that structure and creativity are somehow in opposition, that a messy sort of freedom is a mark of creativity. If you read biographical accounts of creative people, however, you will learn that many of them (probably most) have been well organized. They know when and how they do their best work; they take care of their materials and can find what they need quickly because their tools are always put in the same place. In fact, it is this structured ritual that opens up the genuine freedom to create.

Another misconception held by many students is that there is one tried-and-true set of learning strategies that all successful students must master. Your teachers may, for example, emphasize note-taking, and spend considerable time teaching you how to do it. This may be useful, but you should know that many highly successful students (I was one) take very few notes. If you are listening, fully engaged, you may find note-taking a distraction. While you are writing down some trivial comment, the teacher may go on to something vital, or you may lose an opportunity to think about what was just said. My own preference has always been to use notes sparingly—an occasional name, title, or date. A fully engaged mind has a wonderful capacity for remembering. Find what works for you.

I have one more piece of advice for you on what you should get from school. Learn to speak clearly and grammatically! People make their first judgment about you on the basis of appearance, so you should try to present yourself as clean and appropriately dressed. However, the judgment on appearance is usually held lightly; everyone knows that appearance can change with circumstances. A more lasting judgment is made on the basis of how you speak. If you want to qualify for a decent job and be accepted as an educated person, learn to speak correctly. Lots of good, decent people never acquire and use standard English, and I am not suggesting that standard speech should be used as a test of moral worth. I *am* saying that people will make judgments about your social class, education, capability, and job qualifications—rightly or wrongly—on the basis of your oral language. Use that knowledge to further your occupational and social life.

Thoughts for Teachers

We all know that students will forget much of what we teach in our regular classes. In particular, they will forget many facts and special skills—especially those that are not used over a period of time. However, we hope that students will acquire and retain certain attitudes and habits of mind, that they will remain intellectually curious and grow in their capacity to manage their own time and work.

One of the most powerful qualities students should develop is competence in organizing and structuring their own work. Recognizing this, teachers often teach the techniques of outlining, note-taking, and neatness in presentation. It may be useful to teach these skills, but there is a danger in teaching specific ways of handling issues of organization. If we are too specific, the techniques are likely to join the stack of facts and details doomed to be forgotten. What we should do is to help students analyze their own work habits and experiment a bit with possible approaches to time management, study, and production. To do this, we can draw on biographical accounts, and encourage students to share their own experiences.

Teachers should encourage individual analysis and a detective-like habit of learning from mistakes and trials. Some of the finest lessons in mathematics develop from an examination of wrong answers. What went wrong? Was it a simple mistake, easy to fix? Was it an important misconception that we should talk about in some depth? Was there a promising discovery embedded in the strategy that yielded the wrong answer? Sometimes, with a little tinkering, what seems wrong on the surface may be converted into a powerful strategy and deeper conceptual understanding. We should encourage students to explore, analyze, and make the most of apparent errors.

An attitude of exploration can be encouraged by giving positive credit to things done well instead of subtracting points for mistakes. Students will be more willing to show their work if they know that teachers are looking for points to reward rather than mistakes to penalize. Just marking a problem solution +8 instead of -2 can make a psychological difference. Similarly, continually reminding students that we can learn much from mistakes may increase their willingness to try various strategies and share them with classmates.

Students should also be aware that work has to be put aside now and then. When we have worked for some time at a task and the results are still unsatisfactory, we should probably quit for a while and turn to something else. The great mathematician, Henri Poincaré, described his experience along these lines. He had filled waste baskets with failed attempts to solve a difficult set of mathematical problems, and then he had to leave the work incomplete in order to attend a conference. He wrote, "At the moment when I put my foot on the step [of the bus] the idea came to me. . . ."[10] He recounts several other occurrences of seemingly spontaneous illumination.

Psychologists have since described Poincaré's experience more fully. In working on difficult problems, there is a stage of preparation; we may or may not be successful at this stage, but we cram our heads with ideas. Next, we put the work aside temporarily and turn to other activities; this is the stage of incubation in which, apparently, our subconscious minds continue to work on the problem. Finally, most wondrous, is the instant of illumination. I have found that students love to hear these stories. Of course, some also ask hopefully whether it is possible to skip the stage of preparation and go directly to incubation and illumination. Unfortunately, the answer to this is no.

We acknowledge that there is considerable labor in learning, slogging through routines, experiencing dead-ends with exasperation. However, there are also the wonderful moments when the object we are pursuing speaks to us, and there are many biographical accounts of such experiences that students should hear.[11] Some of the most difficult mental tasks can be turned into adventures.

Message Four to Students

The American philosopher, John Dewey, said:

> An occupation is the only thing which balances the distinctive capacity of an individual with his social service. To find out what one is fitted to do and to secure an opportunity to do it is the key to happiness.[12]

Now, I have already suggested that satisfying human relations are the most significant contributors to human happiness, and I reaffirm that in this message. However, in the public domain, finding a suitable occupation is a strong contender. Too often today, young people think of an occupation as merely a source of income. It is that, of course, but it can be much more than that. Some of us are fortunate enough to find paid work that we love, and such work provides us with genuine happiness. We are doubly fortunate if we maintain satisfying relations in both our private and public activities.

I have argued that teenagers should explore a variety of possibilities for their future occupations. Not everyone needs to go to college, but most people can profit from some postsecondary training, and this is widely available. Today, because so much emphasis is put on preparation for college, many teenagers are convinced that they must go to college or "be nothing." I assure you that this is not true. If you consult the United States Bureau of Labor Statistics, you will learn that the greatest number of job openings in the next decade will be in occupations that do not require a college education. If you decide to try one of these occupations, you should learn how best to prepare yourself for an entry level job, and explore the possibilities for advancement.

There are several reasons for looking at a variety of occupations. First, you may find one that really interests you, and that interest may help you to decide whether or not to go to college. Second, an honest look at a large range of occupations should increase your appreciation for the work done by others. We should all develop a healthy respect for the enormous range of jobs done by fellow citizens. Third, a careful appraisal of possibilities should help you to avoid working at a job for which you are unfit. If you honestly dislike schoolwork, such appraisal may also save you from spending four years at college. Get the preparation you need in the shortest way, a way congenial to your appraised interests.

Although it is admirable to respect all honest work, we should be sensitive to the plight of those who must do jobs that virtually all of us find undesirable—especially when the work is well beneath the capability of the worker. Herbert Kliebard has reminded us that we sometimes speak too glibly about the "dignity" of all work:

> Undoubtedly, satisfaction may be derived from the work of the hands, but I sometimes think that the conviction that all work has dignity regardless of the circumstances has served to inhibit attempts to improve conditions in the workplace and to stave off efforts to somehow humanize it. When all work, even under the most degrading conditions, is declared to be ennobling, the need to reform the workplace somehow seems much less urgent.[13]

Thus, there is much to be learned from a study of occupations. Not the least of these things to be learned is that good citizenship requires us to be concerned with the welfare of our fellow citizens. What can be done to improve conditions for all of our workers? I hope you will find work that you enjoy. If that work requires a college education, I hope that you will also enjoy the studies preparing you for your chosen field. It may happen that you—like many, many other people—will go to college with little idea of what you want to do by way of an occupation. That is fine so long as you enter with a curious mind and the expectation that you may learn something about living a full life as well as making a living. True education at every level is about finding oneself and building a life that is satisfying intellectually, morally, socially, spiritually, aesthetically. . . in every way that marks us as fully human.

Thoughts for Teachers

There is much talk today about preparing *all* students for college, and teachers sometimes lead students to believe that they will be lifelong occupational failures if they do not obtain a college degree. It is true that college graduates generally earn more over a lifetime than peers who do not complete college. However, even on this claim, there is some disagreement. Some researchers argue that the salary benefits accrue largely to students who were in the upper half of their high school classes; those in the lower half either fail to complete a degree or realize very little in salary benefits.[14] College is not the answer for everyone. One must find what he or she is fitted to do.

Teachers can suggest that students examine the statistics on employment and salaries more closely. If we look at *average* salaries, we find that occupations requiring a college education usually yield higher pay than those which do not. However, we should look beyond the average to the full pay range. A youngster who is really talented in a mechanical field might make more money at the top of his job range than he would as a mediocre employee in a field requiring a college education. In addition, he would enjoy his work—a big plus.

School counselors, responsible for guiding far too many students, cannot do an adequate job of occupational counseling. It is up to teachers to discuss various possibilities with teenagers, and this can be done in regular conversations about the point of education. Education should lead to greater satisfaction in both public and private domains. It should broaden and deepen intellectual life, inform citizenship, and enrich our social relations. Kids should not be made to feel that a full adult life depends on their high school GPA and the completion of a college degree.

In the early twentieth century, educators and policymakers argued over the expansion of high school education. Some maintained that all youngsters should go to high school (only about 7% did so at the time); they insisted that the future of the nation depended on a better educated citizenry. Others suggested that most students were not capable of rigorous high school studies—that probably only 25% or so could profit from a high school education. Both groups were partly right. The solution chosen was to change the high school, moving away from traditional classical studies to a wide range of offerings and activities that would characterize the comprehensive high school.

That innovation proved to be a resounding success, with almost 60% of young people graduating from high school by 1950 and about 70% by 1960. Indeed, although arguments persisted throughout the century over how many students were capable of college-preparatory work, many educational thinkers regarded the comprehensive high school as an important foundation of American democracy. Students with all sorts of interests and aptitudes came together in these schools to work, play, and participate in democratic processes.

There remains the possibility that both groups were wrong and that virtually all students were (and are) capable of rigorous college-preparatory studies. I think the weight of evidence is against this.[15] However, even if all students could, with help, meet the demands of such academic courses, why should they be forced to do so? Why can we not provide excellent courses that recognize their intrinsic interests?

The argument persists today, and so does one about what constitutes a "real" college education. It is reasonable to suggest that the idea of post-secondary education be greatly expanded. Just as the whole conception of high school changed at the start of the twentieth century, so might our perspective on education after high school. We need not abandon the traditions of college and liberal arts for those inclined toward such studies, but we should recognize a multitude of promising educational alternatives designed to prepare young people directly for occupations, and we should encourage all students to gain some respect and appreciation for the full range of essential work required in our society. Our democracy is at risk when such respect and appreciation are scorned.

Message Five to Students

I want to talk with you now about a subject that your teachers will probably not discuss—unless you are in a religious school. Even if you are in a religious school, the chances are that you will not have many opportunities to talk freely and critically about religious beliefs. Christian Smith, a sociologist who did a survey of teenagers' beliefs, found that for many of the teens interviewed, "Our interview was the first time that any adult had ever asked them what they believed and how it mattered in their life."[16] Many parents do not want other adults, particularly teachers, to discuss religion with their children. They are afraid that their children will "lose" their religion. It could happen.

Even so, think about it. If there is a God, it is he or she who has given you the mental capacity to ask questions, analyze, and reflect. Surely, this cannot be a bad thing. Asking questions about your beliefs is rather like opening an elaborately packaged gift. When you remove the ribbons, glittery outer wrap, and soft inner wrapping, what will you find? Some investigators find a small, beautiful, eternal gem at the center. They will probably retain their faith—more intelligently and thoughtfully held—although they may discard some (even most) of the wrappings. Others will find nothing or a bit of shiny dust at the center of the package. They may give up belief in God, or they may seek another path to God, or even another God.

There is no reason why any of these questioners should deny the beauty of religiously inspired music, art, architecture, or literature. Many of today's atheists, for example, speak appreciatively of the religious works of Handel, Bach, and Beethoven. Richard Dawkins, an eloquent atheist, expresses regret over the widespread ignorance of religious matters, especially of the Bible, displayed by most of our citizenry. He believes that the Bible should be part of everyone's education because "it is a major source book for literary culture."[17] It is not just unbelievers (atheists and agnostics) who are ignorant about religion. As Smith points out, many believers are ignorant of the doctrines and histories of their own institutions. If you begin to ask questions, you will find a huge, fascinating library of work on religion. You may become captivated by it.

I am not going to tell you what to believe. I only urge you to read, study, *think*. Do you believe in a loving God? If you do, then you cannot logically believe in hell. Loving, earthly parents would not condemn their children to long-lasting punishment. Surely, then, a loving God would not threaten us with eternal punishment. As a parent and teacher, I grieve for the multitudes of teenagers who express fear of angering God and going to hell. Smith's study is loaded with such cases.

Do you need the threat of hell to keep you from doing bad things? You should know that many, many very good people do not believe in God at all. Indeed, several of America's Founding Fathers were unbelievers, and Washington specifically stated that the United States was not founded on Christian principles. (Note that this does not mean that it was founded on principles antagonistic to Christianity.) There are many wonderful biographical accounts of unbelievers who led highly moral lives. In fact, some of them gave up religion because they found it lacking in genuine morality.[18] The heart of morality is the care and compassion with which we meet our fellow human beings and other sentient creatures.

Thoughts for Teachers

We teachers profess to educate, to develop critical thinkers. Even so, we tolerate a system of public education that forbids us to discuss with our students some of life's central concerns: Is there a God? What is the meaning of life? How do we find happiness? What do we owe to nonhuman living beings? How should I live? Where do I belong?

Think about our predicament. We can moderate it some by choosing biographical and fictional material that invites discussion of these fundamental questions. Choosing judiciously and preparing carefully for the discussion to follow should protect us from the complaints that arise when we announce that such topics will be a main aim of our teaching. The questions appear naturally as part of acceptable subject matter. It is sad that we cannot simply include existential questions directly as part of our curriculum, but it is better to include them incidentally than to omit them entirely.

There is another positive feature of addressing these questions as part of our regular subject matter. This approach shows that, in every discipline, careful scholars encounter and discuss existential issues. For teachers, the requirement to prepare for handling life's big questions implies continued study and an ever-widening program of reading. What joy!

QUESTIONS TO CONSIDER

1. Noddings speaks of the cruel behavior and uncaring attitudes that sometimes beset our secondary schools. What does she claim are their causes and sources? Do you agree?

   Why or why not? Give reasons and examples to support your case.

2. How does Noddings conceptualize "friendship," and why does she consider it so broadly important in school and society?

3. What does she pinpoint as some of the leading myths and misconceptions about "good" teaching? What does she recommend as crucial pedagogical strategies? Do you agree?

   Why or why not?

4. Why does Noddings regard the study of occupations as so critical? Does she believe that all adolescents should be college-bound? Why or why not? Do you agree with her argument?

5. What tensions does she see in religious instruction and the development of critical thinking? Do you agree with her position? Why or why not?

Notes

1. A. S. Neill, *Summerhill* (New York: Hart Publishing, 1960), 271.
2. John Knowles, *A Separate Peace* (New York: Macmillan, 1960), 196.
3. See Nel Noddings, *Caring: A Feminine Approach to Ethics and Moral Education* (1984; repr., Berkeley: University of California Press, 2003); and *The Challenge to Care in Schools* (1992; repr., New York: Teachers College Press, 2005).
4. George Orwell, "Such, such were the joys," in Orwell, *A Collection of Essays* (1946; repr. San Diego: Harcourt Brace, 1981).
5. Nel Noddings, *Happiness and Education* (Cambridge: Cambridge University Press, 2003).
6. See Andrew Garrod, Lisa Smulyan, Sally I. Powers, and Robert Kilkenny, *Adolescent Portraits: Identity, Relationships, and Challenges* (Boston: Allyn & Bacon, 2002).
7. See Alfie Kohn, *Punished by Rewards: The Trouble with Gold Stars, Incentive Plans, A's, Praise, and Other Bribes* (Boston: Houghton Mifflin, 1993).
8. Denise Clark Pope, *"Doing School": How We Are Creating a Generation of Stressed Out, Materialistic, and Miseducated Students* (New Haven: Yale University Press, 2001), 37.
9. Knowles, *A Separate Peace*, 46.
10. Henri Poincaré, "Mathematical Creation," in *The World of Mathematics*, ed. James R. Newman (New York: Simon & Schuster, 1956), 20–44.
11. See Nel Noddings, *Critical Lessons: What Our Schools Should Teach* (Cambridge: Cambridge University Press, 2006).
12. John Dewey, *Democracy and Education* (New York: Macmillan, 1916), 308.
13. Herbert Kliebard, *Schooled to Work: Vocationalism and the American Curriculum 1876–1946* (New York: Teachers College Press, 1999), xv.
14. See James E. Rosenbaum, *Beyond College for All: Career Paths for the Forgotten Half* (New York: Russell Sage Foundation Press, 2001).
15. See John W. Gardner, *Excellence* (1961; repr. New York: W.W. Norton, 1984); also Nel Noddings, *When School Reform Goes Wrong* (New York: Teachers College Press, 2007).
16. Christian Smith, *Soul Searching: The Religious and Spiritual Lives of American Teenagers* (Oxford: Oxford University Press, 2005), 133.
17. Richard Dawkins, *The God Delusion* (Boston: Houghton Mifflin, 2006), 341.
18. See Nel Noddings, *Educating for Intelligent Belief or Unbelief* (New York: Teachers College Press, 1993).

Contributors

Bauer, Dan. Dan Bauer is an associate professor of middle grades education and English at Georgia College & State University in Milledgeville. As a cohort mentor leader, he works closely with pre-service middle school teachers in an intense and ambitious undergraduate teacher education program. A former secondary language arts teacher and debate coach, he directs the Central Georgia Writing Project with Linda Golson Bradley. His research interests focus especially on writing assessment, the intersection of composition and epistemology, and the legacy of writers of the Harlem Renaissance. He has published in *College Composition and Communication* and the *Journal of Business and Technical Communication*, among other places.

Beineke, John A. John A. Beineke is a distinguished professor of educational leadership and curriculum and professor of history at Arkansas State University in State University, Arkansas. He has been a middle and high school history teacher, college dean, and foundation program director. He is the author of *And There Were Giants in the Land: The Life of William Heard Kilpatrick* (Peter Lang Publishing, 1998) and *Going over All the Hurdles: A Life of Oatess Archey* (Indiana Historical Society).

Bentley, Mary K. Mary K. Bentley is an associate professor, and she currently serves as the chair of the Department of Health Promotion and Physical Education in the School of Health Sciences and Human Performance at Ithaca College in New York. Her research interests include family health, women's health, international health issues, integrated health and healing, and models and theories of health promotion.

Blake, Brett Elizabeth. Brett Elizabeth Blake is an associate professor of early childhood, childhood, and adolescent education at St. John's University in Queens, NY. She is also a senior research fellow at the Vincentian Center for Social Justice and Poverty at St. John's. Her interests are applied/sociolinguistics, urban education, literacy among diverse learners, alternative pedagogies, and gender studies. Her books include *Understanding Language and Literacy Acquisition: Learning and Teaching* (Allyn & Bacon, 2008); *Teaching All Children to Read* (Rowman & Littlefield, 2007); *Engaging Readers and Writers in Reflective and Authentic Literacy Practices* (Christopher-Gordon, 2006); *Literacy Primer* (Peter Lang Publishing, 2005); *A Culture of Refusal: The Lives and Literacies of Out of School Adolescents* (Peter Lang Publishing, 2004); and *She Say, He Say: Urban Girls Write Their Lives* (SUNY Press, 1997).

Boaler, Jo. Jo Boaler is Marie Curie Professor of Education at the University of Sussex in England. Formerly at Stanford University, she is a fellow of the Royal Academy of Arts and the Center for Advanced Study in the Behavioral Sciences. Her books include *The Elephant in the Classroom: Helping Children Survive, Achieve and Enjoy School Maths* (Souvenir Press, 2009); *What's Math Got to Do With It?* (Viking/Penguin, 2008); *Connecting Mathematical Ideas: Middle School Video Cases to Support Teaching and Learning* (Heinemann, 2005); *Multiple Perspectives on Mathematics Teaching and Learning* (Lawrence Erlbaum, 2002); and *Experiencing School Mathematics: Traditional and Reform Approaches to Teaching and Their Impact on Student Learning* (Lawrence Erlbaum, 2002).

Boyles, Deron. Deron Boyles is a professor of educational policy studies at Georgia State University, where he teaches philosophy of education and social foundations of education. He was president of the American Educational Studies Association in 2010. His scholarly interests include school/corporate connections, epistemology, pragmatism and John Dewey, and critical theory. His books are *The Politics of Inquiry: Education Research and the 'Culture of Science'* (SUNY Press, 2009); *The Corporate Assault on Youth: Commercialism, Exploitation, and the End of Innocence* (Peter Lang Publishing, 2008); *Schools or Markets? Commercialism, Privatization, and School-Business Partnerships* (Lawrence Erlbaum, 2004); and *American Education and Corporations: The Free Market Goes to School* (Routledge, 2000).

Bradley, Linda Golson. Linda Golson Bradley is an assistant professor of literacy in The John H. Lounsbury College of Education at Georgia College & State University, where she coordinates the literacy program. She directs the Central Georgia Writing Project with Dan Bauer. Her research examines the beliefs and practices of exemplary teachers of writing, who make positive differences in the lives of their students each day.

Bryan, Julia. Julia Bryan is an assistant professor of counseling and personnel services in the College of Education at the University of Maryland, College Park. She writes extensively on the role of school counselors in school-family-community partnerships and on urban school counseling issues. She gained interest and experience in those areas while serving as a secondary school counselor in Barbados from 1988 to 1998. She has received a number of faculty research awards, including an Association of Counselor Education and Supervision (ACES) research award to study factors that influence school counselor involvement in school-family-community collaboration. Her published work appears in such journals as *Professional School Counseling* and *Journal of Counseling and Development*.

Carlson, Dennis. Dennis Carlson is a professor of educational leadership in the School of Education, Health and Society at Miami University of Ohio, Oxford. He is a past president of the American Educational Studies Association. His scholarly interests are in curriculum and cultural studies. His most recent books are *Keeping the Promise: Essays on Leadership, Democracy, and Education* (Peter Lang Publishing, 2007); *Promises to Keep: Cultural Studies, Democratic Education, and Public Life* (RoutledgeFalmer, 2003); *Leaving Safe Harbors: Toward a New Progressivism in American Education and Public Life* (RoutledgeFalmer, 2002); and *Educational Yearning: The Journey of the Spirit and Democratic Education* (Peter Lang Publishing, 2002).

Claus, Jeff. Jeff Claus is an associate professor of education at Ithaca College in New York. His research and service interests are in issues of equity, diversity, and social justice in education; service learning; multicultural education; and school-community partnerships for social change. He is a board member and vice-president of Ithaca's Southside Community Center. He co-edited *Service Learning for Youth Empowerment and Social Change* (Peter Lang Publishing, 2001).

Daniel-Tyson, Camille. Camille Daniel-Tyson is principal of the Georgia College Early College (GCEC) in Milledgeville. In her educational career, she has been a high school social studies teacher, an intervention coordinator for at-risk students, and an alternative school principal. She is also an adjunct instructor in The John H. Lounsbury College of Education at Georgia College & State University. ECGC is considered one of America's exemplary early colleges, expanding its "at-promise" students' horizons and growth beyond what many think possible.

Dean, Jana. Jana Dean teaches social studies and science at George Washington Bush Middle School in Tumwater, Washington. She is a member of Olympia Washington's Educators for Social Justice. She is also a regular contributor to *Rethinking Schools.*

Demir, Abdulkadir. Abdulkadir Demir is an assistant professor of science education in the Department of Middle/Secondary Education & Instructional Technology at Georgia State University. He teaches undergraduate and graduate courses in science education. His current research foci include reform-based practices of college science faculty and pre/in-service secondary science teachers and science education in urban settings.

DeVitis, Joseph L. Joseph L. DeVitis is a professor of educational foundations at Georgia College & State University. He is a past president of the American Educational Studies Association, the Council of Learned Societies in Education, the Society of Professors of Education, and the Southeast Philosophy of Education Society. In 2007, he received the Distinguished Alumnus Award from the College of Education, University of Illinois at Urbana-Champaign. His interests as a scholar are wide-ranging, but his special focus is on educational policy and the social foundations of education. His books are *To Serve and Learn: The Spirit of Community in Liberal Education* (Peter Lang Publishing, 1998) and *The Success Ethic, Education and the American Dream* (SUNY Press, 1996).

Dillon, Lindell. Lindell Dillon teaches seventh-grade mathematics at Georgia College Early College in Milledgeville, an initiative of the Bill and Melinda Gates Foundation to improve access to college for first-generation students who have otherwise not enjoyed wide success in grades K-6. He was a participant in the first Invitational Summer Institute of the Central Georgia Writing Project. He now serves on the Leadership Team of that initiative, and he is a leader in several other professional development efforts that help teachers use writing to deepen understanding, fluency, and confidence in content areas.

Domine, Vanessa. Vanessa Domine is an assistant professor of educational technology at Montclair State University in New Jersey. She has worked at P-16 levels with students, teachers, parents, and administrators to explore the critical and creative uses of all forms of media and technology across curricula.

Duncan, Garrett Albert. Garrett Albert Duncan is an associate professor of education, African and Afro-American studies, and American culture studies at Washington University in St. Louis. His research focuses broadly on race, culture, citizenship, democracy, and globalization. He has a special interest in the school-to-prison nexus. His forthcoming book, *School to Prison: Education and the Ceiling of Black Youth in Postindustrial America* will be published by Peter Lang.

Evans-Winters, Venus. Venus Evans-Winters is an assistant professor of social foundations of education at Illinois State University. She teaches courses on the social foundations of education, sociology of education, urban girls, and qualitative research methodology. Her areas of research interest are the interactions of race, class, and gender on educational resilience; urban education; and the role of community organizations in the lives of African-American female youth.

Finders, Margaret. Margaret Finders is a professor of education, director of the School of Education, and associate dean of the College of Liberal Studies at the University of Wisconsin, LaCrosse. She is interested in the sociopolitical dimensions of schooling, language and literacy, adolescents' literacy practices, teacher education, and issues of equity and social justice. Her books are *Language Arts and Literacy in the Middle Grades: Planning, Teaching and Assessing* (Pearson Merrill/PrenticeHall, 2007); *Literacy Lessons: Teaching and Learning with Middle School Students* (PrenticeHall, 2002); and *Just Girls: Hidden Literacies and Life in Junior High* (Teachers College Press, 1997).

Gibboney, Richard A. Richard A. Gibboney has most recently taught at the Graduate School of Education, University of Pennsylvania. A former elementary school teacher in Ferndale, Michigan, he is also a former Pennsylvania deputy secretary of education for research and development and the former Vermont commissioner of education. His books include *What Every Great Teacher Knows: Practical Principles for Effective Teaching* (Holistic Education Press, 1998); and *The Stone Trumpet: A Story of Practical School Reform, 1960–1990* (SUNY Press, 1994).

Goldfarb, Katia. Katia Goldfarb is an associate professor in the Department of Human Ecology, Family, and Child Studies at Montclair State University in New Jersey. Her major area of research is the interconnection of school, community, and families, especially Latino immigrant families.

Goldstein, Rebecca A. Rebecca A. Goldstein is an assistant professor of curriculum and teaching at Montclair State University. Her academic interests include student and teacher identity construction, issues of democracy and social justice on urban schools, urban school reform and teacher preparation, and the impact of No Child Left Behind.

Griffin, Dana. Dana Griffin is an assistant professor of school counseling at the University of North Carolina at Chapel Hill. She has worked as a school counselor in Hampton, Virginia. Her research interests are in the areas of multicultural supervision issues and culturally responsive school-family-community collaboration. She has presented at numerous national and international conferences and has written on multiculturalism, school counselor supervision, parental involvement, and school-family-community partnerships.

Grubb, W. Norton. W. Norton Grubb is professor of policy, organization, measurement, and evaluation in the Graduate School of Education, University of California, Berkeley. His interests are in the economy and education, reform issues in education, poverty and children, school and non-school learning contexts, school to work, and social services and schools. His recent books are *The Education Gospel: The Economic Power of Schooling* (Harvard University Press, 2004); *Working in the Middle: Strengthening Education and Training for the Mid-Skilled Labor Force* (Jossey-Bass, 1996); and *Learning to Work: The Case for Re-integrating Job Training and Education* (Sage Publications, 1996).

Irwin-DeVitis, Linda. Linda Irwin-DeVitis is dean of The John H. Lounsbury College of Education and professor of literacy at Georgia College & State University. She specializes in reading, language arts, adolescent literacy, and critique of political constructions of literacy. She has had extensive teaching experience in New Orleans and Jacksonville-area middle and high schools and in literacy programs in the Mississippi Delta. She has written in such journals as *ALAN Review, Educational Studies*, and *Educational Theory*. Her books include *50 Graphic Organizers for Reading, Writing & More, Grades 4–8* (Scholastic, 1999) and *Graphic Organizers, Grades K-8: Visual Strategies for Active Learning* (Scholastic, 1996).

Jackson, Ryonnel. Ryonnel Jackson is a graduate student at Washington University in St. Louis. He is working on his Master of Arts degree in American Culture Studies. His thesis focuses on the post-civil rights, post-desegregation education of African-American males at an elementary school in metropolitan St. Louis.

Jocson, Korina M. Korina M. Jocson is an assistant professor of education at Washington University in St. Louis. Her research interests include literacy, youth development, ethnic studies, and cultural studies in education, especially issues of equity and globalization. Her work examines the changing nature of literacies and new media technologies in relation to learning, teaching, and communication. She is the author of *Youth Poets: Empowering Literacies in and out of Schools* (Peter Lang Publishing, 2008).

Jones, Melissa M. Melissa M. Jones is an associate professor of special education at Northern Kentucky University with special interests in developing inclusive communities, student empowerment, and postsecondary opportunities for students with cognitive disabilities. She is the author of *Whisper Writing: Teenage Girls Talk About Ableism and Sexism in School* (Peter Lang Publishing, 2004) and *Within Our Reach: Behavior Prevention and Intervention Strategies for Learners with Mental Retardation and Autism* (Division on Mental Retardation and Developmental Disabilities of the Council for Exceptional Children, 1998).

Kelly, Deirdre M. Deirdre M. Kelly is a professor of educational studies at the University of British Columbia. Her research interests include feminist and cultural studies, anti-oppression pedagogies, sociology of education, gender and media issues, children and youth, teacher research, and critical policy studies. Her most recent books are *Pregnant with Meaning: Teen Mothers and the Politics of Inclusive Schooling* (Peter Lang Publishing, 2000) and *Debating Dropouts: Critical Policy and Research Perspectives on School Leaving* (George Scheer & Associates, 1996).

Kharem, Haroon. Haroon Kharem is an associate professor of childhood education at Brooklyn College, City University of New York. He is also a mentor and professor in the New York Teaching Fellows Program and co-supervisor of the Learning Community, District #19, in East New York. His scholarly interests are in urban education, African American history, and African Free Schools. He has published *The Curriculum of Repression: A Pedagogy of Racial History in the United States* (Peter Lang Publishing, 2006).

Koballa, Thomas R., Jr. Thomas R. Koballa, Jr., is a professor of science education at the University of Georgia. He is past president of the National Association for Research in Science Teaching and the recipient of the Association of Science Teacher Education's Outstanding Mentoring Award. His research interests include science teacher learning, mentoring, affective assessment, science literacy, and case-based learning. He has authored or coauthored more than 50 journal articles and chapters. His most recent books are *Science Instruction in the Middle and Secondary Schools*, 6th ed. (Merrill/PrenticeHall, 2006); *Cases in Middle and Secondary Science Education: The Promise and Dilemmas*, 2nd ed. (Merrill/PrenticeHall, 2004); and *Learning from Cases: Unraveling the Complexities of Elementary Science Teaching* (Allyn & Bacon, 2002).

Lewis, Cynthia. Cynthia Lewis is a professor of literacy education and director of graduate studies in the Department of Curriculum and Instruction at the University of Minnesota. She is interested in how literacy is shaped by the social politics of classrooms and communities and how literacy intersects with popular culture and youth identity. Her current research focuses on the responses to literature among early adolescents, their teachers, and on the uses of Internet messaging among teens. She is the author of *Literary Practices as Social Acts: Power, Status, and Cultural Norms in the Classroom* (Lawrence Erlbaum, 2001) and the co-author of *Reframing Sociocultural Research on Literacy: Identity, Agency, and Power* (Teachers College Press, 2007).

Longwell-Grice, Robert. Robert Longwell-Grice is Director of Academic Services in the School of Education, University of Wisconsin at Milwaukee. He was a co-author of the article, "Understanding Adolescent Suicide," in this volume, while a doctoral student in educational and counseling psychology in the College of Education and Human Development at the University of Louisville.

Lounsbury, John H. John H. Lounsbury is a professor and dean emeritus at Georgia College and State University in Milledgeville. Widely regarded as one of the founding fathers of the middle school movement, his distinguished career in education has spanned over 50 years. He still remains active as the Publications Editor for the National Middle School Association and makes himself available to speak to middle school teachers and teacher educators, young adolescents, parents, and policy makers. His most recent books include *Curriculum Integration, Twenty Questions—With Answers* (Georgia Middle School Association, 1999); *Teaching at the Middle Level: A Professional's Handbook* (D. C. Heath, 1995); and *As I See It* (National Middle School Association, 1991).

Lussier, Richard. Richard Lussier is a social studies teacher and lead instructor for administration at Ridge View High School in Columbia, South Carolina. He has an Ed.D. in curriculum and instruction from the University of South Carolina. His academic interests include social studies education and modern language education. He is a contributing writer in Susan Schramm-Pate and Rhonda B. Jeffries, eds., *Grappling with Diversity: Readings in Civil Rights Pedagogy and Critical Multiculturalism* (SUNY Press, 2008).

Nix, Lianna. Lianna Nix teaches sixth- and seventh-grade mathematics at the Da Vinci Academy at South Hall County Middle School in Flowery Branch, Georgia. She taught seventh-grade mathematics and social studies at Georgia College Early College during its initial development as a small school for at-promise youths. She is an impassioned advocate for excellence and equity in middle grades education and for learning communities that transform school experience.

Noddings, Nel. Nel Noddings is Lee L. Jacks Professor of Education, Emerita, at Stanford University. She has had an illustrious and prolific career in philosophy of education, most notably in her pioneering contributions to the notion of caring. She is a past president of the National Academy of Education, the Philosophy of Education Society, and the John Dewey Society. A scholar with wide-ranging interests, she has written on ethics and education, spirituality, feminist issues, constructivism, and the concepts of evil and happiness. Her most recent books include *When School Reform Goes Wrong* (Teachers College Press, 2007); *Critical Lessons: What Our Schools Should Teach* (Cambridge University Press, 2007); *Philosophy of Education*, 2nd ed. (Westview Press, 2006); *Educating Citizens for Global Awareness* (Teachers College Press, 2005); and *Happiness and Education* (Cambridge University Press, 2004).

Ogden, Curtis. Curtis Ogden is a senior associate in the Interaction Institute for Social Change in Boston. He created ImPACT, a model youth service learning program based at The Learning Web in Ithaca, New York. He is an adjunct faculty member at Antioch University/New England and board member of the New England Grassroots Environment Fund. He co-edited *Service Learning for Youth Empowerment and Social Change* (Peter Lang Publishing, 2001).

Peck, Marcia. Marcia Peck is an assistant professor of foundations and secondary education at Georgia College & State University in Milledgeville. She earned her Ph.D. from the Department of Education, Culture and Society at the University of Utah. She has also taught language arts in grades 7–9. Her academic interests include teacher research, qualitative research methodologies, and social justice issues in education. She is the co-author of *Educational Poetics: Inquiry, Freedom, and Innovative Necessity* (Peter Lang Publishing, 2005).

Portes, Pedro R. Pedro R. Portes is The Goizueta Foundation Distinguished Chair of Latino Teacher Education and a professor of counseling and human development services at the University of Georgia. He is the recipient of the American Educational Research Association's Research Award in Human Development for 2005. His interests center on linking primary prevention practices to human development within cultural contexts. He is the author of *Dismantling Educational Inequality: A Cultural-Historical Approach to Closing the Achievement Gap* (Peter Lang Publishing, 2005) and numerous research articles in human development, learning, and home environment and intellectual growth.

Price, Margaret. Margaret Price is an associate professor of curriculum studies and teacher education at Texas Tech University. She teaches both undergraduate and graduate courses in secondary teacher education and qualitative research methodologies. She was a Texas secondary educator for 18 years prior to returning to higher education. Her research interests include professional development schools, teachers' lives, curriculum issues and policy, and constructivist methodologies.

Reio, Thomas G. Thomas G. Reio, Jr., is an associate professor and chair of the Department of Educational Leadership and Policy Studies at Florida International University. His research examines curiosity and risk taking and their roles in learning and development across the lifespan, teacher workplace socialization, emotions, and school-to-work transition. He teaches graduate courses in adult learning and development, educational psychology, and motivation. Editor of *Human Resource Development Review*, he has published in such journals as the *Journal of Genetic Psychology, Personality and Individual Differences, Teaching and Teacher Education*, and *Educational and Psychological Measurement*.

Sandhu, Daya S. Daya S. Sandhu is a professor of educational and counseling psychology at the University of Louisville. His research interests are school counseling, multicultural counseling, career counseling, and spirituality. His most recent books include *Counseling Employees: A Multicultural Approach* (American Counseling Association, 2002); *Faces of Violence: Psychological Correlates, Concepts, and Intervention Strategies* (Nova Science, 2001); and *Elementary School Counseling in the New Millennium* (American Counseling Association, 2001). He is the recipient of numerous awards from professional societies in counselor education.

Schramm-Pate, Susan L. Susan L. Schramm-Pate is an associate professor of instruction and teacher education at the University of South Carolina, Columbia. Her research interests are in curriculum studies, women's studies, historiography, cultural studies, and integrated curriculum.

Her books include *Grappling with Diversity: Readings on Civil Rights, Pedagogy and Critical Multiculturalism* (SUNY Press, 2007); *A Separate Sisterhood: Women Who Shaped Southern Education in the Progressive Era* (Peter Lang Publishing, 2002); and *Transforming the Curriculum: Thinking Outside the Box* (Scarecrow Press, 2002).

Seaton, Elizabeth. Elizabeth Seaton is an assistant professor in the Communications Studies Program at York University in Canada. Her academic interests focus on relations of environment, body, social identity, and globalization. She is currently completing a book on the historical relationships of biological and social reproduction.

Simpson, Douglas J. Douglas J. Simpson is Helen DeVitt Jones Chair in Teacher Education and a professor of curriculum studies and teacher education at Texas Tech University. He served as education dean at the University of Louisville, Texas Christian University, and Tennessee State University. He is a past president of the American Educational Studies Association, the Society of Professors of Education, the Council of Learned Societies in Education, and the Southeast Philosophy of Education Society. His scholarly interests focus on John Dewey, curriculum theory, teacher preparation, and education and ethics. His most recent books include *Ethical Decision Making in School Administration* (Sage Publications, 2008); *John Dewey: Primer* (Peter Lang Publishing, 2006); and *John Dewey and the Art of Teaching: Toward a Reflective and Imaginative Practice* (Sage Publications, 2005).

Smyth, John. John Smyth is a research professor of education at the University of Ballarat in Australia. He has held distinguished visiting professorships at universities in Australia, Canada, New Zealand, and the United States. In 1992, he received the Palmer O. Johnston Award from the American Educational Research Association. His scholarly interests include social justice and policy, sociology of students' lives and teachers' work, socially critical policy ethnographies of communities and schools, and school and community activism. His most recent books are *Activist and Socially Critical School and Community Renewal: Social Justice in Exploitative Times* (Sense Publishers, 2009); *Critically Engaged Learning: Connecting to Young Lives* (Peter Lang Publishing, 2008); *Teachers in the Middle: Reclaiming the Wasteland of the Adolescent Years of Schooling* (Peter Lang Publishing, 2007); and *"Dropping Out," Drifting Off, Being Excluded: Becoming Somebody Without School* (Peter Lang Publishing, 2004).

Teitelbaum, Kenneth. Kenneth Teitelbaum is Dean of the College of Education and Human Services and a professor of curriculum and instruction at Southern Illinois University, Carbondale. His research interests center on school knowledge in current and historical contexts, critical reflection in teacher education, and teachers' work, and school reform as it relates to democracy, social justice, and diversity. He is the author of many journal articles in those areas as well as *Schooling for 'Good Rebels': Socialism, American Education and the Search for Radical Curriculum* (Teachers College Press, 1995).

Thayer-Bacon, Barbara J. Barbara J. Thayer-Bacon is a professor of cultural studies in educational foundations at the University of Tennessee, Knoxville. Her interests are philosophy of education, pragmatism, feminist theory and pedagogy, and cultural studies in education. Her recent books include *Beyond Liberal Democracy in Schools: The Power of Pragmatism* (Teachers College Press, 2008); *Relational "(E)pistemologies"* (Peter Lang Publishing, 2003); and *Transforming Critical Thinking: Thinking Constructively* (Teachers College Press, 2000).

Yu, Tianlong. Tianlong Yu is an assistant professor of foundations of education at Southern Illinois University at Edwardsville. Before coming to the United States, he was an educational researcher in Beijing, China. His research interests are moral education, sociopolitical critique of character education, diversity issues in education, and comparative/international education. He has written a number of articles on those topics and is the author of *In the Name of Morality: Character Education and Political Control* (Peter Lang Publishing, 2004).